Theories and Strategies in Counseling and Psychotherapy

CONTENTS

PART TWO   Psychodynamic Therapy

4   Psychoanalytic Theory and Object Relations Therapy   69

5   Adlerian Therapy   102

10 Cognitive Behavior Therapy   266

PART FIVE   Integrative Therapy

11 Solution-Focused Brief Therapy   307

12 Systems Therapy   336

PREFACE

Writing a textbook on counseling and psychotherapy in the twenty-first century is a daring venture. This is true for three reasons. First, the number and complexity of theories has grown exponentially in the last three decades. The popularity of traditional therapies such as the psychoanalytic and client-centered approaches has declined while other emergent modalities, such as the brief therapies and the constructivist view, have rapidly increased in popularity and use. However, for all therapies and their theoretical approaches, the central axiom continues to be change. Those that cannot change and adapt in a world of managed care and accountability are doomed to go the way of the saber-toothed tiger—no matter how powerful they once were, their influence will wane and they will become a historical footnote.

The second reason is that therapy has moved from the Freudian couch into the community. The people we train work in businesses as big as Federal Express and as small as locally owned real estate agencies. Customer relations personnel at South Central Bell, personnel managers at Tennessee Valley Authority, chaplains at hospitals, officers and NCOs in the armed services, ministers in churches, recruiters for a wide range of organizations, nurses in a variety of health-care settings, and police officers with crisis intervention teams and hostage negotiation units all find utility in the practice and use of the theories and techniques found in this book. Such people use these approaches not only with others, but also for themselves. None of these people would label themselves *therapists* or *counselors*. Yet all of them have found worth, both personally and professionally, in the ideas promoted in this book.

When we move to the helping professions themselves, we find the same diversity in the field. Employee assistance counselors, marriage and family therapists, preretirement counselors, rehabilitation therapists, drug and alcohol counselors, psychiatrists, high school counselors, clinical psychologists, vocational and employment counselors, counseling psychologists, elementary school counselors, student personnel workers in higher education, gerontological counselors, crisis interventionists, mental health agency therapists, social workers, educational psychologists, pastoral counselors, psychiatric nurses, teachers, and corrections counselors all find some utility in the theories and techniques in this book. The list of occupations that are indirectly and directly allied with counseling and psychotherapy is staggering and continues to grow.

The third reason is the profession itself. Since the first edition of this book was published in 1984, we have seen a dramatic increase in the influence of both professional and state accrediting bodies on what constitutes a comprehensive program of study in the field and what a person must do to achieve certification or licensure for mental health work. National legislation has also affected programs and delivery of services. As an example, the 1992 Americans with Disabilities Act ushered in dramatic shifts in the way business and industry must deal with work barriers and disabling conditions of physically and mentally challenged clients. Clearly, mental health plays a major role in what services will be provided to this group and how they will be delivered.

The advent of managed care has had an extraordinary influence on the provision of mental health services. Cost containment has pushed all professionals in the mental health field to be diagnostically clear and behaviorally specific, and to supply the briefest and most efficacious treatment possible. As a result, managed care certainly has an impact on the kind of theoretical modalities used in treatment.

Finally, increased awareness by professional organizations that service providers need to recognize the pluralism of their clientele has resulted in a tremendous amount of discussion and research on the way services should be delivered to populations that do not fit the ethnocentric Western European mold that has long held sway in psychotherapy.

We have opted to approach the several different theories from a practical point of view, to slant them toward entry-level professionals whatever their field, and to include many of our own cases and experiences to reflect the wide and ever-expanding clientele that depicts the current human dilemma. We use the words *counselor* and *therapist* in different places as generic representations of all helping professions. We use other terms to represent the helping professions sparingly, if at all. We hope that other professionals who call themselves by other names will not be offended.

In this fifth edition we have added what we believe are significant new therapeutic techniques and deleted some that seem not to have held up under the demands of practice. First, we have changed the psychoanalytic perspective in Chapter 3 from a somewhat puristic and antiquated Freudian approach to an object relations view that focuses much more on relationships as opposed to sexual drive. Second, in Chapter 7 we have moved a number of rejuvenated behavioral techniques, such as flooding, back into that chapter. Third, we have introduced a new Chapter 11 on solution-focused brief therapy. This specific application of brief therapy best depicts the evolutionary movement of all therapies toward shorter, more precise, and target specific interventions. This trend may be seen through the other chapters in this book with comments and applications of brief therapy approaches that other modalities are attempting to use to compete for the health care dollar and become more consumer friendly. Fourth, we have added a new Chapter 12 on systems theory. While most theories books deal with systems from an intact, family systems–only perspective, this new chapter will deal with how a variety of systems interact and integrate in the total ecological system of the client. This interactive and integrative approach is necessitated by the need to understand and deal with the complexity of multiple systems as they simultaneously impact the client and each other.

Finally, in the fourth edition of this book we introduced what we thought would be a somewhat controversial approach and would probably be a wave of the future: computer-assisted therapy. We now believe we were right on both counts and our only miscalculation was that it would be in the somewhat distant future. That future is rapidly becoming *now,* with professional organizations and licensing bodies scrambling to define what the ethical and legal parameters of cybercounseling should be, as it has proliferated through the World Wide Web. As a result, this chapter has been expanded to include some of the cybercounseling techniques that are rapidly coming online.

To do all of the foregoing, we have closely edited each chapter. We have continued to give case studies a good deal of space because we believe that written examples of what we do and why we do it are as close to real life as a textbook can get. While this approach may be at the expense of more detailed theoretical discussion, our hope is that this book will demonstrate for beginners in the field how theory goes into practice, thus we give somewhat more emphasis to the latter. We hope the result is clear and concise, flows smoothly, and covers theory adequately.

Finally, our different styles of therapy show through in our writing, despite our best efforts to standardize the text. Therapists are not clones, nor are writers of books on therapy. We trust that our different styles, both in techniques and in writing, give an eclectic flavor to this book, which we think represents us. Our choices of theoretical systems, our organization of chapter topics and content, and our depth of coverage are the result of our eclectic view, our experience in teaching beginning students, our formal and informal discussions with colleagues, and our work with clients. We hope the product will help you help your clients. If it does, we will have done our job.

Acknowledgments

We would like to acknowledge two of our outstanding colleagues, Drs. Sue Lease and Dwaine Rice of the University of Memphis Department of Counseling, Educational Psychology and Research, both for their ability to teach students from this textbook and their insightful comments on how to make this a better teaching vehicle. We would like to thank thirty years' worth of our students at the University of Memphis for their helpful comments on making this a better book and their willingness to be the guinea pigs while we try some of this stuff out on them. We would also like to thank Mary Young and Shannon Foreman of Omegatype Typography for their excellent editorial support and coordination. Finally, we wish to acknowledge Virginia Lanigan and Erin Leidel at Allyn and Bacon for their support throughout the writing and publication of this edition.

Dick and Burl

1 Introduction

Purposes of the Book

Our objective in writing this book is to integrate the theory and application of the current major systems of counseling and psychotherapy. Programs in counselor and therapist education are frequently criticized for being too theoretical.

Theories and strategies are often dealt with separately in human service curriculums. Both courses and their content separate theories and strategies. It is as if thinking about psychotherapy has little, if anything, to do with the actual practice of it. We believe that is an ineffective way to learn about theories and about how to do therapy. This book is an attempt to bridge the gap between thinking and doing in the psychotherapy business. To that end, you are going to see techniques welded directly to theories. You are also going to see client and therapist comments that illustrate what the techniques are proposing. The case studies in each chapter will then tie theory and techniques together and explain what, how, and why the therapist was doing with the client. The exercises that we have provided on the website, or the ones your instructor may provide, are designed to put all of the information in this book into action for you.

Overview

We put a good deal of thought and discussion into the selection of the thirteen theoretical positions we discuss in the book. We used three criteria—*applicability* to a broad spectrum of practitioners; a recognized, sound *theoretical foundation;* and *current* usage—and selected the thirteen theories that in our judgment best met those criteria.

We considered several criteria in ordering the chapters—historical development, process similarities, and philosophical kinship. But as we indicated, this is a working theories of counseling and psychotherapy text that attempts to tie theory and strategy together. Therefore, this book is laid out to match our Expanded Eight-Stage Systematic Counseling Model as closely as possible (see the model in this chapter). We suggest that right now you leaf over to the model and speed-read its descriptors so you can get a better idea of what we are talking about in the next few paragraphs.

This book is divided into four parts. In Part One we introduce you to two of the major humanistic-existential approaches, person-centered therapy in Chapter 2 and Gestalt therapy in Chapter 3. We open with these two chapters because they deal with a number of initiating procedures in counseling and psychotherapy. Rogers's person-centered therapy has been influential in making the personal relationship between client and counselor an essential part of almost all counseling strategies. Learning how to create and facilitate a trusting relationship with a client to set the stage for counseling is one of the most critical activities a therapist does and is vitally linked to our own eight-stage model. No other approach does this better than person-centered therapy. It is the single most used therapy in creating trust and establishing rapport in the predisposition and problem exploration stages of the Expanded Eight-Stage Systematic Counseling Model.

Gestalt therapy is inextricably linked to the emotions or affective components of the client. As most beginning students will soon find out, helping clients to start to explore hurtful, conflicting feelings is not easy. Gestalt therapy's use of awareness-evoking techniques is designed to do exactly that. It is typically used in steps two and three, problem exploration and three-dimensional problem definition, to explore affective dimensions of the problem.

Part Two deals with three representative systems of dynamic or psychoanalytic therapy. Chapter 4 begins with a brief introduction to Freudian psychoanalysis. Then the reader is introduced to object relations therapy. Object relations is one of the leading branches of modern psychoanalytic theory and places far more emphasis on the client's relationships with significant others than does classical Freudian drive theory. Chapter 5 explores Adlerian therapy, which originated as a direct alternative to Freudian therapy. However, of all the psychoanalytic therapies, it is undoubtedly the most widely used and practiced approach in current operation. Its positive, social psychology basis has proved to be effective in a wide variety of settings with a wide variety of problems. In Chapter 6 we discuss transactional analysis, which can be seen as the common person's psychoanalytic approach. From its birth in the 1960s, transactional analysis became popular because of its use of common language to demystify therapy. This caused it to take root and grow throughout the world. All of these dynamic theories are useful when working with clients regarding affective, behavioral, and cognitive precursors related to past events and people that influence current functioning. As such, they are helpful in providing insight in Stage 2, Problem Exploration; Stage 3, Three-Dimensional Problem Definition; and Stage 4, Identification of Alternatives. It may also prove useful in Stage 5, Planning, and Stage 6, Action/Commitment.

Part Three begins with Chapter 7, "Behavioral Counseling, Therapy, and Modification." Nothing has revolutionized the field of counseling and psychotherapy more than the advent of the behavioral approaches. Behavioral approaches have single-handedly put accountability into therapy. This is done through methodical planning by behavioral objective, use of proven learning theories to reinforce or extinguish behavior, and measurable data to demonstrate success. Some behavioral component is always present in Stages 4 through 8 (Identification of Alternatives, Planning, Action/Commitment, Assessment and Feedback, and Postdisposition) of our Expanded Eight-Stage Systematic Counseling Model.

Part Three also includes three of the most common cognitive based therapies. Choice theory/reality therapy (Chapter 8), rational-emotive behavior therapy (Chapter 9), and cognitive-behavior therapy (Chapter 10) all have thinking and perception as major mediating factors between events and outcomes. All of these theories use techniques that closely link thinking to behavior change. When added to behavioral techniques, they form the major arsenal of techniques in Stages 4 through 8.

Part Four deals with integrative approaches. All of these approaches seek to provide the most efficacious and efficient treatment for targeted problems. Chapter 11 addresses solution-focused brief therapy, which uses a positive, humanistic, cognitive-behavioral, person-centered approach to immediately impel persons to take action. Systems therapy, which is discussed in Chapter 12, uses an expanded ecological model to bring a variety of forces within the client's system together to operate on issues. In Chapter 13 we look at eclectic therapy, which seeks to pull the best, most efficacious techniques together from all the available therapeutic systems and tailor fit them to specific client needs. Chapter 14 explores cybercounseling and computer-assisted therapy, which use computers to assess and perform therapy with clients. Computers are used both in addition to the human therapist and as stand-alone counseling tools. Each of these integrative approaches may be useful during any of the steps of the Expanded Eight-Stage Systematic Counseling Model.

Each chapter contains the following sections:

1. Fundamental tenets
2. The counseling process
3. Strategies for helping clients
4. Sample case or cases
5. Contributions of the system
6. Shortcomings of the system
7. Therapy with diverse populations
8. Summary
9. Suggestions for further reading
10. References

None of the sections attempt in-depth coverage. This book is a *survey* emphasizing theory and strategy. Readers who wish to study an approach in greater depth are encouraged to begin with our suggestions for further reading. Table 1.1 (on page 4) provides an outline of each chapter's general approach, its personality theory base, its founders and major contributors, and key characteristics.

Focus on Client Growth in Systematic Counseling: Stages in a Systematic Counseling Model

We now introduce you to our systematic model of counseling (Gilliland, James, Roberts, & Bowman, 1984, pp. 274–277). This is an eclectic model (see Chapter 13, "Eclectic Counseling and Psychotherapy," for a complete description) that is readily adaptable to all of the theories used in this book. We have expanded the model for this edition. Originally a six-stage, fluid, linear model, we have added two additional stages—predisposition and postdisposition (see Figure 1.1). We have added these two stages for two reasons. First, there is mounting evidence that setting the stage for counseling success, or *predisposing* the client, may be as critical or even more critical than the counseling itself (de Shazer, 1985, 1988; Hoyt & Miller, 2000; Hubble, Duncan, & Miller, 1999; Miller, Duncan, & Hubble, 1997; Prochaska & DiClemente, 1982, 1984; Prochaska, DiClemente, & Norcross, 1992). Second, the days of long-term, cookie-cutter therapeutic intervention are long gone, due in part

TABLE 1.1 Theoretical Approaches to Counseling and Psychotherapy

General Approach	Chapter and Theoretical System	Personality Theory Base and Founder and/or Major Contributors	Key Characteristics
Humanistic, experiential, existential	2. Person-centered counseling	Person-centered theory *Founder:* Carl Rogers	Humanistic, experiential, existential, organismic, self-theoretical, phenomenological, person-centered, here-and-now-oriented
	3. Gestalt therapy	Gestalt therapy theory *Founder:* Frederick Perls	Existential, experiential, humanistic, organismic, awareness-evocative, here-and-now-oriented, client-centered, confrontive
Psychodynamic	4. Psychoanalytic theory and object relations therapy	Psychoanalytic theory *Founder:* Sigmund Freud *Major contributor:* Ronald Fairbairn	Deterministic, topographic, dynamic, developmental, historical, insightful, unconscious, motivational, In object relations: relational, empathic, and affective
Social-psychodynamic	5. Adlerian therapy	Individual psychology *Founder:* Alfred Adler *Major contributors:* R. Dreikurs D. Dinkmeyer, Sr. H. Mosak	Holistic, phenomenological, socially oriented, teleological, field-theoretical, functionalistic
	6. Transactional analysis	Transactional analysis theory *Founder:* Eric Berne *Major contributors:* R. Goulding M. Goulding	Cognitive, analytic, redecisional, contractual, interpretational, confrontational, action-oriented, awareness-evocative, social-interactive, semantic
Cognitive, behavioral, action-oriented	7. Behavioral counseling, therapy, and modification	Behavior theory and conditioning theory *Major contributors:* B. F. Skinner J. Wolpe	Behavioristic, pragmatic, scientific, learning-theoretical, cognitive, action-oriented, experimental, goal-oriented, contractual
	8. Rational-emotive behavior therapy (REBT)	Rational-emotive behavior theory *Founder:* Albert Ellis *Major contributors:* W. Dryden R. A. DiGiuseppe	Rational, cognitive, scientific, philosophic, action-oriented, relativistic, didactic, here-and-now-oriented, decisional, contractual, humanistic

4

TABLE 1.1   Continued

General Approach	Chapter and Theoretical System	Personality Theory Base and Founder and/or Major Contributors	Key Characteristics
	9. Choice theory/reality therapy	Reality theory *Founder:* William Glasser *Major contributor:* R. Wubbolding	Reality-based, rational, anti-deterministic, cognitive, action-oriented, scientific, directive, didactic, contractual, supportive, nonpunitive, positivistic, here-and-now-oriented
	10. Cognitive behavior therapy	Cognitive theory *Major contributors:* A. Beck, D. Meichenbaum	Cognitive, rational, scientific, goal-directed, systematic, logical, mental and emotive, imaginal, perceptual, stress-, thought-, and belief-managerial
Integrative	11. Solution-focused brief therapy	Constructivist theory *Founder:* Steven de Shazer *Major contributors:* Milton Erickson, Insoo Kim Berg, Members of the Brief Family Therapy Center, Milwaukee, WI	Person-centered, post-structural, constructivist, cognitive-behavioral, humanistic, semantic, positive
	12. Systems theory	Systems theory *Major contributors:* Members of the Mental Research Institute, Palo Alto, CA Gregory Bateson Jay Haley Virginia Satir Uri Bronfenbrenner Cloe Mandanes The Milan, Italy, Group Milton Erickson Salvadore Minuchin	Strategic, multisystemic, ecological, interactive, managerial, integrated, problem-focused, cybernetic, structural, functionalist
	13. Eclectic counseling and psychotherapy	Eclecticism *Contributors:* F. C. Thorne S. Garfield J. Palmer A. Ivey R. Carkhuff, A. Lazarus	Integrative, systematic, scientific, comprehensive, organismic-environmental, cognitive, past-present-future-oriented, behavioral, educational, developmental, humanistic, analytic, decisional
	14. Computer-assisted therapy and cybercounseling	Atheoretical *Major contributors:* K. M. Colby J. H. Greist M. Wagman	Integrative, systemic, programmed, systematic, interactive, electronic, eclectic, decisional, feedback loops, cybernetic

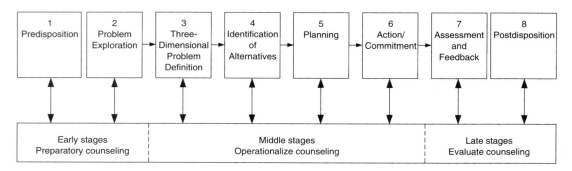

FIGURE 1.1   The Expanded Eight-Stage Systematic Counseling Model

to managed health care's insistence on efficiency and behavioral outcomes. Today clients are far more likely to be given very specific, tailor-made interventions that call for a great deal of outpatient, psychoeducational, consultive treatment approaches. The efficacy and success of specific treatment goals matched to client success have led to managed care's absolute insistence that there must be long-term monitoring of clients after care. Thus, *postdisposition* is now becoming almost mandatory for ethical reasons and for reimbursement by third-party payers (de Shazer, 1985, 1988; Haas & Cummings, 1991; Hoyt & Miller, 2000; Hubble, Duncan, & Miller, 1999; Miller, Duncan, & Hubble, 1997; Stomberg, Loeb, Thomsen, & Krause, 1996; Thompson & Rudolph, 2000).

Stage One: Predisposition

Counselor's Process Goals: Initiating contact prior to the first formal counseling session through telephone, computer, or face-to-face contact; setting the stage for treatment and change; recruitment of client cooperation; stabilizing and restoring equilibrium and homeostasis if in crisis; dealing with issues of client safety if needed; informing the client of treatment process; obtaining specific description of problem; assessing problem severity, coping skills, and attempts at solution; targeting exceptions to the problem; reinforcing help-seeking behavior.

Theoretical Basis: Stage-appropriate change-oriented brief therapy (Hoyt & Miller, 2000, pp. 289–330) to assess commitment and motivation to change, establish pretreatment goals, conduct client self-assessment, prepare client for induction into counseling, and seed client expectations for success; Six-Step Crisis Intervention Model (James & Gilliland, 2001, pp. 31–34) to determine degree and kind of problem, safety issues, and support needs; Triage Assessment Scale (Myer, Williams, Ottens, & Schmidt, 1992) to determine problem severity across affective, behavioral, and cognitive dimensions of the client's functioning; use of Egan (1986, 1990) and Carkhuff (1969) models of helping to provide concreteness, empathy, congruence, and unconditional positive regard to building a trusting relationship.

Stage Two: Problem Exploration

Counselor's Process Goals: Establishing rapport; listening to client concerns; responding in ways that encourage client to explore concerns on a deeper level; devel-

responsibility for others; (7) they frequently view the world in a somewhat mechanical fashion, making it difficult to separate objects from experiences, feelings from facts, and external situations from beliefs about such situations; (8) they may find expressing owner-ship of difficulties and emotions particularly threatening.

As clients successfully move through counseling, their attitudes, feelings, and per-ceptions move forward along a continuum. This movement is characterized by (1) feeling less apprehensive about the counseling, the counselor, and their own participation; (2) beginning to recognize and express previously denied feelings and moving toward a more open, honest mode of communication; (3) gradually gaining awareness of inner experiencing and eventually being able to live freely and to accept the process of experi-encing; (4) moving from a locus of evaluation and valuing outside themselves toward eval-uation and valuing that is consistently owned and internalized; (5) diminishing negativism, anxiety, self-doubt, and blaming of others in favor of optimism, calmness, self-acceptance, and constructive or realistic responses to what others say or do; (6) accepting responsibil-ity for behaviors or choices and, with increasing comfort, ceasing to feel responsible for the acts and choices of others; (7) making sharper distinctions between objects and expe-riences and becoming more able to separate feelings from facts and external situations from beliefs; and (8) expressing ownership of difficulties and emotions with greater ease, openness, and assurance (Rogers, 1965).

The Counselor's Perspective

Person-centered counselors strive to approach the client's world without preconceived notions. They know in advance that their clients are more likely to experience and make positive gains if the client–counselor relationship is one of mutual trust, acceptance, and spontaneity. If counseling is to be of optimum value to clients, counselors will (1) experi-ence inner freedom and congruence and exhibit a willingness for clients to do the same; (2) impose no external values or standards on clients; (3) endeavor to be genuine in their relationships with clients; (4) listen and respond to clients and communicate empathy; (5) communicate through their words, voice, and nonverbal behavior their acceptance, understanding, respect, and prizing of the clients as people; (6) see a new, exciting, positive venture in each new client relationship; (7) endeavor to communicate unconditional posi-tive regard toward clients; (8) trust that their congruence shows; (9) communicate to clients that they are *accurately* and *fully* hearing their verbal messages as well as their nonverbal cues and messages; (10) ensure that their own verbal and nonverbal responses reflect an accurate understanding of clients' feelings and messages; (11) communicate to clients that they trust them to be responsible, self-directing persons; and (12) nurture the conditions (the climate) wherein clients can experiment with new behaviors (Kirschenbaum & Hen-derson, 1989, pp. 239–240).

The Conditions of Growth

There are three main conditions for promoting psychological growth: *genuineness, uncondi-tional positive regard,* and *empathic understanding* (Raskin & Rogers, 1995, pp. 128–138).

Genuineness.   For Rogers, a key component to genuineness is being *transparent*. Transparency means that there are no pretensions about what the counselor is or does. There is no hiding behind a professional demeanor or a false front of personal superiority. What the client sees is what the client gets, with no hidden innuendos, no retreat into psychological jargon, and no defenses to hide counselor inadequacies. The counselor presents him- or herself as he or she is at that moment, with all of the flux and flow of feeling, thought, and behavior that transpires in the relationship. Thus, being transparent means being *congruent*.

Counselors who are congruent are clearly cognizant of what they are experiencing between their gut (feeling) and their head (thinking), how the two blend together in awareness, and how that awareness is expressed to the client as a presentation of their total personhood and investment in the therapeutic moment (Rogers, 1977, pp. 9–10). As Rogers (1969) states, "When I can accept the fact that I have deficiencies, many faults, make lots of mistakes, and am often ignorant when I should be knowledgeable, often prejudiced when I should be open-minded, often have feelings which are not justified by the circumstances, then I can be much more real" (p. 228).

Genuineness means that the counselor opens him- or herself to the emotive experience that takes place in the counseling relationship. Warmth and compassion when the client is in distress, anger when the client is assailed by overpowering forces, boredom when the client is mired down, and fear when the client reacts destructively toward the counselor or others—these are some of the emotional hallmarks that describe the counselor who acts genuinely. The more the counselor can be aware of and give voice to these feelings, whether positive or negative, the more likely it is that therapy will move forward (Rogers, 1977, pp. 9–10).

Owning such feelings is the height of genuineness and takes a special kind of courage and tenacity of purpose not easily attained. It would be far easier for the counselor to pronounce judgments that would put the client on the defensive than to own feelings that might make him or her vulnerable. Yet any judgments about the client are immediately debatable, no matter how expert, and mark the counselor as incongruent with the client's needs in the therapeutic moment. Owning feelings needs to be tempered by judicious use. The therapeutic encounter is the client's time, and not a platform for the counselor to vent his or her frustrations, inadequacies, and irritation over unjust treatment the client has encountered and life in general. Through temperate, well-timed, and targeted owning statements, the counselor provides a living model for the client to take a risk by responding in more congruent and genuine ways and to feel safe in doing so. The extent to which the counselor is deeply in touch with his or her own feelings and attitudes and expresses them in deeply felt ways to the client is the extent to which therapy will be facilitated (Rogers, 1977, pp. 11–12).

Unconditional Positive Regard.   Words such as *prizing, acceptance,* and *caring* are synonymous with an attitude that is positive toward the client. Easily said, unconditional positive regard is far more difficult to demonstrate. At any given time, the counselor needs to be willing to accept the confusion, fear, anger, resentment, courage, sorrow, and multiplicity of other feelings the client may have. Such caring is total and nonpossessive and lacks prior conditions of rightness or appropriateness of the client's feelings. It conveys to the client that the counselor is willing for him or her to legitimately be whatever he or she is at that time. Unconditional positive regard is not an all-encompassing, all-loving approach to the client, nor is it something the counselor "should" do. No one, including the counselor, feels such unconditional caring for everyone all the time. Tempered with genuineness, unconditional positive regard needs to be reasonably frequent in therapy. Research indicates that the more it is present, the more likely therapy will be successful, and the less it is present, the less likely there will be constructive change in the client (Rogers, 1977, pp. 10–11).

Empathic Understanding. Seeing through the client's eyes, walking in the client's shoes, and feeling both the agony and the ecstasy of the client describe empathic understanding. Empathy is realized by the counselor's ability accurately and sensitively to enter into the inner, private world of the client and experience at the deepest levels what the client is feeling. Moment by moment the counselor adapts, comprehends, encounters, and mirrors the client's feeling state.

To be empathic, the counselor must walk an emotional tightrope, moving delicately within the client's realm of experiencing without being *judgmental* or *sympathetic*. Empathy becomes judgmental when the counselor not only reflects the client's feeling state but also applies his or her own emotional yardstick in measuring its appropriateness for the client. Such evaluations do little to convey empathic understanding and a lot to put the client in a closed, defensive posture. Sympathy is equally problematic. Sympathy goes beyond empathy in that the counselor not only feels the emotional state of the client but also assumes that state! Whether consumed with the client's depression or indignant at the way significant others have dealt with the client, the counselor who shows sympathy presents only a facade of understanding. What sympathy really demonstrates is the inability of the counselor to come to grips with the emotion-laden content the client presents and probably says more about the counselor's feelings of inadequacy than the client's.

To be empathic, the counselor must not only sense meanings of which the client may scarcely be aware, but also must not precipitously confront such unconscious feelings, since to do so would be extremely threatening and convey the exact opposite of what empathy means. Empathic understanding means checking frequently with the client to validate perceptions and not being paralyzed by the content the client presents or the meaning of that content for the client. To engage in this balancing act, the counselor needs to be able to look with unfrightened eyes at the fearful things the client sometimes sees. In a sense it means laying aside oneself for the moment, and to do this the counselor must be very secure in stepping out of him- or herself into the sometimes frightening world of the client (Rogers, 1980, pp. 142–143).

By pointing out to the client in tentative terms the possible meaning in what he or she may be experiencing, the counselor provides linchpins to anchor the client's feelings more firmly, bring those feelings to awareness, and allow the client to experience them more fully. Empathic understanding, then, is a complex, strong, and demanding attribute but is also a subtle and gentle way of being in the therapeutic moment (Rogers, 1980, pp. 142–143).

Reciprocity

Encompassing all three of these conditions of psychological growth is reciprocity in the therapeutic relationship. As clients experience genuineness, unconditional positive regard, and empathy in response to even the most hideous aspects of their lives, they begin to experience prizing, caring, and acceptance of themselves; are able to drop defensive facades; and more openly experience themselves as individuals with self-actualizing abilities and unconditional self-regard (Patterson, 1990a; Rogers, 1977, p. 12; Rogers, 1986).

Strategies for Helping Clients

In person-centered counseling the relationship is of the essence—it is the beginning, the main event, and the end. It is important that the client–counselor relationship be one of safety and mutual trust. Even difficult (involuntary) clients who are alienated and highly resistant can be successfully helped by the person-centered counselor. Patterson's (1990a) research demonstrated that such resistive clients—who experience the persistent offering of the core conditions (of empathy, genuineness, and acceptance) by a skilled person-centered counselor—can profit from counseling and make positive change. Once an atmosphere of safety and trust exists, the probability that a facilitative relationship can be developed is greatly enhanced (Bozarth, 1990; Rogers, 1965, 1977, 1980, 1986).

Since person-centered counseling is essentially a "being" and relationship-oriented approach, it is important to note that Rogerian strategies for helping people are devoid of techniques that involve doing something to or for the client. There are no steps, techniques, or tools for inducing the client to make measured progress toward some goal; instead, the strategies are geared to experiential relationships. They occur in the here and now and permit both client and counselor to "live" and experience an ongoing process (Kirschenbaum & Henderson, 1989, pp. 60–152). Rather than intellectualize about the client's concerns, the counselor deals directly with the client's deep concerns of the moment. Person-centered strategies mainly emphasize the three conditions for psychological growth, which are initiated by the counselor. These strategies may be described as follows.

Facilitating Empathic Understanding

As we have seen, empathic understanding means perceiving the world from the client's point of view and communicating these perceptions to the client. Some major counseling strategies that facilitate empathic understanding include attending, verbally communicating empathic understanding, nonverbally communicating empathic understanding, and using silence (Cormier & Cormier, 1991, pp. 74–78; Raskin & Rogers, 1995, pp. 142–143).

Attending.   The counselor cannot achieve empathic understanding without attending to the client in a way that can be sensed by the client from the beginning. Counselor attention to the client involves both an attitude and a skill. Effective counselors put aside their own concerns while focusing fully on the concerns of the client—without sacrificing their own identity and uniqueness.

The physical distance between client and counselor is important. Many clients feel out of contact with a counselor who insists on sitting behind a desk. The client may interpret the desk as the counselor's way of keeping the client a safe distance away or as a condescending gesture (Hall, 1966). Generally, clients and counselors feel better about the interview if they are in comfortable, informal surroundings with no furniture between them. Attentiveness is enhanced when the counselor is facing the client at the distance that is most comfortable to the client. Some clients feel uneasy, threatened, and "hovered over" if the counselor sits too close. The counselor must be sensitive to the personal and cultural variances of clients so that the distance will facilitate rather than distract from the interview.

Voice qualities—modulation, tone, pitch, smoothness, diction, enunciation, and variation (absence of monotone)—tell the client an enormous amount about the attentiveness of the counselor. Choosing words that reflect the client's cultural background and value system helps communicate understanding, as well as acceptance, to the client. To the vision-impaired client, voice quality is the major criterion for judging the counselor's attention.

Many clients come to counseling with feelings of vulnerability, apprehension, fear, caution, or uncertainty. The counselor who cultivates the attitude and the skill of attending can allay these negative feelings. The counselor who focuses totally on the client enters the client's world quickly and empathically and thereby increases the chances of freeing the client to be genuine in the relationship. Effective attending is unobtrusive. The counselor who attends naturally does not call attention to that skill.

Verbally Communicating Empathic Understanding. Empathic understanding means understanding the client's affective and cognitive messages and then letting him or her know that these feelings and thoughts have been accurately understood at the surface level and at a deeper level. At the surface level the counselor limits verbal communication to restating or reflecting what the client has communicated. For example

> CL: I am pretty low after that test. I didn't think I'd do that badly.
>
> CO: You're feeling disappointed about the test. (*restatement*)

At a deeper level of empathic responding, the counselor understands and communicates the inferred, implied, or deeper meaning. For example

> CO: You're feeling surprised and disappointed about how you did on the test, especially since you were expecting more of yourself. (*reflection of a deeper meaning*)

The first response is considered minimally helpful; the latter response is considered more facilitative because it makes the client aware of a wider perspective and a deeper personal meaning. Whereas the first response leaves the client at the "disappointed" or "victim" state of awareness, the latter places self-expectation—something the client was barely aware of and initially only implied—at the forefront, where the client can now grasp and deal with it. The counselor used what Egan (1975, pp. 134–135) describes as *advanced accurate empathy.* This is not to imply that the counselor should pursue a fishing expedition responsiveness, hoping to hit upon the client's hidden motives. Rather, it implies that the counselor attends to the total client, that he or she is fully attuned to all the verbal and nonverbal cues and subtle messages of the client.

Facilitative verbal communication must focus on the client's current affective and cognitive content. Thus the counselor deals *directly with* the client's concerns and is not lured into talking *about* the client's situation. The following dialogue illustrates this important distinction:

CL: My parents just don't trust me. I can never do anything right, according to them!

CO: Your parents don't have any confidence in you—there are many parents like that. (*talking about the situation*)

CO: You're feeling hurt and angry with your parents because you really would like for your parents to show confidence in you—you really would like to prove to them and to yourself that you can do things right. (*dealing with the client's concerns*)

The latter response is better because it focuses right where it should—on the client, facilitating self-exploration—rather than on the parents, who are not present. Also, the second response leaves the next communication squarely up to the client.

Nonverbally Communicating Empathic Understanding. Empathic understanding involves accurately interpreting both nonverbal and verbal messages and cues, which the client and counselor continuously emit. Nonverbal messages may be transmitted through a number of recognizable ways—posture, body movement, body position, facial expression, smiles, frowns, wrinkled forehead, biting of the lip, rate of body movement (quick or slow), gestures, voice quality (tone, pitch, volume, rate), use of hands, use of legs and feet, eye contact, eyebrow gestures, and so on. Omissions, unspoken messages, and the observed energy level of the body also transmit cues. Even the placement of furniture affects social and personal distance and understanding. A client who chooses the seat farthest from the counselor, for example, may be communicating discomfort or distrust. It is important for counselors to observe and be sensitive to clients' nonverbal cues as well as their own nonverbal messages to clients. We can transmit and interpret nonverbal cues such as puzzlement, fear, anger, joy, exhaustion, doubt, avoidance, rejection, and embarrassment through many different body messages. Although the interpretation of nonverbal cues is by no means perfect, attentiveness to those cues in the context of the words being spoken does contribute enormously to our understanding of the affective and cognitive messages of the client (Cormier & Cormier, 1991, pp. 21–24; Cormier & Hackney, 1987, pp. 35–64; Hall, 1966; Knapp, 1978).

Silence as a Way of Communicating Empathic Understanding. In many instances in counseling silence is golden. There comes a time when both counselor and client are busy thinking about what has been said and observed. No words are needed (Raskin & Rogers, 1995, p. 142). Indeed, words might be intrusive at that moment. The observant counselor senses when the client is meaningfully processing feelings or information. Therefore, silence as a strategy can be a deeply empathic response. It communicates to the client, "I see and sense that we need time to deal with this; I respect your ability to handle it, and I'm right here to support you whenever you're ready to continue." Here is an example of the use of silence to communicate empathic understanding:

CL: It's just like he told me—that he can count on one hand the number of times I've told him that I love him.

CO: You feel badly because you perceive that he is hurt because you don't often use the words "I love you."

CL: Yes, but . . . (*three minutes of thoughtful silence*) All right, I don't want to hurt him. But I don't know that I love him—he insists, "It's got to be love." (*thirty seconds of silence*) Sometimes it's like he's no different from my mother. I feel like I've just got to get away—out on my own for a while.

CO: You don't know what you want, but you believe that what you've got now is not what you want.

CL: (*Two minutes of thoughtful silence*) It all goes back to when I was a child. I was a spoiled brat. I got everything I wanted. I wanted this—I got it; I wanted to date that guy—I dated him. I don't want to date him any more! (*thirty seconds of silence*) I always did what my mother wanted. I even married when she wanted me to. (*thirty seconds of silence*) That's just immaturity! I guess I'm just a thirty-two-year-old kid who never grew up!

The periods of silence were not uncomfortable to either client or counselor. The two were deeply in contact with each other—fully sensitive to the nonverbal cues, which were perhaps more powerful than the verbal ones.

Once the client understands that the counselor is comfortable with and accepts the silence, he or she is encouraged to explore more openly. The client senses that the counselor has no need or desire to direct the topic, tone, or focus. Some silent behavior tends to give more emphasis to what the counselor communicates verbally. Also, the modeling effect of empathic silence by the counselor may be to prompt the client to take more time to reflect.

Communicating Genuineness

Egan's (1975) system of helping skills was derived from Rogerian theory. According to Egan, the communication of genuineness includes

1. *Freedom from roles.* Being role-free means that the counselor is genuine in life as well as in the therapeutic relationship, that he or she is professional without hiding behind a professional role, and is congruent in experiencing and communicating feelings (p. 91).

2. *Spontaneity.* The spontaneous person communicates freely, with tact and without constantly weighing what to say. Counselors who are spontaneous behave freely, without being impulsive or inhibited, and are not bound by rules or techniques. Their verbal expression and behavior are based in self-confidence (p. 92).

3. *Nondefensiveness.* The genuine person is also nondefensive. Counselors who behave nondefensively know about their strong and weak areas and how they feel about them. Therefore, they can be open to negative client expressions without feeling attacked. They try to understand this negative expression and facilitate the exploration of it rather than defending themselves (pp. 92–93).

4. *Consistency.* Genuine people have few discrepancies between what they think, feel, and espouse and how they actually behave. For example, counselors behaving genuinely would not think one thing about a client and tell him or her something else, nor would they espouse one value and then act contrary to this value (pp. 93–94).

5. *Sharing of self.* The genuine person willingly self-discloses when appropriate. Thus, counselors behaving genuinely will allow clients and others to know them through open verbal and nonverbal expression of their feelings (p. 94).

A segment from an interview illustrates genuineness in the counseling relationship. The setting was a class in counseling techniques. The client, in a modeling situation, was angry at the professor (who was the counselor). The client readily volunteered to be counseled in the fishbowl.

CL: You cut me off the other day, before I even had a chance to ask you to be my chairman. You threw up the excuse of having too many advisees already. I resented that! You're supposed to be warm, accepting, and understanding!

CO: I can see that you are angry at me because my behavior didn't fit your idea of how I should respond to you.

CL: How can you explain acting like such a caring person here in class and being so callous toward me before I even got a chance to explain my situation?

CO: You see my behavior as inconsistent and maybe hypocritical.

CL: That's right. And at this point I wouldn't ask you to serve as my chairman even if you were the last person in this department.

CO: I'm sorry you feel that way. It seems to me that I'd be in a double bind—and perhaps you would be too—if I tried to chair your committee at this point.

The counselor refused to accept the gauntlet thrown down or to engage in excuses or defenses. By being nondefensive, consistent between thoughts and actions, and owning feelings, he was able to remain free from the manipulative ploys of the client. By owning feelings in a nonthreatening way the counselor let the client know that while the situation may not have been resolvable, the client was still valued as a person and could trust the counselor to be congruent and genuine.

Communicating Unconditional Positive Regard

The third fundamental condition of counselor behavior is the communication of unconditional positive regard to the client. As we have seen, this condition has been variously termed *acceptance, respect, caring,* and *prizing.* Egan (1975) refers to unconditional positive regards as *respect* and states that it is an active value of the high-functioning helper. According to Egan, respect can be communicated in several ways by the counselor's perceived orientation to the client: being "for" a client because of the client's basic humanity and potential for growth; committing oneself to work with the client; supporting the client as a unique individual and helping to develop this uniqueness; believing in the client's potential for self-direction; and assuming the client is committed to change (pp. 95–96). These five attitudes can become operational in the counseling relationship if the counselor engages in the following four behaviors (pp. 97–98):

1. Giving quality attention to the client's concerns and feelings
2. Communicating a nonevaluative attitude toward the client as a person worthy of genuine care
3. Responding to the client with accurate empathy and, as a result, communicating an understanding of the client's frame of reference
4. Cultivating the client's resources and thus demonstrating to the client his or her own potential and capabilities for action

The following counseling segment provides an example of acceptance. The client's presenting problem was her loss of an extended lesbian relationship.

CL: I've debated, inside of me, a long time—whether to share this with you. I have some apprehension—as to how you'll view my love life with my girlfriend.

CO: You're feeling some anxiety over whether I can fully accept your style of love life.

CL: Yes. (*pause*) Even now, I'm wondering if you think I'm strange or abnormal—I'm wondering whether I should be discussing this with you.

CO: I sense the great risk you're taking with me. My real concern is helping you deal with your inner feelings and choices—my esteem of you isn't based on your sexual orientation or lifestyle.

The counselor's words and body language communicated an openness to accepting and valuing the client as a person and were a catalyst for moving the counseling relationship forward. The counselor's accepting response focused on the client's real concerns rather than on the counselor's attitudes about her sexual orientation. The segment reminds us that the act of communicating acceptance must be free from any form of judgment or condescension. The counselor should accept and affirm the client as a person of worth, regardless of the client's personal orientation or lifestyle (Kirschenbaum & Henderson, 1989, pp. 20–23).

Sample Cases

Case of Jackie, Age 30

Even though the following transcript cannot convey voice tones, facial expressions, gestures, and other nonverbal dimensions, it illustrates the style, technique, and process that the typical person-centered counselor displays.

CL: Sometimes I think I must be crazy to put up with what I've gone through. I lived through hell. I could tell you some tales. Nobody would believe it! It would make a good book if anyone would believe it! (*laughs*) I've paid my dues—still paying for it.

CO: You're kind of amazed that you got through it. And now, you're ready to put the frightful mess behind you.

CL: Yeah. I must have been some kind of nut to stay in it that long. (*pause*) You know, I lived with that man twelve years—and all the time he treated me like shit. He didn't care about me. He didn't know me—not really . . . I knew him though. When they made him, they threw the mold away. He had a brilliant mind—about some things. But he was sure dumb about me. (*pause*) I had three kids by him and he didn't even know who I was. Have you ever heard of such a crazy thing? (*laughs*) I don't know why I put up with it. (*pause*) Yeah I do. Religion! Family! My mother! I was just as stubborn as a mule. For a long time, I thought I'd rather die than get divorced.

CO: Even though it's over, you're still feeling an awful lot of emotion—you'd even like to know why you did what you did. I gather from your tone of voice that you are rather pleased with yourself for having the strength to do what you felt you had to do.

CL: It was do or die. You never know what you can do until put to the test. (*laughs*) Well, something had to give. Things kept getting progressively worse. His drinking was getting worse and worse. It was always bad. But I knew I had done all I could do. He couldn't accept help, and the kids were beginning to suffer, I knew it would be rough. I didn't have a job. (*laughs*) To think I was such a kid when I married him—I was just sixteen. I didn't have a dab of sense. (*laughs*)

CO: Your voice communicates anger and regret. But I'm feeling confused about all the laughter that's coming out.

CL: Hmm . . . I guess it's to keep from crying. I guess I've felt like crying for so many years that I've just learned to cover it up with laughter. (*tears; very long pause*) I just hope I can get over it. I've got these three kids to raise all by myself, and I've got to finish the LPN course. I've come this far. It's not easy, but my God! All I've got to do is look back at where I've been. I've got my job at the supermarket—and I've got a roof over my head—and I'm doing okay in school—and I'm rid of the S.O.B. I guess I don't have much time to feel sorry for myself.

CO: It sounds like you're realizing what a great responsibility rests on your shoulders and that, even though you're not very happy, you're betting on yourself to pull through.

CL: Uh-hmm. (*long pause*) We had our first test on clinical nursing practice today! I was scared to death. I knew I had studied. But I was scared! (*pause*) When we got our evaluations in staffing this afternoon my instructor looked at me and said, "Jackie, you did well!" I'd liked to have fainted. I scored a ninety-two.

In the case of Jackie, a divorced mother, the person-centered counselor was attending to the verbal and nonverbal messages—including what appeared to be laughter at inappropriate times. This client was a prolific talker and was also silent for periods of time. These silences were perceived by the counselor to be periods of fruitful processing. Therefore, the counselor did not interrupt or vocally call attention to the silence. The counselor's response to the laughter ("Your voice communicates anger and regret. But I'm feeling confused about all the laughter that's coming out.") demonstrated that the counselor owned the feeling of confusion and also allowed the client to explore herself at a deeper level of understanding. This was a typical person-centered response. A response such as "Why are you laughing at such unfunny things?" could have been perceived as judgmental and might have damaged the relationship.

Case of Vernon, Age 12

The case of Vernon, a very obese sixth grader who was addicted to candy, depicts person-centered counseling with a different kind of client.

CL: (*sits down in chair, slumps, hangs head, looks at floor, doesn't look at counselor or speak*)

CO: Hi, Vernon. I'd like to know what's troubling you.

CL: (*doesn't speak, doesn't look up, shrugs*)

CO: I'd like to understand what that means—what you're really saying to me when you shrug your shoulders.

CL: (*doesn't look up, doesn't move*) Don't matter. Don't nobody care anyhow. (*low, mumbled voice*)

CO: You're feeling alone, that there's just no use going into it—no one can or will do anything that shows they care.

CL: (*glances up, briefly makes eye contact, then resumes looking down, remains slumped*) I didn't want to come in here anyhow. Why don't they just leave me alone? (*low, mumbled voice*)

CO: You don't want to be here. You'd like for people to get off your case—to just forget all about you.

CL: (*glances up again, briefly makes eye contact, then looks down again, remains slumped*) Ain't no use bothering about me. Nobody cares about me.

CO: You feel isolated, that no one cares about you. You believe that things would be better if there was just *one person* in the world who sincerely cared about Vernon.

CL: (*glances up, longer this time, then lowers head*) Ain't got no friends. Everybody hates me.

CO: You're really feeling lonely and abandoned. You wish you had *some* friends.

CL: (*not looking up, eyes getting teary, very long silence*)

CO: It's just so unpleasant to be all alone—to have no friends at all—and to wish that someone would treat you right.

CL: (*glances up briefly, looks down*) Everybody just laughs and pokes fun at me.

CO: And that just makes you feel negative toward yourself. But what you really want, down deep inside, is someone who cares about you—someone who will accept you as the person you are—without putting you down or judging you in any way.

CL: (*looks up, makes eye contact, looks away, but does not look down this time*) They keep calling me names. They all call me names. Some of them call me "fatso," some call me "blimp," some call me "hippo." They do it in the bathroom, they do it in the halls, they do it in the lunchroom. They all laugh. That's what burns me up.

CO: It sounds like you're feeling angry at others because of the names they call you, and maybe you're a little dissatisfied with yourself for putting up with it. Frankly, it makes me a little angry to discover that you're being treated this way, too. Let's you and me look at some things you and I can do to improve on the way people are speaking to you.

Here we see the counselor dealing with an unwilling and, at first, noncommunicative client. There is also evidence that the counselor is attempting to nurture a growth-promoting climate. The genuine and accepting statement "Frankly, it makes me a little angry to discover that you're being treated this way, too" does not judge the client, his tormentors, or the school. It communicates to the client that the counselor is involved. Also, the counselor's anger at the disrespectful treatment of the client was a real part of the relationship and deserved to be openly admitted. That the counselor was genuine and empathic and communicated these qualities served as a model for the client and probably represented a growth-promoting factor for Vernon. As we have noted, we make a sharp distinction between empathy and sympathy. Sympathy is rarely helpful to a client. If the counselor had said "That's terrible! They shouldn't be treating you this way!" Vernon might have been encouraged to continue to feel sorry for himself and to ruminate, and it might have distracted him from examining viable alternatives for himself.

Contributions of the Person-Centered System

The person-centered system has made several notable contributions to counseling and psychotherapy. For one thing, it is applicable to a wide variety of helping situations and settings—individual counseling, group counseling, family counseling, classroom learning, and supervision in education, business, hospitals, clinics, and government. Another strength is that the person-centered counselor consciously avoids taking responsibility for decision making by clients. Therefore, clients come to realize that they are responsible for making their decisions and consequently may develop a feeling of personal power. As Rogers (1977) noted, power "is politically centered in the client" (p. 14). This is a crucial point in facilitating the development of independence in the client.

Person-centered counseling has a history of encouraging inquiry, hypothesis testing, and investigation of its tenets and its outcomes (Bozarth, 1991b; Patterson, 1990b). As a result, the system is supported by a large body of research conducted over a long period. The theory is healthy today because of this research. Person-centered researchers have overcome criticism from detractors by developing effective ways of assessing client progress.

The person-centered approach has done much to remove the helping process from the exclusive control of highly-trained professionals and make it understandable and usable to all people. The fundamental conditions of genuineness, empathic understanding, and unconditional positive regard can be understood and used successfully at some level by any person. The simplicity and understandability of the person-centered approach do not diminish its effectiveness or validity. It is a system that is strengthened by both public and professional use and is therefore a highly "democratic" system of helping. Power, authority, or control over the client is missing; the personal power, autonomy, responsibility, and inner strength of the client are seen as curative outcomes in themselves (Kirschenbaum & Henderson, 1989; Raskin, 1992; Raskin & Rogers, 1995).

Another contribution of the person-centered approach has been to elevate the importance of *listening, caring,* and *understanding* in counseling and in the training of counselors, psychologists, social workers, and other professionals. Listening, responding, and relating skills are part of most helping endeavors and in the training of helpers largely because of the influence of Rogerian principles. In short, the core skills of helping have roots in the person-centered movement (Carkhuff, 1969a, 1969b; Cormier & Cormier, 1979, 1985, 1991, 1998; Cormier & Hackney, 1987; Egan, 1975, 1982, 1986, 1994; Hackney & Cormier, 1979; Ivey, 1988, 1997).

Person-centered counseling and philosophy have pervaded the entire world. At different times in their careers, both Carl Rogers and his daughter, Natalie, traveled, worked, taught, consulted, and practiced in countries all over the world. Natalie Rogers (1997) reported that Rogerian principles proved to be an excellent system for cross-cultural communicating. She recommends the approach as a premier method for providing "a rare quality to be heard" for children, adolescents, adults, groups, couples, and even addicts. As practiced in many countries today, person-centered counseling offers a sense of hope and potential for people to move beyond their immediate dilemmas. It represents, according to Natalie Rogers (1997), almost a "spiritual awakening" in that it builds community among disparate peoples.

Shortcomings of the Person-Centered System

One of the principal shortcomings of the person-centered approach is a deficiency not of the theory itself but rather in the way it is sometimes applied. Some counselors misunderstand or misuse the theory at the practical level. Many practitioners who understand the principles (or think they understand) and philosophically agree with them (or think they agree) have difficulty in effectively applying them. As a result, one frequently hears statements such as "It's a good theory, but it won't work with clients in our setting." Even though the individuals who make such statements are speaking in earnest, their difficulty may lie in a subtle need on their part to control clients, a desire to manage or do for clients, or some institutional practice that limits person-centered relating. Even with much training and modeling, some counselors and therapists find that the system is not congruent with their own beliefs or behavior. In other words, they may find that it is not a part of their being to experience the process, even though they have a thorough knowledge of the principles involved.

A recent critique of person-centered counseling (Kahn, 1999) that we consider archaic but is nevertheless often heard, revolves around the belief or misunderstanding that the person-centered system is nondirective. Even in the 1940s that was a misnomer. But the argument persists that because personal and theoretical biases are unavoidable, it is impossible for a therapist to be consistently nondirective. Furthermore, it is contended, the concept of nondirectivity, with its focus on the psychology of the client, implies that the person-centered system is a one-person rather than a two-person psychology. The inference is that the client's autonomy somehow cannot be fully respected in a one-person psychology and that the counselor's fallibility may be more a relevant factor than nondirectivity.

Another critique, explored by Owen (1999), alleges that person-centered counseling really does deal with unconscious processes. It is proposed that person-centered practice could be enriched and enhanced by reconsidering the differences to and similarities with modern psychodynamic approaches, thereby establishing greater clarity about each form of practice and further defining the boundary between these two systems of relationship and feeling-oriented therapies.

Another possible drawback is that the counselor's own identity may become obscured through deep involvement with clients. This is particularly true of helpers who have strong feelings for their clients. They may tend to submerge their own feelings and concerns into those of their clients and thereby lose some of their own identity and objectivity. Such counselors may become overinvolved with clients and their problems—a situation that is detrimental to their clients as well as to themselves.

A frequent criticism of the person-centered approach is that the counselor is too easily manipulated. This criticism relates to both of the shortcomings just discussed. If the practitioner limits interaction to listening and reflecting, some clients will either manipulate or discount him or her. Some clients may be helped simply by experiencing a relationship with a listening and reflective helper; others may not. The counselor who has a total grasp of the system and brings to the encounter the necessary experiential background and personal qualities is more likely to be helpful. Otherwise, manipulation and ineffectiveness in facilitating client growth may be valid concerns.

Another criticism of the person-centered approach is that it may be adequate for healthy clients, but what about the more severely disturbed clients or clients with less-than-normal intelligence? Although Rogers (1967) and others have reported the use of person-centered counseling with schizophrenic clients, we believe that the approach is least effective with those clients whose contact with reality, ability to communicate, and intellectual functioning are at the lower end of the scale.

Another shortcoming of the person-centered system is the possible tendency of the counselor—especially the inexperienced counselor or the one who does not fully understand the system—to selectively attend to and reflect the client's self-defeating statements. Though not a flaw in the system itself, it is a vulnerable point. After accurate reflection of the client's dilemmas—what then? Do clients simply leave with the understanding that their dilemmas are genuine? This perceived lack of technique to get clients moving out of their negative feelings—the perceived lack of concrete steps for them to take—is one of the most frequent criticisms of the person-centered system.

Person-Centered Counseling
with Diverse Populations

The person-centered system adheres to several conceptual formulations (Patterson, 1996; Zimring, 1992) that promote understanding, accepting, and valuing diversity (Cain, 1987; Natiello, 1990; Rogers, 1980, 1987a, 1987b; Sims, 1989; Zimring, 1990). Unconditional positive regard for each individual and belief in the inherent positive growth tendency of the person are only two such formulations. The person-centered approach is recognized worldwide for its contributions to human relations, cross-cultural empathy, facilitating communication among disparate groups, and nurturing diversity among people who are distinctly different in dimensions such as race, ethnicity, religion, lifestyle, age, sex, sexual orientation, physical disability, and societal status (Kirschenbaum & Henderson, 1989, pp. 433–477).

The person-centered approach has been popularized and used successfully with clients in the developmental disabilities community (Holburn & Vietze, 1999, 2000). It has also been used with conditional success with clients who have profound physical or mental disabilities (Green, Middleton, & Reid, 2000; Reid, Everson, & Green, 1999). Zeman (1999) reported that person-centered treatment was useful in the care of people with Alzheimer's disease. Sinnott et al. (1998) found that, of all treatment modalities available for use with the elderly, person-centered therapy was rated the most acceptable.

O'Leary et al. (1998), reporting on the applicability of person-centered counseling with Gestalt groups in Ireland, reported substantial improvements in experimental groups on the dimensions of self-esteem, interpersonal relationships, empathy, congruence, unconditionality, level of regard, acceptance of others, and various aspects of awareness. The Irish studies yielded definite support for person-centered Gestalt therapy. Landi, Laffranconi, Zoratti, and Tait (2000), studying person-centered counseling with male and female heterogeneous students in Argentina, reported significant improvements in parameters of functionality after participation in counseling.

In his later years, Rogers devoted a substantial amount of energy and influence to the resolution of intercultural concerns (Kirschenbaum & Henderson, 1989, pp. 438–445). He sincerely believed that person-centered concepts could be applied to governments, nations, and community groups as well as to individuals, and that the quest for world peace would be enhanced when people came to use these concepts in their normal interactions (Bozarth, 1992; Raskin & Rogers, 1989, p.183; Rogers, 1987b). Rogers (1987c) facilitated human relations training workshops, consulted with institutions and international groups, and contributed to the literature regarding the reduction of tension among differing groups, including diverse cultural groups. Clearly, a major strength of the person-centered approach is found in the practical application of acceptance, genuineness, and empathic understanding to ameliorate adversities and misunderstandings among diverse national, cultural, or racial groups (Boy, 1990; Bozarth, 1992; Kirschenbaum & Henderson, 1989; Natiello, 1990; Patterson, 1996; Raskin, 1992; Raskin & Rogers, 1989; Rogers, 1977, 1980).

According to Livneh and Sherwood (1991), the central constructs of person-centered theory that apply to understanding the psychological implications of physical disability include "(a) the salience of the phenomenological field, (b) the self-concept, and (c) the denial and distortion of threatening experiences" (p. 529). Person-centered proponents argue that it is not so much the physical disability that psychologically affects clients but rather the subjective meanings, attitudes, and beliefs associated with the personal perception.

Person-centered strategies have definite merits for helping people with physical disabilities, including:

1. Facilitating clients' insight into their perceptions and feelings, especially during the period immediately following the injury or disabling condition and the early phase of rehabilitative treatment
2. Accepting the disability emotionally without devaluing themselves or resorting to defensive behaviors concerning the existence of their condition
3. Moving toward becoming more open to experience and accept the disability
4. Perceiving themselves with disabilities more realistically and less anxiously
5. Viewing themselves as a process characterized by change and fluidity, rather than rigidity and immobility
6. Developing an increased trust in themselves with their disabilities
7. Acting with confidence and assertiveness, as opposed to being nonconfident and passive (Livneh & Sherwood, 1991, pp. 529–530)

For clients with physical disabilities, Livneh and Sherwood (1991) cite See (1985), and identify several limitations in person-centered strategies in rehabilitation counseling. Among these deficiencies are the person-centered system's aversion to

1. Setting goals other than self-actualization
2. Diagnosing and evaluating
3. Giving advice
4. Focusing on the external environment
5. Facilitating process rather than outcome goals
6. Avoiding task-oriented needs, such as facilitating constructive client behavior and skill development

There are some distinct deficiencies in the person-centered approach in working with certain other categories of clients. Some people have limited experience in dealing with their feelings. For those clients whose lifestyles, family mores, cultural heritage, and vocations predispose them to respond to environmental, behavioral, parental, or authoritarian advice or influence, person-centered counseling may seem ineffective or even unsuitable. Some clients may need goal-direction, short-term reinforcement, short-term concrete results, and structured guidance that the person-centered counselor may not be prepared for or comfortable in providing. Clients with severely disadvantaged educational and social experience or limited intellectual capacity may be more responsive to a product-oriented therapy than to the process orientation of person-centered counseling.

Another unique population that is appropriately served by the person-centered approach is people who have suffered loss. Most clients who are in a state of bereavement and grief fare better with an empathic, acceptant, genuine, caring support person rather than a product-oriented helper. Still another population that responds to the techniques of person-centered counseling is the elderly. Reminiscence, validation, and anchoring strategies (Gilliland & James, 1997, pp. 499–500; James & Gilliland, 2001, pp. 501–502) are especially appropriate for gerontology work. These strategies, based on person-centered principles, operate to get clients in touch with their meaningful past, restore them psychologically to more therapeutic periods in their lives, and serve as connecting anchors for recovery of lost emotional security.

Finally, a major strength of the person-centered approach of *all diverse populations* has emerged through the intensive group work developed by Rogers during the 1960s and 1970s (Raskin & Rogers, 1995, p. 153). Such groups can facilitate the basic encounter of nontherapist peers in a group, responding to each other with undivided empathy in mutual understanding, sharing, and not holding back in their quest for personal growth.

Summary

Person-centered counseling is a continually growing, evolving, and changing theoretical system. Its founder, Carl R. Rogers, was in the forefront of its development from its beginning in the 1940s until his death in 1987. As the approach has evolved, it has been called *nondirective, client-centered, experiential,* and *person-centered.* Although it is now evolving toward a more eclectic system, certain fundamental tenets remain. Among these tenets is the assumption that there are three necessary and sufficient conditions that promote positive growth in clients: genuineness, unconditional positive regard, and empathic understanding. Recent applications of the theory emphasize more active participation by the counselor. The theory has long been vulnerable to misuse and misinterpretation by practitioners. Despite this shortcoming, the person-centered counselor is seen as a genuine, caring, empathic person who is fully involved with the client in an ongoing and vital way.

At different times in their careers, both Carl Rogers and his daughter, Natalie, traveled, consulted, practiced, and taught in many different countries and cultures (N. Rogers, 1997). Natalie Rogers reported that Rogerian principles proved to be an excellent system for cross-cultural communicating, understanding, community building, and providing a sense of hope for diverse peoples. She likens it to a spiritual awakening among disparate populations of the world.

SUGGESTIONS FOR FURTHER READING

Boy, A. V., & Pine, G. J. (1999). *A person-centered foundation for counseling and psychotherapy* (2nd ed.). Springfield, IL: Chas. C. Thomas.

Bugental, J. (Therapist). (1997). *Existential-humanistic therapy* (Videotape No. 0-205-32881-4, T. Labriola, Producer). In J. Carlson & D. Kjos,

Existential-humanistic therapy with Bugental: Psychotherapy with the experts. Boston: Allyn & Bacon.

Combs, A. W. (1989). *A theory of therapy: Guidelines for counseling practice.* Newbury Park, CA: Sage.

Kirschenbaum, H., & Henderson, V. L. (Eds.). (1989). *The Carl Rogers reader.* Boston: Houghton Mifflin.

Raskin, N. J., & Rogers, C. R. (1995). Person-centered therapy. In R. J. Corsini & D. Wedding (Eds.), *Current psychotherapies* (5th ed., pp. 155–194). Itasca, IL: F. E. Peacock.

Rogers, C. R. (1951). *Client-centered therapy.* Boston: Houghton Mifflin.

Rogers, C. R. (1961). *On becoming a person.* Boston: Houghton Mifflin.

Rogers, C. R. (1969). *Freedom to learn: A view of what education might become.* Columbus, OH: Chas. E. Merrill.

Rogers, C. R. (1970). *Carl Rogers on encounter groups.* New York: Harper & Row.

Rogers, C. R. (1972). *On becoming partners: Marriage and its alternatives.* New York: Delacorte Press.

Rogers, C. R. (1977). *Carl Rogers on personal power: Inner strength and its revolutionary impact.* New York: Delacorte Press.

Rogers, C. R. (1980). *A way of being.* Boston: Houghton Mifflin.

Rogers, N. (Therapist). (1997). *Person-centered therapy* (Videotape No. 0-205-32885-7, T. Labriola, Producer). In J. Carlson & D. Kjos, *Person-centered therapy with Rogers: Psychotherapy with the experts.* Boston: Allyn & Bacon.

REFERENCES

Bixler, R. H. (1990). Carl Rogers, "Counseling," and the Minnesota point of view. *American Psychologist, 45,* 675–675.

Boy, A. V. (1990). The therapist in person-centered groups. *Person-Centered Review, 5,* 308–315.

Boy, A. V., & Pine, G. J. (1999). *A person-centered foundation for counseling and psychotherapy* (2nd ed.). Springfield, IL: Chas. C. Thomas.

Bozarth, J. D. (1985). Quantum theory and the person-centered approach. *Journal of Counseling and Development, 64,* 179–182.

Bozarth, J. D. (1989). Person-centered therapy with couples. [Special issue: Person-centered approaches with families.] *Person-Centered Review, 4*(3), 280–294.

Bozarth, J. D. (1990). The evolution of Carl Rogers as a therapist. [Special issue: Fiftieth anniversary of the person-centered approach.] *Person-Centered Review, 5*(4), 387–393.

Bozarth, J. D. (1991a). Actualization: A fundamental concept in client-centered therapy. [Special issue: Handbook of self-actualization.] *Journal of Social Behavior and Personality, 6*(5), 45–59.

Bozarth, J. D. (1991b). Person-centered assessment. *Journal of Counseling and Development, 69*(5), 458–461.

Bozarth, J. D. (1992, August). *The person-centered community group.* Paper presented at the symposium on Contributions of Client-Centered Therapy to American Psychology's 100 Years, presented at the Centennial Convention of the American Psychological Association, Washington, DC.

Brent, J. S. (1984). Person-centered apologetics: An empathic approach. *Journal of Psychology and Christianity, 3,* 18–26.

Bugental, J. (Therapist). (1997). *Existential-humanistic therapy* (Videotape No. 0-205-32881-4, T. Labriola, Producer). In J. Carlson & D. Kjos, *Existential-humanistic therapy with Bugental: Psychotherapy with the experts.* Boston: Allyn & Bacon.

Cain, D. J. (1987). Carl R. Rogers: The man, his vision, his impact. *Person-Centered Review, 2,* 283–288.

Carkhuff, R. (1969a). *Helping and human relations. Vol. 1: Selection and training.* New York: Holt, Rinehart & Winston.

Carkhuff, R. (1969b). *Helping and human relations. Vol. 2: Practice and research.* New York: Holt, Rinehart & Winston.

Cormier, L. S., & Cormier, W. H. (1998). *Interviewing strategies for helpers: Fundamental skills and cognitive behavioral interventions* (4th ed.). Pacific Grove, CA: Brooks/Cole.

Cormier, L. S., & Hackney, H. (1987). *The professional counselor: A process guide to helping.* Englewood Cliffs, NJ: Prentice-Hall.

Cormier, W. H., & Cormier, L. S. (1979). *Interviewing strategies for helpers: A guide to assessment, treatment, and evaluation.* Pacific Grove, CA: Brooks/Cole.

Cormier, W. H., & Cormier, L. S. (1985). *Interviewing strategies for helpers: Fundamental skills and cognitive-behavioral interventions* (2nd ed.). Pacific Grove, CA: Brooks/Cole.

Cormier, W. H., & Cormier. L. S. (1991). *Interviewing strategies for helpers: Fundamental skills and cognitive behavioral interventions* (3rd ed.). Pacific Grove, CA: Brooks/Cole.

Cowen, E. L. (1985). Person-centered approaches to primary prevention and mental health: Situation-focused and competence-enhancement. *American Journal of Community Psychology, 13*, 31–48.

deCarvalho, R. J. (1999). Otto Rank, the Rankian circle in Philadelphia, and the origins of Carl Rogers' person-centered psychotherapy. *History of Psychology, 2*, 132–148.

Egan, G. (1975). *The skilled helper: A model for systematic helping and inter-personal relating.* Pacific Grove, CA: Brooks/Cole.

Egan, G. (1982). *The skilled helper: Model, skills, and methods for effective helping* (2nd ed.). Pacific Grove, CA: Brooks/Cole.

Egan, G. (1986). *The skilled helper: A systematic approach to effective helping* (3rd ed.). Pacific Grove, CA: Brooks/Cole.

Egan, G. (1994). *The skilled helper* (5th ed.). Pacific Grove, CA: Brooks/Cole.

Fernald, P. S. (2000). Carl Rogers: Body-centered counselor. *Journal of Counseling & Development, 78*, 172–179.

Gilliland, B. E., & James, R. K. (1997). *Crisis intervention strategies* (3rd ed.). Pacific Grove, CA: Brooks/Cole.

Ginsberg, B. G. (1984). Beyond behavior modification: Client-centered play therapy with the retarded. *Academic Psychology Bulletin, 6*, 321–334.

Glauser, A. S., & Bozarth, J. D. (2001). Person-centered counseling: The culture within. *Journal of Counseling & Development, 79*, 142–147.

Grant, B. (1990). Principled and instrumental nondirectiveness in person-centered therapy. *Person-Centered Review, 5*, 77–88.

Green, C. W., Middleton, S. G., & Reid, D. H. (2000). Embedded evaluation of preferences sampled from person-centered plans for people with profound multiple disabilities. *Journal of Applied Behavior Analysis, 33*, 639–642.

Hackney, H., & Cormier, L. S. (1979). *Counseling strategies and objectives* (2nd ed.). Englewood Cliffs, NJ: Prentice-Hall.

Hall, E. T. (1966). *The hidden dimension.* Garden City, NY: Doubleday.

Harren, V. A. (1977). Client-centered theory of personality and psychotherapy. In D. C. Rimm & J. W. Somerville (Eds.), *Abnormal psychology* (Chapter 17). New York: Academic Press.

Herlihy, B. (1985). Person-centered Gestalt therapy: A synthesis. *Journal of Humanistic Education and Development, 24*, 16–24.

Holburn, S., & Vietze, P. (1999). Acknowledging barriers in adopting person-centered planning. *Mental Retardation, 37*, 117–124.

Holburn, S., & Vietze, P. (2000). Person-centered planning and cultural inertia in applied behavior analysis. *Behavior & Social Issues, 10*, 39–70.

Holdstock, T. L., & Rogers, C. R. (1977). Person-centered theory. In R. J. Corsini (Ed.), *Current personality theories* (pp. 125–151). Itasca, IL: F. E. Peacock.

Ivey, A. E. (1988). *Intentional interviewing and counseling: Facilitating client development* (2nd ed.). Pacific Grove, CA: Brooks/Cole.

Ivey, A. E. (Therapist). (1997). *Integrative therapy* (Videotape No. 0-205-32910-1, T. Labriola, Producer). In J. Carlson & D. Kjos, *Integrative therapy with Ivey: Psychotherapy with the experts.* Boston: Allyn & Bacon.

James, R. K., & Gilliland, B. E. (2001). *Crisis intervention strategies* (4th ed.). Belmont, CA: Wadsworth/Thompson.

Kahn, E. (1999). A critique of nondirectivity in the person-centered approach. *Journal of Humanistic Psychology, 39*, 94–110.

Kahn, E., & Rachman, A. W. (2000). Carl Rogers and Heinz Kohut: A historical perspective. *Psychoanalytic Psychology, 17*, 294–312.

Kirschenbaum, H., & Henderson, V. L., (Eds.). (1989). *The Carl Rogers reader.* Boston: Houghton Mifflin.

Knapp, M. L. (1978). *Nonverbal communication in human interaction* (2nd ed.). New York: Holt, Rinehart & Winston.

Landi, M., Laffranconi, C., Zoratti, S., & Tait, R. (2000). Efectividad de al psicoterapia. Enfoque Centrado en la Persona./Effectiveness in psychotherapy: Person-centered approach. *Acta Psiquiatrica y Psicologica de America Latina, 46*, 267–273.

Lewis, C. M. (1985). Symbolization of experience in the process of group development. *Group, 9*, 29–35.

Livneh, H., & Sherwood, A. (1991). Application of personality theories and counseling strategies to clients with physical disabilities. *Journal of Counseling and Development, 69*, 525–538.

May, R., & Yalom, I. (1995). Existential Psychotherapy. In R. J. Corsini & D. Wedding (Eds.), *Current psychotherapies* (5th ed., pp. 262–292). Itasca, IL: F. E. Peacock.

Meador, B. D., & Rogers, C. R. (1973). Client-centered therapy. In R. J. Corsini (Ed.), *Current psychotherapies* (pp. 119–165). Itasca, IL: F. E. Peacock.

Meador, B. D., & Rogers, C. R. (1979). Person-centered therapy. In R. J. Corsini (Ed.), *Current psychotherapies* (2nd ed., pp. 131–184). Itasca, IL: F. E. Peacock.

Natiello, P. (1990). The person-centered approach: Collaborative power and cultural transformation. *Person-Centered Review, 5,* 268–286.

O'Leary, E., Purcell, U., McSweeney, E., O'Flynn, D., O'Sullivan, K., Keane, N., & Barry, N. (1998). The Cork person centered gestalt project: Two outcome studies. *Counselling Psychology Quarterly, 11,* 45–61.

Owen, I. R. (1999). Exploring the similarities and differences between person-centered and psychodynamic therapy. *British Journal of Guidance & Counselling, 27,* 165–178.

Patterson, C. H. (1986). *Theories of counseling and psychotherapy* (4th ed.). New York: Harper & Row.

Patterson, C. H. (1990a). Involuntary clients: A person-centered view. *Person-Centered Review, 5*(3), 316–320.

Patterson, C. H. (1990b). On being client-centered. [Special issue: Fiftieth anniversary of the person-centered approach.] *Person-Centered Review, 5*(4), 425–432.

Patterson, C. H. (1996). Multicultural counseling: From diversity to universality. *Journal of Counseling and Development, 74*(3), 227–231.

Raskin, N. J. (1992, August). *A revolutionary approach to counseling and psychotherapy.* Paper presented at the symposium on Contributions of Client-Centered Therapy to American Psychology's 100 Years, presented at the Centennial Convention of the American Psychological Association, Washington, DC.

Raskin, N. J., & Rogers, C. R. (1989). Person-centered therapy. In R. J. Corsini & D. Wedding (Eds.), *Current psychotherapies* (4th ed., pp. 155–194). Itasca, IL: F. E. Peacock.

Raskin, N. J., & Rogers, C. R. (1995). Person-centered therapy. In R. J. Corsini & D. Wedding (Eds.), *Current psychotherapies* (5th ed., pp. 128–161). Itasca, IL: F. E. Peacock.

Reid, D. H., Everson, J. M., & Green, C. W. (1999). A systematic evaluation of preferences identified through person-centered planning for people with profound multiple disabilities. *Journal of Applied Behavior Analysis, 32,* 467–477.

Rennie, D. L. (1998). *Person-centered counselling: An experiential approach.* London: Sage.

Rogers, C. R. (1942). *Counseling and psychotherapy.* Boston: Houghton Mifflin.

Rogers, C. R. (1951). *Client-centered therapy.* Boston: Houghton Mifflin.

Rogers, C. R. (1959). A theory of therapy, personality, and interpersonal relationships as developed in the client-centered framework. In S. Koch (Ed.), *Psychology: A study of science, formulations of the person and the social context* (Vol. 3, pp. 184–256). New York: McGraw-Hill.

Rogers, C. R. (1961). *On becoming a person.* Boston: Houghton Mifflin.

Rogers, C. R. (1965). Client-centered therapy (Film no. 1, client named Gloria). In E. L. Shostrom (Ed.), *Three approaches to psychotherapy* (three 16 mm color motion pictures). Orange, CA: Psychological Films.

Rogers, C. R. (1967). *The therapeutic relationship and its impact: A study of psychotherapy with schizophrenics.* With E. T. Gendlin, D. J. Kiesler, & C. Lomax. Madison: University of Wisconsin Press.

Rogers, C. R. (1969). *Freedom to learn: A view of what education might become.* Columbus, OH: Chas. E. Merrill.

Rogers, C. R. (1970). *Carl Rogers on encounter groups.* New York: Harper & Row.

Rogers, C. R. (1972). *On becoming partners: Marriage and its alternatives.* New York: Delacorte Press.

Rogers, C. R. (1977). *Carl Rogers on personal power: Inner strength and its revolutionary impact.* New York: Delacorte Press.

Rogers, C. R. (1980). *A way of being.* Boston: Houghton Mifflin.

Rogers, C. R. (1985). Reaction to Gunnisons' article on the similarities between Erikson and Rogers. *Journal of Counseling and Development, 63,* 565–566.

Rogers, C. R. (1986). Person-centered therapy (Videotape No. 1, client named Kathy). In E. L. Shostrom (Executive Producer), S. K. Shostrom (Producer), & H. Ratner (Director), *Three approaches to psychotherapy II* (three VHS videotapes). Corona Del Mar, CA: Psychological and Educational Film.

Rogers, C. R. (1987a). Inside the world of the Soviet professional. *Counseling and Values, 32,* 46–66.

Rogers, C. R. (1987b). Our international family. *Person-Centered Review, 2,* 139–149.

Rogers, C. R. (1987c). Steps toward world peace, 1948–1986: Tension reduction in theory and practice. *Counseling and Values, 32,* 38–45.

Rogers, N. (Therapist). (1997). *Person-centered therapy* (Videotape No. 0-205-32885-7, T. Labriola, Producer). In J. Carlson & D. Kjos, *Person-centered therapy with Rogers: Psychotherapy with the experts.* Boston: Allyn & Bacon.

Scharff, J. S., & Scharff, D. E. (1998). *Object relations individual therapy.* Northvale, NJ: Analytic Press.

See, J. D. (1985). Person-centered perspective. *Journal of Applied Rehabilitation Counseling, 16,* 15–20.

Sims, J. M. (1989). Client-centered therapy: The art of knowing. *Person-Centered Review, 4,* 27–41.

Sinnott, J. D., Burgio, L. D., Lakein, D., Pappas, K., DeLeonardo, L., & Spencer, F. M. (1998). Acceptability ratings of psychotherapeutic treatments for elderly individuals. *Journal of Applied Gerontology, 17,* 172–185.

Slack, S. (1985). Reflections on a workshop with Carl Rogers. *Journal of Humanistic Psychology, 25,* 35–42.

St. Clair, M. (1996). *Object relations and self psychology: An introduction* (2nd ed.). Pacific Grove, CA: Brooks/Cole.

Willis, R. J. (1985). "The life of therapy": An exploration of therapeutic method. *Psychotherapy in Private Practice, 3,* 63–70.

Zeman, S. (1999). Person-centered care for the patient with mid- and late stage dementia. *American Journal of Alzheimer's Disease, 14,* 308–310.

Zimring, F. M. (1988). Attaining mastery: The shift from the "me" to the "I." *Person-Centered Review, 3,* 165–175.

Zimring, F. M. (1990). A characteristic to Rogers's response to clients. *Person-Centered Review, 5,* 433–448.

Zimring, F. M. (1992, August). *Contributions to the constructs of self, empathy, and experience.* Paper presented at the symposium on Contributions of Client-Centered Therapy to American Psychology's 100 Years, presented at the Centennial Convention of the American Psychological Association, Washington, DC.

3   Gestalt Therapy

Fundamental Tenets

History

Frederick S. (Fritz) Perls is credited with the formulation of Gestalt therapy. Perls first became acquainted with Gestalt psychology through Kurt Goldstein, with whom he worked in 1926, but it was not until the early 1940s that Perls actually incorporated principles of Gestalt psychology into his writing. His book *Ego, Hunger and Aggression* (1947) marked his break from psychoanalysis and a bridge to Gestalt therapy.

Goldstein's theory of holism, with its emphasis on figure-ground formulation, is the basis of one of the major concepts of Gestalt therapy. Sigmund Friedlander, a German philosopher described by Perls as one of his three gurus, provided what Perls later developed into the concept of "working toward the awareness and integration of polarities." Perls was also influenced by the semanticists I. A. Richard and Alfred Korzybski, who were concerned with the effect of language on thought and behavior (Kogan, 1976, pp. 241–242). Perls also seems to have been strongly influenced by the psychodramatic methods of Jacob Moreno, as evidenced by the parallels in the practice of psychodrama and Gestalt therapy.

In the early 1930s, as Hitler came to power in Germany, Fritz and his wife Laura moved to South Africa, where he was engaged in training psychoanalysts from 1934 to 1942 (Kogan, 1976, pp. 237–243). From 1947 until his death, Perls lived in North America, where his work influenced and was influenced by the human potential movement. He and Laura founded the Gestalt Institute of America in New York City in 1951. The term *Gestalt therapy* was first used as the title of a book by Perls, Hefferline, and Goodman (1951). However, Gestalt therapy remained relatively unknown until Perls went to the Esalen Institute in California in 1963. During his six years at Esalen, Perls presented workshops using the hot seat format. (The hot seat is a workshop technique in which one individual at a time sits in "the hot seat," where his or her problems are publicly confronted first by the therapist, then by peer group members.) Ironically, the hot seat work at Esalen that so firmly established Gestalt therapy and Perls as the foremost practitioner represented only a small segment of the approach and of Perls's work as a therapist. Perls died in 1970 (Kogan, 1976, pp. 246–253).

Since Perls's death, Gestalt therapy has broadened from the almost guru focus on Perls's teachings. Two husband and wife teams, Erving and Mariam Polster in San Diego, and Robert and Mary Goulding in Esalen, have been major contributors to the evolution and development of Gestalt therapy. The Polsters (1999) did much to establish a more comprehensive theory base, and they moved Gestalt therapy away from the "MEism" of Perls and the 1970s and toward a more social relationship approach. The Gouldings combined Gestalt with transactional analysis and named the hybrid *redecision therapy* (Gladfelter, 1999; Goulding & Goulding, 1979). Redecision therapy can probably fit equally well in either the Gestalt or transactional analysis camps. In the twenty-first century, Gestalt therapy is moving away from some of the excesses of Perls as the unitary spokesman and is being redefined (Polster & Polster, 1999; Shane, 1999). To that extent some Gestalt adherents have taken the concept of holism and extended it to a number of transpersonal areas such as bioenergy, spirituality, and gender issues (Wolfert & Cook, 1999).

Therapists continue to be trained at major Gestalt centers in San Francisco, Cleveland, New York, Los Angeles, and San Diego. The *Gestalt Journal* is the literary organ that disseminates research, theory, and innovative techniques of the approach. The Gestalt movement and Gestalt centers operate worldwide and may be found from Brazil to Germany to Australia.

Overview of Gestalt Therapy

"*Gestalt* is a German word meaning whole or configuration" (Simkin, 1976, p. 225). Perls used it to mean a unique kind of patterning in which parts are integrated into perceptual wholes. This integration is a basic function of human organisms. For the individual, the organization of the world is defined by the subjective reality of his or her perceptions. Thus, the Gestalt approach is said to be phenomenological. That is, it does not attempt to define an absolute reality. The Gestalt approach is also existential, in that it deals with what is currently happening to the individual. In that sense it focuses on the sources of experiences, such as what an individual is thinking and doing and how he or she is feeling. Understanding of the self and others is based on the totality of experience as expressed in gestures, voice, posture, and breathing as well as unspoken words (Passons, 1975, pp. 47–58; Polster, 1992).

Perls's view of human beings was essentially negative—he believed they were manipulative, not self-reliant, and that they avoided responsibility. As a result, Perls felt that the therapist's job was to directly frustrate and confront attempts by the client to escape the tough job of living effectively. The way that the therapist goes about this is not by analyzing the client to death, as the psychoanalytic therapists do, but by creating awareness of what is going on both intrapersonally and interpersonally with the client and integrating that with his or her contacts with the environment. To effectively do that means not letting the client ruminate about the past or what other people or things may do to him or her, but rather to help the client come to grips with his or her experience with as much impact and immediacy as possible. While the past is important because of unresolved contacts and issues ("unfinished business" or "unfinished Gestalts"), the way to attack those issues is to constantly keep the client operating in the "here and now" of the therapeutic moment. By doggedly doing so, the therapist forces the client to constantly confront and make contact with what he or she is trying most to avoid. The client's past will most likely include avoidance of the hurtful affective components of the unfinished business. As such, Gestalt therapy is relentless in pursuing feelings. The default response for Gestalt therapists who are not sure what to do is, "How do you feel about that?" The bottom line is that in Gestalt therapy, awareness—particularly affective awareness—is curative (Perls, 1969, 1971, 1973; Perls, Hefferline, & Goodman, 1951).

Whereas in the heyday of Perls in the 1960s such awareness was almost entirely egocentric, post-Perls Gestalt is also concerned about the interpersonal and intrapersonal awareness of the client. That is to say that relationships have as much emphasis on the *"thou"* as they do on the *"I."* There is less focus on "me" than there was in Perls's period. In current usage, emphasis is on creating a therapeutic dialogue between the client and therapist. Unlike Perls's paternalistic approach, current Gestalt therapists have little or no need to confront the client. These therapists are interested in creating an effective relationship that will allow the client to become interdependent rather than independent of the environment (Passons, 1975, pp. 47–58; Polster, 1992; Polster & Polster 1999).

The general goals of contemporary Gestalt therapy can be summarized as follows:

1. Create awareness of and freedom to experience the maximum potential for living.
2. Operate in the moment, with a here-and-now perspective.
3. Promote responsibility and responds-ability.
4. Provide the ability to experience meaningful contact with oneself, significant others, and the larger ecosystem.
5. Reduce the bipolar dilemmas that pervade people's lives.
6. Bring closure to debilitating events of the past that hinder growth.
7. Provide a more holistic outlook and a plan of action to achieve integration and balance.

Theory of Personality

Gestalt psychology is based on the notion that the whole is greater than the sum of its parts. That is, an individual cannot be reduced to discrete psychological parts and still maintain the essence of the whole person. Likewise, for Gestalt therapists, understanding the integration of the total person (the self) in his or her own phenomenological field is the core of the Gestalt theory of personality. The Gestalt concepts of homeostasis, holism, the development of the capacity for aggression, and field theory provide the primary structural components of viewing the personality.

Homeostasis.   People are motivated by a continual striving for *homeostasis* (balance). This striving is instinctual: it flows from the natural self-regulating rhythm of the organism between the states of equilibrium and disequilibrium (Walker, 1971, pp. 72–74). This homeostatic principle serves to order individual perceptions. We may think of the perception of a need in terms of a figure emerging from a background (Polster & Polster, 1973, pp. 28–32). When a person perceives a need, such as the need to satisfy a sex urge, hunger, or thirst, he or she is said to be in a state of disequilibrium, and a figure (the need) has emerged from the background. Equilibrium is restored when the person can assimilate something from the environment to satisfy the need. With equilibrium restored, the way is clear for the emergence into awareness of a new figure (need). Thus, the person exists in a constant state of flux as a need emerges into the foreground, a way to satisfy the need is selected, the need recedes into the background, and a new need emerges (Walker, 1971, p. 77).

Holism. Holism entails two relationships important to Gestalt theory. The first is the interdependent, inseparable unity of the human body and spirit; the human is a psychological and physical totality. The second relationship is the unity of human beings and environment through their interdependence (Walker, 1971, pp. 77–79).

Aggression. Human interaction in growthful and creative ways in the environment requires the full development of a capacity for aggression (Walker, 1971, pp. 109–111). Aggression can be understood by referring to Perls's explanation of the child's development of this quality. Perls related the development of aggression to teething, which enables the child to attack his or her solid environment by ingesting solid food (Perls, 1969, pp. 108–111). Here, eating is a destructive process (the taking apart of food) that results in the assimilation of food and causes growth. Likewise, the person can "de-structure" other aspects of the environment, assimilate these aspects, and grow as a result.

Field Theory

Field theory proposes that the individual is inextricably linked and related to the environment, and both the individual and the environment are in a constant state of flux, movement, and process (Perls, 1969, 1973). Gestalt therapists are very much interested in what goes on at the interface or boundary markers between the individual and the environment.

The relationship among homeostasis, holism, aggression, and field presupposes that the person and his or her environment coexist (Perls, 1973, pp. 15–18). Although the individual and the environment are separate, the interaction between them cannot be split; the two are a whole. The *ego boundary* defines this interaction. It is both the person's internal and external definitions of him- or herself when engaged in interactions with the environment. In an ideal sense, the ego boundary is not carved in stone but is fluid and elastic to meet the demand of changing conditions (Perls, 1969, p. 7). Human aggression comes into play between the person and the environment by means of contact or withdrawal at a point called the *contact boundary*. More specifically, when an object has been contacted or withdrawn from in a way satisfying to the individual, both the object and the need associated with it disappear into the background. The situation is finished; another Gestalt is completed. A frightened person runs (withdraws) from a dangerous animal, and the situation is finished. Withdrawal may leave some situations unfinished and thus precipitate further avoidance, but at the time of withdrawal, anxiety is reduced and homeostasis is restored.

Problems occur when boundaries become fused. Fusion occurs when the person's own self-identity becomes lost as he or she tries to fit into the environment. Polster and Polster (1973, pp. 115–116) distinguish between four frames of reference when viewing contact boundaries

1. *Familiarity boundaries* are constantly repeated events that are never considered until they are disrupted. One thinks little of a job or a relationship until one is fired or divorced, and then the boundary loss is devastating.
2. *Body boundaries* may restrict general sensations or make various parts of the body be completely off limits to sensations. Psychological frigidity and impotence are classic examples.

3. *Expressive boundaries* are learned at an early age and set the limits for the amount and kinds of feelings we are allowed to display. Display of feelings is a risky business; thus many people have constricted expressive boundaries. Typically, Gestalt therapy will be given the task of the expansion of expressive boundaries.

4. *Value boundaries* are values we hold that are resistant to change. These values are so rigidly held that they represent some of the most difficult and confrontive work the Gestalt therapist must do if these boundaries are to change.

Nature of Maladjustment

Perls (1969, pp. 59–61) viewed neurosis or "growth disorders" (Perls, 1969, p. 30) as the major manifestation of maladjusted behavior. The development of neurotic behavior is related to the development of aggression, the maintenance of homeostasis, the interaction of a person and the environment, and unfinished business.

The neurotic's rhythm of contact and withdrawal (the striving for homeostasis) is itself out of balance. Neurotics do not know when to participate (contact) and when to withdraw because the many unfinished situations of their lives interfere with their sense of orientation. Therefore, they cannot tell which objects in the environment will satisfy their needs. They have lost the freedom of choice because they cannot see the choices that are available (Perls, 1973, pp. 20–24).

Because a person is both an individual and a social creature, the person's life is an interaction between him or her and the environment, which is constantly changing. The individual must be able to change his or her techniques of manipulation and interaction in response. Growth disorders arise when the individual becomes incapable of doing this. His or her behavior becomes the same regardless of the demands of the situation. People are neurotic when their attempts to maintain equilibrium lead them to withdraw farther and farther from society (Perls, 1973, pp. 25–32).

Although some growth disorders are caused by traumatic events, most are caused by day-to-day interference with growth. The neurosis is born as a defense designed to maintain the integrity of the organism, and the neurotic behavior is an attempt to maintain equilibrium within a defensive system.

There are five major boundary disturbances that lead to neurosis: introjection, projection, retroflection, deflection, and confluence (Perls, 1973, pp. 25–32).

Introjection. Psychologically swallowing whole concepts is called *introjection*. Perls compares it to the biological process of eating, digesting, and assimilating nourishment so that the body will grow. Individuals also accept, digest, and assimilate concepts, facts, ethics, and standards from the environment. When these learnings become part of the person, he or she changes and grows. However, if swallowed whole, without digestion and assimilation, they become foreign bodies within the individual. If enough of these concepts and ideas that are not owned by the person are swallowed intact, the person cannot develop a unique personality (Perls, 1973, pp. 32–35).

Introjectors have difficulty knowing what they believe and what they do not believe. They report seeing themselves as phony, superficial, and distant from others. In therapy, the habit of introjection often makes them compliant clients who swallow what the therapist says without assimilating it. Introjectors are exemplified by the dependent client, who willingly does everything the therapist asks but never quite seems to succeed at the task at hand.

Projection. To project is to make someone or something in the environment responsible for what originates in oneself. The person with a healthy personality is aware of owning assumptions and hunches he or she makes about the world; the person who projects is not. Extreme projection results in paranoia. The projector cannot accept his or her feelings and thus attaches them to others. For example, a man may deplore the sexy way a woman is acting when in actuality he cannot accept his own feelings of sexuality. The result is a split between the individual's actual characteristics and his or her awareness of them (Polster & Polster, 1973, pp. 78–82). Words often used in the projector's speech are *they, them, he, she,* and *you.* This third-person approach to contact with the environment means that such individuals are always looking outside themselves for the sources of their problems. The projector needs to experience ownership of his or her feelings and attitudes or, in Gestalt terminology, the "I" of his or her existence (Harman, 1982).

Retroflection. Retroflection is doing to self what one would like to do to others. The retroflector redirects behavior inward and substitutes the self for the environment. For instance, the retroflector turns anger inward rather than expressing it toward others. This behavior creates stress and a rigid and blocked personality. Energy once available for spontaneous behavior and growth is now used to block the release of the retroflected feelings (Polster & Polster, 1973, pp. 82–89). Retroflection in the extreme is the depressed client who turns his or her rage at the world inward and decides to commit suicide as a way of dealing with his or her repressed feelings of anger and rage.

Deflection. Deflection is a subtle maneuver to avoid contact with the environment. The deflector avoids intense emotions; deals mainly in polite civilities; talks about things rather than people; relates problems from an abstract, intellectual, third-person perspective; talks constantly to avoid experiencing interaction; speaks of the there-and-then rather than the here-and-now; and avoids physical contact (Sharf, 1996, p. 258). From a therapeutic standpoint the deflector is passive–aggressive. The deflector is like cotton candy—there is the appearance of a lot of stuff, but there is little emotional substance for the therapist to sink his or her teeth into because the client seeks to avoid contact in the present therapeutic moment.

Confluence. Confluence is the absence of a boundary between self and the environment. People who are pathologically confluent are unaware of the boundary between themselves and others. Thus they cannot make good contact; nor can they withdraw. In less extreme confluence, the person cannot tolerate differences in others from him- or herself and may instead demand likeness from them. An example of this type of confluent behavior is the parent who considers the child an extension of him- or herself (Perls, 1973, pp. 38–40). The parent becomes so fused with the child that all contact boundaries are lost. The child must act, sleep, breathe, and do what the parent demands. At a minimum, the backstage mom or the grandstand dad both depict a confluent approach. Both are frustrated in missing out on their fantasy career goals and thus project them through their offspring. At a more lethal level, the spurned lover who becomes a stalker, the jealous spouse who becomes a batterer, and the borderline personality disorder who blatantly disregards socially sanctioned boundaries are all individuals with confluence issues.

Unfinished Business.   People have the capacity to tolerate a great number of unfinished situations. These remain in the background, influencing behavior and perceptions. For instance, a hungry person may perceive an ambiguous stimulus as food. A person with an unresolved conflict with a parent will play out this conflict with a spouse or a supervisor. People perceive in the present what was unfinished in the past. The figure that emerges from the background is the material for the Gestalt therapeutic encounter. This figure may change as new aspects of it come into awareness.

People who have growth disorders are overwhelmed by unfinished business and all of the negative affect that goes with it. They expend all of their energy attempting to solve their long-buried and largely unconscious problems and are overwhelmed when the same dilemmas constantly present themselves again and again and are met with the same ineffective responses.

Unfinished business, then, has to do with unfulfilled needs, unexpressed feelings, and uncompleted situations (Thompson & Rudolph, 1996, p. 142) that may be submerged from conscious awareness but are continuously recycled and demand attention. Unfinished business puts the client in an endless feedback emotional loop in which the old problem continuously reemerges, sometimes in the same form and with the same situation (an attempt to rekindle a broken romance), sometimes camouflaged in a slightly altered situation (new person but same doomed romantic tactics as before). The individual may attempt to "get it right" over and over but even if successful (she finally hits the romance lottery and comes up with the grand prize) may still somehow feel unresolved and unfulfilled because the past business (the old romance with all its traps and snares) has not been finished. As a result, unfinished business deals mainly with negative feelings, fantasies, and memories such as abandonment, estrangement, guilt, fear, anger, hatred, remorse, and sorrow (Sharf, 1996, p. 260). One of the major goals of Gestalt therapy is to create awareness of the unfinished business and bring closure to it—in short, to "finish" it.

Major Concepts

Here-and-Now Orientation.   Interventions in Gestalt therapy are built on actual present behavior. Present behavior is not just defined as what the client is talking about, but rather as how congruent or incongruent the body language of the client is with what he or she is saying. For Gestalt therapy, becoming aware of what is going on with one's body is directly related with what is going on with one's self (Clance, Thompson, & Simerly, 1994). Talking about what happened "way back when," whether twenty years or five minutes ago, is a safe way of avoiding contact with the emotionality of the moment and particularly contact with the therapist in the therapeutic environment. Therefore, one of the major tasks of the Gestalt therapist is to aggressively frustrate the client's attempts to break out of the awareness of the "here-and-now" and retreat to the "there-and-then."

Awareness. In Gestalt therapy, awareness is everything. Awareness is the ability of the client to be in full mental and sensory awareness of experiencing the now. As such, it is viewed as curative. Gestalt therapists are not opposed to using humor, sarcasm, dramatics, confrontation, and shock to create awareness. Perls, in particular, was not opposed to using these techniques. Little time is spent by the therapist rehashing the client's history of problems in an attempt to gain insight. Rather, the experimental nature of the therapeutic encounter is to aid the client in becoming aware of present behavior and developing and experimenting with new behaviors (Thompson & Rudolph, 1996, p. 144).

The therapist calls attention to the individual's posture, breathing, mannerisms, gestures, voice, and facial expressions. For example, clients are asked to experience their posture and then to put into words the existential meaning of the posture. A man who speaks with his jaw and chest thrust forward may live his life as a battle. His existence is reflected in his posture. Interventions are almost exclusively in the form of "what" and "how" questions, such as "What are you doing?" and "How are you feeling?" These questions keep awareness centered in the present. The therapist prevents the individual from escaping experience by focusing on present awareness. To this end, he or she instructs the client to complete the basic sentence, "Now I am aware . . . " The word *I* is emphasized because it symbolizes ownership of what is going on with the person (Walker, 1971, pp. 76–93).

Responsibility. Gestalt therapy views the existential meaning of the word *responsibility* as one of its basic concepts. Responsibility means that each individual, and no one else, determines the essence of his or her existence. Further, it means owning one's projections instead of blaming others for one's thoughts, feelings, impulses, and behaviors. Responsibility is also *response-ability,* or the ability to respond. Whenever a person acts, decides, or chooses, he or she is exercising response-ability (Perls, 1973, p. 68).

Polarities. When organismic self-regulation is interfered with, the person may experience internal or interpersonal conflicts. These conflicts occur between thoughts, traits, values, and actions that are polar opposites. Generosity and stinginess, for example, are opposite poles of a "giving" continuum.

Integrating these polarities is a primary therapeutic goal. Whenever an individual recognizes an aspect of him- or herself, the antithesis (the polar opposite) of this characteristic can become powerful enough to emerge from the background as a figure.

Assagioli (1965) has identified five generic polarities that include physical, emotional, mental, spiritual, and interindividual issues. The bipolar dilemmas that generate out of these generic issues are infinite in number and a great deal of time is spent by most of us in figuring out how to get off the horns of these everyday dilemmas. One of the most famous Gestalt techniques is the "empty chair," which is used to let clients literally sit on either side of the dilemma and have a dialogue with the empty chair on the other side. At a deeper level these polarities may be longstanding and deeply embedded in the individual and are part of an unfinished gestalt the client needs to complete. Thus, integrating polarities involves facilitating full awareness of them by experiencing them during therapy (Simkin, 1975, pp. 9–10).

Top Dog/Under dog.   Gestalt therapists frequently use the term *top dog* or *under dog* when they refer to polar opposites. The top dog takes the role of the parental authoritarian who says, "I know what is best for you." The under dog sabotages the top dog by playing helpless: "I don't know how to do that. Will you help me?" The top dog is a righteous, moralist authoritarian. The under dog is the wheedling, excuse-making, defensive, cunning, pleasure-seeking "I want it" part of the person. This polarity is a major player in the person's life and each of its sides is constantly vying for control of the individual. A typical empty chair exercise involving these polarities will have a dialogue between "I should" and "I want" parts of the person (Sharf, 1996, p. 268; Thompson & Rudolph, 1996, p. 146).

Environmental Contact.   "The function that synthesizes the human need for union and separation is contact" (Polster & Polster, 1973, p. 99). Contact is necessary for growth. It is the means for changing oneself and one's experience of the world. When one makes contact with the environment, change is inescapable because of one's assimilation or rejection of what was contacted. Learning that one likes the taste of alcohol upon having one's first mixed drink and embracing a religious belief after hearing a charismatic speaker are examples of change with contact.

The problem is that many of our contacts are not assimilated in positive ways and wind up fragmenting our lives so that we become stuck and immobilized and are able to only make neurotic contact with the environment. According to Perls (1969, 1971) there are five layers of neurotic contact that represent psychological growth.

1. The *phony* layer. Attempting to be somebody one is not, reacting in stereotypical patterns, doling out meaningless platitudes, being insincere, and lying for self-enhancement or gain are some of the activities that make people phony. A great deal of time is spent by many clients building and maintaining these facades.

2. The *phobic* layer. Phobias are set in place as a way to avoid feared psychological pain. As people become more aware of their phoniness, they become more frightened about their own vulnerability and set in place a variety of defense mechanisms to keep them from imagined harm.

3. The *impasse* layer. When the games people play during the first two layers are no longer effective and are dropped or extinguished, they are likely to become stuck because the individuals do not know of a better way to cope with their fears and inadequacies.

4. The *implosive* layer. When all the previous roles are stripped away, people begin to be aware of how they limit themselves and commence experimenting with new behaviors. In essence, they pull themselves together, contracting, compressing, and imploding as they reintegrate into different people.

5. The *explosive* layer. As reintegration occurs and new behaviors are learned, a great deal of pent-up energy becomes available. This energy mushrooms out with a new, more authentic person who is now capable of experiencing and expressing emotions.

Figure–Ground.   Magic Eye prints are an excellent, if not maddening, example of visual figure–ground Gestalts. For many people the background of squiggle lines is meaningless until the perceptual area of their brains can pierce through the lines and have the submerged figure suddenly pop into awareness. Emotional figure-ground configurations are analogous to Magic Eye prints. A past unresolved incident (an argument with one's first love that leads to a broken engagement) gets pushed into a mental file drawer due to the emergence of other pressing matters. As time passes, the squiggle lines of history cover it up, but it is not gone—merely covered! Wheeler (1991, pp. 53–54) cautions that Gestalt therapy is much more than exclusive attention to the emerging figure. To adhere to the holistic nature of Gestalt therapy, therapeutic attention should also focus on the relational context from which the figure emerges. This relational context is the ground of the client's existence and provides the backdrop for the client's behavior. To ignore the ground is to become figure-bound. To attend to the interplay between figure and ground provides a holistic rather than an episodic approach to Gestalt therapy.

The Counseling Process

Central Focus

During the years since Perls's death, the focus of Gestalt therapy has shifted toward a style that is more relational in nature. In this shift, the therapeutic power of the relationship is acknowledged; a trend toward support for and less frustration of the client is advised; a balance between here-and-now emphasis and historical perspective is allowed; and attention to rational thought as well as feeling and sensation is permitted (Hendlin, 1987). This shift in focus has resulted in a more balanced integration of mind/body, emotion/intellect, and individual/relational aspects of therapy.

Within this more integrative brand of Gestalt practice, the therapist will facilitate the individual's awareness of self and all the feelings, behaviors, experiences, and unfinished situations that make up the self. Four aspects of human experience on which awareness can be focused are discussed next.

Sensation and Action. *Sensation* refers to physical experience, such as hunger, itching, heart palpitation, pain, warmth, tingling, and relaxation; *action* refers to behavior. Often sensation and action are related minimally if at all. This means that the individual may be unaware of sensation and not act on it, or feel sensation but still not act on it. At times of union between sensation and action, profound feelings of integration are present. This union, which the Polsters call the *synaptic experience,* is the matrix of creativity. "In this state of aliveness, wholeness, and spontaneous expression, [the individual] is dancing on the edge of awareness" (Polster & Polster, 1973, p. 215).

The Gestalt therapist explores sensation by asking what the person is experiencing while he or she is talking about a concern. A major component of Gestalt therapy in general, and sensation in particular, is the creation of awareness of nonverbal behavior. Gestalt therapy takes much more interest in body language than most therapies. It does so because it believes that individuals whose body language and verbal language are congruent with one another are much more integrated in their functioning. Witness the mother who talks of her daughter's drug addiction, how it is tearing the family apart, utters a nervous laugh, states that she and her husband are now together on how to approach the problem, and things will now be better; as she does so, she changes her body position, crosses her arms tightly against her body, and tucks her legs up to her chest. Clearly the verbal messages of the family's togetherness are not congruent with what her body says about the problem.

Passons (1975, pp. 101–102) believes there are four important reasons for closely monitoring the body language of a client. First, each physical behavior is an expression of a person at that particular instant. Rarely are physical movements in the intensity of a therapeutic situation random events. Second, nonverbal behaviors seldom are preconceived or planned. In that regard, they are a better indicator of the true emotional state of the client. Third, clients are usually far more attuned to what they are saying as opposed to what their bodies are doing. Pointing out what a person's body is doing in relation to what is being said is a powerful way of creating awareness. Fourth, becoming aware of and getting body language congruent with verbal language is a powerful tool in creating awareness and changing behavior, particularly in males (Clance, Thompson, & Simerly, 1994).

Feelings.   Gestalt therapy aims to make room for feelings so that the unfinished situations they are attached to can be integrated into life. This integration is accomplished through awareness in much the same way that sensation is integrated into life. As the client talks, the therapist artfully moves him or her back and forth between awareness and feelings, actions, and verbal expression to emphasize the substance and drama in the story and to fill in gaps in experience. For example, the therapist may ask the client, "What are your feelings now?" or may tell the client, "Stay with that feeling and see where it leads you" or "Get into the feeling of anger as if you were angry" (Polster & Polster, 1973, pp. 222–227).

Wants.   Awareness of wants directs, mobilizes, and channels the individual's actualizing tendencies. Wants link present experience and future gratification. Knowing what one wants motivates action. The Gestalt therapist asks the client, "What do you want?" The goal of this question is to get the individual to define wants so that they emerge as figures in a figure-ground configuration. Then the individual can decide how to attain them (Polster & Polster, 1973, pp. 227–230).

Values and Assessments.   Values and assessments are larger units of experience than sensation, feelings, and wants. One goal of Gestalt therapy is to sort out values and assessments so that actions can be rooted in current needs rather than in evaluations based on behavior that was required in the past. When dealing with values and assessments, the therapist may be tapping a whole range of judgments and internal contradictions that are no longer appropriate to the current situation. Part of the therapeutic process is to help the individual rebuild new values by integrating the person he or she was with the person he or she is now. This may involve focusing awareness on the past by bringing it into present experience. The person is then free to respond differently to old situations because current responses can be based on current evaluations rather than on past evaluations (Polster & Polster, 1973, pp. 230–232).

In summary, sensory awareness of past, present, and future events, feelings, cognitions, beliefs, and perceptions is experienced in the here and now of therapy. A major assumption of Gestalt therapy is that such awareness will bring the unfinished situation into the foreground of the individual's perception. Through active participation in therapy, the client experiences and assimilates experience rather than interrupting it, and thereby reowns alienated parts of his or her personality and reintegrates them into a new conception of self. This part of therapy is called *closure* or *completing the unfinished gestalt.*

Conditions of Growth

The therapist's job is to introduce a new situation in which excitement exists, contact can be made, and growth can occur. The key to the therapeutic endeavor is to keep the level of excitement within manageable limits.

Polster (1985) describes a three-phrase integration sequence in which the therapist uses support to keep the client's excitement within manageable limits. The first phase of this sequence is *discovery.* Discovery involves bringing an issue into the foreground so that it becomes a figure and the client achieves awareness of it. *Accommodation,* the second phase, involves adjusting to the excitement of discovery. This phase has implications for action outside therapy and mobilizes the client's own resources to deal with this excitement. *Assimilation* is the third phase; it involves making a new behavior part of oneself. For a while during this phase, the new behavior will be situation-bound, but later it can become a natural part of the person's behavior.

Strategies for Helping Clients

Probably no other therapeutic modality has developed more techniques, or what Perls calls *games* (Levitsky & Perls, 1970), than Gestalt. In one way or another, all of these techniques are designed to do one thing—to bring emotional awareness and integration of experience to the client.

Confrontation

For any one who has seen Fritz Perls in action, the watchword would be *confrontation.* In fact, one of the stereotypes of Gestalt therapy is its confrontive stance à la Perls. While there are numerous techniques that use confrontation to motivate the client to enactment, most contemporary Gestalt therapists use it parsimoniously to point out incongruencies between what the client says and how the client acts. Confrontation is a useful tool that does not have to be used in a vindictive, scathing, satirical, or narcissistic way. Many times clients cannot or will not see their incongruities. A passive, reflective response is not likely to help them much. A subtle kind of confrontation that invites the client to become involved can be taken from the *Columbo* television series, in which Detective Columbo would plead with a suspect to straighten him out on some detail.

> TH: I am a bit puzzled about this, so I need you to help me straighten it out. On the one hand you said you were through agonizing about getting engaged to Jeff, but just then you started chewing vigorously on your fingernails. What's that all about? I just can't figure that out.

Use of Language

Gestalt therapy is very keen on proper use of language. *Proper* means using language that will promote awareness and integration in the client's experience.

"What" and "How" Questions.   "What" and "how" questions are used a great deal to keep the client in the present moment. "Why" questions typically lead to resistant behavior through intellectualization of the problem; externalization to other people, places, and things; and soliloquies about past injustices.

"I" Statements.   "I" statements encourage clients to own their feelings and experiences rather than talk about other people or events. Clients are continuously encouraged to use "I" statements and confronted when they use disowned messages such as "she made me" or "it was out of my control" or "my mother (God, the police officer, the principal, etc.) hates me."

Present Tense.   Whether clients are talking about past experiences (unfinished business) or the future (catastrophizing), they are encouraged to speak in the present tense. For example, "When I think of how mother treated us all, I get goose bumps all over. I see her getting out the paint paddle for some small infraction and I am terrified." These statements bring the event into real time and let the client experience it as if it were happening now.

Taking Responsibility.   Gestalt therapy has a number of semantic techniques to help clients take responsibility. The "Who told you that?" question is repeated to clients until they run out of others to blame and start taking responsibility for their actions. Clients who continuously make excuses for their behavior are asked to make their implicit feelings explicit by making clear assertion statements about what they will and will not do. Instead of "Yes dear, I'll get on that just as soon as I finish _____," the assertive response is, "I will do that on Monday. Right now I want to relax." Confronting clients about projecting their faults onto others can be accomplished by having the client own the projection. Instead of "I wish he was more romantic," the statement is owned: "I want more romance."

Feeding a Sentence.   The therapist feeds the client a sentence that he or she feels is significant for the client. The client then tries the sentence on for size by saying it. Typically, the statement will generate out of an interpretation of the client's behavior that is unconscious or unobserved by the client.

> TH: As I've listened it seems it's not the sex that is scary, but the intimacy of it. I'd like you to say this statement: "I am scared to death of intimacy with a man because it would turn out just like my mother and father."

Body Work

A great deal of body work is done in Gestalt therapy. The therapist actively manipulates the client's body to make it congruent with what is being said. One way is by having clients exaggerate subtle nonverbal cues they give off.

TH: Every time you get bored and frustrated, I see your foot start to tap. What I would like you to do is to really start to bounce your foot now. Pound it on the floor and tell me what you are feeling.

When clients attest that they feel a certain way but their body says something entirely different, the therapist puts the two into congruence.

TH: You say you want to stand up for yourself when somebody attacks you but you are slumped over as you practice being assertive. Throw your chest out and your shoulders back and get your arms and hands up and out.

Quite often clients will complain that they feel funny or odd when they do these things. Such feelings can be excellent enactment cues that tell them they are changing and integrating actions and feelings.

Another way to point out inconsistencies between what clients' bodies are saying and what is coming out of their mouths is to anthropomorphize the body part.

TH: If the tears that are now welling up in your eyes could talk, what would they say about your agreement to get married?

TH: I noticed you drumming your fingers when you said that your wedding day will be the happiest day of your life. I wonder if you could prop your elbow on the table, turn your hand around to your face, and have a dialogue with those drumming fingers about how happy you are to be getting married.

The Experiment

The experiment is the means by which much of Gestalt therapy is conducted. By playing out feelings and actions in the relative safety of therapy, the individual is mobilized to confront difficulties and emergencies in life (Polster & Polster, 1973, pp. 237–244). Several forms of the experiment are described: (1) enactment, (2) directed behavior, and (3) fantasy and guided imagery.

Enactment.   Enactment is based on the idea that learning requires action. In Gestalt therapy, enactment involves dramatizing some aspect of the individual's existence.

The following dialogue illustrates the use of enactment with a 25-year-old university student struggling to accept his impending blindness. His rehabilitation counselor has recommended preparing for his blindness by participating in mobility training with either a cane or a guide dog. The student is extremely resistant to engaging in any behavior that will call attention to his visual impairment. One of the issues that clearly emerges from this struggle is his strong desire to be viewed as an independent person. His therapist suggests the experiment of engaging in a dialogue between two aspects of himself, the side that is currently functioning independently and the side that will one day require accommodation and assistance in his daily living. In an attempt to concretize the feelings about the bipolar dilemma, the therapist proposes that the client give character names to the feeling states. Polster (1995) proposes that the therapeutic aim of synthesizing alienated aspects of ourselves can be done by construction of heterogeneous characters. Each character should have its own place and voice because within each of us reside a host of characters that, depending on conditions, may be more or less prominent at any given time.

TH: Can you give names to those two feelings, just as if they were real people, but components of yourself?

CL: The independent one would be Iron Mike, the dependent one would be Wimp.

TH: Start out by talking to Wimp.

CL: You won't be able to do anything by yourself. You'll have to rely on other people all the time. You'll have to ask people to help you. You won't be able to read. Somebody will have to drive you to school. You won't be able to take care of yourself, and you'll be a burden to everyone. (*pauses*) You're nothing but a wimp! Useless!

TH: Is there anything else you want to say? (*shakes head no*) Okay, then, switch chairs and answer from Wimp's side.

CL: Well, I don't know what to say. It seems pretty bad to me too. (*Thinks a while, then speaks from dependent side.*) When it comes right down to it, you're either going to have to make some adjustments or just give up.

TH: Change sides and answer from Iron Mike's side.

CL: It just isn't that simple. (*angry tone and fist clinched*) I hate to have to ask anybody for anything. I've always been able to get by on my own. Never needed anyone. I don't want to start now. You can have your adjusting.

TH: Okay. Answer him.

CL: (*long pause and without much energy*) It doesn't seem to me that adjusting is always asking for help. Like the rehab counselor said, you can still do a lot of things on your own even when you can't see. You could learn to use a cane and you could go through that rehab place.

TH: How do you feel as you take Wimp's side?

CL: Sad and frightened. But maybe if I can get Iron Mike to come around we can whip this.

TH: Ask him for help.

CL: Look, if you're so tough then I need your help. I don't know whether I can handle this. (*starts to shake*)

TH: Switch sides. What do you want to say to him?

CL: You can't handle it, what do you think I feel?

TH: What do you feel?

CL: (*jaw clenched*) I feel like I've got to carry the whole load. I always have, but now I'm not so sure I can. It really makes me angry and scared, too.

TH: So what do you want to do with that anger and fear, Mike? If that clenched jaw could talk, what would it say?

CL: By God! Make it work somehow. Get my courage back, but I'm not so sure I can.

TH: Get up from the chairs. (*Client steps out and away from the chairs.*) I'm wondering if one of these sides seems more preferable. Which chair would you choose?

CL: Neither one, really, and both. Wimp is reasonable and Iron Mike is strong, but they're both afraid of going blind. Somehow I need to get the strong and reasonable together so they can both handle the fear.

Although the enactment did not provide an integration of the polarities, there does seem to have been some movement in the client's thinking about his dilemma. There was also considerable awareness that there is more than one side to the argument. As this awareness is internalized and affects feelings, some integration will occur.

By concretizing the independent/dependent feeling states through character names, the client is able to bring abstract feeling states into more realistic terms that can be identified and addressed. As more feelings surface, more names may be added to the character repertoire and their strengths and weaknesses examined for the parts they play in helping or hindering the client as he attempts to come to grips with his approaching disability. The empty chair is not a cure-all. What it will do is resolve the split between the client's top dog and underdog and allow the polarity to come into awareness so that the client can confront his ambivalent feelings and take responsibility for both sides. After this awareness occurs, then the therapist can move the client past the first two neurotic stages of phoniness and phobic responses to the impasse stage where the client is now stuck (Friedman, 1993).

The therapist also uses two techniques that are standard with Gestalt work. She allows the client to experience the polarity and then uses a processing question: "How do you feel?" The continuous use of this question throughout the exercise is designed to keep the client continuously attuned to his feeling state as he moves back and forth. By pointing out to the client his clenched jaw, the therapist also seeks to make the client aware of his body language and how congruent it is with his verbal responses.

Directed Behavior. This strategy involves instructing or guiding the person in something that uncovers or highlights some aspect of behavior that may have been blocked from awareness. For example, a directed behavior experiment may instruct the person to practice behaviors that the person does not recognize as his or her own. A woman who has a little girl's voice but does not realize this may be asked deliberately to talk like a little girl. Another example would be to direct a shy and unassuming person to speak with assertiveness and authority to the group. Both of these experiments can lead to deeper self-awareness in the directed person and can open the way to new and creative behavior.

The following directed behavior was used to help a male client with the issue of unconditional versus conditional acceptance, particularly by his mother. He thought her love was conditional on his achievements. The therapist directed the client to approach each group member, stand in from of him or her, make eye contact, and say "I don't have to do anything for you to like me. I am good enough for you to like me for myself."

CL: (*reluctantly agrees and begins awkwardly with the first group member*) I don't have to do anything for you to like me. I'm okay just as I am.

(*The client stands rather meekly, with shoulders hunched over and arms hanging loosely at his sides.*)

TH: Notice how you're standing and your voice tone. (*The therapist goes over to the client and pulls his shoulders back and puts both hands on his hips.*) How does that feel?

CL: Weird! Like it's not me.

TH: I'd like you to experiment with that weird feeling a bit, because what you're doing verbally isn't you yet either. Perhaps by taking that weird, not you posture, that can serve as a kind of cue for the new you you're trying to build.

As the client proceeded around the group, his tone became more assertive and he received hugs and other nonverbal support from the group.

TH: How was that for you? What was your experience?

CL: I really felt like I didn't have to do anything for them to like me. It's the first time I can remember feeling that way. I hope I can hang onto it.

Fantasy and Guided Imagery.   Fantasy can be used to make contact with a resisted event, feeling, or personal characteristic; an unavailable person; an unfinished situation; or the unknown (Polster & Polster, 1973, pp. 255–265). As in enactment, there is often a tremendous release of emotional energy during the fantasy. One example of fantasy is contacting a parent or significant other who has died. Repressed emotion, unfinished business, and resistance to thinking and talking about the death are likely to be evident. In this experiment the therapist instructs the person to imagine the deceased person sitting and facing him or her (an empty chair is often placed in front of the person) and to engage in dialogue with the deceased person (Field & Horowitz, 1998). During the dialogue the therapist may instruct the client to tell the deceased person what he or she resented and appreciated about him or her and to express guilt for past actions. The client can also be directed to take the role of the deceased and to project what the deceased would say to him or her about resentments, appreciations, and guilts. Then the client and the deceased say goodbye, symbolizing a letting go of each other. This farewell, usually accompanied by a release of emotion, may bring a sense of relief or peace with the closure of the unfinished situation.

The following excerpt depicts a client who has been verbally abusive with his wife and daughter. He has a great deal of trouble expressing his own feelings. The course of therapy has revealed that his father was a cold, emotionally distant parent who was verbally abusive to the client both as a child and an adult. The father died five years ago. The following scenario depicts the use of guided imagery to help the client get in touch with feelings he has for his father and complete some unfinished business with him.

CL: I don't know what to say about my old man. He never beat me but he was pretty cold.

TH: Could you just close your eyes and imagine what that feeling of "cold" would be?

CL: Like his tombstone. Grayish, black granite, hard, and in January with the snow blowing. It sends a chill down my spine.

TH: Where are you in the scene?

CL: Standing off to the side looking at it. Wanting to say or do something, but not sure what.

TH: What would you like to do?

CL: Get rid of it. I hate that thing.

TH: Do that.

CL: I don't know how, it's granite. I need some tools, like a jackhammer.

TH: Put an air hammer and compressor into your image. What's happening?

CL: I start in on it, chipping at it, but it's really hard.

TH: How are you feeling?

CL: Frustrated. Like I always was with him cause he was immobile and wouldn't crack.

TH: What would help you out?

CL: Like, a crane with a wrecking ball and a rock crusher.

TH: They're now in your image, so go ahead and use them. Tell me what's happening.

CL: Man, I knocked a big chunk out of it. How does that feel? Not so tough now. (*smile crosses face*) Now I'll grind that up. There, it's dust. (*continues to work on breaking up tombstone*)

TH: How are you feeling?

CL: (*perspiration on client's face, hands clenched*) Better, but not happy. Really, kind of sad. Like I wished he wouldn't have been that way, but he needed to have that hard rock shell busted off of him.

TH: What would you like to say to your father now that you have busted away the hard rock?

CL: That I miss the times we fished together and I loved him for those times, but despised him for not being there when I needed his emotional support.

TH: Say that to him as if he were here right now.

CL: (*says that to father's gravesite in image and continues talking out his positive and negative feelings toward the deceased parent*)

TH: Can he hear you?

CL: Yes, now that I've got the rock busted away.

TH: Anything else you'd like to do with that image?

CL: Yes, I don't even want that rock dust around, it's gritty and nasty.

TH: How do you want to get rid of it?

CL: Load it up in a dump truck and dump it in the river.

TH: Do that. How do you feel?

CL: Like it's finished, relieved maybe.

TH: Open your eyes and tell me what this experience has meant.

CL: I guess the thing that strikes me the most is I don't want my daughter sitting in an office like this in twenty years doing the same thing I just did, but to me. That scares me, and I'm gonna need to make some changes with her so that doesn't happen.

The guided imagery is used as a way of getting the client in touch with his feelings. Note that it is not the father but the feeling of "cold" that is operationalized in the image, because it is the feeling about the relationship that needs to be finished, not the parent. When the client is at an impasse, the "guided" part of the imagery occurs. The therapist provides the client with the necessary equipment to move the image forward. The therapist also stops periodically and processes how the client is feeling. Indeed, as new feelings emerge, it is not uncommon to symbolize those feelings and bring them out into the foreground. At times, if the image is stuck, the therapist may physically move the client around in the scene so that he can achieve a different perspective. The therapist may have the client assume the role of the tombstone because there is a good deal of evidence that the tombstone is an integral part of the client as well. Finally, the therapist brings the image into real time by asking the client to process the experience. The "aha" experience he has in seeing his daughter in his place is typical of the insights clients gain through this procedure.

Sample Case

Carol is a 33-year-old single parent who how has come to therapy because of anxiety attacks and a variety of somatic problems, including high blood pressure and irritable bowel syndrome. A prevailing theme in her life is attempting to balance the demands of her children, Becky, 13, and Jack, 16, and her semi-invalid mother who is attempting to live independently but is highly dependent on Carol. She reports a recent dream about becoming a lamb. While the dream seems benign, she says she woke up drenched in sweat and very upset. The therapist directs her to engage in a dialogue with the lamb.

A dream can serve as the basis for an experiment that brings the dream material to life in therapy. According to Perls (1973, pp. 73–76), dreams are projections of the person; various parts of a dream represent various aspects of the person's existence. In dream work, the person is instructed to recount a dream or a fragment of a dream, speaking in the present tense as if the dream were happening at that moment. After the dream, or a portion of it, is recounted, the person is instructed to play out the parts of the dream, usually by engaging in a dialogue with those parts.

TH: So why don't we start out with you talking to the lamb.

CL: I don't like to talk to something that can't answer me back, but . . . (*pause*)

TH: Develop that a little.

CL: (*to the lamb*) I'd like to talk to you if you could talk back to me. I think you are kind of cute, fuzzy. I hate to think that you are going to have to grow up because I think you're having more fun right now than when you are grown. Maybe you don't feel like that, but you can't tell me. I see you wanting to get out of the chair and run. You don't seem to have any patience. So just go and run. You don't have to stay here with me because I can still like you when you're way off in the distance and that's kind of nice.

TH: Okay, switch chairs. Now you're the lamb talking back to Carol.

CL: (*voice becomes childlike*) I'm kind of glad you think I'm so cute because I think I'm kind of nice. I like to be fuzzy because when I rub up against a stone it doesn't hurt because I have so much protection. But I really would rather run. I don't like to stay in one place too long. Just let me go and play by myself and then come back and play with all the other lambs.

TH: What is that? (*no answer*) Who is that?

CL: I suppose it's me.

TH: Uh . . . (*client begins to cry*) What's happening? (*pause*) Go ahead and stay with that. (*client cries with more intensity*) Just keep breathing. (*pause*) Can you give a voice to your tears?

CL: (*voice wavering and tears in eyes*) I suppose it's because I feel too much responsibility right now, and I don't want it. I'm in the middle of two generations and most of the time it's very lonely. Right now, I just want to leave it. But if I left it, there would be misunderstanding and sadness. There would be an unsympathetic attitude.

The two sides of this client's existential dilemma have emerged—the part of the client that wants to be free and the part that is trapped by her sense of responsibility for her family. A dialogue is set up between these parts.

TH: What I'd like you to do is put Carol over there (*pointing to the empty chair designated "overly responsible Carol," located opposite from another empty chair designated "responsible Carol"*), the side of Carol who would like to be free, who has too much responsibility. And tell her what the consequences would be if she did what she wanted to do.

CL: (*client takes responsible role instead*) Huh!—you can't believe what would happen—well, if you just took off now, you know how your family would feel. Your daughter would be upset because she wouldn't understand. Your mother would be upset because she would think you had to be there when your daughter needed you or when your son needed you.

TH: You'd let a lot of people down.

CL: Yeah—obviously—I couldn't do it. You could do it, *but* after you had been gone a day or so, you would be miserable. It would be much better to go when everyone understood why you are going. Until you can reach this understanding, I don't think you should (*pauses and laughs*), but anyway . . . (*trails off and seems to realize she is talking to herself*).

TH: Go ahead and give it to her. She's irresponsible.

CL: You can't go until they *understand,* because you *should* care enough about their feelings not to hurt them. When everything is fine, then you can leave.

TH: Talk to the real responsible person who is going to take care of all those people—solid-as-a-rock Carol. And you (*indicating other chair*) are Carol who wants to run in pastures and be free.

CL: (*laughs*) I understand what you are telling me, but right now I think it's a lot of bull (*rapid, firm speech with seemingly decisive tone*). If I want to go and do, I should be able to do so. I have stayed patient for a long enough period of time, and if I want to go away and do something I should be able to do it. I'm old enough to know what to do, and I don't think it's going to upset anyone if I just take off. When I come back I would be easier to live with, feel better, and have a different frame of mind.

TH: What do you resent about Carol over there?

CL: I resent her saying I should be more responsible.

TH: Say that again.

CL: (*stronger tone*) I resent you saying I should be more responsible for my children, for my mother, but you don't say (*cries*) I should be more responsible for me.

TH: Stay with that.

CL: Just let me be me. (*pause*) I want to be me. (*in tears*) I feel I could be more me if I didn't keep hearing how I should be feeling all the time. (*words measured and slower*) I could be more myself if everyone wasn't so demanding of my time.

TH: Plus the family is too demanding.

When the therapist proposed that the family is too demanding, Carol responded by bringing her family into focus. She was then instructed to engage in a dialogue with her family because her energy had seemed to switch toward them and away from herself.

TH: Okay. Let's just do this. Put mom and the kids over there and give them hell. They deserve it.

CL: (*bursts out laughing*) But maybe they don't. Becky, you expect too much of me economically. You expect too much of my time, and I think you expect me to accept whatever mood you're in without caring how I feel.

TH: Tell her what you don't like about that.

CL: I think you should understand from a point of view of economics why some things are not feasible, like a new pair of designer jeans. When you have six pairs, you don't need a seventh pair. I also don't always have time to take you where you want to go, and there are some places that I don't think you should go. Because you upset me this way, that interferes with my time to be myself because I worry about you.

TH: I want a lot for you. (*feeds Carol a line to say to her daughter*)

CL: Mm-hm. I do want a lot for you, but there are limitations.

TH: I want you to respect me. (*feeds another line*)

CL: No. Not so much that. I know it's difficult to live with someone else. There are times when you can like someone and can't love them and times when you love someone but can't like them. I think you should understand that. And Mama (*angrily switches to mother*), I wish you would stop telling me how the children should behave. If I can live with it, then you should be able to live with it. I think it's unfair to always take it out on me when you think the children don't behave the way you think they should. They have a right to like me, love me, or not, and that is their decision.

At this point it seemed appropriate for the therapist to instruct Carol to talk with her son rather than having Mama engage in dialogue with her, because her last sentence to Mama was said with finality.

TH: What do you want to say to Jack?

CL: Jack, I think you know I wish you were a little neater. I think sometimes you are too much alone, but there's nothing I can do for you. If that's how you are comfortable, then that's fine. Other than that, cut your hair. (*laughs*)

TH: Tell Jack what you appreciate about him.

CL: I like your care, your concern. I appreciate your doing what I ask you to do. I appreciate that you care enough for me to be concerned about different things. That you don't cause any waves between Becky and you. I enjoy you because I can talk to you like an adult. I think the times we have together are fun. I appreciate your sense of humor. I really (*voice breaks*) love you. (*cries, pauses*)

In this session Carol's awareness of her existence emerged sharply, as did some self-discovery and some clarification of her feelings toward family members. She also showed awareness of her responsibility for her existence, but seemed barely able to acknowledge any choice in her life. There seemed to be no integration of the polarities of freedom and responsibility during the session.

Contributions of Gestalt Therapy

One of the major contributions of Gestalt therapy is its experiential nature. Talk about the problem, conflict, or issue is minimized and actual experiencing of its existential meaning for the individual is maximized. Whereas some therapies attempt to change behavior directly without changing the person, Gestalt therapy uses clients' behavior to make them aware of their creative potential to discover for themselves and to facilitate their own change.

One of the toughest problems in therapy is getting clients to open up to their affect. Although Gestalt groups became notorious for their hot seat approach and encounter group format in the 1960s and 1970s, no therapy has served the cause of increasing emotional awareness better than Gestalt. The techniques used in Gestalt to get at denied and shunted emotions are without parallel and work when no others will.

Another contribution of Gestalt therapy is its practice of using body and other nonverbal language to help clients become aware of their conflicts and choices. Other therapists do recognize the importance of attending to the client's nonverbal behavior for the purpose of adding nuance to what the client is saying. But Gestalt therapy acknowledges nonverbal behavior as one of the keys to discovering meaning.

The creative stance of Gestalt therapy is a major contribution to the therapy field in general. Most therapies, with the exception of Gestalt and person-centered, are technique rather than process oriented. And even person-centered counseling, which emphasizes process, is oriented around the technique of reflection. In theory, Gestalt therapists approach each therapeutic session as an existential encounter.

Probably the greatest compliment an approach can receive is from those who use it to build their own theories. Self-psychology, object relations, transactional analysis, and neurolinguistics have all borrowed heavily from Gestalt to enhance their own approaches (Jacobs, 1992; Polster & Polster, 1993).

Shortcomings of Gestalt Therapy

The Gestalt approach is not without limitations. The techniques of Gestalt therapy often lead to the intense expression of emotion. The therapist must have the experience and emotional presence to guide the individual through the expression of this affect and through the cognitive and affective integration of what he or she experienced during the therapy session. Otherwise the individual can be left feeling unfinished and less integrated than before the experience.

Gestalt therapy has been somewhat a victim of the times (Miller, 1997; Thompson & Rudolph, 2000). It is not a very acceptable approach for dollar-conscious health care agencies that want specific, measurable treatment goals. Gestalt therapy is about as far away from the diagnostic criteria of the *Diagnostic and Statistical Manual of the American Psychiatric Association* or any type of behavioral contracting or prescripting as we can imagine, although Melnick and Nevis (1998) propose that it can be done. Gestalt's only concern with specific behaviors is how they fit into the bigger picture of the individual's Gestalt. The problem is that health care organizations are loath to pay off completed Gestalts and do not see incomplete Gestalts as mental health problems.

Another issue is brevity. Although many times the high impact of Gestalt appears to generate miraculous, instantaneous cures, and a one-step Gestalt therapy has been promoted (Harman, 1995), the business of integration is generally not a quick business. We find it difficult to fit Gestalt therapy into the "brief" category based on its lack of identifiable and quantifiable behavioral goals and the amount of time it takes to get the job of integration done.

A final limitation of traditional Gestalt therapy is its emphasis on the individual as sole master of his or her fate without regard to the functioning of society or the day-to-day influences of other people. The individual who takes on the philosophy of individual responsibility wholeheartedly will experience considerable frustration and even intolerance of the way things are in the real world.

Gestalt Therapy with Diverse Populations

Gestalt therapy's primary focus on process (what is happening to the person internally) rather than on content (verbal material and external events being discussed) is an advantage for its use in multicultural counseling.

Some of the gender issues that people bring to counseling are feelings of powerlessness, lack of trust in their capacity to find self-direction, difficulties in maintaining firm interpersonal boundaries, reluctance to express bottled-up feelings, and meeting others' needs to the exclusion of their own (Enns, 1987). Gestalt techniques can be empowering to both women and men who present gender issues such as these by focusing on self-awareness, providing avenues for acknowledging feelings, identifying and integrating disowned aspects of the personality, and finding ways of exercising autonomy and power.

Livneh and Sherwood (1991, pp. 530–531) report that Gestalt therapy strategies provide rich opportunities for helping clients with disabilities. Prototypical examples of appropriate use of Gestalt techniques in rehabilitation settings are enhancing self-awareness, encouragement of client responsibility for self, and enabling clients to deal with impasse and attain closure of unfinished needs and concerns. The Gestalt concepts considered most critical for understanding the psychosocial adaptation to physical disability are the holistic view of the person, the emphasis on self-awareness and the here and now, personal responsibility, and the principles of polarities and closure.

The emphasis of Gestalt therapy on existential living, aggression, and conflict makes it well suited for clients who have AIDS (Hardy, 1999; Klepner, 1992; Siemens, 1993) or other terminal diseases. Not only can Gestalt deal with the issues of hurt, grief, and anger that undergird the psychological foundations of these diseases, it also can provide a format for transcending them and living life in full contact with the world.

There is little doubt that Gestalt is about the individual taking responsibility for oneself and then acting to meet his or her own needs. That notion certainly flies in the face of any culture that relies on group consensus. Yet, there are numerous places in the world where Gestalt therapy is practiced and used by cultures that place a great deal of reliance on group consensus (Ciornai, 1998; Colombo, 1998; Philippson, 1999). For these cultures the total integrated mind/body concept of Gestalt and its interface and contact with the environment is a way of meeting this problem.

Cultures that don't give voice to emotions will have a lot of trouble with Gestalt. There are some real ethical dilemmas in using some Gestalt experiments with individuals who have never vented their emotions or are not permitted to do so by their culture. The fact is, though, that very few cultures *do* give permission to vent emotions and that is the very reason people tend to get into psychological trouble. For people who deny emotions as an integral part of their lives, the confrontive style of Gestalt therapy can be extremely threatening and may drive them away from both individual and group therapy.

It should be clearly understood that Gestalt therapy is not a good choice for clients who are experiencing a crisis, who are mentally ill, or who are otherwise emotionally fragile. Gestalt is far too volatile and threatening for clients who are struggling to keep a tenuous grasp on reality.

Gestalt therapy works well for over-socialized, emotionally-constricted individuals who shunt or deny the part that emotions play in their lives. Clients who no longer feel they are living their lives fully, or are living them for someone else or some other thing, can profit from Gestalt. Clients who end up with a somatoform disorder due to their repressed emotions should also be able to profit from Gestalt because of its emphasis on body congruence (Seligman, 2001, p. 272).

Corey (2001, p. 222) makes an interesting point about bicultural clients (we will also add biracial clients because they appear to experience many of the same pushes and pulls). We cannot think of a therapy better suited to the difficulties these individuals face—the empty chair and other Gestalt techniques are designed specifically for bipolarity problems.

The clients who benefit the most from therapy are those who have a well-developed sense of symbolizing, imaging, and fantasizing in their personal lives. Clients who have difficulty symbolizing or articulating in symbolic terms may not fare well with a purely Gestalt therapist. For cultures that use indirect speech as the norm, body language is a key to understanding. Certainly, no approach does as well as Gestalt at dealing with nonverbal expression.

Summary

Gestalt therapy was developed by Frederick Perls from a background of training and experience that included psychoanalysis, Gestalt psychology, semantics, psychodrama, and the human potential movement. The therapy is based on a personality theory that stresses the organism's innate striving toward homeostasis; the holistic nature of the person and the environment; and the organism's development of a capacity for aggression that facilitates contact with the environment. It is the failure to develop this aggression in a wholesome and complete manner that leads to maladaptive behavior, or what Perls termed *neurosis*. During therapy, the client's maladaptive behavior is directly dealt with through the creative utilization of experiments that facilitate the development of awareness. Several key concepts govern the nature of the therapeutic encounter, and their embodiment in therapy contributes to the development of the client's awareness. These concepts are the experiential nature of Gestalt therapy, here-and-now orientation, awareness, responsibility, polarities, top dog/underdog, environmental contact, figure-ground, and unfinished business. Specific Gestalt therapeutic strategies include enactment, directed behavior, fantasy, and dream work.

SUGGESTIONS FOR FURTHER READING

American Association of Gestalt Therapy (AAGT) Homepage. Available: http://www.aagt.org

The Center for Gestalt Development, Inc. Available: www.gestalt.org

The Gestalt Therapy Page. Available: http://www.gestalt.org/index.htm

Perls, F., Hefferline, R., & Goodman, P. (1951). *Gestalt therapy: Excitement and growth in the human personality.* New York: Dell.

Polster, E., & Polster, M. (1973). *Gestalt therapy integrated.* New York: Brunner/Mazel.

Polster, W., & Polster, M. (1999). *From the radical center: The heart of Gestalt therapy: Selected writings of Erving and Miriam Poster.* Cleveland, OH: Gestalt Institute of Cleveland Press.

REFERENCES

Assagioli, R. (1965). *Psychosynthesis.* New York: Viking Press.

Ciornai, S. (1998). Paths for the future: From a culture of indifference toward a Gestalt of hope. *Gestalt Review 3*(3), 178–189.

Clance, P. R., Thompson, M. B., & Simerly, E. D. (1994). The effects of the Gestalt approach on body image. *Gestalt Journal, 17*(1), 95–114.

Colombo, D. (1998). Back to Africa: The contribution of Gestalt therapy for an integrated culture in psychotherapy. In S. N. Madu & P. Kakubeire (Eds.), *Quest for psychotherapy for modern Africa* (pp. 235–239). Sovenga, South Africa: Ateneo.

Corey, G. (2001). *Theory and practice of counseling and psychotherapy* (6th ed.). Belmont, CA: Wadsworth/Thompson.

Enns, C. Z. (1987). Gestalt therapy and feminist therapy: A proposed integration. *Journal of Counseling and Development, 66,* 93–95.

Field, N. P., & Horowitz, M. J. (1998). Applying an empty chair monologue paradigm to examine unresolved grief. *Psychiatry: Interpersonal & Biological Processes, 61*(4), 279–287.

Friedman, N. (1993). Fritz Perls's layers and the empty chair: A reconsideration. *Gestalt Journal, 16*(2), 95–119.

Gladfelter, J. (1999). Redecision therapy. In J. R. Price & D. R. Hescheles (Eds.), *A guide to starting psychotherapy groups* (pp. 119–131). San Diego, CA: Academic Press.

Goulding, M., & Goulding, R. (1979). *Changing lives through redecision therapy.* New York: Brunner/Mazel.

Hardy, R. E. (1999). Gestalt therapy, hypnosis, and pain management in cancer treatment: A therapeutic application of acceptance and adjustment to disability. In G. Gandy & D. E. Martin (Eds.), *Counseling in the rehabilitation process: Community services for mental and physical disabilities* (2nd ed.). (pp. 251–257). Springfield, IL: Chas. C. Thomas.

Harman, R. (1995). Gestalt therapy as brief therapy. *Gestalt Journal, 18*(2) 77–85.

Harman, R. L. (1982). Gestalt therapy theory: Working at the contact boundaries. *Gestalt Journal, 5,* 39–48.

Hendlin, S. J. (1987). Gestalt therapy: Aspects of evolving theory and practice. *Humanistic Psychologist, 15,* 184–196.

Jacobs, L. (1992). Insights from psychoanalytic self-psychology and intersubjectivity theory for Gestalt therapists. *Gestalt Journal, 15*(2), 25–60.

Klepner, P. (1992). AIDS/HIV and Gestalt therapy. *Gestalt Journal, 15*(2), 5–24.

Kogan, G. (1976). The genesis of Gestalt therapy. In C. Hatcher & P. Himmelstein (Eds.). *The handbook of Gestalt therapy* (pp. 235–257). New York: Jason Aronson.

Levitsky, A., & Perls, F. S. (1970). The rules and games of Gestalt therapy. In J. Fagan & L. L. Shepard (Eds.), *Gestalt therapy now* (pp. 140–149). Palo Alto, CA: Science and Behavior Books.

Livneh, H., & Sherwood, A. (1991). Application of personality theories and counseling strategies to clients with physical disabilities. *Journal of Counseling and Development, 69,* 525–538.

Melnick, J., & Nevis, S. M. (1998). Diagnosing in the here and now: A Gestalt therapy approach. In L. S. Greenberg & J. C. Watson (Eds.), *Handbook of experiential psychotherapy* (pp. 428–447). New York: Guilford Press.

Miller, M. V. (1997). The emptiness of Gestalt therapy. *Gestalt Journal, 20*(2), 55–73.

Passons, W. R. (1975). *Gestalt approaches in counseling.* New York: Holt, Rinehart & Winston.

Perls, F. (1947). *Ego, hunger and aggression: The beginning of Gestalt therapy.* New York: Random House.

Perls, F. (1969). *Gestalt therapy verbatim.* New York: Bantam Books.

Perls, F. (1971). *In and out of the garbage pail.* New York: Bantam Books.

Perls, F. (1973). *The Gestalt approach and eyewitness to therapy.* New York: Bantam Books.

Perls, F., Hefferline, R., & Goodman, P. (1951). *Gestalt therapy: Excitement and growth in the human personality.* New York: Dell.

Philippson, P. (1999). Cultural action for freedom: Paulo Freire as Gestaltist. *Gestalt Review 3*(3), 251–258.

Polster, E. (1992). The self in action: A Gestalt outlook. In J. K. Zeig (Ed.), *The evolution of psychotherapy: The second conference* (pp. 143–154). New York: Brunner/Mazel.

Polster, E. (1995). *A population of selves: A therapeutic exploration of personal diversity.* San Francisco, CA: Jossey-Bass.

Polster, E., & Polster, M. (1973). *Gestalt therapy integrated.* New York: Brunner/Mazel.

Polster, E., & Polster, M. (1993). Frederick Perls: Legacy and invitation. *Gestalt Journal, 16*(2), 23–25.

Polster, M. (1985). Gestalt therapy: Evolution and application. Paper presented at the Evolution of Psychotherapy Conference, Phoenix, AZ.

Polster, W., & Polster, M. (1999). *From the radical center: The heart of Gestalt therapy: Selected writings of Erving and Miriam Poster.* Cleveland, OH: Gestalt Institute of Cleveland Press.

Seligman, L. (2001). *Systems, strategies, and skills of counseling and psychotherapy.* Upper Saddle River, NJ: Prentice-Hall.

Shane, P. (1999). Gestalt therapy: The once and future king. In D. Moss (Ed.), *Humanistic and transpersonal psychology: A historical and biographical sourcebook* (pp. 49–65). Westport, CT: Greenwood Press.

Sharf, R. S. (1996). *Theories of psychotherapy and counseling: Concepts and cases.* Pacific Grove, CA: Brooks/Cole.

Siemens, H. (1993). A Gestalt approach in the care of persons with HIV. *Gestalt Journal, 16*(1), 91–104.

Simkin, J. (1975). An introduction to Gestalt therapy. In F. D. Stephenson (Ed.), *Gestalt therapy primer* (pp. 9–10). Springfield, IL: Chas. C. Thomas.

Simkin, J. (1976). The development of Gestalt therapy. In C. Hatcher & P. Himmelstein (Eds.), *The handbook of Gestalt therapy* (p. 225). New York: Jason Aronson.

Thompson, C. L., & Rudolph, L. B. (1996). *Counseling children.* Pacific Grove, CA: Brooks/Cole.

Thompson, C. L., & Rudolph, L. (2000). *Counseling children* (5th ed.). Belmont, CA: Wadsworth/Thompson.

Walker, J. (1971). *Body and soul: Gestalt therapy and religious experience.* Nashville: Abingdon.

Wheeler, G. (1991). *Gestalt reconsidered: A new approach to contact resistance.* New York: Gardner Press.

Wolfert, R., & Cook, C. A. (1999). Gestalt therapy in action. In D. J. Wiener (Ed.), *Beyond talk therapy: Using movement and expressive techniques in clinical practice* (pp. 3–27). Washington, DC: American Psychological Association.

4 Psychoanalytic Theory and Object Relations Therapy

In the fourth edition of this text we dealt with psychoanalytic therapy largely as a singular entity based on the concepts of Freud. We are infusing in this fifth edition an example of one of the leading applied therapies among the family of modern psychoanalytic approaches.

Object Relations: A Major Evolution of Psychoanalytic Therapy

It is not by accident or random selection that we have highlighted *object relations therapy* as the representative choice from among several similar, competing, and deserving psychoanalytically-oriented modalities. The impressive and widely recognized philosophical and clinical work of a number of contributing object relations theorists, scholars, and clinicians appropriately demonstrates and represents the flavor of the newer analytic approaches. The seminal and foundational investigations and practices of theorists such as the following (all of whom had deep roots in classical psychoanalysis) are offered in support of our choice to include an abbreviated version of object relations therapy in this chapter: W. Ronald D. Fairbairn, Melanie Klein, Donald W. Winnicott, Otto F. Kernberg, David E. Scharff, Jill S. Scharff, and many others (Gomez, 1997; Scharff & Scharff, 1998; Skolnick & Scharff, 1998; St. Clair, 1996). In addition, the influence of *attachment theory* (also founded on psychoanalytic concepts) as espoused by both John Bolby and Mary Ainsworth (each professing to have begun work under the classical psychoanalytic umbrella), has proven to be a substantive factor in support of object relations as a viable theory (St. Clair, 1996, p. 2).

In the first part of this chapter we present a very condensed sketch of classical Freudian psychoanalytic theory. (Readers who are interested in a broader and more comprehensive review of psychoanalytic theory may wish to visit our website for an addendum to the theoretical approaches contained in this book.) Although Freud's concepts clearly laid the foundation for most of the modern forms of psychoanalysis and psychotherapy, classical psychoanalysis is now substantially outdated because several of Freud's basic constructs, such as his drive theory, are no longer considered valid (Mitchell, 1988, p. viii; Scharff & Scharff, 1998). That is our main rationale for devoting the bulk of this chapter to a more current system of applied therapy—the object relations approach.

Fundamental Tenets of Psychoanalytic Theory

History

Psychologists in the United States virtually ignored psychoanalysis from the 1890s to the 1920s and then vigorously opposed it from the 1920s until about the 1950s. By the middle of the twentieth century, psychologists were subjecting psychoanalytic concepts to rigorous experimental tests (Shakow & Rapaport, 1964), and subsequently many of the psychoanalytic principles were incorporated into mainstream psychology (Hornstein, 1992, p. 254). By the 1990s, psychoanalytic theory was considered a cornerstone of modern counseling and psychotherapy (Fine, 1990; Hornstein, 1992). Of the several hundred therapies in use from the 1970s to 2000, most derived some fundamental formulation, technique, or impetus from the psychoanalytic system (Fine, 1979, 1990; Goldman & Milman, 1978; Gunderson & Gabbard, 1999).

Several contemporary psychoanalytically-oriented therapies have been developed based on Freudian and neo-Freudian formulations (Arlow, 1995). A few representative examples of systems or approaches that might be called contemporary descendants of classical psychoanalysis are ego psychology, interpersonal psychoanalysis, existential psychoanalysis, time-limited dynamic psychotherapy, object relations therapy, self-psychology, autonomous psychotherapy, depth psychology, dynamic psychotherapy, dynamic psychiatry, and psychodynamic theory.

Overview of Freudian Psychoanalytic Therapy

Freudian psychology is a psychology of the conflicting forces inherent in the dualistic nature of humankind. The conflicting dualism of the mind may be dichotomized into *conscious* and *unconscious*. The dualism of humans in society may be dichotomized into the person as a biological animal and the person as a social being (Arlow, 1979, p. 1). It is through conflicts between the conscious and the unconscious and between the biological motivating forces in people and the social tempering forces in the environment that the personality develops, acculturation occurs, and values are acquired. Freud described this human motivation as being governed by the tendency to seek pleasure (a biological drive) and to avoid pain. He called this tension-reducing force the *pleasure principle* (Arlow, 1995, p. 16; Freud, 1958, pp. 213–227).

Freud's conception of the development of neurosis grew from his studies of hysteria and hypnosis. In these studies he found that certain unacceptable events and thoughts people had consciously experienced were sometimes repressed into an area of the mind he called the *unconscious*. These experiences, which were of a sexual nature, directly influenced the person's behavior and caused hysterical symptoms. These ideas were the basis of Freud's theory of the development of neurosis (Fancher, 1973). Thus, the hysterical neurotic became the accepted prototype for the early Freudians' understanding, diagnosis, and treatment of maladjusted patients.

Auld and Hyman (1991, p. 17), citing Rapaport (1967), identified seven postulates or assumptions that characterized psychoanalytic therapy from the middle of the twentieth century to the 1990s:

1. Access to unconscious functioning comes through the *associative process.*
2. Later mental structures have to be explained by earlier experiences, by turning back to the past.
3. Psychic continuity is a lifelong process.
4. Mental life has meaning.
5. Determinism, the conviction that nothing that happens is accidental, is an accepted principle.
6. Instinct as the source of motivation in bodily processes is an accepted concept. (This postulate is sometimes referred to as Freud's *drive theory.*)
7. The assumption of the concept of the unconscious is necessary because conscious experiences leave gaps in mental life that unconscious processes bridge.

Auld and Hyman hold that postulate one (which they added to the other six assumptions developed by Rapaport), is the guiding rationale for psychoanalytic technique.

According to Arlow (1989, 1995), effective psychoanalytic treatment can best be understood by examining *empathy, intuition,* and *introspection* (1989, pp. 39–40). Arlow explains that empathy is a form of "emotional knowing," central to the psychotherapeutic process, whereby a therapist exercises the ability to identify with and share the client's experiences both affectively and cognitively. He describes intuition as the organization, in the therapist's mind, of the myriad of data communicated by the client "into meaningful configurations outside the scope of consciousness" of the therapist (1989, p. 40), yet made conscious through unconscious mental operations. The therapist becomes aware of such unconscious material through introspection, a process using mental free association, in which the therapist consciously synthesizes the client's accumulated communications. These introspections are not communicated to the client but rather are used to understand and help the client finally attain the insight and ego strength needed to cope with whatever emotional traumas or dilemmas brought him or her to therapy in the first place. The communication of *empathy* directly to the client has been recognized and recommended by many modern psychoanalysts as a prerequisite to effective psychotherapy (Bacal, 1995; Feiner & Kiersky, 1994; Josephs, 1994; Kohut, 1995; J. S. Scharff, 1997; Scharff & Scharff, 1998; St. Clair, 1996; Summers, 1999; Warren, 1994).

Theory of Personality

According to Arlow (1995), personality "evolves out of the interaction between inherent biological factors and the vicissitudes of experience." Psychoanalytic personality theory is based on several fundamental principles cited by Arlow (pp. 23–24):

1. *Determinism.* Mental events are not random, haphazard, accidental, unrelated phenomena. They are causally related chains of events.
2. *Topography.* All mental elements are judged according to accessibility to consciousness.
3. *Dynamic viewpoint.* The interaction of libidinal and aggressive impulses is biologically based and is more correctly defined by the term *drives* than by the more common but acceptable term *instincts.*

4. *Genetic viewpoint.* Psychoanalysts have empirically linked later conflicts, character traits, neurotic symptoms, and psychological structures to childhood events, wishes, and fantasies.

Freud proposed that the personality consists of three major parts—the id, the ego, and the superego (Hall, 1954).

The Id.   The id exists at birth and is the source of psychic energy and the instincts, the most important of which are sex and aggression. Energy in the id is mobile and can be readily discharged through action and wish fulfillment. One function of the id is to fulfill the pleasure principle, which is a basic motivating force that serves to reduce tension by seeking pleasure and avoiding pain (Arlow, 1995, pp. 21–22; Fine, 1973, p. 14). The id is the newborn's reservoir of emotional energy. A basic function of the id is to maintain the organism in a state of tension-free comfort.

The Ego.   The ego is a complex psychological organization that acts as an intermediary between the id and the external world. It has both defensive and autonomous functions. It is not present at birth but is developed as the person interacts with the environment. To function as this intermediary, the ego operates by the *reality principle*. The reality principle postpones the discharge of energy until an object that will satisfy the need, or reduce tension, is found. Unlike the id, the ego is able to tolerate tension and thus delay gratification. The ego has been called the executive of the personality because it controls and governs the id and the superego and maintains interaction with the external world (Fine, 1973, p. 15; Giovacchini, 1977, p. 21; Hansen, Stevic, & Warner, 1982, p. 29).

The Superego.   The superego is the moral, social, and judicial branch of the personality; it represents the ideal rather than the real. The superego strives for perfection rather than pleasure or reality. It develops as a result of the need to control the aggression that results when needs are not immediately satisfied. The superego develops from the ego by assimilating parental standards and eventually substitutes parental authority with its own inner authority. It takes over the governance of the psyche and mediates between the person and the environment. It acts as the moral and social gatekeeper and keeps the person's baser instincts from running rampant (Fine, 1973, pp. 15–16; Giovacchini, 1977, p. 21).

The Development of Personality

Childhood sexuality plays an important role in the development of the personality (Freud, 1961a, pp. 141–149). The infant is capable of receiving sexual gratification from rhythmic stimulation of any part of the body; Freud termed this *polymorphous perversity.* As the infant matures, the generalized ability to receive sexual gratification decreases as certain parts of the body become preferred sites for gratification. In other words, the possibilities for gratification of the sexual instinct narrow as the infant develops. Freud postulated a series of developmental stages that describe this narrowing process of sexual gratification. These stages, now referred to as the stages of psychosexual development, are as follows.

Oral Stage.   This stage occurs during the first year of life and develops from the act of feeding in which the mouth and lips naturally come to receive more stimulation than other parts of the body. Because oral responses had been demonstrated to have strong sexual connotations in perversions, neuroses, and latent dream content, Freud thought that the nonnutritive components of an infant's oral behavior were sexual. Conscious and unconscious memories of oral experiences have a central position in the psychological life of the infant, and new experiences are organized around these memories (Arlow, 1995, p. 25; Wolman, 1968, pp. 67–69).

Anal Stage.   The anal stage develops during the second and third years of life as the anal area begins to assume a central position in the child's sexual development. This area becomes more strongly associated with sexual gratification than the mouth. As children become capable of voluntary muscle control and eventual bowel control, they discover that sexual stimulation occurs from voluntarily retaining and expelling feces. Anal ideas and memories involve such activities as elimination, retention, smearing, or cleaning. Just as with the oral stage, the prototypes of later personality characteristics develop during the anal stage.

Phallic Stage.   This stage occurs after mastery of the tasks of toilet training. At approximately age three or four the child discovers the pleasures of genital manipulation and another shift of the zone of sexual stimulation occurs. Because of increased dexterity, the child can now have regular and intense pleasure by stimulating the genitals. It is during this stage that the Oedipus complex develops. Freud named this stage for its parallels with the Greek play *Oedipus Rex,* in which Oedipus kills his father and marries his mother. The Oedipus complex develops when the child has intense sexual feelings for the parent of the opposite sex. The male child fears castration by the powerful father and subsequently represses his desires for the mother and identifies with the father. The female child thinks she has already been castrated and thus suffers from penis envy and is not as fearful of her mother as the male is of his father. Difficulties in the resolution of the Oedipus complex may lead to problems of sexual identity (Arlow, 1995, pp. 25–27; Wolman, 1968, pp. 71–72).

Latency Period.   The first stages constitute the *pregenital* stages. Fixation at any one of these stages may produce oral, anal, or phallic character types in later life. These stages are precursors to the fourth stage of psychosexual development, the latency period, which extends from age five or six to puberty. At about age six, the sexual instinct diminishes and the child enters a stage of sexual quiescence. During this stage, children enter school and apply themselves to the tasks of learning. Although the sexual instinct is repressed, the sexually charged memories of the previous stages are still intact and will influence personality development (Arlow, 1995, pp. 27–28; Freud, 1961a, pp. 141–149).

Genital Stage.   This fifth stage of psychosexual development occurs at puberty and is characterized by nonnarcissistic behavior that develops in the direction of biological reproduction. Characteristics of this stage are an attraction for the opposite sex, socialization and group activities, marriage and the establishment of a family, and vocational development. The genital stage becomes fused with the pregenital stages as kissing, caressing, and sexual intercourse satisfy pregenital impulses. This stage lasts from puberty to death or senility, whichever comes first (Babcock, 1983, pp. 37–44; Wolman, 1968, pp. 81–82).

As the person proceeds through these stages, propelled by inherent forces and molded by the environment, he or she acquires various components of personality. Fixation at any of the first three stages may produce certain personality types, such as the oral, anal, or phallic character. Although there are two further stages of psychosexual development, the basis for the individual's personality in later life is determined during the first three stages.

Nature of Maladjustment

A basic theme of Freudian psychology is that human development requires the suppression of "impure" childish impulses. Adults continue to fight these antisocial and disruptive impulses. In Freud's time a common manifestation of the attempt to repress these "loathsome" childhood wishes was hysteria. It was through Freud's work with hysterical clients that he discovered the relationship between sexual fantasies and impulses and hysterical symptoms. He first thought that childhood seduction and sexual trauma were the cause of hysterical symptoms, but he eventually proposed that his client's "memories" were the products of wish fulfillment rather than actual traumatic events. He found traces of childhood sexuality in himself, and from these observations concluded that the unsuccessful resolution of the Oedipus complex was responsible for neurotic symptoms (Freud, 1961b, pp. 173–183).

Basically, what precipitates the neurosis is that the impulses of the Oedipus complex have a strong need for satisfaction. Most people can satisfactorily resolve these impulses. The most common and significant conflicts arise from wishes during the Oedipal phase. Childhood neuroses are usually manifested through nightmares, phobias, tics, mannerisms, ritualistic behaviors, and general apprehensiveness. Childhood behavior disorders are generally related to repressed neuroses. Adult neurosis is generally interpreted as a resurfacing of childhood neurosis (Arlow, 1995, pp. 29–30).

Freud proposed that the psychic processes in neurosis and psychosis had a fundamental unity. The symptoms of the psychotic are explainable by the same unconscious mental processes that give rise to the symptoms of the neurotic client and the dreams of a normal person. The principal difference between psychosis and neurosis is the change in the psychotic's relationships with people and the environment: the psychotic withdraws from the world and people, often thinking that the world has changed and that people are unreal. Thus the psychotic, unlike the neurotic and the normal person, has a break with reality (Arlow & Brenner, 1964).

Major Concepts

Psychoanalytic theory embodies a host of formulations, assumptions, and concepts. The major Freudian concepts that we will mention are the unconscious, instincts, identification, displacement, the Freudian symbol, defense mechanisms, transference, and free association.

The Unconscious. The unconscious is an actual entity of the mind, the lowest of its three layers. The preconscious is the middle layer and the conscious is the upper layer (Wolman, 1968, pp. 6–11). The contents of these three layers of the mind vary in their degree of availability to conscious awareness. Some are readily accessible, because resistance to their expression is weak; others are not available except through psychoanalysis. What seems most important about unconscious content is the influence it exerts on the behavior of the consciously unaware individual. Its effects range from forgetfulness, slips of the tongue, and accidents to neurosis manifested in hysterical symptoms. Freud explained that the unconscious stores material that is unavailable to awareness because of incompatibility. The incompatibility is between certain unacceptable ideas and the ego, which represses those ideas (Wollheim, 1971).

Wolman (1989) introduced the concept of the *protoconscious* rather than the preconscious. The protoconscious is described as a bridge between conscious and unconscious phenomena. For example, many altered states of consciousness such as lucid dreams, posthypnotic states, meditation, and parapsychological phenomena are observed on the protoconscious level when individuals are neither totally conscious nor totally unconscious. Fluctuating modes and shifts from the unconscious to protoconscious states of mind, and vice versa, may be observed in schizophrenics and autistic children.

Instincts. Instincts are organic motivational forces, or *drives* (Wolman, 1968, pp. 39–40). Freud recognized two classes of instincts—the life instincts, which he labeled *libido,* and the death instincts, or *thanatos.* The seat of the instincts is the id. Instincts direct psychological processes and function as the motivational forces in people. Each instinct has a source (energy), an aim (removal of a need), an object (such as food), and an impetus (strength) (Hall, 1954).

Identification. Identification is an ego mechanism that is important in personality development (Wolman, 1968, p. 68). One form of identification is the incorporation of the qualities of another person into one's personality. According to Hall (1954), there are four types of identification:

1. *Narcissistic identification* is identification with others who possess the same trait as the identifier, such as athletic ability.
2. *Goal-oriented identification* is identification with someone who has a trait the identifier hopes to acquire. A male child wanting to be strong like his father is an example.
3. *Object-loss identification* occurs when someone attempts to regain a lost object by identifying with it. The child who tries to regain parental love through attempts to please his or her parents by adopting their values and standards is an example.
4. *Authority identification* is identification with the prohibitions set down by parents and other authority figures. This type of identification leads to the development of the conscience.

Displacement.   This is the process by which psychic energy from the instincts can be rechanneled from one object to another. Only the object of the instinct varies; the source and the aim of the instinct remain the same. Through this process a major portion of the personality is formed. The development of the personality through displacement is a complex process by which multiple tensions can be reduced, and the object chosen may be far removed from the drive that started the process. For example, the original drive for oral gratification, which is first satisfied by sucking the nipple, will undergo several displacements—thumb sucking, candy sucking, cigarette smoking, beer drinking, eating, talking, oratory, and so forth (Hall, 1954; Wolman, 1968, pp. 147–152).

The Freudian Symbol.   The Freudian symbol is a socially acceptable representation, usually in dreams, of an unconscious and objectionable thought, wish, or object. For example, the penis may appear in dreams as an elongated object or an object capable of penetration, such as a knife, gun, snake, statue, spire, or cigar. The vagina is represented by objects capable of being receptacles, such as a cave, box, tunnel, or pocket. In psychoanalytic treatment, the symbols in dreams, which may represent a wide range of unconscious thoughts, are analyzed as a means to make unconscious material conscious (Hall, 1954).

Defense Mechanisms.   Defense mechanisms are used by the ego to reduce anxiety associated with threatening situations and feelings. Anxiety is generated by the instinctual demands of the id and the pressures of the superego. In contrast with realistic measures for dealing directly with the source of the threat, defense mechanisms distort, deny, or falsify the reality of the anxiety-producing situation. These protective mechanisms are used by most people, and at times, particularly when the ego is developing, may prevent the person from being overwhelmed by parental and societal demands. Such demands may become so excessive that the defense mechanisms employed thwart the natural development of the person and thereby become unhealthy. Some of the more important defense mechanisms are as follows (Wolman, 1968).

   1. *Repression.*   Repression forces a threatening memory, thought, or perception out of consciousness and prevents it from returning. Repression may prevent a person from seeing an object that is actually in view, or it may allow distortion of objective reality in order to protect the ego from the danger associated with the perception. Freud attributed hysterical disorders to repression. Repression may contribute to a conversion reaction resulting in so-called psychosomatic disorders such as asthma, arthritis, and ulcers (Wolman, 1968).

   2. *Projection.*   When forces from the id or the superego threaten a person, the ego sometimes attributes those forces to an external source. The ego is attempting to convert internal anxiety into an objective external anxiety that is easier to handle. Thus, projection is the attribution of one's feelings or characteristics to people in general. One who is unhappily married may reduce the anxiety associated with that condition by concluding that all marriages are unhappy (Wolman, 1968, p. 146).

   3. *Reaction formation.*   Reaction formation occurs when the ego sidetracks the expression of a threatening impulse by prompting the person to behave in the opposite way. A person who crusades against vice and corruption may be doing so (unconsciously) to deny an urge to participate in these same activities. The principal features of reaction formation are an exaggerated demonstration of the opposite feeling and an inflexibility of expression of that feeling. Reaction formations are also employed against external threats, as in the case of exaggerated friendliness toward or obedience to someone or something that is feared (Wolman, 1968, p. 146).

4. *Fixation.* Fixation is a psychological stunting whereby the person fails to proceed from one developmental stage to another. People generally experience anxiety when faced with the prospect of engaging in a new behavior; they worry about performing adequately, are afraid of being ridiculed for failure, or fear punishment. Most people will take the risk in order to grow. However, some people feel such great anxiety at the thought of the antic-ipated situation that they refuse to engage in the new behavior and thus remain fixated at an earlier developmental level. This fixation, a fear of leaving the old for the new, is called sep-aration anxiety (Wolman, 1968, pp. 140–141).

5. *Regression.* Regression is a retreat to a previous stage of development. Some forms of regressive behavior are so common they are viewed as childish. The college freshman regresses when he or she returns to the security of the parental home every weekend or drops out of school rather than face the anxiety of confronting the world "alone." A more severe expression of regressive behavior is withdrawal into a world of daydreams and fan-tasies to the exclusion of independent functioning in society (Hall, 1954).

Transference.　　Transference is a key concept in psychoanalytic therapy. It occurs when the client's feelings are directed toward the therapist as though the therapist were the source of the feelings. The therapist's analysis helps the client distinguish between the fantasy and the reality of the feelings transferred from some previous significant person to the therapist (Arlow, 1995). Also, the client is helped to gain an understanding of how he or she "mis-perceives, misinterprets, and relates to the present in terms of the past" (p. 32). Since most transferee's feelings are unconscious, the skill of the therapist is needed to help the client realign these distorted relationships.

Free Association.　　Free association is a technique that encourages the client to report to the therapist without bias or criticism whatever enters his or her mind. Such reports enable the therapist to uncover repressed material. The analysis of hidden conflicts helps the client gain the insight that is the core of growth (Fine, 1973, p. 21). According to Auld and Hyman (1991, p. 243), *"free association is the primary method (perhaps the only one) by which the therapist and the patient gain access to unconscious conflict* [emphasis added]. Thus, free association becomes the defining element of psychoanalytic therapy."

For further coverage of psychoanalytic theory, we refer the reader to our Allyn & Bacon website at www.ablongman.com/james5e. On this site we cover the history and background of psychoanalytic theory as if it were a stand-alone chapter in this text. We fur-ther address topics such as the counseling process, strategies for helping clients, brief psy-chotherapies, a sample case, contributions and shortcomings of the psychoanalytic system, and psychoanalytic therapy with diverse populations.

We now shift the focus, for the remainder of this chapter, to one of the systems of therapy that grew out of classical psychoanalysis. *Object relations therapy* enjoys a wide degree of acceptance as a premier, modern, therapeutic modality with roots reaching back to the Freudian as well as to the Neo-Freudian era (Gomez, 1997; Scharff & Scharff, 1998; St. Clair, 1996; Summers, 1999).

Fundamental Tenets of Object Relations Therapy

History

Drive versus Relational Theories.   Over the course of several decades, Freud's formulations provided the impetus and conceptual basis for several competing analytical philosophies and clinical approaches. Concomitant with the current conceptual disarray among the psychoanalytical approaches are two broad, competing perspectives—Freud's drive theory and a cluster of *relational* models that include object relations theory, interpersonal psychoanalysis, and self psychology. Although drive or instinct (sometimes simply called *biology*) theory is systematic, unified, and comprehensive, it is also obsolete because it does not account for major aspects of human motivation that modern theorists attribute to environmental factors (Mitchell, 1988, p. viii; Scharff & Scharff, 1998). Relational theories are proliferating and more consistent with applied psychoanalytic practice today, and a number of object relations–oriented analytical clinicians (including many in North America) are working toward developing the newer theories (especially object relations) into a more coherent, comprehensive, and systematic framework (Blanck & Blanck, 1986; Corrigan & Gordon, 1995; Ganzarian, 1989; Gomez, 1997; Klein, 1990; Kumin, 1996; Mitchell, 1988; Rogers, 1991; J. S. Scharff, 1997; Scharff & Scharff, 1998; Skolnick & Scharff, 1998; St. Clair, 1996; Summers, 1999).

Object relations therapy is one of several different psychoanalytically oriented schools that cluster around the concept of relational theory rather than Freudian biological or drive theory. Even so, all of the relational models are grounded in Freud and are derivations of the basic foundations that were laid down by Freud. Mitchell (1988, pp. 8–9) regards the family of relational models as valuable correctives (checks and balances) for each other. He considers the cluster of emergent relational psychodynamic approaches to be a *multifaceted relational matrix* which takes into account self-organization, attachments to others (objects), interpersonal transactions, and the active role of the client in the continual recreation of his or her subjective world. We believe that an appropriate and useful way for entry-level learners to view psychological reality is by operating within the relational or interpersonal realm of object relations psychology.

The Attachment Theory Connection.   The research and clinical work of a large group of attachment theorists are similar, related to, and complementary of the studies of object relations theorists. The work of attachment theory figures such as Bolby and Ainsworth lends credence to and supports many of the theoretical underpinnings and clinical practice of object relational work. As an interesting example, one major conclusion of Bolby's studies, grounded in rigorous empirical evidence, was that to grow up mentally healthy, the infant and young child should experience a warm, consistent, caring, intimate, and continuous relationship with his or her mother (or permanent mother substitute) in which both find satisfaction, security, and enjoyment (Bretherton, 1992, p. 6).

Ainsworth's research supports the connection between attachment theory and object relations. Two of her core emphases are that (1) the mother–infant relationship is the start of personality development, and (2) substantial elements of that early personality development carry forward through all stages of life. An example of special note, derived from Ainsworth's studies, involved the evaluation of maternal sensitivity to infant signals. Securely attached infants had mothers who were rated as highly sensitive and spontaneous. In contrast, insecurely attached infants had mothers who were rated as inattentive and/or imperceptive of the nuances of infant behavior. The latter babies were significantly less content. The securely attached babies cried little and seemed content to explore in the presence of mother. But insecurely attached babies of inattentive and/or imperceptive mothers cried much more frequently, even when being held by their mothers, and did little or no exploring. Infants not yet attached manifested no differential behavior toward the mother (Ainsworth & Bolby, 1991, p. 7; Bretherton, 1992, pp. 10–11).

In another investigation, Ainsworth and Bolby (1991, p. 3) reported that "when children become uneasy or frightened while exploring, they are nevertheless secure if they can retreat to a parent figure, confident that they will receive comfort and reassurance. Thus the parent's availability provides the child with a secure base from which to explore and learn." The enormous volume of work in the attachment theory arena appears to validate much of the theoretical framework of the relational theorists (Ainsworth & Bolby, 1991; Bretherton, 1992; Fraley & Shaver, 2000; Lopez & Brennan, 2000; Pietromonaco & Barrett, 2000). Both object relations and attachment theories were developed out of the heritage of classical psychoanalytic theory by clinicians and scholars who were themselves well grounded in Freudian psychology. In fact, object relations theorists consider themselves within the psychoanalytic mainstream, but they frequently alter that mainstream in important ways (St. Clair, 1996, p. 2).

Biology versus Psychology.　　Gomez (1997, p. 49) credits Melanie Klein with making the important leap from biology to psychology in psychoanalytic theory. Rather than believing that the mind works as a fundamental aspect of the body, the Kleinian psychology view is that meaning, relationship, and subjective experience are the primary criteria for understanding human beings. It might be said that classical psychoanalytic theory gained emotional vividness at the expense of the more systematized relational theories. (A Biblical analogy might be thought of, by people of the Christian faiths, as the Old Testament representing classical psychoanalysis and the New Testament emerging in the form of the relational theories.) Although Kleinian theory perpetuates the mind-body dichotomy, it replaces a physical predicate with a mental bias. Object relations formulations were a direct outcome of this crucial shift of focus.

The British Connection.　　In view of the foregoing, rather than attempting to address all of the different types and variants of the analytic approach's descendants from Freud, we are concentrating on one prominent, British-connected (but becoming somewhat Americanized), widely recognized, and extensively used relational prototype—object relations therapy—that was representative of the psychoanalytic system at the beginning of the twenty-first century (Blanck & Blanck, 1986; Corrigan & Gordon, 1995; Ganzarain, 1989; Gomez, 1997; Klein, 1990; Kumin, 1996; Mitchell, 1988; Rogers, 1991; J. S. Scharff, 1997; Scharff & Scharff, 1998; Skolnick & Scharff, 1998; St. Clair, 1996; Summers, 1999; Theweleit, 1994). Object relations therapy was developed by analysts who were interested in the interactions between themselves and their clients or patients (J. S. Scharff, 1997). Fairbairn (1954) is credited with coining the term "object-relationships," which came to be known as "object relations theory." Scholnick and Scharff (1998) and J. S. Scharff (1997) acknowledge Fairbairn as having played a major role in establishing the *relational* rather than the instinct thrust on which object relations theory is based. They consider Fairbairn to be a major founder of that theory.

The full-fledged object relations theoretical framework was variously rather than collectively developed by British Freudian psychoanalytic clinicians and scholars who became convinced that human beings were more than systems of biological drives. They were unanimous in placing relationship at the heart of what it means to be fully human (Gomez, 1997, p. 1; J. S. Scharff, 1997). Consequently, in modern psychoanalytic terms, *object* is no longer rooted solely in the instinct theory from which it evolved. That is, the object is no longer defined as being the exclusive "vehicle of instinctual gratification and discharge or as the energic investment of the mental images of other people." Instead, object relations have also become the "crucial organizers of the emotional, cognitive, and psychosomatic needs of the infant, child, adolescent, and adult" (Kumin, 1996, p. 19).

Theory of Personality

Clinical evidence and research show that human motivation does not originate in the tension reduction drive theory of classical psychoanalysis (Summers, 1999). Moreover, interpersonal relating cannot be reduced to instinctual need gratification. Humans are born with autonomous motivation to relate to other people rather than being forced to do so in order to attain tension reduction. Summers states that "This theoretical shift raises the question of what is to replace drives as the basis for human motivation. The autonomous nature of the need for others has led some analysts to believe that the formation of relationships is the most fundamental human motivation" (p. 32).

According to Summers's (1999, pp. 53–63) description of object relations theory, humans are born with a wide range of affects, possibilities, and capacities. Whenever the mothering caregiver allows the child to experience his or her inborn affective tendencies and responds to them, the child then has opportunities for the creation of meaning from experience. If the mothering figure interacts with the infant with genuine love and affection in a way that the infant trusts the mother object enough to feel safe, secure, affirmed, and prized, the child has a good chance of internalizing positive affects, developing inherited capacities, organizing experiences, and learning to do voluntarily what has been only innately reflexive. The object relations model described by Summers (1999, p. 61) views the "development of the self as a creative outcome borne of the inborn maturational process and relationships to objects." He further states (p. 62) that, ". . . the generalized categories created from these interactions, is encoded in the form of object relationships, connections between self and object, that guide navigation through the world." This viewpoint shows how the child's needs for self-realization and relatedness are the motivational bases of personality development.

The Development of Personality

In object relations terms, the early personality development in humans, as explained by Fairbairn (1954) and later described by Scharff (1997), begins with essential "other relationships" in the infant's world. Instead of thinking of the other as the object of the infant's drive or basis for motivation, we think of the infant's *need*—the object vested in the other that fulfills the infant's need. It is not necessarily the need for attention, emotional release, sexual drive, or aggressive instincts, but rather the other person who provides two fundamental things: context and focus. *Context* is described by J. S. Scharff (1997) as that arms-around holding relationship that the mother (or other significant caregiver) provides for the infant. It is a relationship of security in which the baby can go on existing in a secure and relaxed way. *Focus* refers to the direct eye-to-eye relationship that the mother (or other significant caregiver) offers in which the infant subjectively learns to both relate to and think about that experience. Summers (1999, p. 38) speaks of an infant's inborn affective tendencies, in addition to the need for relatedness, that play a vital role in personality formation.

Given the above context and focus, the caregiver (mother, housekeeper, babysitter, father, sibling, aunt, grandparent, or any significant other) becomes the object that nurtures the infant's relational attachment, enabling the baby to internalize meaning. We think of the child's primary need as an instinctual need for relatedness—a need to exist in an affective relationship. Without a caregiver, the infant is nothing. Without attachment formation experience the infant will die. Whenever such context and focus relationships are appropriately provided, the seeds of a healthy personality are planted (J. S. Scharff, 1997). Essentially, personality is formed through interaction with significant others.

Melanie Klein described the infant's basis for the formation of a healthy sense of self in terms of *splitting* (Gomez, 1997, p. 37). Infants, existing in an environment of high intensity and stress under the sway of absolute impulses, have little life experience to modify the extremes they encounter. With the perceived threats and fears in new and unfamiliar surroundings, the infant may find it impossible to trust and love. By separating everything bad from everything good (splitting), the infant has the chance of experiencing total goodness and can take in this goodness (good object) as a basis for organizing a secure sense of self.

D. E. Scharff (1998, pp. 255–261) points out that the need for relationships throughout life is at the center of personality development. It is a lifelong process that includes infancy, adolescence, and the various stages of adulthood. But development does not occur in a straight, smooth progression. It has bumps, false starts, chaotic episodes, moments of order and stability, accelerated phases, and periods of near dormancy.

Nature of Maladjustment

Mental disturbance, psychological illness, or pathology is viewed by object relations theorists in terms of developmental arrest rather than conflicts between different parts or structures of the personality (St. Clair, 1996, pp. 3–4). Developmental arrests result in unfinished, disorganized, and unintegrated structures of the personality. Such arrests denote basic damage to object relationships of the individual or to the structures of the self. Fairbairn understood pathology in relational terms—the bad internal objects that are disruptive within the ego. Such bad internal objects, which are in relation to different portions of the ego, are repressed and represent the badness inside the person (St. Clair, 1996, p. 65).

Mitchell (2000) found that individuals can become traumatized by early attachment disturbances in the primary caregiver. For example, tenacious, unsatisfying love attachments, as seen in sexual addictions and obsessional love, may result from internalization of an absent or intermittent object relationship—a morbid attachment to the missing object during infancy. Such individuals often demonstrate depressive or addictive traits and schizoid defenses and typically they have difficulty forming an attachment bond with the therapist because they perceive the therapist as a dangerous, rejecting agent who will recapitulate the original trauma. In everyday life, such an individual typically manifests love relationships marked by chronic, repetitive infidelity and obsession. According to Mitchell (2000), the lover will be enamored with that which he or she cannot have. Without undergoing therapy, he or she may suffer from loss of psychological development which may be characterized by recurrent traumatization during adulthood.

From the object relations perspective, several primary symptoms such as maladjustment, self-defeat, chronic underachievement, emotional explosiveness, and self-sabotage are rooted in early object relationships with others—usually with one or both parents (Summers, 1999, pp. 14–19). Since most humans are born with the potential to relate, if we are somehow deprived of the opportunity to relate, we suffer from psychological withering (Scharff & Scharff, 1998, pp. 183–184). In a broad sense, the object relations view of maladjustment is that we have a need for people with whom we can have intimate relationships. We need for them to not only respond to us but also to care for us by holding us in mind. If what we want does not matter to others who matter to us, we will be deprived of normal development and thereby develop in maladjusted ways.

Major Concepts

Description of Objects.   According to St. Clair (1996, pp. 5–6), the *object* in object relations is a technical term that refers not so much to some inhuman entity but identifies or symbolizes someone or something that provides a specific gratification. Essentially, an object is that with which the human relates. Feelings and affects may have objects—for example, I love my *children,* I fear furry *animals,* I am angry with my *sibling.* Human drives may have objects, too. The object of the hunger drive is food, the object of the sex drive may be a sexually attractive person or a thing (object representation of a person). An infant's objects might be first the mother's breast, then the mother herself, and later other people or things that gratify the baby.

It should be noted that the term *representation* is used to define how the individual internalizes and represents an object. An example of representation might be the case of a famous business tycoon who marries and divorces several beautiful women. An object relations theorist might view this man's inner world as being filled with distorted, idealized representations of nurturing women, which in turn creates a fantasy world that disturbs his actual relationships with actual women. In his distorted representations of both himself and women, he may feel quite needy and have cravings or yearnings to be cared for by these temporarily idealized women. In his fantasies he projects that each woman, in turn, will fulfill his unmet yearnings or needs. But alas, the painful discrepancy between his inner world and his actual wives results in disappointments, more divorces, and the need for new relationships (St. Clair, 1996, p. 4).

The Meaning of Being Human. At its most fundamental level, object relations theory is based on the assumption that the human being is essentially social and that the need for relationships is at the central core of the definition of the self. Our innate need for contact with others is primary and cannot be adequately explained in terms of drives, other needs, nor can it be reduced to something more basic (Gomez, 1997, pp. 1–2).

External–Internal Dichotomy. Ganzarain (1989, p. 10) reminds us that the concept of object relations theory presents a confounding observation that humans exist "simultaneously in an external and an internal world, and that the relationship between the two ranges from the most fluid intermingling to the most rigid separation." Object relations theory is concerned with studying the "relationship between real, external people, and internal images and residues of relations with them, as well as the possible significance of these residues for psychic functioning" (p. 10).

Motivation and the Role of Objects. According to Fairbairn (1954) and discussed in St. Clair (1996, p. 56), people have an inherently basic drive toward relating with other humans. Libido is a highly directional object-seeking mechanism. The object that libido is constantly seeking is another human. Motivation is understood in terms of striving for a relationship with a human (the object), not merely seeking drive reduction through satisfaction.

The Structure and Influence of Objects. An object relations theory view of the ego's inner structure can best be understood in terms of the way a child must handle various unpleasant or cruel situations that life presents. For instance, a child who is abused or who receives harsh parental treatment believes that the only option for changing or improving the situation is to change him- or herself. The child may seek to solve the object-related dilemma by mentally splitting the object into good and bad components and then mentally internalizing the bad aspect (Gomez, 1997, pp. 37, 65; St. Clair, 1996, pp. 56–57). The likely result is that the child mentally constructs the environment (or object) as good and him- or herself as bad and deserving of abuse or punishment. Because objects internalized within the psyche become dynamic structures, the ego becomes intertwined with the objects. Consequently, the ego and the object become inseparable. For example, following a commonplace childhood error or accident, the child is unfairly punished and arbitrarily demeaned by a powerful and domineering parent or caregiver. The child, striving to please the caregiving figure, internalizes the belief that he or she is bad and not only deserves to be treated harshly but also can never be worthy of love and affection.

For substantive or affective meaning to be incorporated into the ego, the thing, event, or person must become merged with the ego. Internalized objects are fluid and are capable of acting as independent entities within the mind. Therefore, in object relations theory, objects are more than merely internal figures or representations. They are agencies that produce dynamic psychological activity. For example, an abused child may love and cling to the abuser but hate him- or herself, and may later in life make choices that result in becoming revictimized (St. Clair, 1996, pp. 56–57). Gomez (1997) refers to such love–hate phenomena in terms of the infant's splitting off his or her unbearable neediness in a withdrawal from external object relationships. This neediness implies that the original object of the child's need—the person who excited the child beyond what he or she could endure—becomes repressed and emerges from the repression in intense dependency cravings. As an adult, "at a more conscious level, it merges into the central ego/ideal object, as painful yearning in situations such as waiting endlessly by the phone for the lover who had promised to ring, but who we know from experience will not" (p. 62). This example underscores a primary issue in object relations theory that the concepts of splitting and yearning, referred to by St. Clair (1996, pp. 3–4), center on the discrepancy between the person's inner world representations and the situations of the actual environment.

Influence of Attachment Theory.   Commenting on the positive attributes of Bolby's theories and their applicability and adaptability to object relations therapy, Lopez and Brennan (2000, p. 283) stated that "Attachment theory effectively juxtaposes personality and developmental themes within a broad lifespan framework. In particular, we contend that the literature in adult attachment is contributing to an increasingly comprehensive understanding of the healthy and effective self."

Lopez and Brennan further state that persons possessing the healthy and effective self, which is derived through positive object attachments, are "resilient in adapting to the vicissitudes of life, and they have a remarkable capacity to develop, maintain, and enlarge their networks of supportive, intimate relationships" (p. 283). Other attachment theory studies have also supported the interplay of object attachment and care giving behavior in infancy and early childhood with attachment functions in adult relationships (Bolen, 2000; La Guardia, Ryan, Couchman, & Deci, 2000; Pietromonaco & Barrett, 2000). Individuals who experienced overall attachment security as infants may be predicted to positively experience the basic needs of autonomy, competence, and relatedness during adulthood.

The Counseling Process

Definition and Meaning of Object

St. Clair (1996, p. 219) defines *object* as "The 'other' involved in a relationship or, from an instinctual point of view, that from which the instinct gets gratification." The term *object* can denote other relationships, memorable events, or impressionable things. Object relations is largely based on the individual's relational need of important others from infancy to the present. How people obtain their need fulfillment through others speaks to the essence of adaptive (healthy) or maladaptive (pathological) functioning. Thus, object relations therapy provides clients with at least part of the psychological nurturing that they did not receive in early infancy and childhood (J. S. Scharff, 1997). To provide such nurturing, Scharff and Scharff (1998, pp. 10–13) describe object relations theory as more of an art than a science. In object relations therapy, we try to assess the client's internal perceptions of other groups or individuals as objects and seek to determine what effect the client's perceptions have on us as counselors in the immediate setting of the therapeutic encounter. It is more than simply monitoring the client–counselor relationship to maintain a healthy alliance. We do not avoid confrontation or empathic failures. We provide a safe space for thinking, feeling, and making ourselves available for clients to use as current, realistic, and therapeutic object attachments, the goal being to transport or transfer that therapeutic experience to relationships outside of the therapy setting. We view the counseling session as an evolving and ongoing laboratory for sharing experiences, examining motivations, and exploring viable options. In summary, the therapeutic relationship is at the core of clinical practice.

Crucial Role of the Client–Therapist Relationship

Regarding the primacy of relationship over impulse, Fairbairn believed that the single most important factor in facilitating therapeutic movement in clients is not the transference relationship but the person-to-person relationship with the therapist (Gomez, 1997, p. 74). That does not mean that the transference relationship is ignored or is considered obsolete. It means that the quality of the client–therapist relationship takes precedence over transference as the primary emphasis in object relations clinical practice. Melanie Klein and other object relations clinicians also suggest that counselors and therapists seek to help clients understand the relationships between their unconscious or forgotten infant and childhood object relations and to assess the impact of those objects on present emotions and motivations (Gomez, 1997, p. 49).

Focus on the Client

According to J. S. Scharff (1997) the therapeutic process in the object relations approach entails the therapist's genuine acceptance of all clients who present themselves for help. Every client is different, even if they happen to look similar or have similar backgrounds. The therapist must create psychological space by allowing his or her own internal object representations to reverberate with the client's. Initially, it may help if the therapist keeps an impartial or neutral position and allows the client to affect the therapist. The therapy is managed in such a way that the deep empathy and focus is on the client, especially on the client's internal world. Such a focus will usually allow the client and the therapist to affect each other. This is highly desirable. The therapist follows the client's affective lead. Client affect may be a signal of a deeper conflict, perhaps stemming from an earlier experience that the therapist will want to explore. The therapist will be especially sensitive to an expressed wish, dream, or fantasy that sheds light on an inner need or constitutes a representation of an important internalized object relational issue.

Strategies for Helping Clients

Objectives of the Therapist

The casual observer of an object relations therapist at work would notice little difference between that therapist's strategies and those of other psychoanalytical, dynamic, or even humanistic therapies. The main difference is in the object relations therapist's thinking or attitude—in how the therapist is conceptualizing what is transpiring in the therapeutic relationship. In early interviews with the client the therapist conducts a subjective assessment to gain a sense of the client's inner being and to get a feel for being in the room with that client. The therapist wants to know something about the client's family background, career goals, current living conditions, perceptions of the past and present, fears, hopes, dreams, and fantasies. Initially object relations therapy tries not to be too directive of the therapist's self or of the patient or client, but attempts to let things develop and to tolerate chaos. The therapist is highly interested in the positive value of chaos, of allowing meaning to emerge from the relational experience in its own time (J. S. Scharff, 1997). During the get acquainted phases of the therapy, the therapist operates with empathic listening, concern, and acceptance, doing lots and lots of listening for meaning in the client's inner world.

The Therapeutic Climate

Object relations therapy is really a way of being with a person. It is not a precise, scientific, intellectual process. It is an intensely personal, in-the-moment, you-and-me kind of relationship. The therapist strives to do whatever must be done to create a space for the client to truly be him- or herself—to be as natural as possible. It is very important that the therapist facilitate the conditions whereby the client gains and maintains autonomy. In the initial interviews, the therapist purposefully avoids being intrusive or assaulting the client's ego in a way that impedes the development of trust. The relational aspects of object relations therapy depend upon a high level of mutual trust (J. S. Scharff, 1997).

Once a bond of trust has developed and the client's tolerance level has been established, the therapist will operate with more directness and authority, moving into matters that may be more sensitive, painful, and defended by the client. The therapist will assertively go after such guarded and sensitive material because it must be confronted by the client if progress toward self-understanding is to be attained by the client. After all, the client is coming to therapy for help. Whenever a sufficient rapport and trust level have been attained, the therapist welcomes the opportunity to deal with chaos. It is as if during therapy the therapist is covertly saying to him- or herself and to the client, "I can better understand your pain whenever you openly disclose to me your prior chaotic episodes. That disclosure and mutual understanding will enhance our ongoing relationship and therefore strengthen our therapeutic alliance." Such a trustful and constructive alliance increases the chance of enabling the therapist and the client to reach a clearer understanding of the client's unconscious and conscious material and examining alternative choices that the client may wish to pursue (J. S. Scharff, 1997).

Therapeutic Technique

As the therapy unfolds, usually during interviews succeeding the initial interview, the therapist carefully attends to the client's dreams, fantasies, wishes, and needs. Following up on these kinds of inner-world dimensions gives the therapist opportunities to explore in depth the kinds of object relational and representational issues that are likely to be bothering the client. The therapist does not go off on intrusive tangents or into fishing expeditions and information gathering just to make conversation. All of the follow-up questions, insightful confrontations, and information sharing are geared to what the client says, how the client reacts, what the client omits, how the client relates to the therapist, how the therapist is feeling about the client, and the mutual object relations and transference issues that are arising in the moment of the therapeutic laboratory. The interview is considered to be a microcosm of the client's and the therapist's lives. What we learn about each other, how we feel about each other, and how we respond to each other in the interview becomes grist for our examination of the meaning of life and the meaning of relations outside the therapy session (J. S. Scharff, 1997).

Object relations techniques, as practiced by Fairbairn and others, essentially established the primacy of relationship over impulse as the central psychoanalytic rationale (Gomez, 1997, p. 74). That rationale holds that the single most important factor in facilitating change in clients is the real relationship—not the transference relationship—with the therapist. If clients are going to become empowered to release their attachments to their internalized bad objects, there must be a genuine relationship with the therapist to replace such bad objects. Also, the relationship with the therapist is far more important than the accuracy and correctness of any interpretations offered by the therapist.

Object relations technique abandons the conventional analytic interview setting. The client sits in a comfortable chair facing the therapist and the therapist also sits in a comfortable chair—not behind a desk or seated or standing above the client. Removal of all barriers to the development of a trusting and therapeutic relationship is an important conceptual change. To have the client lying down, with the therapist located behind or out of sight, is perceived to perhaps replicate the client's early traumas of abandonment, deprivation, and bad object images. The purpose of these conceptual changes is to enable the client and the therapist to experience each other more fully and more truthfully (Gomez, 1997, pp. 74–75; J. S. Scharff, 1997).

Another fundamental rationale in object relations therapy is that the client's internalized objects or attachments are important and must not be summarily expunged by the therapist. The most powerful resistance to change is the client's loyalty to and need for these internal objects or attachments. Humans have a propensity for holding on to their inner world of unsatisfying relationships. That tendency leads us to view the external world in the same terms. Gomez (1997, p. 74) states that "the risk of disregarding our normal way of being, with its familiar judgments and predictions, feels extraordinarily dangerous because of our absolute need as children to reserve our external relationships through the only means available to us." Therefore, if the therapist opens up the client's closed systems, the client is at risk of an acute fear of falling into a spinning vacuum of emptiness, disorientation, or humiliation in a resurgence of early trauma. That is why a real, trusting, secure client–therapist relationship is absolutely essential. Without such a secure trust in the therapist, clients cannot risk abandoning their internal objects or attachments to turn more fully to the therapist. Both Gomez (1997, pp. 74–75) and J. S. Scharff (1997) support Fairbairn's basic purpose of therapy: to help clients, through genuine concern, understanding, and challenge, to re-own their split-off capacities for anger and need and to integrate them into their central ego/ideal object. Clients will then be able to relate to others with more richness and their inner world will be less divided and conflictual. Clients can then experience themselves, the therapist, and other people more fully and more truly. Broadly speaking, the primary outcome goals of object relations therapy are to make clients aware of relationship deficits and to help them discover ways to improve their interpersonal functioning.

Sample Case

Precursory Information

During one of the early interviews in his therapy, Darald, a 30-year-old man, regained a memory in which he, as an 8-year-old boy, had just returned from an overseas trip to Germany with his father. Darald had been born in Germany but immigrated to the United States with his parents when he was 18 months old. His hard working, serious-minded, humorless father, a descendant from a long line of patriarchal Prussian forebearers, had served in the German military during World War II and had been taken as a prisoner of war during that conflict. The father had been brought to the United States and had been confined to prisoner of war camps in several different parts of the United States before being repatriated back to Germany at the termination of the war. The father subsequently married his German sweetheart, fathered a son (Darald), and immigrated to the United States six years after having been repatriated.

Early Memories and Trauma

As a child, Darald had accompanied his father on his first trip back to Germany since immigrating to the United States. Later, at age 30, after he entered therapy, Darald began to remember the difficult and emotional trip. He had tried to please his father by being a dutiful and devoted son in a land where he had minimum understanding of the language and customs and little recall of the numerous and doting relatives they had encountered. During the trip to the "fatherland," Darald had been enormously tense, confused, and stressed, but he had covered up his emotional feelings by acting in the role of a subservient son who expended every ounce of psychic energy in his efforts to please his father and make a good impression on relatives. As they returned to the United States, Darald felt rather pleased with himself for having survived the trip without displeasing or embarrassing his father. However, Darald had no recollection of his experiencing trauma during that event in his early life.

Mother as Confidante

As the course of therapy unfolded, Darald vividly remembered how his anxious, controlling, and over-solicitous mother had showered him with love and attention. At that time,

Darald went into explicit detail, telling his mother not only about his many exciting experiences during the journey but also about the hardships, emotional wounds, and extreme psychological stress he had endured during the trip—his difficulty with the language, his strivings to keep up a front to please his father and relatives, his feelings of guilt during the trip because he believed his acting made him a fraud. During his confidential and close conversations with his mother, Darald found it pleasurable to garner her undivided attention, profound compassion, and sympathy, which she obligingly lavished upon him.

A Second Traumatizing Event

Later in therapy, Darald remembered one sad and frightful occasion when, as a lad, he was mowing the lawn at his father's request. The weather was exceedingly hot. His mother came outside, served him a glass of cool lemonade, wiped his brow with a soft towel, and admonished him to slow down, cool off, and spend a little time resting in the shade. The father, noticing the interaction out on the lawn, came bursting out of the den and yelled demeaning remarks at Darald. "Lazy," "sissy," "stupid," "no good," "slow," "sorry," "weak," and "worthless" were words that came back to Darald's consciousness as he clearly recalled the incident. But the most devastating aspect of the traumatic occasion for Darald was the vivid mental image of his father's facial expression and body language during the tirade. Darald could not seem to shake that stressful and overwhelmingly burdensome image from his mind.

> **DARALD:**   I had always wanted and hoped to hear, just one time, from my dad's lips, "I love you, regardless of what you do or don't do." But I guess I was just disillusioned. When he came out of the house on that hot day and attacked me like he did, it devastated me! I never felt so empty and betrayed in all my life. I guess at that moment I hated them both. Him for his unfair, controlling, take-no-prisoners attitude. And her for her veiled overprotective coddling of me to curry my favor. I was so confused. I didn't know what was going on. I still don't, I guess. But at that moment I didn't care what happened to me. I felt that I was the most worthless piece of humanity that ever lived.

> **THERAPIST:**   So, as you now remember, that was a moment when you lost hope of obtaining expressions of love from your father. And, at the same time, you realized a love–hate feeling toward your mother that just heaped more trauma on your overburdened psyche than you, as a young son, could bear. And you judged yourself to be bad, indeed! How about now?

> **DARALD:**   I can see that better now. But it certainly wasn't as clear to me then. And I had just forgotten about it for many years, I guess. But dad was so scary, rigid, uncompromising, and lacking the ability to show caring. That's what hurt so much.

> **THERAPIST:**   It sounds like it is still hurting you, deeply. It also sounds like you're still carrying a heavy burden of hurt over your relations with your father and also a lot of remorse and anger in relation to your mother's behavior during that time.

> DARALD: Yes, both. I resented her but I loved her, too. But I can't think of anything she could have done to shield me from his rage or from my fear and my need to be thought of as worthwhile in his eyes.

> THERAPIST: How about your feelings right now, as we sit here together talking about it? How do you see yourself, including our relationships in this room now, affected by it today?

> DARALD: Well, I'm just sitting here with you and wondering how I forgot about it for all those years. I was just a kid, and I don't think I deserved that treatment. I was really feeling horrible then. It's not too pleasant to think about it now. I guess I just buried it in my soul a long, long time. As for us now, I guess it's OK. I'm not as scared to discuss it with you now as I was for a long time.

Splitting the Object

The foregoing dialogue is an example of what Scharff and Scharff (1998, pp. 44–47) referred to as *splitting and repression*. In object relations terms, young Darald's traumatic event was so internally painful to his ego that he had generated the defense of splitting of the object (the *object* being a symbolic representation, within his psyche, of the earlier traumatic conflict with his dad) as a fundamental unconscious defense against the pain he felt. This was also a way of avoiding negatively judging his all-powerful and all-knowing father. Through a mental trick Darald internally split the father object into good and bad and assumed the bad split for himself. ("It must be *me* that is bad, since I dare not judge dad as bad. *He* must be the good one.")

In the case of the mowing incident, young Darald's unconscious projection and splitting of the mother object may be explained by his attempt to purge the traumatic and unpleasant experience and affect from himself by projecting it onto his mother, whom he had rationalized as bad for the moment. His rationale for this anger toward his mother seemed to stem from such internalized, self-constructed, and extremely ambivalent emotional splitting that the therapist postulated the following explanation:

> THERAPIST (*privately, reading from her post-evaluative written notes*):   The purpose of this note to myself is to record, in the case of Darald, what appears to be a typical case of *double splitting* and *repression*. Darald appears to have such an intense internal craving for some sort of overt indication of love, acceptance, affection, and affirmation from his dad. But, realizing that such response will never happen, he has written off his dad completely. At the same time, his mother's pandering and attempting to protect and shield him, as a means of both compensation and intercession, seems to be an effort to demonstrate (1) to Darald that he is, in fact, loved and valued, and (2) to the father that Darald is worthy of the father's esteem, that the father should change and show some overt love and affection for his son, and that the father should lay off the son's case. By overplaying the protective and pandering role, it seems to me, the mother has unwittingly imparted to Darald that he is still a weak and helpless boy and victim who

is unequal to the task of manhood. Thus, Darald, feeling diminished and powerless, has directed anger toward his mother, effectively splitting the mother object into bad and good.

The Difficulty in Uncovering Unconscious Memories and Motivation

Although it finally began to dawn on Darald that nothing he did or could have done would have won his father's unconditional favor, and that his mother's futile ministrations appeared to have been intended as emotional shields for her son, the effects of these memories left Darald with strong psychic wounds. He had feelings of dependency and anger toward his mother and feelings of worthlessness in the eyes of his father, accompanied by rage toward his father. His strongly negative, self-deprecating feelings of loneliness, emptiness, and devastation became core issues as his therapy continued. But Darald appeared to be largely oblivious to many of the connections between early traumatic incidents and the multitude of problems that seemed to follow him throughout his adolescence and adulthood.

Even when Darald described to his therapist the details of his many failures and disappointments, he seemed to be unable to face or recognize the internal psychic damage he sustained as a result of his distorted object relations. He related instances in which he had continually sought to gain his father's approval through hard work. During his high school years, he worked as a bag boy in a grocery store. His diligent efforts and obsession to achieve were noticed by his supervisors, and soon he progressed to stock clerk, cashier, and, by the time he graduated from high school, to department manager. That was not good enough for Darald or his father! Furthermore, before he graduated from high school he impregnated and married a ninth grade female. He was 18 and the girl was 14. He lost his job at the grocery store, but quickly obtained another position with another chain, worked hard, and received several raises and promotions. By the time he was 26, he was appointed manager of a large new supermarket that opened up in the neighborhood. That was still not good enough for Darald or his father!

Darald enrolled in the local university as a part-time evening student. That didn't work out, so he dropped out of the university. Darald was unaware of the debilitating influence (latent trauma) of his unfulfilled and conflicted internal father object, and he unknowingly projected this onto his corporate supervisors. He was also charged with having an affair with one of his store employees. Because of these things, Darald soon lost his job as manager of the new store. This loss of a good job confirmed to the dad that Darald was a worthless jerk. By the time Darald's spouse was 21, they had five young children. That wasn't good enough either. Soon after he lost his job, Darald and his wife were divorced. Darald's parents effectively divorced their grandchildren. Darald moved to another state and took another job, but that did not work out. Before long he was again living with his parents, to the delight of his mother and the chagrin of his father. He was constantly in financial trouble due to job instability and alimony and child support payments. He went from job to job and from failed love relationship to failed love relationship. His object relations–oriented therapist could sense any number of debilitating and maladaptive aspects of Darald's life that he himself seemed unable to recognize, even though he knew that he had problems. That knowledge brought him to the point of presenting for therapy in the first place.

Surviving a Complicated and Traumatic History

Darald manifested multiple and complex problems: developmental arrests, relational problems with others, vocational difficulties, loneliness, interpersonal conflicts, unintegrated thinking, unsatisfying and failed love attachments, underachievement, consistent fear in social situations, feelings of inadequacy, intermittent periods of depression, and obsession about being a fraud.

>   **DARALD:**   Like I've been telling you during all these sessions, I have more problems than I ever recognized or admitted I had. I know I am capable. I'm capable of successfully handling a career or of relating to women, coworkers, and people in general. But I haven't been very successful at it. Maybe I just compulsively shoot myself in the foot. I don't know.

>   **THERAPIST:**   What strikes me is that what you're saying is encouraging from the standpoint that right now you may be in a state of readiness to really examine yourself and work on putting your capabilities to work. I get the feeling that you are beginning to want to change the direction of your life and that you realize that you are capable of doing just that! But I am a bit worried about how you just discounted yourself, and I'd like to explore with you where that kind of negative self-evaluation is coming from.

In his later sessions Darald's object relations work brought to light what appeared to be a history of progression from symptoms of Fairbairn's *schizoid position* to indication of the *schizoid state* (as described by Gomez, 1997, pp. 59–67). In a nutshell, the schizoid position is characterized by having intense needs for objects but with fear of closeness with the same objects, similar to an approach-avoidance feature. The schizoid state is ascribed to the person whose personality manifests isolated, meaningless, and withdrawn characteristics (St. Clair, 1996, p. 220). It would appear that Darald's pathology may be described, again in Fairbairn's paradigm, in terms of bad internal objects that are disruptive within the ego. Such internalized objects are repressed and are the bad elements inside Darald. In pure psychological terms, Darald's schizoid state is a self-generated self-protection mechanism intended to repress and compensate for the badness that his ego had long ago encountered in his environment (St. Clair, 1996, pp. 65–66). What can the therapist do to help Darald ameliorate his distress and developmental deficit? After much diligent and intensive work with Darald, the following is something that the therapist wrote in a journal entry following a typical object relations session:

>   **THERAPIST** (*writing in summary notes*):   I now believe that Darald's difficulties in relationships with others must involve restoring his direct and forceful capacity at making and sustaining contact with others. My goal for him is to facilitate the

release of bad objects from his unconscious mind. When we can rid his unconscious of these bad objects, he can effectively dissolve the residual distorted emotional constructs that have sustained his pathology over the years. His bad objects were internalized in the first place because they once seemed indispensable, and they were repressed because they were painfully intolerable to his ego. As I read in St. Clair (1996, pp. 66–67), I am made more aware of my role as therapist to take care to avoid strengthening his guilt, fear, and feelings of worthlessness. I must not side with Darald's superego (antilibinial ego or internal saboteur), because guilt, fear, and feelings of worthlessness may strengthen his resistance and keep the bad objects repressed (these are defenses and can sustain his resistance). I believe that Darald's resistance may be fear of releasing the bad objects from his unconscious and that such fear runs the risk of partially returning these bad objects to his psyche. So, for future therapy sessions, I must definitely assist Darald in restoring and structuring his positive and constructive relationship competencies.

Relationship, Transference, and the Essence of Therapy

As Darald's personal interaction with the therapist continued, his life adjustment slowly changed. So did his life situation. He obtained management training and employment with a large national firm. He moved from his parent's home into an apartment of his own. His relationships with women improved to the point where he could sustain and enjoy them. Then, his father died. Shortly thereafter, Darald moved back into the family home in order to care for his aging and ailing mother. At this writing, Darald continues therapy. He is still employed by the national firm. He has begun to interact socially, and his relationships with women are still satisfactory.

The status of Darald's progress, as advised by his therapist, is positive and encouraging. Darald's therapeutic journey to this point has been long, hard, and often painful to both himself and the therapist. The relationship between Darald and the therapist has evolved into one of hard work, strong commitment, and mutual trust. The therapist has been acutely but sensitively aware of the concepts of both relationship and transference in her work with Darald. In terms of comparing the therapeutic relationship to transference-countertransference in object relational therapy, the therapist points out that the differences are quite subtle but important (J. S. Scharff, 1997). The therapeutic relationship is based on shared affective meaning, mutual empathy and trust, subjective experience, and unconditional acceptance of the client's personhood, problems, perceptions, feelings, and life goals. *Transference* refers to the feelings the client projects onto the therapist, whereby *countertransference* denotes the ways in which the therapist is influenced by the client's projections. The therapist has emphasized the therapeutic relationship as taking precedence over the phenomenon of transference without diminishing the value of the latter.

THERAPIST (*again writing in summary notes*): After several months of work with Darald, I am confident that he has come to understand himself better and that the therapeutic relationship we have forged together has played a substantial role in facilitating his emotional maturation. Environmental changes have been factors that have been important. And I cannot determine the extent they might have influenced him. But, in object relations terms, I have attempted to provide the kinds of consistent, trusting, caring, supportive relationships that would encourage him to trust himself more. Many times I sensed and was aware of the transference/countertransference phenomenon in our relationship. I recognized that, but deliberately chose not to go there with Darald because I felt that doing so would negatively affect our therapeutic relationship. I observed that the more I fully trusted and shared myself honestly with him, the more he gradually came to trust me and began to interact with others outside of the therapy setting in more trusting and effective ways. He progressed to the point where he could appropriately relate to his mother and revise his memories and hostility toward his deceased father. I believe that his overall functioning and relational abilities have substantially improved and that the therapy played an important part in assisting him to do so. I am quite confident that Darald will succeed in his challenging quest to re-own his split-off bad objects and integrate them into his central ego/ideal object.

For his part, Darald writes an evaluative response to his therapeutic experiences. "I'm now feeling better about myself. I feel fortunate to have found a therapist that I can trust and understand and who truly understands me. She has allowed me to progress at my own pace. In a way, I have discovered that a good therapist is someone who cannot and will not do anything *for* you. I have also discovered that I must keep working at this for the rest of my life, and that is as it should be. I am responsible for my own mental health. Best of all, I feel that our relationship is for keeps, and that is starting to provide me with an object of security."

Contributions of the Object Relations System

Most of the humanistic systems of counseling and psychotherapy have been enriched and improved as a result of the object relational–conceptual framework that deepens the understanding of what it is like to be a person as well as the meaning and personal development that counseling and psychotherapy provide (Gomez, 1997, p. 4). Object relations teachings enhance spontaneity; authenticity; openness; attention to clients' own feelings; and attention to others' affects, thoughts, sensations, attitudes, and hunches. Its honest focus on internal and interpersonal unconscious processes enhances the work and understanding of counselors, psychotherapists, social workers, teachers, pastoral counselors, nurses, and other human service workers (Gomez, 1997, p. 5).

Object relations has had a revolutionary impact on Western societies in general, as well as in the limited world of psychotherapy. Because the critical importance of a close, consistent, and continuous relationship has been recognized, social policy has been transformed. More legal and social efforts and resources are now being focused on preventing the separation of young children from their parents. Medical institutions such as hospitals and clinics are more prone to encourage than to forbid parents from staying with young children. In the vast majority of cases, children who are wards of the public are placed with foster families rather than being remanded to impersonal institutions. Insofar as possible, refugee children are kept with their parents rather than being rescued and reared in institutions that are foreign to them. The closure of so many psychiatric hospitals nationwide has shown some recognition of the shortcomings of sterile and impersonal institutional care for vulnerable adults. The key-worker system with its nurturance of caring relationships has spread throughout the welfare system (Gomez, 1997, p. 5).

St. Clair (1996, pp. 175–176) credits object relations theory with becoming a revolutionary catalyst for changing how psychoanalysts think about the person. Rather than viewing the human mind as a set of predetermined, inherited structures emerging from within the individual (the classical drive model), the emphasis has now been shifted to the relational model. Mitchell (1988, p. 17) commenting on that shift, states that "the very boundaries around the subject matter of psychoanalysis have been redrawn, and that broad reframing has had profound implications for both theory and clinical practice." Mitchell supplied italicized emphasis to the following statement, which makes a cogent point: *"Mind has been redefined from a set of predetermined structures emerging from inside an individual organism to transactional patterns and internal structures derived from an interactive, interpersonal field"* (p. 17). In terms of the effects on counseling and psychotherapy, St. Clair (1996) asserts that many of the creative, innovative, and influential contributions of the past several decades have flowed from the relational model (p. 176).

The emergence of the relational models, such as object relations therapy, has made a dramatic contribution toward transforming traditional psychoanalytic therapy into a more interactive and personable process. For example, Wilner (1999) points out that psychoanalysis has progressed from its original classical base toward the positivistic tradition of observing and understanding the client. Wilner states

> The interpersonal and relational positions, with their emphasis on intersubjectivity, have brought additional foci to our attention. Psychoanalysis now attends to subjective feelings, fantasies, sensations, and the like in order to see more clearly the influence of patient and analyst upon one another in this expanded context. This new movement has led to a democratization of psychoanalysis, making pertinent such concepts as interpersonal mutuality and symmetry, and to a different constructivistic and perspectivistic view of reality. . . . (p. 617).

Another contribution of the relational theories has been the injection of such emotional components as affects and joy into the psychoanalytic experience. As an example, Heisterkamp (1999) calls our attention to the positive influence of the affect of joy and affects in general to current psychoanalytic therapy. He states that, "Whereas anxiety reflects structuring in the psyche, joy is the expression of successful (re)structuring in whatever form, and marks the dawn of a new beginning" (p. 1247). Heisterkamp notes that although joyful phenomena, including jokes and humor (accounts of observed therapeutic incidents or events of an interesting or amusing nature), have scarcely appeared in professional journals, such relational affects enhance the value, quality, and tone of psychoanalytic therapy (p. 1247).

Shortcomings of the Object Relations System

Probably the most obvious deficit in the object relations model we have been describing has to do with the model's failure to account for certain needs of the client, such as the need to be alone or to regress (Summers, 1999, pp. 33–38). Since object relations clinicians have made a shift from a one-person to a two-person model, it is assumed that all free associations are reactions to the therapist. It is also assumed that transference is not only the client's experience of the therapist but also includes the therapist's participation in the client's pattern of relating. Therefore, it is opined that the subjectivities of client and therapist are indistinguishably commingled (p. 34). If the object relational therapist adheres rigorously to the model, the subjective interviewing approach positions the therapist in a strategy of inextricably being with the client every step of the way, in every object representation and in every therapeutic moment (J. S. Scharff, 1997). Consequently, the client's needs, such as the need for pure autonomy, to be alone, or to regress cannot be separated from the subjectivity of the therapist (Summers, 1999, p. 35).

Object relations therapy works best with individuals who are interested in gaining psychological understanding through the relationship with the therapist (J. S. Scharff, 1997). Therefore, this may not be the first treatment choice for mandated therapy clients such as individuals who come in for court-ordered therapy.

Since the early development of object relations theory occurred in British and European cultural settings, many of the ideas have been considered culture-bound and founded on white, mostly male, middle-class subjects. Formulations which may resonate with a certain cultural group cannot automatically be applied to all cultural groups. Therefore, there is an urgent need for more diverse influences to be brought to current theory and clinical work by object relations practitioners (Gomez, 1997, p. 5).

Another shortcoming of object relations therapy that has been pointed out by students of therapy is that the writings of some of the experts in object relations and other relational theories use unique words (vernacular terms) that seem to be difficult to understand. The seemingly exclusionary terminology of such writings seems to often make the material more confusing than if it had been clearly stated in plain language. This shortcoming appears to be unfortunate because the writings of these experts have much to teach us about the innovative, refreshing concepts and strategies of the object relations viewpoint.

Some therapists still cling to the notion that symptoms such as extreme childhood trauma related to sexual abuse should be relived through the process of permanent interpretation of transference. Hirsch (1997) stated that transference and countertransference alone do not always sufficiently work through the guilt feelings, shame, and mourning to permit separation from the traumatic objects. Rather, a supporting, confirming, and valuing therapist activity is indicated.

Object Relations Therapy with Diverse Populations

Regarding work with difference and diversity, object relations cannot and should not be expected to take the place of social and political involvement (Gomez, 1997, p. 201). But object relations theorists and clinicians hold in common a belief in the centrality of relationships between and within people. Working against prejudice, discrimination, and scapegoating is a difficult task that all societies and all systems of therapy, including object relations, must continually confront. At least three elements of the object relations approach provide insight into the dynamics of prejudice: (1) Klein's bad object concept, (2) Fairbairn's exciting and rejecting dichotomy, and, (3) Bolby's system of insecure or avoidant attachment patterns (Gomez, 1997, p. 200).

Because object relations therapy as it is practiced in the United States today was derived from the study of relationships, it is claimed by many clinicians to transfer effectively across populations and modalities. It is said to be ideally suited for work with couples, families, groups, and communities. In current U.S. usage, the object relations theoretical modality is also universal in its way of looking at things. It bridges the gap among age, race, gender, nationality, socioeconomic status, and other divergent cultural dimensions (J. S. Scharff, 1997). For example, if an educated, white, middle-aged, female therapist works directly with either a female or male of another race and culture, the therapist is faced with the differences between them. The therapist may be unsure of how the client perceives him or her, what it is like for the client to come to therapy, and what the client expects to gain from the therapy. "The clients certainly cannot assume that they will receive understanding on the basis of similarity of background alone" (J. S. Scharff, 1997). Clients must test it out in the therapy setting. The way to test it out is for the client to experience the therapist as he or she is—to be able to openly talk about fears and fantasies while regarding the therapist as an object. Is the therapist like other objects that the client is familiar with? Can the client feel safe and fully accepted by the therapist? The diversity or cultural difference between the therapist and client is openly talked about in the beginning. No hidden attitudes, beliefs, feelings, or other factors are put aside until later. The therapy setting is considered a part of real, ongoing life. It is a laboratory of life. The client is not left hanging and wondering about any different object representations that might be lurking in the therapy room, and therefore the honesty, ethics, and openness of the situation encourage the development of a trusting relationship in which other object relational and therapeutic issues may be more effectively and comfortably addressed. According to J. S. Scharff (1997) that is the way object relations works with difference and diversity.

Summary

For the sole purpose of providing a cursory introduction to a more up-to-date system of analytic therapy (object relations), this unique dualistic chapter began with a very brief background sketch of classical Freudian psychoanalytic theory. Although almost all of the modern, analytically-oriented therapists claim to adhere to Freud's fundamental theories, most of them have developed and used substantial and fundamental additions and revisions to Freud's tenets. That is especially true in the case of the relational approaches, including object relations, which the remainder of the chapter described.

The object relations approach was first developed by British classical psychoanalytic clinicians and scholars who became convinced that people were more than systems of biological drives. They also placed relationship at the heart of what it means to be fully human.

Consequently, in modern analytical terms, *object* is no longer rooted solely in the Freudian instinct theory from which it evolved. In terms of personality theory, clinical evidence and research have overwhelmingly shown that human motivation does not originate in the tension reduction drive theory of classical psychoanalytic theory. Nor can interpersonal relating be reduced to instinctual need gratification. Object relations theory holds that people are born with an autonomous motivation to relate to other people as opposed to being forced to do so in order to attain tension reduction. This autonomous nature of the need for others has led object relations therapists to believe that the formation of relationships is the most fundamental human motivation.

Since the need for relationships throughout life is at the center of the formation of the self, personality development is considered to be a continuous lifelong process including infancy, adolescence, and the various stages of adulthood. Healthy object attachments early in life are needed to produce a healthy personality. But maladjustment is broadly viewed in terms of developmental arrest rather than conflicts between different parts or structures of the personality. Such developmental arrests result in unfinished, disorganized, and unintegrated structures of the personality.

Some of the important concepts of object relations that were described in the chapter included: (1) The object or the other is that from which the instinct gets gratification or that with which the human relates. Powerful and impressive object attachments are often formed during infancy. (2) Human beings are essentially social creatures. The need for relationships is at the central core of the definition of the self—of what it means to be truly human. (3) The primacy of relationships over instincts is unequivocal in object relations theory. (4) Splitting of internal object attachments early in life may result in the person forming a sense of self as being either bad or good, and that sets the stage for maladjustment or mental health problems.

The therapeutic process in object relations does not follow a step-by-step cookbook formula. Rather, it entails the therapist's genuine acceptance of all clients who present themselves for help. Therapists try to create or allow psychological space by allowing their own internal object representations to reverberate with the client's. The therapy is managed in such a way that there is deep empathy and focus is on the client, especially on the client's internal world. Such a focus will usually allow the client and the therapist to affect each other. That is highly desirable. The first goal is to do no harm. There is often little noticeable difference between object relations strategies and those of other psychoanalytical, dynamic, or even humanistic therapies. The main difference is in the object relations therapist's thinking or attitude—in how the therapist is conceptualizing what is transpiring in the therapeutic relationship.

Object relations therapy is really a way of *being* with a person. It is not a precise, scientific, intellectual process. It is intensely personal. The therapist strives to do whatever must be done to create a space for the client to truly be him- or herself. It is very important that the therapist facilitate the conditions whereby the client gains and maintains autonomy. The client has the capacity within the self to discover what is bothering him or her. The therapist uses a variety of strategies to help the client gain knowledge of his or her unconscious world and to discover therapeutic choices (J. S. Scharff, 1997). The outcomes of successful object relations therapy are simply this: clients will become aware of their relationship deficits and they will discover ways to improve their interpersonal functioning.

The chapter included a sample case involving Darald to depict some of the theoretical and therapeutic strategies that object relations advocates. We pointed out some of the ways object relations therapists work with diverse populations. Also, a discussion of the strengths and weaknesses of object relations was provided.

SUGGESTIONS FOR FURTHER READING

Gomez, L. (1997). *An introduction to object relations.* New York: New York University Press.

Klein, R. S. (1990). *Object relations and the family process.* New York: Praeger.

Kumin, I. (1996). *Pre-object relatedness: Early attachment and the psychoanalytic situation.* New York: Guilford Press.

Mitchell, S. A. (1988). *Relational concepts in psychoanalysis: An integration.* Cambridge, MA: Harvard University Press.

Rogers, R. (1991). *Self and other: Object relations in psychoanalysis and literature.* New York: New York University Press.

Scharff, J. S. (1997). *Object relations therapy* (Videotape No. 0-205-32913-6, T. Labriola, Producer). In J. Carlson & D. Kjos, *Object relations therapy with Scharff: Psychotherapy with the experts.* Boston: Allyn & Bacon.

Scharff, J. S., & Scharff, D. E. (1998). *Object relations individual therapy.* Northvale, NJ: Jason Aronson.

Skolnick, N. J., & Scharff, D. E. (Eds.). (1998). *Fairbairn: Then and now.* Hillsdale, NJ: Analytic Press.

St. Clair, M. (1996). *Object relations and self psychology: An introduction* (2nd ed.). Pacific Grove: CA: Brooks/Cole.

Summers, F. L. (1999). *Transcending the self: An object relations model of psychoanalytic therapy.* Hillsdale, NJ: Analytic Press.

REFERENCES

Ables, N. (1979). Psychodynamic theory. In H. M. Burks & B. Stefflre (Eds.), *Theories of counseling* (pp. 132–171). New York: McGraw-Hill.

Ainsworth, M. D. S., & Bolby, J. (1991). An ethological approach to personality development. *American Psychologist, 46,* 333–341.

Arlow, J. A. (1979). Psychoanalysis. In R. J. Corsini (Ed.), *Current psychotherapies* (2nd ed., pp. 1–43), Itasca, IL: F. E. Peacock.

Arlow, J. A. (1989). Psychoanalysis. In R. J. Corsini & D. Wedding (Eds.), *Current psychotherapies* (4th ed., pp. 18–62), Itasca, IL: F. E. Peacock.

Arlow, J. A. (1995). Psychoanalysis. In R. J. Corsini & D. Wedding (Eds.), *Current psychotherapies* (5th ed., pp. 15–50), Itasca, IL: F. E. Peacock.

Arlow, J. A., & Brenner, C. (1964). *Psychoanalytic concepts and the structural theory.* New York: International Universities Press.

Auld, F., & Hyman, M. (1991). *Resolution of inner conflict: An introduction to psychoanalytic therapy.* Washington, DC: American Psychological Association.

Babcock, R. (1983). *Sigmund Freud.* New York: Tavistock.

Bacal, H. A. (1995). The essence of Kohut's work and the progress of self psychology. *Psychoanalytic Dialogues, 5*(3), 353–366.

Blanck, R., & Blanck, G. (1986). *Beyond ego psychology: Developmental object relations theory.* New York: Columbia University Press.

Bolen, R. M. (2000). Validity of attachment theory. *Trauma, Violence, & Abuse, 1*(2), 128–153.

Bretherton, I. (1992). The origins of attachment theory: John Bolby and Mary Ainsworth. *Developmental Psychology, 28,* 759–775.

Corrigan, E. G., & Gordon, P. E. (Eds.). (1995). *The mind object: Precocity and pathology of self-sufficiency.* Northvale, NJ: Jason Aronson.

Fairbairn, W. R. D. (1954). Endopsychic structure considered in terms of object-relationships. In W. R. D. Fairbairn, *An object-relations theory of the personality* (pp. 82–136). New York: Basic Books. (Original work published in 1944)

Fancher, R. E. (1973). *Psychoanalytic psychology: The development of Freud's thought.* New York: W. W. Norton.

Feiner, K., & Kiersky, S. (1994). Empathy: A common ground. *Psychoanalytic Dialogues, 4*(3), 425–440.

Fine, R. (1973). Psychoanalysis. In R. J. Corsini (Ed.), *Current psychotherapies* (pp. 1–33). Itasca, IL: F. E. Peacock.

Fine, R. (1979). *A history of psychoanalysis.* New York: Columbia University Press.

Fine, R. (1990). *The history of psychoanalysis.* New York: Jason Aronson.

Fraley, R. C., & Shaver, P. R. (2000). Adult romantic attachment: Theoretical developments, emerging controversies, and unanswered questions. *Review of General Psychology, 4*(2), 132–154.

Freud, S., (1958). Formulations on the two principles of mental functioning. In J. Strachey (Ed. and Trans.), *The standard edition of the complete psychological works of Sigmund Freud* (Vol. 12, pp. 213–227). London: Hogarth Press. (Original work published 1911)

Freud, S. (1961a). The infantile genital organization: An interpolation into the theory of sexuality. In J. Strachey (Ed. and Trans.), *The standard edition of the complete psychological works of Sigmund Freud* (Vol. 19, pp. 141–149). London: Hogarth Press. (Original work published 1923)

Freud, S. (1961b). The dissolution of the Oedipus complex. In J. Strachey (Ed. and Trans.), *The standard edition of the complete psychological works of Sigmund Freud* (Vol. 19, pp. 173–183). London: Hogarth Press. (Original work published 1924)

Ganzarain, R. (1989). *Object relations group psychotherapy: The group as an object, a tool, and a training base.* Madison, CT: International Universities Press.

Giovacchini, P. L. (1977). Psychoanalysis. In R. J. Corsini (Ed.), *Current personality theories* (pp. 15–43). Itasca, IL: F. E. Peacock.

Goldman, G. D., & Milman, D. S. (Eds.). (1978). *Psychoanalytic psychotherapy.* Reading, MA: Addison-Wesley.

Gomez, L. (1997). *An introduction to object relations.* New York: New York University Press.

Gunderson, J. G., & Gabbard, G. O. (1999). Making the case for psychoanalytic therapies in the current psychiatric environment. *Journal of the American Psychoanalytic Association, 47,* 679–704.

Hall, C. S. (1954). *A primer of Freudian psychology.* New York: World.

Hansen, J. C., Stevic, R. R., & Warner, R. W., Jr. (1982). *Counseling theory and process* (3rd ed.). Boston: Allyn & Bacon.

Heisterkamp, G. (1999). Zur Freude in der analytischen psychotherapie. [Joy in psychoanalytic therapy]. *Psyche: Zeitschrift fuer Psychoanalyse und ihre Anwendungen, 53,* 1247–1265.

Hirsch, M. (1997). Psychoanalytische therapie bei sexuell missbrauchten jugendlichen. [Psychoanalytic therapy with adolescent victims of sexual abuse]. *Praxis der Kinderpsychologie und Kinderpsychiatrie, 46,* 681–695.

Hornstein, G. A. (1992). The return of the repressed: Psychology's problematic relations with psychoanalysis, 1909–1960. *American Psychologist, 47,* 254–263.

Josephs, L. (1994). Empathic character analysis. *American Journal of Psychoanalysis, 54*(1), 41–54.

Klein, R. S. (1990). *Object relations and the family process.* New York: Praeger.

Kohut, H. (1995). Introspection, empathy, and psychoanalysis: An examination of the relationship between mode of observation and theory. *Journal of Psychotherapy Practice and Research, 4*(2), 163–177.

Kumin, I. (1996). *Pre-object relatedness: Early attachment and the psychoanalytic situation.* New York: Guilford Press.

La Guardia, J. G., Ryan, R. M., Couchman, C. E., & Deci, E. L. (2000). Within-person variation in security of attachment: A self-determination theory perspective on attachment, need fulfillment, and well-being. *Journal of Personality & Social Psychology, 70,* 367–384.

Lopez, F. G., & Brennan, K. A. (2000). Dynamic processes underlying adult attachment organization: Toward an attachment theoretical perspective on the healthy and effective self. *Journal of Counseling Psychology, 47,* 283–300.

Mitchell, L. (2000). Attachment to the missing object: Infidelity and obsessive love. *Journal of Applied Psychoanalytic Studies, 2*(4), 383–395.

Mitchell, S. A. (1988). *Relational concepts in psychoanalysis: An integration.* Cambridge, MA: Harvard University Press.

Pietromonaco, P. R., & Barrett, L. F. (2000). Attachment theory as an organizing framework: A view from different levels of analysis. *Review of General Psychology, 4*(2), 107–110.

Rapaport, D. (1967). The scientific methodology of psychoanalysis. In M. M. Gill (Ed.), *The collected papers of David Rapaport* (pp. 165–220). New York: Basic Books.

Rogers, R. (1991). Self and other: *Object relations in psychoanalysis and literature.* New York: New York University Press.

Scharff, J. S. (Therapist). (1997). *Object relations therapy* (Videotape No. 0-205-32913-6, T. Labriola, Producer). In J. Carlson & D. Kjos, *Object relations therapy with Scharff: Psychotherapy with the experts.* Boston: Allyn & Bacon.

Scharff, J. S., & Scharff, D. E. (1998). *Object relations individual therapy.* Northvale, NJ: Jason Aronson.

Scharff, D. E. (1998). Object construction, object sorting, and object exclusion: Implications of family and marital therapy for object relations theory. In N. J. Skolnick & D. E. Scharff (Eds.), *Fairbairn: Then and now* (pp. 255–274). Hillsdale, NJ: Analytic Press.

Shakow, D., & Rapaport, D. (1964). *The influence of Freud on American psychology.* New York: International Universities Press.

Skolnick, N. J., & Scharff, D. E. (Eds.). (1998). *Fairbairn: Then and now.* Hillsdale, NJ: Analytic Press.

St. Clair, M. (1996). *Object relations and self psychology: An introduction* (2nd ed.). Pacific Grove: CA: Brooks/Cole.

Summers, F. L. (1999). *Transcending the self: An object relations model of psychoanalytic therapy.* Hillsdale, NJ: Analytic Press.

Theweleit, K. (1994). *Object choice (All you need is love . . .): On mating strategies & a fragment of a Freud biography.* London: Verso.

Warren, M. P. (1994). The missing link: The role of empathy in communicative psychoanalysis. *International Journal of Communicative Psychoanalysis and Psychotherapy, 9*(2), 35–39.

Wilner, W. (1999). The un-consciousing of awareness in psychoanalytic therapy. *Contemporary Psychoanalysis, 35,* 617–628.

Wollheim, R. (1971). *Sigmund Freud.* New York: Viking.

Wolman, B. B. (1968). *The unconscious mind: The meaning of Freudian psychology.* Englewood Cliffs, NJ: Prentice-Hall.

Wolman, B. B. (1989). The protoconscious. *Dynamische Psychiatrie, 22*(1/2), 22–30.

5

Adlerian Therapy

Fundamental Tenets

History

The history of Adlerian therapy can be divided into three eras: (1) its origin in Europe, where it split off from Freudian psychoanalytics in the early 1900s under its namesake, Alfred Adler; (2) its rooting and fledgling growth in America through the advocacy of Rudolf Dreikurs—writer, therapist, and editor; and (3) the growth and dissemination of Adlerian concepts and techniques in the elementary school guidance movement through the work of Don Dinkmeyer.

In 1902, Alfred Adler was invited to join Freud's inner circle, probably because of articles he had written in defense of Freud. However, it was not long before theoretical divisions started to separate the two men. The schism widened, and in 1912 Adler and others of Freud's circle split to form the Society for Free Psychoanalytic Thought and started publishing the *Journal for Individual Psychology*.

More than any other early psychologist, Adler envisioned a social psychology that reached out into the community. The most notable example of such outreach programs was the child guidance centers he started in the Vienna public schools in 1922.

One of the major precepts of Adlerian psychology, that of inferiority and superiority, may be traced to Adler's own early life. His childhood was marked by sickness, accidents, and failure in school, all of which contributed to a compensatory drive to become superior. Adler's determination culminated in a medical degree, publication of over three hundred books and articles, worldwide lecture tours, and the naming of a therapeutic modality after himself by the time of his death in 1937.

If not for Rudolf Dreikurs, the fledgling Adlerian movement might have ceased to exist. Dreikurs pushed hard for the adoption of child guidance centers in America. His prolific writing about Adlerian psychology and his own innovations, such as group therapy, the modeling of real-life counseling sessions before audiences (Dreikurs, 1959), multiple therapist procedures, and a comprehensive counseling approach to children (Dinkmeyer, Pew, & Dinkmeyer, 1979, p. 3), did much to bring Adlerian psychology to the attention of the general public. Dreikur's editorship of the *Journal of Individual Psychology* and the *Individual Psychology Bulletin* and his founding of the Alfred Adler Institute in Chicago and the North American Society of Adlerian Psychology have played a crucial part in revealing

Adlerian therapy as a comprehensive therapy for humankind and not merely an approach good for "talking to kids." Dreikurs died in 1972.

It was not until the emergence of Don Dinkmeyer, an acolyte of Dreikurs, that Adlerian concepts became widespread. Two excellent commercial enterprises, *Developing Understanding of Self and Others* (DUSO) (Dinkmeyer & Dinkmeyer, 1982) and *Systematic Training for Effective Parenting* (STEP) (Dinkmeyer & McKay, 1976), have enabled thousands of children, parents, and human service workers to profit from the basic tenets of Adler and Dreikurs.

The use and success of Adlerian psychology and therapy have probably been most pronounced in educational settings (Allen, 2000; Dinkmeyer & Sperry, 2000, pp. 127–149; Pryor & Tollerud, 1999). A constant theme of Adlerian therapy over the years has been in working with children, parents, teachers, and significant others in their social context, and clearly one of the major social contexts of most children is school. It is the rare elementary school counselor who will not have some familiarity with or use some techniques that are Adlerian in nature. The "common-sense" basis of the Adlerian approach has resulted in many of Adler's ideas being appropriated by other theorists without due credit to Adler (Ansbacher, 1977, pp. 77–78). Such concepts as inferiority and superiority complexes, goal orientation, lifestyle, the will to power, dependency, and overprotection have become so widespread that few realize they were originated by Adler.

While many other theories have and still are "borrowing" from Adler, the Adlerians themselves have not been idle in evolving their approach. Due to the current focus on brevity in the therapeutic world, an analytic therapy such as Adlerian would seem to have little chance of survival. As a result, Adlerians have changed and adapted their analytic approach to become more parsimonious and efficient without giving up their analytical base (Carlson, 1997; Carlson & Sperry, 2000; Slavik, Sperry, & Carlson, 2000; Watts, 2000a; Watts & Carlson, 1999).

Overview of Adlerian Therapy

Humans are constantly *becoming*—moving toward fictional goals that they think lead to superiority. At times such behavior is self-defeating. The pursuit of unrealistic and unattainable goals—the result of inferiority feelings—leads to discouragement. In its most severe forms such discouragement fosters neurosis, psychosis, substance abuse, perversions, problems in children, criminal behavior, and suicide (Adler, 1956, p. 158). The role of the counselor is to apprise the client of mistaken goals that lead to self-defeating behavior and to help the client broaden his or her social interest so that self-centeredness, egotism, and isolation are expunged in favor of sincere, meaningful, and positive interpersonal relationships. A holistic view of the client is taken by the counselor, and the concept of discrete traits, factors, attributes, typologies, indexes, and so forth, becomes secondary to the unity of the individual (Mosak, 1989, p. 73).

However, no person is merely a clone of some perfect human model that exists in society. Personhood is perceived to be phenomenological, which means that each individual is unique. Society is viewed as teleological, meaning that humans exist for a definite purpose or design in the natural scheme of things. Adlerian theory holds that people are not pushed by the objective past or controlled by mechanistic or external forces (although they may think they are), but rather, they are pulled by the future and controlled by themselves (even though they may occasionally need help from a counselor).

In a contemporary sense, Adlerians may be considered *technical eclectives.* That is, they use a variety of cognitive, behavioral, and experimental techniques within their analytical framework. This approach operates in a flexible manner and is based on the individual needs of the client (Watts, 2000a). Therefore, at any given time, and depending upon a variety of factors that impact the client, Adlerians may range in operation from a psychoeducational approach that provides information, an analytical framework that seeks to achieve insight, a cognitive view that seeks to change perception, and a behavioral contract to promote behavior change. The therapist can overlay all of these with the confrontation of mistaken goals of belonging and encouragement for adapting a better lifestyle (Dinkmeyer, Dinkmeyer & Sperry, 1987).

Theory of Personality

Adlerian psychology is both an individual and a social psychology—individual in the sense that the person is viewed as a unified organism (Mosak, 1989, p. 73); social in the sense that humans are seen as being motivated primarily by social interest. Because individual psychology was developed in reaction to Freudian psychoanalytic psychology, the Adlerian position on personality differs from the psychoanalytic view in several important ways. First, social urges take precedence over sexual urges in personality development. Second, consciousness rather than unconsciousness is the primary source of ideas and values. Third, the determinants of behavior consist of more than just one's genetic endowment or early sexual impressions. Fourth, normal psychological development is the model of choice rather than varying degrees of mental illness (or the lack thereof) (Dinkmeyer, Dinkmeyer, & Sperry, 1987).

From birth (when we are utterly dependent on others for our survival) to adulthood (when to be fully functional we must learn to cooperate with others), all behaviors may be construed to have social meaning (Dinkmeyer, Pew, & Dinkmeyer, 1979, p. 7). *Social meaning* may be defined as "wanting to belong." Whether belonging is in terms of family, significant others, or professional or social groups, "no man is an island unto himself."

Life Tasks.   The goals of belonging are embedded in life tasks. There are three major life tasks—friendship, occupation, and love (Dreikurs, 1981). Life tasks are aimed at the development of a feeling of responsibility to the commonweal. If one of the tasks is evaded, difficulties in fulfilling the others will be expressed sooner or later (Dreikurs, 1981, p. 34).

The life task of friendship is probably the best indicator of a person's social interest because one's relationships with significant friends express one's attitude toward the whole community (Dreikurs, 1981, p. 40). Because work consumes the greater portion of our waking moments, occupation is a prime life task. Only the most discouraged people evade work, which is why the inability to work is often regarded as a serious illness and why nonfulfillment of this task threatens the very maintenance of one's life (Dreikurs, 1981, p. 34). The importance of the occupational task weighs most heavily on those who have failed in the life tasks of love and friendship, because these individuals have no other effective way of keeping in touch with society (Dreikurs, 1981, pp. 35–36).

Love is seen by Adlerians not in terms of libidinal drives but rather as a matter of role. The major task of love is understanding and relating to another person. Fulfillment of this task demands a maximum of social interest because it involves the closest of all contacts between two humans. It tests their capacity for cooperation to the limit and eliminates the distance that can be maintained in occupational and social relationships (Dreikurs, 1981, p. 40). To achieve such a capacity, fully functioning individuals do not see men or women in stereotypical or antagonistic roles, but rather as equal and contributing partners. Adlerians, then, have much to say about equal rights between the sexes.

Two other life tasks have been added to the first three. Humankind needs to deal with its relationship to the spiritual (Mosak & Dreikurs, 1967). Because religion and man's search for transcendental meaning play such an important part in the social fabric of the individual, spirituality is a key life task (Cheston, 2000; Gold & Mansager, 2000; Mosak & Dreikurs, 2000; Watts, 2000b). People do not live by bread alone and "must" (according to Adler) define a spiritual self in relation to the cosmos, God, and universal values and how to relate to these concepts to obtain a spiritual centeredness such that the other life tasks all take on meaning (Mosak, 1989, p. 68; Witmer, 1989, pp. 33–46).

Finally, humans need to understand their individual selves—the "I" and the "me" (Dreikurs & Mosak, 1967). Being able to define and affirm ourselves means that it is imperative that good relations exist between the "I" and the "me" as well as between the "I" and other people (Mosak, 1989, p. 68; Witmer, 1989, p. 33).

None of these life tasks stands apart from the others. A solution to one helps provide a solution to the others. All of the life tasks deal with the same problem—the necessity for humankind to persevere in the contemporary environment.

Nomothetic Principles.   Yet, basic questions remain. Why are people different? Why do some become law-abiding citizens and others criminals? Why do some become neurotics, others psychotics, and the rest, by degrees, well-adjusted? In essence, what makes us what we are? For Adler, the answer to this question lies in four parts. Three of the parts are *nomothetic* (they apply to humankind in general) but they include many exceptions.

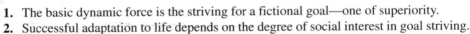

1. The basic dynamic force is the striving for a fictional goal—one of superiority.
2. Successful adaptation to life depends on the degree of social interest in goal striving.
3. Goal striving may be considered more or less active and can be considered according to type (Ansbacher & Ansbacher, 1956, p. 172).

Fictional Goals.   Fictional goals are the outcome of unconscious notions that have no counterpart in reality. These fictional goals, then, are generated in an unreal world. However, this makes them no less important than the objective facts of the real world. This unrealistic world becomes the individual's real world of values (Vaihinger, 1956, p. 77). Fictional goals are concerned with the future. However, this future is not objective because it is expressed and wished for by the individual in the present. According to Adler, because individuals are seldom, if ever, aware of their fictional goals, such hidden goals make up the essential content of the unconscious (Vaihinger, 1956, p. 89).

These fictional goals are mental constructions which take the place of reality (Bruder, 1998). As the individual filters reality through his or her personal lens, it becomes reconstructed to fit what the individual believes will enhance his or her sense of belonging, style of life, and goal striving.

Fictional goals start early in life. A newborn child enters an environment that is by no means neutral. That environment is represented by the family constellation. Through observation, exploration, trial and error, and feedback from this primary environment, the child quickly learns what will and will not work (Dinkmeyer, Dinkmeyer, & Sperry, 1987, p. 34). As children attempt to carve out a territory in the family constellation, they generate goals that they hope will lead to a feeling of self-worth. Problems arise because children make erroneous judgments and do not always think logically. This makes no difference, for they accept such judgments and thoughts as if they are true, even though they have no basis in fact (Mosak, 1979, pp. 56–57). In the young child, fictional conceptualizations form the first far-reaching goals of what is to become the lifestyle. These form at such a young age that they are submerged by the individual (Dinkmeyer, Pew, & Dinkmeyer, 1979, p. 26). Nevertheless, they survive, carrying the individual forward into his or her fictional future.

Fictional goals are not necessarily bad, evil, or debilitating. They are merely an attempt at belonging and striving for a piece of significance in the eyes of others—in other words, being somebody (Rule, 1985). If people did not have such goals, there would be no striving for perfection and society would not progress.

The individual who learns to deal in socially acceptable compensatory ways with life's problems will strive for the commonly acceptable individual goal of perfection. However, the individual who cannot navigate life's shoals is likely to seek an exaggerated goal of personal superiority. Taken to the extreme, these private, dysfunctional goal fictions lead to neurosis, psychosis, substance abuse, perversions, suicide, and criminal behavior (Ansbacher & Ansbacher, 1956, pp. 165–166). It is from individuals with such fictional notions that all human failures come; this is the human "flotsam and jetsam" the notions counselor is most likely to encounter.

Striving for fictional goals can be considered according to the degree and type of activity. Individuals tackle their problems with varying degrees of activity, and the degree of activity acquired in childhood becomes a thread that runs true into adulthood. Adlerians are reticent to classify people. However, to demonstrate people's attitudes and behavior toward external problems, Adlerians have proposed the following types of people and their degree of social interest:

1. *Ruling.* The individual is dominant in relationships. Much activity but little social interest is shown.
2. *Getting.* The individual expects things from others and is dependent on them. Little activity and little social interest are demonstrated.
3. *Avoiding.* The individual shies away from problems. Again, little activity and little social interest are shown.
4. *Driving.* The individual wants to achieve. Total success or nothingness are the only alternatives. Much activity and little social interest are shown.
5. *Controlling.* The individual likes order, but it must be his or her order. A great deal of activity is expended in keeping the unexpected to a bare minimum. Social interest is minimal because others in the system are constantly disrupting the individual's plans.

6. *Being victimized or martyred.* Both types are similar in their suffering. However, victims have diminished activity and interest, whereas martyrs have increased activity and interest.
7. *Being good.* The individual satisfies his or her sense of superiority by being more competent, more useful, more right, and "holier than thou." Heightened activity and interest characterize this club, to which very few can belong.
8. *Being socially useful.* The individual cooperates with others and contributes to their social well-being without self-aggrandizement. Activity and social interest are both great and positive (Adler, 1956, pp. 126–162; Mosak, 1971).

None of the foregoing types is inherently bad. The behavioral outcome of each will depend on what the individual does with his or her convictions. Very seldom will the counselor see these pure types; a blend is much more common (Dinkmeyer, Dinkmeyer, & Sperry, 1987, p. 39).

Idiographic Principles.   The fourth part of Adler's answer to why people are different is *idiographic* (it applies to the individual and no one else). It is the wholeness and uniqueness of the individual in implementing the three nomothetic laws discussed earlier (Ansbacher & Ansbacher, 1956, p. 172). In simple terms, it is the style of life. One's lifestyle is the overall pattern that influences one's feeling, thinking, and behaving (Rule, 1985). This plan is unique to each individual, is created early on in childhood as a blueprint for action, is embedded in the individual's social context, and is refined throughout life (Watts, 2000a).

We tend to behave according to how things appear to us, and when our perception changes our behavior changes accordingly. Thus, *perception* of the situation often determines behavior and belief more than the *reality* of the situation (Dinkmeyer, Dinkmeyer, & Sperry, 1987, p. 18). Individual psychology, then, draws its conclusions not from a person's possessions but from his or her use of those possessions. These applications and, more important, the manner in which the individual "experiences" them are the bricks and mortar with which an attitude toward life is built (Adler, 1956, pp. 250–256).

Nature of Maladjustment

Adler's approach to maladjustment can be best explained by his approach to neurosis. All the behavior disorders, mental and physical incapacities, delinquent and criminal acts, and psychoses are directly related to what Adler has to say about the neurotic. For Adler, the obsessive-compulsive person is the prototype of all neurosis. The obsessive-compulsive's indecisiveness and doubt, deprecation of others, godlike strivings, and focus on minutiae are all routine safeguards that exclude him or her from the social mainstream (Dinkmeyer, Dinkmeyer, & Sperry, 1987, p. 47).

Adler (1956, p. 239) depicted neurosis as follows:

1. An individual has a mistaken opinion of self and the world.
2. The individual will resort to various forms of abnormal behavior aimed at safeguarding his or her opinion of self.

3. Such safeguarding occurs when the individual is confronted with situations he or she feels will be met unsuccessfully.
4. The mistake consists of being self-centered rather than taking humankind into account.
5. The individual is not consciously aware of these processes.

Inferiority Complex.   These five components of neurosis issue from the wellspring of maladjustment—the inferiority complex. Inferiority feelings should be distinguished from an inferiority complex. All of us have inferiority feelings, since we all find situations we wish to improve (Adler, 1958, p. 51). However, inferiority becomes pathological (a complex) only when the individual is overwhelmed by a sense of inadequacy and becomes incapable of development (Adler, 1929, pp. 78–79).

Inferiority is one horn of a dilemma. The person with an inferiority complex seeks escape through a compensatory move toward superiority. However, such compensation is aimed no longer at solving problems but rather at preserving the useless side of life (Adler, 1958, p. 52).

Neurotics vacillate between inferiority and superiority. They are highly ambitious but lack courage. Avoidance, displacement, projection, retreat, helplessness, and detouring all describe how they save face when confronted with the ultimate threat—being seen as a failure. Neurotics are constantly putting psychological distance between themselves and people, environments, and tasks. They can be characterized as "yes, but" personalities. They know what should be changed but cannot or, more likely, will not change (Dinkmeyer, Dinkmeyer, & Sperry, 1987, p. 44).

Family Constellation.   Whence does the twisted logic of the neurotic come? For the Adlerians, the family constellation and atmosphere are the axes on which most other factors in the development of the child turn. The family constellation mediates the genetic and constitutional factors the child brings into it and the cultural factors the child learns from it. The personality characteristics of each family member, the birth order of the child, the sex of siblings, and family size all influence how the child finds his or her niche. Depending on the prevailing family atmosphere, the child can develop in the direction of accepting attitudes shared by the family, in the direction of rejecting them, or somewhere in between (Dinkmeyer, Pew, & Dinkmeyer, 1979, p. 24). As long as the family shares trust, confidence, mutuality, love, work, and social interest in equitable ways, the child will likely find a wholesome niche for potential growth.

However, there are a variety of family atmospheres that are anything but equitable. Those that reject, suppress, overprotect, and disparage the child (Dewey, 1971) are breeding grounds for discouragement, and the discouraged child becomes the maladjusted child (Mosak, 1979, p. 57). Such children find their place in the family constellation by striving for the mistaken goals of attention, power, revenge, and inadequacy (Dreikurs, 1953). Shulman (1973) has noted three common mistakes of adaptation in the growing child: (1) distorted attitudes of self, people, and the world ("I, others, and the world are all rotten"); (2) distorted goals and operating methods ("I must be perfect, and I will ignore, reject, or fight anything that interferes with belonging"); and (3) distorted ideas and conclusions ("I must be the best, so I'll look out for number one"). These distorted ideas may be a small part of every normal child's passage into adulthood. However, if they become concrete ideas, serious problems can occur in later life.

Safeguarding. The adult neurotic is a veritable draft horse in creating ways of safe-guarding the fictional goal. Safeguarding becomes so consuming that the task the neurotic is threatened by is almost forgotten. No problem can be solved because neurotics become so skilled at safeguarding that they generate symptoms that they use to delude themselves and divert others from focusing on the core of the neurosis. These symptoms become obsta-cles the neurotic can hide behind, feeling secure from the horrible life tasks that are "out there just waiting" to terrorize him or her.

Although the symptoms may relieve the neurotic of responsibility or help him or her gain power over others, safeguarding calls for more and more maladaptive responses. Excuses channel the maladjusted individual into even narrower behavior modes. The neurotic vows to do anything to get rid of the symptoms that hinder and debilitate life at every turn. But this is a lie because the fictional cost—loss of prestige—is too high. Depre-ciation, accusation, guilt, martyrdom, anxiety attacks, psychosomatic illness, and restric-tion of physical perimeters are but a few of the items on the smorgasbord of maladaptive safeguarding behaviors the neurotic relishes.

The Counseling Process

Adlerian counseling has four phases: establishment of the relationship, investigation of the lifestyle, interpretation of the lifestyle, and reorientation (Rule, 1985). Overarching these phases is a cooperative effort by counselor and client to ferret out the client's goals and faulty beliefs about life tasks and reeducate him or her. Mosak (1979, p. 64) has described the objectives of this reeducation as follows: (1) fostering social interest; (2) decreasing inferiority feelings and overcoming discouragement; (3) changing the person's lifestyle; (4) changing faulty motivation or values that underlie even acceptable behavior; (5) encour-aging the individual to recognize his or her equality among fellow humans; and (6) helping the client to become a contributing human being. Incorporating these objectives, psy-chotherapy deals with the changing of one's lifestyle and counseling deals with behavior change within the existing lifestyle. Adlerians, although interested in changing behavior, have as their major goal not behavior modification but motivation modification (Mosak, 1989, pp. 66, 79, 82).

The Client–Counselor Relationship

The client–counselor relationship in Adlerian therapy can best be viewed as collaborative, egalitarian, respectful, and cooperative (Watts, 1998). Indeed, Watts (1998) has drawn some very clear parallels between the social interest modeled by Adlerians and the core facilita-tive conditions that Rogers proposed person-centered counselors should have. That does not mean the counselor is a doormat for a client's every wish or whim. Two hallmarks of Adlerian therapy, encouragement and confrontation, may seem paradoxical on first view. However, if the therapist and the client are to be true partners, then the therapist must be as resolute in confronting mistaken goals as he or she is in encouraging the client to move forward toward perfection. To that end, the Adlerian therapist is anything but passive in therapy and takes a direct and active role in it (Nicoll, Bitter, Christensen, & Hawes, 2000, p. 222).

The client, though hurting enough to seek therapy, perceives both therapy and the counselor as dangerous. As a result, the client is less than likely to be open and honest or to follow prescribed treatment (Shulman, 1973, p. 105), even if he or she avows just the opposite. The client may see dangers such as these in the counselor and the therapeutic situation (Shulman, 1973, pp. 106–109):

1. *Being defective.* The client will not be able to live up to the counselor's expectations and requirements.
2. *Being exposed.* The client cannot allow the counselor to see his or her faults.
3. *Being disapproved of.* The client is dependent on the good will of the counselor.
4. *Being ridiculed.* The client will not report symptoms for fear of this.
5. *Being taken advantage of.* The client distrusts the counselor.
6. *Not being able to get help.* The client cannot have confidence in the counselor.
7. *Submitting to order.* The client is determined to have his or her own way and will not submit to any order except his or her own.
8. *Facing responsibility.* Courage fails the client, who is appalled at the task the counselor requires of him or her.
9. *Unpleasant consequences.* The client is excessively fearful and habitually anticipates dire results from counseling.

The dangers clients see in the counselor and therapy are microcosms of how they live their total lives. The counselor's foreknowledge of these perceived dangers and the understanding that they are dynamics of the inferiority–superiority continuum are the opening wedge in the counselor's attempt to understand the client's defenses. If the counselor understands that the client brings all of these safeguarding behaviors into counseling, fully armed and prepared to fight, and if the counselor can accept this, one of the basic conditions for accepting and understanding the client has been met.

Understanding the Client

Understanding the client's behavior occurs at three levels (Nicoll et al., 2000, pp. 225–227). First, the counselor attempts to determine the client's precise actions and emotions and the social context in which the issues occur. This is the "how" of the client's behavior. Second, the counselor attempts to determine the function of the behavior, or its "what for." Symptoms are assumed to serve some function of the client's fictional goals. Third, the counselor attempts to determine the client's idiosyncratic rules of interaction. These rules tell "why" the client handles life in this manner. It should be noted that *why* here is not about causation but rather is to tease out the rationale of the logic system underlying the presenting behaviors or the *rules of interaction* under which the client operates. Understanding the rules of interaction is critical to understanding the reason for the client's maladaptive behavior and the possible solutions to it. Rules of interaction undergird all systems whether it be for the individual, a family, an organization, or an entire community. These rules are the unique, unwritten "contract of expectations" (Hawes, 1989) that governs how the system operates. Once these rules are understood then behavior becomes understandable and fairly predictable.

Everything the client says and does—how he or she relates with significant others (including the counselor), what symptoms he or she presents, and what action or inaction he or she has taken to alleviate these symptoms—has social as well as therapeutic significance. As Adler (1956) has indicated, we can start wherever we choose. Every expression, word, thought, or feeling leads to the motives and goals around which the individual's lifestyle is built. Nonverbal behaviors—the way people stand, sit, walk, and sleep—are all indicative of the way people approach their goals (p. 220). Even physical symptoms—the client's *organ dialect,* whereby the client speaks with his or her bladder, head, stomach, and so on—emphasize the goal (pp. 222–223).

Assessment and Analysis

Adlerians are divided on psychological testing. Because Adlerians are concerned with process, little diagnosis is done in terms of nomenclature (Mosak, 1989, p. 68). Most avoid diagnosis except for nontherapeutic purposes, such as filling out insurance labels. Labels are static descriptions and ignore the movement of the individual. They describe what the individual has, but not how he or she moves through life.

Reliable and valid standardized lifestyle inventory measures can be collected and used as quick screening devices (Kern, 1982; Wheeler, Kern, & Curlette, 1991). When combined with other intake data, such as family atmosphere and constellation, birth order, earliest childhood memories, dreams, and therapist observations, lifestyle inventories yield a comprehensive profile of the family lifestyle and the client's role in it (Sweeney, 1989, p. 211). Combined with past and present ecological factors, these are all important data for understanding the client's present condition and future course of action in regard to basic mistakes and self-defeating behaviors (Dinkmeyer, Pew, & Dinkmeyer, 1979, pp. 31–32).

Family Atmosphere and Constellation. Another facet of the client's lifestyle is obtained using a family-constellation questionnaire (Dinkmeyer, Pew, & Dinkmeyer, 1979). The client is asked to describe, among other things, his or her parents' personalities, their ambitions and relationships with their children, and their marital relationship. Detailed information is obtained on the client's siblings including birth order; who was most different or most like the client; and who had unusual talents, sickness, or physical, sexual, or social development. Finally, a variety of attributes are listed, and the client is asked to write the names of the siblings who (in the client's judgment) rate the highest and lowest for each attribute (pp. 265–267). Retrieval of this information allows the client to relive deeply emotional moments in his or her first contact with society—contact with the family. Of all the questions on the form, probably none has caught the public's attention more than birth order.

Birth Order.   Adlerians believe that psychological position in the family (rather than chronological position) is probably as important as the parents' method of child rearing (Dinkmeyer, Pew, & Dinkmeyer, 1979, p. 87). Even so, Adlerians such as Mosak (1979, p. 57; 1989, p. 77) qualify their use of the child's psychological position with words like "most likely" and "perhaps" and do not recognize causal, one-to-one relationships between family position and sibling traits. Whatever relationship exists between ordinal position and traits is idiosyncratic to the atmosphere, stability, and total configuration of factors in the family constellation. Further, not only birth order but gender also plays a part in each sibling's psychological position in the family (Singh, 1990).

Birth order by itself is meaningless, since it does not reflect the child's attitude and movements, the formation of alliances within the family, or the unique ways in which the child approaches the family system (Dinkmeyer, Dinkmeyer, & Sperry, 1987, pp. 26–27). No two children are ever born into the same family situation, because the family environment changes: parents become older, wiser, and wealthier or poorer; move and change jobs; divorce, remarry, and die (Pepper, 1971). At best, birth order by itself denotes general traits that are only statistical probabilities.

Early Recollections.   Another major component of the lifestyle inventory is early recollections. These are used as an index of social interest and provide a great deal of diagnostic data about the client (Allers, White, & Hornbuckle, 1990; Slavik, 1991). First memories show the individual's fundamental view of life. Clients will usually discuss first memories because they appear to be innocuous. Yet no memories are chosen by chance. The client, however unconscious the choice may be, remembers only those memories that bear on his or her goal and lifestyle and are significant to the individual in understanding, managing, and controlling life experiences (Dinkmeyer, Dinkmeyer, & Sperry, 1987, p. 36; Sweeney, 1989, pp. 217–218). Thus, early recollections are the story of the client's life and permit the derivation of the client's "basic mistakes" (Mosak, 1989, p. 87). These early memories are much like other projective techniques in that they allow the client to relate affective perceptions to what he or she believes is an objective event (Ansbacher & Ansbacher, 1956, p. 350).

Important components of early recollections that the counselor should typically take note of are: Is the client active or passive? Is he or she an observer or a participant? Is the client giving or taking, approaching or avoiding? Who else is in the scene, and does that person or gender continuously reappear in the same manner? Is the client alone or with others? Is a person who should typically be in the scene left out? What items or things are in the scene? Where does it typically take place? What relationship does the client have with others? What feeling, tones, and states are conveyed? Are the recollections positive or negative? Is there a great deal of color, detail, and embellishment or is the scene barren and devoid of everything except the bare essentials? What themes appear again and again to form an overall pattern of striving? How does the family constellation support the early recollections? How are the early recollections currently played out? Recording the age of the recollection can be helpful, especially if the client had no recollections until a significant family event occurred, such as the birth or death of a sibling or a move. No standard set of questions exists for the lifestyle inventory. Rather, most practitioners modify questions such as these to gain as panoramic a view as possible of the client's current functioning and fictional goal striving (Sweeney, 1989, pp. 217–218).

Dreams. Dreams are much like early memories in that they help the counselor under-stand and define problem areas, predict the near-future direction of the client's lifestyle, alert the counselor to the client's therapeutic movement in the counseling relationship, and teach the client to understand his or her own personality dynamics (Shulman, 1973, p. 71). Dreams may be seen as a short-term problem-solving process that serves as a "stop-or-go" function in regard to immediate dilemmas, whereas early recollections serve as a "stop-or-go" function for lifestyle and long-range issues (Mosak, 1992).

Priorities. The objective in the counselor's lengthy assessment is to establish the number-one priority in the client's lifestyle. Priorities are listed in the lifestyle interview under two headings: "Important to my belonging" and "To be avoided at all costs." Priorities that are important to the client's belonging are divided into four categories by Kefir (1972):

1. *Superiority*—Being competent, right, useful, victimized, martyred. The price paid is overinvolvement, overresponsibility, fatigue, stress, and uncertainty about one's rela-tionship with others.
2. *Control*—Either of others or oneself. Controllers constantly work on their goals. Con-trollers of others pay the price of distancing themselves from others. Self-controllers pay a price of diminished spontaneity and creativity.
3. *Comfort*—Pleasures without waiting. People with this priority get what they want but hurt others in the process. The price paid is diminished productivity and reduced pos-itive social interaction.
4. *Pleasing*—Without respect for oneself or for others. If relationships continue any length of time, rejection, disgust, frustration, despair, and exasperation are the out-comes. The price paid is stunted growth, alienation, and retribution.

According to Dinkmeyer, Pew, and Dinkmeyer (1979, p. 82), stress for the com-forter, rejection for the pleaser, humiliation for the controller, and meaninglessness for the superiority type are to be avoided at all costs. Two basic questions are generated from the establishment of the number-one priority: "How do I use my number-one priority to belong?" and "What must I avoid at all cost when using my number-one priority?" (Dinkmeyer, Dinkmeyer, & Sperry, 1987, p. 99). The answers to these questions apprise the counselor of the client's mistaken beliefs and goals and allow more viable alternatives to be considered.

Insight and Interpretation

Adlerians do not believe in delaying action on problems while the client becomes intellec-tually insightful about them. People who come for therapy have no intention of giving up their number-one priorities. The only reason they come is that the price they pay behav-iorally has gotten too steep. Therefore, a major goal of counseling is to help the client see his or her number-one priority, accept it for what it is, and decide whether the price is really worth paying (Dinkmeyer, Pew, & Dinkmeyer, 1979, p. 83).

The client gains insight through the counselor's interpretation of his or her ordinary communications, dreams, fantasies, behavior, symptoms, transactions with the counselor, and other interpersonal transactions. The emphasis in interpretation is on purpose rather than cause, on movement rather than description, on use rather than possession. Past to present is related only to indicate the continuity of the maladaptive lifestyle, not to demonstrate causal connection (Mosak, 1989, p. 89).

Yet initial interpretations, however accurate, are rarely accepted by the client. On-target interpretations are invariably resisted. Adlerians see resistance only as a lack of courage by the client to return to useful living and a discrepancy between the goals of the client and the counselor (Dreikurs, 1967, p. 65). Such a lack of courage and goal disparity may be manifested by the client's expression of doubt and criticism, special requests, forgetfulness, tardiness, silence, and persistent symptoms. Whatever form the resistance takes, the counselor can be sure that it is the way the client generally acts toward people he or she sees as important, influential, and possibly dangerous (Ansbacher & Ansbacher, 1956, pp. 336–337).

Reorientation

Reorientation is the final action-oriented stage of counseling. The counselor offers alternative ideas or beliefs for the client's consideration (Dinkmeyer, Dinkmeyer, & Sperry, 1987, p. 70). Reorientation is the attempt to persuade the client, by means that range from gentle to forceful, that change is in his or her best interest.

The first step in reorienting the client is to clarify what he or she wants and determine whether it is realistic. The second step involves realigning inappropriate and self-defeating beliefs, perceptions, feelings, and goals with common sense. The third step is to move from insight to outsight—to take what is learned in counseling and move it into the world at large. The fourth step involves dealing with lack of progress. Any failure to progress is seen in terms of the mistaken purpose and payoff of continuing the self-defeating behavior. The counselor has the client evaluate alternative behaviors by asking, "What is the worst thing that could happen if I changed?" Reorientation is primarily a motivation-modification rather than a behavior-modification approach. The Adlerian thesis is that if client beliefs, attitudes, and perceptions are changed, then behavior will soon follow (Dinkmeyer, Dinkmeyer, & Sperry, 1987, pp. 119–121).

Prescribing New Behavioral Rituals

New behavioral rituals are tasks assigned outside of therapy. The client is assigned homework that is designed to engage him or her in regular, repeated actions that reaffirm and reinforce the client's new belief system, behaviors, and rules of interaction. In instituting these new rules, two different types of therapeutic tactics may be used—compliance based or noncompliance based. With compliance-based tactics the assumption is that the client is willing to try out a variety of new behavioral interactions. The therapist may then prescribe restoring previous positive rituals, connecting rituals, desensitizing rituals, and boundary making rituals. If the client is suspected of sabotaging efforts, then noncompliance-based tactics (which Adlerians are fairly famous for employing) are used. Noncompliance-based techniques involve paradoxical prohibitions by the therapist against doing anything to solve the problem. These prohibitions place the client in a double bind. On the one hand the client may want to defy the therapist's requests, but to do that the client would have to engage in some proactive behavior or solution to the problem, which is exactly what the therapist wants to happen (Nicoll et al., 2000, p. 237–240).

Strategies for Helping Clients

Adlerian techniques for helping clients are many and have certainly become more eclectic since Adler started individual psychology. Adlerians use basic listening and responding skills in much the same way that person-centered counselors do.

Restatement

CL: I heard you were the best, and since I'm getting out of the joint in a little while, I thought you'd be the guy to help me get my act together. I'm a little hinky about this.

CO: The yard talk is that I've helped some people out—particularly short-timers. You're also a little nervous—about what, though, I'm not sure.

Reflection

CL: I'm fed up with being controlled by her, but I do love her!

CO: You're angry with her, yet your deep feelings for her make you want to stick with the relationship. Perhaps under the anger you're afraid you might lose her.

Guesses, Hunches, Hypotheses

CL: I really get angry, but then she can make me feel so damn good!

CO: Sounds as if she can really get to you with those conflicting feelings.

Questioning

Questioning in Adlerian therapy operates not only to obtain a more complete understanding of what is going on but is also about reframing the client's perspective of the symptoms (Nicoll et al., 2000, p. 230). Questions posed do *not* allow the client to possess a trait.

CO: How long have you been depressed?

CL: I guess ever since I was about 12 and my mother left for good.

Rather, questions are posed in action terms so that the client stops thinking about what he or she *has* and starts thinking about what he or she is *doing* in the situation.

CO: What happens when you start feeling down?

CL: I kinda get withdrawn, quiet, maybe even sullen.

Interpretation

Interpretation takes guesses, hunches, and hypotheses a step further. Through interpretation the counselor tries to tease out the reasons for a person's behavior. The counselor's response is tentatively phrased so that the client will not become resistant. Interpretation focuses more on the "whys" of behavior than other counseling techniques. Interpretation must be timed appropriately—when the client is ready for it, can accept it as congruent with his or her fictional goals, and can use it to consider new ways of behaving (Dinkmeyer, Dinkmeyer, & Sperry, 1987, p. 102).

> CL: I dunno, I really get confused about the anger and the love.
>
> CO: Seems like it's not so much confusion, rather that "I want her to love me but I must be in control . . . I must be *the man.*"

Nonverbal Behavior

Adlerians may not interpret nonverbal behavior to the extent that Gestalt therapists do, but they are well aware of it and are willing to at least bring it to the client's conscious awareness and to interpret it. Further, Adlerians may suggest that the client use nonverbal behavior as a fail-safe mechanism (Dinkmeyer, Dinkmeyer, & Sperry, 1987, pp. 90–91).

> CL: I thought to myself, "If I can't have her, nobody will."
>
> CO: As you say that, I notice that you're wiping your hands on your pants. My guess is that they're sweating and you're starting to feel tense. I wonder if you can monitor that, kinda use it as a checkpoint about your emotions. My guess is when those physical kinds of things happen your emotions are starting to take over.

Immediacy

Immediacy means dealing with what is going on right here and right now. It is helpful in pointing out to the client how his or her verbalizations may run counter to his or her behavior, and how what happens in counseling is a microcosm of the larger, real world (Dinkmeyer, Dinkmeyer, & Sperry, 1987, p. 123).

> CL: I'd really like to take that drafting course, but the warden, the unit counselor, and my case manager all have to approve it. What's the use?
>
> CO: The way you say it, it's like you can't fight all that authority. Sounds kinda like those excuses you use on the outside and kinda like you want me to know this is already gonna fail before you start.

Active Wondering

Active wondering is a somewhat self-deprecating technique that proposes alternatives to the presenting problem (Nicoll et al., 2000, p. 236).

CO: I don't quite know about this, but could it be that when you lose control you're scared and you need to feel secure, but you don't know how to go about asking for support . . . or you feel that if you do, you'll be told to go away?

Confrontation

The counselor catches discrepancies between what the client says and what the client does and nonpunitively challenges the client on them. Dinkmeyer, Pew, and Dinkmeyer (1979, pp. 110–111) have gleaned four areas of confrontation from Adlerian literature.

Confronting Subjective Views. The client is confronted with the private logic he or she used to make a certain behavior acceptable in his or her own mind. The confrontation technique used here pins the client down on what was going on at the moment of that behavior.

CL: Well, I only tried dope once because this guy talked me into it. I'm really against it.

CO: So what was going on with you at that time? What were you saying to yourself to make taking the dope okay?

Confronting Mistaken Beliefs and Attitudes. The client is confronted with the mistaken beliefs and attitudes that poison his or her attempts at positive social adaptations.

CL: I don't know about women. They gripe when the man takes over and gripe when he doesn't.

CO: It's not the women so much, but you who doesn't know how to respond. At times it seems like you issue them an invitation to get on you so you can show them who's really in control.

Confronting Private Goals. The client is confronted with his or her denial of feelings that the counselor suspects are being hidden.

CL: Maybe, but women really do confuse me.

CO: Confused . . . or could it be that if you don't show them that you're in control, you think they'll see you as a real wimp!

Confronting Destructive Behavior. Clients may become self-destructive by avoiding the issue (passive aggression) or by acting out (active aggression) toward the counselor.

CL: Hey, haven't you ever felt like if you didn't stand up to a woman, she'd run all over you?

CO: When you start attacking my manhood, it makes me wonder if what I just said doesn't strike pretty close to home.

Paradoxical Intention

Adlerian therapy is an effective framework for using paradox to resolve impasses in therapy (Kopp & Kivel, 1990). Paradoxical intention involves having the client attempt to increase his or her debilitating thoughts and behaviors. The client practices enlarging the symptoms out of proportion to the reality of the situation. By becoming acutely aware of how ridiculous such behavior is in terms of a satisfying lifestyle, the client will either change or give up the behavior. The technique is used for a specific period and is treated as an experiment (Dinkmeyer, Dinkmeyer, & Sperry, 1987, pp. 124–125).

> CL: Every time I get with her, things go okay as long as I'm in control, but when she starts to take control I can really fly into a rage in a hurry.
>
> CO: Why not work on that anger? How about nurturing that rage and practicing those behaviors when you're in control? I mean really work at getting angry when everything is going your way.

Creating Images

Images of the neurotic defenses may be extremely helpful in clarifying for clients how absurd their behavior can be. Closely allied to paradoxical intention, imaging involves the client imagining a farcical scene as he or she enters a threatening social situation (James & Myer, 1985).

> CL: If I could just get off this inferiority–superiority merry-go-round.
>
> CO: Let's try an experiment. Every time you're about to see Karen, I'd like you to stand in front of the mirror, flex your muscles, and repeat the words "Macho Man!" three times. Then when you're with her and you start to feel the need to control things, flex, and repeat the words to yourself. Do that every time you feel yourself getting into that situation.

Asking "The Question"

Asking "the question" is generally regarded as a tool for determining whether a client's problem is physical or psychological. But it also has therapeutic value, in that the client's response can be reflected or interpreted. Here are two examples, one that would indicate a physiological basis for the symptom, the other a psychological basis (Dinkmeyer, Dinkmeyer, & Sperry, 1987, pp. 102–103):

> CO: If I had a pill that would make the headaches go away, how would things be different in your life?
>
> CL: (*physical basis*) I would feel better, like I wouldn't want to drive a railroad spike through my forehead to release the pressure.
>
> CL: (*psychological basis*) I would feel better and wouldn't wind up making my visiting time with Karen a real bummer!

CO: (*response to psychological basis*) Hmm! The headaches really affect you, but what you just said didn't emphasize headaches so much as time with Karen. I wonder about that.

Catching Oneself

When the client understands the fictional goals he or she pursues and wants to do something about them, the counselor provides a checklist of mental "stop signs." Such "stop signs" allow the client to catch him- or herself in the irrational behavior. The technique takes practice, because at first clients generally catch themselves too late (Dinkmeyer, Dinkmeyer, & Sperry, 1987, pp. 126–127).

CL: When I start to work up to that uncontrollable rage, I notice my hands sweat and I get really confused.

CO: Yes, and I notice you actually use the word *confused.* So why not use those as stop signs? When you first notice your hands sweating or you say to the person, "I'm confused," *stop!* Think to yourself, "I know what's about to happen; I've got to go to the alternate game plan."

Acting As If

Many clients use the ploy "If only I could. . . ." At such times the client is instructed to act out the role as if he or she could do it. By trying out the role, clients often find they not only can act out a part but also become a different person in the process (Dinkmeyer, Dinkmeyer, & Sperry, 1987, p. 126).

CL: If only I could deal straight up with the lieutenant every time he stops by my home [cell].

CO: For the next week, I'd like you to try this out. Treat anybody, particularly staff personnel, that stops by your home as if they were your guests that you invited in for a cup of coffee and they are there at your invitation.

Spitting in the Soup

By unveiling the hidden motivation for the client's self-defeating behavior the counselor sets up an approach-avoidance situation. By "spitting in the soup" of the client's behavior, the counselor makes it extremely unpalatable. The client may still try to eat the soup (practice the behavior), but there will never be quite the relish there was before. In short, the counselor spoils the soup (game) of the client (Dinkmeyer, Dinkmeyer, & Sperry, 1987, p. 126).

CL: I don't know, so many years in here, I just feel like giving up.

CO: You certainly have the choice of doing that.

CL: What? You're supposed to be supportive.

CO: Right now you'd like me to say something like, "You've got to keep at it; you'll prevail." Yet, I believe that's kind of a game you play so you can be dependent on others and then blame them when things go wrong. If you want to play that, okay!

Encouragement

Encouragement is one of the essential constructs of Adlerian psychology. It was Adler's conclusion that when extrinsic reinforcement and punishment were replaced by encouragement, individuals would gain the ability to develop insight into and start to evaluate their mistaken beliefs. By doing so they would become much more concerned about self-evaluation rather than being concerned about others' self-evaluations (Carns & Carns, 1998).

This is a primary technique throughout the counseling process. The basic Adlerian notion that clients are not sick but rather discouraged means that the counselor's primary task is one of encouragement. However, encouragement does not mean rewarding the client materially. It means investing in clients a feeling of self-worth and accepting clients for what they are and not for what they should or could be (Dinkmeyer, Dinkmeyer, & Sperry, 1987, p. 214).

Use of encouragement as a therapeutic tool should be judicious and with clear forethought about what the counselor is encouraging and the reasons for doing it. Care should be taken to ensure that encouragement does not become misconstrued as sympathy, appeasement, bribery, or rewarding and it should not invite other forms of dependency or manipulation from the client. To provide encouragement, the following points should be considered (Sweeney, 1989, p. 110):

1. *What* one is doing is more important than *how* one is doing.
2. The present is more the focus than the past or the future.
3. The deed is what is important, not the doer.
4. The effort, rather than the outcome, is to be emphasized.
5. Intrinsic motivation, such as satisfaction, enjoyment, and challenge, is more worthwhile than extrinsic payoffs.
6. What is being learned is more important than what is not being learned.
7. What is being done correctly is more important that what is being done incorrectly.

CL: How could I have done that . . . killed that woman . . . what a loser I am. (*cries*)

CO: It really hurts as you think back on it and experience those feelings now, and you wonder whether I see you as that same person who did that. What I see is a person who has worked hard in therapy, who can start to catch himself when he feels put down and not act out in violent ways. Right now I see a person trying to get his life together by going to school and learning and by practicing what you have learned in therapy. You are thinking straighter and staying out of trouble a lot more than when you started counseling two years ago.

Midas Technique

This involves exaggerating the client's neurotic demands. Originated by Shulman (1973, p. 191), the technique is based on King Midas, who discovered that his consuming desire for gold and his ability to have all he wanted soon became a curse rather than a blessing. Like Midas, the client gets what he wants from the counselor. The counselor treats the client in overbearingly sympathetic ways by catering to his or her demands. Such a confrontive approach should be carried out with humor so that the behavior, not the client, is held up for satire.

> CL: The rotten phone company. They wouldn't put my collect call through.
>
> CO: That's terrible! That's catastrophic! The phone company is criminal for not putting your call through to Karen, and we all know the meaning of the word *criminal.*

Pleasing Someone

Since loss of social interest is one of the main factors in client discouragement, the counselor enjoins the client to go out and do something nice for someone. The client is thereby propelled back into the social mainstream (James & Myer, 1985).

> CL: I just want to be left alone. I don't even wanna talk to my best friend, Joe . . . and I'm afraid he's gonna get bent out of shape.
>
> CO: I wonder if you could catch Joe and tell him some of the things that are going on for you now and tell him you really appreciate his support and friendship.

Avoiding the Tar Baby

Dinkmeyer, Pew, and Dinkmeyer (1979, p. 118) describe the tar baby as the perceptions on life the client carries into counseling and attempts to fit into the counselor. Anger, discouragement, seductiveness, martyrdom, and a host of other traps are set for the unwary counselor as the client resists change. To avoid those traps the counselor must respond in ways that are contrary to what the person expects.

> CL: It's up and down. I've been at this twelve weeks and I don't see us any further than where we were when I started.
>
> CO: You'd like me to get discouraged and give up. The work has been getting tougher lately and you'd really like to have an excuse for not getting into some of those treacherous waters.

Summary

As may be seen from the foregoing sample of Adlerian techniques, the counselor is not passive, but highly active in encouraging the client. Throughout therapy the Adlerian counselor remains free to have feelings and opinions and to express them. The therapist is not a blank slate as in the Freudian sense. Such a stance would promote social distance. In the egalitarian and human relationship of counseling, Adlerians seek to help a client regain or increase social interest through a close and personal interactive approach (Mosak, 1989, pp. 99–100).

Sample Case

Initial Interview to Establish Lifestyle[1]

Al is a 28-year-old white man who is serving a life sentence for murdering his girlfriend when he was 20 years old. He has come to counseling because he has realized that something is wrong with the way he thinks and behaves. Al has become especially concerned with his lifestyle for two reasons. The first is a woman, Karen, whom he met through the prison volunteer program. Though at first he was deeply in love with her, he now has questions about the relationship. The second reason is that Al's court case was reopened and he won a reduction in sentence. He will be up for parole in three years and is extremely concerned that once free he will become violent again.

On a scale of satisfaction with current life tasks ranging from 1 (things are going very well) to 5 (things are very dissatisfying) Al rates himself as follows:

occupation—2	meaning—3
friendship—4	leisure—2
opposite sex—5	parenting—3
self—3	

In terms of occupation, Al has taken numerous prison courses in engineering technology and is now certified to be an engineering technologist. He hopes to continue his education and receive a B.S. in civil engineering.

In terms of relationships, Al has only one fairly close friend inside the prison and no friends outside except for Karen. His relationship with the opposite sex, in his own words, is poor. The woman he murdered was his first love. She was rather controlling and demanding, but initially he saw her actions as manifesting concern and love. However, as the relationship progressed, it also deteriorated. He felt himself losing control of the situation and became suspicious and paranoid about her actions toward him. This stormy relationship lasted eight months and was punctuated by verbal battles, threats of suicide on Al's part, all-night vigils outside her house, sabotage of her car, an aborted murder attempt, and finally a calmly planned and carried out murder.

---

[1]The interview format is based on Don Dinkmeyer, W. L. Pew, and Don Dinkmeyer, Jr., "Appendix A: Guide for Initial Interview for Establishing the Life Style," *Adlerian Counseling and Psychotherapy* (Monterey, CA: Brooks/Cole, 1979), pp. 265–274.

Al's present concern with Karen is that he sees their relationship moving in the same direction. He has started to experience the same kinds of thoughts that occurred in the first relationship, which culminated in murder. In regard to himself and the meaning he obtains from life, Al vacillates between optimism and extreme pessimism. He stated that he has been like this for as long as he can remember. Al related feeling good about his leisure time, which he uses for self-study through reading. He also takes every extension course he can obtain through the university prison program. Al would very much like to have a family. In fact, one of the things he found attractive about the woman he murdered was that she had a two-year-old daughter: "A ready-made family and the girl was calling me Daddy." Al had a poor family life as a child. He has no brothers or sisters. His parents were divorced when he was eight. There were many verbal and physical battles between his parents. His mother was an alcoholic. He stated that after the divorce he never saw his mother again and did not miss her. He and his father lived with his father's sister and mother. Al hated his aunt, who ridiculed both him and his father. He loved his grandmother and indicated that the last time he cried was at her funeral. He was eleven at the time. He and his father have never been close. As a child he was afraid of his father because of the beatings he received from him. Al now feels that his father cared about him but is still not able to communicate with him.

Al described himself as a loner who had few relationships—even casual ones—during grade school and high school. He reported very little difficulty with school, but generally he did little work, was often truant, and barely obtained his high school diploma. His sexual life was minimal until he graduated from high school. Although his sexual fantasies were rather exotic, he felt intimidated by women his own age. Upon graduation from high school he started forming casual relationships with women, invariably older ones. He stated he "just felt secure with an older woman who knew her way around." He further related that he feared nothing as a child or a teenager and could hold his own in any fight. This has held true to the present. Al is pretty much left alone by some very tough people in a very tough prison. Al's work experience before incarceration was erratic. He held a variety of menial jobs and usually quit or was fired after a short time because he "lost interest" or the work was "beneath him." Al's earliest recollection was going to his grandmother's house, sitting in a chair stacked with telephone books so he could reach up to the table like a grown-up, and eating ginger cookies she had made. He recalled this as being very pleasant and loved being spoiled by his grandmother.

Al's number-one priority appears to be control flavored with superiority. He fights very hard to deny his feelings and emotions. Although Al is attracted to women and idealizes a family life, he invariably chooses women who are controlling. At first, Al mistakes control for caring and falls deeply in love with "the perfect woman." Over time, Al's own fictional goal of control distorts any chance of a meaningful relationship occurring. The result is a breakdown in the relationship and humiliation, which Al cannot tolerate because of his need to be superior. To rectify this dilemma, Al acts out, defending his fictional goals with catastrophic results. Al's assets are his intelligence and his desire to understand himself. He is energetic both in the jobs he is assigned in the prison and in his college coursework. He has voluntarily sought counseling and has contracted to work hard at rearranging his life.

Excerpts from Al's Counseling Interviews

Session 1

CL: I don't get hurt or feel insecure. You, nobody can hurt me.

CO: Is that true? I feel hurt and insecure at times.

CL: (*smiles nervously*) No, it's a crock. I put up a front.

CO: So what you're giving me is an image you show the world. My guess is you defend yourself with those images. In the short run they seem to meet your needs, but in the long run they leave you vulnerable and stressed. . . . The work we'll be doing in here will mostly be probing at and attacking those defenses. You can accept or reject my guesses, but I want you to know they're gonna keep coming. It's going to be hard work and scary at times, and that's the last lecture you get from me, okay?

CL: Okay! That's what I came for—to get straightened out. Let's go!

Session 3

CL: She was running around on me, very immature, so I'd follow her around, mess up her car . . . cut her brake line.

CO: You wanted to hurt her . . . show her who was boss.

CL: No . . . I . . . uh . . . wanted her attention. I'd sleep in the car in front of her house. For what reason I don't know. Maybe to protect her.

CO: You protected her by cutting her brake lines. What was your purpose in that? To show her your love? See how you delude yourself?

CL: I do? (*long silence*)

CO: One of the reasons you were fighting was because she was possessive of you and then the roles changed, she wanted out, you lost control, became insecure, more possessive, kinda like a whirlpool.

CL: I guess I wanted to be sure she couldn't control me.

CO: Guess?

CL: Yeah, I know.

CO: See how you fool yourself?

CL: (*silence, deep in thought, hand tremors*) I was confused.

CO: Your image of yourself was confused.

Session 5

CO: Listening to the tapes is there anything you want to go over?

CL: Reviewing things I feel real depressed. Don't do that to me again!

CO: I don't do anything. You do those things. When those hurtful feelings come out there's going to be some depression.

CL: It's tough, not like I thought it'd be in therapy. Scary.

CO: When you feel that way, what happens?

CL: I get moody . . . short with people . . . confused . . . don't know what I want. Although I felt good after I got some of that stuff out in the open with you.

CO: That was one of your goals in coming here, but you avoid those upsetting feelings. Those feelings you avoid come out in moods and actions.

CL: It really got to me Saturday night when my girl came down. She's an only child and her parents wanted her to do something. She didn't know if she could come. I feel like I'm competing for her attention. I got really uptight and so did she. Then we had an argument.

CO: You have to be the center of attention.

CL: Yeah, I want attention, to feel good, accepted. I mean like Jean waited on me hand and foot. I felt like a king. Real caring.

CO: What extremes do you go to to get people to feel the way you want them to about you? Like with your girlfriend that you murdered [Jean] you lied about your age and sexual experience—these things made you feel important when you first met her.

CL: I wasn't feeling important.

CO: Right. That's why you lied.

CL: I was confused. I mean I wasn't real sure of myself, about sex, especially, like I was a fag or something.

CO: Okay! When you felt that way what thoughts went through your head?

CL: I really blew it, but then Jean said a little later that I'd make a good father for her daughter. *Wow,* did that blow my mind.

CO: So it wasn't the way she looked that made her attractive. Nineteen and a father, pretty heavy stuff, feeling important. Sounds like some needs your own family never met.

CL: (*silence, avoids interpretation*) She started getting more and more demanding, and I started lying . . . car broke down, couldn't get to a phone. She started throwing other guys up to me. She knew how to get to me.

CO: You talk a lot about how you behaved, not how you felt.

CL: I couldn't live with her or without her. Jealousy.

CO: My guess is that everything you do has something to do with that goal of control, being top dog. Can you start checking those feelings, those behaviors that lead to that?

Session 8

CL: I realize those lies I make up to cover my feelings. I think I should impress somebody. My thoughts get me in trouble.

CO: The way I interpret things is the way I make myself feel and act.

CL: I won't admit what I did to the other cons.

CO: What is the reason you won't admit it?

CL: I said I killed a man in a fight. To kill a woman you're not much of a man. I couldn't admit I was irrational or lost control.

Session 12

CL: She was taking advantage of me and I loved her and it hurt that she'd do that.

CO: Hurt, insecure.

CL: I didn't want to deal with those feelings so I killed her. . . . She played with dynamite and it blew up.

CO: Sounds like a real nice way of not being responsible. Being vulnerable and not owning it. See, you still make it her fault!

CL: Yeah, it's a defense. I was trying to be a lot of things I couldn't be. I think I understand what went on. I've grown up some emotionally. All those years I couldn't let it out, wanted to cry but couldn't. (*sobs*)

CO: That fits an image.

CL: Yeah, real men don't cry! What a crock! Stupid!

Session 13

CO: Is it possible to be perfect?

CL: No way! I play the game.

CO: The game worked so well for you that it helped you murder—and it still goes on. So if you get rejected, will you die on the spot?

CL: I don't think I put Karen up on a pedestal like Jean. If she were to go, I'd feel bad, but I'm starting to believe there'd be other fish in the sea.

CO: What makes you think you can handle it better now than then?

CL: Because the games scare the hell out of me now.

CO: The games are part of your insecurity. Do you still feel insecure?

CL: I don't know, it's confusing to narrow it down.

CO: You use the word *confused* a lot. Every time you seem to start to feel insecure you use that word. Do you realize that?

CL: Maybe it's a habit.

CO: A habit that needs to be broken. That word, *confused,* is a checkpoint. When you use it, notice how you feel. It may be a warning that you're feeling stress.

Session 14

CO: We talked about checkpoints, particularly your confusion. I wonder, were you able to put that into practice?

CL: Yeah, I did. I could have gotten into it with the lieutenant, but I remembered *CONFUSED* and stopped myself, just shrugged it off, thought about the bad time I'd get and how my number-one priority is getting out of here with no more time added on. And I have not lost control once with Karen on the phone or in visitation. To tell you the truth, I'm not so sure she and I are right for each other. Not feeling the need to be in control is giving me more control. Weird!

Session 20

CL: In the past I couldn't handle the rejection. I was afraid. Now, you either accept me or you don't. I'm not in competition. I don't have to put on an act.

CO: With Karen?

CL: If I'm feeling apprehensive with her I work it out. It's funny, she's a lot more scared of Al the human being than Al the manipulator. She said she was a lot more secure with Al the "man." That didn't bother me. I didn't need to go back to that. If she needs that, she doesn't need me.

CO: Is this another delusion, this new way of thinking? Are you just fooling yourself?

CL: It's not a delusion. Hard to explain. I'm really at peace. I can see problems a lot clearer. A lot of other guys in here say I'm different.

Summary

In the beginning, Al personified the fictitious goals of control and superiority. Those goals are extremely crystallized, though. Al comes to therapy seeking change. His words in the opening session say it all: "My girl is a counselor and tries that stuff on me and it doesn't work, but with you it's okay." The counselor is a retired professional football player and is the essence of the macho man, so at least on the surface he meets Al's need to deal with "real men."

The counselor tenaciously attacks Al's mistaken attitudes, fictitious goals, and defended feelings. The counselor catches Al safeguarding and points it out both by interpretation and confrontation. Things are moving slowly. At times Al denies the interpretations, but later he accepts them. The insight gained from the counselor and from playbacks of the counseling sessions moves Al slowly but surely toward awareness of the way he deludes himself. The checkpoints he establishes with the counselor allow him to start recognizing his emotions and controlling them rather than vice versa. The excerpts from the sessions demonstrate Al's progress from a highly defensive client who admits to little feeling to a person who is able to look at the past, make sense of its psychological meaning, and use the insight he has gained to deal in more congruent ways with his present self.

You may wonder if Al's progress was really just another con, a distorted way of achieving control and superiority over the counselor, the institution, and society. A subsequent report leads us to believe Al's therapeutic gains were real. He had been on extremely good behavior for the nine months preceding the report and had been permitted to move to a prison where he could complete his degree. He had established a number of checkpoints that he monitored both with the counselor and with a counseling group he had joined. Feedback from other inmates indicated he was no longer a loner. He had become involved in a number of positive relationships. The counselor also worked with Al's girlfriend, Karen, helping her change some of her attempts to control the relationship. Although much work remained to be done by both Al and Karen, they were continuing, with several starts and stops, to explore their new relationship.

Contributions of the Adlerian System

Adlerian therapy, as it is promoted and practiced, is a therapy for all society. Its emphasis on human perfectibility through increased social interest makes it a unique counseling theory.

Because Adlerian theory views people as being pulled by the future, its practitioners care what generations to come will inherit in a comprehensive ecological sense. A keystone of Adlerian therapy is encouragement, and because of their inherent belief in the perfectibility of humankind Adlerians do not hesitate to be encouraging. The approach, then, focuses on mental health rather than mental illness.

Because it is phenomenological, the Adlerian view does not consider humans predestined by their genetic or environmental endowment. Each individual has the distinctive qualities to be whatever he or she chooses to be. The Adlerian approach is, indeed, a psychology of use and not of possession.

The Adlerian approach has extended therapy from the patient on the couch to a variety of procedures in the real world. Group counseling, parent education, and family-system procedures can all be traced to Adlerians.

Because it has been an outreaching system, the Adlerian approach has had great impact on the public domain. Nowhere has this been more apparent than in education. From Adler's work in the Vienna school system in the 1920s to the advent of Dinkmeyer's developing understanding of self and others (DUSO) program in the 1970s, individual psychology stands above all other therapeutic modalities in its attempts to humanize education. Finally, perhaps the greatest contribution of individual psychology has been its integration into so many other modalities—and, indeed, into the mainstream of America—that many of its concepts have come to be understood as what Adler would have called "common sense" (Dinkmeyer, Dinkmeyer, & Sperry, 1987).

Shortcomings of the Adlerian System

A major problem has been the rather awesome amount of family constellation and lifestyle information typically collected by Adlerians. Although Adlerians vigorously promote collection of this information as fluid and flexible, persistent stereotypes exist among counselors that these protocols are inscribed in stone. Perhaps the most abused and confused of these stereotypes, especially for the neophyte counselor, is birth order. Although Adlerians maintain that they do not stereotype by birth order, this perception still exists and is difficult to put to rest.

If the beginning counselor can wade through these difficulties, there is still the problem of interpretation of early recollections and dreams. The notion of interpretation has long been vigorously debated in therapeutic circles. We have no hope of resolving that issue here.

We wonder if Adlerian theory, like all approaches that rely heavily on verbal erudition, logic, and insight, is not limited to clients who are a cut above those of normal intellect. Sadly, not all of our clients fit into that intellectual category.

Like many other therapies fighting for survival in a managed care world, Adlerians promote themselves as capable of delivering the goods in a brief therapy format. However, in order to do that the number of sessions ranges from one to twenty. Therein lies the problem. Twenty sessions is not going to be seen as brief by behavioral health-maintenance organizations and they are not likely to pay for that much insight. A further problem is the reluctance of Adlerians to codify for mental illness. While their positive view of the individual is laudable, behavioral health-maintenance organizations regrettably only pay for classifiable problems.

Adlerian Therapy with Diverse Populations

Adlerians discussed and promoted equality and sensitivity for diversity long before multiculturalism and diversity issues were raised in the counseling professions. In fact, the undergirding and driving force in Adlerian therapy and theory is social involvement and the equitable participation of everybody (Dreikurs, 1946, 1971).

Adlerian therapy's emphasis on building equitable relationships, cooperation and responsibility skills, empathy for others, and encouragement makes it one of the preeminent therapies of choice for elementary school counselors and others who work with groups of children in multicultural settings (Herring & Runion, 1994).

Because perceived or actual inferiority status plays such a central part in how persons acclimate to primary socializing agents such as families, neighborhoods, schools, cities, and countries, Adlerians understand clearly the general dynamics of disenfranchised individuals and groups who see little opportunity for a productive lifestyle and are alienated and discouraged. Thus, their major therapeutic tools are weighted heavily in favor of gaining insight into reasons for having a positive social interest and encouraging broad and equal participation in society. Particularly in regard to their long-standing emphasis on sexual equality, Adlerians have much to offer feminist therapy (Rigby-Weinberg, 1986).

The Adlerians also have much to say to those who see spirituality as a key component to living. Studies comparing Adlerian theory to Native American views of life show a common ground (Kawulich & Curlette, 1998; Roberts, Harper, Tuttle-Eagle Bull, & Heideman-Provost, 1998).

Although Adler's writings proposed that homosexuality was a neurotic lifestyle, many contemporary Adlerians see utility in using the approach to help gays and lesbians gain self-acceptance and broadened social interest. The Adlerian view of egalitarianism crosscuts all populations and is uniquely suited to help gays and lesbians combat stigmatization, feelings of inferiority, and discouragement (Chandler, 1995; Chernin & Holden, 1995; Fisher, 1993; Kottman, Lingg, & Tisdell, 1995).

Further in the Adlerians' favor, their approach should make a great deal of sense and have credibility to those cultures that highly value the family system and honor of one's parents. Unlike Freudians or transactional analysts, Adlerians do not specifically vilify parents.

For those clients who are alienated from society, Adlerian therapy is probably perceived as one of the bigger scams in therapy: Why would anyone want to attempt to gain a greater social interest in society when that society is not worth much to begin with?

Although social inferiority has replaced organ inferiority as the cornerstone of Adlerian personality theory (Mosak, 1989, p. 81), Adlerians still have much to say to clients with physical disabilities. The concepts of lifestyle, compensation, and striving for superiority are primary in understanding those with physical disabilities.

Summary

Individual psychology was developed by Alfred Adler as a denial of Freud. Adler forged a psychotherapy that directly related the individual's mental health to degree of social interest. The life tasks of social, occupational, and sexual relationships are primary to the development of a wholesome and fulfilling lifestyle. Through Rudolf Dreikurs, the Adlerian approach took root in America. Group therapy, child guidance centers, and parent training programs are among its major contributions to society. The modality is marked by its great concerns for the individual's relationship with his or her total environment. Adlerians are optimistic about humankind and value the well-being of the individual and society over that of organizations and institutions. Adlerian theory is, then, a functional and operational social psychology.

Adlerians believe the original socializing agent, the family, plays a large part in the adjustment or maladjustment of the individual. Thus, they spend a great deal of time trying to make sense of the client's family constellation and childhood in attempting to assess what his or her present fictional goals are and how those goals are translated into feelings of inferiority and superiority.

Practitioners of the approach use a variety of counseling techniques, from basic restatement and reflection skills to specific Adlerian techniques such as "spitting in the soup" and "avoiding the tar baby." All techniques provide encouragement as clients work to realign their goals with those of society and attempt to find more satisfying lifestyles.

Although individual psychology has been criticized as being just "common sense," its practicality in everyday living would seem to be just what Adler wanted. Although its identity may be obscure, its theoretical concepts, such as inferiority and superiority complexes, birth order, lifestyle, and acting "as if," have become so ingrained in contemporary vocabulary that it is indeed a psychology of social usefulness both in theory and practice.

S U G G E S T I O N S F O R F U R T H E R R E A D I N G

Adler, A. (1958). *What life should mean to you.* A. Porter (Ed.). New York: Putnam's Capricorn Books.

Ansbacher, H. L., & Ansbacher, R. R. (Eds.). (1956). *The individual psychology of Alfred Adler: A systematic presentation in selections from his writings.* New York: Harper & Row, Harper Torchbooks.

Carlson, J. (Speaker). (1997). *Psychotherapy with the experts: Adlerian therapy.* (Videocassette). Boston: Allyn & Bacon.

Dinkmeyer, D. Jr., & Sperry, L. (2000). *Counseling and psychotherapy: An integrated, individual psychology approach.* Upper Saddle River, NJ: Prentice-Hall.

REFERENCES

Adler, A. (1929). *The science of living*. New York: Greenberg.

Adler, A. (1956). (1) The neurotic disposition; (2) Psychology of use; (3) Social interest. In H. L. Ansbacher & R. R. Ansbacher (Eds.), *The individual psychology of Alfred Adler: A systematic presentation in selections from his writings* (pp. 126–162; 205–262). New York: Basic Books.

Adler, A. (1958). *What life should mean to you*. New York: Putnam's Capricorn Books.

Adler, A. (1970). Superiority. In H. L. Ansbacher & R. R. Ansbacher (Eds.), *Superiority and social interest* (p. 257). Evanston, IL: Northwestern University Press.

Allen, T. W. (2000). An Adlerian renaissance in education? *Individual Psychology 56*(1), 115–119.

Allers, C. T., White, J., & Hornbuckle, D. (1990). Early recollections, detecting depression in the elderly. *Individual Psychology: Journal of Adlerian Theory, Research, and Practice, 46,* 61–66.

Ansbacher, H. L. (1977). Individual psychology. In R. J. Corsini (Ed.), *Current personality theories* (pp. 45–82). Itasca, IL: F. E. Peacock.

Ansbacher, H. L., & Ansbacher, R. R. (1956). (1) Degree of activity; (2) Early reflections and dreams; (3) Individual psychology in its larger setting; (4) The style of life; and (5) Understanding and treating the patient. In H. L. Ansbacher & R. R. Ansbacher (Eds.), *The individual psychology of Alfred Adler: A systematic presentation in selections from his writings* (pp. 1–18; 163–203; 326–365). New York: Basic Books.

Bruder, K. J. (1998). Die aufloesung der fesseln der fiktionen im analytischen sprechen. *Zeitschrift fuer Individualpsychologie, 23*(3), 244–259.

Carlson, J. (Speaker). (1997). *Psychotherapy with the experts: Adlerian therapy*. (Videocassette). Boston: Allyn & Bacon.

Carlson, J., & Sperry, L. (Eds.). (2000). *Brief therapy with individuals and couples*. Phoenix, AZ: Zeig, Tucker, & Theisen.

Carns, M. R., & Carns, A. W. (1998). A review of the professional literature concerning the consistency of the definition and application of Adlerian encouragement. *Individual Psychology, 54*(1), 72–89.

Chandler, C. K. (1995). Guest editorial: Contemporary Adlerian reflections on homosexuality and bisexuality. *Individual Psychology: Journal of Adlerian Theory, Research, and Practice, 51,* 82–89.

Chernin, J., & Holden, J. M. (1995). Toward an understanding of homosexuality: Origins, status, and relationship to individual psychology. *Individual Psychology: Journal of Adlerian Theory, Research, and Practice, 51,* 90–101.

Cheston, S. E. (2000). Spirituality of encouragement. *Individual Psychology, 56*(3) 296–304.

Dewey, J. (1971). Family atmosphere. In A. G. Nikelly (Ed.), *Techniques for behavior change* (pp. 41–48). Springfield, IL: Chas. C. Thomas.

Dinkmeyer, D. C., & Dinkmeyer, D. C., Jr. (1982). *Developing understanding of self and others, DUSO-1 revised, DUSO-2 revised*. Circle Pines, MN: American Guidance Service.

Dinkmeyer, D. C., Dinkmeyer, D. C., Jr., & Sperry, L. (1987). *Adlerian counseling and psychotherapy* (2nd ed.). Columbus, OH: Chas. E. Merrill.

Dinkmeyer, D. C., & McKay, G. D. (1976). *Systematic training for effective parenting*. Circle Pines, MN: American Guidance Service.

Dinkmeyer, D. C., Pew, W. L., & Dinkmeyer, D. C., Jr. (1979). *Adlerian counseling and psychotherapy*. Monterey, CA: Brooks/Cole.

Dinkmeyer, D., Jr., & Sperry, L. (2000). *Counseling and psychotherapy: An integrated, individual psychology approach*. Upper Saddle River, NJ: Prentice-Hall.

Dreikurs, R. (1946). *The challenge of marriage*. New York: Hawthorn Books.

Dreikurs, R. (1953). *Fundamentals of Adlerian psychology*. Chicago: Alfred Adler Institute.

Dreikurs, R. (1959). Early experiments with group psychotherapy. *American Journal of Psychotherapy, 13,* 882–891.

Dreikurs, R. (1967). *Psychodynamics, psychotherapy, and counseling*. Chicago: Alfred Adler Institute.

Dreikurs, R. (1971). *Social equality: The challenge of today*. Chicago: Henry Regnery.

Dreikurs, R. (1981). The three life tasks. In L. Baruth & D. Eckstein (Eds.), *Lifestyle: Theory, practice and research* (2nd ed., pp. 34–41). Dubuque, IA: Kendall/Hunt.

Dreikurs, R., & Mosak, H. H. (1967). The tasks of life II. The fourth life task. *Individual Psychologist, 4,* 51–55.

Fisher, S. K. (1993). A proposed Adlerian theoretical framework and intervention techniques for gay and lesbian couples. [Special issue: Marriage and couples counseling.] *Individual Psychology: Journal of Adlerian Theory, Research, and Practice, 49,* 438–449.

Frankl, V. E. (1970). Fore-runner of existential psychiatry. *Journal of Individual Psychology, 26,* 38.

Gold, L., & Mansager, E. (2000). Spirituality: Life task or life process? *Individual Psychology, 56*(3), 266–276.

Hawes, E. C. (1989). Therapeutic interventions in the marital relationship. In R. M. Kern, E. C. Hawes, & O. C. Christensen (Eds.), *Couples therapy: An Adlerian perspective* (pp. 77–114). Minneapolis, MN: Educational Media.

Herring, R. D., & Runion, K. O. (1994). Counseling ethnic children and youth from an Adlerian perspective. *Journal of Multicultural Counseling, and Development, 22,* 215–226.

James, R., & Myer, R. (1985). Using Adlerian confrontation with children. Paper presented at the National/ Elementary Middle School Guidance Conference, Normal, IL.

Kawulich, B. B., & Curlette, W. L. (1998). Life tasks and the Native American perspectives. *Individual Psychology, 54*(3) 359–267.

Kefir, N. (1972). Priorities. Manuscript.

Kern, R. (1982). *Lifestyle scale.* Coral Springs, FL: CMTI Press.

Kopp, R. R., & Kivel, C. (1990). Traps and escapes: An Adlerian approach to understanding resistance and resolving impasses in psychotherapy. *Individual Psychology: Journal of Adlerian Theory, Research, and Practice, 46,* 139–147.

Kottman, T., Lingg, M., & Tisdell, T. (1995). Gay and lesbian adolescents: Implications for therapists. *Individual Psychology: Journal of Adlerian Theory, Research, and Practice, 51,* 114–128.

Mosak, H. H. (1971). Lifestyle. In A. G. Nikelly (Ed.), *Techniques for behavior change* (pp. 77–84). Springfield, IL: Chas. C. Thomas.

Mosak, H. H. (1979). Adlerian psychotherapy. In R. J. Corsini (Ed.), *Current psychotherapies* (2nd ed., pp. 44–94). Itasca, IL: F. E. Peacock.

Mosak, H. H. (1989). Adlerian psychotherapy. In R. J. Corsini & D. Wedding (Eds.), *Current psychotherapies* (4th ed., pp. 65–116). Itasca, IL: F. E. Peacock.

Mosak, H. H. (1992). The "traffic cop" function of dreams and early recollections. *Individual Psychology: Journal of Adlerian Theory, Research, and Practice, 48,* 319–323.

Mosak, H. H., & Dreikurs, R. (1967). The life tasks III. The fifth life task. *Individual Psychologist, 5,* 16–22.

Mosak, H. H., & Dreikurs, R. (2000). Spirituality: The fifth life task. *Individual Psychology, 56*(3), 257–265.

Nicoll, W. G., Bitter, J. R., Christensen, O. C., & Hawes, C. (2000). Adlerian brief therapy: Strategies and tactics. In J. Carlson & L. Sperry (Eds.), *Brief therapy with individuals and couples* (pp. 220–247). Phoenix, AZ: Zeig, Tucker, & Theisen.

Nystul, M. (1999). Problem solving counseling: Integrating Adler's and Glasser's theories. In R. E. Watts & J. Carlson (Eds.), *Interventions and strategies in counseling and psychotherapy* (pp. 31–42). Philadelphia, PA: Accelerated Development.

Pepper, F. C. (1971). Birth order. In A. G. Nikelly (Ed.), *Techniques for behavior change* (pp. 49–54). Springfield, IL: Chas. C. Thomas.

Pryor, D. B., & Tollerud, T. R. (1999). Applications of Adlerian principles in school settings. *Professional School Counseling, 2*(4), 299–304.

Rigby-Weinberg, D. N. (1986). A future direction for radical feminist therapy. *Women and Therapy, 5,* 191–205.

Roberts, R. L., Harper, R., Tuttle-Eagle Bull, D., & Heideman-Provost, L. M. (1998). The Native American medicine wheel and individual psychology: Common themes. *Individual Psychology, 54*(1), 135–145.

Rule, W. R. (1985). An Adlerian perspective. *Journal of Applied Rehabilitation Counseling, 16,* 9–14.

Shulman, B. H. (1973). *Contributions to individual psychology.* Chicago: Alfred Adler Institute.

Singh, A. (1990). Toughmindedness in relation to birth order, family size, and sex. *Individual Psychology: Journal of Adlerian Theory, Research, and Practice, 46,* 82–87.

Slavik, S. (1991). Early memories as a guide to client movement through life. *Canadian Journal of Counseling, 25,* 331–337.

Slavik, S., Sperry, L., & Carlson, J. (2000). Efficient Adlerian therapy with individuals and couples. In J. Carlson & L. Sperry (Eds.), *Brief therapy with individuals and couples* (pp. 248–263). Phoenix, AZ: Zeig, Tucker, & Theisen.

Sweeney, T. J. (Ed.). (1989). *Adlerian counseling: A practical approach for a new decade* (3rd ed.). Muncie, IN: Accelerated Development Inc.

Vaihinger, H. (1956). Fictionalism. In H. L. Ansbacher and R. R. Ansbacher (Eds.), *The individual psychology of Alfred Adler: A systematic presentation in selections from his writings* (pp. 77–100). New York: Basic Books.

Watts, R. E. (1995). How I remember my family: A premarital and marriage counseling questionnaire. *The Family Journal, 3,* 155–157.

Watts, R. E. (1998). The remarkable parallel between Rogers's core conditions and Adler's social interest. *Individual Psychology, 54*(1), 5–9.

Watts, R. E. (2000a). Adlerian counseling: A viable approach for contemporary practice. *TCA Journal, 28,* 11–23.

Watts, R. E. (2000b). Biblical based Christian spirituality and Adlerian psychotherapy. *Individual Psychology, 56*(3), 316–328.

Watts, R. E., & Carlson, J. (1999). *Interventions in counseling and psychotherapy.* Philadelphia: Taylor & Francis.

Wheeler, M. S., Kern, R. M., & Curlette, W. L. (1991). Life style can be measured. *Individual Psychology: Journal of Adlerian Theory, Research, and Practice, 47,* 229–240.

Witmer, J. M. (1989). Reaching toward wholeness. In T. J. Sweeney (Ed.), *Adlerian counseling: A practical approach for a new decade* (3rd ed., pp. 31–80). Muncie, IN: Accelerated Development Inc.

6 Transactional Analysis

Fundamental Tenets

History

Eric Berne (1910–1970), trained as a psychiatrist and psychoanalyst, began developing the essence of transactional analysis (TA) theory in the 1950s. Berne's discovery and naming of the parent, adult, and child ego states (1955–1962) is considered to be the first phase in the development of TA.

As a theory, TA began to gain notoriety in the 1960s with the publication of two widely read books: *Games People Play* (Berne, 1964) and *I'm OK—You're OK* (Harris, 1969). With the advent of the *OK* book, which sold over 15 million copies in eighteen different languages, TA became *the* self-help psychological approach of the 1970s.

In the second phase of its development (1962–1966), TA focused mainly on games. Berne's interest in communication theory helped him to understand that in many instances, two types of messages (social and psychological) were originating at the same time from one communication source. Berne observed that the covert psychological meaning of such messages differed from the overt social meaning. This finding resulted in his concept of games—a series of these two-level transactions leading to a predictable outcome or payoff.

The dominant force in TA during the third developmental phase (1966–1970) was script analysis. The concept of scripts emerged in response to the question "Why do different people play the same games over and over?" Techniques for analyzing and understanding scripts (Berne, 1966, 1972; Steiner, 1967, 1974) were developed and put to use in treatment (Goulding & Goulding, 1978; Schiff, 1970). Thus, TA began to shift away from a passive, intellectual-insight approach to a more proactive regimen in which the therapist intervenes and changes client scripts.

In the 1970s, TA gained additional prominence through such popular publications as *Born to Win* (James & Jongeward, 1971) and *What Do You Say After You Say Hello?* (Berne, 1972), published two years after Berne's death in 1970. After Berne's death, TA continued to incorporate new if somewhat idiosyncratic treatment techniques, such as Dusay's "energy distribution and action" and "egogram" (1972, 1977; Dusay & Dusay, 1989, p. 416) and Schiff's "reparenting" approach (1970). This splitting off after Berne's death resulted in a variety of different factions espousing their own particular brand of TA, which led to a decline in its status as *the* therapy of the seventies.

The fourth influence on TA was the hybridization of TA and Gestalt into *redecision therapy* by the Gouldings (1978, 1979; Goulding, 1997). Redecision therapy ferrets out the affect that links past to present and allows the client to challenge his or her beliefs about the self in the past. In challenging those beliefs comes the opportunity to reconsider old scripts and replace them with newer, more functional ones (McClendon & Kadis, 1995). It would appear that in the twenty-first century TA has shifted and evolved so that it embraces all three mainstreams of psychology—behavioral, analytic, and humanistic—and as a result has become more eclectic in nature (Allen & Allen, 2000; Clarkson, 1992; Goulding, 1997; Jacobs, 2000; Schlegel, 1998; Summers & Tudor, 2000).

Overview of Transactional Analysis

Transactional analysis has several identifying characteristics. First, it is *contractual:* the therapist is guided by a therapeutic contract in working with clients.

Second, TA is *decisional* and views *responsibility* as a key issue in therapy. Clients are assisted in tracing here-and-now behavior and feelings back to some basic decisions they made regarding how to get along in the world.

A third major characteristic of TA is that its practitioners share a *common vocabulary* of well-defined terms easily understood by clients. *Education* of clients in the essential concepts of TA is viewed as a necessary component of counseling. Books explaining TA theory, such as *Born to Win* (James & Jongeward, 1971), are often assigned to clients as an adjunct to therapy.

Finally, Woollams and Brown (1979) have pointed out two other distinguishing characteristics of TA. All TA therapists apply concepts of *ego states* and *life scripts* and follow a treatment approach based on the assumption "I'm OK—You're OK."

TA's theory of personality and its therapeutic principles are operationalized by collecting and analyzing four different types of information:

1. *Transactions*—what people say and do to one another
2. *Scripts*—endless feedback loops of behavior generated in early childhood and continuing to the present
3. *Games and cons*—transactions (often maladaptive) that are played with others and that lead to payoffs (also often maladaptive)
4. *Structures*—the differential composition of ego states specific to each individual.

Theory of Personality

Transactional analysis is a humanistic, existential, dynamic theory of personality and a therapeutic modality whose practitioners believe humans are born in an "OK" state, that each person is unique, and that people ultimately are responsible for their own behavior and destinies. Transactional analysis theorists understand personality development in terms of several key concepts: ego states, strokes, injunctions, decisions, script formation, games, transactions, and life positions (Berne, 1964; Goulding, 1989; Goulding & Goulding, 1979; Woollams & Brown, 1979). Given Berne's psychoanalytic roots, all of these concepts have a distinct Freudian flavor (Novellino & Moiso, 1990). However, whereas the Freudian constructs of the superego, ego, and id exist in the unconscious, the constructs of TA are behavioral realities (Goldhaber & Goldhaber, 1976, p. 9). The basic personality premise of TA is that all of us are three people in one—a child, an adult, and a parent (Harris & Harris, 1985, p. 12). These constructs are shown in Figure 6.1.

The Parent Ego State.   In terms of function, the parent ego state may be divided into the nurturing parent (NP) and the critical parent (CP). In most cases, someone functioning as an NP behaves in a caring, concerned, and protective manner but may sometimes appear overprotective. Someone functioning as a CP is experienced as an oppressive, prejudiced, powerful, intimidating, and controlling person who demands yes and no answers. Trusting neither self nor others, the CP calls on external authority to enforce his or her demands (Harris & Harris, 1985, pp. 223–224). Too much of a CP results in aggression, while too little results in passivity. Too much NP results in an overbearing and inhibiting personality, while too little means an inconsiderate and uncaring personality (Dusay & Dusay, 1989, p. 408).

In the parent ego state is recorded a modeled and taught concept of life. This unerasable-tape concept is composed of events that actually happened in childhood. The problem is that the individual internalizes this tape in a distorted fashion, recording both the distorted and the objective realities of what one's parents were. Because the child is dependent on its parents, it is unable to comprehend that they were not God, but human, and thus made mistakes. As a result, the child grows to adulthood with a commingled but ultimately right parent ego state that is filled with demands, directions, and dogmatic decisions. The parent ego state, then, is the externally derived "have to" of the personality (Harris & Harris, 1985, pp. 14–18).

The Adult Ego State.   The adult ego state is the referee between the demands of the parent ego state and the wants of the child ego state. The adult ego state adds the thought concept to the taught concept of the parent ego state and the felt concept of the child ego state. It provides the "how to" for the personality by asking "why" questions and considering consequences. The adult ego state is not only a functioning part of the personality but also an observable state, and it is internally derived. One of its major functions is to update the values of the parent ego state (Harris & Harris, 1985, pp. 17–18).

The adult ego state is not divided because it is unemotional and functions solely as a computer (Dusay & Dusay, 1989, p. 409). Therefore, too much adult results in a technically

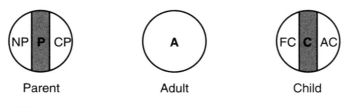

Parent   Adult   Child

FIGURE 6.1   Ego States

rational but boring individual, while too little adult results in an illogical and irrational individual (Dusay & Dusay, 1989, p. 437).

The Child Ego State. The child ego state consists of "impulses, feelings, and spontaneous acts." It contains the "recordings of the child's early experiences, responses, and the 'positions' taken about self and others" (James & Jongeward, 1971, p. 18). The child ego state has two basic functional states—the free child (FC) and the adapted child (AC). The FC is spontaneous, playful, eager, joyful, and curious. However, individuals who stay in their FC state too long may be considered "out of control" or "irresponsible." In contrast, individuals in their AC ego state may be described as compliant, compromising, rebellious, or industrious and act as if a parent may be watching or listening. The important distinction between FC and AC behavior is that the AC state is an adaptation to others whereas the FC state is a spontaneous expression of feelings and behavior without regard to the reactions of others (Dusay & Dusay, 1989, p. 438). Throughout one's life, the child ego state is both an influence and a state of being that is internally derived. It provides the "want to" of the personality and is the force that motivates the individual (Harris & Harris, 1985, p. 17).

Strokes. In TA theory, the need for strokes is considered the basic motivation for any human social interaction and necessary to an individual's healthy functioning (Dusay & Dusay, 1979, p. 377). The most positive strokes come from parents who unconditionally accept their children (Harris & Harris, 1985, p. 45). As children grow, they receive strokes that may be either positive—"I love you!"—or negative—"I hate you!" Although naturally preferring positive strokes, children consider negative strokes better than no strokes at all (Woollams & Brown, 1979, p. 43). On the basis of parental messages and in order to obtain strokes, children may decide to adapt to what they perceive their parents desire, even though such behavior may be detrimental to their long-term health and overall well-being. Although parental strokes are probably the strongest and most enduring for the child, strokes in adulthood may also be obtained from peers, bosses, spouses, and children and from our own realization that we did a good job (Harris & Harris, 1985, pp. 47, 87). When straightforward, direct strokes are not available, people may opt to play games and rackets to obtain them (Woollams, 1978). In summary, the strokes one receives or gives to others reinforce one's life position and furthers his or her script, ego functions, transactions, rackets, and games (Cassius, 1980, p. 216).

Life Positions. Life positions are a result of decisions made in response to how parent figures react to the child's initial expressions of his or her feelings and needs (Woollams & Brown, 1979, p. 108). There are four basic life positions an individual may adopt (Cassius, 1980; Harris, 1969; Woollams & Brown, 1979):

1. *I'm OK—You're OK.* This is probably the position reflecting how the child entered the world. As long as the child's emotional and physical needs are met in a loving, accepting way the infant retains this position and maintains a "winner's" script.

2. *I'm OK—You're not OK.* If a child is mistreated, he or she may decide others are not OK, which is essentially a defense against a more basic feeling of being "not OK." People in this position often blame and distrust others and react to the world with frustration or anger (sometimes called the "paranoid" position).

3. *I'm not OK—You're OK.* If the child's needs are not met, the child may decide that it is his or her fault for being "lacking" in some fundamental way. This is the most common position and is sometimes called the "depressive" position. People who are frequently in this position commonly experience guilt, depression, inadequacy, and fear.

4. *I'm not OK—You're not OK.* If stroking is lacking or extremely negative, the child may decide, "I'm not OK—You're not OK." Since there is no source of positive stroking, the infant may give up and feel hopeless. Persons who adopt this position are more likely to end up in mental institutions, jail, or the morgue.

Script Formation.   Berne (1972, p. 31) stated that in early life, individuals decide how they will live and how they will die, and this plan, "ever-present" in their heads, is called a script. Scripts have a variety of components, including decisions, life positions, fantasy characters, games, payoffs, physiological attributes (body language), and parental injunctions (Cassius, 1980, p. 214; Steiner, 1967, pp. 38–39). Scripts often incorporate specific elements from fairy tales and myths in which the person may be seen as playing different dramatic roles (Karpman, 1968).

Parents may send children two types of messages that influence the formation of their life position: permissions and script messages. Permissions—positive strokes given unconditionally—are growth-promoting messages. In contrast, script messages are negative, growth-restricting, and destructive injunctions.

After the child incorporates early messages from the parents, a script develops into a strong belief system, which is staunchly defended as an adult (Dusay & Dusay, 1989, p. 409). Negative, long-term, global injunctions and attributions do little for the child's physical and mental health. There are two types of such messages. First are those messages that come from the critical parent, a pseudoparent who is in reality operating in the child ego state. The critical parent may give several injunctions phrased in a variety of "don't" messages: "Don't do (be, love). . . ." Stated in all-inclusive, nonspecific terms, these messages stultify discrimination between growth-promoting and growth-restricting activities and lead to a pathological child ego state that carries into adulthood (Steiner, 1974, p. 60).

Another component of the critical parent is the use of attributions to form script messages in the child (Laing, 1971). These are "do" messages that may be set from birth through myths such as "You were born on Martin Luther King's birthday, so do be a great man." Even names subtly suggest attributional states: Cliff, Jr., will follow in his father's footsteps, Biff will raise hell, Lydia will be elegant, and Billie Jean will be the boy her father never had. Attributions or counterinjunctions are "driver" statements that set what the child must, should, or will do, whereas injunctions tell the child what he or she must, should, or will not do in order to gain the parents' favor (Steiner, 1974, pp. 62–64).

Counterscripts.   To complicate matters, the nurturing parent also contributes contradictory "do" messages that may have problematic consequences for the child. Called a *counterscript,* these parental messages demand acquiescence to the social and cultural expectations of society. The nurturing parent makes a positive verbal demand—"Be a caring person"—which is contradicted by the hypocritical action of the critical parent who says, "I won't give any money to that charity; they're just a bunch of welfare parasites." In other words, "Do as I say, not as I do!"

Transactions. A transaction is the basic unit of behavior in TA theory. It is the actual line of communication among the parent, adult, and child ego states of two people and determines whether communication is likely to continue, stop, or be dishonest.

A transaction is "an exchange of strokes between two persons, consisting of a stimulus and a response between specific ego states" (Woollams & Brown, 1979, p. 65). A conversation involves a series of linked transactions. There are three kinds of transactions— complementary, crossed, and ulterior. The vectors of these transactions are illustrated in Figure 6.2. In a *complementary transaction* the response comes from the same ego state to which the stimulus was directed and is directed back to the same ego state that sent the stimulus. Thus, it is a parallel transaction. For example, Bob asks (from his adult ego state), "How much does this cost?" and Joan (from her adult) responds, "Five dollars." Or Bob says (from his child), "I can't find my tie!" and Mary responds (from her parent), "I'll help you find it; don't worry." In complementary transactions, communication may continue without breaking down (Woollams & Brown, 1979, pp. 66–68) as long as the vectors stay in parallel, as demonstrated by the lines in Figure 6.2.

A *crossed transaction* occurs when communication lines are not parallel and the receiver responds to the sender in an ego state different from the one to which the message was directed. For example, Bob asks (from his adult) "How much does this cost?" and Joan responds (from her free child), "None of your business, nosy!" This crossed adult–defiant child transaction is illustrated by the vectors in Figure 6.3. Whenever a crossed transaction occurs, a breakdown in communication is likely to follow (Woollams & Brown, 1979, pp. 66–68).

An *ulterior transaction* is one that contains two levels of communication—a social level and a psychological level—and always involves more than two ego states. The psychological message is the ulterior message; it is aimed at an ego state different from the one

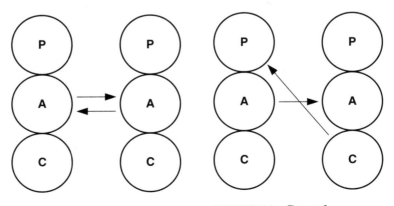

FIGURE 6.2   Complementary Transaction

FIGURE 6.3   Crossed Transaction

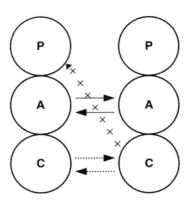

FIGURE 6.4   Ulterior Transaction

the social message is aimed at. For example, Leona, a real estate saleswoman, sends a psychological message to the customer's child: "You're not big enough to play with us!" although ostensibly it is sent as a social adult-to-adult transaction: "While this is a really fine home, its payment schedule may be a little rough to handle on your salary; we'll have to really work to make this deal go!" The psychological response may trigger the customer's child into thinking, "Oh, yeah, well I'll show you I'm big enough to make payments. I want this house, so gimme it *now*!" Such an ulterior transaction is demonstrated by the dotted vectors in Figure 6.4, where the double message from the salesperson is transmitted to both the adult and the child of the purchaser, and the purchaser's response comes back as a defiant child to the critical parent of the salesperson as illustrated by the crosshatched vector.

Nature of Maladjustment

Overview.   According to TA theory, emotional disturbance reflects learned behaviors based on early decisions children make. One possible choice is an "I'm OK—You're OK" life position, in which case the child has chosen a "winner's" script. On the other hand, the child may decide "I'm OK—You're not OK," "I'm not OK—You're OK," or "I'm not OK—You're not OK," all of which are unhealthy life positions leading to "loser" scripts. Such "loser" script decisions commonly take three general forms, according to Dusay and Dusay (1979, p. 405):

1. "I'm sad"—a depressive decision by persons who believe they are "not OK" in relation to others
2. "I'm mad"—a paranoid decision by persons who have decided they will be "OK" at the expense of others being "not OK"
3. "I'm scared"—a schizophrenic decision by persons who have decided that they are "not OK," nor is anyone else

Thus, one way of viewing pathology is to consider the maladjusted individual as having opted for a "loser's" script.

Injunctions. Most humans live in a state of stroke scarcity, and thus spend much of their waking hours seeking to obtain strokes—if not in positive then in negative ways. Besides social taboos that militate against the indiscriminate obtaining and giving of strokes, a variety of parental "don't" and "do" tapes keep people from getting strokes from significant others. If these strokes are not obtained from humans, then they may be obtained from alcohol, drugs, fast cars, gambling, work, or any other of a variety of negatively addicting substances or objects (Steiner, 1971).

Injunctions come to the child ego state in a number of formats; culled by the Gouldings (1976, 1979), the Harrises (1969, 1985), and Kahler and Capers (1974), they form a recipe book for maladaptive behavior. Here are the major "don'ts" and "dos" of maladjustment and some typical decisions the child makes in response to them:

1. *"Don't."* This generic junction may be given by frightened parents who send the message "Don't do anything risky—the world is a dangerous place." As a result, the child may come to believe that no possible course of action is right or safe.

2. *"Don't be"* or *"Don't exist."* This "don't" message is considered the most lethal. Often parents send this message in a subtle manner by suggesting "If it weren't for you, our lives would be better." Children who interpret messages as "don't be" messages may make very different decisions in response. One child may decide, "You're wrong; I'm valuable"; another may create a fantasy parent who really cares. However, if the child totally accepts this injunction, he or she may decide, "If things get too bad, I'll kill myself or somebody else."

3. *"Don't be close."* If a parent figure discourages physical closeness or positive stroking, a child may interpret this as a "don't be close" message. Children may also give themselves this injunction upon losing a parent through death or divorce, concluding, "What's the use of getting close; I just lose them in the end" or "I'll never trust anyone again."

4. *"Don't be important."* If children are discounted in some way, they may experience this message as "don't be important." In response, a child may decide, "Everyone else counts first around here," "I'll never amount to anything," or "I may become important but I can never let anyone know."

5. *"Don't be a child."* This script message is given most often to the eldest child, who is expected to be responsible for younger siblings. Some decisions that children may make in response to this injunction are to deny their needs; to grow up always to take care of others; or to "go crazy" in order to get their needs met.

6. *"Don't grow."* Parents may say, "Don't grow beyond infancy," "Don't grow beyond a certain age," "Don't be sexual," and/or "Don't leave me." It is most often the youngest child who is given these injunctions. Two common responses are deciding to remain in the "cared for" position and deciding to fight back and prove themselves.

7. *"Don't succeed."* The parent may communicate "If you are more successful than I am, I will not love you" or "You can't do anything right," which may be translated as "Don't succeed" by the child. Some typical decisions children make in response to this message are to work extra hard to succeed; to succeed and yet not enjoy success; or to accept the injunction totally and fail.

8. *"Don't be you"* (the sex you are). Parents or others may send a child messages that they value the opposite sex more highly. Thus, girls may adopt "tomboy" behaviors while boys become "girlish" to conform to parental expectations, or continue to engage in sex-appropriate activities but feel bad about themselves for violating parental injunctions.

9. *"Don't be sane"* or *"Don't be well."* Parents may give children strokes for being sick and withhold them when they are well. If the parents reward, tolerate, or model "crazy" behavior, the child may receive a "don't be sane" message. If children accept these injunctions, they may remain sick or "crazy" to keep getting strokes.

10. *"Don't belong."* If parents communicate that they should be somewhere else, such as in another country, a child may interpret this as a "don't belong" message. In response, the child may decide, "I'll never belong to anyone" (or any group or any country) or "Nobody will ever like me, because I don't belong."

Counterinjections.   To obtain strokes, the child believes that he or she will be "OK" if one or more of the following "do" messages can be accomplished (Harris & Harris, 1985, p. 36). These counterinjunctions, however, are also restrictive and, like injunctions, also prevent growth (Goulding & Goulding, 1979, p. 38).

1. *"Do be perfect."* If a B grade is obtained, an A is better. If an A grade is obtained, then an A+ is better. Obtaining a medical degree is not as good as getting a specialty in neurosurgery. No defects are allowed.

2. *"Do be the best."* Winning isn't everything, it's the only thing. No strokes are given for effort or accomplishment.

3. *"Do try hard."* "You are not living up to your potential" is the broken record the child hears over and over. "Idle hands are the devil's workshop," but superhuman efforts will still not get the job done.

4. *"Do hurry up."* Taking time to process events and "smell the daisies" is unacceptable. If one hurries, a multitude of activities can be accomplished. It doesn't matter if the efforts are slipshod.

5. *"Do be strong."* "Bearing up under the load" without complaining or feeling is the mark of an emotionally strong individual who is able to take the world on in equal terms and give and ask it no quarter.

These "driver" messages are all impossible to evaluate or accomplish and thus are open-ended, one-way contracts that may never be brought to successful closure. Using counterinjunctions to overcome injunctions has two results. First, injunctions are much more likely to prevail and remain firmly in place, culminating in a no-win situation. Second, many counterinjunctions are the direct antitheses of injunctions, are impossible to follow, and put the individual in a double bind (Goulding & Goulding, 1979, pp. 38–39).

Driver statements given by parents, such as "be perfect" "hurry up," "try hard," and "be strong," each generate specific kinds of fears, which lead to compensatory defensive responding in the form of a specific type of righteous behavior. For example, "be perfect" people are besieged by guilt and worry. In a vengeful child state they are anything but perfect and make a mess of things. Their script consists of "I am worthless/shameful" and their neurotic and psychotic tendencies range from being organizational fanatics to having psychiatric disturbances of the obsessive-compulsive type (Klein, 1992).

Mundy's (1994) discussion of American slang and colloquialisms is particularly instructive of how common statements can be used as subtle drivers. An interesting example (particularly to teachers) is the badly overused and irritating "You know;" used as a statement, an exclamation, or a question. Mundy proposes that "you know" is actually a subconscious "please me" miniscript message because it allows the speaker to not have to process thoughts, be unclear as to meaning, and trap listeners into having to assume what the speaker actually means or wants, if indeed the speaker does know.

Games.   Games are a recurring set of transactions, often repetitious, superficially plausible, but with a concealed motive (Berne, 1964, pp. 48–50). Games may be played at a variety of levels and intensities: some are socially acceptable; in others feelings are hurt without any permanent damage; and still others are played for keeps (Goldhaber & Goldhaber, 1976, p. 139).

Structurally, a game is a series of duplex (social–psychological) transactions that lead to a well-defined predictable payoff that justifies a not-OK, or discounted, position (Woollams & Brown, 1979, p. 117). A game begins with an outwardly straight stimulus; contains a covert or ulterior message that is responded to overtly; and ends with a payoff in which at least one person may be hurt (Goulding & Goulding, 1979, p. 30). Games are defense mechanisms as well as transactions, and everyone plays them 60 to 70 percent of the time (Cassius, 1980, p. 215).

The general advantage of a game is that it is a stabilizing influence. Homeostasis is promoted by the stroking one receives, and psychological stability is reinforced by the confirmation of one's position (Berne, 1964, p. 56.) Whatever their product—self-castigation, justification, reassurance, absolution, revenge, alleviation of guilt, sexual gratification, vindication, and so on—games are a way of saying from the child ego state, "I too am OK!" (Harris & Harris, 1985, p. 210).

Rackets.   The payoff in which individuals have some favorite negative feeling that they use to confirm their life position is termed a *racket.* This collection of bad feelings is usually learned from a parent figure to whom the child ego state has become accustomed (Cassius, 1980, p. 215; Goldhaber & Goldhaber, 1976, p. 138).

Stamps.   People prefer to collect their own brand of racket feelings, such as guilt, anger, inadequacy, or depression, that reinforce their script. These feelings are called *trading stamps,* and they represent the kind of emotional reaction that marks the end of a game. When enough stamps are collected, they may be turned in for psychological prizes. Some prizes are minor, such as hitting, screaming, crying, and laughing; some are much bigger, such as murder, suicide, divorce, and job loss (Cassius, 1980, p. 215; Goldhaber & Goldhaber, 1976, p. 138).

Drama Triangle.   Karpman's (1968) drama triangle is an enclosed system with a *persecutor* (I am better than you; you are inferior), a *rescuer* (I know more than you; you are inferior), and a *victim* (I am helpless) at its corners. In terms of strokes, the persecutor discounts others with negative strokes, the rescuer discounts others with conditional positive strokes, and the victim discounts him- or herself with negative strokes. An individual may move into a game or racket from any of the three basic positions by "exaggerating or devaluating the worth of himself or herself or the other person" (Woollams & Brown, 1979, p. 122). Individuals switch positions as the game or racket progresses.

When the other person refuses to continue to play, such individuals switch drama triangle positions and play games in order to continue receiving strokes. Thus, a person may begin as a victim, complaining about "how unfair life is," and as long as he or she has a sympathetic audience—"Yeah, life is rotten" (a complementary transaction)—the racket can continue. However, if the "rescuer" responds by switching to the victim position—for example, "I'm stupid—I've run out of suggestions"—the original victim may switch to the persecutor role and respond, "You selfish clod. You're just like all the others. You care only about yourself!" By switching positions, each person can collect a stroke payoff—the racket feeling—and justify his or her life position.

Discounting.   Discounting occurs at the following four levels of severity (Mellor & Schiff, 1975; Woollams & Brown, 1979, p. 103):

1. A person may discount the *existence* of a problem. A woman may deny that her family is sick even though her spouse is having an affair, a child has attempted suicide, and she is anesthetizing herself with martinis and tranquilizers.
2. One may discount the *significance* of the problem. The family may be sick, but it is not important to do anything about it. Things always work out, so the person may invest no energy in solving it.
3. One may discount the *change possibilities* of the problem. Operating out of this external locus of control, the person may believe, "It is out of my hands and only God can deal with it."
4. One may discount his or her *ability* to solve the problem but acknowledge that others may have the ability to do so. The person may decide that Dr. Krane, who runs that radio show for people with marital problems, should be called.

Ego State Pathology.   An emotionally healthy person can choose the ego state that appears to be most useful in a given situation. One kind of ego state pathology occurs when a person's ego state boundaries break down and his or her adult state becomes contaminated by the child state and/or parent state. For example, a parent contamination occurs when the person mistakes parent information, such as prejudices and opinions, for fact, as in "Women are no good." A child contamination occurs when old childhood experiences are used to assess current reality inaccurately, as in "I never step on a crack because something bad will happen."

Another type of ego state pathology, *exclusion,* "occurs when one or two ego states dominate a person's behavior. When a single ego state dominates, that ego state is called *constant* or *excluding*" (Woollams & Brown, 1979, p. 36). A constant parent may be authoritarian; a constant adult may function like a "computer"; and a constant child may be irresponsible.

Ego State Imbalance.   Whereas the concepts of ego state contamination or exclusion and the "loser's" script relate to the "what and where" issue of maladjustment, they do not address the issues of "degree" of disturbance. Dusay and Dusay (1979) discuss the concept of the egogram (Dusay, 1972, 1977), a tool used to assess the amount of energy invested in the forces of the three ego states—the critical parent, nurturing parent, adult, free child, and adapted child (see Figure 6.1). A person who is well-adjusted will have an egogram in which no ego state is extremely low or particularly high (Dusay & Dusay, 1979, p. 393). The advantage of the egogram, besides its reflection of the strengths and weaknesses of an individual's personality, is that "it provides a personal map for growth and change" for the individual (Dusay & Dusay, 1979, p. 391).

Because each person has a distinct and unique personality, these five psychological forces are aligned in different amounts and balance in each individual. A bar graph may then be constructed to demonstrate to the client how much of each of these psychological forces is present and what they are doing (see Figure 6.5 of Billie Jean, the case study for this chapter). Egograms remain fairly fixed unless the person actively decides to change the energy balance (Dusay & Dusay, 1989, p. 409). Many TA practitioners believe this is a more effective way to view diagnosis because it suggests a direction for treatment. Individuals are considered "cured" when they are able to strengthen their "low-energy" ego states and achieve a "harmonious balance" among their ego states (Dusay & Dusay, 1979, p. 412).

Ego State Oppositions.   "Energy distribution action" therapists support the concept of *ego state oppositions.* Through techniques of ego state opposition, clients learn to transfer their ego state energies from those states considered too high to those considered too low. In the case of Billie Jean, she has almost no critical parent (others dictate to her), an extremely high nurturing parent (she can be smothering), little adult (she cannot think), little free child (she is too responsible), and an extremely high adapted child (she feels depressed and guilty and worries about what others will think) (see Figure 6.5, Billie Jean's egogram).

Dusay (1976) hypothesizes that a rule of constancy operates with the ego states: when one state increases, another must decrease in a complementary way because of the finite

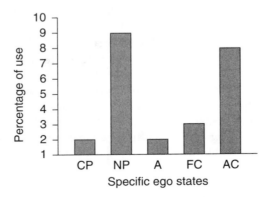

FIGURE 6.5   Billie Jean's Egogram

amount of psychic energy that may be expended (p. 65). The ideal egogram for Billie Jean would be an increased critical parent, a greatly decreased nurturing parent, a greatly increased adult, a somewhat increased free child, and a severely decreased adapted child. However, this is easier said than done.

The Counseling Process

Goals

In life, individuals write their own scripts rather than being scripted. In therapy, clients rewrite their scripts "with the help of a strong parent that clients build for themselves rather than incorporating it from the counselor" (Goulding & Goulding, 1979, p. 42). Berne (1964) implies that the overall goal of the therapeutic process may be autonomy, which he defined as "the recovery of three capacities: awareness, spontaneity, and intimacy" (p. 178). To achieve this autonomy, clients must come to realize that they have the power to understand and change the early decisions they made in response to parental injunctions.

In the redecision process, clients reexperience these early-life decisions and make new, healthier decisions. Some TA theorists speak of this change as adopting a "winner's script" (James & Jongeward, 1971); others believe it involves becoming "script-free" (Woollams, 1978).

The Therapist's Perspective

Transactional analysis emphasizes a therapeutic approach based on the assumption "I'm OK—You're OK," which means that everyone has a lovable part and is capable of change (Woollams & Brown, 1979, p. 221). Through contracting, therapist and client are made "equal partners." It is the client's job to decide what he or she wants to change and the therapist's job to lend his or her expertise to accomplish those changes (Steiner, 1968).

In accomplishing therapeutic changes, TA therapists are commonly involved in four kinds of rational analysis: structural analysis (the analysis of individual personality); transactional analysis (the analysis of what people say and do to one another); game analysis (the identification of games and the resulting racket feelings); and script analysis (the analysis of the overall life plans people follow) (James & Jongeward, 1971, p. 16).

A basic philosophical difference exists between some schools of TA theorists. According to Dusay and Dusay (1979), theorists such as Berne, Steiner, Dusay, and Karpman have suggested that change can best be accomplished when the therapist takes a strong parent role, giving potent well-timed counterinjunctions to counter the original parental injunctions. In contrast, other theorists (Goulding & Goulding, 1979; Woollams & Brown, 1979) emphasize that clients must get in touch with their own power to redecide, rather than rely on the parent ego state of the therapist. A key task of the therapist is to help clients get in touch with their own potency, to protect themselves, and to give themselves permission to change. Both groups agree that clients are responsible for their own actions and decisions (Goulding & Goulding, 1978; Steiner, 1968).

While working as a partner for change, the therapist also helps clients learn the language and concepts of TA so that they may apply them in analyzing their own behavior. As a case in point, one can purchase a dictionary of terms devoted exclusively to TA concepts (Tilney, 1998). Transactional analysts are also great believers in using pictures to illuminate what happens to increase understanding and demystify the therapeutic process. Concepts are not only expressed verbally but also drawn as symbols, and these graphic representations of transactions and changes in ego state energy are shown to the client (Dusay & Dusay, 1989, p. 406).

The Client's Perspective

Clients are asked by the therapist to decide specifically what they want to change. If they are unclear about this, the therapist will help them get in touch with these goals through such techniques as experiencing here and now a recent, fantasized, or early situation in which they had negative feelings like those that motivated them to seek therapy. Although the therapist assists clients in defining the contract, clients essentially make the contract with themselves while the therapist serves as a witness and facilitator (Goulding & Goulding, 1979, p. 50).

Clients must be willing to take the risk of revealing themselves and to carry out assignments the therapist might recommend. In other words, clients might be assigned to engage in some behaviors that are inconsistent with their script-reinforcing behavior but that are congruent with their overall treatment contract.

Strategies for Helping Clients

Woollams and Brown (1979, pp. 228–233) outlined seven stages of therapy: motivation; awareness; the treatment contract; deconfusing the child; redecision; relearning; and termination. In the following sections, the strategies and techniques applicable to these stages are discussed as they apply to the case of Billie Jean Overton.

Billie Jean Overton, 44, oscillates between depression and hyperactivity. She is married to John W. Overton, a successful real estate developer and insurance broker. Until recently, Billie Jean immersed herself in rearing her two daughters (Johnie Ruth, 22, and Stephanie, 19), serving her church, and functioning as John's perfect wife. Billie Jean reared Johnie Ruth and Stephanie to follow in her footsteps by teaching them to be alluring and enticing princesses who achieve recognition and attention from men through skillful coquettish behavior. While the younger daughter, Stephanie, has accepted a princess role, Johnie Ruth has rebelled violently.

John Overton is extremely busy and is away from home most of the time. He has alternated between addiction to his businesses and younger women. Billie Jean knows about some of John's escapades with younger women. Sometimes she has been made so angry and jealous by John's infidelity that she has contemplated divorce. But when she consulted her own father (now deceased), she took his advice to keep a stiff upper lip, live up to her marriage vows, be a dutiful wife, remember what an excellent provider John is, and to work to keep the family together—just as he did.

Billie Jean is now distressed and deeply depressed that Johnie Ruth is planning to leave the United States for the Far East to study with a guru. Billie Jean has also returned to college after a twenty-year hiatus, and is now a senior. However, she recently experienced such severe academic problems that she may not graduate. Her academic failures have shaken her to her foundations, and now she believes that her best opportunity to become her own person and move out from under John's shadow is in serious jeopardy. She vows that money and a very comfortable lifestyle mean little to her and is extremely angry when John uses financial power to control her behavior by providing her with unlimited charge accounts, vacations, servants, and a magnificent home. However, she is not willing to give up her material comforts with John even though the emotional part of their marriage has long been dead.

As Billie Jean presents herself for therapy, her body language is rigid. In contrast, her speech is disorganized, scattered, ambivalent, and replete with pleas to the therapist to "fix" things for her and help to get her life straightened out.

The TA therapist's analysis of Billie Jean's injunctions indicate that she has carried deep within her since early childhood the following "don'ts:"

1. "Don't be important!" (You're only important in regard to how you look and what kind of social contacts you can make to enhance the importance of your husband.)
2. "Don't grow!" (As a youngster, be the ideal daughter—be daddy's perfect little girl; later, be the dutiful all-giving wife.)
3. "Don't be you!" (Be alert to sensing what others, especially male authority figures, want you to be, and strive to meet their expectations; put others' needs ahead of your own.)
4. "Don't think!" (Think what your parents thought; think what your husband thinks; don't have your own thoughts.)
5. "Don't feel!" (You may emote, but do not feel; don't manifest any of the emotions underlying feelings; don't act on feelings; either deny having feelings or ascribe them to external causes, such as your husband's wishes, social peers, God, or your children's dilemmas.)

Billie Jean's "do" counterinjunctions, also transmitted by her parents and ingrained in her adapted child state, include the following:

1. "Do be perfect!" (You must always appear to be perfect in looks and behavior.)
2. "Do please me!" (Please mommy and daddy; please your husband; please your daughters.)
3. "Do be strong!" (Never show weakness; keep your chin up and keep a stiff upper lip, with a pleasant smile; be assured that you will be well taken care of.)

Billie Jean's principal games are IWFY and Peasant.

■ *IWFY (If It Weren't for You).* ("I could _____ if I didn't have to be at home and take care of things for John," or "I would never wear clothes like that or fix my hair like that, because he wouldn't allow that," or "Johnie Ruth might not have been so quick to follow that guru if John hadn't been so stern about cutting off her support)." IWFY (Berne, 1964, pp. 50–58, 103–104), the most common game played between married couples, typically originates in the initial choice of marriage partners. The woman associates with women who feel they are likewise victimized, and that reinforces her IWFY beliefs. She plays IWFY in her marital role, in her social life, and in her vocation. She refrains from doing things she really doesn't want to do, but pretends that she wants to do them and complains that she could do them if it weren't for her husband.

> **JOHN:** Billie Jean, you stay here and take care of the house while I'm on my business trip to Florida.
>
> **BILLIE JEAN:** I could finish my degree and get a job of my own if it weren't for you and all those trips you take.

■ *Peasant* (Berne, 1964, pp. 151–154). ("Gee, you're a wonderful _____ [husband, father, doctor, daughter, delivery person, etc.].") In Billie Jean's case, Peasant, in the form of GYWH (Gee you're a wonderful husband), is played on two levels. First, by romanticizing and praising John's attributes, Billie Jean publicly obligates him to be well-behaved socially. Second, once she has him convinced that she believes he is wonderful, she can make herself look saintly or make him look foolish. The simplest way for the GYWH player to win is to not get better.

> **BILLIE JEAN:** (at John's office party) Look what a beautiful turquoise bracelet John brought me from Arizona. I guess it was worth staying home and minding the answering machine after all. He's such a wonderful husband!

Strategies for Increasing Client Motivation and Awareness

Typically, in order for clients to enter therapy they must be in touch with their own pain enough to feel a need or desire to change. This awareness of their own unhappiness or discomfort drives the *motivation* (stage one) necessary to work toward change.

> **CL:** (*very stiff posture; speaking dramatically*) I need help. I think I'm going to flunk out of school. It's making me a nervous wreck, and I can't sleep. I don't know what to do. I've struggled so hard to get this far and I've really tried, plus I've got a lot of other problems right now with my daughter, and my father's death on my mind. He's been gone only two years, and my husband and I aren't getting along well and he is gone all the time selling. They suggested that I get psychological help at my internship site, so here I am, but I think they are wrong. They made me feel so bad, like I wasn't worth anything. What do you think?

Billie Jean's initiating behavior illuminates the verbal and nonverbal transactions that provide interpersonal communication hooks to ensnare others into her games and rackets. Her monologue is replete with disowned messages. Others make her the way she is. Indefinite pronouns and global externalized "theys" are not "I" statements of what the child in her wants (Goulding & Goulding, 1979, pp. 5–6). She follows the parental injunction "Don't think." She turns to external authorities, such as the therapist—an "expert," much in the model of what she believes her father was to her and what her husband has failed to be in regard to "fixing" her tremendous number of emotional needs. Even though the therapist is a woman, she will have to be very careful and aware of the strokes she delivers and what reinforcement her responses have for the client's script (Clarkson, 1992). The therapist now asks a number of here-and-now questions while listening very closely to the client's responses and carefully monitoring her body language. Throughout therapy the therapist avoids falling into the jargon of TA, because this in itself would embellish the "expert" status that the needy client seeks and also would undoubtedly play into the hands of more indirect transactions that would not facilitate awareness or change (Goulding & Goulding, 1979, p. 49).

TH: What are the feelings that go with this?

CL: I'm angry at my supervising teacher. I really did a good job.

TH: What other feelings?

CL: I'm really scared. What will happen to me if I don't graduate?

TH: What *will* happen?

CL: I don't know. I'd like to be my own person, not just somebody's wife, except that if he cared for me I wouldn't have to do this now. I really want a good relationship with him which I don't have now, and I can't understand that because I've tried to be everything he's ever wanted, but it's never enough.

TH: So are you saying you've had enough or you've not had enough?

CL: I keep thinking that perhaps he'll change, really come back and love me. I've devoted all my energy to him and the kids and it's all fallen apart. I need to feel like I'm somebody. I've failed with them and now it looks like I've failed with school. (*starts sobbing*)

TH: (*indicates tissues on table*) What is it you want?

The client makes a number of indirect behavioral transactions that are designed to bring the therapist to her assistance. The therapist wisely does not respond to these indirect pleas for help, but rather pushes forth very direct statements that seek to put the transactions on an adult-to-adult level (Goulding & Goulding, 1979, p. 28).

Once individuals are in touch with their dissatisfaction enough that they are willing to commit to change, they are ready to enter stage two of therapy—*awareness.* In the awareness stage, although clients may be aware that they are dissatisfied with what is occurring in their lives, they may not be clear about what exactly they want to change. So in this stage the therapist assists clients in deciding what it is, in concrete, specific terms, that they want to change through therapy.

CL: If I could get this degree it'd make me somebody. I mean I could go out and get a professional job, I wouldn't be so dependent.

TH: What do you want to change so you won't be dependent? And what are you willing to do to make that change to being independent?

CL: This degree would do it.

TH: Be factual. How would the degree "do it"? I don't know what "it" means. What do you want?

CL: (*rather icily*) To be loved and appreciated and feel like I am somebody. Is that specific enough?

TH: No! How do you want to be loved, appreciated, and felt for so that you are somebody to you?

CL: (*head back, eyes deflected up to the right and away, with a sad smile*) Like my father. He was wonderful. It was perfect when he was alive. I adored him and he me.

TH: But your father is now dead.

CL: (*tears return to eyes*) Yes, and I miss him terribly, he took care of me. I don't know why my husband can't be like him, caring and loving and all that.

TH: What you are saying is that you now want to be independent and the degree would somehow do that for you. You don't want to be victimized by the whims of somebody else and you want to be your own boss. You also say that you want to be cared for just like your father did for you. Also it sounds as if you spend a lot of time rescuing or trying to fix things for your daughters and husband, but that hasn't worked very well either, yet you still go about doing it. How do those notions hook up with being independent?

The therapist makes this interpretation because of the drama the client plays out that keeps her at an impasse. She is operating under both injunctions and counterinjunctions. She responds to the injunctions from her father's parent ego state ("Be nice") and child ego state (Don't think . . . particularly angry thoughts"). Her decision then becomes, "If I show how smart I can think, I'm uppity and men will put me in my place. I can't be nice and smart at the same time and still get strokes. Therefore, I'll be nice and make myself helpless."

The client is vacillating between two points, victim and rescuer, on Karpman's (1968) drama triangle. As long as she is bound to this script pattern, it is going to be very difficult for her to assume independence. Certainly a degree by itself will no more make her her own person than being married, bearing children, or having a Mercedes. It is apparent that there are some very strong parental injunctions and counterinjunctions in her life, given the extremely strong emotional influence her dead father still has on her. However, on the positive side she has moved toward some "dos" in her life, such as returning to college and coming to therapy.

CL: I don't know.

TH: Don't or won't?

CL: I am really trying to get my act together. I just don't know what to do. I need to get on with my life.

TH: As a result of this there seem to be a lot of "don'ts" in your life. There also seem to be some vaguely defined "dos." You say you *need* to do some things, but will you change that to a *want*? Very specifically, I'd like you to state the differences you want in your life, how far you want to go in making those changes, what the gain and loss will be, and what you will do to achieve those differences.

The therapist is setting up some clear behavioral plans for change. Whereas thinking one wants to do something is a prerequisite for change, action steps specifically put the client's adapted parent on notice that change is imminent and provides the concrete motivation for change (Harris & Harris, 1985, pp. 186–187).

CL: (*wistfully, wringing her hands*) If my husband could just pay attention to me. If things were like they were when we got married; he adored me then. Perhaps I could get him in here and we could both work things out. It's the same with the oldest girl. If I could just make her see the light, then she might get out of that horrible sect she's in.

TH: Perhaps? If things were like they were? Might? That's magical thinking. Things will never be like they were. Indeed, you yourself propose to change things by going to school and becoming independent. What do you want to change about you and not them right now, and I mean today, in this room?

Billie Jean uses a number of cop-out words—*might, perhaps, try,* and *work*. These qualifiers do not indicate a real commitment to risk change. They leave the person an out because one can always try to do something and can continue to work forever without changing. By saying "What do you want to change?" the therapist puts the onus squarely on the client to decide not only what she wants but also what she is willing to do (Goulding & Goulding, 1979, p. 73). The therapist catches the client's words that are based on the magical thinking she has scripted for herself and confronts her tentativeness. The therapist's confrontation is intended to disturb the client's egogram energy imbalance and cause the client to start making energy shifts toward more balanced ego states (Dusay & Dusay, 1989, p. 441).

CL: (*whining*) But I don't want to be alone. I hate that.

TH: Becoming independent does not mean going it alone. It does mean broadening your social support base, not putting all your eggs in one basket. Are you willing to do that, take a risk that goes with freedom?

While seeking to create awareness and motivation in the client, the therapist also *reparents*—she brings attention to how the client discounts the present and to the assertive action that is needed for change in the future.

CL: (*avoiding the question*) I just wish she'd listen. I just want what's best for her. I know she despises me for interfering, but . . . my husband keeps after me to take care of it and get her straightened out, and it's my Christian duty.

TH: Do you see how you have attempted to placate, even rescue, others, as much as you have placated and fooled yourself by allowing others to rescue you and by giving them permission to think for you?

The therapist pushes this aspect of the client's "don't think" injunction that she attempts to carry over from her adapted child into her own parental role with the daughter. While Billie Jean may sound as if she is speaking from a nurturing parent ego state because of her concern for her daughter, there is much in her worry over her daughter that comes from a script she wrote many years ago. Thus, it is within the adapted child that the redecision process must start, for it is that ego state that made the original decision (Goulding & Goulding, 1979, p. 212).

Strategies for Establishing the Therapeutic Contract

The therapeutic contract sets the focus for treatment. The client decides in terms of beliefs, emotions, and behaviors what she plans to change about herself to reach her goals (Goulding & Goulding, 1979, p. 50). A good contract should be brief, stated in words that are understandable to the child ego state, and as behaviorally specific as possible. Although the contract is basically an adult-adult agreement, all of the client's and therapist's ego states need to approve and be involved in the contract and end up at an OK position (Woollams & Brown, 1979, pp. 223–224).

CL: I want to gain respect . . . like from my professors, that I'm really not a bundle of fluff.

TH: Give me an example. A recent time when you wanted respect but didn't get it. Imagine yourself in that scene and the professor there in that empty chair. What do you say to him to get respect?

CL: I feel kinda dumb doing this.

TH: "Dumb" is a judgment. Tell me how you feel when you are dumb.

CL: I felt dumb with my professor.

TH: You were making yourself dumb. How did you feel?

CL: Like I was going to come apart. I knew the material, but when I opened my mouth a bunch of nonsense spilled out and I just couldn't focus on the topic. I was angry . . . I guess at myself.

TH: What were you angry with yourself about?

CL: That I knew the answer but couldn't respond and then had to ask for help, as if I'd never had an ounce of sense. It's sort of the way I am around John.

TH: You just had an incisive insight, that you give up any wits (power) to important men in your life. So, clearly, you are not dumb. What would you then change about yourself?

CL: Stop thinking I'm dumb. Dumb people don't deserve respect and I am *not* dumb!

TH: Fantastic! That's right! So are you willing to make a contract to be smart and be respected for what you know and not how you look?

Billie Jean conveys a part of her life script ("You can't think!"). As she encounters a new, unorthodox, and risky situation she plays dumb with the therapist. If the therapist lets her get away with being dumb with her, she and Billie Jean will have made an *ulterior contract,* a pact between therapist and client to prevent the client from reaching her goals (Goulding & Goulding, 1979, p. 85). Billie Jean's acknowledgment of also acting this way with her husband indicates her "Think dumb" is at least one of the scripts in her life drama of being a victim, a script acted out in front of her family, peers, and professors.

If the contract comes only from Billie Jean's parent ego state (for example, "I can't be angry" because of the counterinjunction "be nice") it will be difficult to achieve because the motivation to change comes from Billie Jean's free child ("Oh yes, I can be angry, and I can stand up for my rights and that's tough noogies for any of you guys who try to put me down.") (Woollams & Brown, 1979, p. 229). If Billie Jean had made a contract not to be dumb and not to be angry with her professor, it would not be acceptable because her child ego state would have no investment in it (Goulding & Goulding, 1979, p. 71).

A further complication may arise if Billie Jean tries to negotiate a *contract to change others.* All too commonly, the client initially attempts to continue a game and a racket by getting others, rather than herself, to change (Goulding & Goulding, 1979, p. 75).

CL: I would like to change the way I relate to men.

TH: Be specific when you say "relate."

CL: I'd like to be able to be open enough to be myself.

TH: Are you unopened?

CL: Well, yes! Right now I am but if. . . .

TH: Are you disabled?

CL: Well, ah, no.

TH: So then you are able. You are able to open, whatever that may be. Again, be specific as to what you want to change in you.

CL: I want to become so assertive that all the important men in my life will have to pay attention to me.

TH: To do that you will have to become assaultive. You cannot make others do that unless you plan to hold a .357 magnum to their heads. Is that your goal?

CL: Certainly not.

TH: Then you have not made a contract for you; you've made it for others. What will you do for you to make yourself think smart and not be dictated to in a fawning, chauvinistic way?

Billie Jean manifests the type of life script that holds another potential problem for contracting. Because she operates a great deal of the time out of a victim stance, she is a past master at playing a component of the game "look how hard I'm trying." Thus, if not careful, the therapist may agree to a *forever contract.* Such a contract allows the client to work hard forever toward some nebulous goal but keep the secret goal of remaining unhappy. This game will allow the adapted child to continue to receive the same strokes that were achieved in childhood—working hard and suffering (Goulding & Goulding, 1979, p. 80).

The TA therapist must be very skillful at monitoring both the client's games and her own so that she doesn't get caught up in transference and countertransference issues that can lead to therapeutic rackets (Summerton, 2000). This would be very easy to do with a client like Billie Jean. Again and again the therapist will have to be watchful so as not to implicitly enter into bad therapy contracts that Billie Jean will unconsciously attempt to negotiate.

> CL: If men were just like my father—he was truly a wonderful man. The greatest man I have ever known. And I miss him terribly.
>
> TH: He has been dead now for two years?
>
> CL: Yes.
>
> TH: So the greatest person in your life is dead. How can one compete against a dead person?
>
> CL: (*face flushes and tears start to well up in her eyes*) I don't understand. I cherish his memory, it's still hard to cope without him.
>
> TH: You still cherish him, not his memory, as if he were alive, which he is not. That deal you have cut about relationships is with a dead person who will be that way forever. As long as you do that no man can ever measure up and you will continue to contract relationships in the same way you did with your dead father. I will not accept a forever contract.

While the approach of the therapist may seem unnecessarily cruel, the client needs to accept her father's death and the unfinished business she has with him by keeping him alive (Goulding, 1997; Goulding & Goulding, 1979, pp. 174–184). Under no circumstances would the therapist pursue the death of Billie Jean's father or uncover the kinds of intense emotions that underlie it unless she knew exactly how to promote a successful conclusion (Goulding & Goulding, 1979, p. 149). One of the most vicious, and justified, criticisms of TA is that in the hands of amateurs, confrontation may be used injudiciously to strip away the defenses of the client and leave nothing in place.

If the therapist allows Billie Jean to continue to hunt for her Prince (Father) Charming, she will be allowing her to engage in a *game contract*. Game contracts are those in which the client asks the therapist's approval to do that which will continue to hurt his or her chances of redeciding and changing the game (Goulding & Goulding, 1979, p. 78).

> CL: I've thought about what I would do, and a divorce seems best, to get me out on my own, but I did promise my father I'd stay with this.
>
> TH: I am not here to affirm your decision about a divorce one way or another. I am here to say that the implicit message is that if you do that, you are a failure to a rather awesome cast of characters and most particularly to yourself. So are you building a new life by deciding to start as a failure?
>
> CL: So you're saying that I shouldn't get a divorce?

TH: I am saying that if you do that, you will continue to perpetuate the rotten feelings you have. I would like you to look at what the best and worst possible outcomes would be if you decided to take such action, not only in terms of being independent, but also in terms of your feelings.

Strategies for Deconfusing the Child

Woollams and Brown (1979) describe this stage as one in which clients learn to accept responsibility for their decisions and discover how they use their present behavior to maintain their scripts. The two major goals for this stage of therapy are to (1) deconfuse the client's child ego state by helping him or her become aware of and express unmet needs and feelings; and (2) help the client "develop an internal sense of safety sufficient to make a redecision."

To get to the here and now, the therapist asks the client to imagine a scene from his or her past, most likely from early childhood, and conduct an interview with a parent or significant other as if it were happening in the *present moment* in therapy (Goulding, 1997). The goal is to uncover early injunctions and counterinjunctions that parents give to their children. It is not uncommon for the client to ignore certain contextual parts of the image to justify the old scripts (Goulding & Goulding, 1979, pp. 204–205).

TH: Billie Jean, I want you to take a little trip down memory lane. I want you to go back in time when you were with your father and felt like he was being wonderful.

CL: That's easy. It was my tenth birthday. We had a party at my house, and I was all dressed up. It was a great party. He took lots of pictures and told everybody how cute and what a precious little peach I was. He nicknamed me Peaches. He got me my first pony for my birthday. It was a pinto and I named him Scooter.

TH: I want you to bring that scene up to present time and have a conversation with your father. Tell him how wonderful he is.

CL: Daddy, you're the greatest! The party was just grand and I love Scooter to pieces. When can I ride him?

TH: Take the role of your father. What does he say?

CL: (*as father*) Right now, if that's what you want, Billie. There's nothing too good for daddy's little girl. You know that, don't you, Peaches?

TH: How does that make you feel as you say that, particularly as that soft, fuzzy little fruit?

CL: My dad got me everything I wanted, and he put me on a pedestal. Looking back on it though, I was a spoiled brat, I guess.

TH: You may have been, but how do you feel as you listen to your father talking to you?

CL: It's odd but I somehow feel cheated, and powerless, like I was dependent on him for everything. Like I am with John.

TH: Change that first *was* to *am*.

CL: I *am*. I don't like that. It's like he's still doing it.

TH: How do you feel right now?

CL: I'm starting to realize that I'm an emotional midget. It would have been better if I would have got a healthy dose of independence when I was a kid. I was pretty capable, but I never got credit for it.

Strategies for Redecision

Woollams and Brown (1979) comment that redecisions involve the client changing some aspect of his or her script. Billie Jean's last sentence, stated in a benign way, is a clue to her script. No place prior to this in therapy has she mentioned having any worth other than being cute. The therapist immediately recognizes this slight perceptual shift and probes it.

TH: How were you capable?

CL: Momma always had a bad case of nerves and I had to look after her because daddy was gone a lot in the cotton business.

TH: Nerves?

CL: (*twisting her hair and wringing her hands*) Well . . . ah . . . actually she was . . . I guess . . . an alcoholic. And there were pills too! God! I'd mix her drinks, get dinner ready, dress my little sister Kate, pack her a lunch, and get her off to school and do the same for me. I never said a word about that. I was really the woman of the house since I was nine. (*in a muted, but hard and angry voice*) And he never said a word about that and he knew it.

TH: So things were not so wonderful as they seemed, for either you or your mom.

CL: It was like . . . I mean . . . this is terrible . . . I was like his wife! (*breaks into sobs*)

TH: So the fact of the matter is you had to be a thinking, grown-up person when you were only a child. On the one hand you were your dad's pretty little girl, but also you were his wife. I wonder if he could ever come to admit that. As a result, he discounted you and kept you little so he'd never have to come to grips with his lousy relationship with his wife.

CL: (*regains some composure*) I guess so. He couldn't have ever really handled that. Everything had to be nice and peaceful at home, but it wasn't. It was like a big secret.

The therapist immediately shifts Billie Jean back to a scene where she is taking care of her mother.

TH: Put your mother right in front of you and tell her how you feel as you do all those things she should be doing.

CL: I hate it.

TH: You can't hate an it. Who or what precisely do you hate. Her? Yourself? Your father? Your life? Tell her specifically what you hate.

CL: I hate you for being so weak and caving in to daddy. I also feel sorry for you and pity you for giving up. You've got no way out. You're a prisoner, and so am I!

TH: So, is your dad still wonderful?

CL: No, he isn't. I shouldn't have been put in the middle. He hamstrung momma and he hamstrung me. But I didn't realize it then.

TH: Now you put yourself in the same position of being hamstrung again—a victim like your mom. You also attempt to hamstring your daughter, only she won't allow you to do it to her. How are you different from your mother who prostituted herself to your father's checkbook just as you prostitute yourself to John's?

CL: My God! (*yelling*) *That's right!* That *is* right! They both should have been horsewhipped.

TH: Yet, it's you who gets horsewhipped now. What do you want to do about redeciding who gets whipped? You can decide what you want.

Transactional analysts have taken a good deal or interest in anger (Clark, 1995; Frazier, 1995; Garcia, 1995; Hyams, 1994; Joines, 1995). Anger, or the repression of it, is often an overlay for the person's true emotional state. Other negative feelings that are not being resolved undergird and support the anger. Different types of anger (Garcia, 1995; Joines, 1995) signal different ego states and developmental stages in operation and are part of the client's disowning of self. As Billie Jean interacts with the therapist in ways that were missing in childhood, she may experience what Garcia (1995) calls responsive anger. Learning how to use responsive anger will allow her to be effective in setting boundaries and making contact when others are intruding on, or alienating themselves from her, such as her wayward and controlling husband and her oppositionally defiant daughter. By understanding and learning to use her anger in productive ways rather than stuffing it in her adapted child, she is much more likely to solve the problems that she is now experiencing.

The client is now asked to play her father as she imagines the role to be. She may play her father as she remembers him, but as traumatic material emerges she must not change him to fit her maladaptive script or game. She may fight with him, understand him better, and change herself, but her father's role is fixed in the script (Goulding, 1997; Goulding & Goulding, 1979, p. 206).

TH: See yourself alone with your father right after the birthday party. Go back to that time and tell your dad what your feelings are based on these injunctions you were given and the decisions you made. First, be your dad.

CL: (*as her father*) I don't want you to grow up because then I'd have to admit that you are the woman I love and not your mother.

CL: (*as herself as a child*) Well, I am not your wife. I am your little girl. Sometimes I have to act like your wife and I really get angry, particularly when you don't acknowledge all that I do and treat me like a little girl because of your own crap.

TH: Don't be the sex you are.

CL: (*as her father*) I treat you like a little girl, but I didn't even name you a girl. I really wanted a boy, but your mother let me down again.

CL: (*as herself*) Nobody let you down except your own chromosomes. I'll take my name, but I'm not a boy, I'm a girl, and you can't deny that. Plus I'm a very capable little girl who has to think like a woman, but always gets discounted.

TH: Don't think. Particularly about our little secret.

CL: (*as her father*) It would kill me if you really knew what was going on here.

CL: (*as herself*) Well, I do know what's going on, I deal with it every day. You're the one who won't 'fess up to it. I am not stupid. You are going to have to deal with your wife.

The therapist now moves to a recent scene to problem solve. In such scenes the client is being herself at her current age and thus may use her adult ego state.

CL: John is telling me I've got to take care of this crazy business with Johnie Ruth and I'm trying to think but I don't know what to do.

TH: Trying . . . don't know. Bring your dad into the scene. What does he say?

CL: He's saying "There, there . . . you need to do what John says."

TH: What in the world does he know about it? He never handled knotty problems like that.

CL: Nothing. He never, ever dealt with those tough family problems.

TH: Are you ready to fire him as your interpersonal supervisor?

CL: Yes. "Dad, you are fired. Further, John, I'm fixing to fire you too if you don't take some responsibility. She's your kid, too."

TH: Victory!

In a typical empty chair exercise in Gestalt therapy the therapist might be very noncommittal as the client moves back and forth between viewpoints. Here, the TA therapist is very active throughout the process because she does not want the client to slip back into parental injunctives that easily lead to racket feelings, game behavior, and old life scripts (Goulding, 1997).

The use of imagery is a clear blending of TA redecision therapy's use of Gestalt approaches to resolve impasses (Gladfelter, 1995; Goulding, 1997). Here, the imagery is particularly useful in bringing insight about how a past ego state applies to a present ego state and motivating the client to action. The key component of this redecision drama is having the client achieve success and not have the play end in tragedy. The therapist knows what baggage from the past the client needs to set aside and writes in some lines that will help Billie Jean expunge the maladaptive tapes transmitted to her by her father (Goulding & Goulding, 1979, pp. 211–212).

Redecision and Change.   It may be necessary early in therapy to focus on the shortcomings of others, such as parents, to clarify early injunctions and decisions. Later in therapy, however, it is important for clients to realize that their parents, are, after all, only human and no longer responsible for their offsprings' mental health. Finally, for a successful redecision, it is crucial that the scene end "victoriously" for the client. To accomplish this, the therapist helps clients to recognize or find something new in the scene or, more important, to discover some hidden power in themselves (Goulding & Goulding, 1979, pp. 207–211).

Woollams and Brown (1979) comment that after the redecision process, it is important that the therapist remain available to clients to provide information and strokes for changing, as well as to confront residual script behaviors (p. 231). Follow-up sessions will constantly review the therapeutic contract by asking what the client has done since the last session, what has worked and what hasn't, and what needs to be done differently now (Goulding, 1997).

Contributions of Transactional Analysis

One of the strengths of TA is its emphasis on the therapeutic contract to guide the direction of the therapeutic process (Harper, 1975). Since therapist and client work together in achieving the goals of the contract, they function more as partners than as doctor and patient, thus lessening the power differential existing in some other therapeutic approaches. Furthermore, a contract enables both client and therapist to better assess whether the outcome of therapy has been successful.

From a dynamic viewpoint, TA has done much to demystify the psychodynamic approach to therapy. Its use of common, everyday language and metaphors to label its techniques and theoretical principles simply makes sense and is understandable to most clients.

TA is one of the most widely used therapies in this book. Its principles, concepts, and techniques are widely used in organizations, business, and education (Gregoire, 1998; Goulding, 1997). The International Transactional Analysis Association has a strong membership and active organizations throughout the world. Interestingly, its membership presently is probably weakest in the United States. A tribute to its international flavor is that its convention is held in a different country every year (Goulding, 1997).

Shortcomings of Transactional Analysis

Transactional analysis has been criticized as being simple, superficial, and palliative. We disagree with this criticism. However, in some instances, TA practitioners overemphasize diagrams and "cutesy" jargon (e.g., "pig parent," "witch mother," "warm fuzzy").

A major limitation of TA applies more to possible misuses of the approach rather than to TA itself. Some of the techniques of TA, such as Schiff's Reparenting approach (1970), are extremely confrontational, can strip clients of needed defenses, and can create tremendous dependency on the therapist. The International Transactional Analysis Association's ethics committee has looked into the ethics of this and other techniques that might put clients at risk (Weiss, 1994). However, the fact remains that in the hands of therapists who do not have a strong ethical foundation, TA's ease of use makes it extremely susceptible to misuse.

Because of its simple vocabulary and game approach, TA became a self-help hit in the 1970s. Many professionals in the human service field were left with a bitter taste as they saw the harm inflicted on gullible and maladjusted individuals by the psychobabble of self-appointed gurus. This acid professional view is aptly characterized by Gholson's (1973) satire "I'm OK, You're So-So" and still prevails to a great extent in professional therapeutic circles.

Although the terminology is simple, there is a lot of it. Understanding "transactionalese" is not easy for anyone not initiated into TA's vast array of metaphors. The reading required may be too time-consuming or difficult for some individuals who have not made a habit of reading.

For those with diminished mental capacity, TA may have little utility because of its reliance on cognition. The welter of crossed transactions, ego states, and energy distribution can become mind-boggling, especially if the therapist is not competent enough to keep from relying on the verbiage of TA to impress the client with his or her expertise.

While Goulding (1997) proposes that TA is a brief therapy and can be done in six hour-long sessions, her definition of brief therapy also includes marathon sessions of all day for up to a month! The research that has been done on TA's efficacy as a brief, time-limited therapy does not support that notion (Novey, 1999). Our belief is that because of all of its trappings of analytic therapy, it takes time to unravel all of the dynamics that are important to TA. It is hard to see how it can truly be brief.

Transactional Analysis with Diverse Populations

Transactional analysis is becoming one of the world's most multicultural therapies, with rapid growth in Western and Eastern Europe, the former Soviet Union, and South America (Cassius, 1992). In an issue of the *Transactional Analysis Journal,* the editor spoke to the international flavor of the approach by noting that four of the six major articles were from England, South Africa, and India. Such cultural diversity provides practitioners in North America a much broader therapeutic perspective as they are increasingly exposed to clients with different cultural backgrounds (Douglass, 1992).

For many transplanted ethnic groups, reliance on and respect for one's family is a primary survival technique. Injunctions such as "Don't shame the family" and "Don't put your interests ahead of the family's" are ironclad rules for preserving the sanctity and authority of the family system—no matter how pathological or how much that system may be out of touch with what is occurring in the contemporary world around it. From cultures such as these, generational transmission of scripts make sense. Transactional analysis may be helpful in ferreting out parental messages that culturally different clients have received and that may conflict with their present living conditions.

However, for those cultures that place a great deal of respect in parental authority, delving into parental injunctions may cause problems. Confronting injunctions and scripts obtained from one's parents without respecting the client's belief system about loyalty to family can generate all kinds of guilt feelings in the client.

As an example, Cassius (1992) reports in his training of Brazilian therapists that they have enthusiastically adapted the fundamental tenets of TA to their own cultural milieu. Because of the preeminent role tight-knit families play in that culture, Brazilian therapists have placed a good deal of emphasis on Schiff's (1970) reparenting techniques. Parental injunctions are not so much seen as being malevolent, but rather reframed as statements delivered under stress.

The use in TA of simple and concrete terminology and metaphors such as *stamps, discounts, rackets,* and *games* makes it ideally suited to work with clientele without the sophistication or desire to put up with more complex analytic or cognitive strategies. The parent, adult, and child ego states can be understood by anyone. TA's emphasis on rackets, games, and transactions strikes a responsive chord in individuals whose existence may be tied to how well they can engage in games and complete ulterior transactions—for example, prison inmates.

Transactional analysis also works well with those who are shackled to a nonnurturing, pathological childhood, such as adult survivors of child sexual and physical abuse and adult children of alcoholics. For survivors of these dysfunctional families, unraveling the ego/genograms of family functioning may be extremely helpful in coming to grips with the past, repressed material.

For clients with physical disabilities, TA may play an extremely important role in helping them come to grips with problems in relationships that have resulted from early scripts they have written for themselves because of their disabilities (Champeau, 1992). From a dynamic point of view, physical disability occurring in early childhood has an adverse impact on ego development because of the severe impact it has on the family system and how that system reacts to the disabling condition. Parents may engage in overindulgence and overprotection or may neglect the child. The outcome may be a physically and emotionally disabled adult who plays passive-aggressive, dependent, and narcissistic games (Livneh & Sherwood, 1991). Unless these individuals become aware of the manipulative games they play, they will have difficulty forming equitable relationships with others.

TA concepts are readily adaptable to children. "Warm pink fuzzy" and "cold grey prickly" are TA terms that would be understood in practically every elementary school in North America. TA's use of simple analogies and figural drawings to make therapy as concrete as possible for children is exemplified in *TA for Kids* (Freed & Freed, 1974a) and *TA for Tots* (Freed & Freed, 1974b).

Finally, when therapists are challenging the life scripts of ethnically distinct and culturally diverse clientele, they need to understand how those scripts differ from their own cultures. For example, the normative life script for a fifth-generation American Caucasian whose ancestors have lived on the family farm for over one hundred years may be radically different from a Vietnamese boat person disenfranchised from her homeland, a Hispanic migrant worker who lives a nomadic existence for most of the year, or a homeless African American from the inner city who was raised in an extended family with few positive male images present. To attempt to apply generic scripts to all of these individuals without understanding the environmental context within which they operate is poor judgment at best, and at worst, unethical.

Summary

Transactional analysis, originated by Eric Berne in the 1950s, is contractual and decisional in its approach to treatment. It considers emotional difficulties to be the result of inappropriate decisions made in response to early, "unhealthy" parental messages and contends that individuals have the capacity and the responsibility to make new, more appropriate decisions.

One characteristic of TA is that its concepts and the vocabulary to describe them are shared by TA practitioners. Such terms include *parent, adult, child, script, game, racket, discount, stamp, stroke, contract, decisions,* and *redecision.* Transactional analysis therapists emphasize a treatment approach based on the assumption "I'm OK—You're OK."

Transactional analysis attacks maladaptive behavior by examining ego states, uncovering parental driver and injunction messages, detecting games and rackets, rewriting scripts, and redistributing energy distribution between ego states. It is an equitable therapy that involves the client as a full and contributing partner through the therapeutic contract.

Although TA has a variety of divergent international camps as far as its theory and practice are concerned, many TA theorists (Cassius, 1980; Clarkson, 1992; Dusay & Dusay, 1989; Goulding, 1997) believe that TA will continue to integrate techniques from other therapeutic approaches into its constantly evolving frameworks. From that standpoint, while it still adheres to its analytic roots, its use of cognitive, behavioral, Gestalt, and rational-emotive and bioenergetic techniques makes it much more eclectic than it was early in its development.

SUGGESTIONS FOR FURTHER READING

Berne, E. (1964). *Games people play: The psychology of human relationships.* New York: Grove Press.

Goulding, M. (Therapist). (1997). Transactional analysis therapy (Videotape Recording No. 0-205-32931-4, T. Lariola, Producer) In J. Carlson and D. Kjos, *Transactional analysis with Mary Goulding: Psychotherapy with the experts.* Boston: Allyn & Bacon.

Harris, T. A. (1969). *I'm OK—You're OK.* New York: Harper & Row.

James, M., & Jongeward, D. (1971). *Born to win: Transactional analysis with Gestalt experiments.* Reading, MA: Addison-Wesley.

REFERENCES

Allen, J. R., & Allen, B. A. (2000). Every revolution should have dancing: Biology, community organization, constructionism and joy. *Transactional Analysis Journal, 30*(3), 188–191.

Berne, E. (1964). *Games people play: The psychology of human relationships.* New York: Grove Press.

Berne, E. (1966). *Principles of group treatment.* New York: Oxford University Press.

Berne, E. (1972). *What do you say after you say hello?* New York: Grove Press.

Cassius, J. (1980). Bodyscript release: How to use bioenergetics and transactional analysis. In J. Cassius (Ed.), *Horizons in bioenergetics: New dimensions in mind/body psychotherapy* (pp. 212–224). Memphis: Promethean.

Cassius, J. (1992). *The future of TA and the multicultural issues involved in its use* (Cassette Recording No. 7581-92-1). Memphis, TN: Memphis State University, Department of Counseling and Personnel Services.

Champeau, T. (1992). Transactional analysis and rehabilitation: An integrative approach to disability. *Transactional Analysis Journal, 22*(4), 234–242.

Clark, F. C. (1995). Anger and its disavowal in shame-based people. *Transactional Analysis Journal, 25*(2), 129–132.

Clarkson, P. (1992). *Transactional analysis psychotherapy: An integrated approach.* London: Routledge.

Douglass, J. (1992). Letter from the editor. *Transactional Analysis Journal, 22,* 64–65.

Dusay, J. M. (1972). Egograms and the constancy hypothesis. *Transactional Analysis Journal, 2,* 37–40.

Dusay, J. M. (1976). Egograms and the "constancy hypothesis." in G. M. Goldhaber & M. B. Goldhaber (Eds.), *Transactional analysis: Principles and applications* (pp. 62–67). Boston: Allyn & Bacon.

Dusay, J. M. (1977). The evolution of transactional analysis. In G. Barnes (Ed.), *Transactional analysis after Eric Berne* (pp. 32–52). New York: Harper's College Press.

Dusay, J. M., & Dusay, K. M. (1979). Transactional analysis. In R. J. Corsini (Ed.), *Current psychotherapies* (2nd ed., pp. 374–427). Itasca, IL: F. E. Peacock.

Dusay, J. M., & Dusay, K. M. (1989).Transactional analysis. In R. J. Corsini & D. Wedding (Eds.), *Current psychotherapies* (4th ed., pp. 405–453). Itasca, IL: F. E. Peacock.

Frazier, T. (1995). Anger: Don't express it and don't repress it. *Transactional Analysis Journal, 25*(2), 123–128.

Freed, A., & Freed, M. (1974a). *TA for kids.* Sacramento, CA: Freed.

Freed, A., & Freed, M. (1974b). *TA for tots.* Sacramento, CA: Freed.

Garcia, F. N. (1995). The many faces of anger. *Transactional Analysis Journal, 25*(2), 119–122.

Gholson, B. G. (1973). I'm OK, you're so-so. *Playboy,* December, p. 213.

Gladfelter, J. (1995). Imagery in redecision therapy. *Transactional Analysis Journal, 25*(4), 319–320.

Goldhaber, G. M., and Goldhaber, M. B. (1976). *Transactional analysis: Principles and applications.* Boston: Allyn & Bacon.

Goulding, M. (Therapist). (1997). Transactional analysis therapy. (Videotape Recording No. 0-205-32931-4, T. Lariola, Producer). In J. Carlson and D. Kjos, *Transactional analysis with Mary Goulding: Psychotherapy with the experts.* Boston: Allyn & Bacon.

Goulding, R. (1989). Teaching transactional analysis and redecision therapy. *Journal of Independent Social Work, 3*(4), 71–86.

Goulding, R., & Goulding, M. (1976). Injunctions, decisions and redecisions. *Transactional Analysis Journal, 6,* 41–47.

Goulding, R., & Goulding, M. (1978). *The power is in the patient: A TA/Gestalt approach to psychotherapy.* San Francisco: TA Press.

Goulding, R., & Goulding, M. (1979). *Changing lives through redecision therapy.* New York: Brunner/Mazel.

Gregoire, J. (1998). Criteria for defining the boundaries of transactional analysis fields of application. *Transactional Analysis Journal, 28*(4), 311–320.

Harper, R. (1975). *The new psychotherapies.* Englewood Cliffs, NJ: Prentice-Hall.

Harris, A. B., & Harris, T. A. (1985). *Staying OK.* New York: Harper & Row.

Harris, T. A. (1969). *I'm OK—you're OK.* New York: Harper & Row.

Hyams, H. (1994). Shame: The enemy within. *Transactional Analysis Journal, 24*(4), 255–264.

Jacobs, A. (2000). Psychic organs, ego states, and visual metaphors: Speculation on Berne's integration of ego states. *Transactional Analysis Journal, 30*(1), 10–22.

James, M., & Jongeward, D. (1971). *Born to win: Transactional analysis with Gestalt experiments.* Reading, MA: Addison-Wesley.

Joines, V. S. (1995). A developmental approach to anger. *Transactional Analysis Journal, 25*(2), 112–118.

Kahler, T., & Capers, H. (1974). The miniscript. *Transactional Analysis Journal, 4,* 26–42.

Karpman, S. B. (1968). Fairy tales and script drama analysis. *Transactional Analysis Bulletin, 7,* 39–43.

Klein, M. (1992). The enemies of love. *Transactional Analysis Journal, 22,* 76–81.

Laing, R. D. (1971). *The politics of the family and other essays.* New York: Pantheon.

Livneh, H., & Sherwood, A. (1991). Application of personality theories and counseling strategies to clients with physical disabilities. *Journal of Counseling and Development, 69,* 525–538.

McClendon, R., & Kadis, L. B. (1995). Redecision therapy: On the leading edge. *Transactional Analysis Journal, 25*(4), 339–342.

Mellor, K., & Schiff, E. (1975). Discounting. *Transactional Analysis Journal, 5,* 295–302.

Mundy, W. L. (1994). "You know": Or do you? *Transactional Analysis Journal, 24*(3), 216–219.

Novellino, M., & Moiso, C. (1990). The psychodynamic approach to transactional analysis. *Transactional Analysis Journal, 20*(3), 187–192.

Novey, T. B. (1999). The effectiveness of transactional analysis. *Transactional Analysis Journal, 29*(1), 18–30.

Schiff, J. L., with Day, B. (1970). *All my children.* New York: Evans.

Schlegel, L. (1998). What is transactional analysis? *Transactional Analysis Journal, 28*(4), 269–287.

Steiner, C. M. (1967). A script checklist. *Transactional Analysis Bulletin, 6,* 38–39.

Steiner, C. M. (1968). Transactional analysis as a treatment philosophy. *Transactional Analysis Bulletin, 7,* 61–63.

Steiner, C. M. (1971). The stroke economy. *Transactional Analysis Journal, 1,* 9–28.

Steiner, C. M. (1974). *Scripts people live: Transactional analysis of life scripts.* New York: Grove Press.

Summers, G., & Tudor, K. (2000). Cocreative transactional analysis. *Transactional Analysis Journal 30*(1), 23–40.

Summerton, O. (2000). The development of game analysis. *Transactional Analysis Journal, 30,* (3), 207–218.

Tilney, T. (1998). *Definitions and concepts in transactional analysis.* London: Whurr.

Weiss, L. (1994). The ethics of parenting and reparenting in psychotherapy. *Transactional Analysis Journal, 24*(1), 57–59.

Woollams, S. (1978). The internal stroke economy. *Transactional Analysis Journal, 8,* 194–197.

Woollams, S., & Brown, M. (1979). *TA: The total handbook of transactional analysis.* Englewood Cliffs, NJ: Prentice-Hall.

7 Behavioral Counseling, Therapy, and Modification

Fundamental Tenets

History

The history and practice of the behavioral approach can be divided into three components. The first, *classical* or *respondent conditioning,* is based on the work of Pavlov (1960) and Hull (1943). In practice, respondent conditioning is called *behavior therapy* (Chambless & Goldstein, 1979, p. 230) and traces its human application to Watson and Rayner's (1920) and Jones's (1924) work in sensitizing and desensitizing children to small furry animals. The first large-scale clinical application of these principles occurred in the late 1950s, when Wolpe (1954, 1958, 1961) introduced systematic desensitization by reciprocal inhibition.

The second component is *operant conditioning.* It is based on the work of B. F. Skinner (1953) and in practice is called *behavior modification* (Chambless & Goldstein, 1979, p. 230). Skinner practiced behavior modification with individuals (1953) and groups (1948, 1958). While different in theory, in practice behavior therapy and behavior modification are often used in tandem and are difficult, if not impossible, to distinguish (Kaplan, 1986).

Because behaviorists find their roots in learning theory, two works are particularly important to understanding how behaviorism got out of the laboratories and into therapy. The first is *Personality and Psychotherapy,* by Dollard and Miller (1950). This book translated psychoanalytic theory and practice into learning theory terms and laid the foundation for behaviorists to enter the field of therapy. The second work is *Case Studies in Behavior Modification* by Ullmann and Krasner (1965). This book brought a variety of behavioral techniques, previously known only to the back wards of mental hospitals and a few behavioral therapists, to the forefront of psychology. Ullmann and Krasner's brilliant introduction to the book clearly stated the theory, use, and efficacy of a psychological model as opposed to the customary medical or disease model of therapy.

The third and latest component is *cognitive behavior therapy.* This therapy represents the convergence of two different streams of therapeutic thought. For all its startling appearance and promise as it came onto the therapeutic stage in the 1960s, the pure behavioral approach to treatment did not become the panacea its advocates originally thought it would be. Although rats could be conditioned to run the same way every time in a Skinner box, it soon became apparent that strict application of respondent or operant procedures would not guarantee the same results in the treatment of humans, even though the laws of conditioning would seem to dictate otherwise. Even early operant procedures, such as Wolpe's

(1958) desensitization techniques, could not be called a pure behavioral approach because of the use of the client's thinking processes to modify noxious stimuli. As behaviorists struggled to come to grips with this perplexing issue, the question of cognition as a mediating variable continued to surface.

Borrowing equally from the respondent and operant precepts of Pavlovian and Skinnerian behavioral psychology and from the cognitive precepts of Ellis's (1962) rational-emotive behavior therapy (REBT), innovative theorists such as Ellis and Grieger (1977), Lazarus (1977), Beck (1976), Kazdin (1974, 1976), and Meichenbaum (1977) welded behavioral and REBT approaches into cognitive behavior therapy in the late 1970s. In the 1980s, cognitive behaviorism moved beyond the respondent and operant approaches of behaviorism and the philosophical systems of REBT and became distinctly broader than either. Therefore, cognitive behaviorism as a specific therapeutic modality is dealt with separately, in Chapter 10.

To date, behavioral approaches view the client as both the producer and the product of the environment (Kazdin, 1978), capable of imagining which behaviors are desirable (Meichenbaum, 1977) and then working to make those images a behavioral reality (Watson & Tharp, 1981, 1989). Thus runs the brief but phenomenal history of the behavioral system of counseling and psychotherapy. If one remembers that 90 percent of the work in the field has been accomplished in three decades, its development is impressive indeed.

Since the heyday of Skinner and other radical behaviorists, the two approaches—traditional behavior therapy and cognitive behavior therapy—have tended to overlap and develop similar clinical approaches, but not necessarily similar philosophies. Both systems, under certain conditions, use strategies such as systematic desensitization, modeling, flooding, contracting, assertion, imagery, role playing, and reframing. Whereas behavior therapy, under the influence of Skinnerian principles, held that behavior was an exclusive function of its consequences, neobehavioral thinking came closer to the social cognitive viewpoint that private (internal psychological) events such as imagery and systematic desensitization constituted integral components of behavior therapy (Wilson, 1995, pp. 198–214). In terms of the comparative effectiveness of traditional behavior therapy and cognitive behavior therapy—in counseling with obsessive-compulsive clients in groups—McLean and associates (2001) found, for example, that there was little difference in outcome measures between the two approaches. Both treatments were shown to be superior to the control condition in symptom reduction, with traditional behavior therapy being marginally more effective than cognitive behavior therapy.

Overview of the Behavioral Approach

The concepts and techniques presented in this chapter demonstrate the two initial thrusts of the behavioral approach: respondent and operant. A variety of commonly used strategies are discussed, but it is beyond the purview of any one chapter or book to treat the world of behavioral counseling exhaustively. The suggestions for further reading at the end of the chapter provide a starting point for further exploration of the many facets of behavioral theory and practice.

The case study touches on the two respondent and operant processes of the behavioral approach. The chapter portrays the counselor in a personal and collaborative mode, helping the client generate corrective learning experiences. This view of the behavioral counselor refutes many of the erroneous descriptions of the approach that present it as too mechanistic and impersonal.

Theory of Personality

No single theory of personality has been exclusively identified with behaviorism. Behaviorists have given more attention to learning theory than to the development of a behavioral model of human personality. Behaviorists assume that individuals develop those consistencies known as personality through maturation and the laws of learning (Chambless & Goldstein, 1979, p. 237). Therefore, for behaviorists, what most nearly fits a personality theory is actually learning theory.

Major theorists who could be classified as behavioristic personality theorists include Bandura (1991, 1995), Dollard and Miller (1950), Eysenck (1960), Krumboltz (1966), Lundin (1961, 1972, 1977), Mowrer (1950, 1973), Skinner (1948, 1953, 1971, 1974), and Wolpe (1982, 1991). Behavioral theorists have explained human personality in a variety of ways. However, there are a few general tenets of behavioral theory and personality:

1. The *behavior* of organisms, not *mental phenomena,* determines learning, attitudes, habits, and other aspects of personal development.
2. Personality development is deterministic. That is, the environment and experiences determine how the personality develops.
3. Individual differences are derived from different experiences.
4. Dualisms such as mind–body, body–spirit, and body–soul have no scientific validity in the development, prediction, and control of human behavior.
5. Although personality development has certain genetic limitations, which are fixed, the effects of environmental and internally generated stimuli play the dominant role.

Lundin (1977) has elaborated on twelve basic Skinnerian principles that form the basis for an *operant reinforcement* view of personality development. Such a view holds, essentially, that given a specific genetic endowment limit, the personality of the organism is determined by antecedent conditions. That is, operant reinforcements shape the personality. For Skinner (1953) the concept of self represents a functionally integrated system of responses, and one's knowledge of self is a description of one's own behavior. What other theorists see as traits, Skinner sees as differences in the processes or independent variables to which persons are exposed. This concept is important because if traits are not set in stone, but are ongoing behavioral processes, then there is the possibility for treatment intervention and change (Chambless & Goldstein, 1979, p. 239). Lundin (1977) has specified eight principles of operant reinforcement that pertain to personality *development* (1–8) and four principles that pertain to personality *maintenance* (9–12).

1. In the development of a theory of personality, prediction and control of behavior are paramount. There is no such thing as free will. Environmental variables determine responses. Once the variables are known, the behavior can be predicted and controlled (p. 183).

2. All behavior can be divided into operant and respondent classes. That is, the individual responds to, or operates on, the environment. Since all behavior falls under the control of environmental stimuli, there is no such thing as voluntary behavior (p. 184).

3. One's personality is acquired through the use of reinforcers. Besides the primary positive reinforcers—food, water, and air—certain conditioned positive reinforcers, such as money and social approval, shape personality. Negative reinforcers that strengthen a behavior when a stimulus is removed also shape personality. Turning the air conditioning up to cool off and stopping at a traffic light are examples of negative primary and conditioned reinforcers that help people avoid aversive stimuli (pp. 184–185).

4. Behavior may be changed by weakening or withholding reinforcement—a process called *extinction.* An example of changing behavior by extinction is ignoring the tantruming, attention-seeking behavior of a small child. In practice such procedures may take a long time if the behavior has had a long history of reinforcement or if attempts to extinguish the behavior have been interspersed with intermittent reinforcement (p. 185).

5. Personality develops by a process of discrimination from a generalization of responding. When a response has been conditioned to a particular stimulus, other stimuli similar to the conditioned stimulus can produce the conditioned response. Discrimination occurs as differentiations are made between stimuli that closely resemble one another. Selective reinforcement, in which the presence of certain stimuli is reinforced and not others, develops discrimination (p. 186).

6. Personality is shaped or differentiated by the variability of responding. Differentiation also involves selective reinforcement. Initial efforts to accomplish a task or learn a skill usually have large variable-ratio schedules of reinforcement. As the individual differentiates which responses are reinforced and which are not, skill and accomplishment are gained. From learning how to talk to performing brain surgery, differentiation and shaping of responses to obtain less variability is the end goal. However, even in tasks well learned there is some variability, otherwise all individuals would be B. F. Skinners, Arnold Palmers, or Katharine Hepburns (p. 187).

7. Modeling develops many aspects of personality. Behavior is acquired by watching significant others and is reinforced the more the behavior approximates that of the significant others. The use of role playing to teach assertiveness is modeling (p. 187).

8. Besides positive reinforcement, personality is controlled by aversive stimuli that can result in escape, avoidance, punishment, or anxiety (p. 188). (This assertion is dealt with at length in the section on maladjustment.)

9. Personality is maintained by a series of conditioned reinforcers. Conditioned reinforcers start out as neutral stimuli, but by pairing with primary reinforcers they can later strengthen behavior in their own right. Some conditioned reinforcers are specific to individuals; others are general to all people. Approval and affection are examples of intrinsic conditioned reinforcers, and tokens in the form of money are extrinsic conditioned reinforcers. If conditioned reinforcers are not paired with primary reinforcers from time to time they lose their power. If money, even gold, could not be exchanged for other primary or conditioned reinforcers, it would soon lose its potency as a reinforcer (p. 190).

10. Behavior can be maintained by reinforcers delivered regularly or intermittently. Regular or continuous reinforcement means every response is followed by reinforcement. Taken to the extreme, continuous reinforcement causes satiation and loses its power. Intermittent reinforcement means behavior is reinforced on schedules. Intermittent reinforcement schedules develop strong behavior. There are four types of schedules:

   a. *Fixed-interval reinforcement* occurs at regular intervals, such as receiving a weekly paycheck.
   b. *Variable-interval reinforcement* occurs on a time schedule that varies but averages out to a specified time. The automatic change makers at convenience stores are set up on this schedule to foil robbery attempts.
   c. *Fixed-ratio reinforcements* are delivered at a specified rate that depends on how many responses are made. Being paid by the number of "widgets" turned out on an assembly line exemplifies this schedule.
   d. *Variable-ratio reinforcements* are obtained irregularly but average out to a given figure. Duck hunting in miserable weather and shoving quarters into slot machines are outstanding examples of how powerful this schedule can be (pp. 190–191).

11. Depriving or satiating an individual with some kind of reinforcement is a *motivator.* Deprivation of primary reinforcers affects all people in about the same way. People who are deprived of food become hungry. However, conditioned reinforcers may substantially alter what is considered deprivation. The absence of chocolate cake, potato chips, and ice cream to a person on a diet may constitute deprivation of the severest kind. The other side of the coin is satiation. Reinforcement occurs so often and in such quantity that a response no longer occurs. A typical example is the between-meals snacker who, to the chagrin of the cook, is not hungry when dinner is served (pp. 191–92).

12. Behavior can be maintained or altered by motivation-like operations, in which something other than deprivation or satiation affects the behavior of the individual. The most common, and addictive, examples of motivation-like operations are alcohol and cocaine (p. 192).

Throughout these twelve basic tenets is the overarching concept of overt observable responses and the identifiable stimuli that go with them. Nowhere among respondent or operant behaviorists will attempts at dynamic explanations of personality be found. For these behaviorists, behavior is the explanation of personality.

Nature of Maladjustment

Although respondent and operant theories of maladjustment will be distinguished for purposes of clarity, they are intermingled in terms of behavioral outcomes (Ullmann & Krasner, 1965, p. 22). Maladaptive behaviors, like adaptive behaviors, are learned. This being the case, they can also be unlearned (Chambless & Goldstein, 1979, p. 230). The implications of these statements are that there are few if any disease pathologies present in maladjusted individuals (Ullmann & Krasner, 1965, p. 20).

Maladjustment is specific to the culture, time, social class, and situation. What may be maladjustive in one culture may be adjustive in another. The distinction is that the individual is able to obtain reinforcement from the significant others that control reinforcement (Ullmann & Krasner, 1965, p. 20).

The times we live in have a great deal to do with what is construed to be maladjusted behavior, and the very nature of maladjustment may change from one generation to the next. St. Vitus's dance—the frenzied gyrations of mobs of people that occurred in Europe in the Middle Ages—might be viewed in an entirely different manner if it occurred on the main street of a midwestern town in the United States today.

Each social class has its own definition and particular ways of acting out maladjustive behavior. Myers and Roberts (1959) found considerable difference in symptoms between neurotics and psychotics from different social classes. Middle-class individuals were inhibited, self-deprecating, and guilt-ridden, whereas lower-class individuals were aggressive, rebellious, violent, self-indulgent, and lawbreaking.

Combat is an excellent example of what may be situation-adjustive or maladjustive behavior. To subject oneself voluntarily to being killed or maimed would seem to be the height of insanity. Yet, to escape such circumstances in combat may have consequences that are considered extremely maladaptive. Even if a soldier manifests combat-related psychosomatic symptoms, this may not be an acceptable maladjustment in terms of the safety needs of his or her combat unit. As a result, the sick soldier may suffer some very aversive consequences from his or her peer group. The major implication of these examples is that there is no discontinuity between *healthy* and *sick* behavior except in terms of what a particular society in a particular time and place perceives the malady to be.

How, then, do people become sick? Because behaviorists believe that people learn by either respondent or operant means, it follows that maladaptive behavior is learned to either increase positive reinforcement or decrease an aversive stimulus (Chambless & Goldstein, 1979, p. 239). The client in psychotherapy is an excellent example of the person who obtains positive reinforcement for maladaptive behavior. He or she receives treatment (attention) and causes considerable consternation (attention) among significant others. Conversely, the aversive stimuli the client encounters may play an even greater part in the development of maladjustment. By escaping or avoiding a situation, one strengthens behavior by removing the aversive stimuli. If enough aversive stimuli are presented early in the client's conditioning history, then the client's continued avoidance of those stimuli will lead to withdrawal into a fantasy world where the stimuli are not present (Lundin, 1977, p. 188).

If an individual cannot escape or avoid aversive stimuli, punishment occurs. For Skinner (1953), most emotional problems are reactions to overcontrolling, punitive environments. Fear is a conditioned outcome to punishment and elicits such environmentally conditioned emotions as guilt, depression, and anger.

Guilt and depression lead to a state of anxiety. Anxiety may be defined behaviorally as an autonomic response to noxious stimuli and is maladaptive in circumstances where objectively there is no threat (Wolpe, 1954). In respondent terms, anxiety reactions may change physiological reactions such as heart rate, blood pressure, and perspiration; from an operant standpoint they may elicit nervousness, feelings of being upset, and hyperactivity (Lundin, 1977, p. 189). Because learning leads to the ability to anticipate an event, when a real or imaginary aversive stimulus is perceived, anxiety preceding the punishing event may be worse than the punishment itself. Excessive conditioning in this manner can lead to neurotic anxiety attacks in which the individual is paralyzed with fear or panic. On the opposite end of the behavioral continuum, interpersonal relationships may be impeded by displaced aggression against persons or objects not originally responsible for the punishment (Azrin, 1966).

In summary, both behavior therapy and behavior modification treat maladjustive behavior directly. There are no underlying causes. Second, changing maladjustive behavior is the major focus; insight is not. As Eysenck (1959) puts it, "there is no neurosis underlying the symptom, but merely the symptom itself. Get rid of the symptom and you have eliminated the neurosis." Contemporary cognitive behaviorists, though, have come to see this premise as too simplistic. Cognitive behaviorists assume that the symptom is not the entire problem but part of the larger problem of thoughts, feelings, actions, and interactions with other people and the environment (see Chapter 10). Yet Eysenck and Martin (1987) have made a strong case to disprove the notion that the underlying tenets of conditioning and cognition are contradictory. They present considerable experimental evidence that even though conditioning and cognitive theories have oppositional aspects, a formidable body of theory undergirds both.

The Counseling Process

In behavioral counseling, as in any system of counseling or psychotherapy, it is essential that the counselor demonstrate accurate listening, concern, caring, acceptance, and understanding of the client as a unique person. A positive relationship between client and counselor is necessary to ensure that the counselor thoroughly understands the client's problem before intervention strategies are begun and to provide the client with enough motivation to succeed in the difficult and often complex process of acquiring adaptive behaviors. Most modern behavioral counselors approach the helping process from a much broader perspective than was the case a few years ago. Rather than viewing the counselor as the expert who scientifically develops and imposes behavior-modifying processes on the client, the modern approach strives to involve the client in the analysis, planning, process, and evaluation of his or her behavior-management program. Modern behavioral counselors seek to help the client extinguish a wide range of maladaptive behaviors and learn adaptive behaviors needed to establish and maintain targeted goals and consequences. The counselor collaborates with the client. The counselor is expected to have training and experience in human behavior modification and also to serve as consultant, teacher, adviser, reinforcer, and facilitator. The counselor even instructs and supervises noncounseling personnel (paraprofessionals, technicians, and volunteers) who function as counselor extensions and support persons. The qualities of the counselor are understanding, friendliness, caring, and being personal in the relationship. Such a description is a far cry from the earlier stereotype of the behavioral counselor as an indifferent, mechanical, manipulative technician.

In counseling or psychotherapy, the initial concern is to help the client analyze behavior, define problems, and select goals. This process is facilitated if the counselor and the client develop effective communication, trust, and cooperation. These relationship factors are also valuable throughout the client–counselor involvement. The counselor is more than a caring helper, however. He or she is skilled in applying scientific knowledge and experimental techniques in helping clients define and solve a wide range of human problems, which the client alone would not be able to do. Behavioral counseling and therapy have evolved from a mechanistic and reductionist system that viewed clients as responding to their genetic histories and to environmental influences that controlled them, toward viewing clients as agents who operate on and influence their environments. That evolution has included the active involvement of clients in every phase of counseling, from the definition of their problems through the evaluation and maintenance of their adaptive behavioral patterns (Watson & Tharp, 1989; Williams & Long, 1983; Wilson, 1995).

Strategies for Helping Clients

Most of the strategies presented in this section are aimed at entry-level professional human services helpers. Some should be useful to professionals in developmental or preventive counseling with individuals. In the main, the strategies presented emphasize the collaborative effort of counselor and client. Since clients are both regulated by and regulators of their environments, the counselor's role as facilitator or mentor of their self-management is emphasized.

We have included eleven representative strategies that are associated with *overt* behavioral change: behavioral contracting; role playing; assertion training; aversion therapy; flooding and implosion therapy; satiation; token economies; self-management, self-monitoring, and self-reinforcement; systematic desensitization; behavioral modeling; and behavior rehearsal. Thumbnail sketches of each are provided. Readers who desire more detail are invited to begin with the suggested readings at the end of the chapter.

Behavioral Contracting

Also called *self-contracting* or simply *contracting,* this is a self-management strategy wherein the client enters into an agreement with one or more persons to perform or attain specific predetermined responses or goals. The contract usually contains specified consequences related to the time and level of performance or nonperformance (Cormier & Cormier, 1991, pp. 320–321). Extensive and varied use of contracting has been made in group and individual counseling to address such issues as weight management, drug and alcohol treatment, smoking cessation (Klesges, Haddock, Lando, & Talcott, 1999), and monitoring physical fitness. The contract may serve as the primary behavior-change strategy or it may simply be an evaluative tool. Contingency contractual consequences may vary from requiring the client to deposit a considerable sum of money or an object of value to merely giving his or her word by affixing a signature to the agreement. Behavioral contracts allow for virtually unlimited flexibility and creativity. Rarely are any two alike. If a contract is to be of optimum help to the client, it should contain several basic features identified by Cormier and Cormier (1979, p. 507; 1991, pp. 320–321).

1. The contractual terms should be clear to every person involved. The behavioral goals and performance levels should be specific.
2. Rewards and sanctions should be specific and appropriate to the contracted behavior.

3. The contract should be written in a positive mode and may include a bonus clause.
4. Another person or persons should be included as positive supports. Their supportive role should be specified.
5. Commitments, through signatures at appropriate places, should be obtained from all persons involved.
6. Provision should be made for a progress chart, log, or other visible means of monitoring progress toward goal attainment, rewards, and sanctions, and if possible there should be verification by one other person.
7. An informed consent statement should contain a descriptive paragraph and a place for the date and both client and counselor signatures.

The applied behavioral principles found in contracting provide effective strategies for counseling clients in all age and social groups. Contracting has proved highly effective with many types of clients, particularly with children in school settings. The guidelines in Figures 7.1, 7.2, and 7.3 for using contracting with clients should prove useful to counselors interested in employing behavioral contracting to help clients attain their goals. These guidelines are based on behavioral principles and suggestions found in Alberto and Troutman (1982, pp. 188–200), Homme (1970, pp. 18–20), and Krumboltz and Krumboltz (1972).

The effectiveness of contracting depends on the particular use, user, and situation. Many clients like having something formalized, on paper, specific, and positive. A written contract appears to have some reinforcement value in itself. The contract should be a tangible symbol, for the client, of the counseling relationship and of the targeted behavioral goals. The case of Peggy Smith in this chapter contains an example of a written behavioral contract for an adult.

Role Playing

Role playing with clients has been used by behavioral counselors in assertiveness training, covert modeling, career counseling, rehearsal, and aversion therapy (Krumboltz & Thoresen, 1969, 1976). Role play is an excellent technique for expanding client awareness and showing the client alternative behaviors. For example, in the counseling session an incarcerated client can role play and develop effective social behaviors before having to use them alone on the streets. Another client may discover, in role play, that he or she cannot confront a strong-willed parent and must therefore learn assertion skills prior to attempting a confrontation in real life. The uses of role play are limited only by the counselor's resourcefulness and skill in using the technique and by the client's need for viewing, hearing, and experiencing a particular role in the risk-free environment of the counseling session.

Assertion Training

The fundamental goals of assertion training are (1) to empower clients actively to initiate and carry out desired choices and behaviors that do not harm other people physically or emotionally, and (2) to teach clients alternatives to passive, helpless, dependent, and stifled ways of dealing with life situations.

FIGURE 7.1 Contracting Guide

1. Select one or two behaviors that you want to work on first.
2. Describe those behaviors so that they can be observed and counted.
3. Identify rewards that will help provide motivation to do well. Utilize a reinforcing-event menu. Build in specific and varied contract payoffs:
   a. Rewards should be immediate.
   b. Initially, contract should reward *successive approximations*—small approximations that progress toward the target behavior.
   c. Payoffs should be frequent and in small amounts.
   d. The contract should call for and reinforce attainment rather than obedience.
   e. Payoffs should be made *after* attainment occurs.
   f. To reinforce a client with a previously ineffective reward, use the *substitution principle:* present the reward just before (or as close as possible to) the time the more effective reward is given.
   g. To stop a client from behaving in a particular way, build in the *incompatible-alternative principle:* reward an alternative action that is inconsistent with (or cannot be performed at the same time as) the desired act.
   h. To condition a client to remember to act at a specific time, use the *cueing principle:* arrange for the client to receive a cue for the correct performance immediately prior to the expected behavior rather than after the client has performed the act incorrectly.
   i. To help the client overcome fear, use the *fear-reduction principle:* gradually increase the client's exposure to the feared situation while the client is otherwise comfortable, secure, or rewarded.
4. Locate people who can help you keep track of the behaviors being performed and who can perhaps give out the rewards.
5. Write the contract so everyone can understand it and the method is used systematically.
6. Collect the data.
7. Troubleshoot the system if the data do not show an improvement.
8. Rewrite the contract if the goal is not achieved.
9. Continue to monitor, troubleshoot, and rewrite until there is improvement in the behaviors that were troublesome.
10. Select another behavior to work on.

FIGURE 7.2 Negotiating a Contract and Putting It on Paper

A contract is *negotiated.* Imposing a contract on a student or client will not work. Imposed agreements are not contracts because one party has not had the freedom to determine the terms and may have been forced to sign or accept it. The exact form of the contract is not very important if you include these items:

1. Date the agreement begins, ends, or is renegotiated
2. Behavior targeted for change (must be clear, honest, positive)
3. Amount and kind of rewards or reinforcers to be used
4. Schedule of delivery of reinforcers
5. Signatures of all parties involved
6. Schedule for review of progress (optional, but strongly suggested)
7. Bonus clause for sustained or exceptional performance
8. Statement of the penalties that will be imposed if the specific behavior is not performed

FIGURE 7.3   Behavioral Contract Troubleshooting Guide

1. Was the target behavior clearly specified?
2. Did the contract provide for immediate reinforcement?
3. Did it ask for small approximations to the desired behavior?
4. Was reinforcement frequent and in small amounts?
5. Did the contract call for and reward accomplishment rather than obedience?
6. Was the performance rewarded after its occurrence?
7. Was the contract fair?
8. Was the contract honest?
9. Were the terms of the contract realistic?
10. Was the contract positive?
11. Was the contract, as a method, being used systematically?
12. Was the contract mutually negotiated?
13. Was the penalty clause too punitive?
14. Was the bonus clause motivational, reasonable, and attainable?

Many counselors find their clients need to develop assertion skills to strengthen their overall coping and problem-solving behaviors (Bellack & Hersen, 1977). Clients may lose self-esteem by allowing others to take advantage of them, may be unable to confront parents, employers, spouses, or other important persons in appropriate ways, or may elicit unwanted responses from others by using aggression instead of assertion. Assertion training is usually accomplished by role playing and modeling of passive, aggressive, and assertive situations the client faces regularly. Through problem exploration and definition, assertion goal development, repeated role play, role reversal, and progressive and successive approximation of the desired behaviors, the client learns appropriate (assertive) ways of expression. In the safety of the client–counselor encounter, the client not only forms new behaviors but also has an opportunity to participate, with the counselor, in analysis and critique of successive approximations of the behaviors the client seeks to develop. Counselors who employ both assertion training and the use of audiovisual feedback are able to provide their clients with immediate documented feedback on client progress. Clients can then try out the techniques in the real world and return for further training (Alberti & Emmons, 1978).

Aversion Therapy

Aversion therapy is a controversial technique that is infrequently used by counselors and is not recommended for most school situations with children. It is sometimes used in clinics by highly skilled therapists to help clients who want to be helped and whose maladaptive behaviors are not amenable to intervention through other strategies. Aversion therapy employs procedures such as electric shock, emetics, stimulus satiation, unpleasant mental or visual imagery, or unpleasant sounds or verbal descriptions to inhibit unwanted behaviors. Competent behavior therapists have treated difficult problems such as drug and alcohol addiction, sexual deviation, and smoking by combining aversive techniques with other behavioral procedures (Franks & Wilson, 1973, p. 193). The goal of this therapy is to get the client to "associate an undesirable behavior pattern with unpleasant stimulation or to make the unpleasant stimulation a consequence of the undesirable behavior" (Franks, 1969, p. 280).

An example of the use of aversion therapy with an alcoholic client is to encourage the client to see, smell, and drink alcoholic beverages containing an emetic drug—one that causes illness, retching, and vomiting. The treatment is continued until the client associates the smell, sight, and taste of alcoholic beverages with extreme discomfort. At the same time, the client is provided with desirable, pleasant, and comforting reinforcements for nondrinking cravings and behaviors. The counselor who seeks to use aversion therapy should be thoroughly trained and experienced in the technical, therapeutic, philosophic, and ethical issues involved in using the technique with clients (Morrison & Bellack, 1987; Poling, 1986).

Flooding and Implosive Therapy

Flooding (Stampfl & Levis, 1967) is a technique in which fear-evoking stimuli are presented continuously, usually during long therapy sessions. It may use *in vivo* or covert imagery formats. The rationale is that if the client is literally flooded with anxiety-provoking cues for several periods of from one to two hours, the client will discover that there is no basis for fear. An example of *in vivo* flooding was a case in which the client exhibited an irrational fear of getting into and riding elevators. The counselor accompanied the client during several prolonged elevator riding sessions. During the rides the counselor continuously presented the most anxiety-provoking stimuli that the client had been able to identify as associated with fear of elevators. As the client's anxieties associated with elevators steadily diminished, the client was able to risk trial runs alone and, finally, to ride on elevators as part of the daily routine.

Another example of flooding was the use of covert imagery with a client who feared entering a room full of people. The client was first exposed to photographs and then to mental imagery of herself entering a familiar room full of people. The counselor continuously presented the most fearful aspects of the entry to the client ("You see everyone glaring at you; they're turning and whispering to each other while glancing in your direction; you feel sweat popping out all over you; you feel sick; you spot only two chairs, in the far corner; you start toward them; your feet are clumsy and heavy; you stumble over something on the floor and everyone laughs out loud; you continue toward the two chairs, even though you are terribly embarrassed; the room becomes quiet; everyone is staring at you; you see that the two chairs are full of umbrellas and purses; you feel scared and repugnant; you'd like to turn around and flee; your neck and face are looking flush; you can feel yourself looking ridiculous; everyone starts laughing again. . . ."). As the procedure continued over a period of several sessions the client's fear diminished and the client was able to progress, in a graduated sequence, to independent entrance into that room and then to rooms full of people in general. The objective was to continuously expose the client to strong fear-evoking aspects of entering the room and to force the client to become acclimated to the anxiety and to discover that she could stand it.

Implosive therapy (Stampfl & Levis, 1967) is similar to flooding. The technique is used to confront the client with fear-evoking stimuli. It is based on the theoretical principle that if the client continues to repeat a response without reinforcement, the strength of the tendency to perform that response will progressively diminish. Implosive therapy has been used to intervene in a wide number of client problems such as sexual dysfunction, compulsive use of obscene words, phobias, marriage and family counseling, test anxiety, fear of speaking in public, obsessional neuroses, rehabilitation counseling, hysteria, and a number of neurotic responses. Implosive techniques may employ mental imagery and sound tape recordings of implosion material to achieve extinction of unwanted fears. The procedure requires the client to experience a full measure of anxiety and to discover that the basis of the fear or phobia is groundless. It is essential that the rationale of implosion be understood by the client before proceeding with therapy and that the client has a commitment to extinguishing the unwanted fears and anxieties. It is also important that the client have alternatives available to take the place of the imagined fears and anxieties. Client ownership and understanding of the procedure and the desired changes increases the probability of success.

One example of the use of implosive therapy was with a young mother who constantly screamed at her young children for no apparent reason. She was given a tape recorder and instructed to continuously scream into the microphone as if she were haranguing her children. She then listened to the tape of herself until she was repulsed at her own screaming behavior. She was also taught adaptive verbal responses to her children and she was reinforced in using the alternatives. The experience resulted in her stopping the maladaptive responses with her children.

In recent years a great many behavioral researchers and practitioners have made substantial strides in learning about and using flooding techniques in clinical treatments (DeRubeis & Crits-Christoph, 1998; Gauthier, 1999; Showers & Kevlyn, 1999; Tarrier, et al., 1999; Thom, Sartory, & Johren, 2000; Turner, Beidel, & Jacob, 1994). The term flooding has been used interchangeably with the terms *exposure therapy, imaginal flooding,* and *imaginal exposure* (DeRubeis & Crits-Christoph, 1998). The flooding technique has been perfected and used successfully with a wide array of mental disorders in adult clients in both individual and group treatment programs. For example, DeRubeis and Crits-Christoph (1998) and Turner et al. (1994) found flooding to be a superior strategy in extinguishing the ill effects of social phobia. We know of no substantive research where flooding has been shown to be appropriate for children and we do not recommend such use.

DeRubeis and Crits-Christoph's (1998) National Institutes for Mental Health (NIMH)–funded empirical studies subjected flooding and exposure strategies to enormous and rigorous investigation. They reported that these techniques proved to be effective in treating clients with obsessive-compulsive disorders, agoraphobia, panic disorder, posttraumatic stress disorder (including Vietnam veterans suffering from PTSD), and a number of other phobias. Also, Gauthier's (1999) investigations found that combining flooding with several other cognitive techniques succeeded in treating clients with severe panic disorders. Practically all mental disorders have been subjected to flooding and imaginal exposure techniques. We found over 400 recent psychological research reports that focused on flooding alone. These reports included structuring clients with purely positive self-beliefs to counteract negative self-beliefs (Showers & Kevlyn, 1999), successful treatment of dental phobias (Thom et al., 2000), chronic stress disorders, and many other mental disorders (Tarrier et al., 1999). The resurgence of flooding as a viable behavioral counseling strategy has shed a new light on behavioral theory as well as provided an effective brief therapy technique at a time when clients, counselors, and the entire managed health care environment sorely need it.

Satiation

Satiation is a mild aversive technique that uses an excessive amount of reinforcement to make the undesired reinforcer lose its effectiveness. The reinforcer is emitted by the subject or given by another person in such quantities that the individual not only tires of the reinforcer but also becomes repelled by it. Smoking, eating, and acting-out behaviors have been amenable to this technique. One of the most famous uses of satiation occurred with the towel-hoarding behavior of a long-term hospital patient (Allyon, 1965). A weekly average of nineteen to twenty-nine towels were found in the patient's room despite attempts by the ward nurses to retrieve the towels. Stimulus satiation was introduced without comment by the nurses, who gave the patient seven towels daily. This rate was increased until, by the third week, the number had increased to sixty. When the total number of towels reached 625, continuing to receive towels became noxious. Verbal responses of the patient in the first week were positive. "Oh, you found it for me. Thank you." By the fourth, fifth, and sixth weeks verbal responses were extremely negative: "Get these dirty towels out of here. I can't stay up all night folding these. I can't drag any more of these out of here, I just can't do it." No more towel hoarding was reported. A major problem is that if satiation does not occur, the behavior becomes entrenched because of all the reinforcement.

Token Economies

Another widely used behavioral strategy is the token economy (Chambless & Goldstein, 1979). It is a systematic procedure in which tokens are given as immediate tangible reinforcers for appropriate behaviors. The tokens can be poker chips, scrip, points, or other concrete items that can be cashed in by the holder for articles of value or for privileges. Token economies have proved successful in institutional settings such as hospitals, schools, clinics, day care units, and prisons. The procedure is amenable to almost any setting, and the options for creative employment are virtually infinite.

In an institutional setting, behavioral planners can develop token economy structures to reinforce patients or inmates for performing positive acts or to invoke penalties or loss of tokens for infraction of rules or failure to carry out assigned responsibilities. The strategy is powerful in dealing with either simple or complex behaviors; it is effective in extinguishing maladaptive behaviors or shaping adaptive ones.

One important question raised about the token economy has been, "How does it move from laboratory reinforcement to changes in the real world?" Although the strategy is amenable to wide application and creative innovation by professionals and lay personnel alike, maintenance of modified behavior may pose problems. Behavior planners can generally improve retention by:

1. Obtaining the commitment of all personnel (professionals, clients, aides, lay workers, and volunteers) to the goals and concepts of the token economy
2. Selecting behaviors that are likely to receive natural social and environmental reinforcement
3. Adhering to proven laboratory principles of behavior modification (for example, providing for giving out tokens in an immediate, fair, and consistent manner)
4. Ensuring that tokens maintain their reinforcement value and that clients have frequent opportunities to redeem tokens for desired payoffs
5. Pairing material reinforcers (tokens) with social reinforcers (verbal praise), so that the value of intrinsic motivation is learned
6. Fading out material reinforcers (tokens) and fading in social reinforcers (verbal praise) so that long-term results can be maintained solely by intrinsic motivation
7. Focusing on behaviors that affect both long-term and short-term quality of life, thereby demonstrating to clients and staff that the program means more than simply controlling unruly behavior
8. Ensuring that behaviors modified will transfer to client requirements outside the institution
9. Maintaining sound assessment and feedback procedures so that necessary strategy changes can be made when problems occur (for example, when the reinforcement value of certain rewarded behaviors diminishes)

Self-Management, Self-Monitoring, and Self-Reinforcement

The terms *self-management, self-monitoring,* and *self-reinforcement* embody a trend toward expecting the client to be an active collaborator in the counseling and psychotherapeutic process (Cormier & Cormier, 1991, pp. 518–549, 1998, pp. 530–578; Watson & Tharp, 1981, 1989). These terms suggest a mode of coping on the part of the client that avoids the concepts of inhibition and restraint often associated with the mechanisms of external control, regulation, other-directedness, and manipulation by experts other than self (Cormier & Cormier, 1998, p. 530). According to Bandura (1976, 1991), human behavior is extensively regulated, motivated, and energized by the element of self-influence. Cormier and Cormier (1998, p. 530) identify four major subfunctions that drive self-management processes: "(1) self-monitoring of one's behavior, its components, and its effects; (2) judgment of one's behavior; (3) affective self-reactions; and (4) self-efficacy." Compared with earlier views of many theorists, the self-management/self-monitoring/self-reinforcement movement contains some notable shifts: (1) clients play an active role in every phase of counseling—they are far less passive; (2) clients augment the introspective and didactic aspects of counseling by developing specific action steps and/or action skills; (3) client thought processes are considered internal events and are dealt with in counseling; (4) clients assume greater responsibility for therapeutic outcomes; (5) clients learn self-reinforcement techniques (Bandura, 1976; Cormier & Cormier, 1991, pp. 538–547, 1998, pp. 555–560);

(6) clients are called on to observe, monitor, record, self-reinforce (Cormier & Cormier, 1991, pp. 520–533), and sometimes interpret their own behavioral data; and (7) counselors and therapists take on greater mentor and educator roles and lesser expert roles. The self-management/self-monitoring/self-reinforcement strategies described by Cormier and Cormier (1998, pp. 530–577), Watson and Tharp (1981, 1989), and Williams and Long (1979, 1983), provide a framework whereby *any* of the different behavioral strategies can be used in the client's own behavioral plan.

Self-management, self-monitoring, and self-reinforcement strategies have been used extensively, appropriately, and effectively in a wide variety of counseling settings with a great many client problem areas. For example, Cormier and Cormier (1998, pp. 532–567) cite dozens of research and clinical studies where investigators used these techniques with such disparate problem areas as alcohol abuse and weight loss. Marcus and associates (2000) demonstrated that self-management strategies were effective in helping physically healthy adult clients to establish and maintain vigorous and intense physical activity to sustain health benefits for preventive purposes. These investigations also highlighted the benefits of self-monitoring in support of physical activity behavior in adults and youth and how physical activity relates to other health behaviors such as smoking and other debilitative habits.

Wilson and Vitousek (1999) reported that self-monitoring techniques can play a key role in helping clients with eating disorders. They indicated that adherence to self-monitoring should be practiced by counselors who are skilled in using a collaborative therapeutic alliance. In terms of the maintenance of dietary behavior change, Kumanyika and associates (2000), studying nutrition risk factors in clients, reported that behavioral counseling approaches, such as self-management, are appropriate for use in nutritional counseling. They advise that various nutrition education and behavioral counseling strategies have been shown to facilitate lasting and healthy changes in the intake of fat, fiber, sodium, and fruits and vegetables primarily in highly motivated clients. A similar investigation by Bouton (2000) studied the maintenance of behavior change in clients referred for cardiovascular risk. Self-management was one of several techniques used to help clients deal with obesity, smoking, diet, and exercise. As indicated by Cormier and Cormier (1998, pp. 530–578), there are very few problem areas in human existence that are not amenable to alleviation through self-management, self monitoring, or self-reinforcement strategies.

Following is an adaptation from several sources, including the previously mentioned citations from self-management/self-monitoring/self-reinforcement literature, outlining five important steps and sample counselor–client dialogue for guiding the client through each successive step of generating his or her own self-management/self-monitoring/self-reinforcement plan. (The terms identified with an asterisk are defined in the next section.)

Step 1: Conceptualizing and Defining the Problem and Selecting Appropriate Outcome Goals in Behavioral Terms

A. Establish one target outcome goal* at a time

B. Goal should be:

1. Understandable, important, and of value to the client
2. Measurable in objective and analyzable terms
3. Realistic and attainable
4. Positive and constructive

C. Statement of target outcome goal should include:
  1. Client's desired and attainable level of performance or extinction
  2. Successive approximations of projected milestones and targeted goal attainment dates

CO: So, Peggy, what you've *really* decided to do is attain your goal of getting some weight off and then, this time, keeping it off.

CL: That's exactly right, because my health is my greatest concern.

CO: So, since you're fully committed to it and you're wanting to start work on it now, let's determine exactly how many pounds you're aiming at losing and also plan a realistic and medically safe timeline and target date for attaining that weight.

Step 2: Managing and Monitoring Target Behavior

A. Select appropriate target process goals* based on client objectives
B. Initiate baseline assessment* of targeted behaviors prior to implementing behavior-change strategies
C. Begin monitoring and recording data on behaviors related to process goals
  1. Record behavior immediately after it occurs
  2. Use paper and pencil, wrist counter, knitting-stitch counter, stopwatch, wristwatch, biofeedback monitoring device, or other appropriate recording system or technique to record or document behavioral data
  3. Do a frequency count,* time duration,* or product assessment,* or use some other accurate monitoring strategy to document the behavior

CO: Peggy, how are you going to change the way you record and monitor your behavior this time so that you make sure you stay on your timeline and achieve your desired weight on schedule?

CL: Well, I've figured out all the weights, calories, exercises, and ways to keep track of what I do each day. And I have decided on some ways to monitor my behavior so that I don't cheat on myself.

CO: You say, "Some ways to monitor." Peggy, precisely what are those procedures? I want you to have a no-fail system. I really do want you to succeed this time. I want us to go over every detail of what you're planning to do and how you're going to do it.

CL: OK, let me show you what I've written down so far.

CO: (*looks at the list*) That's a pretty good list. Let's examine it and perhaps brainstorm together for some more specific but simple and effective monitoring devices or strategies you might employ that either of us alone might overlook.

Step 3: Changing Precipitating Conditions and Setting Events* and Generating Appropriate Action Steps

Continue recording the targeted behaviors.

A. Initially avoid environments and situations that are certain to produce undesirable or maladaptive behaviors

B. Alter environments, conditions, and situations to ensure that you
   1. Become aware of what you're doing
   2. Limit the stimuli that evoke the bad behaviors
   3. Make it easy and satisfying to emit desired behaviors
   4. Specify alternatives or substitute behaviors that are incompatible with maladaptive behaviors

CO: Peggy, this is the step at which you determine what you're going to do differently. If you keep following the previous patterns you've established for yourself it will be hard to change setting events, and you may simply keep on eating and doing the physical activities you've been used to. That will make it harder. It seems to me you've got to make some pretty drastic changes if you intend to ensure that you reach your goals.

CL: Well, I know some of the things I must do. The first thing I thought of was to prepare my low-fat, low-calorie lunch for the next day each evening before I go to bed.

CO: OK, anything else?

CL: I was thinking about figuring out some way to make sure I do my dancercises every day—maybe even every morning!

CO: Good! Now, let's together examine that and also some more ways you might change your setting events to make sure your plan succeeds this time.

Step 4: Generating Appropriate Reinforcement Contingencies* and Establishing Consequencies That Are Meaningful and Effective for the Client

Continue recording the targeted behaviors.

Continue maintenance of changing of precipitating conditions and setting events and generating appropriate action steps.

A. Identify reinforcers or consequences that would be positively reinforcing or aversively punitive to the client
B. Implement reinforcement contingencies such that
   1. Appropriate behaviors are immediately reinforced
   2. Criteria for reinforcement are realistic and readily attainable
   3. Significant others will support attainment of desired behavioral goals
   4. A graduated (approximated) time frame is established for reinforcing behavior leading to process goals
   5. Extrinsic* as well as intrinsic* reinforcers are available and included
   6. Reinforcers have enough valence or power to be effective
   7. Reinforcements are scheduled to provide maximum short-, medium-, and long-term incentives
   8. An accurate system for graphing, displaying, and examining behavioral data is continuously used
   9. A specific behavioral contract may be written

C. Consider use of aversive consequences if reinforcement contingencies fail to produce desired changes in behavior
  1. Write in and make commitments to penalize yourself in the event of noncompliance (perhaps contract with a support person to forfeit something of real value to you in the event of noncompliance)
  2. Use mechanically induced pain or aversive consequences
  3. Induce a state of stimulus satiation*

CO: I want your rewards to be strong enough to ensure your compliance with your plan. But I don't want to see you go off the deep end and make them unrealistically high. Nor do I want you to rely only on yourself to administer your rewards. I would like to know who will serve as support persons—persons who have a stake in your meeting your goals—to increase the chances that you will succeed.

CL: I am sure my husband will be glad to be a key support. I thought about asking my supervisor. I would trust her to be fair but firm with me. She would certainly know if I cheated at lunch, and she'd certainly call my hand on it.

CO: Good! Put those names down on your pad and let's devise a strategy whereby you can enlist them in a way that will be good for both you and them. Also, I'd like to suggest that we figure out some short-range, medium-range, and long-range rewards that will be fair, effective, and sure to work for you.

CL: OK, I want to fix it so that I definitely get this weight off this time and keep it off!

Step 5: Maintaining and Consolidating Gains

Continue recording targeted behaviors.

Continue maintenance of precipitating conditions and setting events and generating appropriate action steps.

Continue generation of appropriate reinforcement contingencies and establishing consequences that are meaningful to the client.

A. Establish an effective system of assessment/feedback to ensure that self-management/self-monitoring/self-reinforcement can be altered, redefined, or redirected to achieve and maintain target outcome goals
B. Maintain natural consequences
  1. Phase out self-recording
  2. Provide for natural, continuous self-monitoring/self-reinforcement
  3. Maintain most changes in setting or precipitating events
  4. Phase out artificial reinforcement contingencies
  5. Enlist social support
  6. Apply self-management/self-monitoring/self-reinforcement in other areas in which the client wants to effect behavioral change

CL: One thing I can do is to get my husband involved and invested in my maintaining my safe and healthy weight—once I'm on it.

CO: You think there's any chance he might somehow sabotage it and subtly reinforce your previous behavior?

CL: No way! He's as concerned about my health as I am.

CO: Then I'd certainly recommend that you use him as a maintenance support. Let's compile a list of the additional maintenance strategies and perhaps additional support persons you will use to make sure you never again have to face the task of losing this much weight and that you remain alive to enjoy the fruits of your goal attainment.

CL: OK.

CO: Also, I want to work with you as you develop your behavioral contracts. Written and signed contracts are vital to both you and your support persons. I want your contracts to be clear and specific and to accurately reflect your action goals and commitments as well as to clearly specify those behaviors your support persons have pledged to provide to help ensure your compliance and success.

Definitions of Terms in the Self-Management Behavior Model

Baseline assessment. The initial appraisal of behavior—it more clearly defines the problem and serves as a basis of comparison for assessing the effectiveness of treatment.

Extrinsic reinforcer. A reward or payoff that increases the probability of a particular response and comes from the environment (i.e., is external to the individual emitting the response).

Frequency count. Tabulating the number of times a particular behavior or event occurs (e.g., a procedure was interrupted three times).

Intrinsic reinforcer. A reward or payoff that increases the probability of a particular response and comes from within the individual emitting the response—for example, inner thoughts and feelings.

Product assessment. Evaluating behavior in terms of its products—for example, number of completed assignments, grade point average attained, number of cavities reported at a dental checkup.

Reinforcement contingencies. The conditions under which a schedule of reinforcers or punishers is administered (e.g., "You can have ice cream only after you clean your room").

Setting events. Stimuli in the environment that precipitate or trigger behavior—for example, seeing a vending machine may trigger an eating binge.

Stimulus satiation. A strategy of continuously repeating a reinforcing activity until the activity becomes no longer reinforcing (e.g., eating candy until one is repulsed at the sight or taste of candy).

Target outcome goal. A statement of the aim of a behavioral plan in terms of a specific product such as grades, weight, money saved, number of miles jogged per day.

Target process goal. A statement of the aim of a behavioral plan in terms of responses that either facilitate or hinder achievement of the desired outcome (i.e., the target outcome goal). For example, fifty situps per day may contribute to the desired amount of weight loss.

Time duration. A method of assessing behavior by recording the amount of time devoted to the behavior (e.g., she studies for four hours or he cried for five minutes).

Self-management, self-monitoring, and self-reinforcement not only emphasize great responsibility on the part of the client but also place confidence and trust in the client. The behavioral model presented here is recommended as a general guide rather than a narrow prescription for solving all behavioral problems. A client often finds that completion of Steps 1 and 2 is sufficient to produce desired changes. Also, clients who experience success in using self-management, self-monitoring, and self-reinforcement often find that the successful consequences of changing one specific behavior transfers to other similar behavioral situations. Such transfers may translate into something akin to habit and thus eliminate the need to apply a comprehensive behavioral change model singularly to every debilitative problem they may encounter.

Systematic Desensitization

Wolpe (1958, 1961, 1982) and Lazarus (1968, 1982) developed and perfected techniques for systematically using clients' internal mental processes to help them control their own adverse responses to aversive stimuli and inhibit undesirable behaviors. They used both cognitive and behavioral concepts and strategies to teach clients to desensitize themselves to debilitating phobias. Many writers classify systematic desensitization as a purely behavioral strategy. However, we believe it represents one of the earliest behavioral procedures that clearly extended traditional behavioral principles to include internal cognitive events as behavioral data to be used in therapy. Both Wolpe (1982) and Lazarus (1968) used clients' mental processes as rich sources for connecting thinking and behaving. Both called for the client mentally to generate pictures or images and to use reciprocal images to inhibit, counterbalance, or dispel anxieties. With the advent of the incorporation of emotional (emotive) images in the therapeutic process, we are even more sure that systematic desensitization belongs squarely in the cognitive camp (Cormier & Cormier, 1991, pp. 480–507).

Although systematic desensitization was originally based on the learning principles of classical conditioning, it has become the treatment of choice for many problems such as phobias, irrational fears, and anxieties in which there are no obvious external dangers and in which the main source of the phobias is internal. An example of an appropriate use of systematic desensitization is the treatment of a client who has an irrational fear of bridges. The therapy would incorporate three basic steps: (1) muscle relaxation and relaxation therapy, (2) construction of a hierarchy representing the anxiety-producing situations the client typically faces and needs to overcome, and (3) graduated and progressive pairing through emotive imagery of the anxiety-producing situations with the relaxed state of the client (Wolpe, 1982). The desensitization sessions would be continued until the client could stand, without debilitating anxiety, to be presented with bridge scenes and finally could ride or drive alone across bridges without discomfort.

Behavioral Modeling

Modeling is the overt and explicit demonstration of appropriate behavioral choices available to the client (Bandura, 1976, 1991, 1995). Modeling can be done by the counselor, by a group, by peers, by significant others, by videotape, or by audiotape. The old adage "actions speak louder than words" is quite correct. Many clients have great difficulty emitting desired behaviors until they actually see, hear, and compare acceptable and unacceptable responses. Whenever modeling is combined with other procedures such as emotive imagery, desensitization, and relaxation it is even more valuable. Modeling through structured emotive imagery is called *covert modeling* (Cormier & Cormier, 1979, p. 307). Often a combination of covert modeling and live, or *in vivo,* modeling makes a stronger and more efficient action plan. The role of the counselor in modeling is to help the client define and analyze the needed responses, provide the modeled experience and practice, and follow up with client progress until the client has developed a sufficient repertoire of appropriate responses to cope at a level that is satisfactory to the client. Positive reinforcement by the counselor or by others increases the probability and rate of acquisition of behaviors learned through modeling.

Two specific types of behavioral modeling and two distinct types of cognitive behavioral modeling are described by Cormier and Cormier (1998, p. 300). The behavioral modeling types are *symbolic modeling* and *participant modeling.* The two types of cognitive behavioral modeling are known as *cognitive modeling* and *covert modeling.* In symbolic modeling, the client behavior that is to be imitated (and learned or habituated) is presented in the form of a film, videotape, computer image or program, written material, cartoons, charts, graphs, photographs, overhead projections, or live enactments such as role play or psychodrama. Participant modeling is accomplished by presenting *in vivo* behaviors to the client during the counseling process. In vivo presentations are managed in such a way that the client is guided through successive performances of the desired behavioral sequence (Cormier & Cormier, 1998, p. 300).

Cognitive modeling is usually performed by exposing the client to desired thoughts or emotional feelings through self-talk (in which the counselor verbally models and the client repeats the counselor's words) or through some other means of inducing symbolic learning. In covert modeling, the client imagines him- or herself or others engaging in desired behavior that is to be imitated and learned. Covert modeling is usually enhanced through the use of guided imagery or emotive imagery. *Guided imagery* is a procedure in which the client mentally focuses on positive thoughts or images while imagining a discomforting or anxiety-arousing activity or situation (Cormier & Cormier, 1998, p. 319). Similarly, *emotive imagery* is a procedure in which the client focuses on positive thoughts, images, and emotions while imagining a discomforting or anxiety-arousing activity or situation, paying particular attention to and contrasting both positive and negative emotional images felt by the client (Cormier & Cormier, 1991, p. 350).

Modeling techniques are powerful tools that have multiple applications in behavioral counseling and psychotherapy. They have been used successfully in treating generalized anxiety disorders, panic disorders, eating disorders, and alcohol dependence (Haaga, 2000), and in understanding and dealing with false memory dilemmas (de Rivera, 2000). In terms of general behavioral counseling, therapy, and modification, the different types of modeling we have described provide an enormous array of alternative ways to learn for both clients and counselors. An individual can acquire new and desired behaviors from several different types of modeling. Modeling can assist a client in performing already acquired behaviors in more appropriate ways or at more opportune times. Modeling strategies can be used to extinguish or reduce fears and phobias, control anxiety, decrease stress, enhance weight management protocols, control smoking and alcohol use, and change self-perspectives (Cormier & Cormier, 1998, p. 299). In an age when accountability throughout the health care system is mandatory, modeling is especially valuable as a brief therapy technique. It is being used in sports psychology, preventive and behavioral medicine, and industrial psychology work, as well as in clinical counseling settings.

Behavior Rehearsal

Behavior rehearsal is quite similar to modeling. In fact, it is frequently used in connection with modeling, coaching, and structured practice with clients (Cormier & Cormier, 1991, pp. 310–314). Both rehearsal and modeling may be used to complement each other (McFall & Lillesand, 1971). The difference is that in rehearsal the desired response has been preselected by the client and counselor. The counselor serves as mentor and coach while the client practices, adjusts, and improves the response. The role of the counselor in behavior rehearsal is to help the client practice and perfect the goal behaviors that are similar to the situations that occur in the client's environment (Cormier & Cormier, 1979, p. 264). The most important goal of rehearsal is to help the client develop generalized response patterns independent of the counselor's coaching sessions.

Rehearsal techniques may be accomplished either covertly or overtly. Cormier and Cormier (1991, p. 310) recommend that clients rehearse *covertly* by imagining and reflecting on the desired behavior to be acquired. In *overt* rehearsal clients may verbalize and act out the behaviors that have been deemed desirable. Coaching involves providing instructions to the client regarding the purposes and principles involved in satisfactorily performing the desired behavior. The coach can provide verbal or written cues to assist the client in making discriminations about the appropriate use of target responses. Cue cards, visual media, and other props are commonly used in the rehearsal and coaching procedures (Cormier & Cormier, 1991, p. 311). Behavior rehearsal is a practical, sensible, effective, and efficient behavioral strategy.

Sample Case

The case of Peggy Smith, age 56, illustrates a fairly typical use of the self-management/self-monitoring/self-reinforcing procedure. The counselor is in a *collaborative* role—working *with* the client instead of doing something *to* or *for* the client—to facilitate change. Typical of the case management in behavioral systems, Peggy's counselor places a great deal of autonomy and responsibility on the client. The terms *counselor, consultant,* or *mentor* seem to accurately capture the flavor of what the counselor does.

Background

Peggy's presenting problem was her concern over her excessive weight. She saw it as a longstanding, recurring, very serious problem. The counselor worked with Peggy for several weeks in the development of her plan for losing weight. Rather than summarizing the counseling techniques used with Peggy during the sessions, we present the plan itself, written in the first person by the client.

> Baseline Statement. *Two years ago I was informed by my doctor that I had developed mild congestive heart disease. In no uncertain terms I was told to go on a salt-free diet and lose weight or suffer the consequences. Although I had lived fifty-four full and interesting years, I was not yet ready to depart this planet, so I did what I was told.*
>
> *I went on a 750-calorie low-salt diet, signed up for a class in yoga, memorized a list of low-salt foods, and learned to think thin. In four months I lost twenty-five pounds, my lungs were free of fluid, I felt and looked better, and I was on my way.*
>
> *Alas, my good intentions went awry; I changed jobs, and one of the benefits of my new job was free lunch in the employees' dining room. Lunch was always a full-course meal, and, being free, it was extremely hard to pass up.*
>
> *I now have more than my twenty-five pounds back, like an unwelcome guest. Thinking about it does not help; telling myself to do something about it does not help; my only recourse is to set up a behavioral plan to lose weight, with positive and negative consequences and just DO IT! Steps one through five contain a description of my behavioral plan, with attendant data-collection provisions, and a behavioral contract signed by myself and the parties involved in helping me keep my commitment.*

Discussion

In behavioral counseling and behavior modification, the counselor does not look for deep underlying causes or hidden emotional disturbance. The theoretical assumption in Peggy's case was that the most direct and efficient way to help Peggy was to focus on overt behaviors and consequences.

Peggy Smith's plan was unique to her. Even though the plan was lengthy, improvements could have been made. For example, she could have strengthened her incentives by availing herself of social supports, such as a weight-management group. She might have chosen more powerful rewards and consequences. For instance, her husband might sabotage her plan if his incentive for getting money is stronger than his desire to see her lose weight. Perhaps a better plan would have allowed the husband to give the money to an organization that she deplores. Another improvement might have been for Peggy to include other people in her recording and data-keeping plan.

On the plus side, Peggy's plan was systematic, based on behavioral principles, thorough, and problem-centered. Her target goals were specific, important, measurable, attainable, realistic, and positive. She used support persons who had a stake in her success. Finally, the self-management method provided Peggy an opportunity to learn not only weight control but also a self-action strategy for similar problems.

Self-Management/Self-Monitoring/Self-Reinforcement Plan

Losing Weight by Peggy Smith (May 23)

Step 1.   *Goal selection.* I must lose weight for my health and for my own satisfactory self-image. My plan, therefore, is to lose 48 pounds in 12 months to achieve my ideal weight of 127 pounds.

Step 2.   *Monitoring target behavior*

Step 2a.   *Process goal selection*

1. I will establish a 750-calorie low-salt diet of three meals per day with low-calorie snacks.

2. I will establish a regular routine of a minimum of six exercises to be done daily, reaching a minimum of two fifteen-minute sets per day.

3. I will establish a regular routine of walking, working up to a minimum of two miles per day, rain or shine.

Step 2b.   *Baseline assessment*

1. I now weigh 175 pounds.

2. I now take in between 4,000 and 5,000 calories per day.

3. I engage in no regular exercise.

4. Since I have the money to buy clothes whenever I want, I don't worry about size.

5. I eat a large free lunch in the employee dining room every day.

Step 2c.   *Recording behavior related to process and outcome goals*

1. Weight will be recorded biweekly on a graph.

2. I will keep a daily calorie count.

3. Exercises will be done daily and when each daily series has been completed, it will be checked off on a calendar.

4. Walking will be done daily. After completion of a scheduled daily distance, it will be checked off on a calendar.

5. My supervisor will validate on her desk calendar each day I bring my diet lunch. She will praise me for compliance and criticize me for noncompliance.

Step 3.   *Changing precipitating conditions and setting events*

1. I will not go to bed until I have made my low-calorie lunch for the next day and put it in the refrigerator with a sign on the door reminding me not to forget it.

2. When I watch television or study, I will have available at my side a bowl of carrot and celery sticks to munch on.

Self-Management/Self-Monitoring/Self-Reinforcement Plan (*Continued*)

3. I will set a timer on my stereo so that at 7:00 A.M. every morning my dancercise CDs will start playing.

4. Before I leave in the morning, I will set my jogging shoes in the entranceway so that they will be the first thing I see when I come home after work.

5. In lieu of going straight to the employee dining room at lunch, I will go to my supervisor's office, where my lunch will be monitored by my supervisor.

Step 4. *Generating appropriate reinforcement contingencies and effective consequences*

1. Any month that I meet my four-pound goal, my husband will contribute another $50 to my account. Any month that I do not attain my goal, I forfeit $50 to my husband.

2. Any time that I have a bowl of carrot and celery sticks by my side, I may continue watching television or studying. If not, I will stop studying or watching television immediately. My husband has agreed to monitor this.

3. Each time I do my exercises, I will enjoy a twenty-minute warm bubble bath. Each time I do not exercise, I will take a cold shower with Lava soap.

4. Each time I complete my walking, I will take fifteen minutes to tend my flowers, an activity I thoroughly enjoy. If I do not, I will clean my husband's aquarium.

5. I will bring my diet lunch to my supervisor, who will praise me publicly in the dining room. If I do not, my supervisor will criticize me publicly in the dining room.

6. If I successfully meet my target outcome goal on the specified date, I will receive my $600 plus $600 of matching funds from my husband to be used to visit a friend in California. If I do not, I forfeit all the money to my husband.

7. My husband has agreed to praise me whenever he sees me following the provisions set forth in this plan.

Step 5. *Maintaining and consolidating gains*

Step 5a. *Evaluation*

1. If at any biweekly weighing period I have not lost at least two pounds, my counselor and I will review the components of this plan and make the necessary adjustment.

2. My husband has agreed to give me feedback regarding any behaviors or events he observes that may be deterring my progress.

Step 5b. *Maintenance*

1. Upon reaching 127 pounds, I will continue to maintain a weight chart for evaluating my weight. If at any month my weight goes above 130 pounds, the full behavioral plan will be reinstated.

Continued

2. All clothes I have above a size 10 will be given to Goodwill.

3. My husband will install a full-length mirror in our bedroom so I can appreciate my new figure.

4. I believe my new behaviors will become so much a part of my life that I will feel good when I do them and guilty when I do not.

Behavioral contracts. I, Peggy Smith, agree to carry out a weight reduction and exercise plan as outlined in the foregoing document, in which I shall lose forty-eight pounds during the twelve months from June 1 this year to June 1 next year.

I further agree to abide by all the stipulations as described in my behavioral plan and to forfeit $600 to my husband, Oscar Smith, if I fail to fulfill the terms of this contract.

_____
(Signature—Peggy Smith)

_____
(Date)

I, Oscar Smith, agree to abide by the stipulations described in the attached document. I also agree to refrain from remarking about the diet and exercise plan or referring to it in any way except in the manner described in said document.

I further agree to provide matching funds of $600 if the terms of the contract are successfully met by Peggy Smith. I agree to accept $600 from Peggy Smith if she does not fulfill the conditions of the above contract.

_____
(Signature—Oscar Smith)

_____
(Date)

I, Annie Mae Jones, Peggy's supervisor, agree to monitor Peggy's diet at lunch time. I further agree to provide praise and criticism as described in the attached document.

_____
(Signature—Annie Mae Jones)

_____
(Date)

(*Note:* Four attachments to Peggy Smith's behavior plan have been omitted: weight chart, salt-free diet, schedule of exercises, and exercise charts.)

Contributions of the Behavioral System

The growth of behavior therapy has been characterized by the system's movement from focusing on a few simple problems (such as phobias and obsessions) to attending to a wide "range of the most complex social neuroses and so-called existential problems" (Wolpe, 1981, p. 162). It is unique in that it is the only system of therapeutic intervention that "does what had been predicted on theoretical grounds" (Wolpe, 1981, p. 161).

Another contribution of the behavioral system is its accountability. No system is better suited for accountability. Funding sources have increasingly demanded tangible evidence that psychotherapy produces positive results (Garfield, 1981, p. 181). Behaviorism's rigorous insistence on identifying success in terms of measurable gains in objective data has given the system a great deal of credibility with funding agencies and legislatures.

Related to accountability is specificity (Cormier & Cormier, 1991), one of the most important characteristics of behavioral counseling. Other systems have adopted and attempted to adapt some of the typical behavioral methods, such as identifying and defining problems in objective terms and specifying target goals, reinforcement contingencies, outcomes, feedback, assessment, and follow-up in objective and measurable terms (Wilson, 1995, pp. 200–201).

Another strength of the behavioral system is its insistence on defining and directly attacking problems (Goldstein, Heller, & Sechrest, 1966). Clients and funding sources alike have come to appreciate the fact that everyone knows, up front, what is being worked on, what the goals are, and when and to what extent gains or changes are expected. Since the approach is centered in a specific problem there are few deep-seated mysteries within the client that require an outside expert to reach in, understand, analyze, interpret, prescribe, and fix without the client being aware, involved, and responsible. The behavioral system's premise that the proof is in the data (and the evidence that such proof generalizes to similar events) has given other counseling systems incentives to move from the mystical toward the scientific.

Shortcomings of the Behavioral System

Behavioral counseling has received extensive criticism from proponents of other systems. Behavioral counseling may change simple, overt behavior, but it does not deal with deep-seated emotions and feelings. Further, it fails to provide the client with insights and deep understanding of the problem. Behavioral counseling focuses mainly on symptoms; as a result, when one symptom is fixed another appears. Behavioral counseling ignores the historical roots of present maladaptive behaviors. Behavior modification strategies are applicable only to a narrow range of anxieties and phobias, and they are too effective in that they program clients into rigid, manipulative behavioral responses that rob them of their autonomy and freedom of choice. Behavioral systems largely ignore the higher levels of human cognition or functioning and program clients toward minimum or tolerable levels of behaving, reinforce conformity, stifle creativity, and ignore client needs for self-fulfillment, self-actualization, and feelings of self-worth. Behavior therapy requires too much education and experience in behavior analysis to provide enough therapists to be of practical value to the multitudes needing help. Behavior modification does not really work. There may be short-term effects, such as habit changes, but no appreciable lasting changes accrue. Behavioral strategies are dangerous to society in that they take away freedom. If control is in the wrong hands, large numbers of people may be manipulated into doing things they don't really want to do (much like being subjected to unwanted brainwashing).

Some forms of behavioral counseling have been shown to actually reinforce deviant behavior. Dishion, McCord, and Poulin (1999) explored developmental and intervention evidence relevant to iatrogenic effects (outcomes caused by the therapy experience itself) in adolescent peer groups. Two experimentally controlled intervention studies included adolescents in deviancy training groups. Findings of both studies suggested that behaviorally-based peer-group interventions increased adolescent problem behavior and negative life outcomes in adulthood, compared with control youth. The data from both experimental studies suggested that high-risk youth are particularly vulnerable to peer aggregations, compared with low risk youth. The researchers suggested that under some circumstances peer aggregation during early adolescence inadvertently reinforces problem behavior. Research further suggests that out of hundreds of controlled intervention studies examined, 29 percent show negative effects on youth. Further, researchers suspect that this may be an underestimate, given that intervention researchers are unlikely to publish null or negative effects. The finding that group counseling and behaviorally-guided group interaction produced a negative effect on delinquent and antisocial behavior is disturbing, indeed. Dishion et al. (1999, p. 1) challenge the scientific community in general and behavioral researchers in particular to "cull iatrogenic interventions from the social policy armamentarium in the effort to improve the outcomes for children and families in communities."

Practically every rival system has attacked behavior therapy, behavior modification, and behavioral counseling. The charge regarding loss of freedom has probably been the most persistent and formidable criticism.

Behavioral Counseling with Diverse Populations

In recent years, counselors of all persuasions have come to recognize the critical importance of competencies that guide interpersonal counseling interactions with attention to culture, ethnicity, race, and other diverse populations. Most leading proponents of behavioral and cognitive behavioral counseling recognize and recommend that *all* counselors and therapists be trained and become competent in multicultural counseling theory, philosophy, and technique. Many leading proponents of behavioral and cognitive approaches, such as Cormier and Cormier (1998, pp. 579–597), reproduce multicultural competency components in their writings and advocate for the Association for Multicultural and Counseling and Development's (AMCD) published statement "Operationalization of the Multicultural Counseling Competencies." Support for the contents of that document epitomizes the essence of how modern behavioral counselors respond to diversity issues.

Because behavioral counseling derives from learning theory and focuses on modification of behavior rather than feelings and self-disclosure, it has definite advantages over some of the other therapies in helping clients from diverse ethnic, cultural, lifestyle, and racial backgrounds. Because its conceptual structure is easy to understand and its application is concrete and makes sense to ordinary people in every walk of life, it enjoys wide usage and popularity by counselors with such disparate populations as special groups of children, mental health clients, prisoners, nursing home residents, and other institutionalized clients. The straightforward steps such as setting goals, changing setting events, monitoring performance, and establishing rewards have wide appeal to people who are oriented toward concrete behavioral performance as opposed to abstract symbolizing, or focusing on the personhood of the client.

According to Wilson (1995, pp. 200–204), behavioral approaches offer a broad range of heterogeneous procedures with different theoretical rationales for systematically assessing and treating a wide variety of disorders. The approach's scientific method of changing behaviors and developing problem-solving skills is suited for diverse cultural populations whose members are sometimes offended by catharsis and the open expression of personal feelings and concerns. Eysenck, Eysenck, and Barrett (1995) noted that the behavioral system views and responds to client gender, age, and socioeconomic differences in unique and appropriate ways.

The objective, organized, systematic, contractual nature of the behavioral approach tends to minimize the counselor–client relationship as a factor in the equation. Much of the counseling process is a rational stimulus–response formulation that does not place blame or demand perfectionism. It is easy for anyone to understand because its programmed-by-the-numbers approaches provide immediate feedback and place responsibility on the client for performance. Behavioral counseling works for mentally limited clients because of its behavior modification and management techniques that successively approximate their goals and do not rely heavily on the cognitive domain of that clientele. The approach also works for many parents and students of inner city schools and rural environments where clients are conditioned to operate on short-term contingencies and where concrete, clear, structured formats are desired. In these cases, the client is not dependent on the counselor. Progress is visible and evident because clients can tell when beds are made, cigarette consumption is diminished, pounds are lost, and money is saved. They may have real trouble discerning when they are doing better, thinking straight, or improving their attitudes. Measurable goals and attainments put immediate and short-term reinforcements within the grasp of clients who can neither wait for long-term rewards nor delay gratification.

People of color as well as people from other diverse backgrounds, such as those with language disadvantages, physically disabling conditions, economic and educational disadvantages, and diverse sexual orientations often face social, political, and other environmental influences and problems that require more than one-to-one talk to resolve (Sue, 1992). The behavioral system of counseling offers many alternatives for the counselor of diverse clientele. The counselor can scientifically examine what needs to be done; involve clients in the planning, goal setting, and employing techniques needed to effect behavioral or environmental change; and guide, mentor, and teach clients how to alter both their behaviors and their environments in positive and constructive ways. Counselors can assist and empower clients from lower socioeconomic, disadvantaged, and/or disenfranchised backgrounds to obtain the services they need or attain goals that have been denied them by the dominant culture. Perhaps more important, behavioral counselors can assist clients to become more autonomous and independent by learning ways to get past dependence on artificial or nonsubstantive reinforcers.

Livneh and Sherwood (1991, pp. 534–536) describe how the behavioral approach can provide the practicing counselor with numerous concepts and strategies for helping clients with physical disabilities. The intervention strategies they cite for helping clients with physical disabilities include eliminating maladaptive behaviors and replacing them with positive, constructive, and adaptive behaviors; approximating learning new skills needed to cope with their personal limitations and environmental restrictions; strengthening their self-concept and power of positive thinking through covert conditioning and cognitive restructuring; and establishing effective self-management procedures for more independent living through systematic operant conditioning.

In summary, it is clear that the behavioral approach has much to commend it to counselors of diverse clientele (Livneh & Sherwood, 1991, pp. 534–536; Wilson, 1995, pp. 197–222). Structurally, behavioral counselors draw from the fundamental precepts of classical, instrumental, and operant conditioning as well as from cognitive behavior modification. Counseling strategies run the gamut from simple stimulus-response to cognitive restructuring. Since it is uniformly goal- and behavior-centered, it is personally nonthreatening to clients. That is its greatest asset in dealing with diverse clientele.

Summary

Behavioral counseling is not a single system of helping. It is a family of systems, formulations, and strategies. There are no clear-cut distinctions among behavioral counseling, behavior therapy, behavior modification, operant conditioning, and so forth. Generally, one could say that the main thrust of behavioral counseling has been preventive (keeping healthy clients healthy) and that the main thrust of behavior therapy has been restorative (to make unhealthy clients healthy again). That, however, is an oversimplification.

Behavioral systems of counseling have been evolving since the days of Pavlov and Watson, making the behavioral family broader and more pragmatic each year. In both theory and strategy behavioral counseling encompasses the simple to the complex, the short-term habit and the long-term social problem, tally marks on a card and networks of computers, self-regulated breathing and sophisticated biofeedback systems, the paraprofessional who charts the number of behaviors emitted and the highly educated (and skilled) behavior analyst. Behavioral counseling offers a wide range of strategies for clients with diverse backgrounds and problems. The effectiveness of these strategies depends on many factors including the knowledge, training, and skill of the counselor and the motivation, expectation, and cooperation of the client. Behavioral counseling has progressed from a simplistic, structured, counselor-controlled activity applied to clients toward a collaborative, consultative, facilitative process of participating with clients in their own growth-promoting activity. The strongest thread of behaviorism remains its adherence to a scientific base. The data have become broader and more complex. Strategies have expanded exponentially, bringing trends such as cognitive behavior techniques, self-managed and self-directed procedures, and greater counselor–client collaboration. But the scientific base has remained at the core.

SUGGESTIONS FOR FURTHER READING

Alberto, P. A., & Troutman, A. C. (1982). *Applied behavior analysis for teachers: Influencing student performance.* Columbus, OH: Chas. E. Merrill.

Cormier, S., & Cormier, B. (1998). *Interviewing strategies for helpers: Fundamental skills and cognitive behavioral interventions.* Pacific Grove, CA: Brooks/Cole.

Eysenck, H. J., & Martin, I. (Eds.). (1987). *Theoretical foundations of behavior therapy.* New York: Plenum.

Franks, C. M., Wilson, G. T., Kendall, P., & Brownell, K. D. (1984). *Annual review of behavior therapy: Theory and practice* (Vol. 10). New York: Guilford Press.

Gambrill, E. D. (1977). *Behavior modification: Handbook of assessment, intervention, and evaluation.* San Francisco: Jossey-Bass.

Goldfried, M. R., & Merbaum, M. (Eds.). (1973). *Behavior change through self-control.* New York: Holt, Rinehart & Winston.

Goldstein, A. P., & Foa, E. (Eds.). (1980). *Handbook of behavioral interventions: A clinical guide.* New York: Wiley.

Kazdin, A. E. (1978). *History of behavior modification: Experimental foundations of contemporary research.* Baltimore: University Park Press.

Kazdin, A. E. (1980). *Behavior modification in applied settings* (Rev. ed.). Homewood, IL: Dorsey.

Krumboltz, J. D., & Thoresen, C. E. (Eds.). (1976). *Counseling methods.* New York: Holt, Rinehart & Winston.

Lazarus, A. A. (1977). *In the mind's eye: The power of imagery for personal enrichment.* New York: Guilford Press.

Lazarus, A. A. (1989). *The practice of multimodal therapy.* Baltimore: Johns Hopkins University Press.

Lazarus, A. A. (1995). Multimodal therapy. In R. J. Corsini & D. Wedding (Eds.), *Current psychotherapies* (5th ed., pp. 322–355). Itasca, IL: F. E. Peacock.

Lundin, R. W. (1972). *Theories and systems of psychology.* Lexington, MA: Heath.

O'Leary, K. D., & Wilson, G. T. (1987). *Behavior therapy: Application and outcome* (2nd ed.). Englewood Cliffs, NJ: Prentice-Hall.

Skinner, B. F. (1953). *Science and human behavior.* New York: Macmillan.

Skinner, B. F. (1971). *Beyond freedom and dignity.* New York: Knopf.

Skinner, B. F. (1974). *About behaviorism.* New York: Knopf.

Watson, D. L., & Tharp, R. G. (1989). *Self-directed behavior: Self-modification for personal adjustment* (5th ed.). Pacific Grove, CA: Brooks/Cole.

Williams, R. L., & Long, J. D. (1983). *Toward a self-managed life style* (3rd ed.). Boston: Houghton Mifflin.

Wilson, G. T. (1995). Behavior therapy. In R. J. Corsini & D. Wedding (Eds.), *Current psychotherapies* (5th ed., pp. 197–228). Itasca, IL: F. E. Peacock.

Wolpe, J. (1958). *Psychotherapy by reciprocal inhibition.* Stanford, CA: Stanford University Press.

Wolpe, J. (1981). Behavior therapy versus psychoanalysis. *American Psychologist, 36,* 159–164.

Wolpe, J. (1991). *The practice of behavior therapy* (4th ed.). Elmsford, NY: Pergamon.

REFERENCES

Alberti, R. E., & Emmons, M. L. (1978). *Your perfect right: A guide to assertive behavior* (3rd ed.). San Luis Obispo, CA: Impact.

Alberto, P. A., & Troutman, A. C. (1982). *Applied behavior analysis for teachers: Influencing student performance.* Columbus, OH: Chas. E. Merrill.

Allyon, T. (1965). Intensive treatment of psychotic behavior by stimulus satiation and food reinforcement. In L. Ullmann & L. Krasner (Eds.), *Case studies in behavior modification* (pp. 77–84). New York: Holt, Rinehart & Winston.

Azrin, N. H. (1966). Sequential effects of punishment. In T. Verhave (Ed.), *The experimental analysis of behavior* (pp. 186–189). New York: Appleton-Century-Crofts.

Bandura, A. (1976). Self-reinforcement: Theoretical and methodological considerations. *Behaviorism, 4,* 135–155.

Bandura, A. (1991). Social cognitive theory of self-regulation. [Special issue: Theories of self regulation.] *Organizational Behavior and Human Decision Processes, 50*(2), 248–287.

Bandura, A. (1995). Comments on the crusade against causal efficacy of human thought. [Special issue: Cognition, behavior and causality: A broad exchange of views stemming from the debate on the causal efficacy of human thought.] *Journal of Behavior Therapy and Experimental Psychiatry, 26*(3), 179–190.

Beck, A. T. (1976). *Cognitive therapy and the emotional disorders.* New York: International Universities Press.

Bellack, A. S., & Hersen, M. (1977). *Behavior modification: An introductory textbook.* Baltimore: Williams & Wilkins.

Bouton, M. E. (2000). A learning theory perspective on lapse, relapse, and the maintenance of behavior change. *Health Psychology, 19,* 57–63.

Chambless, D. L., & Goldstein, A. J. (1979). Behavioral psychotherapy. In R. Corsini (Ed.), *Current psychotherapies* (2nd ed., pp. 230–272). Itasca, IL: F. E. Peacock.

Cormier, S., & Cormier, B. (1998). *Interviewing strategies for helpers: Fundamental skills and cognitive behavioral interventions.* Pacific Grove, CA: Brooks/Cole.

Cormier, W. H., & Cormier, L. S. (1979). *Interviewing strategies for helpers: A guide to assessment, treatment and evaluation.* Monterey, CA: Brooks/Cole.

Cormier, W. H., & Cormier, L. S. (1991). *Interviewing strategies for helpers: Fundamental skills and cognitive behavioral interventions* (3rd ed.). Pacific Grove, CA: Brooks/Cole.

de Rivera, J. (2000). Understanding persons who repudiate memories recovered in therapy. *Professional Psychology: Research & Practice, 31,* 378–386.

DeRubeis, R. J., & Crits-Christoph, P. (1998). Empirically supported individual and group psychological treatments for adult mental disorders. *Journal of Consulting and Clinical Psychology, 66,* 37–52.

Dishion, T. J., McCord, J., & Poulin, F. (1999). When interventions harm: Peer groups and problem behavior. *American Psychologist, 54,* 755–764.

Dollard, J., & Miller, N. E. (1950). *Personality and psychotherapy: An analysis in terms of learning, thinking, and culture.* New York: McGraw-Hill.

Ellis, A. (1962). *Reason and emotion in psychotherapy.* Secaucus, NJ: Lyle Stuart.

Ellis, A., & Grieger, R. (Eds.). (1977). *Handbook of rational-emotive therapy* (Vol. 1). New York: Springer.

Eysenck, H. J. (1959). Learning theory and behavior therapy. *Journal of Mental Science, 105,* 61–75.

Eysenck, H. J. (1960). *The structure of human personality.* London: Methuen.

Eysenck, H. J., Eysenck, S. B. G., & Barrett, P. (1995). Personality differences according to gender. *Psychological Reports, 76*(3), 711–716.

Eysenck, H. J., & Martin, I. (Eds.). (1987). *Theoretical foundations of behavior therapy.* New York: Plenum.

Franks, C. M. (1969). *Behavior therapy: Appraisal and status.* New York: McGraw-Hill.

Franks, C. M., & Wilson, G. T. (Eds.). (1973). *Annual review of behavior therapy, theory, and practice.* New York: Brunner/Mazel.

Garfield, S. L. (1981). Psychotherapy: A forty year appraisal. *American Psychologist, 36,* 174–183.

Gauthier, J. G. (1999). Bridging the gap between biological and psychological perspectives in the treatment of anxiety disorders. *Canadian Psychology, 40,* 1–11.

Goldstein, A. P., Heller, K., & Sechrest, L. B. (1966). *Psychotherapy and the psychology of behavior change.* New York: Wiley.

Haaga, D. A. F. (2000). Introduction to the special section on stepped care models in psychotherapy. *Journal of Consulting and Clinical Psychology, 68,* 547–548.

Homme, L. (1970). *How to use contingency contracting in the classroom.* Champaign, IL: Research Press.

Hull, C. L. (1943). *Principles of behavior.* New York: Appleton-Century-Crofts.

Jones, M. C. (1924). A laboratory study of fear: The case of Peter. *Pediatric Seminar, 31,* 308–315.

Kaplan, S. J. (1986). *The private practice of behavioral therapy: A guide for behavioral practitioners.* New York: Plenum.

Kazdin, A. E. (1974). Comparative effects of some variations of covert modeling. *Journal of Behavior Therapy and Experimental Psychiatry, 5,* 225–231.

Kazdin, A. E. (1976). Assessment of imagery during covert modeling of assertive behavior. *Journal of Behavior Therapy and Experimental Psychiatry, 7,* 213–219.

Kazdin, A. E. (1978). *History of behavior modification: Experimental foundations of contemporary research.* Baltimore: University Park Press.

Klesges, R. C., Haddock, C. K., Lando, H., & Talcott, G. W. (1999). Efficacy of forced smoking cessation and an adjunctive behavioral treatment on long-term smoking rates. *Journal of Consulting and Clinical Psychology, 67,* 952–958.

Krumboltz, J. D. (1966). *Revolution in counseling: Implications of behavioral science.* Boston: Houghton Mifflin.

Krumboltz, J. D., & Krumboltz, H. B. (1972). *Changing children's behavior.* Englewood Cliffs, NJ: Prentice-Hall.

Krumboltz, J. D., & Thoresen, C. E. (Eds.). (1969). *Behavioral counseling: Cases and techniques.* New York: Holt, Rinehart & Winston.

Krumboltz, J. D., & Thoresen, C. E. (Eds.). (1976). *Counseling methods.* New York: Holt, Rinehart & Winston.

Kumanyika, S. K., Van Horn, L., Bowen, D., Perri, M. G., Rolls, B. J., Czajkowski, S. M., & Schron, E.

(2000). Maintenance of dietary behavior change. *Health Psychology, 19,* 42–56.

Lazarus, A. A. (1968). Variations in desensitization therapy. *Psychotherapy: Theory, Research and Practice, 5,* 50–52.

Lazarus, A. A. (1977). *In the mind's eye: The power of imagery for personal enrichment.* New York: Guilford Press.

Lazarus, A. A. (1982). *Personal enrichment through imagery.* Workbook (audio tape). New York: BMA Audio Cassettes.

Livneh, H., & Sherwood, A. (1991). Application of personality theories and counseling strategies to clients with physical disabilities. *Journal of Counseling and Development, 69,* 525–538.

Lundin, R. W. (1961). *Personality: An experimental approach.* New York: Macmillan.

Lundin, R. W. (1972). *Theories and systems of psychology.* Lexington, MA: Heath.

Lundin, R. W. (1977). Behaviorism: Operant reinforcement. In R. J. Corsini (Ed.), *Current personality theories* (pp. 177–202). Itasca, IL: F. E. Peacock.

Marcus, B. H., Dubbert, P. M., Forsyth, L. H., McKenzie, T. L., Stone, E. J., Dunn, A. L., & Blair, S. N. (2000). Physical activity behavior change: Issues in adoption and maintenance. *Health Psychology, 19,* 32–41.

McFall, R. M., & Lillesand, D. B. (1971). Behavior rehearsal with modeling and coaching in assertion training. *Journal of Abnormal Psychology, 77,* 313–323.

McLean, P. D., Whittal, M. L., Thordarson, D. S., Taylor, S., Soechting, I., Koch, W. J., Paterson, R., & Anderson, K. W. (2001). Cognitive versus behavior therapy in the group treatment of obsessive-compulsive disorder. *Journal of Consulting & Clinical Psychology, 69,* 205–214.

Meichenbaum, D. (1977). *Cognitive-behavior modification: An integrative approach.* New York: Plenum.

Morrison, R. L., & Bellack, A. S. (Eds.). (1987). *Medical factors and psychological disorders: A handbook for psychologists.* New York: Plenum.

Mowrer, O. H. (1950). *Learning theory and personality dynamics.* New York: Ronald Press.

Mowrer, O. H. (1973). *Learning theory and behavior.* Huntington, NY: Robert Kreiger.

Myers, J. K., & Roberts, B. H. (1959). *Family and class dynamics in mental illness.* New York: Wiley.

Pavlov, I. P. (1960). *Conditioned reflexes.* New York: Dover.

Poling, A. (1986). *A primer of human behavioral pharmacology.* New York: Plenum.

Showers, C. J., & Kevlyn, S. B. (1999). Organization of knowledge about a relationship partner: Implications for liking and loving. *Journal of Personality and Social Psychology, 76,* 958–971.

Skinner, B. F. (1948). *Walden two.* New York: Macmillan.

Skinner, B. F. (1953). *Science and human behavior.* New York: Macmillan.

Skinner, B. F. (1958). Teaching machines. *Science, 128,* 969–977.

Skinner, B. F. (1971). *Beyond freedom and dignity.* New York: Knopf.

Skinner, B. F. (1974). *About behaviorism.* New York: Knopf.

Stampfl, T. G., & Levis, D. J. (1967). Essentials of Implosive therapy: A learning-theory-based psychodynamic behavioral therapy. *Journal of Abnormal Psychology, 72,* 496–503.

Sue, D. W. (1992, Winter). The challenge of multiculturalism: The road less traveled. *American Counselor, 1,* 6–14.

Tarrier, N., Pilgrim, H., Sommerfield, C., Faragher, B., Reynolds, M., Graham, E., & Barrowclough, C. (1999). A randomized trial of cognitive therapy and imaginal exposure in the treatment of chronic posttraumatic stress disorder. *Journal of Consulting and Clinical Psychology, 67,* 13–18.

Thom, A., Sartory, G., & Johren, P. (2000). Comparison between one-session psychological treatment and Benzodiazepine in dental phobia. *Journal of Consulting and Clinical Psychology, 68,* 378–387.

Turner, S. M., Beidel, D. C., & Jacob, R. G. (1994). Social phobia: A comparison of behavior therapy and Atenolol. *Journal of Consulting and Clinical Psychology, 62,* 350–358.

Ullmann, L. P., & Krasner, L. (1965). *Case studies in behavior modification.* New York: Holt, Rinehart & Winston.

Watson, D. L., & Tharp, R. G. (1981). *Self-directed behavior: Self-modification for personal adjustment* (3rd ed.). Monterey, CA: Brooks/Cole.

Watson, D. L., & Tharp, R. G. (1989). *Self-directed behavior: Self-modification for personal adjustment* (5th ed.). Pacific Grove, CA: Brooks/Cole.

Watson, J. B., & Rayner, R. (1920). Conditioned emotional reactions. *Journal of Experimental Psychology, 3,* 1–14.

Williams, R. L., & Long, J. D. (1979). *Toward a self-managed life style* (2nd ed.). Boston: Houghton Mifflin.

Williams, R. L., & Long, J. D. (1983). *Toward a self-managed life style* (3rd ed.). Boston: Houghton Mifflin.

Wilson, G. T. (1995). Behavior therapy. In R. J. Corsini & D. Wedding (Eds.), *Current psychotherapies* (5th ed., pp. 197–228). Itasca, IL: F. E. Peacock.

Wilson, G. T., & Vitousek, K. M. (1999). Self-monitoring in the assessment of eating disorders. *Psychological Assessment, 11,* 480–489.

Wolpe, J. (1954). Reciprocal inhibition as the main basis of psychotherapeutic effects. *Archives of Neuro-logical Psychiatry, 72,* 205–226.

Wolpe, J. (1958). *Psychotherapy by reciprocal inhibition.* Stanford, CA: Stanford University Press.

Wolpe, J. (1961). The systematic desensitization treat-ment of neuroses. *Journal of Nervous and Mental Disease, 132,* 189–203.

Wolpe, J. (1981). Behavior therapy versus psychoanaly-sis. *American Psychologist, 36,* 159–164.

Wolpe, J. (1982). *The practice of behavior therapy* (3rd ed.). New York: Pergamon Press.

Wolpe, J. (1991). *The practice of behavior therapy* (4th ed.). Elmsford, NY: Pergamon Press.

8 Choice Theory/ Reality Therapy

Fundamental Tenets

Since William Glasser's 1965 book *Reality Therapy* was published, the original therapy has undergone considerable refinement, improvement, and transformation. In the 1970s he began to refer to *control theory* as the underlying theory. But since 1996, with his creation of *choice theory*, there have been substantial changes in the way reality therapy is practiced (Glasser, 2000c, 2001). That does not mean, however, that the counseling strategies have totally changed. Glasser's (2000b, 2000c) new reality therapy is still very much the same reality therapy in that it deals almost exclusively with present problems and does not focus on symptoms. Since this chapter is about both choice theory and the new reality therapy, we selected the title, "Choice Theory/Reality Therapy" to depict the currency, importance, influence, and power of Glasser's innovative formulations.

History

Doubts about the traditional psychoanalytic approach led William Glasser, under the tutelage of G. L. Harrington, to start formulating his ideas about reality therapy while completing his psychiatric residency at the University of California, Los Angeles, in 1956. Reality therapy first gained recognition for its positive therapeutic outcomes through Harrington's use of it with chronic psychotics and Glasser's use of it with delinquent adolescent girls (Glasser & Zunin, 1979, p. 309). Glasser's first book, *Mental Health or Mental Illness?* (1961), spelled out the basic tenets and application of reality therapy. The term *reality therapy* was coined in 1964 (Glasser, 1964) and resulted in the formal presentation of the approach in a book of the same name (Glasser, 1965). The book, while refining the theory and practice of the approach, also attempted to refute the basic concepts of conventional therapy and to promote a system of teaching clients how to fulfill their needs in responsible ways without the stigma of mental illness.

Following the publication of *Schools without Failure* (Glasser, 1969), the reality therapy approach received an enormous amount of acceptance in school systems. The recognition and success in schools led to the establishment by Glasser's Institute for Reality Therapy of the Education Training Center (ETC) and the William Glasser LaVerne College Center, both with the purpose of eliminating academic failure in Los Angeles. For several years the Los Angeles–based Institute for Reality published the *Journal of Reality*

Therapy. This journal provided a comprehensive repertoire of training programs for a diversity of human services workers in addition to its strong emphasis on schools. Glasser continued to focus on school improvement as evidenced by his books *Control Theory in the Classroom* (1986) and *The Quality School: Managing Students without Coercion* (1990a, 1990b).

With the publication of *Stations of the Mind* (Glasser, 1981) reality therapy took a new turn. Glasser launched an in-depth examination of personality called Behavior: The Control of Perception Psychology (BCP). The basic premise of this theory is that the brain operates to gain the perception of what is wanted from the environment. To express this idea another way, people control what they perceive, not what actually exists. Building on the theory presented in *Stations of the Mind,* Glasser wrote *Taking Effective Control of Your Life* (1984), published subsequently as *Control Theory: A New Explanation of How We Control Our Lives* (1984). The advent of the publication of *Control Theory* signaled a conceptual expansion of reality therapy that eventually led to the approach's becoming *control theory/ reality therapy,* or *control theory* for short, and the Institute for Reality Therapy being changed to The Institute for Control Theory, Reality Therapy, and Quality Management. *Staying Together* (Glasser, 1996) not only focused the power of control theory on keeping marriages healthy, it also emphasized the overarching axiom for all human endeavors: "The only person we can control is ourself," not others (p. 8).

Control Theory was a self-help work that expanded the basic psychological needs to include survival, love and belonging, power, fun, and freedom (Glasser, 1984, 1986, 1989; Wubbolding, 1997). Yet another conceptual expansion of reality therapy transpired with the advent of Glasser's 1998 book, *Choice Theory: A New Psychology of Personal Freedom,* in which Glasser contended that human beings *choose* essentially *everything* we do, including the behaviors that are commonly referred to as mental illnesses and the miseries we feel. The application of *Choice Theory* principles in clinical work with a variety of client problems was later explained in detail in Glasser's (2000a) book, *Reality Therapy in Action* (later retitled in a paperback edition to *Counseling with Choice Theory: The New Reality Therapy*) and Wubbolding's (2000) book, *Reality Therapy for the 21st Century.* In the foreword to Glasser's (2000a) book (p. xiii), Peter Breggin, M. D., stated that "Dr. Glasser's therapy is based on inescapable truths: Meaningful relationships are central to the good life, the choices we make will determine their quality, and we can create them only if we take responsibility for ourselves without controlling other people." That brief sentence constitutes the current central core of choice theory/reality therapy.

After many years of clinical practice and refinement of his therapeutic and theoretical formulations, Glasser (2000a, p. 2) stated that his 1965 book, *Reality Therapy,* lacked a clear theoretical base and that the advent of his 1998 book, *Choice Theory,* fulfilled that void. With the publication of the 2000 book, *Reality Therapy in Action,* Glasser (2000a) demonstrated a pattern of continually refining, improving, and keeping current the system of therapy that has steadily gained in popularity since its inception. It is noted that, for purposes of variety, Glasser uses the terms *counseling, therapy,* and *psychotherapy* interchangeably because he believes they are different ways of describing the same process or activity (Glasser, 2000a, p. 2, 2000b, p. 7, 2001). We do that in this chapter also.

Concomitant with the metamorphosis of reality therapy into CT/RT, the former Institute for Reality Therapy was transformed into The William Glasser Institute in Los Angeles, with Glasser serving as its president. The Institute serves the public through its membership and it benefits members in many ways. It conducts various and extensive training and practica formats; disseminates information about CT/RT; publishes books and materials; makes available audiotapes, videotapes, and other media; encourages research; publishes the *International Journal of Reality Therapy;* and provides certification of educational experiences for reality therapists worldwide. The Institute also provides a voice for its members through regional representatives and international liaisons.

Overview of Choice Theory

Primacy of Relationships. Choice theory holds that if people are not sick, poverty stricken, or suffering the ravages of old age, the main problems they struggle with— namely violence, crime, child abuse, spousal abuse, alcohol and drug addiction, the proliferation of premature and unloving sex, and emotional distress—are a result of unsatisfying or unfulfilled relationships (Glasser, 1998, p. ix, 2000b, 2001). The first and foremost single factor in effective counseling and psychotherapy is that therapists connect with the inner quality worlds of their clients in ways that establish meaningful and trusting relationships with these clients (Glasser, 1998, 2000a, 2000b, 2000c, 2001; Wubbolding 1997, 2001).

Expanded View of Needs. In the formulation of both control theory (Glasser, 1984) and choice theory, Glasser (2000a, p. 226) expanded the two fundamental needs of love and worth (Glasser, 1965) to five basic needs of survival, love and belonging, power, freedom, and fun. According to Glasser (1998, 2001), Glasser and Glasser (1999), and Wubbolding (1997, 2000), everyone has these five needs which are equated with drives. Both Glasser (1998, 2000a, 2001) and Wubbolding (1997, 2000) explain that everything we do is an attempt to fulfill these five basic human needs. *Survival* includes the need for life, sex, procreation, and the struggle to preserve the human species. *Love and belonging* incorporate not only our need for nonsexual love but also for loving sex, caring relationships, self-worth, and some proof that we are valued or prized by others. *Power* for the sake of power is probably unique to the human species. People need power in order to succeed in life. They may come to exercise too much power over others to the detriment of everyone. But our personal empowerment enables us to contribute to society and lead happy, creative, and productive lives. *Freedom* usually concerns us most when others threaten to take it away. Glasser (1998, p. 40) states that the more we are able to freely satisfy our needs in responsible ways that do not infringe upon the ability of others to fulfill their needs, the more we are able to use our creativity not only for our own benefit but also for the benefit of others. The principles manifest in the golden rule are examples of what Glasser views as the essence of freedom. Glasser (1998, p. 41, 2001) likens *fun* to the genetic reward for learning. The need for fun is seen as genetically encoded into human beings. Play, laughter, creativity, the joy of discovery, and the experiencing of novelty seem to be rewarding to people. The need for fun is stronger in some individuals than in others, but we all have the need for it. Laughter, humor, and learning are fundamental to all successful long-term relationships. Glasser says that fun is the easiest need to satisfy because there are so many things we can do to have fun, and rarely does anyone stand in our way.

Role of Choice in Human Existence.   Choice theory informs us that people are infinitely more in control of their lives than they realize. Common sense has long held that how we feel and what we do are dictated by people and events outside ourselves. But choice theory refutes that notion and explains that people choose almost everything they do, think, and feel, including misery they feel (Glasser, 1998, pp. 3–7, 2000a, pp. 225–230, 2000c, 2001; Wubbolding, 2001). Contrary to what many people believe, other people cannot make us feel guilty, happy, miserable, anxious, or angry. We choose these feelings for ourselves. We choose all our actions and thoughts and, indirectly, practically all of our emotions and much of our physiology (Glasser, 1998, pp. 3–4; 2000a, pp. 225–226).

Choice Theory as a New Psychology.   The advent of choice theory ushers in a psychology that is radically different from what Glasser (2000a, 2000c, 2001) calls *external control psychology*. External control psychology operates on the premise of many of the world's prevalent beliefs in and uses of external controlling strategies such as criticizing, labeling, discriminating, punishing, rewarding, judging, failing, blaming, disapproving, correcting, forcing, nagging, coercing, pressuring, compelling, manipulating, bossing, badgering, rating, withdrawing, complaining, and denying. Choice theory teaches that we must replace the old, external control psychology mechanisms with behaviors and strategies that promote, strengthen, and sustain relationships. Glasser (1998, pp. 3–24, 2001) maintains that we must replace these destructive and debilitative behaviors by choosing to care, listen, support, negotiate, encourage, love, befriend, trust, accept, welcome, and esteem, because the old external control mechanisms are more attuned to destroying relationships than nurturing and preserving them.

The Quality World as a Unique Window into Individual Differences.   From birth we human beings begin to create in our memories, and we recreate throughout our lives, a small group of pictures that portray within our inner beings the best ways we know to satisfy our needs. According to Glasser (1998, pp. 44–61, 2001) these inner mental pictures represent our quality world and they fall into three categories: "(1) the *people* we most want to be with, (2) the *things* we most prize or want to own or experience, and (3) the *ideas or systems of belief* that govern much of our behavior." Whenever we feel good, we are choosing to behave in ways that cause someone, something, or some belief in the real world to match a picture of that person, thing, or belief in our quality world. Choice theory teaches that every individual has his or her own unique quality world. This quality world is at the core of our lives. The choice theory concept of quality world is similar to the idea of worldview that is contained in some systems of counseling and psychotherapy. The difference, however, is important. *Worldview* usually denotes an acquired general view of the world and life events that are held in common by different groups of people. Glasser (1998, pp. 44–61, 2001) views the *quality world* as an inherent attribute created in and by each person starting at birth. The quality world is unique, powerful, and individually defines our ability to fulfill our basic needs, to make choices, and to engage in relationships. Indeed, our individualized quality worlds are similar to unique psychological DNAs.

It follows then that if therapists are to understand any client they must first listen, interact, and relate to the person in ways that help them fully grasp the client's quality world. Only then can effective therapy begin to take place. Glasser (1998, p. 53, 2001) states that it is especially difficult for powerful people (external control individuals) to be tolerant of the quality worlds of less powerful people. Regardless of how much we threaten, punish, or coerce people to change the pictures that they have created in their quality worlds, we cannot make them change their internal pictures. Only they can alter or change the internal pictures imbedded in their quality worlds. Our quality worlds are defining internal assets that we have uniquely created and own. And nobody can change or take them away (Glasser, 1998, p. 55).

Total Behavior.   *Total behavior* means that all behavior is chosen and is composed of four inseparable components: acting, thinking, feeling, and physiology. (It is noted that choice theory and reality therapy, in contrast to some other systems of therapy, classify feeling as a part of total behavior.) Glasser's (2000a, p. 226, 2001) explanation of total behavior is that people can only directly choose their actions and thoughts. However, they have indirect control over most of their feelings and some of their physiology. Their chosen actions and thoughts are inseparable from the feelings and physiology that go with them. One fundamental goal of clients who feel badly and present themselves for reality therapy is to choose more need-satisfying actions and thoughts as two of the four components of more effective and appropriate total behavior.

Theory of Personality

A fundamental philosophical tenet of choice theory is that people are ultimately self-determining. Internal and external psychosocial pressures may relate directly to present emotional functioning of clients, but in the long run clients are autonomous, selective, responsible people who can control their own behaviors, thinking, and destinies.

Need Fulfillment.   Because choice theory teaches that the development of human personality is an attempt to fulfill our five basic innate needs of love and belonging, power, freedom, physical survival, and fun from birth onward, we generate choices and behaviors. As we continually experiment throughout our lives to satisfy these needs, we discover that some choices satisfy our needs, whereas other choices threaten our needs. As our experimental quests influence the external environment, we discover that other people, events, objects, and situations are either need-satisfying, need-threatening, or neutral (Glasser & Wubbolding, 1995, pp. 299–300). The strength of each of the five basic needs (or drives) that we previously described are believed to be, in part, written into our genes at birth (Glasser, 1998, pp. 91–92, 2001). Each person is born with varying needs strength. For instance, one person may possess an innately high need for power and a low need for love and belonging, whereas another person may possess a low need for power and a very high need for love and belonging. In essence, each person is born with his or her own individual needs strength profile.

Normalcy.   Very few individuals have needs strength profiles that propel them into pathologies such as sociopathic behavior. The vast majority of people have genes whose needs strength lie well within three standard deviations of the norm. That is a wide range, indeed, but it is still considered statistically normal. Most individuals have the capacity to generate quality worlds that function satisfactorily in society and are strong enough to create for themselves an effective life with good relationships. But human functioning is limited by factors such as age, sex, size, looks, physical health, disposition, and talent. We are also somewhat limited by the circumstances and location of our birth. But considering these real world limits, people have far more choices than most of them conceive of using. People are much more constrained by external control psychology than by their genes (Glasser, 1998, p. 113).

Personality Development

Role of Innate Needs.   The differences between and among individual personalities are striking. From birth onward, CT/RT views different people's brain systems as mechanisms that seek to manipulate the external world. Glasser explains the development of human personality as an attempt to fulfill the five basic needs of survival, love and belonging, power, freedom, and fun (Glasser, 2001; Glasser & Wubbolding, 1995, pp. 299–300). Some personalities, even among siblings in the same family, appear to be diametrically opposite to each other. Some are outgoing, gregarious, optimistic, liberal, compliant, and fun loving whereas others are introverted, sober, quiet, conservative, pessimistic, controlling, and gloomy (Glasser, 1998, p. 92). The variations are endless because our personalities are created out of our genetic needs-strength profile, which is unique for every person.

Throughout our lives we humans generate behaviors and refine our quality worlds, and through experimentation, we find them to be either need-satisfying or need-threatening. As these behaviors and quality worlds influence the external world we discover that other people, events, objects, and situations can be need-satisfying, need-threatening, or neutral (Glasser & Wubbolding, 1995, pp. 299–300). The ways that we find to fulfill our needs tend to shape the context of our interactions and therefore have an enormous effect on our development of relationships with others.

Role of Choice and Discovery.   Choice theory teaches that we choose virtually all of our behaviors and that in the process of choosing we discover whether our choices produce desirable or undesirable results. We therefore discover whether our behaviors were effective or ineffective in attaining need satisfaction (Glasser, 2001). We also discover whether specific components of the external world are pleasurable (need satisfying), painful (not need satisfying), or neutral. When we are infants, we choose the only behaviors available to us—survival options such as the satisfaction of hunger, obtaining safety, and comfort. As we grow and develop physically we discover that other behaviors—commensurate to our age, maturity, and stage of development—are available to satisfy our needs (Glasser & Wubbolding, 1995, p. 300).

Role of Identity Development.   Choice theory identifies two general types of human personality: (1) people who view themselves from their own internal frames of reference and quality world, and (2) people who perceive of themselves as others see them (Glasser, 1972, 1998; Glasser & Wubbolding, 1995). As we seek to accomplish our various developmental tasks and fulfill our five basic needs, we may either succeed or fail. As a result, we develop either a *success identity* or a *failure identity.* The latter is described by Glasser and Wubbolding (1995, p. 300) as ineffective and out-of-control behavior.

Success Identity.   Success identity is characterized (Glasser, 1972; Glasser and Wubbolding, 1995; Wubbolding, 1988) as our development of health and success as evidenced through our coming to possess a willingness as well as a repertoire of skills for attaining our basic needs of survival, love and belonging, power, freedom, and fun in positive and constructive ways. Wubbolding's (1988) model of success identity describes the positive stages we may experience as we learn to be successful and positive. If we are fortunate enough to attain a full measure of positive addiction, we might view ourselves at *stage one* through fulfilling our needs in responsible ways without infringing on the rights of others. At *stage two* we cope with life through positive and constructive symptoms such as (1) altruistic activities; (2) effective thinking; (3) positive affect such as self-confidence, enthusiasm, and trust; and (4) effective behaviors, such as choosing a healthy diet and exercise. We reach *stage three,* the optimal stage of success identity, when we become positively addicted to life-enhancing choices and activities that are so valuable, positive, and constructive that our lives and the lives of those around us are enhanced, and if we ceased doing the positively addictive activities we would feel pain and discomfort. Glasser (1976) proposes that two examples of positively addictive behaviors are meditation and noncompetitive exercise. Examples of *pure positive addiction* identified by Glasser and Wubbolding (1995, p. 301) include such activities as travel, reading, walking, and other habitual enjoyment-related behaviors.

Failure Identity.   Failure identity is synonymous with pathology or failure to attain one's needs in responsible ways. If we develop a failure identity we might seek to fulfill our needs through negative and destructive behaviors and make choices that infringe on the rights of others and, inadvertently, keep us from getting what we really want in life. The three stages of failure identity development proposed by Glasser and Wubbolding (1995, p. 300) are the following:

- *Stage one, giving up.* We give up when we perceive that we cannot attain our needs or that something external keeps us from doing so.
- *Stage two, choosing negative symptoms.* As a result of having given up we may choose antisocial activities, negative thinking, debilitative feelings, and negative physiological conditions such as psychosomatic disorders. While we are engaging in these negative choices, we believe that we are doing the best we can to fulfill our needs at the moment and that we are either constrained by the environment or are not competent to make more effective choices.
- *Stage three, negative addictions.* When we regress to the point that we believe that our negative symptoms, behaviors, and choices are need-satisfying, then we have developed negative addictions. We then have the delusion that the negative, destructive, and needs-aversive activities are really positive and that such activities provide for our immediate belonging, power, fun, and freedom.

Glasser and Wubbolding (1995, pp. 300–301) list several negatively addictive identifiers such as alcohol, drugs, gambling, food, and addiction to work. If we develop a failure identity we might have a distorted and momentary sense of popularity, power, excitement, enthusiasm, or liberation from stress and pain. Such distortions rob us of the ability to fulfill our needs in responsible ways.

Nature of Maladjustment

Glasser rarely speaks of maladjustment and he does not believe in mental illness. He is more likely to use terms such as *unhappiness, lack of satisfactory relationships,* or *ineffective and unsatisfying choices.* According to Glasser (2000b, pp. 1–2), CT/RT's theory of how the human brain functions directly challenges the traditional view of mental illness. His theory holds that when we are unable to figure out how to satisfy one or more of the five genetic basic needs that are the source of all human motivation, we sometimes behave in ways that are commonly labeled as mental illness. These behaviors that we choose are ineffective and unsatisfying and lead to unhappiness. We not only choose all our unhappy behaviors, but also every behavior we choose is composed of four components (acting, thinking, feeling, and physiology), one of which is how we feel as we behave. When we choose a behavior that fails to fulfill our needs, we feel badly. But our choice to be unhappy is not mental illness (Glasser, 2001).

Choice theory teaches that people's brain structures are neither psychologically nor chemically so abnormal that they cannot choose happiness. Many people who were previously unhappy (diagnosed as mentally ill) found ways, either on their own or through counseling, to fulfill their needs and become happy again (Glasser, 2000b, p. 2, 2001). Further, Glasser (2000b) states

> It is not a sick brain that is the cause of their unhappiness; it is their present inability to figure out more effective behaviors than the ones they are using. While the brain chemistry of a happy person differs from the brain chemistry of an unhappy person, that difference is not the cause of their unhappiness. It is the result of the choice or choices they are making. And it is no more permanent than the chemistry of any choice. The brain chemistry returns to normal as soon as the "sufferer" has figured out, with or without help, how to satisfy his or her needs more effectively (p. 2).

Many people choose anxious, fearful, depressive, obsessive, crazy, hostile, addictive, and withdrawn behaviors. They are all very unhappy. But many mental health professionals who believe in mental illness don't believe that these unhappy individuals are capable of helping themselves or benefiting from therapy. They may turn to the *DSM-IV* (American Psychiatric Association, 1994) labels and adjudicate their clients as suffering from some kind of brain pathology that requires drug therapy. They may not even consider that time-consuming counseling or psychotherapy might help. Brain drugs, as Glasser calls them, may help some individuals to feel better as long as they take them. But being on prescription drugs for years is not unusual. Few people on brain drugs judge themselves to be happy. Only improved choices and more effective behaviors can solve such unhappiness (Glasser, 2000b, p. 2, 2001).

In its most rudimentary form, Glasser (1998, p. 136; 2001) views maladjustment as the destructive creativity most often seen when we want good relationships and are not able to obtain them. The maladjusted personality is equated with what Glasser (1972, pp. 72–101; Glasser & Wubbolding, 1995, pp. 299–303) calls a *failure identity*. Persons who develop failure identities tend to be lonely, critical of themselves, and irrational. Their behaviors are likely to be rigid and ineffective. They often exhibit weakness, irresponsibility, and lack of confidence. Failure-identity persons may be prone to giving up, exhibiting maladaptive symptoms, or even negative addiction. They may expend their energies attempting to reduce their pain by giving up, denying failure, or even finding pleasure in failure.

Choice theory holds that maladjustment generally begins during the very early years of life when the individual cannot or does not learn to fulfill a substantive amount of his or her five basic needs, most importantly the need to experience love and self-worth. The inability to acquire or maintain self-worth comes from the absence of the experience of success or doing something worthwhile. The absence of love and a feeling of worthlessness cause disinvolvement and lead to a failure identity (Glasser, 1972, pp. 72–101).

In choice theory all behavior, including maladjusted behavior, is an attempt to control perceptions. However, maladjusted behavior results in losing *effective* control over our perceptions, and consequently our lives (Glasser, 1981, p. 44). Glasser states that people choose their misery—such as depression, anxiety, or guilt—to keep anger under control, to get other people to help them, to gain control over others, and to excuse their unwillingness to do something more effective (1981, pp. 56–62). Glasser says that rather than being in a state of depression, anxiety, or guilt, people engage in "depressing, anxietying, or guilting." He uses the *-ing* form of the word to designate feeling behaviors and to show that people are doing something to choose their misery. A few other examples of feeling behaviors are paining, headaching, migraining, psychosing, and obsessing.

These feeling behaviors are the result of an attempt to maintain control of our lives (Glasser, 1981, pp. 154–155). Although these behaviors provide some control, they are not effective in the long run. Furthermore, the person is just as responsible for this crazy behavior, such as compulsive handwashing, as he or she is for a more reasonable and effective way to gain control (Glasser, 1981, p. 98).

Basic Concepts

Axioms that Drive Personal Freedom.   Choice theory is really about personal freedom. Glasser persistently contends that people can enjoy much more personal freedom if we are willing to replace external control psychology with choice theory in our lives. It is through what he calls *ten axioms of choice theory* that personal freedom can be defined, redefined, and encouraged (Glasser, 1998, pp. 332–336). Understanding these axioms is vital for both therapists and clients who are in quest of replacing external control psychology with choice theory.

Axiom 1. The only person whose behavior we can control is our own. No one can make us do anything we don't want to do. When we are threatened with punishment or any kind of coercion, we rarely do well. When we actually begin to realize that we can control only our own behavior, we immediately start to redefine our personal freedom and find, in many instances, that we have much more freedom than we realize.

Axiom 2. All we can get from other people is information. How we deal with that information is our choice or their choice.

Axiom 3. All long-lasting psychological problems are relationship problems. A partial cause of many other problems, such as pain, fatigue, weakness, and some chronic diseases—commonly called autoimmune diseases—is relationship problems.

Axiom 4. The problem relationship is always part of our present lives.

Axiom 5. What happened in the past that was painful has a great deal to do with what we are today, but revisiting this painful past can contribute little or nothing to what we need to do now—improve an important relationship.

Axiom 6. We are driven by genetic needs: survival, love and belonging, power, freedom, and fun.

Axiom 7. We can satisfy these needs only by satisfying a picture or pictures in our quality worlds.

Axion 8. All we can do, from birth to death, is behave. All behavior is total behavior and is made up of four inseparable components: acting, thinking, feeling, and physiology.

Axiom 9. All total behavior is designated by verbs, usually infinitives and gerunds, and named by the component that is most recognizable. For example, I am choosing to depress or I am depressing, instead of I am suffering from depression or I am depressed.

Axiom 10. All total behavior is chosen, but we have direct control over only the acting and thinking components. We can, however, control our feelings and physiology indirectly through how we choose to act or think.

Premises that Drive External Control Psychology.   When we try to externally control people they uniformly resist (Glasser, 2001). There are three premises inherent in external control psychology that invariably cause resistance that damages the forming or sustaining of healthy relationships. These premises, stated in simplified form, are:

1. The attempt to control other people through the "I'm going to try to get you to do what I want you to do" tactic
2. The overwhelming evidence that external control harms and kills relationships
3. The belief in the idea that "I know what's right for other people"

Glasser (2001) contends that the whole *DSM-IV,* which is growing by leaps and bounds, is an example of a document that describes the behaviors that people choose to use in their unsuccessful attempts to resist external control. The above premises are the direct antithesis of the truism in choice theory's principle that "the only person I can control is myself." Glasser asserts that as long as we continue to use external control psychology we will destroy relationships and do great harm to ourselves and other people.

Qualities of the Effective Reality Therapist

Though the bulk of the training and certification of reality therapists is focused on knowledge and skill building, the personal and professional qualities of therapists are factors that clearly affect their competency. Wubbolding and Brickell (1998) reviewed several qualities or characteristics that contribute to the effectiveness of reality therapists as well as to other professionals in the health and human services arena.

Personal Qualities

1. *Manifesting empathy, congruence, and positive regard.* Reality therapists subscribe to, endorse, and aspire to practice the Rogerian attributes that enhance the conditions for client growth. Such practice enables the therapist to focus on the client's needs from the client's point of view.

2. *Possession of energy.* Having an abundance of strength, stamina, enthusiasm, and vigor empowers the reality therapist to go the extra mile with clients, to stay focused, and to never give up.

3. *Ability to view everything as an advantage.* A talent for perceiving something positive in almost every situation enables the therapist to model optimism to clients and to help them discern that choosing can lead to positive and constructive action.

4. *Having a positive but not naïve view of human nature.* Reality therapists can be of optimum help to their clients whenever they, themselves, are in touch with the wide range of opportunities as well as the dangers, drawbacks, and pitfalls of the real world (Wubbolding & Brickell, 1998, pp. 47–48).

Professional Characteristics

1. *Having a sense of paradox and the ability to reframe.* Paradoxing, thereby enabling clients to view, accept, and cope with life's contradictions and inconsistencies, and helping them to redefine problems to opportunities are skills that are enormously valuable for reality therapists.

2. *The ability to communicate hope.* The retention of hope for the future, regardless of how dire the circumstances may appear to the client, is an important quality for therapists to impart.

3. *Being skillful in defining problems in solvable terms.* Helping clients to consider problems and alternative solutions in specific, measurable, doable behaviors goes a long way toward assisting them to become decision, action, and success oriented.

4. *Using competency in the use of metaphors.* Expanding metaphoric statements and meanings to encompass greater significance than was originally intended can be instructive to clients who are seeking to clarify their problems. For example, the client statement "I'm out on a limb with this situation" might be rephrased to "What does it look like out on that limb?" "What would being off that limb be like for you?" "What can you do today to begin to get yourself safely off that limb?"

5. *Willingness to work within the boundaries of professional guidelines, standards, and ethics.* People who work as therapists, human services workers, or in other helping roles need to acquire the necessary credentials and competencies to be accepted by their clients, the public, their colleagues, and their professions. It is also incumbent upon them to know how to deal with crises, avoid dual relationships, work within their limitations, practice the limits of confidentiality, recognize conflicts of interests, provide informed consent regarding referral to other client systems, disclose openly their professional credentials, and to accurately and ethically represent the services of other professionals.

6. *Demonstrate cultural sensitivity.* In an increasingly pluralistic world, effective therapists must appreciate their own culture and recognize that what is appropriate in one cultural setting or in another part of the world may not be acceptable in the present setting. In terms of a multicultural worldwide society, the ability to adapt the principles of therapy to cultures other than that in which they originate requires study, flexibility, consultation, and a willingness to adjust one's beliefs and ideas to encompass a broad worldview (Wubbolding & Brickell, 1998, pp. 48–49; Wubbolding, Al-Rashadi, et al., 1998).

In Quest of Competency Assurance.   The personal qualities and professional characteristics previously described must be carefully considered by persons endeavoring to enter CT/RT or related professional human services work. It is absolutely necessary that these qualities be taught, learned, modeled, and practiced by trainers, educators, and trainees. The importance of self-awareness, knowledge, and experience in achieving multicultural awareness and adapting personal beliefs and behaviors in the application of CT/RT is an imperative in today's world (Wubbolding, Al-Rashadi, et al., 1998). Agencies and boards that certify and license workers have a responsibility to ensure that individuals who work with clients are fully qualified and competent to function in their declared areas of service. Excellence in education, training, experience, and supervision accompanied by the personal qualities and professional characteristics described above are all necessary for ensuring that therapists and related human services workers are qualified to counsel clients in the diverse, pluralistic society in which we live.

The Counseling Process

Choice theory/reality therapy is a unique system of counseling that has cognitive-behavioral aspects (containing thinking and acting components of behavior) composed of two interrelated parts: (1) the counseling environment, and (2) procedures for change. Previously, these two parts were known as the eight steps of reality therapy. These steps have been incorporated into the two parts of the counseling process so students of CT/RT can conceptualize choice theory as a process rather than a series of lock steps. In this process of counseling, the overall therapeutic objective is to help the client feel better. This is accomplished when the client is able to meet needs by learning to make choices that ensure effective control of his or her life (Glasser, 1998, 2000a, 2000b, 2001; Wubbolding, 1988, 1990, 1991a, 1991b, 1992, 1997, 2000, 2001). In choice theory work, Glasser uses the words *counselor* and *therapist* interchangeably. We also interchange the terms.

The Counseling Environment

The Therapeutic Alliance.   Choice theory teaches that the counselor–client relationship is the first priority. The counseling environment can be characterized by authenticity, warmth, empathic listening, caring, acceptance, and involvement—a mutual alliance. Trust and rapport are established by listening to the client's story. This signals to the client that the counselor believes in their personal worth, competence, ability to make appropriate choices, succeed, and behave responsibly. In this supportive environment, the counselor focuses on present acting and behaving, and redirects talking about the past except when a connection can be easily related to present concerns. It is necessary for the client to become aware of his or her acting and thinking because these are the two components (the other two being feeling and physiology) of the person's total behavior, which he or she can directly control (Glasser, 1998, p. 72, 2000a, p. 65; Wubbolding, 1988, pp. 10–21). In keeping with the present-oriented counseling focus, the counselor helps the client become aware that feelings and physiology may be related to current actions and thoughts. Therefore, if the client talks about feelings as separate from action and thought, the counselor will direct the client to examine what he or she is doing and thinking to maintain such feelings (Glasser, 1998, pp. 62–88, 2000a, pp. 65–66; Wubbolding, 1997).

Client Responsibility.   Other important characteristics of the counseling environment concern the counselor's attitude about client choice, responsibility, consequences of behavior, and demonstrating support. The counselor accepts no excuses for irresponsible choices or behavior because ultimately the responsibility is the client's. In addition, there is no punishment or criticism for bad choices or irresponsible behavior. Allowing natural consequences of choices to impact the client is a strong enough message. Instead of punishment, criticism, or negative comments, Glasser's (1998, p. 212) choice theory recommends that counselors, parents, teachers, or other helpers respond with a message such as *"I want you to learn from your mistakes. My job, if either of us is dissatisfied with what you chose to do, is to get together and help you figure out a better way."* Finally, the counselor imparts his or her belief in the client's ability to take effective control of his or her life by never giving up. These choice theory attitudes build trust and confirm to the client that the counselor genuinely cares (Glasser, 1998, p. 211).

Procedures for Change

The procedures that lead to change continue to convey the supportive atmosphere of the counseling environment and are construed as integral parts of that environment. These procedures include (1) exploring needs and perceptions, (2) exploring and evaluating total behavior, and (3) planning and commitment (Wubbolding, 1997).

Exploring Needs and Perceptions.   The focus of this procedure is to help the client become aware of what he or she wants (Wubbolding, 1997). These wants can be as specific as obtaining material possessions or as broad as projecting a lifestyle. For most people not all needs are equal—they compete with each other—and their fulfillment involves negotiation because they often conflict (Glasser, 1984, pp. 16–18). Because of these factors, exploring needs and perceptions is critical in helping the client sort out values and determine priorities as depicted in the brief dialogue segment below.

TH: You say your wife complains because you don't spend much time with your family. How do you spend your time?

CL: Well, I work long hours so I can get ahead in the company and provide more for my family. I stop off after work a few nights a week with my supervisor for happy hour, and my family has finished eating when I get home. This makes my wife mad. On weekends I like to have some time to myself to fish, hunt, and play golf. I do try to attend church with them when I don't have too much yard work.

TH: Well, tell me this. How much of a priority is your family?

CL: You may not believe this, but I've always thought they were number one. I've worked hard to give them things I didn't have. At times, I've thought my wife should be happy I'm such a good provider. On the other hand, she did say something that kind of got to me . . . that I was missing out on my kids growing up and that they wondered why I worked so much.

TH: Well, what do you think is the most important? Your work, your family, your leisure?

CL: I think it's a toss-up between family and work. I get a lot of satisfaction and recognition at work. On the other hand, my family is important because they're the closest people I have, and I don't think I could get along without them. The hobbies aren't as important, but I do need time to relax.

TH: So let's talk about what you are willing to do to have more time for your family.

Exploring and Evaluating Total Behavior. Glasser and Wubbolding (1995, p. 305) describe client self-evaluation as the core of the reality therapy process. It is essential that clients evaluate their own behavior and make a value judgment about whether what they are doing is fulfilling their needs. The therapist is active and objective in helping the client openly evaluate the behavior. The client is the one who must judge the rightness or wrongness of the choice or behavior. The therapist is neither judge nor moral guide.

Exploring the client's behavior can usually be facilitated by asking "What are you doing?," "What do you do?," or "What did you do?" questions (Glasser & Wubbolding, 1995, pp. 304–309; Wubbolding, 1988, pp. 28–38). Examples include "What did you do when your mother grounded you?," "What are you doing to contribute to the stressful situation?," "What do you do when you are depressing?," or "What can you do right now to begin to alleviate the stressful situation?" These questions and others like them can be asked until the client has provided specific information about his or her total behavior. Behaviors can then be examined and evaluated by the client for their potential to fulfill his or her stated needs. Further questions are asked to help the client evaluate his or her total behavior: "Are your actions helping or hurting you?," "Is what you are now doing getting you what you want?," "Does the way you talk to your mother help you to relate to her the way you said you want to?," "Does what you are doing now violate the rules or is it illegal?," "Does it help or hurt you to respond that way to your teacher?," or "Is what you are doing acceptable behavior?"

Clients who have been habitually exhibiting behavior that is self-defeating do not always recognize what they are doing. They may strongly deny their problem behavior and erect valid-sounding excuses for continuing to engage in it. An example is a client (a teacher) who continues to teach even though he or she clearly has a medical need for hospitalization and medical treatment. The teacher might make excuses such as "my students need me," to the detriment of his or her own immediate health and to the ultimate detriment of the students. It may be difficult for the client to make the value judgment that what he or she is doing is really not good for them or their students. But such a value judgment is critical. It is not up to the therapist to say "Look, what you're doing is killing you and hurting your students." If the client has difficulty evaluating the behavior objectively, the therapist can intervene with genuine, caring, but confrontational responses.

TH: How is what you're doing going to help you and the students? Can you tell me how putting off the operation that you badly need is helping you to get what you want?

CL: That's true. It's really not good for me to put off the operation.

TH: Then putting off the operation at this time is *wrong* for you; it won't get you what you want.

CL: That's right. I'm worried about what will happen to the students while I'm gone. But when I think about it, I know they will be taken care of—they'll be okay. And I'm scared for me too. But I know, too, that putting off surgery may really injure my health even more.

TH: So, you have almost concluded that going ahead with the operation is the best course of action for you right now.

CL: Yes. There's no really sensible reason to put it off.

Here the therapist is forceful and facilitative by actively pursuing the client's own evaluation (Glasser & Wubbolding, 1995, pp. 304–309; Glasser & Zunin, 1979, p. 319).

To summarize, choice theory teaches that clients must judge their own behavior, identify what they are doing to contribute to the difficulty or problem, and decide what they must do to begin to choose and behave in more responsible and positive ways (Glasser & Wubbolding, 1995, p. 305).

Planning and Commitment.   Once the client has decided that his or her behavior is not fulfilling needs and that he or she is willing to behave in more responsible ways, the therapist helps him or her develop a realistic plan. The plan should be a positive, constructive plan of action—need fulfilling, simple, realistic, attainable something to do (not stop doing), something dependent on the client, something specific, and something the client does or can do every day (Wubbolding, 1988, pp. 58–72). Client ownership of and commitment to the plan is vital. No matter how much the therapist wants the client to buy into a plan, the success of the plan must rest with the client. The action the client commits to doing should be of manageable size and complexity to ensure a high probability of success. If the client proposes to develop a plan that obviously has little chance for success, the therapist points that out and tries to help the client make a more realistic plan (Glasser & Wubbolding, 1995, p. 306). As an example, an overweight client who is enthusiastically anticipating a weight loss may want to lose too many pounds too fast.

CL: I'm so excited about this idea of losing weight. I figured it out last night. If I go on a 600-calorie diet, jog two miles a day, and go to aerobics class three times a week, I can lose five pounds a week. In three months that would be sixty pounds.

TH: I can see you're really enthusiastic about doing something about your weight. I've learned from experience with weight-loss programs that motivation is important, and you certainly have that. What I'd like you to consider is a more moderate approach.

CL: You don't think I should lose the weight so fast.

TH: That's right. My experience says that people like you are more likely to stick to diet and exercise programs that are much less stressful than what you are thinking about.

CL: Well, maybe you're right. I sometimes have the tendency to jump into things full force and later burn out quickly.

A formal commitment enhances the client's motivation to successfully carry out the plan (Glasser, 1972, pp. 125–126). Commitment to the plan binds the client both to the plan and to personal involvement with the person helping him or her. Commitment encourages and reinforces the client to take positive and constructive action. Such commitment stimulates the client to think and do the things that the inertia of ordinary living would usually cause one to ignore (Glasser & Wubbolding, 1995, pp. 306–309). The commitment is to the self, to the agreement, and to the helper (the therapist or counselor). An example of a verbal commitment follows.

TH: When do you plan to get the operation?

CL: I don't know. I'll have to see my doctor about it.

TH: When can you see your doctor about it?

CL: Oh, I could call him tomorrow to set up an appointment to talk about it. He'll want to see me in his office to examine me before setting a time to go into the hospital.

TH: What time can you call him tomorrow?

CL: Oh, I guess in the morning.

TH: What time in the morning do you intend to call him?

Another way to foster commitment to the plan is to put the essential parts into a written form such as a behavioral contract. The written plan is not only a tangible reminder, but also a symbolic shift toward an action by the client. The very act of writing the plan becomes the first action that predisposes the client to anticipate some degree of success. It also gives the therapist an opportunity to encourage and reinforce the client verbally for making the plan. Thus, an important goal of reality therapy "is to help clients perceive some inner control and realize that they can increase it by consciously generating the feeling that they are in charge and then changing their behavior" (Glasser & Wubbolding, 1995, p. 305).

TH: What would be a more moderate version of the plan you thought up, one you think you would maintain?

CL: Well, what do you think of a 1500-calorie diet, walking two miles a day, and maybe putting off aerobics until I see how that works?

TH: That seems reasonable to me and a lot less stressful. How much would you lose a week on that plan?

CL: From all the diets I've been on, I think I would lose about two pounds a week.

TH: So it would take about seven and a half months to lose sixty pounds. Do you think you could commit to a program that long? If you do, let's put something down on paper, kind of like a contract.

For many clients, a commitment in writing is of great importance. A written and signed contract or document can serve as a memory jog and a catalyst to take action not previously taken. Many clients keep a pocket-sized notebook or battery-operated electronic planner containing the written plan, contract, or performance diary. Such recorded plans enable the therapist and client to agree on specific wording of goals and actions, instill a much needed sense of hope in the client, and to identify target dates, times, places, and activities that will result from goal attainment. The commitment also can be expressed in other ways, such as shaking on it and telling other people about the specific goals the plan entails.

Strategies for Helping Clients

Overarching Goal

The overall goal of the CT/RT practitioner is to facilitate more effective need fulfillment by the client. The mechanism for attainment of this goal is through behavior on the part of clients. Therapists seek to empower clients to meet their five basic needs by helping them realize that they can *choose* the behaviors that lead to effective and satisfactory need fulfillment. Even though most clients may not be able to instantly choose to make radical changes in their thoughts or feelings, they can make small, progressive, incremental changes in their behaviors. And with continued support and encouragement by therapists, clients can autonomously effect changes in their thinking, feelings, and at times even physiological or health-related behaviors. It is through clients' choosing to own and make behavioral changes that reality therapists teach clients that they are not victims of external stimuli or events but that they are agents in charge of their own need fulfillment (Glasser & Wubbolding, 1995, p. 303).

Emphasis on the Relationship

Counselors who practice CT/RT first seek to establish and sustain positive and trusting relationships with their clients. It is the relationship that is most crucial. Counseling is not usually done in steps. It is a fluid process. Counselors must focus on what choice theory holds to be the source of almost all clients' unhappiness—their failure to act and think in ways that would lead them to more satisfying relationships (Glasser, 2000b, p. 3; 2001). Glasser says that in all the clients he has counseled he has never seen any problem that was not directly related to clients' failure to act and think in ways that bring them closer to the people they need in their lives. It may take a great deal of listening to develop a trusting relationship with the client and to uncover the real source of unhappiness, but invariably the core psychological problem will turn out to be at least one very unsatisfying relationship or no relationships at all (Glasser, 2000b, p. 4). Wubbolding (1997, 2000, 2001) reiterates that it is the relationship, more than any other one factor, that enables the counselor to connect with the client, establish a trusting relationship, and thus, create the climate in which the client can learn to connect or reconnect with other important people in his or her life. With an improved relationship experience, the client can then begin to learn choice theory, fulfill basic needs in more responsible ways, choose better alternatives, and use CT/RT strategies to attain autonomy from the external control psychology that has been contributing to his or her misery, disconnectedness, and unhappiness.

Influence of Effective Listening

Both Glasser (1998) and Wubbolding (1997) emphasize that counselors must focus their total mental energy on listening to the client in order to find out the true source of the client's unhappiness, which will invariably turn out to involve either the lack of or loss of a relationship. Clients will not usually recognize or admit that it is a relationship issue. Most clients will believe that the problem is centered in their symptoms such as pain or unhappiness caused by some external person, situation, or event that is beyond their control. Concentrated or focused listening to the client will usually enable counselors to find out not only what is troubling clients but also what clients really want to have happen. Then counselors can introduce the concepts of total behavior (including the role of acting, thinking, feeling, and physiology) and choice theory. Also, the complex but necessary process of leading clients to act and think in ways that result in more satisfying current relationships can begin (Glasser, 2000b, p. 3; 2001; Wubbolding, 1997, 2000).

Emphasis on the Here and Now

Since nothing we can do will change the past, and choices can only be made in the present, CT/RT emphasizes current and recent lifestyle behaviors (Glasser & Wubbolding, 1995, p. 303). Although it may be true that our present lives are clearly connected to our past and that we love to ruminate about the trials and tribulations that we have endured, focusing on past events and problems rarely, if ever, helps us find choices that are currently need satisfying. Discussing past behaviors and problems should only occur in therapy if it impacts present choices and future behaviors.

Positiveness

The CT/RT practitioner talks about, focuses on, and reinforces positive and constructive planning and behaving. Clients who have been exposed to other therapies may believe that the therapist wants to hear about their miseries, problems, failures, disappointments, and debilitating situations over and over again. Such negative discussion leads the client to do more depressing and cannot contribute to the improvement of the client's thinking and behaving (Glasser, 1998, pp. 63–88; 2001). The facilitative strategy is to accept the fact that the client truly feels miserable (or depressed, defeated, disappointed, or helpless) and to encourage him or her to break the negative pattern and focus on something constructive and positive in the here and now (Glasser & Zunin, 1979, pp. 317–318). For example, a client might say "I just have this hopeless feeling about what she did to me yesterday." Instead of saying "She really made you feel hopeless and depressed," a better reply by the therapist would be, "What are you doing to produce this hopeless thinking inside yourself?" The latter statement focuses on changing the client's perceptions about the hopeless feeling into ownership of the thinking and on taking responsibility for the acting aspect reflected in the statement. These are the two aspects of the client's total behavior that can be controlled (Glasser, 1998, p. 72–73).

Controlling Perceptions

In CT/RT practice, behavior is an attempt to control perception. That is, people act in such a way as to reduce the discrepancy between what they want and what they perceive they are getting. Positively addicting behaviors, or *meditations,* as Glasser calls them, are activities that people can undertake, usually by themselves, to reduce their discrepancies and gain a feeling of choice in their lives. Glasser categorizes a wide variety of behaviors as meditations, ranging from relatively weak ones, such as regularly taking a vitamin pill, to strong ones, such as regularly running (Glasser, 1981, pp. 247–262). Other examples are transcendental meditation, working out in a gym or on an exercise machine, biofeedback, visualization and imagery, chanting, hiking, swimming, bicycling, gardening, writing, and sewing. Glasser states that it is not the activity that is of utmost importance in the meditation behavior, but that the person believes in the process of meditation and that it has some value, that it is personally fulfilling in some way, and that it can be easily accessed by the person (Glasser, 1981, p. 249).

For positive addiction to be of optimum benefit, the person must pursue the activity for about an hour each day until an addictive state is achieved—that is, until the person experiences some discomfort or withdrawal if the activity is omitted. Positive addictions enable clients to overcome their negative addictions and lead more constructive, integrated, and rewarding lives (Glasser, 1976). As a counseling strategy, nurturing regular meditation activity is consistent with the choice theory concept that what a client *does* has the most potential for establishing more effective need satisfaction.

Confrontation

Because CT/RT emphasizes client responsibility, no excuses, and no punishment, it is natural that confrontation is a necessary and effective strategy. Confronting clients in ways that are helpful yet nonpunitive requires concentration, caring, and skill in zeroing in on excuses or irresponsibilities. A caring confrontation can reinforce the belief that the therapist values the client. Confronting client excuses, explanations, or rationalizations is necessary to facilitate client movement toward responsible choices and behaviors (Glasser, 1998, pp. 212–214). Glasser and Zunin (1979, pp. 325–326) emphasize the role of compassionate confrontation as an intentional strategy. This strategy pertains to the reality of the client's current behavior, not to the therapist's personal or emotional feelings triggered by the client. Below is an example of appropriate confrontation of an excuse.

> CL: I was going to face up to him, but . . . after he gave me the roses . . . and we were so rushed for time . . . well, I just didn't want to cause any hard feelings.
>
> TH: Evelyn, I have two questions about what you've just said. When you change your mind about facing him, what are you doing? And how is this going to help you get what you want?

An inappropriate confrontation follows.

> TH: Evelyn, I have two things to say to you. It bugs me to hear about you doing this to yourself again and again. Why can't you learn to say what's on your mind? It's time you grow up.

Plans and Contracts

Setting limits for the therapy in such matters as the number of sessions and their cost, therapist and client responsibilities, intermediate and long-term goals, and specific plans for goal attainment establishes a structural and rational process for gaining success identity and making choices that fulfill needs. Moreover, it is important that the plan be made in writing—a contract or self-managed behavioral plan such as those described in the chapter on behavioral counseling. The written plan should carry the specific action needed to move the client toward need satisfaction.

Specifying and Pinning Down

This strategy is related to confrontation in that it may prevent the client from coming up with excuses for failing to follow through with plans. Suppose the therapeutic session has begun to focus on the client's intention to apply for a job. The client has stated that he intends to put several applications on file next week. The therapist pins the client down by asking the following questions: "What day next week will you do this? What time of the day? What will you wear? How are you going to get there? Are you going to call for an appointment? What will you *do* if the interview is not successful?" The most important benefit of these questions is to cement the client's commitment to do something positive to attain a goal. With each affirmative answer to a pinning down question, the client moves closer and closer to doing a specific positive behavior. Each answer is a verbal commitment to the therapist and to him- or herself about what will be done. Then the therapist can reinforce each verbal commitment by saying "So on Wednesday at 9:00 A.M. you are going to file an application with the A & I Nut and Bolt Company. You plan to wear a sport coat, a tie, dress pants, and a pair of dress shoes. You will ride the number 16 Metro bus and leave home at 8:00 A.M. to allow ample time to arrive before your 9:00 A.M. appointment. Is that correct?"

Resolving Conflicts

Glasser (1984, pp. 146–158) says there are two types of conflicts—true and false. The true conflict is one that develops from an attempt to change the behavior of persons who do not want to change because the condition of control does not satisfy them. The reason this is a true conflict is that no single behavior can solve it; there is no solution to it, and a major part of the stress in it comes from repeated frustrating attempts to do something to resolve it. Glasser recommends reducing the stress by doing nothing, choosing to be passive, or just waiting. In the meantime, some aspect of the conflict may change without intervention. During the interim, Glasser recommends expending energy to satisfy oneself in a nonconflict area.

Glasser (1984, pp. 149–150) says that most situations that people construe as conflict are in reality false conflicts. In these situations, there is a behavior the person can do to resolve the conflict, but the person is unwilling to engage in the behavior. Glasser cites an example of the overweight person who would like to be thinner but doesn't want to diet. One solution would be to jog or exercise daily to burn calories while maintaining the same caloric intake. Although exercising may be hard work and time-consuming, it is a solution. Glasser says that doing something in these situations is necessary because hoping and complaining are not effective behaviors (1984, p. 154).

Sample Case

The case of Evelyn, age 34, illustrates a CT/RT practitioner working with a client in planning concrete, responsible action. It illustrates several important strategies typical to the application of reality therapy.

CL: I've been so unhappy lately. I've tried to talk to Bill, but it's hard to pin him down. I've been his fiancée for over four years, but we never get around to discussing our marriage or setting a date. I get the feeling he wants it that way. He's a very strong and forceful person. I guess he intimidates me. I don't want to risk losing him by pushing him. His job keeps him so tied that up I rarely see him. When I do see him, we do lots of neat things. Sometimes I wonder if we'll ever get married. I feel so helpless.

TH: You say you hope to get married to Bill, but he won't discuss it or set a date. What are you doing to contribute to his not discussing it?

CL: I don't know. (*pause*) Yes, I do too. I guess I'm doing something. I'm being patient. Not pushing him. I'm being his steady girlfriend who doesn't ask questions and who doesn't nag him.

TH: Is this waiting getting you what you want? What are your present actions doing for you?

CL: (*pause*) Gosh! I hadn't thought of it that way. What's it doing for me? (*pause*) Hmmm, I don't think it's doing anything *for* me. It's certainly doing something *to* me. Making me feel low. Making me worry all the time.

TH: What do you want to see happen in the relationship?

CL: I want us to get married. I want us to get together. I want us to talk about it, to set a definite date. Oh, I'm willing to wait—a while. Even several months. As long as it's set. I want to know where I stand.

TH: What can you do to bring that about?

CL: I don't know. I don't know that *I* can make it happen. I don't know if I can confront him. He is very logical, very convincing. I'm afraid I'd just melt away.

TH: You don't think you are ready to stand up to him, then.

CL: I know I've got to. Nobody else can do it for me.

TH: You want to confront him but are afraid you'll fail. I gather you don't think it's very realistic that you would walk right up to him right now and get an answer.

CL: I wish I could. I think if I practiced it or something maybe I could. I don't know.

TH: Would it help if we practice it now?

CL: I don't know.

TH: What have we got to lose by practicing?

CL: Okay, if it'll help. I'm willing to try practicing.

TH: To help you practice more realistically, could you tell me how he'll likely respond to you when you talk about your future plans together?

CL: Oh, he'll be calm, cool, and collected. He'll handle it just like a business deal. He'll not raise his voice—in fact, he'll lower it. He's likely to say, "Honey, I've been thinking that as soon as I wrap up these next four important business deals, I have got to sit down with you and map out some definite plans. You know you're important to me, sugar. I know you don't mind waiting a little longer." That's about the way he would be. Except he wouldn't be meek like me.

TH: That was helpful. Are you ready to practice?

CL: I guess so. I just hope I can be strong enough.

TH: Let's talk about it a little—how do you want to be in your session with him?

CL: Well, I want to be able to be me—to command respect, and to get my ideas across without threatening him and without harming our relationship. And I want to be strong enough to do it without getting put off and without going away feeling like a helpless child.

TH: Can you rehearse with me now what you'd like to say to him if you had the opportunity and the conditions were right?

CL: I'll try.

TH: Now, I'll be Bill. We're all alone and it seems like a good time for you to bring it up.

TH: Well, Evelyn, you look like you have something important on your mind.

CL: Hmmm. Well, Bill, there's something I've been wanting to talk with you about.

TH: Okay, shoot, sugar.

CL: It's about us—our relationship. You tell me you care about me, and I certainly care about you a whole bunch. And I'm still thrilled every time I look at my engagement ring. But every time the subject of definite planning comes up, it gets put off. I'm wondering if it's ever going to happen. Bill, I don't want you to think I'm pushy, but I really would like to know where I stand.

TH: Evelyn—dear! You know I love you. You know you're the most important thing in my life. We'll get it together, believe me! Just trust me! You know how confining my work is and how much stress I'm under. Sugar, it wouldn't be fair to you for me to try to finalize plans for us with all this unfinished business hanging over our heads. Just a few more months and things will be right for us.

CL: I . . . Oh my gosh—you're just like him. I don't know what to say.

TH: Okay, cut! You think my playing the part of Bill was too strong for you right now to be able to get your point across successfully.

CL: You were almost like he'd be, all right. I wonder if I can ever do it.

TH: Let's talk some more about what you want to do and try to figure out how you can succeed in doing it if you decide you really want to do it.

A discussion, an assertiveness training session, and more planning followed, and another rehearsal episode proved to be quite successful for Evelyn. She was able to decide what she wanted to say; she was able to hold her ground and stand up to the therapist even though the therapist was being as persuasive as possible. Evelyn was obviously pleased with herself and felt good about having taken such a definite and assertive stand. Her posture, voice, and facial expression showed confidence and a more positive outlook.

TH: Evelyn, I'm pleased with your performance in our practice session, and you are apparently feeling positive about the way you handled yourself.

CL: I felt really good about myself. I really surprised myself. I couldn't believe it was really me, saying those things.

TH: Then it is realistic to assume that you will be able to be just as strong, just as self-assured with him as you demonstrated with me.

CL: I think so. I am really a very strong person when I really want to be. Yes, I can do it.

TH: You *can* do it. Does that mean you *will* do it?

CL: Well, yes. I've got to do it. I don't intend to live the rest of my life feeling miserable.

TH: You seem quite certain about wanting to get this thing settled. When do you plan to confront him?

CL: I don't know. Soon. Before the summer's over.

TH: It's now June twenty-first. *When* this summer do you plan to do it?

CL: I won't see him again until the middle of July.

TH: What day in July will you see him?

CL: I'll be with him the weekend of the fifteenth—Friday, Saturday, and Sunday.

TH: What day will it be?

CL: Friday—Friday evening at dinner will be the best time to do it. That will give us the whole weekend.

As the session continued, the client made a written commitment to carry out her plan followed by an appointment with the therapist to discuss it after July seventeenth. The therapist gave Evelyn verbal reinforcement for her successful rehearsal and for having developed a reasonable written plan, and let her know that he would be genuinely interested in hearing how she did in the real meeting with her fiancé.

Contributions of Choice Theory

From the time of its inception in the mid-1960s to the present, choice theory has made a number of important contributions to the helping professions. It has had a substantive influence in challenging the medical model of client treatment in counseling and psychotherapy. Another major contribution has been the application of its principles to a variety of educational institutions. These principles have proved successful in educational settings from kindergarten through graduate school. Starting with *Schools without Failure* (Glasser, 1969) and continuing through *Every Student Can Succeed* (Glasser, 2000d), Glasser's many books, workshops, consultations, and training models on schooling, education, and quality schools have had a profound and positive influence on teaching, discipline, grading, counseling, and improving the ways schools are organized and managed (Glasser, 1998, pp. 234–282, 2000d).

CT/RT represents both a positive and an action therapy. The direct, frank, realistic, straightforward, and refreshingly different process that it brings to the counseling relationship is among its foremost contributions. Choice theory's introduction and emphasis of the concepts of total behavior and quality world place the responsibility for choice directly on clients. The theory also teaches that the source of almost all clients' unhappiness stems from their present failure to act and think in ways that would lead them to more satisfying current relationships. It also teaches that external control psychology is the root cause of 99 percent of the people of the world's difficulty in getting along with others (Glasser, 2000b, pp. 3–6). The facilitation and empowerment of clients to choose and act in ways that fulfill their five basic needs (survival, love and belonging, power, freedom, and fun) provide ways for clients to form satisfying relationships and rid themselves of the misery and unhappiness that they previously chose (Glasser 1998, pp. 25–43).

CT/RT has proved to be an appropriate and effective approach for dealing with a wide variety of client problems that have traditionally been classified as difficult to help. Such difficult types of clients have included families with problems; people experiencing workplace or employment problems; delinquents; offenders; drug and alcohol addicts; angry and violent people; depressed and suicidal individuals; survivors of assault; grieving people; physically disabled persons; and people suffering from maladies such as anxiety, compulsions, delusions, fears, guilt, loneliness, chronic misery, neurosis, obsessions, panic, phobias, post-traumatic stress disorder (PTSD), anorexia, powerlessness, psychosis, psychosomatic symptoms, and schizophrenia (Glasser, 1998, 2000b). Commenting on the strengths of CT/RT, Glasser (2000b, p. 3) states that "people, no matter what their diagnoses, can be helped to live their lives more effectively through a psychotherapy that leads to their making better choices."

In recent years, Glasser's theories have branched out through involvement in far more areas than the counseling office and school room (Glasser, 1998). Choice theory has made considerable contributions to solving complex and distressing problems in the areas of (1) love, marriage, and the family (pp. 163–233), (2) different kinds of workplaces (pp. 283–305), and (3) community relationships (pp. 309–331). Such successes and versatility as those attained by the total application of choice theory have elicited comments from people like Peter Breggin, M.D., who, in the foreword to Glasser's book (2000a, p. xi) represents CT/RT as "a beacon that can lead people into the brighter land of fulfilling relationships based on personal responsibility and conscious choice."

Shortcomings of Choice Theory

Some of the underlying assumptions of choice theory are questionable. For example, the assumption that mental illness is equated with irresponsibility of the client and that a failure identity and unsatisfying relationships stem from lack of need fulfillment seem to be oversimplifications. Even though these assumptions may be valid in a large number of cases—and Glasser (1998, 2000a, 2000b, 2000c, 2001) argues persuasively in their favor—their narrow view may limit the full range of therapeutic interventions, especially when we consider the environmental, sociological, physiological, and biochemical precursors to human functioning in modern life. A larger view of the causes of maladaptive behavior, coupled with the use of a global, multidisciplinary helping approach, appears to be more defensible.

Focusing on the here and now and staying away from the client's past history are generally appropriate and commendable. However, humans are products of their past, and there are instances in which helping clients to find their roots—their connectedness—may be of great importance to them in fulfilling their need to become whole. Taking stock of where we have been may at times be a helpful strategy for use with clients from some cultural backgrounds and may serve as both an instructional and a motivational impetus toward their making better choices for the future.

Another shortcoming is that the simple, efficient methods employed in choice theory may lend themselves to surface-level, symptom-oriented problems that can be quickly attacked and show noticeable results. This may give the fix-it-quick therapists (especially beginning therapists) a sense of accomplishment, but it could also permit deep-seated emotional dilemmas in the client to go unexamined.

Questions about CT/RT, sometimes posed by students and new professionals, concern issues such as "Who decides which reality is valid—the therapist, the client, or both? Doesn't this system encourage therapists to impose their choices, values, and moral beliefs on clients? Who is to say what choices are responsible and what are irresponsible? Which is right—society's norms or the individual's norms? How do we know that people's pasts or unconscious thoughts aren't crucial to them?" Questions such as these can be bothersome from both a practical and philosophical point of view and have not been adequately addressed by proponents of choice theory.

LaFontaine (1994, 1995) judges choice theory to be lacking in information and awareness of issues related to homosexuality in general and to gay, lesbian, bisexual, and transsexual youth in particular. She recommends a more diversified framework for CT/RT if the approach is to adequately serve the needs of the underserved population of clients of diverse sexual orientations.

Cunningham (1995) expresses similar concerns regarding choice theory's sensitivity to the ten most frequently encountered examples of cultural bias in counseling. These assumptions (examples) of cultural bias included the supposition that normal behavior does not vary across cultures. An inferred shortcoming of choice theory was that the approach places too much emphasis on Western world individualism, fragmentation by academic disciplines, dependence on abstract words, linear thinking, and neglect of the client's traditional cultural support systems. Glasser (2001) and Glasser and Wubbolding (1995, pp. 302–303) counter Cunningham's criticism by pointing out that such alleged cultural bias is more a function of the *use* of CT/RT than a flaw in the theory. Glasser and Wubbolding point out that when using CT/RT with clients from different cultures and different parts of the world, the therapy must be adjusted to meet the needs, style, experience, manner of expression, thought patterns, total behavior, and specific wants of members of various cultures. Obviously Glasser and Wubbolding view choice theory as sufficiently flexible to meet the needs of diverse clients. Glasser (1998, pp. 337–340) also clearly asserts that practitioners who are trained and certified under the auspices of the William Glasser Institute, or its nationwide or worldwide affiliates, are recognized as qualified to conduct reality therapy. The indications are that persons who were not trained or certified by the Institute may not have had the training and experience to be technically competent in the conduct of CT/RT practice, and this would, presumably, include deficits in use of the theory in regard to multicultural counseling and sensitivity.

Choice Theory with Diverse Populations

Universal Applicability

Choice theory/reality therapy embraces several important characteristics that are held in common among cultures. The CT/RT system's formulation of five basic needs are purported to be prevalent among people throughout the world (Glasser, 1998, 2000a, 2001; Glasser & Glasser, 1999; Wubbolding, Al-Rashidi, et al., 1998). Wubbolding, Al-Rashidi et al. (1998) emphasizes that trainers, supervisors, and practitioners of CT/RT should value and demonstrate competencies in multicultural awareness, knowledge, and experience. They further point out that, even though choice theory ideas apply to all people everywhere, the content of each individual's quality world is circumscribed by that person's cultural experience. The choices available to people depend upon their experience and environment which are restricted by culture, and wants are limited by each individual's experience and his or her worldview (p. 5).

Attributes of the Quality World

Glasser's (1998, pp. 44–61) quality world concept is choice theory's most positive, potent, and commendable quality for dealing with people from diverse backgrounds. Remember that each person's individual, internal quality world consists of specific pictures that portray, more than anything we know, the best ways that that person knows to satisfy his or her basic needs. What these pictures portray, in three different categories, resonates directly to the understanding of the person's cultural background and beliefs. These pictorial categories define the *people* we most want to be with, the *things* we most want to own or experience, and the *ideas* or *belief systems* that govern much of our behaviors, thinking, and emotions (p. 45).

Glasser (1998, p. 53) notes that it is especially difficult for individuals to be tolerant of the quality worlds of people who are less powerful. The essence of choice theory's teaching is that *my* quality world is the unique core of *my* life and no one else's. This is a difficult lesson to learn for people who are steeped in external control psychology, but it is a valuable trump card in the repertoire of CT/RT practitioners who seek to counsel with people of different races, colors, religions, cultures, physical abilities, nationalities, sexes, ages, socioeconomic statuses, sexual orientations, and other divergent circumstances or worldviews.

Impact of Total Behavior

Another attribute of CT/RT that is supportive of work with people of diverse backgrounds is Glasser's (1998, pp. 62–88) total behavior. Glasser states that choice theory expands the single word *behavior* to two words, *total behavior,* which always consists of the four components of acting, thinking, feeling, and the physiology associated with all our actions, thoughts, and feelings (pp. 72–73). Every moment of our lives we humans are behaving, and we choose essentially all that we do. Therefore, we try to behave in ways that give us the most effective control over our lives. In choice theory terms, having effective control means actually possessing the ability to reasonably satisfy the pictures in our quality worlds regardless of our cultural backgrounds (Glasser, 2000a, pp. xvii–xviii, 225–226). When practitioners of CT/RT teach clients the essence of choice theory and the concept of total behavior and then proceed to conduct the counseling accordingly, clients of all cultural backgrounds are clearly focused on their own quality worlds. It is in that sense that CT/RT appropriately informs the counselor's work with diverse populations.

Multicultural Adaptations

The application of CT/RT to clients in different parts of the world, of course, requires the counselor to be sensitive to, possess a knowledge of, and adjust the therapy in accordance with the client's cultural values, wants, and manner of expression (Glasser & Wubbolding, 1995, p. 302–303; Wubbolding, Al-Rashidi, et al., 1998). For example, in cultures such as those in the Pacific Rim (such as the Philippines, China, Taiwan, Vietnam, and Singapore), counselors are likely to be perceived as authority figures. Appropriate work with typical clients from such backgrounds necessitates a delicate balance among counseling; accurately and authentically teaching choice theory; and sensitively adapting to the social, economic, historical, political, familial, and psychological processes of the specific culture. Glasser and Wubbolding (1995, pp. 302–303) illustrate and contrast examples of helping students evaluate their own behaviors. To a student from the United States, the counselor might emphasize questions such as "Is what you're doing helping or hindering you? Do your current choices have a realistic chance of getting you what you want?" In contrast, when working with a Chinese student from Singapore, more culturally appropriate questions might be "What does your family think about your actions? Do they approve or disapprove? Do your actions bring shame or honor to your parents or grandparents?"

In helping clients from diverse cultures, the CT/RT counselor is sensitive, responsive, flexible, and adaptive to the style, personality, manner of expression, quality world, total behavior, and specific wants and needs of members of the culture from which the client emerges (Glasser & Wubbolding, 1995, p. 303; Wubbolding, Al-Rashidi, et al., 1998).

Summary

Born because of William Glasser's disenchantment with classical psychoanalysis theory and clinical practice, reality therapy made its debut in 1965. Since that time, the reality therapy of the 1960s has been refined and transformed into a twenty-first century new reality therapy based on choice theory. For brevity's sake we refer to it as CT/RT. CT/RT is based on several innovative but important propositions.

1. We humans choose essentially everything we do.
2. Most people's unhappiness is rooted in the lack or absence of satisfying relationships.
3. The resolution of our problems depends on our ability to satisfy our five basic needs.

4. External control psychology convinces us that our problems are caused by external factors.
5. Each of us is born with the ability to create our own internal quality world that governs how we perceive things and events and allows us to control our total behavior.
6. It is the quality of the client–counselor relationship that is the main catalyst driving effective therapy.
7. The concept of mental illness obfuscates, distorts, and falsifies the reality that people's problems are a result of poor or ineffective choices.

The choice theory mechanisms that undergird the development of human personality include the ability to fulfill five innate or basic needs and are the preeminent role of choice in the development of who we are and become. Our choices ultimately determine whether we develop either a success or a failure identity. Maladjustment is viewed as the lack or absence of a satisfactory relationship.

We have briefly described the basic concepts of CT/RT and summarized the qualities of the effective therapist. The counseling process and strategies for helping clients depict a therapist–client alliance that relentlessly focuses on facilitating clients to think and act in ways that lead them to establish and sustain satisfying relationships and to fulfill their basic needs in responsible ways. The overarching assumption is that clients possess the ability to choose better relationships and ways to satisfy their needs. Representative examples of how the CT/RT practitioner plies the art and science of counseling are described and a sample case expands the portrayal of the therapist's work.

The contributions and shortcomings of CT/RT are discussed and several perspectives on work with diverse populations are examined. The overall description of CT/RT represents it as a modern, progressive, evolving, modality that is gaining in recognition and acceptance.

SUGGESTIONS FOR FURTHER READING

Glasser, W. (1965). *Reality therapy.* New York: Harper & Row.

Glasser, W. (1969). *Schools without failure.* New York: Harper & Row.

Glasser, W. (1972). *The identity society.* New York: Harper & Row.

Glasser, W. (1976). *Positive addiction.* New York: Harper & Row.

Glasser, W. (1986). *Control theory in the classroom.* New York: Harper & Row.

Glasser, W. (1986). *The quality school.* New York: Harper & Row.

Glasser, W. (1998). *Choice theory: A new psychology of personal freedom.* New York:HarperCollins.

Glasser, W. (2000). *Reality therapy in action.* New York: HarperCollins. (This book, reissued in paper edition format without change in content, is also titled *Counseling with choice theory: The new reality therapy*).

Glasser, W., & Glasser, C. (1999). *The language of choice theory.* New York: HarperCollins.

Glasser, W., & Glasser, C. (2000). *Getting together and staying together: Solving the mystery of marriage.* New York: HarperCollins.

Wubbolding, R. E. (Therapist). (1997). *Reality therapy* (Videotape No. 0-205-32886-5/2886L-9, T. Labriola, Producer). In J. Carlson & D. Kjos, *Reality therapy with Wubbolding: Psychotherapy with the experts.* Boston: Allyn & Bacon.

Wubbolding, R. E. (2000). *Reality therapy for the 21st century.* Philadelphia: Taylor and Francis.

The Glasser Institute's website (www.wglasserinst.com) also provides information on training and certification in choice theory and reality therapy; the William Glasser Institute Newsletter; books, videotapes, and audio tapes on reality therapy and choice theory; conferences and workshops pertaining to reality therapy and choice theory; and new developments in choice theory and reality therapy.

REFERENCES

American Psychiatric Association (1994). *Diagnostic and statistical manual of mental disorders* (4th ed.). Washington, DC: Author.

Breggin, P. R. (2000). Foreword. In W. Glaser, *Reality therapy in action* (pp. xi–xiii). New York: Harper-Collins.

Cunningham, L. M. (1995). Control theory, reality therapy, and cultural bias. *Journal of Reality Therapy, 15,* 15–32.

Glasser, W. (1961). *Mental health or mental illness?* New York: Harper & Row.

Glasser, W. (1964). Reality therapy: A realistic approach to the young offender. *Crime & Delinquency, 10,* 135–144.

Glasser, W. (1965). *Reality therapy.* New York: Harper & Row.

Glasser, W. (1969). *Schools without failure.* New York: Harper & Row.

Glasser, W. (1972). *The identity society.* New York: Harper & Row.

Glasser, W. (1976). *Positive addiction.* New York: Harper & Row.

Glasser, W. (1981). *Stations of the mind: New directions for reality therapy.* New York: Harper & Row.

Glasser, W. (1984). *Control theory: A new explanation of how we control our lives.* New York: Harper & Row.

Glasser, W. (1986). *Control theory in the classroom.* New York: Harper & Row.

Glasser, W. (1989). *Control theory in the practice of reality therapy: Case studies.* New York: Harper & Row.

Glasser, W. (1990a). *The control theory-reality therapy workbook.* Canoga Park, CA: Institute for Reality Therapy.

Glasser, W. (1990b). *The quality school: Managing students without coercion.* New York: Harper & Row.

Glasser, W. (1996). *Staying together: The control theory guide to a lasting marriage.* New York: Harper-Collins.

Glasser, W. (1998). *Choice theory: A new psychology of personal freedom.* New York: HarperCollins.

Glasser, W. (2000a). *Reality therapy in action.* New York: HarperCollins. (This book, reissued in paper edition format without change in content, is also titled *Counseling with choice theory: The new reality therapy*).

Glasser, W. (2000b, May 28). *Reality therapy in the year 2000.* Paper presented at The Evolution of Psychotherapy Conference, Anaheim, CA. (From the William Glasser Institute Web site: www.wglasserinst.com).

Glasser, W. (2000c, Winter). The new reality therapy. *The William Glasser Institute Newsletter.*

Glasser, W. (2000d). *Every student can succeed.* Chatsworth, CA: The William Glasser Institute.

Glasser, W. (2001, March 19). *Counseling with Choice Theory: The new Reality Therapy.* Paper presented at the 2001 Convention of the American Counseling Association, San Antonio, TX.

Glasser, W., & Glasser, C. (1999). *The language of choice theory.* New York: HarperCollins.

Glasser, W., & Glasser, C. (2000). *Getting together and staying together: Solving the mystery of marriage.* New York: HarperCollins.

Glasser, W., & Wubbolding, R. E. (1995). Reality Therapy. In R. J. Corsini & D. Wedding (Eds.), *Current psychotherapies* (5th ed., pp. 293–321). Itasca, IL: F. E. Peacock.

Glasser, W., & Zunin, L. M. (1979). Reality therapy. In R. J. Corsini (Ed.), *Current psychotherapies* (2nd ed., pp. 301–339). Itasca, IL: F. E. Peacock.

LaFontaine, L. (1994). Quality schools for gay and lesbian youth: Lifting the cloak of silence. *Journal of Reality Therapy, 14,* 26–28.

LaFontaine, L. (1995). Basic needs and sexuality: Is something missing in reality therapy/control theory? *Journal of Reality Therapy, 15,* 32–36.

Wubbolding, R. E. (1988). *Using reality therapy.* New York: Harper & Row.

Wubbolding, R. E. (1990). Evaluation: The cornerstone in the practice of reality therapy. *Omar Psychology Practitioner Series, 2,* 6–27.

Wubbolding, R. E. (1991a). *Understanding reality therapy.* New York: HarperCollins.

Wubbolding, R. E. (1991b). *Using reality therapy in group counseling* (videotape). Cincinnati, OH: Center for Reality Therapy.

Wubbolding, R. E. (1992). *Reality therapy training manual.* Cincinnati, OH: Center for Reality Therapy.

Wubbolding, R. E. (Therapist). (1997). *Reality therapy* (Videotape No. 0-205-32886-5/2886L-9, T. Labriola, Producer). In J. Carlson & D. Kjos, *Reality therapy with Wubbolding: Psychotherapy with the experts.* Boston: Allyn & Bacon.

Wubbolding, R. E. (2000). *Reality therapy for the 21st century.* Philadelphia: Taylor and Francis.

Wubbolding, R. E. (2001, March 19). *Bringing out the best in the human spirit: Reality therapy in groups.* Paper presented at the annual convention of the American Counseling Association, San Antonio, TX.

Wubbolding, R. E., Al-Rashidi, B., Brickell, J., Kakitani, M., Kim, R. I., Lennon, B., Lojk, L., Ong, K. H., Honey, I., Stijacic, D., & Tham, E. (1998). Multicultural awareness: Implications for reality therapy and choice theory. *International Journal of Reality Therapy, 17*(2), 4–6.

Wubbolding, R. E., & Brickell, J. (1998). Qualities of the reality therapist. *International Journal of Reality Therapy, 17*(2), 47–49.

9 Rational-Emotive Behavior Therapy

Fundamental Tenets

History

Albert Ellis, a clinical psychologist and, at the time, a practicing psychoanalytically oriented psychotherapist, initiated the development of rational-emotive behavior therapy as a separate therapeutic system in 1955. Ellis had become disillusioned with traditional psychoanalytic therapy because clients rarely gave up their presenting symptoms or they developed new ones. This lack of progress occurred even though his clients could achieve insight by connecting the events of early childhood to their present emotional disturbances. Ellis came to realize that the problem was that clients continued actively to reindoctrinate themselves with the irrationalities they had invented and learned in childhood (Ellis, 1979a, p. 191). Influenced by behaviorists such as Watson, Ellis reacted strongly in a series of papers (1949, 1950, 1956, 1958) to the passivity and antiempirical stances of the Freudians and Rogerians. Ellis's early practice and thinking culminated in a book on the psychotherapeutic principles of REBT—*Reason and Emotion in Psychotherapy* (Ellis, 1962).

Ellis's early and continuing interest in philosophy pervades REBT and may be best characterized in Epictetus's words, "Men are not disturbed by things, but the view they take of them." Related to this viewpoint are the Buddhist and Taoist concepts that human emotions originate from human thinking and that to change emotions, one must change one's thinking. These ideas fit nicely into Ellis's notion of how people get into psychological trouble (Ellis, 1979a, p. 190). From a psychotherapeutic standpoint Ellis has taken much from Alfred Adler, who believed that an individual's emotional reactions were generated by his or her attitudes, beliefs, and perceptions and were therefore cognitively created (Ellis, 1970, 1971).

As REBT has developed, it has been termed *rational therapy* (RT), *semantic therapy, cognitive behavior therapy* (CBT), and *rational behavior training* (RBT) (Ellis & Harper, 1979, p. 202). For many years the name *rational-emotive therapy* (RET) was commonly used to identify the approach. Recently, however, Ellis (1995) proposed that the name be changed to *rational-emotive behavior therapy* (REBT) because behavior is and always has been an essential part of the theory.

Today *general* REBT is virtually synonymous with cognitive behavior therapy (CBT; see Chapter 10), but *preferential* or *elegant* REBT, as Ellis calls it (1984, p. iii, 1997), seeks a deeper, philosophical change in the client and is used whenever the client is capable of profiting from it.

Ellis has maintained his empirical scientific view of psychology and therapy throughout his life and has just as enthusiastically attacked nonscientific, nonrational, "it must be taken on faith or intuition" approaches (Ellis, 1986b, 1989a). He has long taken umbrage with Freudian psychoanalytics and has not been enamored with the "new age" transpersonalists who may combine a good deal of mysticism, religion, and spirituality into their therapy (Keegan, 1989).

Currently, the focal point for REBT is the Albert Ellis Institute in New York. It is a multifaceted not-for-profit organization that promotes REBT. The Institute is worldwide and undertakes a variety of endeavors that range from in-depth training programs, clinical fellowships, consulting services, workshops, and courses to sales of books, audio and videotapes, and even T-shirts! *The Journal of Rational-Emotive & Cognitive-Behavior Therapy* is the official institute journal that publishes articles on the research, theory, and practice of REBT and cognitive-behavior therapy. Albert Ellis is actively involved in running the organization and is still busily writing, conducting workshops, and promoting REBT.

Overview of Rational-Emotive Behavior Therapy

REBT is a comprehensive approach to treatment and education that is based on the view that thinking, feeling, and behaving are integrated, interactive, and holistic processes of human functioning. REBT holds that human disturbance is complicated by biological and environmental factors that exacerbate irrational beliefs (Dryden, Neenan, & Yankura, 1999; Ellis, 1999). One of the fundamental tenets of REBT is that human problems stem not from external events or situations but from people's views or beliefs about them. More specifically, people's emotions stem from their beliefs, evaluations, interpretations, and philosophies about what happens to them, not from the events themselves (Ellis, 1999).

Ellis suggests that an individual's belief system may consist of both a set of rational beliefs and a set of irrational beliefs. The irrational beliefs are the principal origin of emotional disturbance, and the main therapeutic goal of REBT is to change them. Through the therapeutic process, clients develop skills that allow them to first identify and then dispute their own irrational beliefs, a process they can then apply to other problem areas in their lives. In addition, effective therapy involves teaching clients to replace their problematic thinking and behavior with vitally absorbing interests aimed at long-range fulfillment rather than short-range hedonism (Dryden et al., 1999).

It is this concern with long-range fulfillment that demarcates elegant REBT from the general type, or CBT. Where CBT frequently concentrates on practical problem solving, REBT much more frequently focuses on solving the emotional problem about the practical problem and then, if required, helps the client with the original problem (Ellis, 1986c, p. 37). The elegant approach calls for realigning one's thinking and indeed one's philosophy about life in broad-based ways. Whereas CBT may include such comprehensive changes, in elegant REBT philosophical change is central to personality change (Ellis, 1986c, p. 37, Ellis, 1997). Ellis proposes that, to be "elegant," a theory of psychotherapy should offer economy of time and effort, rapid symptom reduction, effectiveness with a large percentage of different kinds of clients, depth of solution to problems, and lasting effects. A good deal of research finds that REBT's cognitive behavioral approaches meet these tough criteria (Dryden & Ellis, 2001; Dryden et al., 1999; Ellis, 1989b; Engles, Garnefski, & Diekstra, 1993; Lyons & Woods, 1991; Silverman, McCarthy, & McGovern, 1992).

Theory of Personality

Biological Basis.   Rational-emotive behavior therapy, unlike most other systems of psychotherapy, suggests that there is a biological basis for human behavior (Dryden, 1994). Ellis (1976) hypothesized that probably 80 percent of the variance of human behavior can be accounted for by biological makeup and only about 20 percent by environmental training. Rational-emotive behavior therapy proposes that humans teach themselves irrational beliefs and are biologically prone to do so, as characterized by such attributes as inertia, negativism, habituation, moodiness, comfort striving, and excitement seeking, all of which interfere with productive thinking and planning and result in errors of judgment and self-defeating behavior (Dryden, 1984, p. 2; Ellis, 1991b). Ellis (1976) offers the following points to substantiate this controversial view:

1. Virtually all humans show evidence of major irrationalities.
2. No social or cultural group is devoid of irrational behavior.
3. Many irrationalities run counter to teaching by significant others and society at large.
4. Irrationality is not exclusive to those with mental disabilities; bright and gifted humans can act irrationally.
5. Those who may oppose irrational activity and be most aware of it may also fall prey to it.
6. People often adopt new irrationalities after giving up old ones or go back to an irrational activity after working hard to overcome it.

Summarizing this pessimistic view, Ellis suggests that "humans are born with an exceptionally strong tendency to want and to insist that everything happens for the best in their life and to soundly condemn (1) themselves, (2) others, and (3) the world when they do not immediately get what they want" (Ellis, 1979a, p. 195). In this sense humans continue to think "humanly" all their lives, and only with great effort are they able to think and behave rationally. The saving grace of this dilemma is that humans also have powerful tendencies toward growth and self-actualization. Each person has the potential to effect change by changing his or her cognitive and behavioral processes, and can do so while overcoming gigantic barriers (Dryden, 1984, pp. 2, 44). This perspective puts REBT squarely in a secular humanistic operating mode that emphasizes flexibility and scientific outlook, self-acceptance instead of self-esteem, and long-range self-satisfaction and pleasure in one's activities, flexibility and alternative-seeking behavior, individualism and sociality, and accepts nothing—particularly religious dogma—on blind faith (Ellis, 1991a, 1992).

Social Basis.   People spend much of their lives attempting to live up to others' expectations. They become "other-directed" and neglect to spend time developing the interpersonal skills they need to succeed socially and develop a healthy self-concept (Ellis, 1977, p. 196). For Ellis, however, the notion that one learns from the environment is nonsense. In his view, a more appropriate term is that people *teach* themselves as they aspire to succeed socially and live comfortably (Dryden, 1984, p. 43).

Psychological Basis.   People who develop healthy personalities have an internal locus of control founded on self-enhancing and efficient thinking. However, movement toward psychological growth and self-actualizing behavior is often sabotaged by self-defeating thoughts (Ellis, 1979a, p. 196). People become emotionally distraught by upsetting themselves *about* external events. Convinced that the trouble is outside themselves, they complicate matters by condemning others and the world in general. If they continue this faulty belief in an external locus of control, they eventually come to view themselves in the same despicable way (Ellis, 1977, p. 199). The way this twisted and convoluted thinking, emoting, and behaving occurs can be explained by the ABC theory (Ellis 1958, 1962).

ABC Theory.   At point A there occurs an event, behavior, feeling, or attitude termed an *activating event.* For example, Dr. James, a rational and mild-mannered counselor, is caught in the express lane at the supermarket behind a person who has nine items (three over the limit), who is debating the check-out clerk over the price of an item, has coupons to turn in, and wants to write a check for $3.95 though the lane clearly says "cash only." All this occurs when the good doctor is already late for a therapy appointment.

At point C there is an emotional and/or behavioral *consequence.* Dr. James turns purple, swears under his breath, has visions of carving the miscreant with a chainsaw, and slams his microwave gourmet dinner down on the check-out counter while glaring at the clerk. Because of the close proximity between the activating event (A) and the emotional consequence (C), our agitated counselor may falsely assume that A causes C and conclude, "I am righteously indignant at this cretin for holding *me* up. I'll have to speed to get to my therapy session. Further, it's my lazy, good-for-nothing wife's fault for not taking care of *me* and getting these frozen dinners in the first place!" (A subsequent speeding ticket will link A to C even more closely.)

However, REBT theory asserts that A (the hang-up in the check-out line) does not cause C (the doctor's minipsychotic break and speeding ticket). Instead it asserts B (one's *belief* about A) causes C. If Dr. James were to tell himself, "It's inconvenient that I'm stuck here, but it's not the end of the world, and the next time I've got to budget my time better," then he would tend to feel disappointment, chagrin, and a bit of guilt. In reality, however, Dr. James tells himself, "Here is another example of stupidity and incompetency insinuated on *me,* and it is a major catastrophe that this jerk is now making *me* late for *my* therapy session." Indignation, anger, and outrage predominate, and Dr. James suffers some very aversive consequences that reinforce his irrational belief about what others *ought* to do to make his life easier. The result is that the doctor has a lousy therapy session, gets in a quarrel with his wife about who has what responsibilities, and gets slapped with a divorce decree! In this not-so-extreme example of irrational statements and their consequences, the individual stays so absorbed in nurturing these beliefs that he spends no time working out what contributed to the situation and constructing a more realistic schedule. If no *disputation* (D) by the doctor or some significant other takes place, then he will be doomed to repeat the process and no new cognitive or behavioral *effect* (E) will occur.

This example illustrates a key aspect of REBT: cognition, emotion, and behavior are never considered in a monolithic sense. Although the ABCs of a situation may be viewed as distinct entities, they also transact with and include one another (Ellis, 1984, p. iii). In particular, thought and emotion are not two different processes, but essentially the same thing. Like the other two basic life processes, sensing and acting, they are interrelated. Thus, if a person senses, acts, emotes, or thinks, he or she is also consciously or unconsciously involving him- or herself in the other behavioral processes (Ellis, 1962, pp. 38–39).

Components of ABC. Many times the ABC paradigm presents a semantic rat's warren of interlocking passages that are a confounding maze. To clarify and properly categorize statements, Wessler and Wessler (1980) developed the emotional episode and partitioned the ABC paradigm into eight distinct parts (Wessler, 1986, pp. 13–14). A is composed of (1) an internal or external *objective stimulus,* which starts the sequence. The person then becomes (2) *aware* of its existence and (3) *defines* and *describes* it. Then a cognitive (4) *interpretation* is inferred about unobservable and unknown aspects of the objective event. This inference has the potential to lead to irrational ideation because there is no factual evidence to support it.

The B component is (5) an *evaluation* of the objective stimulus as positive, negative, or neutral. Further complicating matters, Wessler (1986) proposes that there are at least four objects of evaluation—the action, its intent, the consequences of the action, and the actor. Typically, individuals do not separate these entities and make singular, all-inclusive evaluations among them. When the belief is irrational this singular evaluation becomes all-inclusively catastrophic.

The resulting C may be divided into (6) *affective* arousal and (7) overt *behavior* that may or may not follow arousal. However, for the emotionally disturbed individual, negative affective arousal and negative overt behavior are almost always guaranteed. This circular cognitive chain is completed by (8) *reinforcing consequences* that may influence and strengthen future episodes of the event (Wessler, 1986, pp. 13–14).

Belief Categories. Observations, descriptions, evaluations, inferences, and conclusions become commingled in the person's belief system and, depending on how they are cognated, have much to do with whether the individual will behave in a rational or an irrational manner. The following categories demonstrate how observations and inferences get tangled with one another and, based on the degree and kind of evaluation, lead to irrational beliefs and problem behavior (Ellis, 1984, pp. vi–vii; Ellis & Bernard, 1986, pp. 12–13):

1. *Nonevaluative observations or descriptions of what is happening:* "I see I'm going to be held up in this check-out line."
2. *Nonevaluative inferences about what is happening:* "I'm probably going to be late for my appointment because of this delay."

3. *Positive evaluative absolutistic inferences about what is happening:* "Because of this delay I'm going to be late. Since my clients are utterly dependent on me, these people should make way for me due to my importance. I will now have to speed to get to my appointment and save my client."

4. *Negative evaluative absolutistic external inferences about what is happening:* "People and events must not interfere with my life. It is wretched of these rotten swine to do so. The callous customer, the officious cop, my indignant client, and my uncaring wife all prove I am not given the due consideration I should have. I hate them and this burning feeling in my gut that *they* gave me!"

5. *Negative evaluative absolutistic internal inferences about what is happening:* "How many times will I try to cram too much in and not plan my time effectively? I am doomed to repeat this sloppy planning as long as I live. No professional would be so inefficient. I am an incompetent dirtbag!"

Consequences of Beliefs

Consequences about the foregoing ways of evaluating beliefs from an unpleasant activating event may also be partitioned according to their outcome (Ellis & Bernard, 1986).

1. *Desirable emotional consequences:* "Rats! You've once again crammed too much in and you wind up suffering the consequences." Appropriate bad feelings of frustration and irritation are manifested by the guilty doctor.

2. *Desirable behavioral consequences:* "You're just going to have to shape up and plan more effectively—particularly on Monday. Don't forget your appointment book next time!" Determination and planning to do better are self-contracted by the resolute doctor.

3. *Undesirable emotional consequences:* "If I had an Uzi submachine gun right now I'd make Rambo look like Mother Theresa and clean this #@&^*@! grocery store out!" Anger takes over the now running amok doctor.

4. *Undesirable behavioral consequences:* The Indianapolis 500 doctor roars out of the grocery store and is immediately picked up for going forty-five in a thirty-mile-per-hour zone. Undesirable anger consequences are manifested in wildly inappropriate driving and a hefty fine—not to mention alimony payments to come later.

Healthy, Growth-Promoting, Self-Actualized Personalities. As may be seen from these cognitive states, people largely create their own emotional disturbances. Because people have a measure of self-determination, they can choose to indoctrinate themselves in disturbed or undisturbed ways. Rational-emotive behavior theorists believe people have the power to change their self-defeating habits, but such change requires actively working at modifying thoughts, behaviors, and feelings (Dryden, 1984, p. 2; Ellis, 1986c, p. 32). Easily said, the ABCs of living one's life profitably often become as indecipherable as hieroglyphs, and without a psychological Rosetta stone to translate one's erroneous beliefs, maladjustment is the inevitable outcome.

Nature of Maladjustment

Precursors.   Although emotional disturbance is acquired through the combined influence of one's biological tendencies and one's life experiences, it is maintained by self-indoctrination. Ellis believes that children, much more than adults, lack the ability objectively to assess themselves and their environments and therefore tend to internalize the critical attitudes of their parents. Even if a child's parents are not exceptionally critical, Ellis suggests, children will tend to adopt the negative and perfectionistic attitudes from others in their surroundings, such as teachers, peers, and the media. However, children become emotionally disturbed *not only* because of parental attitudes toward them but also because of their "own tendency to take these attitudes too seriously, to internalize them, and to perpetuate them through the years" (Ellis, 1973, p. 34). It is this self-propagandizing that keeps the original irrational beliefs alive.

Psychological problems stem from the way people think about things: it is one's belief system (B) that leads to inappropriate emotional consequences (C) such as rage, depression, and extreme anxiety. This belief system (B) consists of two sets of beliefs. One set consists of rational beliefs (rBs), such as "How unfortunate it is that I have been fired, because it will be inconvenient to look for a new job." The other set of beliefs, those that lead to emotional disturbance, are irrational beliefs (iBs), such as "I must not be fired! How terrible and unjust! It will be catastrophic if I cannot find another job immediately!" (Ellis & Abrahms, 1978, p. 14). It is this limited set of irrational beliefs and their variations that underlie most emotional disturbance. These irrational beliefs typically occur in the form of simple declarative sentences that exist on a conscious or a preconscious level and are therefore readily accessible to conscious thought.

Musturbation.   Rational-emotive behavior therapy's most important and basic premises about irrational beliefs spring from unconditional "shoulds," "oughts," and "musts" people say to themselves about events. These explicitly commanding and demanding words generate what Ellis calls *musturbation.* Musturbation occurs when one moves from preferences, desires, and wishes about what is happening to absolutes and necessities about what is happening. Musturbatory thinking leads to three irrational beliefs (Ellis, 1984, p. viii):

1. *Awfulizing:* "I have no job. I'm 45 years old. I can't get another job. My family will starve. This is not just awful, it is catastrophic."
2. *Self-damnation:* "I am no good at my job. I am no good to my family. I am no damn good for anything."
3. *I-can't-stand-it-itis:* "I will not tolerate them firing me. I am totally destroyed by this and I will get even if it's the last thing I do."

Cold, Warm, and Hot Cognitions.   *Cold cognitions* are generally descriptions, observations, and nonevaluative inferences: "I lost my job. Tomorrow I'll have to start looking for another one." Cold cognitions are unemotional evaluations of facts. *Warm cognitions* emphasize preferences and nonpreferences rather than necessities and absolutes: "I sure don't like the fact that I lost my job after all these years. I'll have to start looking for another one. At my age, I wonder how tough that'll be." Warm cognitions may be seeded with mild or intense emotions, but as long as they indicate preference, they do not fall in the realm of emotional disturbance. *Hot cognitions* emphasize commands and demands: "I must get another job equal to what I lost. If I don't I'm a miserable failure." Hot cognitions are heavily laden emotional-demand statements that usually lead to dysfunctional behavior such as anxiety or depression (Ellis, 1984, p. vi; Zajonc, 1980). Hot cognitions may take a variety of forms—overgeneralizing, catastrophizing, magnification, non sequiturs, personalizing, labeling, and all-or-none thinking. These are all unrealistic statements because no empirical evidence exists to substantiate them (Ellis, 1984, p. ix). It is these hot cognitions with which REBT is mainly concerned.

Ego and Discomfort Anxiety.   Either or both of these anxiety types are generally present in emotional disturbance. *Ego anxiety* is a dramatic, powerful feeling that is accompanied by feelings of guilt and inadequacy in regard to a person's ability to perform: "I couldn't do that; therefore I'm a bum." Thus, the person's personal worth is threatened (Ellis, 1991b). *Discomfort anxiety* is often less dramatic, but it is more common, tends to be specific to "dangerous" situations, and is inherent in most phobias: "I've got to get out of this claustrophobic room or I'll die!" It is emotional tension that occurs when one's comfort is threatened (Ellis, 1986a, pp. 105–106). When the two types commingle, emotional disturbance is exponentially more profound (Ellis, 1986a, p. 110).

Secondary Symptoms.   An emotionally disturbed person will typically experience both primary and secondary symptoms. A secondary symptom occurs when the individual starts musturbating and develops irrational beliefs about the primary symptom. An ego-anxious person may start feeling depressed not only about a broken love affair but also about the depression state itself: "Oh God! I can't stand to think about that wave of depression washing over me, and even as I think of that I'm becoming even more depressed!" The discomfort-anxious person may feel threatened not only by the prospect of getting in a crowded elevator but also by the anxiety state itself: "When I remember how I felt, all sweaty, shaky, and queasy, those feelings start to come up again" (Ellis, 1986c, pp. 37–38).

Discomfort anxiety may become a secondary symptom of ego anxiety: "I must be comfortable about my performance around men." And ego anxiety may become a secondary symptom of discomfort anxiety: "This time I must be cool when I go out on a date; that way I won't feel like I'm in a torture chamber" (Ellis, 1984, p. xiii). Such circular, irrational thinking becomes a self-fulfilling prophecy and pulls the individual deeper and deeper into a vortex of dysfunctional behavior.

Low Frustration Tolerance.   People who fail to change their problematic behavior have largely their low frustration tolerance (LFT) to blame (Ellis, 1979b). LFT is central to understanding a variety of emotional disturbances ranging from procrastination to agoraphobia. The ability to tolerate discomfort, not for its own sake but so that psychological changes may be made, is a primary criterion of good mental health (Dryden, 1984, p. 8). Low frustration tolerance is a predictable consequence of a person holding on to one or more of the following ideas in the face of difficult circumstances: (1) "The world has to be arranged so that I do what I want, when I want, without hassle"; (2) "It is horrible to be presented with such difficult circumstances, and this must stop immediately"; (3) "I can't stand it when things go wrong" (Ellis, 1976b). Therefore, such people avoid short-term discomfort that may result in long-term benefit and opt for comfortable discomfort in the present and probably in the future (Ellis, 1979b).

Major Concepts

Self-Actualizing Behavior.   The main purpose of humans is to stay alive, but staying alive is not just moving from day to day in a "veil of tears" or "do-what-feels-good" world. The idea is to maximize happiness in a long-term investment program that operates within a social context (Dryden, 1984, p. 1).

Holistic Functioning.   Ellis proposes that humans have four basic processes necessary to survival and happiness; perceiving or sensing; feeling or emoting; moving or acting; and reasoning or thinking. He suggests that these processes are interrelated; human beings rarely experience any one of them in isolation. Thus, human beings function holistically—perceiving, moving, thinking, and emoting simultaneously (Ellis & Harper, 1979, p. 16). For example, when a person says, "I am thinking about this test," it would be more accurate to say, "I am perceiving, moving, feeling, and thinking about this test," for when one perceives a test, one also feels (e.g., anxious), thinks ("this looks difficult"), and acts (picks up a pen and writes).

Rational versus Irrational Thinking.   Rational thinking has five main characteristics. A person who thinks rationally (1) derives thoughts from objective fact rather than subjective opinion; (2) will be more likely to preserve life and limb; (3) will define his or her personal goals more quickly; (4) will produce a minimum of personal conflict and turmoil; and (5) will prevent him- or herself from getting into personal conflict with significant others (Ellis & Harper, 1979, p. 73).

The three main barriers to effective thinking and emoting are (1) lack of intelligence; (2) lack of knowledge about how to think intelligently; and (3) inability, because of neurotic behavior, to put intelligence and knowledge to good use. Ellis quips that neurosis "consists of stupid behavior by nonstupid people" (Ellis & Harper, 1979, p. 37).

Comprehensive Approach.   Rational-emotive behavior therapy openly employs cognitive, emotional, and behavioral approaches on the theoretical grounds that because human beings function in a holistic way, it is desirable to employ a diversity of techniques in treatment (Ellis & Abrahms, 1978, p. 39). Because REBT does not limit itself to a few particular disorders but takes on a wide range of clients, many of whom are, in Ellis's words, "tough customers," REBT and Ellis in particular have not been bashful about adapting techniques from other modalities to fit client needs. Thus, as long as the basic REBT framework is used, almost any effective therapeutic technique may be employed, and in this respect, REBT is perhaps the most eclectic system of all (Wessler & Wessler, 1980, p. 185).

Goals of Psychotherapy.   Ellis (1979a, p. 205) has stated that the overall goal of REBT involves "minimizing the client's central self-defeating outlook and acquiring a more realistic, tolerant philosophy of life." Two other central goals are reducing the client's anxiety (self-blame) and hostility (blaming others and the world) and teaching clients a method of self-observation and self-assessment that will ensure that this improvement continues (Ellis, 1973, p. 147). Thus, a primary goal of counseling is to teach clients to detect and dispute irrational beliefs.

Humanism.   Ellis asserts that "REBT is one of the most humanistically oriented of all therapies" in that it emphasizes that humans can fully accept themselves just because they are alive, just because they exist; they do not have to prove their worth in any way. Thus, humans can create their own meaningful purposes and therefore they need neither "magic nor gods on whom to rely" (Ellis, 1973, p. 63; Ellis 1986b; Ellis, 1989a).

Educational Model.   In essence, REBT involves teaching clients effective self-analysis. Rather than holding that its principles are the sole province of trained therapists, REBT advocates learning its principles through any available source. Therefore, within and outside of individual therapy, REBT uses a number of education-oriented techniques and resources, such as bibliotherapy, lectures, tape recordings, stories, seminars, demonstrations, and other mass presentations (Ellis & Harper, 1979, p. x).

Scientific Method.   Ellis has stated that there are two kinds of psychotherapy: scientific and nonscientific. Rational-emotive behavior therapy may be viewed as scientific in two ways. First, it strongly advocates the use of controlled experiments to test its efficacy. Second, clients are taught to test their theories about themselves and others and to question their own ideas, retaining those that have beneficial results and discarding those that have self-defeating consequences (Ellis & Abrahms, 1978, p. 13).

Semantic Approach.   Ellis has described REBT as a form of semantic therapy. Because individuals tell themselves both "sane" and "insane" things and because these beliefs take the form of internalized sentences, or "self-talk," one of the most powerful and elegant modalities for change consists of understanding, disputing, and acting against these internal verbalizations (Ellis & Harper, 1979, p. x).

Therapeutic Relationship.   Although empathy and unconditional positive regard are encouraged (Ellis, 1984, p. xi), rational-emotive therapists "do not believe a warm relationship between client and therapist is a necessary or a sufficient condition for effective personality change" (Ellis, 1979a, p. 186). On the contrary, Ellis suggests that too much personal warmth and empathic understanding may foster client dependence and the need for the therapist's approval. Ellis suggests that REBT principles work "with clients who think you dislike them, who actively hate you, who feel you are only lecturing to them, who blindly follow exercises you give them, and who otherwise maintain a minimal, and often unpleasant, relationship with you" (Ellis, 1973, p. 410). If a positive therapeutic relationship is engendered, it will most likely be because of the REBT therapist's authority and confidence in the approach; the absolute certainty he or she indicates concerning the cause of problems; constant monitoring of client progress through homework assignments; and the therapist's encouragement, compliments, focus on current meaningful problems, and use of down-to-earth language (Garfield, 1995).

Insight.   The following five insights are critical to REBT and, collectively or individually, may need to be discovered by clients before progress can occur. The client (1) understands that current ideas and beliefs play an important role in causing his or her problems; (2) knows that feeling upset and disturbed today is caused by continued self-indoctrination with the irrational beliefs he or she learned in the past; (3) needs to have awareness, acknowledgment, and appreciation of his or her irrational beliefs, because awareness without acknowledgment and appreciation is nonmotivating; (4) learns to accept him- or herself without guilt, even though no one but the client has caused the problem; and (5) sees that he or she has practiced self-propagandization for so long that the irrational beliefs have become incorporated as fact and that only hard work at detecting and disputing these irrationalities will rectify the problem. Clearly, understanding the first four insights will do little good if the client does not come to understand the fifth (Grieger, 1986, pp. 207–208).

The Counseling Process

Overview

The REBT therapeutic process is active, direct, confrontational, and based on the use of the logicoempirical method of scientific questioning, challenging, and debating (Ellis & Grieger, 1977, p. 20). During initial sessions, therapists confront their clients with evidence of their irrational thinking and behavior. Therefore, therapists teach clients the ABC theory and other basics of REBT. To accomplish this goal of reeducation, the therapist explains, persuades, lectures, teaches, confronts, and uses humor in disputing clients' irrational beliefs. Typically, therapists do not "tread lightly" in confronting, nor do they believe it is necessary to delay interpretations to later stages of therapy (Ellis, 1973, p. 90).

Three initiating procedures are necessary in REBT intervention. First, the therapist attempts to form a bond with the rational part of the client's personality against the irrational part. There is no one way to develop such bonds, and initiating procedures may range from a familiar to an expert role (Dryden, 1984, p. 17; Young, 1986b).

Second, agreement on desired outcome goals is reached. The therapist develops a problem list jointly with the client. The therapist must be careful at this juncture not only to avoid falling into the abyss of the external and environmental events (As) the client believes are causing the problem, but also to avoid disputing these events so vigorously that the client has no hope of success. Thus, the therapist suggests that for the moment the client assume that external events or people are beyond his or her control, and that various options might be viewed in that light (Dryden, 1984, pp. 18–19).

Third, the therapist solicits agreement on tasks to be undertaken in pursuit of the desired goals. Periodic review of progress and renegotiation of goals are assumed, because what the client initially believes to be the problem As may change dramatically as his or her iBs unfold.

Inherent in these three procedures is a clear and constant understanding by the client of what is occurring. Therefore, the language the therapist uses must clearly communicate what is planned—no small chore given the complexities involved in unraveling the client's iBs (Dryden, 1984, p. 19).

It should be clear from this overview that REBT makes no pretense about being value-free or entirely objective (Ellis & Bernard, 1986, p. 7; Young, 1986c). As a result, REBT strategies vigorously confront the twisted values and irrational belief systems of clients. The three broad categories of REBT techniques—cognitive, emotive, and behavioral—are all designed to jar the client's crooked thinking, feeling, and acting.

Cognitive REBT deals with the shoulds and oughts in clients' lives that lead them to perfectionist and absolutist thinking and behaving. It works on semantic precision in that it continuously asks clients to evaluate whether what has happened is as bad as they melodramatically make it (Ellis, 1989b, p. 213).

Emotive-evocative REBT dramatically emphasizes the difference between preferences and musts so clients can distinguish between the two. By use of modeling, humor, role playing, and unconditional acceptance, REBT therapists demonstrate how clients can actively dispute and distinguish between preferential and musturbatory thinking (Ellis, 1989b, p. 213).

Behavioral REBT employs various types of operant conditioning not only to change undesirable behavior and reinforce the client for more adaptive ways of behaving, but also to change the client's cognitions about the behavior. Clients may be asked to perform risk-taking activities in which they may intentionally set themselves up to fail to see that the results are not as fearsome as they imagined. They may be given hard tasks so that they can engage in tough activities and learn not to be upset or scared by them (Ellis, 1989b, p. 214).

Strategies for Helping Clients

Rational-emotive behavior therapists view cognitive interventions as the heart of therapy. Specifically, emotional disturbance can be traced to a finite number of irrational beliefs and their corollaries. The therapist, therefore, seeks to identify any of the following irrational beliefs or their variations to which the client subscribes (Ellis & Harper, 1979):

1. The idea that you must have love or approval from all people you find significant.
2. The idea that you must prove thoroughly competent, adequate, and achieving.
3. The idea that when people act obnoxiously and unfairly, you should blame and damn them and see them as bad, wicked, or rotten.
4. The idea that you have to view things as horrible and catastrophic when you get seriously frustrated, treated unfairly, or rejected.
5. The idea that emotional misery comes from external pressures and that you have little ability to control or change your feelings.
6. The idea that if something seems dangerous or fearsome, you must preoccupy yourself with it and make yourself anxious about it.

7. The idea that you can more easily avoid facing many life difficulties and self-responsibilities than undertake more rewarding forms of self-discipline.

8. The idea that your past remains all-important and that because something once strongly influenced your life, it has to keep determining your feelings today.

9. The idea that people and things should turn out better than they do and that you must view life as awful if you don't find good solutions to its realities.

10. The idea that you can achieve maximum human happiness by inertia or inaction or by passively or uncommittedly enjoying yourself.

Strategies for Detecting Irrational Beliefs

Problem Exploration.   A mistake often made by beginning therapists is not to gain a panoramic vision of all the things that brought the client to therapy. Boring right in to challenge the client's first irrational thought is likely to be counterproductive, even though it may be theoretically correct. Therapists need to hear the client out completely in regard to his or her ABCs, what part environmental circumstances play in them, and how the client's values contribute to his or her belief systems (Young, 1986b, p. 95).

One of the most important procedures in REBT is assessing A to the extent that a complete cognitive description of the event is obtained. Without all of the client's forecasts, predictions, assumptions, expectations, and interpretations of A, the therapist has little knowledge of the client's beliefs about and ways of prioritizing the numerous noxious stimuli within the "bad" event. Therapists new to REBT often do not spend enough time tracking the client's chain of inferences that led to the irrational beliefs and resulting emotional disturbances and negative behavioral outcomes. A simple procedure that will allow for complete exploration of A is to use two questions: "Then what?" and "Why's that?" (Moore, 1986, p. 6).

Once the client outlines the presenting problem, the therapist poses a continuous series of "Then what?" questions. Because the client will invariably mix a few B and C statements in with A, the therapist needs to respond to these statements by getting the client back on track with "Why's that?" questions. The interrogation stops when the client's inference chain of responses is exhausted. Typically the client will say, "That's all there is!" The therapist may then attack any part of the inference chain to which the client has reacted most strongly or that the therapist feels is most critical (Moore, 1986, pp. 6–12).

Subsequent sessions will begin with a request for a problem or a review of homework on a problem. Because many clients have such a constellation of problems that they cannot settle on one, the therapist may decide on one problem so that corrective measures can be started as soon as possible. Each session typically is limited to working on one or two problems (Young, 1986b, p. 99).

Ferreting Out B.   On the surface REBT seems ridiculously simple, yet digging out B in the ABC sequence drives many of our students crazy. A therapist may identify A and C but have a great deal of difficulty identifying B, and more difficulty identifying the irrational component of B. As Moore (1986, p. 3) has indicated, clients' thoughts are not the disturbance causing the irrational ideation. If Dr. James thinks he is about to have coronary arrest and has a dull burning stomachache, thinks his client will believe he is unprofessional and leave because he is late, believes his wife is an incompetent dolt and berates her for it, and flies into a rage because of the hold-up in the check-out line, none of these thoughts necessarily belongs in the B category.

Complicating things further, all of these thoughts may be valid and rational. If Dr. James's cholesterol level doesn't get within reasonable bounds he is a candidate for a heart attack—a possible C consequence. His stomachache is an immediate psychosomatic C consequence. His B belief about his wife, while unkind, may or may not be true, but it has little to do with irrationality. His rage is the resulting emotional C consequence of his hot cognitions. Further, all of these C consequences can just as reasonably do double duty as secondary effects of his original A event because they are reactions that have become chained to the original "stuck in the grocery line" event (Moore, 1986, p. 4). The irrationality of the rather long linkage of events and consequences from "stuck in the check-out line" to "appearance in divorce court" hinges not on any of the foregoing and what may be inferred or predicted from them so much as absolutes like "awful," "should," "must," and "completely worthless" that are pinned to them (Moore, 1986, p. 5).

Ellis & Grieger (1977, p. 10) have made some helpful suggestions for detecting irrational beliefs.

1. Look for "awfulizing" and ask the person, "What is awful about this situation?"
2. Look for beliefs such as "I can't stand it!" and examine what about this situation the person believes is unbearable.
3. Look for musturbating thoughts and determine what "shoulds," "oughts," and/or "musts" the person is telling him- or herself about the situation.
4. Look for blaming or damning of self or others and ask, "What does the person view as damnable or unforgivable about this behavior?"

Another simple way of detecting irrational beliefs is to look for them under one of three major musturbating belief systems.

1. "I am no good unless I always do well and receive complete acceptance for my performance." (I *must* behave perfectly and be loved and accepted by everyone.)
2. "You are no good unless you always act fairly and kindly toward me." (You *must* behave in ways that please me.)
3. "Life is no good unless it always provides me what I want or what I believe I deserve." (Life *must* be the way I believe it *should* be.)

Almost all irrational beliefs are related in some way to one or more of these three irrational beliefs (Ellis, 1984, p. viii).

A third way of detecting iBs is to listen for client problems about problems. Secondary symptoms are key signals of emotional disturbance: "I get nauseous every time I even think about asking a good-looking woman out for a date, not to mention how screwed up I get on the date." These secondary symptoms have nothing to do with the primary event (going out on a date) and everything to do with feelings, thoughts, and behaviors antecedent to the event (fear, terror, inadequacy, incompetence, stomachache, etc.) (Grieger, 1986, pp. 204–205).

Strategies for Disputing Irrational Beliefs

To dispute clients' irrational beliefs once they have been identified, the therapist uses three processes: debating, discriminating, and defining (Ellis & Grieger, 1977, p. 20). Ellis and Grieger describe *debating* as asking such questions as "What evidence is there to support this belief?" or "What makes this belief so or not so—in which way does it have truth or falseness?" In debating, the therapist often plays devil's advocate by putting such rhetorical questions squarely in the path of the client's illogical inferences and absolutist evaluations about events (Grieger, 1986, p. 210).

Discriminating helps the client to distinguish clearly between wants and needs, desires and demands, rational and irrational ideas, absolute and nonabsolute values, and behavior and personhood (Grieger, 1986, p. 210).

Defining consists of helping clients choose their terms more precisely. Therapists do this by reflecting the following logical principles: (1) just because one may act in certain ways at certain times, it does not follow that one will *always* act in this way; (2) just because one feels a certain way at a given point in time, it does not follow that one will feel that way forever; and (3) just because one has behaved in a certain way over a period of time, it does not follow that one is a failure (or any other descriptive term that attempts to define one's being or essence). The concept of being implies that one behaves this same way all the time and under all conditions both now and in the future (Ellis & Grieger, 1977, pp. 20–21).

Suppose a client who lost a job thinks, "I behaved awfully in that situation. I should never have behaved in that way. Therefore, I am a worthless clod, both now and in the future, who deserves to be punished!" In response, the REBT therapist might make the following challenges (Ellis & Grieger, 1977): First, assuming that one did behave stupidly, how can one substantiate the awfulness of that behavior? One cannot substantiate this because behaving badly does not mean that one behaved *totally* badly, as *awfulness* would imply. Second, viewing one's behavior as totally bad and viewing this as awful also implies that one lacks the capacity to do better in the future. However, poor past performance does not prove one can never make progress, which in any event is an unprovable assumption. Third, behaving totally badly implies that one could *not* have acted worse. This is also an invalid assumption, because no matter how badly one behaves, one could always have done worse. Fourth, assuming one should not have acted in this way is also unempirical, because no reason exists that one should not have acted in a certain way. Though it might have been preferable to have acted differently, it is not a necessity. By implying that one should have acted differently, one implies that there is a law of the universe that commands that one must have acted differently. This is clearly an impossibility, because if such a law existed, one would have been forced to have acted differently. Fifth, believing that one is a rotten person for behaving badly is also unprovable, because it suggests that one would forever behave rottenly in relation to everything. It is impossible to prove that one will always continue to act badly.

At the conclusion of this disputing process, the client acquires a new enactment or effect (E) that enables him or her to think about self, others, and the world more rationally in the future. This effect (E) involves a new cognitive effect (cE), a new emotive effect (eE), and a new behavioral effect (bE) as well. For example, a client will begin to feel less depressed (although still concerned) about not having a job at present. Also, instead of avoiding looking for a job, the client will actively begin to seek a new one and to work on correcting whatever problems contributed to the loss of the old one (Ellis & Grieger, 1977, pp. 22–31).

Solution-Focused Brief REBT

Huber (2000) has welded the principles of REBT with those of solution-focused brief therapy (SFBT) (see Chapter 11 for a complete description of SFBT). In Huber's approach, the focus is on the exceptions to the problem rather than the problem itself. The *exception* concept comes directly from SFBT and is founded on the notion that clients tend to believe that the noxious event *always happens the same way without exception.* The client is so immersed in the current problem that he or she fails to see exceptions (p. 79).

Huber's (2000) A'B'C' brief REBT approach is a variation on the standard ABC paradigm in which:

A's are detailed descriptions of successful solutions that were employed by the individual during times when he or she was functioning in a more competent manner under similar circumstances. This is an example of an exception.

B's are the client's more rational beliefs that accompanied the successful solution as opposed to the irrational beliefs that would have accompanied a typical problem event.

C's are the positive emotional and behavioral consequences accompanying A' and B'. These indicate that the individual functioned more competently, resulting in an exception (p. 79).

The task of the therapist is to first get the client to recount one of these exceptions. This is much like SFBT, but with one variation. Rather than focusing on the activating event of the exception, Huber focuses on the rational beliefs that caused the event to be an exception. That is, what and how the client thought so that he or she did not fall into hot, absolutistic, musturbatory thinking, but rather engaged in a cool, preferential, conditional decision-making process that resulted in positive behavioral and emotional outcomes (Huber, 2000, pp. 71–77).

The D' of Huber's (2000) system has three components. The therapist first creates a great deal of cognitive dissonance by comparing the two belief systems and then piling up evidence that confirms the benefits of the rational belief system. The therapist then engages the client in exploring the exception, and the rational beliefs that accompany it, in such a way that the greater benefits of the rational exception are affirmed. The third task is to review and confirm how the irrational belief contributed to distressful emotional and behavioral consequences while likewise confirming that the rational belief had much more positive emotional and behavioral payoffs. The E' (or effect) phase involves rehearsing, reviewing, and confirming the step-by-step manner in which the client uses a rational B' approach to prepare for upcoming events in which the irrational B would have typically been the norm (pp. 79–81).

Cognitive Techniques

Although its core cognitive technique is disputing irrational beliefs, REBT employs a variety of verbal procedures to enhance disputation. The following techniques demonstrate the broad array available.

Interpretation of Defenses.   Unlike psychoanalysis, REBT assumes that defenses stem largely from self-condemnation. Thus, if clients condemn themselves for having a symptom they will often use various defenses to keep this symptom out of their conscious awareness (Ellis & Abrahms, 1978).

> TH: Yep! It sure sounds like your wife is an interfering nag. Yet, you did marry her. You did make that choice, and I wonder if blaming her for the rotten marriage isn't a subtle way of condemning yourself for all those crummy decisions you indicate you've made.

Analogies, Parables, and Metaphors.   In REBT, cognitive restructuring involves altering the language and meaning that clients apply to their situations and problems so that abstract beliefs become clear and concrete. Metaphors, analogies, and parables can play an important role in reframing the problem so the irrational ideation can be seen more easily (DiGiuseppe & Muran, 1992; Wessler & Wessler, 1980).

> TH: So you are the little Dutch boy with his finger in the dike, courageously holding back the sea of problems for your children. But in your protecting them, I wonder if you're really Pinocchio and it's your nose and not your finger that's involved when you tell yourself that you must protect them from everything in an evil world. By telling yourself that it becomes easy to believe that you are absolutely necessary to their existence and survival.

Paralinguistics.   The therapist may dramatically emphasize the irrationality of a situation by drawing out the emotionally hot cognitions a client makes by acting both verbally and behaviorally in a flamboyant manner (Walen, DiGiuseppe, & Wessler, 1980, p. 178).

> TH: (*doubling over in feigned pain*) Ohhh, my Gawwwwd! (*whining*) How hoooorible! How (*gasp*) awwwwful.

When the therapist wishes to change from a hot to a warm cognition, he or she may speak slowly and distinctly in a controlled, calm, but powerful voice.

> TH: (*straight up in chair, head up, chest out*) It is unfortunate (*shifts to slumped position*) but not awwwful.

Therapeutic Markers.   Before launching into an irrational diatribe, clients often make antecedent statements that activate their belief systems. The therapist may ask the client to restate such cues (Dryden, 1984, pp. 78–79).

TH: I'm going to stop the tape. I want you to hear that last statement you made and how it leads into those chiseled-in-stone evaluations you make. But first I'd like you to give it back to me with all the emotion you just put into it.

Reduction to Absurdity. The therapist appears to accept the illogical premise of the client. Then he or she carries the faulty premise to its logical extreme (Ellis, 1971). Care must be taken with this technique so that clients do not believe they are being held up to ridicule.

TH: Okay! You want people to leave you alone and quit bugging you. That sounds reasonable. How could you do that and really be alone? Lock yourself up in your room? That wouldn't work very well because you'd have to get food and water and have some minimal contact with the other folks. Perhaps you could go be a survivalist and live in the Rockies. You could be alone there, grow your own food, trap, fish, and hunt. Oh, you say you don't know how to do that and you would starve to death? Excellent! Then you could really be alone, couldn't you! I believe we stumbled onto something here!

Contradiction with a Cherished Value. The therapist introduces a dissonant situation for the client by demonstrating that a particular cognition is incongruent with a valued belief or quality (Crabb, 1971).

TH: You've stated that your word is your bond. Yet do you not keep a bond with yourself? It appears not when you go back on the promises you make to yourself.

Pragmatic Disputes. One way of encouraging clients to surrender their irrational beliefs is to indicate rather dramatically their continued adherence to one such belief (Dryden, 1984, p. 79).

TH: If you continue to behave in that way, you will be miserable for the rest of your life. So have a miserable forever!

Paradoxical Intention. Here the therapist prescribes the symptom and asks the client to practice it repeatedly or to exaggerate the problem (Nardi, 1986, p. 279). Specifically, this technique may be helpful with a resistant client with whom all else has failed. However, care must be taken in its use because of its caustic and regressive nature.

TH: I can see that the anger you feel toward her is the only thing that's keeping you going. I couldn't possibly ask you to give that up since it's so important. I really understand why you'd want to bring that emotion into therapy and try it out in here.

TH: Therefore, I'd suggest you reserve some time for it. Take an hour every morning just to harp and brood on that anger. It deserves at least that much quality time.

TH: Anger has served you well in your present marriage of twenty years. So if you really are getting a divorce, that's certainly something you need to take into your next marriage to keep it going.

Humor.   Almost all neurotic resistance comes from taking things too seriously. One of the antidotes to irrational thinking is a strong dose of therapeutic humor (Ellis, 1986a, p. 34). Humor helps to clarify clients' self-defeating behavior in a nonthreatening manner and to show them the absurdity, realism, hilarity, and enjoyability of life (Ellis & Abrahms, 1978, pp. 145–149). Incredulous responses and irony are typical ways REBT therapists attempt to get clients to laugh at their irrationalities and thus take responsibility for them (Ellis, 1986d, p. 264).

> TH: Uh-huh! That pecan pie jumps out of the refrigerator and demands that you devour it.
>
> TH: That's right. It's all a plot. It's the Wall Street term paper trust. They've gobbled up every good idea and have all those term papers locked up in a big vault and will only sell them for your firstborn.
>
> TH: I have this image of you in your coffin, dead from lung cancer, the undertaker nailing the lid shut, and you rising up and asking if he couldn't stop and everybody have a cigarette break.

Semantic Precision.   Rational-emotive behavior therapists pay particular attention to the language their clients use because they believe language shapes thinking and vice versa. Therefore, the REBT therapist, following the principles of general semantics founded by Alfred Korzybski, assists clients in making the following changes in their language usage (Ellis & Abrahms, 1978, pp. 133–135).

1. Instead of using "must" or "should," clients learn to use "It would be preferable" or "It would be highly desirable."
2. Instead of using "I can't" or "It's impossible," clients learn to use "I can, but I find it difficult to do so" or "So far I haven't, but that doesn't prove it is impossible."
3. Instead of using "I always do badly," clients learn to use "I usually do badly, but that does not mean it is impossible to do better."
4. Instead of saying "It would be awful or terrible if . . . ," clients learn to use "It would be disadvantageous or inconvenient if . . . ."
5. Instead of stating, "I am a bad or worthless person because . . . ," clients learn to say "I cannot legitimately rate myself on the basis of my actions."

As a result of changing the language in their thinking process, clients think and behave differently. Consequently, they also feel differently.

Emotive Techniques

This second broad category of therapeutic techniques is termed *evocative-emotive* because of its emphasis on coming to grips with debilitating affects (Ellis & Abrahms, 1978). Uncovering affect is important for two reasons. For some clients, identifying emotions and beliefs by verbal means is extremely difficult. Other clients may be able to identify their feelings and cognitions but have trouble anchoring them to events. When this occurs, the

REBT therapist can use *vivid imagery* to generate images of activating events. Focusing on such images enables the client to anchor emotions with events and gain access to cognitions below the level of awareness that might not be reached by verbal methods (Dryden, 1984, p. 60). Some representative techniques of vivid imagery follow.

Negative Imagery.   Ellis believes dramatic intrusion into the aversive event is much more likely to influence clients' irrational ideas than slowly desensitizing them to it (Ellis, 1986a, p. 43). In negative imagery, clients are asked to imagine one of the worst things that could happen to them, intensely imagine themselves feeling their most feared inappropriate emotions, implode these feelings, and visualize themselves changing them to appropriate feelings, such as regret or determination (Ellis, 1986d, p. 270).

> **TH:**   Picture yourself up on the podium speaking to the audience. You are scared to death. You start to stumble over words, you feel yourself breaking into a cold sweat, the room starts to reel, and you think you are going to faint. You want to sink into the floor you are so embarrassed and ashamed. This is horrible and catastrophic. You are a complete fool with no place to hide. Now *stop*! You stumble over the words. You grimace sheepishly, and then smile and say to your audience, "And for my next attempt at perfect elocution I will say Peter Piper picked a peck of pickled peppers." You breath deeply twice, compose yourself and continue with a feeling of calmness and satisfaction.

Stepping Out of Character.   The client identifies ways of emoting or behaving that he or she would like to adopt but that involve stepping out of character to do so. Often, imagining how a significant other would act in the situation is used as a model (Dryden, 1984, pp. 34–35).

> **TH:**   Suppose you are Reverend Jesse Jackson making a speech to the church deacons. How would he come across? What would he believe about what he had to say? How would he say it? What would he be feeling as he did it? What would he be saying to himself as he stood before his audience?

Future Imaging.   Extreme anxiety is often generated by forecasting negative consequences about a future event and starting to live as if the catastrophic image were occurring in the present (Dryden, 1984, p. 60). The client is asked to imagine the feared situation as if it were happening in the present. As the image occurs, the therapist processes the anxiety and the irrationality that form the basis of the fear.

A converse approach may be applied when a client is having extreme distress with what is happening in the present. The client is asked to imagine what the event would appear to be in the distant future. Events viewed as terrible in the present usually take on a less dramatic hue when seen from a chronological distance (Dryden, 1984, p. 26).

> **TH:**   Let's take apart each one of those awful things that you believe are going to happen, put them under the intense power of a rational microscope, and see all those irrational bugs that infect you with anxiety and self-doubt.

Labeling.   When clients continue to generalize and assign global ratings to themselves or others, they are asked to describe some of their behaviors, attitudes, talents, interests, and so on by writing them on sticky notes and pasting them all over their bodies. Clients can thus begin to see the futility of ascribing a generic label to themselves or to others (Wessler & Wessler, 1980; Young, 1986b).

> **TH:**   So far I have counted forty-seven negative, killer statements you've made about yourself in the first twenty minutes of our session. If you don't mind, I'm going to start labeling some sticky notes and let you start wearing those around. You can put them on your body wherever it feels appropriate.

Rational Role Reversal.   A variation of role playing is *rational role reversal.* Once the client has gained some sophistication with ABC theory, the therapist takes the role of a rather naive client with a problem much the same as the client's. The client then takes on the role of the therapist and actively disputes the therapist's beliefs. This procedure gives clients excellent practice in detecting, debating, defining, and, it is hoped, inoculating themselves against their irrationalities (Kassinove & DiGiuseppe, 1975).

> **TH:**   I want to be the client today and behave irrationally. You be the therapist. Of course, now it's your job to catch me when I start musturbating and scold me for engaging in the self-gratification of saying "ought" and "should."

Emotionally Charged Language.   Rational-emotive behavior therapists often use emotionally toned words, phrases, and sentences that their clients can then use with themselves. Ellis suggests that strong language often has more impact and hence is more powerful in inducing clients to change their irrational beliefs (Dryden, 1984, p. 82).

> **CL:**   I should be able to stay in control.
>
> **TH:**   You should! You should shit! Particularly every time you start into thinking, "I should be cool, this date should be perfect, he's the only guy left, I'll never get married, I'll be an old maid in a rest home with the oatmeal drooling down my chin. I'm sooo alone and I'm sooo depressed! I shouldn't be like this and absolutely shouldn't end up like that!" Every time those mental billboards run through your head, you ought to give yourself a psychological enema, run right to the bathroom and flush that crap out.
>
> **CL:**   I don't know. The way you say that, it's really crude and vulgar.
>
> **TH:**   Maybe, but all those shoulds, those absolute ways you evaluate each relationship are pretty shitty in what they do for you. In fact, I wonder if you might not interject, in big capital letters, the word "S-H-I-T" into those statements. If the word is really that distasteful, it may just make the shoulds pretty distasteful too!

Behavioral Techniques

This third broad category of therapeutic techniques may also be described as *behavioral-active-directive* (Ellis & Abrahms, 1978, pp. 102–123). Indeed, REBT draws on many techniques that behavior therapists employ, although its objectives are different in that it uses behavior modification and management as means to reinforce cognitive change rather than as ends in themselves.

Homework Assignments.   One of the central REBT techniques is action-oriented homework assignments. Usually, a rational-emotive behavior therapist will assign something that the client fears or finds difficult to do. Rational-emotive behavior therapy is one of the first therapeutic modalities to use homework as an effective reinforcer. Homework helps ensure that what goes on in the safe haven of therapy is carried out and taken into the "dangerous" world of the client. Homework assignments are applied directly and forcefully to the problem rather than in incremental approximations, as in behavioral approaches. The reasoning is that many clients would see setting up an elaborate incremental plan as merely creating another problem, rather than solving the original problem (Young, 1986b, p. 117).

Flooding.   This philosophy of aggressive proactivity ranges throughout REBT techniques and comes from Ellis's belief that graduated approaches only confirm client fears that the assignment is too risky to attempt. Sudden, repeated, and maximum effort is much more effective, not only in desensitizing clients to the pain of taking action, but also in extinguishing ideas that they can't perform the behavior and that it will destroy them if they do (Ellis, 1984, p. xiii; Ellis, 1986c, p. 43). Therefore, no matter what excuses or rationalizations clients make about not doing the fearsome behavior, REBT pushes hard to convince them they can do it.

CL: Look, I'm telling you I'll come apart. I know what happens when I walk into a crowded room with all those classy people. I become so terrified I may even throw up.

TH: That's what you did before we rolled over all those belief rocks and those slimy little irrational musturbations came crawling out. Now you've got all kinds of new armor-plated self-statements to carry you through this. Even if you did puke in front of everybody it would only be embarrassing. The coroner does not check out people who vomit. You will not die! You will have the opportunity to enjoy the hell out of yourself, and maybe even have a chance to meet an attractive person. You can harp and brood about being the consummate social ass for the rest of your life or you can start enjoying yourself right now. So you choose!

Penalization.   What Ellis has to say about punishment flies in the face of what most humane therapists and behavioral researchers might accept as a legitimate therapeutic procedure. However, the low frustration tolerance of Ellis's "tough customers" invariably prompts them to go for immediate reinforcement as opposed to long-term gains. Therefore, the counterpoint to immediate gratification is often immediate and drastic penalization of a repetition of the problem behavior (Ellis, 1986c, p. 42).

TH: Okay! If you chicken out of the reception at the Peabody Hotel that the Junior League is giving for Senator Phoghorn, I'd like to propose that you immediately avail yourself of getting a date with that guy you refer to as a casting reject from the *Hunchback of Notre Dame*. You know, the guy that keeps asking you out, the one with the garlic breath and industrial-grade musk ox cologne. The one that really makes you want to throw up. How about making a little contract that you'll do that?

Practicing and Reinforcing Positive Cognitions.   Like cognitive behaviorists, practitioners of elegant REBT make extensive use of rational, positive, coping statements. The REBT Self-Help Form (Sichel & Ellis, 1983) is a paper-and-pencil version of what goes on in the disputational process in therapy. The generic rational beliefs presented previously in this chapter are listed with space for the client's own irrational beliefs. The client is asked to circle each irrational belief that applies to him or her and then write a disputational statement and a corresponding rational belief next to it. For example:

Irrational Belief
I must be approved or accepted by people I find important.

Disputes (client statements)
Why must I? And who is to say these people are more important than I am?

Effective Rational Beliefs (client statements)
While it would be grand if everyone thought I was great, that's not going to happen, particularly if I'm me. And if I am me and people like me, I'll know they really like me for what I really am and not for what I pretend to be. Furthermore, I'm only anxious about this. It isn't dangerous. It's a bit uncomfortable right now, but risk in any new situation is distressing.

These statements are not only written down but also may be audio- or videotaped for the client to use at home to "rewire" his or her cognitions. The client is then given the mission of building a complete menu of the disputational and positive coping statements to introject when irrational beliefs and their attendant behavior start to crop up (Dryden, 1984, pp. 30–34). (This procedure is examined in extensive detail in Chapter 10.)

Sample Case

Rafael Munoz, 21, is a senior finance major in college. He is a good-looking, well-built young man with jet black hair and coal black eyes. On first appearance, he could melt the heart of any woman, but as he speaks, a quite different story unfolds in this condensed therapeutic encounter.

CL: (*looking askance*) I'm embarrassed to talk about this problem. Nobody knows about it but me. Err . . . that's not quite right . . . some other people . . . women . . . they know about it. I feel . . . well . . . inadequate . . . if you know what I mean . . . and I thought . . . ah . . . maybe I could use some help.

TH: I understand how difficult it is to come to counseling, particularly when the problem is personal, but I wonder if you could just spell it out and for right now not worry about how embarrassing it might be.

While being accepting and empathic, the therapist immediately sets the REBT stage by asking the client to hook some self-statements (beliefs) into the problem.

CL: (*gazes off into the distance*) Well, okay. I've been pretty decent with women. Not any great playboy, but holding my own while playing the field. However, the last couple of women I've been close to, I really wanted a relationship, but when we'd get serious I'd start to get really uptight. Worst of all, this last girl, Maranda, is someone I really like a lot, I mean we've even thought about maybe marriage. But a month ago, we started making out and I started to get actually . . . well . . . sick, sweating, stomach churning, and I had . . . um . . . ah . . . an erection, and it just melted. I made an excuse that I wasn't feeling well, but I had to get out of there right away. I think it was maybe one of those panic attacks I read about in psych class. It was awful and it makes me break out in a sweat just to talk about it. The more I think about it the more nervous I get. I keep telling myself, "You've got to get over this, there's nothing wrong and this is the woman of your dreams," but the more I think about it the worse it gets and I'm starting to think it'll go on forever and I'm nuts or something. Maranda will get sick of this, and then what? Who'd want some eunuch?

TH: So now you know that you cannot possibly have a relationship with any woman you care about and pretty soon every woman who is worth anything on this campus will know about it. Just thinking about it makes you uptight. Notice how your belief about this one instance gets generalized to every other relationship. So now you are a complete sexual wimp and that is absolutely intolerable.

CL: Maybe not a total wimp, but for sure sexually and you're right about the intolerable. I couldn't stand that.

The therapist, while listening to the client's description of the activating event (a date that was getting intimate) and consequences (nonperformance, anxiety attack, and flight), is much more concerned about his beliefs (inadequate, laughed at, worrying about future events). The therapist continues to tap the client's beliefs about the event by finding out what negative self-talk he practices when in the intolerable situation.

TH: For a moment just shut your eyes and imagine you're back on the couch in Maranda's apartment and all of what you just told me is starting to happen. What are you saying to yourself?

CL: (*shuts eyes and starts to squirm and fidget*) Oh Mother of Mary. This can't be happening again. Come on, get with it. She's so foxy. Hell! You love this woman. You've got to cut it now. Get hold of yourself, but I can't! Man, if I can't make it with her, I'll never do it. I've gotta get outta here. Look at how I'm shaking and in a cold sweat. How can this be happening?

By setting the client in the event, the therapist now has several insane statements that the client uses to pursue his irrational beliefs and the bad consequences that issue from those beliefs. The "can'ts," "got tos," and "nevers" are all absolutistic evaluations and inferences that the therapist seeks to counter-propagandize by first showing the client what these musturbatory thoughts do to him. He does this by using warm cognitions and nonabsolutistic inferences through an analogy using the client's favorite pastime, soccer.

TH: You said you play on the soccer team. Let me make an analogy to that. Let me propose what you might say if you performed poorly and missed an easy shot. You'd probably say, "Hell, I blew that snap shot on goal. Man, I've got to get another shot." You'd feel disappointed and maybe even a bit angry and embarrassed, but you surely wouldn't say, "Because I missed this shot, I'll *never* make another" or "Because I can't perform in this situation, I can't perform in any other." But that's what I hear you saying about your relationship with Maranda.

CL: That's true enough. So why is this bugging me?

TH: I'm also saying your so-called failure is not your real problem. It is more what you're saying to yourself and have probably been saying for a while, even before you started having performance anxiety. It would appear that as you get closer and closer to really thinking about an enduring relationship, there's anxiety about all the responsibility concerned with that. Since you can't even handle a little intimacy with someone who might be a potential partner, how can you handle all the other responsibilities of a relationship? I see these billboards flashing through your head:

1. I am a worthless and incompetent person when I don't do well with intimate relationships.
2. My miserable feelings come from external pressures (women who want commitments, or worse, want to get married). I have little ability to control my feelings of anxiety and panic.
3. Because this is so fearsome, all my time has to be spent thinking about and obsessing on my pitiful and terrifying inadequacies.
4. Things are awful and catastrophic when I believe I will have to assume responsibility for someone else.

The therapist uses some interpretation to propose what the client's deep, philosophical beliefs about responsibility are and how they are entangled in the problem. He then proposes the major irrationalities that drive the client into hot inferences and evaluations. This lengthy discourse is typical of the psychoeducational approach used by REBT to reprogram client thinking.

CL: I think you're right about all that performance and responsibility stuff. That sure goes through my head and I get sick thinking about both those things, but . . . I don't know, it really is awful. I don't know if I can handle it. Doesn't make me feel like much of a man, I can tell you.

TH: Do you like being out on a date with her? Does it make you feel good to be able to get a date with her? To be seen with her? To talk with her? To hold her and kiss her?

CL: Sure . . . it's . . . ah . . . was great . . . but not the end . . . and now I don't know. . . .

TH: So you get pleasure from it. You like soccer too. It makes you feel good, a real man, right?

CL: Well, sure.

TH: If you blew your knee out and couldn't play any more, then what?

CL: I'd hate it. I love that game.

TH: Would you be a eunuch? Not a real man?

CL: Of course not. I mean I'd miss it, but lots of guys don't play soccer.

TH: Why then would you think yourself more inadequate if one satisfaction is taken away as opposed to another? Do you see how that self-value is generated in your head? Even if your condition of impotence were permanent—which it is not—all that would have happened is that you would be without one major satisfaction in your life. It would sure not be fun and it would certainly be a bummer, but you would be no less of a man. I mean, would you go into the women's locker room to change?

CL: (*laughs*) That's really crazy, of course not.

TH: So you see how in the one instance a particular disappointment allows you to talk yourself into being crazy—"not a man"—while another disappointment would not.

CL: When you put it that way it makes sense, but the bigger thing you said, the relationship stuff—I don't know if I could handle that responsibility.

TH: Who told you you can't? Where is it written that Rafael is inadequate to the task of handling a meaningful relationship? Have you a crystal ball that allows you to predict the future?

The therapist directively confronts the client by engaging him in a Socratic dialogue. The client is asked to query himself as to the evidence of these irrational beliefs. Of course there is no evidence. A technique from Young (1986c, p. 154) is used that compares favorite satisfactions and asks the client to equate them to his overall self-worth. The foregoing is typical of what Young (1986c, p. 151) calls "less me" thinking, in which clients believe they have some kind of inborn or built-in value, and that disappointment in the form of failure or disapproval somehow lessens that value.

CL: Well, no. I guess there isn't any real proof that I couldn't. But what am I going to do about making love if I am in love, or worse, when I am married?

TH: Forget about the event, the sex, and concentrate on replacing all those "shoulds" and "oughts" with some sentences such as "It would be nice if we made love, but who I am is not contingent on my being a stud. Maranda liked me before I got scared, so there's some little bit of me that she finds attractive. Nobody is making me do this, so if I really don't feel like going out on a date tonight, or making out, or making some kind of commitment, that's okay. It is something I prefer to do. This is a superfine woman and maybe it will work into something and maybe not. I'd like to go out on a date with her again, but if I don't, there are 9,742 other women on this campus. What I really want to do is enjoy being with a woman like Maranda."

By replacing the negative, self-defeating thoughts with positive, enhancing ones, the therapist promotes a way to change beliefs and subsequent maladaptive behavior. The therapist does this by replacing hot demand statements with cooler preferential statements.

CL: That all sounds fine, the power of positive thinking and all, but I don't know if I've even got the courage to face her again.

TH: You're probably right. She's probably too good for you. I wouldn't want you to have to go through that trauma. I'd propose you lower your sights on the kind of a girl you really want. That way you wouldn't have to feel so inept.

CL: Now wait, I didn't mean that. I'd just kinda like to ease back into this.

TH: If you do that, then you only give yourself more time to harp and brood and anxious yourself. By backing away from the problem you continue anxiousing yourself, which feeds into your insane ideas about what this is all about and just piles more insane thoughts onto what the wretched consequences are for you. Picture yourself as a Dagwood Bumstead sandwich, with all those beliefs packed in there, and see if you don't have some gastric distress as you keep trying to eat it.

When the client backs away from dealing with the problem, the therapist uses a bit of paradox and humor to call into question the behavior of what the client really wants. Further, the therapist uses *anxious* as a verb to demonstrate to the client that his thinking, and not a crippled libido or an exceptional woman, makes him suffer these behavioral outcomes.

TH: I am going to propose a homework assignment to you, but first I want to tape a session with you in which you use all those killer statements. Then we'll shift and replace them with positive, coping thoughts. For example, "Because I didn't respond as I liked once, it doesn't necessarily mean I never will. Just because getting into a deep relationship seems scary doesn't mean it will be life-threatening. There is absolutely no evidence at all to substantiate that notion." (*turns the recorder on, relaxes the client, and then floods him with the aversive thoughts, feelings, and behaviors of the situation; sets the image up to confirm the client's worst nightmare about the event in the most noxious manner, plugging in what the client says to himself and also what he believes Maranda might be saying to herself about him*)

CL: Whew! That was rough! But I can see how I get myself into that state, and it really burns me up.

TH: Well if it really burns you up, then are you willing to use some of that angry energy to try using some of those coping thoughts I used? If this is going to work, you've got to do your homework and then take it out there and see if you've learned anything.

CL: All right. I'll give it a go.

The therapist now builds and enhances the coping statements as the tape is made, hammering relentlessly at each irrational statement the client makes and putting a new positive statement in its place.

TH: Indeed, now that we've got that down on tape, I want you to go home and listen to it every day for a week. Then I want you to take what you've learned and try it out on a date with Maranda.

This case demonstrates two components of REBT. First, general REBT is used to deal with the problem—overcoming performance anxiety and panic. Second, elegant REBT seeks to change the client's beliefs about the far deeper problem of assuming responsibility in a relationship. This second problem, if successfully resolved, will mean the client attains not only a behavioral change but a philosophical change as well, one that will have meaning across and throughout his life.

Contributions of Rational-Emotive Behavior Therapy

One of the most valuable contributions that REBT has emphasized, as well as clarified, is the relationship between human thinking and emotion. It is abundantly clear that an effective way to approach changing one's emotions is to change the content of one's thinking.

Another contribution of REBT is its comprehensive, eclectic approach to treatment that includes cognitive, behavioral, and emotive components. In addition, REBT principles have contributed to the development of some important therapeutic innovations. For example, REBT's cognitive-emotive imagery is one of the foundations of modern cognitive-behavior therapy.

A third contribution of REBT is its emphasis not on past events or traumas themselves as creating human disturbances but on one's interpretation of them. Ellis, with his ABC theory, has clearly delineated how this process might occur and how it can be changed. Thus REBT has reinforced the concept that the therapist needs to focus on clients' internal processes rather than on the situation itself in searching for the roots of clients' problems.

Another strong point of REBT is its emphasis on action-oriented homework. REBT can be credited with being one of the first therapeutic approaches to make homework a standard part of the therapeutic regimen.

Another valuable aspect of REBT is its educational, preventive, "democratic" stance toward treatment. Rational-emotive behavior therapy does not insist that the therapist be the "keeper of secret knowledge" but instead advocates that people can learn and change through a variety of means, including impersonal methods such as tape recordings, films, and lectures.

Shortcomings of Rational-Emotive Behavior Therapy

One possible shortcoming of REBT is its de-emphasis of the therapeutic relationship as well as the therapeutic conditions of empathy and therapist–client rapport. Ellis claims that therapeutic change may occur even when the client actively dislikes the therapist. If a client feels "not understood," "not listened to," or "not cared about," it is quite possible that he or she may terminate therapy before obtaining the benefits of the REBT approach.

A related concern is REBT proponents' suggestion that it is desirable to confront clients immediately with their irrational thinking and to make interpretations in the initial session despite client defensiveness. Yet research on counseling outcomes shows over and over that establishing trust and building rapport are critical to therapeutic outcome. It is hard to see how initially confronting a defensive client is going to do that.

Another limitation is the belief that it is effective for the therapist to talk, persuade, and be highly active during the initial as well as later therapeutic sessions. One danger of this approach is prematurely defining and hence "misdefining" or limiting the problem. Once the problem is erroneously defined, the therapist may convince the client that this off-target definition is indeed the root of the problem.

A possible limitation of REBT is its almost total emphasis on changing emotion by changing one's thinking to a more rational perspective. As Hendricks (1977) and other Gestalt therapists suggest, in some cases the most effective way to change emotion is by letting oneself completely experience the emotion rather than trying to block the expression of it. Sometimes more energy is expended trying to change or block the feeling, as in the case of experiencing grief, than simply letting oneself fully experience and work through, rather than against, the feeling.

Also, as Corey (1982, p. 812) points out, "because the REBT therapist has a large degree of power by virtue of persuasiveness and directiveness, psychological harm is more possible in REBT than in the less directive client-centered approach." Thus, it is crucial that the REBT therapist be sensitive and knowledgeable in the application of REBT techniques so as to avoid misusing REBT to browbeat clients into confused and angry individuals who feel misunderstood, frustrated, and powerless. Another possible danger is that clients may accede to the therapist's authority without really internalizing the belief system necessary for change to occur.

Although REBT may at first glance seem as simple as the ABCs, it is not. No theory we teach gives students a harder time when they attempt to put it into practice. The reason is twofold. First, digging out belief systems is not a simple matter. The deductive form of reasoning that REBT calls for requires the ability to grasp the basic premises of the client's syllogisms (Cohen, 1987). Doing so is long, tough detective work, and time and again neophytes get tangled in the activating event or the consequences without ever nailing down the belief. This problem is also true for many clients who may not have the intellectual capacity or language development to comprehend the cognitive intricacies of elegant REBT.

Rational-Emotive Behavior Therapy with Diverse Populations

Human beings are reared in social groups and spend much of their lives trying to impress, live up to the expectations of, and outdo the performances of others. Emotional disturbance is frequently associated with people caring too much about what others think and stems from their believing they can accept themselves only if others think well of them. Thus, cultural as well as family influences tend to play a significant part in bolstering people's irrational thinking (Ellis, 1989b, pp. 206–209).

As a result, REBT therapists have not shied away from diverse populations (Mitchell & DiGiuseppo, 1997) or what Ellis has sometimes called "tough customers." Rational-emotive behavior therapy is an excellent therapeutic vehicle for incarcerated individuals who typically have had little positive guidance in the development of their belief system or little awareness that their thinking may play a substantive part in what negative behavioral outcomes occur for them.

Young's work (1986a, 1986b, 1986c) with lower-class clients, bible-belt Christians, and other tough customers is likely to raise the hackles on a variety of therapists ranging from the very liberal to the archconservative. Young makes no pretense on who is the boss and who is responsible for blowing away irrational beliefs. Put bluntly, the role of the therapist is that of a manipulator who uses the interpersonal relationship to maneuver the client to act in positive and beneficial ways.

Young's philosophy and descriptions of command and friendship power would likely horrify client-centered therapists. His view is that clients in a lower socioeconomic class expect the therapist to be an authority, provide expert advice, teach them what they need to know, and be sure of themselves while doing so. Such clients have little use for an egalitarian, self-actualized, client-centered relationship and would be uneasy with and probably view such a therapeutic approach as a sign of weakness on the therapist's part (Young, 1986b, pp. 88–89).

On first glance, Young's approach may seem outrageous in its condescending view of clients and portrayal of effete therapists willfully manipulating disadvantaged clients like so many sheep to a psychological shearing pen. However, Young takes great pains to differentiate between authoritarian and authoritative roles. His emphasis on acknowledgment and empathy for the environmental constraints and cultural barriers that may militate against the success of lower socioeconomic class clients goes far in establishing trust and an empathic relationship.

REBT's ability to tolerate value differences in child rearing, religious beliefs, marital relationships, and work attitudes without subtly attaching biases and negative evaluations to values different from the therapist's enhances the therapist's credibility with such clients. Under no circumstances does the therapist assume a godlike image or start to feel omnipotent. The therapist's role is to maintain a strong position of leadership while at the same time remaining empathic and responsive to client needs (Young, 1986b, pp. 89–92). Like it or not, believe it or not, our own work in conducting groups of chemically dependent prison inmates and adolescents with behavioral problems and child-rearing classes for lower socioeconomic parents convinces us there is more than a grain of therapeutic truth in what Young is saying.

From the perspective of many Asian clients, the logical thinking, cognition as the origin of emotion, therapist as teacher, paternalism, and expertness of the therapist that are characteristic of REBT have much to recommend it and seem effective when applied with such populations (Chen, 1995; Waxer, 1989; Yang, 1992).

For gays and lesbians, Mylott (1994) believes that REBT is effective in dealing with their irrational beliefs about such issues as love, rejection, growing old alone, approval, sexuality, and issues surrounding AIDS.

From a feminist perspective, REBT is a nonexclusive theory and is a powerful therapeutic tool to depropagandize and dispute many stereotypes that female clients may believe (Shibles, 1991). Wolfe's (1995) twenty-year review of REBT women's groups provides strong evidence of its utility with females in providing powerful corrective socialization experiences and dealing with dependency, power, and risk-taking issues.

If the REBT therapist cannot take into consideration the possible impact of societal racial dynamics on both the client's and therapist's thinking processes, then there is a risk of the therapist oversimplifying or mislabeling the "rationality" or "irrationality" of the client. The racial or cultural minority who has been discriminated against may have a view of *rational* that is very different than the therapist's because of the reality of the discrimination they have suffered (Wohl, 2000, p. 87). Conversely, if employed with sensitivity to injustices the racial minority may have suffered, REBT may also work well for such clients because it allows for an honest examination of real, external racial or cultural factors that may contribute to clients' self-defeating cognitions (Helms & Cook, 1999, pp. 154–155).

The awfulizing thinking engaged in by clients who have experienced a profoundly disabling physical condition is ideally suited for REBT (Gandy, 1995; Kelly, 1992; Sweetland, 1990; Zaborowski, 1997). For example, while certainly a traumatic event by any standard, a disability such as paralysis or blindness is not catastrophic to the extent that the individual's life is completely hopeless and useless because the person can no longer walk or see (Ostby, 1985; Zaborowski, 1997). Rather, emotions such as frustration, anger, depression, and the host of other negative feelings attributed to the disability can psychologically paralyze and blind the individual even more than his or her physical immobility or lack of vision. REBT is without parallel in its ability to change the all-or-none thinking that accompanies such traumatic physical onsets by vigorously attacking it and disputing its seemingly catastrophic effect on the client (Mitchell & DiGiusieppe, 1997).

Summary

Rational-emotive behavior therapy advocates the application of cognitive, behavioral, and emotive approaches to treatment. Because REBT places more emphasis on cognitive and behavioral techniques, it is most often classified as a cognitive-behavioral approach to therapy. It is geared toward the use of logic and the scientific method, but it also emphasizes human values such as growth and happiness. Hence, it is humanistically as well as empirically oriented.

Rational-emotive behavior therapy theory contends that people are born with the predisposition to think distortedly and irrationally but also with the ability to reason and thus are able to transcend some of their own limitations. However, even the most rational of persons are subject to emotional overload that takes the form of hot cognitions about events. Combined with low frustration tolerance and the desire to avoid immediate discomfort at the expense of long-term gain, humans engage in crooked, illogical thinking and become emotionally disturbed.

Rational-emotive therapy theory suggests that emotional disturbance may be explained by the ABC theory. This theory states that when an unpleasant event (activating event) occurs at point A, an individual may react in two ways. One is to conclude, at point B, that this event is unfortunate and disadvantageous (a rational belief) and therefore have at point C (the consequence) an appropriate feeling, such as regret or annoyance. These appropriate feelings stimulate the person to do something to change the unpleasant situation. However, individuals often react to unpleasant situations in a different manner: they may conclude at point B that circumstances are terrible or even catastrophic and therefore should not exist (an irrational belief). As a result, at point C they inappropriately feel depression, anxiety, rage, or lethargy. Such feelings, instead of facilitating constructive action, often interfere with problem-solving behavior.

The main goal of REBT is to teach clients how to detect the irrational beliefs that underlie their emotional disturbance and how to dispute these beliefs, replacing them with beliefs constituting a "more rational philosophy of life." This detecting and disputing of irrational beliefs is typically done by the therapist in a very active, directive, confrontive, and didactic manner.

In conclusion, Ellis has observed that REBT is a psychotherapy "uniquely designed to enable the individual to observe, to understand, and to persistently attack irrational, grandiose, perfectionistic *shoulds, oughts,* and *musts*" (1979a, p. 226).

SUGGESTIONS FOR FURTHER READING

Albert Ellis Institute. (2000, May). The rational emotive behavior therapy website. Available: http://www. rebt.org.

Dryden, W. (1996). Trends in rational emotive behavior therapy, 1955–1995. In W. Dryden (Ed.), *Developments in psychotherapy: Historical perspectives* (pp. 213–237). London: Sage.

Dryden, W., & Ellis, A. (2001). Rational emotive behavior therapy. In K. S. Dobson (Ed.), *Handbook of cognitive behavior therapies* (2nd ed.) (pp. 295–348). New York: Guilford Press.

Dryden, W., Neenan, M., & Yankura, J. (1999). *Counseling individuals: A rational emotive behavioural handbook* (3rd ed.). London: Whurr.

Yankura, J., & Dryden, W. (Eds.). (1997). *Special applications of REBT: A therapist's casebook.* New York: Springer.

REFERENCES

Chen, C. P. (1995). *Journal of Rational Emotive and Cognitive Behavior Therapy, 13*(2), 117–129.

Cohen, E. D. (1987). The use of syllogism in rational-emotive therapy. *Journal of Counseling and Development, 66,* 37–39.

Corey, G. (1982). *Theory and practice of counseling and psychotherapy* (2nd ed). Monterey, CA: Brooks/ Cole.

Crabb, L. J. (1971). *Sensible psychotherapy.* Manuscript, University of Illinois, Champaign-Urbana.

DiGiuseppe, R. A., & Muran, J. C. (1992). The use of metaphor in rational-emotive therapy. *Psychotherapy in Private Practice, 10,* (1–2), 151–165.

Dryden, W. (1984). *Rational-emotive therapy: Fundamentals and innovations.* London: Croom Helm.

Dryden, W. (1994). Reason and emotion in psychotherapy: Thirty years on. *Journal of Rational Emotive and Cognitive Behavior Therapy, 12*(2), 83–89.

Dryden, W., & Ellis, A. (2001). Rational emotive behavior therapy. In K. S. Dobson (Ed.). *Handbook of cognitive behavior therapies* (2nd ed.) (pp. 295–348). New York: Guilford Press.

Dryden, W., Neenan, M., & Yankura, J. (1999). Counseling individuals: *A rational emotive behavioural handbook* (3rd ed.). London: Whurr.

Ellis, A. (1949). Towards the improvement of psychoanalytic research. *Psychoanalytic Review, 36,* 123–143.

Ellis, A. (1950). *An introduction to the scientific principles of psychoanalysis.* Provincetown, MA: Journal Press.

Ellis, A. (1956). An operational reformulation of some of the basic principles of psychoanalysis. *Psychoanalytic Review, 43,* 163–180.

Ellis, A. (1958). Rational psychotherapy. *Journal of General Psychology, 59,* 35–49.

Ellis, A. (1962). *Reason and emotion in psychotherapy.* Secaucus, NJ: Lyle Stuart.

Ellis, A. (1970). Humanism, values, rationality. *Journal of Individual Psychology, 26,* 37–38.

Ellis, A. (1971). *Growth through reason.* Hollywood, CA: Wilshire Books.

Ellis, A. (1973). *Humanistic psychotherapy: The rational-emotive approach.* New York: Crown.

Ellis, A. (1976). The biological basis of human irrationality. *Journal of Individual Psychology, 32,* 143–168.

Ellis, A. (1977). The basic clinical theory of rational-emotive therapy. In A. Ellis & R. Grieger (Eds.), *Handbook of rational-emotive therapy* (Vol. 1, pp. 185–202). New York: Springer.

Ellis, A. (1979a). Rational-emotive therapy. In R. Corsini (Ed.), *Current psychotherapies* (2nd ed., pp. 185–229). Itasca, IL: F. E. Peacock.

Ellis, A. (1979b). The theory of rational-emotive therapy. In A. Ellis & J. M. Whiteley (Eds.), *Theoretical and empirical foundations of rational-emotive therapy* (pp. 1–27). Monterey, CA: Brooks/Cole.

Ellis, A. (1984). Foreword. In W. Dryden, *Rational-emotive therapy: Fundamentals and innovations* (pp. i–xv). London: Croom Helm.

Ellis, A. (1986a). Discomfort anxiety: A new cognitive behavioral construct. In A. Ellis & R. Grieger (Eds.), *Handbook of rational-emotive therapy* (Vol. 2, pp. 105–120). New York: Springer.

Ellis, A. (1986b). Fanaticism that may lead to a nuclear holocaust. *Journal of Counseling and Development, 65,* 146–150.

Ellis, A. (1986c). Rational-emotive therapy and cognitive behavior therapy: Similarities and differences. In A. Ellis & R. Grieger (Eds.), *Handbook of rational-emotive therapy* (Vol. 2, pp. 131–135). New York: Springer.

Ellis, A. (1986d). Rational-emotive therapy approach to overcoming resistance. In A. Ellis & R. Grieger (Eds.), *Handbook of rational-emotive therapy* (Vol. 2, pp. 246–274). New York: Springer.

Ellis, A. (1989a). Dangers of transpersonal psychology: A reply to Ken Wilber. *Journal of Counseling and Development, 67,* 336–337.

Ellis, A. (1989b). Rational-emotive therapy. In R. J. Corsini & D. Wedding (Eds.), *Current psychotherapies* (4th ed., pp. 197–238). Itasca, IL: F. E. Peacock.

Ellis, A. (1991a). Achieving self-actualization: The rational-emotive approach. *Journal of Social Behavior and Personality, 6,* 1–18.

Ellis, A. (1991b). The philosophical basis of rational-emotive therapy. *Psychotherapy in Private Practice, 8,* 97–106.

Ellis, A. (1992). Secular humanism and rational emotive therapy. *Humanistic Psychologist, 20*(2–3), 349–358.

Ellis, A. (1995). Changing rational-emotive therapy (RET) to rational emotive behavior therapy (REBT). *Journal of Rational Emotive and Cognitive Behavior Therapy, 13*(2), 85–89.

Ellis, A. (1997). Extending the goals of behavior therapy and cognitive behavior therapy. *Behavior Therapy, 28*(3), 333–339.

Ellis, A. (1999). Why rational-emotive therapy to rational emotive behavior therapy? *Psychotherapy 36*(2), 154–159.

Ellis, A., & Abrahms, E. (1978). *Brief psychotherapy in medical and health practice.* New York: Springer.

Ellis, A., & Bernard, M. E. (1986). What is rational-emotive therapy (RET) In A. Ellis & R. Grieger (Eds.), *Handbook of rational-emotive therapy* (Vol. 2, pp. 3–31). New York: Springer.

Ellis, A., & Grieger, R. (Eds.). (1977). *Handbook of rational-emotive therapy* (Vol. 1). New York: Springer.

Ellis, A., & Harper, R. A. (1979). *A new guide to rational living* (Rev. ed.). Hollywood, CA: Wilshire Books.

Engels, G. I., Garnefski, N., & Diekstra, R. F. (1993). Efficacy of rational-emotive therapy. *Journal of Consulting and Clinical Psychology, 61,* 1083–1090.

Gandy, G. L. (1995). Disputing irrational beliefs in rehabilitation counseling. *Journal of Applied Rehabilitation Counseling 26*(1), 36–40.

Garfield, S. L. (1995). The client-therapist relationship in rational-emotive therapy. *Journal of Rational Emotive and Cognitive Behavior Therapy, 13*(2), 101–116.

Grieger, R. M. (1986). The process of rational-emotive therapy. In A. Ellis & R. Grieger (Eds.), *Handbook of rational-emotive therapy* (Vol. 2, pp. 203–212). New York: Springer.

Helms, J. E., & Cook, D. A. (1999). *Using race and culture in counseling and psychotherapy: Theory and process.* Boston: Allyn & Bacon.

Hendricks, G. (1977). What do I do after they tell me how they feel? *Personnel and Guidance Journal, 55,* 249–252.

Huber, C. H. (2000). Rational-emotive family therapy: ABC, A'B'C', DE. In J. Carlson & L. Sperry (Eds.), *Brief therapy with individuals and couples* (pp. 71–105). Phoenix, AZ: Zeig, Tucker, Theisen.

Kassinove, H., & DiGiuseppe, R. (1975). Rational role reversal. *Rational Living, 10,* 44–45.

Keegan, A. (1989, February). A Guidepost interview: Albert Ellis: On psychotherapy, psychology, and science. *Guidepost, 31,* 1, 4.

Kelly, L. J. (1992). Rational emotive therapy and aural rehabilitation. *Journal of the Academy of Rehabilitative Audiology, 25,* 43–50.

Lyons, L. C., & Woods, P. J. (1991). The efficacy of rational-emotive therapy: A quantitative review of the outcome research. *Clinical Psychology Review, 11*(4), 357–369.

Mitchell, R. W., & DiGiuseppe, R. (1997). "Shoya moya ik baraba": Using REBT with culturally diverse clients. In J. Yankura & W. Dryden (Eds.), *Special applications of REBT: A therapist's casebook.* (pp. 39–67). New York: Springer.

Moore, R. H. (1986). Inference as "A" in rational-emotive therapy. In W. Dryden and P. Trower (Eds.), *Rational-emotive therapy: Recent developments in theory and practice* (pp. 2–12). Bristol, England: Institute for RET.

Mylott, K. (1994). Twelve irrational ideas that drive gay men and women crazy. *Journal of Rational Emotive and Cognitive Behavior Therapy, 12*(1), 61–71.

Nardi, T. J. (1986). The use of psychodrama in REBT. In A. Ellis & R. Grieger (Eds.), *Handbook of rational-emotive therapy* (Vol. 2, pp. 275–280). New York: Springer.

Ostby, S. S. (1985). A rational-emotive perspective. *Journal of Applied Rehabilitation Counseling, 16,* 30–33.

Shibles, W. (1991). Feminism and the cognitive theory of emotion: Anger, blame and humor. *Women and Health, 17,* 57–69.

Sichel, J., & Ellis, A. (1983). *RET self-help form.* New York: Institute for Rational Living.

Silverman, M. S., McCarthy, M., & McGovern, T. (1992). A review of outcome studies of rational-emotive therapy. *Journal of Rational Emotive and Cognitive Behavior Therapy, 10*(3), 111–186.

Sweetland, J. D. (1990). Cognitive behavior therapy and physical disability. *Journal of Rational Emotive and Cognitive Behavior Therapy, 8*(2), 71–78.

Walen, S., DiGiuseppe, R., & Wessler, R. L. (1980). *A practitioner's guide to rational-emotive therapy.* New York: Oxford University Press.

Waxer, P. H. (1989). Cantonese versus Canadian evaluation of directive and non-directive counseling. *Canadian Journal of Counseling, 23,* 263–272.

Wessler, R. A. (1986). Value judgments and self-evaluation in rational-emotive therapy. In W. Dryden and P. Trower (Eds.), *Rational-emotive therapy: Recent developments in theory and practice* (pp. 12–23). Bristol, England: Institute for RET.

Wessler, R. A., & Wessler, R. L. (1980). *The principles and practice of rational-emotive therapy.* San Francisco: Jossey-Bass.

Wohl, J. (2000). Psychotherapy and cultural diversity. In J. F. Aponte & J. Wohl (Eds.), *Psychological intervention and cultural diversity* (pp. 75–91). Boston: Allyn & Bacon.

Wolfe, J. L. (1995). Rational emotive behavior therapy women's groups: A twenty year perspective. *Journal of Rational Emotive and Cognitive Behavior Therapy, 13*(3), 153–170.

Yang, R. (1992). Rational emotive group therapy applied to sense of inferiority among university students. *Chinese Mental Health Journal, 6*(2), 74–76, 83.

Young, H. S. (1986a). Practicing RET with bible-belt Christians. In W. Dryden and P. Trower (Eds.), *Rational-emotive therapy: Recent developments in theory and practice* (pp. 122–142). Bristol, England: Institute for RET.

Young, H. S. (1986b). Practicing RET with lower-class clients. In W. Dryden and P. Trower (Eds.), *Rational-emotive therapy: Recent developments in theory and practice* (pp. 85–121). Bristol, England: Institute for RET.

Young, H. S. (1986c). Teaching rational self-value concepts to tough customers. In W. Dryden and P. Trower (Eds.), *Rational-emotive therapy: Recent developments in theory and practice* (pp. 143–170). Bristol, England: Institute for RET.

Zaborowski, B. (1997). Adjustment to vision loss and blindness: A process of reframing and retraining. *Journal of Rational-Emotive & Cognitive Behavior, 15*(3), 215–221.

Zajonc, R. B. (1980). Feeling and thinking: Preferences need no inferences. *American Psychologist, 35,* 151–175.

CHAPTER

10 Cognitive Behavior Therapy

Fundamental Tenets

History

This chapter presents a form of psychotherapy based on the formulation that the way individuals structure and interpret experiences determines their moods and subsequent behaviors. Seeing and perceiving negatively are purported to cause negative feelings and debilitative behaviors. Changing the manner in which people conceptualize things lies at the heart of the therapeutic process (Reber, 1995, p. 135).

Developmental Highlights. When the first edition of this textbook was published in 1984, *cognitive therapy* was in the formative stages of development. It had been only twenty-two years since Albert Ellis's (1962) *Reason and Emotion in Psychotherapy* emerged on the scene. It had also been only twenty-one years since Aaron T. Beck's (1963, 1964, 1967) seminal investigations and writings about thinking and depression began to expand our horizons and permanently alter the landscape of cognitive therapy. Although many of the early ideas and elements of the cognitive viewpoint had roots reaching deeply into the historical evolution of psychology, it was largely Ellis's ideas and Beck's research findings that propelled and coalesced the fragmented components into what was later coined the "cognitive" therapy movement. For example, Ellis's premise, inspired from as far back as the Roman philosophers (that it is not what happens to us that causes our misery, but it is what we believe and tell ourselves about it that upsets us), is only one cogent instance of many precursory concepts that led to the development of the brand of cognitive theory and therapy that we now take for granted. Another foundational and almost identical example is Beck's belief derived from the Greek Stoic philosophers—that how one thinks largely determines how one feels and behaves (Beck & Weishaar, 1995, p. 229). Clearly, cognitive ideas and cognitive processes predated even the field of psychology.

According to Beck and Weishaar (1995, p. 233), modern cognitive therapy's theoretical underpinnings sprang from three primary sources: "(1) the phenomenological approach to psychology, (2) structural theory and depth psychology, and (3) cognitive psychology." They further explain that the phenomenological approach assumes that the human view of self and the personal world are primary factors that drive behavior. Kant's (1798) emphasis on conscious subjective experience, based on Greek Stoic philosophy, is cited as relevant to the phenomenological view. The influence of the individual's conscious subjective experience may also be seen in the writings of Adler (1936), Moore (1939), Alexander (1950), Horney (1950), Sullivan (1953), and May and Yalom (1995).

Regarding structural theory and depth psychology, Sigmund Freud's (1958) concepts are primary examples of precursors to the development of cognitive theory. Here we are talking about the hierarchical structuring of cognition into primary and secondary components. In terms of cognitive psychology, Kelly's (1955) personal constructs formulations are credited as being among the first of the modern theoretical underpinnings of cognitive therapy (Beck & Weishaar, 1995, p. 233). In more recent years, the emotional components of cognitive psychology have been more fully developed and explained by a number of theorists and clinicians, including Beck (1976, 1986), Ellis (1962, 1984), Krumboltz (1997), Meichenbaum (1977, 1997), and Walker (1997).

In this chapter we include under the heading of cognitive therapy all systems, strategies, and techniques that have come to be recognized as belonging in the therapeutic purview of the cognitive processes. The boundaries between cognitive therapy and cognitive behavior therapy are becoming more and more blurred. *Cognitive therapies* have been evolving since the 1960s and 1970s into a formidable system of counseling and psychotherapy that has experienced phenomenal growth and has gained widespread recognition and clinical application. If we examine the total set of formulations of both cognitive therapy and cognitive behavior therapy, we find a combined system that is quite eclectic in that it incorporates so many valid elements of therapy into a holistic, systematic, and integrated approach. In a survey of influential psychotherapists, Warner (1991) reported that one in three respondents identified eclecticism as their primary theoretical orientation. A close second was cognitive behavioral orientation, which was strongly preferred to the third ranked psychoanalytically oriented theories. Warner's findings were indicative that the cognitive therapies had clearly emerged as a family of potent treatment modalities.

As Albert Ellis (1982, 1984) has reminded us throughout his career, the concepts and principles you will find in this chapter have been handed down through many generations of helpers and philosophers. Knapp (1985) has highlighted the career of T. V. Moore, author of *Cognitive Psychology* (1939), which described many of the therapeutic perspectives that cognitive psychologists have owned as new developments in the field. Moore and other psychologists of his time, such as E. C. Tolman, recognized the centrality of perception, imagery, memory, and consciousness as topics worthy of investigation. George Kelly's (1955) personal constructs psychology was an early precursor to cognitive therapy. His cognitive model was among the first to emphasize the role of beliefs in the controlling and changing of thoughts, feelings, and behaviors.

Cognitive therapy has been formulated on many separate but important building blocks. Although no one person is credited with being the specific therapeutic founder or architect of the distinct structure of applied cognitive psychotherapy, as previously indicated, we consider two theorists—Albert Ellis (1962, 1984) and Aaron Beck (1963, 1964, 1967)—to represent the most important catalysts and spearheads of the movement. These two figures are closer to our definition of founders than anyone else we have found. But a whole host of important contributors to the evolution, theoretical, and clinical structure of cognitive therapy should clearly be recognized and credited.

Important Contributors.   A long line of researchers, clinicians, and scholars have both separately and collaboratively, over time and in disparate settings, made substantive contributions to the structure of cognitive therapy. There have been hundreds, perhaps thousands, of bits and pieces or components that evolved into solving the jigsaw puzzle of the emergent cognitive modalities. These components came from many geographical areas and disciplines. While undoubtedly leaving out many major figures, we nevertheless acknowledge several important contributions to the total structure that we now define as cognitive therapy (see Figure 10.1).

FIGURE 10.1   Important Contributions to the Sequential Development of the Cognitive Therapies

Contributor(s)	Cognitive Component Identification
A. Ellis (1962, 1984)	Rational emotive and rational emotive behavior therapies (REBT)
A. Beck (1963, 1964, 1967, 1976)	Cognitive models of depression and emotional disorders
L. Homme (1965)	Covert conditioning
J. Cautela (1966)	Covert sensitization
J. Cautela (1969)	Cognitive imagery and cognitive self-control
D. Meichenbaum & J. Goodman (1971)	Self-instructional/self-administered training
R. Suinn & F. Richardson (1971)	Anxiety management training
T. D'Zurilla & M. Goldfried (1971)	Problem-solving theory and therapy
H. Benson (1976, 1987)	Muscle and cognitive relaxation techniques
G. Spivack, J. Platt, & M. Shure (1976)	Problem-solving therapy
M. Mahoney & C. Thoresen (1974)	Cognitive self-control
D. Meichenbaum, D. Turk, & S. Burstein (1975)	Stress inoculation theory and training
A. Beck & G. Emery (1979, 1985)	Cognitive models of anxiety and phobias
A. Beck, A. Rush, B. Shaw, & G. Emery (1979)	Cognitive restructuring
A. Bandura (1985)	Cognitive social learning theory
T. Rosenthal & B. Steffek (1991)	Symbolic and participant modeling
J. Overholser (1991)	Guided imagery
J. Gorrell (1993)	Cognitive modeling
D. Meichenbaum (1993)	Stress inoculation training
E. Gendlin (1996)	Cognitive reframing
J. Krumboltz (1997)	Cognitive-behavior therapy
D. Meichenbaum (1997)	Cognitive-behavior therapy
L. Walker (1997)	Cognitive-behavioral feminist therapy
D. Watson & R. Tharp (1997)	Self-management and self-directed behavior
S. Cormier & B. Cormier (1998)	Comprehensive cognitive behavioral interventions

Overview of Cognitive Therapy

Fundamental Postulations and Processes.   Cognitive therapy is based primarily on the formulation that how one thinks largely determines how one feels and behaves (Beck & Wieshaar, 1995). Ellis (1962, 1984) describes cognitive formulation in terms of the person's belief system—that is, it is not so much what happens to the individual in the external world that affects him or her, but what one believes and tells oneself about those external events that causes emotional disturbances. Cognitive therapy is a collaborative process of empirical investigation, experimentation, reality testing, alliance building, and collaborative problem solving between therapist and client (Beck, 1986). The client's maladaptive conceptions, interpretations, distortions, and conclusions are subject to scientific scrutiny and hypothesis testing in the immediacy of the ongoing therapy session. The therapist is supportive and empathic, yet strong, objective, consistent, nonjudgmental, and rigorously scientific in assisting the client to sort out false beliefs and unfounded conclusions that may be distorting the client's thinking and acting or non-acting. Cognitive and behavioral experiments as well as verbal techniques "are used to explore alternative interpretations and to generate contradictory evidence that supports more adaptive beliefs and leads to therapeutic change" in the client (Beck & Weishaar, 1995, p. 229).

Typical Clinical Applications.   Cognitive therapy is used in the treatment of a large number of mental disorders. Some of the best known applications have been Beck, Rush, Shaw, and Emery's (1979) treatment of depression and Beck and Emery's (1979, 1985) use of the approach in helping clients experiencing anxieties and phobias. Kush and Fleming's (2000) group cognitive therapy research findings showed significant improvements on measures of depression, anxiety, and dysfunctional attitudes from pre- to post-test. But cognitive therapy's scope is by no means limited to these disorders. Beck and Weishaar (1995), Cormier and Cormier (1991, 1998), and Freeman, Simon, Beutler, and Arkowitz (1989) have clearly demonstrated that cognitive procedures are effective with an array of human dilemmas. Cormier and Cormier (1998) identify and describe, in considerable detail, appropriate uses of cognitive therapy procedures in an enormous number of examples of clinical treatments of psychological disorders that encompass a vast number of client problem categories and situations.

Theory of Personality

Cognitive theory views personality as reflecting the individual's cognitive organization and structure, which are based on both genetic endowment and social influence (Beck & Weishaar, 1995, pp. 236–242). Cognitive therapy recognizes the centrality of cognitive processing in emotion and behavior. The emotional and behavioral responses people emit are largely determined by how they perceive, interpret, and ascribe meaning to situations and events (Beck, 1986). Core beliefs and basic assumptions called *schemas* have a substantial influence on one's cognitive operations. Schemas affect the way an individual structures reality, makes assumptions about the self, interprets past experiences, organizes vicarious learning, makes behavioral choices, and develops expectations about the future (Beck & Weishaar, 1995, pp. 236–239).

Schemas may be either adaptive or dysfunctional, depending on how the individual's cognitive structures are formed and maintained. The person may have competing schemas, some of which are adaptive and some of which are dysfunctional. *Cognitive vulnerability* is the term Beck and Weishaar (1995, p. 237) use to describe how a person's beliefs and assumptions predispose him or her to a particular psychological distress. Thus, the ways people form, organize, and interpret their basic cognitive structures determine how they will perceive and behave.

Differences between CBT and REBT.   Although the theoretical and philosophical underpinnings of cognitive behavior therapy and rational-emotive behavior therapy (REBT) are closely related and the two systems have more commonalities than differences, there are some noteworthy distinctions, as reported by Dryden (1984, pp. 42–49) and Beck and Weishaar (1995, pp. 236–245). The two systems are summarized in Figure 10.2.

In critically comparing cognitive behavior therapy and REBT, Dryden (1984) has argued that although REBT has a more thoroughly developed philosophical framework, CBT's strengths lie in the explicit practical guidelines it offers therapists (p. 40). In a nutshell, Beck (1970) views personality development as founded more on a progression of learned cognitions than on biological predispositions. That is why the cognitive therapies tend to be less philosophical than REBT and have more kinship with the scientific psychology of behaviorism than Ellis usually ascribes to REBT. As indicated in Figure 10.2, REBT views every individual as capable of overcoming great odds to cope with life's maladaptive obstacles, whereas the cognitive therapies propose no clear theoretical position, leaving the data concerning human dilemmas to speak for themselves.

Nature of Maladjustment

Beck and Weishaar (1995, pp. 231–242) maintain that maladjustment stems not so much from irrational beliefs (as REBT contends), but from distorted cognitions. One of the systematic errors in cognitive reasoning they identified is selective abstraction (viewing the event or situation out of context). Beck and Weishaar take the position that a great deal of client behavioral dysfunction derives from systematic errors, distorted thinking or expectations, and/or maladaptive cognitions.

Maladaptive cognition, as described by Mahoney (1974), springs from several cognitive deficits: (1) selective inattention—ignoring relevant stimuli and attending to irrelevant stimuli; (2) misperception—mislabeling certain stimuli, both internal and external; (3) maladaptive focusing—focusing on irrelevant external events or stimuli; (4) maladaptive self-arousal—focusing on irrelevant internal cues; and (5) repertory deficiencies—limited or maladjustive behavior caused by deficiencies in cognitive (covert) and/or behavioral (overt) skills. These deficiencies go beyond traditional behavioral views because such views cannot account for vicarious learning, semantic generalization, imagined response patterns, and symbolic processes, all of which are exclusively human functions (Lazarus, 1977a).

Cognitive behavior therapy, cognitive therapy, and cognitive behavior modification are based on the assumptions that (1) maladaptive cognitions lead to maladaptive, self-defeating behaviors; (2) adaptive, self-enhancing behaviors can be induced through the client's learning to generate positive, self-enhancing thoughts; and (3) clients can be taught to shift from covert, self-defeating thoughts and attitudes to self-enhancing thoughts, attitudes, and behaviors.

FIGURE 10.2 Comparison of Cognitive Behavior Therapy and Rational-Emotive Behavior Therapy

Criterion	CBT	REBT
Major contributor(s)	Beck, Meichenbaum	Ellis
Development	Experimentally and academically based; reaction to psychoanalytic therapy	Therapeutically and practice-based; reaction to psychoanalytic therapy
Diagnosis	Much data retrieval through lengthy diagnostic interviews	Verbal uncovering of irrational beliefs and integrated with therapy; diagnosis per se not carried out
Client type	Clinical focus on depression and anxiety disorders	No clinical focus; broad spectrum
Therapeutic outcome	Rigorously controlled pre–post empirical studies	Minor emphasis on systematic study
Acquisition of disturbance	Premorbidity with some biological predisposition and early learning of dysfunctional assumptions	Biological predisposition engendering irrational beliefs
Potential for psychological growth	Substantial; no clear philosophy	Great, given its humanistic, positive philosophy
Nature of emotional disturbance	Cognitive; with feelings and behavior underlying cognitive structure and rooted in inferential cognitive distortions; no clear distinction between evaluation and inference	Cognitive; related with feelings and behavior underlying cognitive structure and rooted in musturbatory ideologies; clear distinction between evaluation and inference
Basic themes of emotional disturbance	Idiosyncratic processing of cognitive distortions; no clear generic processes; disturbance about disturbance in anxiety disorders only	Ego disturbance, discomfort disturbance; thematic irrationalities generic to many disturbances
Perpetuation of emotional disturbance	Cognitive schemata and faulty informational processing edit and distort problems and generate dysfunctional beliefs and maladaptive behavior	Low frustration tolerance; comfort seeking through short-term self-defeating goals
Emotionally healthy personality	Scientifically tests own hypotheses and generates functional beliefs and adaptive behaviors	Scientific and humanistic; atheistic
Psychopathology	Pathological disorders each characterized by a different set of cognitive deficits or distortions	All pathologies have a similar set of underlying irrational beliefs
Distorted client beliefs	Faulty cognitive processing that is self-corrective	Philosophically incongruent with reality

(continued)

FIGURE 10.2 Continued

Criterion	CBT	REBT
Goal of therapy	Help individuals to identify, reality test, and correct maladjusted conceptualization and dysfunctional schema underlying cognitions; little concern with philosophical change	Profound philosophical change; work on self-enhancing life goals, which are specified
Therapist role in change process	Force not advocated; collaborative, empiricist role; confrontation used as a last resort	Forceful and energetic; didactic, directive, confrontive
Client role in change process	Try out new behaviors in a graded fashion negotiated equal to expectations of client	Try out new behaviors by immediate maximum flooding and exposure beyond immediate expectations of client
Therapeutic strategies	1. Initial task is to identify and correct automatic thoughts 2. Tentative hypotheses developed concerning both secondary and primary assumptions underlying automatic thoughts 3. Hypotheses confirmed or rejected depending on data 4. Therapeutic process based on *induction,* since therapist does not know at outset the nature of the client's cognitions related to the disturbance	1. Determine absolutistic evaluations couched in "musts" or in grossly exaggerated negative conclusions 2. Considerable amount of freelancing 3. Go straight to evaluative thinking; therapeutic process operates on *deduction*
Therapeutic techniques	1. Uses Socratic dialogue: inductive questioning of client at length 2. Asks for evidence concerning client inferences (hypotheses), where data can be gathered from outside world to corroborate or falsify the hypotheses 3. Daily record of dysfunctional thoughts (DRDT) kept by client 4. Wide range of imagery used 5. Behavioral assignments used to test faulty inferences 6. Against flooding because it would threaten the therapeutic alliance 7. Little use of flamboyant and dramatic interventions 8. Cannot use paradox because to do so would require explanation of rationale to client 9. Pragmatic throughout 10. Graded assignments used progressively to approximate goal attainment successively	1. Uses Socratic dialogue; inductive questioning of client as long as it is fruitful 2. Often asks for evidence when the therapist knows a priori that evidence does not exist because clients may believe these irrational beliefs are facts 3. REBT self-help form kept by client 4. Variable use of imagery 5. Behavioral assignments used to change evaluations 6. Flooding used to raise levels of frustration tolerance 7. Frequent use of risk taking, humor, and a wide range of educational and social-psychological methods 8. Uses paradoxical intention 9. Pragmatic and philosophical 10. Against graded assignments because that says client can't tolerate the discomfort

The Counseling Process

Eclectic Leanings

Cognitive behavior therapy (Beck, 1976; Beck & Emery, 1985; Beck & Weishaar, 1995) and cognitive behavior modification (Mahoney, 1974; Meichenbaum, 1977) use a variety of procedures to assist clients in changing negative, self-defeating responses to positive, self-enhancing, successful behaviors. Cognitive behavior therapy goes beyond operant and respondent thinking in asserting that the client's negative beliefs, thoughts, attitudes, images, and self-dialogue are all generated internally. It further assumes that the therapist can gain access to these data and help initiate positive thoughts, images, and self-dialogue that promote a restructuring of the client's thinking, coping, and behaving.

Depending on the particular client situation, the therapist might operate in a variety of modes—from directive to unconditionally acceptant; from scientific to empathic; from systematic to open; from suggestive to instructive. Indeed, our view of cognitive therapy is that it is highly eclectic within the parameters of the client's thought processes. In cognitive therapy the therapist takes full advantage of everything we know about cognitive and behavioral psychology.

Collaborative Qualities

During the helping interview the therapist typically employs a combination of cognitive and behavioral strategies (Gilliland & James, 1983). Therefore, therapy incorporates the collaborative involvement (Dryden, 1984, p. 50) of both therapist and client in (1) working together hard and persistently as mentor/facilitator and student/helpee to enable the client to gain permanent cognitive and behavioral control over the presenting problem; (2) imaging and observing different models of behavior that are positive/negative and successful/unsuccessful; (3) vicariously thinking about human emotions and behaviors and learning to convert such thoughts into action; and (4) successively practicing new cognitive and behavioral patterns until new self-enhancing thoughts and performance approximate the levels desired by the client. The entire therapeutic process is viewed not as being done *to* or *for* the client, but as being done *with* the client (Beck & Weishaar, 1995; Dryden & Trower, 1986; Gilliland & James, 1997, p. 53; Gilliland & Myer, 1985).

Strategies for Helping Clients

A great many procedures fall within the purview of cognitive helping strategies. We will comment briefly on the following major techniques:

1. Beck's cognitive psychotherapy
2. Relaxation training and relaxation therapy
3. Mental and emotive imagery
4. Cognitive and covert modeling
5. Thought stopping
6. Cognitive restructuring, reframing, and stress inoculation

   7. Meditation and relaxation
   8. Biofeedback
   9. Neurolinguistic programming
  10. Eye movement desensitization and reprocessing (EDMR)

Beck's Cognitive Psychotherapy

The goals of Beck's cognitive therapy are to correct faulty information processing and help clients modify assumptions that maintain maladaptive behaviors and emotions (Beck, 1986, 1989; Beck & Emery, 1985; Beck & Weishaar, 1995). The first and most important strategy is to develop a trustful and collaborative relationship through the use of accurate empathy, warmth, and genuineness (Beck, 1986; Beck & Weishaar, 1995). A collaborative relationship enables the therapist to assess the client's expectations regarding therapeutic success (Beck, 1986; Beck & Emery, 1985; Beck & Weishaar, 1995).

Once the therapeutic relationship is established the therapist uses collaborative empiricism, Socratic dialogue, and guided discovery in an attempt to get clients to recognize their erroneous assumptions, identify their cognitive distortions, and counteract their dysfunctional behavioral and emotional responses (Beck, 1986, 1989; Beck & Emery, 1985; Beck & Weishaar, 1995).

Collaborative Empiricism. This requires the therapist and client to become coinvestigators, scientifically examining the evidence to support or reject the client's distorted cognitions. The collaborative relationship facilitates the mutual determination of treatment goals, eliciting and providing feedback, and demystifying therapeutic change. Biased thinking is corrected and adaptive alternatives are jointly developed. Brief segments taken from the case of Myra (whom we shall follow through this chapter), a woman undergoing chemotherapy following a mastectomy, illustrate the eclectic leanings of cognitive therapy.

> **TH:**   Myra, you say you can't stand thinking about it and can't possibly face it. Yet, you've described how in the army you handled some of the toughest problems of panic at the firing range among the young soldiers in your platoon. What's the fundamental difference between facing that stress and what you're facing now?
>
> **CL:**   Well, I guess I knew all the soldiers were looking up to me and somehow I mustered up the strength to do it.
>
> **TH:**   What are some similarities between that tough situation and your ability to muster up strength in your present situation?
>
> **CL:**   (*pause*) Well, this is different, but I still have the same strengths of character that I had then. I haven't really lost that.

Socratic Dialogue. In Socratic dialogue (Beck & Young, 1985), careful questioning by the therapist promotes new learning in the client. The objectives are to catalyze the client's exploration and definition of problems; identification of assumptions, thoughts, and images; evaluation of the meanings of situations and events; and assessment of the consequences of maintaining maladaptive thoughts and behaviors (Beck & Weishaar, 1995, pp. 244–245).

CL: At a rational level, I know that this malignancy will likely be arrested and I will probably go on with my life. So far, the tests are quite encouraging. But at the emotional level, I feel robbed or cheated, especially of a very special part of my womanhood. I also realize on some level that I'm choosing to feel that way.

TH: Myra, let's explore the consequences of your continuing to think and feel that way. What will happen if you keep focusing your energy on that one aspect of yourself, as if all of your negative and erroneous assumptions are true—even though right now there is no medical evidence to support those assumptions?

Guided Discovery. This enables the client to reassess and modify maladaptive beliefs and assumptions. Through collaboration with the therapist the client is guided in designing and carrying out experiments that result in the client's discovery of new and adaptive ways of thinking that, in turn, translate into improved cognitive and behavioral choices for the client (Beck & Weishaar, 1995, p. 245).

CL: Ever since my lab tests came in this morning I've felt relieved—kind of like I've been given a new lease on life.

TH: So, what does that tell you about your previous unfounded assumptions and premature fears?

CL: Well, it says that all this worry about how bad things are liable to be is really wasted worry.

TH: Myra, it seems to me you may have identified a key ingredient in your own healing process. Now, if what you've discovered is true, let's you and me set up an experiment to test whether your assumptions and fears can be altered before you encounter your next hurdle—which, incidentally, is tomorrow morning, when your prosthesis consultation is scheduled to occur.

We have found that the therapeutic application of each of these strategies is enhanced through the use of audiotape and/or videotape techniques. Our clients consistently report that their learning and retention of the relaxation, cognitive imagery, modeling, and practice activities engaged in during the therapy interview are greatly strengthened by either listening to the audiotapes of our sessions or watching the videotapes. They frequently report that the audio or video reviews, reexperienced as homework assignments, are more powerful and lasting than the initial therapy sessions. We believe this is true because the time lapse allows them to process mentally what went on during the sessions and because they are instructed to watch or listen to playbacks in a state of complete relaxation in their own homes, with no interruptions from the telephone, television, or any other source.

As a part of the video or audio helping strategy, we ask our clients to bring their own cassettes for use during therapy. That provides them with ownership of both the process and the media and with a repository of their own therapeutic progress. Our clients report that the audio or video enhancement is enormously valuable to them. We believe that because most people have access to standard VCR or audio equipment in their homes, the use of audio or video media is a valuable adjunct to many therapy situations. However, this strategy should be used with great care, discretion, and ethical and professional judgment. It requires a great deal of risk taking by both therapist and client.

Relaxation Training and Relaxation Therapy

The development of effective relaxation strategies has played an important role in the emergence of cognitive therapy as a viable system of helping. Some of the noteworthy contributors have been Benson (1976); Bernstein and Borkovec (1973); Carrington (1978a, 1978b); Cautela and Groden (1978); Jacobson (1964); Lehrer (1982); Lehrer, Woolfolk, Rooney, McCann, and Carrington (1983); Shapiro (1980); Southam, Agras, Taylor, and Kraemer (1982); and Woolfolk, Lehrer, McCann, and Rooney (1982).

Modern problems commonly amenable to remediation through relaxation training and relaxation therapy include stress, anxiety, physiological problems (such as headaches or other pain not traceable to organic causes), and pressures related to the workplace and the fast pace of modern lifestyles. A great number of procedures have been developed to help clients relax both mind and body, meditate, and manage their stress and the pressures of life. Beginning with Jacobson in 1929 and proceeding through the 2000s, much sophisticated work has taken place to empower therapists to use their mental and emotive talents to help clients learn to relax, meditate, and restore equilibrium to their hectic lives.

One example of the effective use of relaxation therapy would be helping a client with no organic disorders whose presenting problem is headaches and vomiting attributed to severe test anxiety. Relaxation therapy would be used to teach the client how to (1) relax all muscle groups and put the whole body in a state of complete physical relaxation, (2) relax mentally (cognitively), (3) reduce anxiety while being totally relaxed, (4) keep out extraneous background cognitions while working on the test anxiety, and (5) use self-relaxation permanently to control not only test anxiety but also other debilitating stresses.

The theoretical principle underlying relaxation therapy is that it is not possible for the human organism to be in a state of complete physical relaxation and at the same time be emotionally anxious. Conversely, it is not possible for the organism to be totally relaxed mentally and at the same time physically uptight. Thus, the therapist applying the cognitive strategy of relaxation assumes the client is physically relaxed in a way that associates that relaxed feeling and image with being cognitively relaxed in the examination room. It is further assumed that the client will transfer that mentally relaxed state to the real testing situation.

Mental and Emotive Imagery

Mental imagery is a process through which a person focuses on vivid mental pictures of experiences or events—past, present, or future. Mental imagery can be useful to the therapist in both the assessment of clients' problems and the therapy process. Boswell (1987) calls it *abstract imaging.* He finds it useful in assessing the relationships between clients' emotional and intellectual experiences and their presenting symptoms and in determining how those experiences become exaggerated and intensified in clients' minds. He uses mental imagery as a primary therapeutic strategy for helping clients forget the past and focus on the here and now (p. 175).

Emotive imagery is a procedure developed by Lazarus and Abramovitz (1962) in which the client imagines, in a covert but vivid way, the emotional sensations and feelings of an actual situation or behavior. Since the early 1960s the use of imagery as a therapeutic strategy has gained wide acceptance and use (Horan, 1976; Kazdin, 1979b; Lazarus, 1977b, 1982; Lazarus & Abramovitz, 1962; Mahoney, 1974; Maultsby, 1984; Sheikh, 1983; Shorr, Sobel-Whittington, Robin, & Connella, 1984). A mental image becomes emotive whenever the person imagines an emotional or feeling state paired with a specific image. For example, a person may clearly imagine dealing with a very abusive person and, at the same time, imagine feeling a growing sense of strength, confidence, calmness, and security.

Emotive imagery is a derivation of systematic desensitization in that it extends and applies systematic desensitization's strategy of maximizing the use of client-generated cognitive images and pictures to cope with problems. In emotive imagery the client focuses on safe, positive, and pleasant images as a strategy for blocking and coping with many anxiety-provoking situations in real life (Cormier & Cormier, 1991, pp. 349–366).

The case of a practicum student who was threatened and emotionally paralyzed by a verbally abusive client vividly demonstrates emotive imagery. The student's practicum supervisor borrowed an idea from Lazarus's (1977b) use of superheroes or superheroines with children (pp. 106–107). The supervisor had previously noticed that the student always wore large bunches of bracelets on her wrists. The student was told to imagine herself as Wonder Woman and use her magic bracelets to fend off the verbal bullets of the abrasive client. Armed with her bracelets, at the next therapy session she was able to confront the client with his inappropriate behavior. The student used emotive imagery to prepare for the session by imagining herself as Wonder Woman and at the same time vividly envisioning herself exercising a strong sense of control, strength, self-confidence, and poise.

In therapy that uses any form of imagery, if the client has trouble or shows reluctance in imaging, another technique may be more appropriate. Clients who are psychotic or who have generalized anxiety neuroses are not appropriate subjects for the procedure because they may lose touch with reality or become extremely threatened.

Cognitive and Covert Modeling

In the section on behavioral modeling in Chapter 7, we defined both cognitive and covert modeling to distinguish them from the behavioral modeling strategies of symbolic modeling and participant modeling. Since we view both cognitive and covert modeling as more in the cognitive than the behavior therapy realm, we are therefore presenting them here in greater detail than in Chapter 7.

Cognitive Modeling.　Initially, cognitive modeling entails working with the client to determine what debilitating (maladaptive or bad) thoughts or emotions the client wishes to correct. Then, collaboratively with the client, the therapist identifies what specifically desired (adaptive or good) thoughts or feelings the client wishes to acquire to replace the bad ones. The therapist usually facilitates the modeling process by employing self-talk (the therapist verbalizes thoughts to be repeated by the client) to enable the client to think about, understand, and acquire the adaptive thoughts or emotions.

Cognitive modeling was developed by a number of therapists (Beck, 1970, 1976; Kazdin & Mascitelli, 1982a; Mahoney, 1974; Sarason, 1973) who wanted to find ways to help clients learn what to say to themselves to ensure that they would avoid self-defeating thoughts and behaviors while performing tasks that they wanted to complete. Cognitive modeling (Beck, 1976) is a combination of overt and covert strategies. Therapist and client work collaboratively to change the client's beliefs, self-statements, or mental attitudes toward a task, behavior, or situation.

Covert Modeling.   Covert modeling is a procedure during which clients imagine themselves engaging in desired behaviors that they want to learn and adopt. The therapist usually employs guided or emotive imagery to facilitate client learning and acquisition of the desired cognitions that represent or symbolize behaviors but are not the behaviors themselves. Covert modeling, initiated by Cautela (1971), has been used extensively to teach clients to mentally envision a model (preferably themselves performing an imaginary task) successfully accomplishing a desired goal (Bornstein & Devine, 1980; Bry & Blair, 1979; Cautela, 1971, 1976; Kazdin, 1979a, 1980; Kazdin & Mascitelli, 1982b; Watson, 1976).

Covert modeling is applicable to helping clients develop assertive behaviors, reduce avoidance behaviors, treat alcoholism, and deal with obsessive-compulsive anxiety. Covert modeling has been used in combination with cognitive modeling and observational learning as an effective method of in-service training of school counselors in the use of cognitive procedures (Cormier & Cormier, 1991, pp. 354–375; Gilliland & Johnston, 1987; Johnston & Gilliland, 1987).

One example of an appropriate use of covert modeling was with a 45-year-old woman who complained of the fear of possible encounters with her ex-husband. In a series of covert modeling scenes, followed by audiotaped homework assignments, the client was able to (1) visualize herself feeling frightened and intimidated; (2) experience, initiate, and use appropriate assertion skills; (3) successfully confront her ex-husband at a social gathering; and (4) demonstrate positive, self-enhancing actions and feelings that she remembered from the covert modeling. While the woman was physically and mentally relaxed with her eyes closed, the therapist verbally presented to her all of the scenes, images, and cognitive and emotive descriptions of herself performing the task she had told the therapist she wanted to be able to do.

In completing her homework assignments, the client reported that her fears and apprehensions were reduced to tolerable levels and that, to her surprise, the exercises provided self-enhancing carryover in her long-term troubled relations with her mother. This report was not unusual. Covert modeling and other cognitive strategies frequently generalize to desensitize and improve the effects of client fears and anxieties that were similar to, but not the specified target of, the structured therapy program.

Thought Stopping

Thought stopping was introduced by J. G. Taylor in 1963. Since then it has been widely used to help clients control unproductive, debilitating, and self-defeating thoughts and images through both sudden and progressively systematic elimination of maladaptive thoughts and emotions (Martin, 1982; Rimm, 1973; Tryon & Pallandino, 1979; Wolpe, 1982).

Thought stopping is initially directed by the therapist. The rationale is that if unwanted thoughts are consistently interrupted whenever they occur, their occurrence will eventually be inhibited (Cormier & Cormier, 1985, pp. 385–390). Because thought stopping enables clients to inhibit unwanted and troublesome thoughts, the procedure involves instructing clients to focus on the unwanted thoughts ten to twenty times daily for several days and shouting "stop" to end each trial. After several days of practice the client can maintain control covertly by shouting "stop" each time the unwanted thought occurs (Williams & Long, 1979, p. 285). As soon as the client becomes familiar enough with the strategy to exercise self-control autonomously, he or she is given homework assignments of practicing self-control through thought stopping in situations outside therapy (Cormier & Hackney, 1987, p. 155).

Cognitive Restructuring, Reframing, and Stress Inoculation

A major development in the cognitive therapy movement has been what Cormier and Cormier (1985, pp. 403–447) have described as influencing or mediating the client's cognitions through cognitive restructuring, reframing, and stress inoculation.

Cognitive Restructuring. Cognitive restructuring (Cormier & Cormier, 1991, pp. 402–415; Ellis & Grieger, 1986, pp. 286–289; Meichenbaum, 1977; Mitchell & Krumboltz, 1987) is a rapidly growing systematic strategy whereby clients are taught to replace negative, debilitating cognitions with positive, self-enhancing thoughts and actions. The strategy assumes (1) that self-defeating behaviors flow from either the development of defective cognitions or irrational thinking and/or self-defeating self-statements; and (2) that a person's defective thinking or self-defeating self-statements can be changed by altering his or her cognitions or views about them. To the extent that the therapist is actively involved in and models self-enhancing thinking and behavior appropriate to the client's stressful situation, the procedure is didactic and directive (Gilliland & Johnston, 1987). However, such a directive approach is derived from the client's unique cognitive deficits, stresses, problems, and accompanying negative self-talk. It should be clearly understood that the therapist does not impose his or her own agendas on the client.

Cormier and Cormier (1991, pp. 402–415) recommend six steps for therapists to follow in cognitive restructuring with a client:

1. Verbal set, which includes the rationale (purpose and overview) of the procedure
2. Identification of client thoughts during problem situations
3. Introduction and practice of coping thoughts
4. Shifting from self-defeating thoughts to coping thoughts
5. Introduction and practice of positive or reinforcing self-statements
6. Homework and follow-up

Typically, the therapist works collaboratively with the client through the six steps. The therapist's role is that of consultant, facilitator, mentor, and coach. It is quite important that clients understand the process, that they want to change, and that they be willing to commit to a plan of action developed cooperatively by themselves and the therapist.

It is our view that cognitive restructuring represents the mainstream of cognitive behavior therapy because it makes full and appropriate use of all the cognitive strategies. In using cognitive restructuring we typically involve the client in relaxation, imagery, modeling, reframing, rehearsal, stress inoculation, and thought stopping. The case of Myra, presented in this chapter, is focused primarily on cognitive restructuring.

Reframing.   The objective of reframing (also called *reformulating* or *relabeling*) is to modify or restructure a client's view or perception of a problem or behavior (Bandler & Grinder, 1982; Cormier & Cormier, 1991, pp. 415–432). Cormier and Hackney (1987) defined reframing as "the gentle art of viewing a situation differently" (p. 233). Reframing is a valuable therapeutic technique for cases in which redefining, reformulating, or relabeling the problem situation, the behavior or motives of others, or the attitudes of the client changes the view or perspective of the problem so that it is more understandable, acceptable, or solvable (Borysenko, 1987, pp. 137–157).

Cormier and Cormier (1998, pp. 395–396) describe the strategy of reframing as exploring with a client how an incident or situation is typically perceived, then offering an alternative view or frame of the situation. Reframing helps clients alter their emotions, meanings, and perceived options. A reframe may be used to change clients' everyday conscious mental sets and perceptions of their personal limitations. Gendlin (1996) advises that to gauge whether the reframing is successful the therapist must sense whether the client manifests a bodily change or not. This can be done by immediately asking the client (as demonstrated in the dialogue below) what bodily responses or sensations he or she feels while experiencing the moment of the reframe.

CL: My oldest sister . . . she's so bossy. We call her the manager . . . the family's manager. If she doesn't get her way in all matters, she flips and upsets all of us. She thinks she is the anointed one to take care of all of us. She'd do anything for us, though. She's good to us, but she acts like she owns us. Kinda mothers us. Whenever we have get togethers, she just ruins things. Bosses us around! Gets her way! Sets the agenda! Manages to get the prime focus of attention on her and her kids. I always leave the gatherings upset and stay that way for a day or two. Our holidays are nightmares because of her. I just hate it!

TH: You really seem upset now, just talking and thinking about her. I wonder if you can just relax, take a few deep breaths, and get in touch, deeply inside your body, with the core of exactly what's driving those feelings and emotions that you're describing.

CL: (*pauses, breathes*) Well, that's been going on so long that I should be used to it by now. I should have just turned it loose a long time ago, like both my other sister and my husband said. Now I'm so worried about her, my oldest sister. She has horrific heart trouble. Really serious! She's scheduled to have a multiple bypass. She's obese and I fear that she might not make it. Her doctors give her about a 50/50 chance. I feel so conflicted and concerned! Like we've been too mean to her all these years. Mostly talking about her behind her back. Complaining, gossiping, and bitching about her to each other. I just don't know. I'm beginning to feel rotten. No, maybe guilty. Or maybe both guilty and rotten.

TH: (*using a reframing-type response*) It seems to me you've been saying that you can't accept your sister or maybe even that you can't stand her the way she is. Now that you fear that her very existence may be in jeopardy, you're feeling guilty, perhaps two-faced, and maybe disloyal toward her. (*client nods in agreement*) Let me ask you a question. Would you rather have her and accept her *as she is* . . . with all of her faults and flaws that you describe, or not have her at all? Assume, right now, that those are your only two choices.

CL: (*appearing somewhat startled*) Oh my gosh! This is awful! Since you put it that way, there's no contest. I'll take her as she is, any day, and feel thankful and blessed to have her! To keep her! Oh my goodness!

TH: (*evaluating the effectiveness of the reframe*) I sense by observing your bodily response that something occurred deeply inside you just then. Can you do a quick body scan to get in touch with any profound sensations or feelings that may be present, and driving your emotions and thinking, as you consider not having your sister?

CL: (*exhibiting an ah ha type of facial and bodily response*) This really is strange! A good type of strange, though. An entirely different way of looking at it. This is good! Wow . . . I never dreamed I could think about her in this way!

Another typical example of the use of reframing is in counseling with persons who are either addicted to substances or are enablers or codependents for persons who are addicted. Whenever clients can reframe the problem to redefine, reformulate, or relabel themselves as either addicts or enablers, it sheds a different light on the whole situation by allowing them to perceive themselves as part of the problem and solution rather than being a victim or blaming the victim.

As Cormier and Cormier (1998, p. 396) point out, therapists reframe whenever they ask or encourage clients to view an issue from a different perspective. Reframing is used frequently in family counseling as a means of reformulating presenting problems for the purpose of shifting the focus away from an identified problem member or scapegoat and onto the family as a whole, in which each person is an interdependent part. This use of reframing enables the family to change the way it encodes an issue or conflict. In individual therapy, reframing may serve many purposes. It can often reduce defensiveness and mobilize the client's resources and motivation to change.

Stress Inoculation. This technique is designed to give clients confidence and skill in dealing with future problems (Feindler & Fremouw, 1983; Meichenbaum, 1985). Stress inoculation is the process of teaching clients both cognitive and physical skills for autonomously coping with future stressful and distressing situations. It is a cognitive approach to teaching clients (1) to discriminate between alternative thoughts, actions, choices, and situations that lead to stress and options that lead to effective coping with stress; and (2) to use alternative cognitive and behavioral skills to successfully manage the stresses and pressures in their lives (Cormier & Cormier, 1985, p. 423). Stress inoculation has been used since the early 1970s to prepare clients to deal with anticipated stresses, anxieties, or tensions caused by a wide variety of traumatic psychological or physical debilitations (Holcomb, 1986; Schwartz, 1986; Wells, Howard, Nowlin, & Vargas, 1986; Wertkin, 1985). Meichenbaum and Turk (1976) view stress inoculation for protection from psychological tensions as analogous to medical inoculation for defending the physical body against disease.

Cormier and Cormier (1998, pp. 402–403) recommend seven steps in the stress inoculation procedure: (1) rationale, (2) information giving, (3) acquisition and practice of direct-action coping skills, (4) acquisition and practice of cognitive coping skills, (5) application of all coping skills to problem-related situations, (6) application of all coping skills to potential problem situations, and (7) homework and follow-up. The primary difference between the steps in cognitive restructuring and stress inoculation is that in stress inoculation the emphasis is proactive and future-oriented. The problem material, imaging scenes, cognitive and direct-action rehearsals, and homework assignments are derived explicitly from the client's descriptions of stress-evoking situations.

The application of stress inoculation is illustrated in the case of a 55-year-old woman enrolled in graduate school many years after completing her bachelor's degree. Although she was quite successful in her business and family life and performed well on graduate school admissions tests, she experienced panic and periods of excessive stress and anxiety as she contemplated statistics class, performance in graduate school, and the thought of not achieving a 4.0 average. The therapy focused on teaching the woman stress inoculation so that she could (1) inoculate herself against the stress of talking to her statistics professor about her fear of statistics and need for tutoring; (2) convince herself, through inoculation, that her anxiety level could endure earning a B in the statistics course and that she would not suffer from guilt for receiving that grade; and (3) prepare herself to cope with her own negative self-evaluation and self-rejection in the event that she found schoolwork too difficult as an adult returning to the university.

Four stress inoculation sessions were recorded on audiotape. The woman was asked to listen to each session at home, in a relaxed state with no interruptions, as part of her homework. She reported that listening to the tapes at home enhanced her understanding of stress inoculation and reinforced what she learned during the therapy sessions. In a three-week follow-up contact she reported that she had had no more recurrences of panic and that her stress levels were quite tolerable. At the end of the semester she reported that her stress inoculation program was keeping her anxieties at tolerable levels and that she had made 98 on her research proposal and a 91.4 (B) for her term grade in statistics. She was quite happy with the B.

Meditation and Relaxation

Recently many types of meditation and relaxation procedures have been developed to help busy and stressed-out people in the industrial societies of the world cope with the responsibilities and pressures of modern, fast-paced employment and hectic daily living. Cognitive therapists have been quick to recognize and adapt these procedures to help clients deal with stress, anxiety, conflict, crisis situations, medical and physical difficulties, business and financial failures, and many other human dilemmas. Jacobson (1929) originally introduced *progressive relaxation*—probably the first relaxation strategy to be recognized professionally. There followed many different types of relaxation, such as Benson's (1976) relaxation response, Lazarus's (1977b) muscle relaxation techniques, and Borysenko's (1987) loving-kindness or *metta* meditation.

The principles, processes, benefits, procedures, and uses of meditation have received a great deal of attention among cognitive theorists and practitioners (Borysenko, 1987; Cormier & Cormier, 1998, pp. 424–458; Epstein, 1995; Fontana, 1991; Levine, 1991; Long, 1995; Simpkins & Simpkins, 1996). Fontana (1991, p. 17) described what meditation is and also what meditation isn't. Meditation *is* "keeping the mind alert and attentive, keeping the mind focused and concentrated, becoming aware of the world, becoming more human, knowing where you are." Meditation *isn't* "falling asleep, going into a trance, shutting yourself off from reality and becoming unworldly, being selfish, doing something 'unnatural,' becoming lost in thought, forgetting where you are."

The term *meditation* has traditionally been associated with the centuries-old mystical techniques of the Far East whereby one achieves high levels of relaxed introspection and altered states of consciousness. Examples are Zen (Zazen) breath meditation and transcendental meditation (TM) (Shapiro, 1980). Cormier and Cormier (1991, pp. 447–456) indicate that a great deal of commonality exists among the different types of meditation, self-hypnosis, and relaxation techniques such as Benson's (1976) relaxation response. They are similar in that each technique helps the client relax, sharply focus the entire mental apparatus on one important idea or thought, and keep all extraneous thoughts and/or stimuli out of the present cognition. Many kinds of meditation are used by cognitive therapists in various settings (Cormier & Cormier, 1991, pp. 447–456).

Meditation as a therapeutic technique typically helps the client concentrate on some internal or external stimulus that serves to focus the client's attention away from aversive stimuli. Borysenko (1987) characterizes meditation as "nothing more than anchoring your attention in the present" (p. 39). She recommends meditation as the method of choice for regaining control over overwhelming stress and anxiety (pp. 29–53). It is a strategy designed to help clients consciously concentrate on positive, self-enhancing thoughts as opposed to dwelling on negative, self-defeating thoughts—especially ruminations on the past (Carrington, 1978b; Shapiro, 1980). Cormier and Cormier (1985) characterize meditation strategies as useful in treating "both cognitive and physiological indexes of stress, including anxiety, anger, pain, and hypertension." They further state that the most effective use of meditation focuses on prevention as well as remediation of stress-related symptoms (p. 448).

An example of the use of meditation was in helping a 35-year-old man whose job as a commodities broker made his ulcer worse and exacerbated his physical and emotional stress, which increased whenever his job pressures increased. The meditation strategy focused on helping the client learn to relax both his mind and his body, concentrate vividly and completely on the positive successes and the stress-free times at the brokerage firm, and keep job-related worries and past and future risks from intruding on his present thinking. The meditation was successful because the client was willing to learn, to use the audiotapes made during therapy sessions as homework, and to consistently practice the meditation technique.

Biofeedback

The development of *biofeedback training* (BFT) was an unprecedented event in the merging of the psychological and medical aspects of controlling one's own body (Brown, 1977). Essentially, biofeedback is a method of using technology to communicate to a person what his or her body is doing and teaching that person to use mental processes to control bodily functions (Brown, 1974). Biofeedback offered new ways to help clients control stress, anxiety, and tensions through the control of blood pressure, temperature, and other physiologic functions.

Biofeedback has been described as "the feedback of biological information to the person whose biology it is" (Brown, 1974, p. 4). The reasons BFT works are not clearly known. What is clear is that the mind exerts a considerably greater influence over bodily functions than many behavioral scientists formerly assumed was the case. In fact, it can be said that the human mind can exert control over any known function of the autonomic nervous system, provided it has accurate data on the level and direction of the internal physiologic events it wishes to monitor.

Some BFT clinics use sophisticated electronic equipment, such as electroencephalographs (EEGs) to monitor changes in the electric potential in the brain and central nervous system; electromyographs to provide audio and visual records of the electrical responses of muscle tissue to nerve stimulation; and electronic devices and technology to measure blood pressure, rate of heartbeat, galvanic skin reaction, and so forth. The essence of the therapeutic use of BFT procedures is that all involuntary bodily responses that can be accurately measured and monitored can be changed.

Used in conjunction with other techniques, BFT can be effective and efficient in helping clients with physiologically related problems such as hypertension, disorders of motor functioning, gastrointestinal difficulties, chronic pain, Raynaud's syndrome, tension headaches, and stress-related disorders (Hatch, Fisher, & Rugh, 1987). Further, BFT has been used to help athletes treat physiological deficits and improve their performance in their sport (Sandweiss & Wolf, 1985).

The range and complexity of BFT instrumentation and procedure are great. A simple indoor–outdoor thermometer can be an acceptable device for monitoring skin temperature and blood flow to the extremities. Instrument choice depends on the client's problem and the therapist's level of training and experience with BFT techniques. One relatively simple strategy, for example, was the use of a skin thermometer to help a secretary decrease her anxiety (and increase her low score) on a civil service typing examination. The client could not perform the task because she would get anxious and the muscles in her arms and hands would cramp. Through BFT the secretary was taught to raise the skin temperature in her arms and hands by cognitively focusing on an appropriate image to increase the flow of warmth to that body area. After several abortive attempts to pair an image with the desired physiologic behavior (soaking in a hot tub, reclining in a warm meadow, and so on), the secretary found that she could elevate her extremity skin temperature by concentrating and imagining warm, glowing spots on the insides of her elbows. She subsequently was able to increase the blood flow to her arms and hands, relax her muscles, and remain free of cramps while she successfully passed her typing test.

Neurolinguistic Programming

Neurolinguistic programming (NLP) is the name derived from a communication theory (Bandler & Grinder, 1975; Grinder & Bandler, 1976) whereby people wield five sensory channels, referred to as *representational* (R) systems, to process information. These channels are termed visual (sight), auditory (hearing), kinesthetic (feeling), olfactory (smell), and gustatory (taste). For communication and therapy purposes, the visual, auditory, and kinesthetic channels are the most important.

Neurolinguistic programming is a powerful tool for the therapist to use in effectively establishing rapport and maintaining an empathic relationship with clients. Lankton (1980) found that when the therapist can identify and utilize the sensory channel that the client predominantly uses, he or she can match or pace the client's inner experience. For example, different clients might use different predicate verbs to indicate sensory ways of communicating (mapping) their inner experience: (1) visual ("I see that . . . ."); (2) auditory ("I hear that . . . ."); or (3) kinesthetic ("I feel that . . . ."). Lankton notes that the therapist who can match the predicates of clients "will literally be speaking the client's language" (p. 19). Cormier and Hackney (1987) describe how NLP can be effectively used to pace the client's verbal and nonverbal cues, thus allowing the therapist to understand more fully the client's internal experiencing and to mirror those cognitive experiences for the client (pp. 45–48). Pacing involves synchrony between the therapist and the client's verbal and nonverbal behavior. Cormier and Cormier (1991, p. 559) advise that timing and pacing enhance the efficiency of the interview by decreasing client resistance and enabling the therapist to avoid taking a stand prematurely.

The use of neurolinguistic programming is illustrated by a therapist doing career counseling with two different clients. One client wants to change from primary teaching to a career that affords travel; the other client cannot visualize herself as a gainfully employed person. The therapist uses visual channeling with the first client and auditory channeling with the second, having discovered that each client has different ways of mapping experiences and of processing and interpreting internal and external information. The therapist works with the first client by paying particular attention to his adjectives and adverbs and then uses sensory words to match, pace, and channel therapeutic responses to him. Thus, to program the client to examine new career choices, the therapist uses and models visual words and expressions such as *see, clear, focus, picture, view, perspective, plain, bright, colorful, glimpse, watch,* "now look," and "Can you picture this?" Concomitantly, to program the second client to explore paid positions, the therapist employs auditory terms and expressions such as *listen, yell, tell, told, talk, hear, discuss, shout, loud, noisy, call,* "now listen," "sounds like," and "I can tune into this" (Cormier & Hackney, 1987, p. 47).

Eye Movement Desensitization Reprocessing (EMDR)

Eye Movement Desensitization (EMD) was developed by Francine Shapiro (1989a, 1989b) to combat post-traumatic stress disorder (PTSD). The "R" was later added by Shapiro

(1991) to indicate a reprocessing of information along with changing to more positive cognitions and desensitization of the traumatic memory. EMDR has been used mainly to treat traumatic memories, but Shapiro maintains that it has utility in working with a variety of negative self-attributions that have occurred at some earlier point in time, are held in the nervous system in state-specific form (as they occurred at the time of the noxious event), and continue to plague clients (Shapiro, 1995, pp. 14, 41–42).

Although EMDR has a therapeutic basis in both psychodynamic and behavioral approaches, one of its major axioms is that a cognitive reassessment or negative thought needs to occur and positive new injunctions about the event and the person are incorporated by the client so that the memory is redefined (Shapiro, 1995, pp. 22–24). From that standpoint, it is our belief that EMDR most closely fits a cognitive behavioral approach, although its incorporation of a variety of techniques could place it as a self-contained eclectic or multimodal approach as well.

EMDR treats negative memories by requiring that the client maintain an awareness of one or more of the following:

1. An image of the memory
2. A negative self-statement or assessment of the trauma
3. The physical anxiety response

Shapiro (1989a, 1989b) proposes that it is best when all three conditions are held at the same time, but she acknowledges that the presence of any one is sufficient for desensitization to occur. Anxiety level is assessed by Wolpe's (1982) subjective units of discomfort scale (SUDS) (0 equals no anxiety; 10 is the highest anxiety possible). Because negative self-cognitions are also part of the disorder, shifts in the client's cognitive view of the traumatic event are also assessed by a validity of cognition (VOC) scale that Shapiro (1989a) developed (1 means the cognition is completely untrue; 7 means the cognition is completely true). The client is asked to focus on the noxious memory and then isolate the most traumatic point while he or she builds a picture of it in his or her mind's eye. The client then states which words best describe the picture and rates him- or herself on the SUDS and VOC scale, indicating the physical location of the symptoms (Shapiro 1989a, 1989b).

The client is next asked how he or she would like to feel and is told to generate a new positive self-statement that reflects the desired feeling; he or she is then asked to judge how true that new statement is (Shapiro 1989a, 1989b). Shapiro (1989b) then gives the client a standard set of instructions designed to diminish performance anxiety and performance demands. She explains the instructions are important because clients may also have difficulty accepting the initial changes they feel in themselves. Her instructions are the following:

> What we will be doing is often a physiology check. I need to know from you exactly what is going on, with as clear feedback as possible. Sometimes things will change and sometimes they won't. I may ask you if the picture changes—sometimes it will and sometimes it won't. I may ask if something else comes up—sometimes it will and sometimes it won't. There are no "supposed to's" in this process. So just give as accurate feedback as you can as to what is

happening, without judging whether it should be happening or not. Just let whatever happens, happen (p. 213).

The client is told to generate the scene, the negative statements, and the noxious feelings, and visually follow the therapist's finger, which is moved rapidly and rhythmically back and forth about one foot in front of the client's face at a rate of approximately two back-and-forth movements per second across a sweep of about 12 inches. For clients who have trouble with this approach, Shapiro uses a slightly different format, in which the therapist's fingers are to the side of the client's field of vision and are alternately moved up and down. The movement is repeated 12 to 24 times for one set (these movements are called a *saccade,* which means a sort of a pulling or pressing movement). After each set of saccades, the client is asked to erase the scene from his or her mind and take a deep breath. The client is then told to bring up the noxious image again and ascribe a SUDS level to it. After two sets of saccades, if the image has not changed, the client is asked if the picture has changed or if anything new has come into the image. If so, the new image is desensitized before returning to the old image. Periodically, the client is asked to assess image, cognition, and memory. The answers are used to determine new insights, perceptions, or alterations.

If the cognition fails to change after two sets of eye movements, there may be a mismatch between the cognition and the image, or vice versa. In each case image and cognition must be congruent with one another. If they are not, then one or the other needs to be replaced.

The client may also be instructed to think of a physical location of anxiety in the body if the SUDS level remains high. He or she is asked to concentrate on the bodily sensation while new saccades are given. When the focal point of physical discomfort subsides, the client is asked to return to the original picture of the trauma and the standard EMDR procedure is resumed (Shapiro 1989a, 1989b).

When the SUDS level reaches 0 or 1, the client's belief in the validity of the desired cognitions is self-assessed by his or her giving a VOC rating to the original cognition. Regardless of what that rating is, the client is then asked to visualize the original picture along with the positive self-statement and another set of saccades is instituted. Shapiro (1989b) reports that it is not uncommon for different traumatic events and cognitions to be uncovered as the client moves through the procedure. When no new events or negative cognitions are elicited, the EMDR procedure is terminated.

Shapiro (1989b, 1995, pp. 328–338) reports that a 60 to 90 percent rate of removal of symptoms of one to three traumatic or negative memories can occur in as little as one session with well-selected and adequately prepared clients. This success rate is supported by other independent sources (Boudewyns, Stwertka, Hyer, Abrecht, & Sperr, 1993; Cocco & Sharpe, 1993; Forbes, Creamer, & Rycroft, 1994; Montgomery & Ayllon, 1994; Silver, Brooks, & Obenchain, 1995; Thomas & Gafner, 1993; Vaughan, Armstrong, Gold, & O'Connor, 1994; Vaughan, Wiese, Gold, & Tarrier, 1994). However, we want to caution that EMDR involves a good deal more than waving a finger in front of a client's face. As with all cognitive behavioral approaches, we urge any therapist to obtain specific and intense training for the techniques in this chapter. In unskilled hands, many of these techniques are dangerous and may create even more trauma in the client than is already present.

Sample Case

The following case study incorporates excerpts from two different sets of cognitive restructuring therapy sessions. The purpose is to provide examples of a therapist working with a client on two different presenting problems related to one major life-threatening problem. In both sets of excerpts, the client is experiencing cognitive deficits about her situation, and in both sets the therapist uses cognitive behavior therapy with primary emphasis on cognitive restructuring.

Example One

The first set of excerpts demonstrates the therapeutic use of cognitive restructuring in the case of Myra Malik, an army veteran in her early thirties who had developed the belief, following a mastectomy, that her body was unacceptably impaired and that she was destined to have a life of physical pain and emotional stress as a result. Therapy followed the six steps of cognitive restructuring.

> TH: (*verbal set*) Myra, the main thrust of our sessions will be to assist you in identifying the self-defeating thoughts and self-talk you're giving yourself about the operation and to help you develop and learn to use self-enhancing thoughts in a way that will lead to freeing you from stress and pain. As an example of some of these negative self-thoughts you've expressed, I'm going to state what I heard you say *prior* to going into the hospital, *during your stay there,* and *after* you came out. *Before* you went in you said, "This can't be happening to me. I can't stand this horrible situation. I know I'll never be able to stand it. I can't stand to give up part of my body." *During* your stay, you said things like "Now no man will ever want me; I know I can't stand the chemotherapy treatments; what's going to happen to me now? I'm alone and I'm scared to death." *After* you came out, your statements were something like, "Now I'm only half a woman; next time it may get me; I dread going out in public; maybe it would be better for me now if I didn't wake up so I wouldn't have to face this again."
>
> Now let me change to positive self-talk about the same situation. I want you to imagine, as vividly as you can, saying these things *before* you went into the hospital: "This is happening to me, but I can handle it; I've been in bad situations in the army—if I could stand that, I can stand this; I may give up part of my body but I won't give up the good part—I'll only give up the diseased part." *During* the stay in the hospital, you could have said, "If no man wants me because I've had breast surgery, he isn't much of a man; if I can stand OCS basic, I can stand chemotherapy; I didn't realize I had so many friends; now I know what friendship really means." *After* you left the hospital, you could have said to yourself, "The pictures and explanations of the cosmetic surgery they showed me thrilled me; now, there's no reason why I can't live a normal, happy life; I'm young, I've got a lot to live for, and I have more friends than ever!"
>
> TH: (*identifying client thoughts in problem situations*) Tell me exactly what you're thinking when you say, "I'm not going back to chemotherapy." What are those

cues, ideas, et cetera, that start you off? Is it the pain? Is it fear? Is it lack of self-confidence? Lack of guts? Tell me precisely what the emotions are that make you want to behave in self-destructive ways. Imagine you have on a headset and you're hearing a very rational little announcer in your head: "The treatments are painful and inconvenient; I don't look good now; I'm sick, but the tests are coming out good, and I'm going to live—not only that, I'm going to enjoy living."

Now that you know what those negative thoughts sound like, I suggest you listen to the tape recording of this session each day for the next four days. Listen to it while you are relaxed on a couch or bed so that you've got a good idea of the difference between your negative and positive self-talk. Make a diary of the times each day you engage in both positive and negative thoughts and self-talk so we can get a handle on the length, times, and conditions in which they occur.

TH: (*introduction and practice of coping thoughts*) We are now going to do something that's really important to whipping this problem. We're going to replace that self-defeating, negative talk with positive, coping talk. I've already modeled what you could say in those situations that wind up being bad. You may have some other, better thoughts you can use. If so, that's fine. Either way, the idea is to conjure up some thoughts that will deal positively with the situation, plan on how to get out of the situation, relax while you're doing it, and use positive reinforcers that encourage you to keep attacking those self-defeating thoughts. Once we have those, you can go back over the tape and practice saying them to yourself.

TH: (*shifting from self-defeating to coping thoughts*) I'm going to demonstrate how you can shift those self-defeating thoughts around to really positive thoughts that attack the problem, so just tune that headset in and listen. Here we go! "God! I'm here in my apartment alone and that fear is just starting to sweep over me. (*anxiety*) Stop that nonsense! (*cue*) Now go over to the telephone, pick it up, and call Gayle. She said she wanted to get a pizza." (*proactive coping response*) Now that you know when those thoughts occur and how to change them, we're going to practice controlling and changing them until it's so automatic it'll be like water off a duck's back. So put yourself into that situation and let's give it a try.

TH: (*introduction and practice of positive or reinforcing self-statements*) Hey, Myra! You've really gotten into this and have done a super job of sticking with the game plan. You've really learned how to beat those killer statements into the ground. So why not give yourself credit where credit is due? I'd like you to add one more kind of statement to what we've already done. That is, I want you to learn how to give yourself a payoff. Just sit back, put your earphones on and listen. "Now, I'm out here at the pizza parlor. I'm having a great time, particularly since Gayle introduced me to that cute graduate student in engineering. The way he's been giving me the eye and hanging on my every word, I really feel good! I may even decide to put some moves on that cute guy myself! Moping around at home is for dummies and wallflowers. I am a woman! I am unconquerable!" If you'll do this and really buy into it, there's no way those killer statements will get to you. So I'd like you to think up some really potent reinforcing statements, and we'll practice those until you become your own best reinforcing agent.

TH: (*homework and follow-up*) Myra, you've done really well implementing the techniques. I believe you're ready to go full blast! What I'd like you to do is practice it for one week without any further help from me. Keep your log up to date on your thoughts and listen to the tapes of our practice session every day. I'm sure you'll succeed at this, but if there are problems, we'll go back and troubleshoot the system.

These excerpts illustrated the therapist in a didactic mode. Of course, the client was involved along the way. The point is that this first set of excerpts gives the details of the procedures directed by the therapist toward solving one presenting problem containing clear cognitive distortions by the clients.

Example Two

Rationale and Overview.   In the second set of excerpts with Myra, the therapist again demonstrated cognitive behavior therapy techniques, primarily cognitive restructuring. Myra was seen in therapy following a radical mastectomy performed in a VA hospital. The following excerpts are from audiotaped interviews with Myra at the hospital.

CL: I guess they told you how upset and depressed I get when I think about how disfigured I'm gonna be. The women from the Cancer Society are coming in tomorrow to explain the implant and prosthesis to me. I'm about to panic just thinking about their coming.

TH: Myra, I'm glad we're having this talk today! The procedure we're going to do today will help you to identify the things you're thinking when you begin to feel panicky, depressed, or anxious about dealing with the prosthesis. Before we're through, you will learn that what causes the panic and depression is simply unfounded thinking, not facts. We will begin right now to work on more realistic ways for you to think about the implant and prosthesis, and this will help you to gain control of your own unproductive and panicky emotions.

The therapist was explaining to Myra the purpose and rationale of cognitive restructuring. The therapist had noted that Myra is an educated and articulate person. She is a captain in the Army Reserve as well as a veteran of four years' active service in the U.S. Army. Therefore, the therapist's language reflects structuring the therapy according to the client's level of functioning, and the therapist's focus on the client's sensory channel of feeling and on language pacing that indicates the therapist's awareness of the value of neurolinguistic programming as practiced by Lankton (1980).

CL: I feel better already. What you've said makes sense. I hope you can help me get rid of some of this fear and panic.

TH: I sense that you're really ready to work on your thoughts. That's good! We'll do three things to help. First, we will identify the kinds of things you're thinking before, during, and following consultations about your breast implant. Second, we'll teach you how to stop a self-defeating thought about the implant situation and replace it with a positive, self-enhancing thought. Third, we will help you learn how to give yourself credit for changing your own self-defeating thoughts.

[Here the therapist was providing Myra a brief overview of the procedure.]

CL: I guess I somehow know that my anxiety and panic are caused by my exaggerated thinking, but that doesn't seem to help.

TH: That's precisely the reason it's important for us to work together on your thinking right now, Myra. You're really talking about your own self-defeating thoughts about the implant. Such self-defeating thoughts about the implant, or any other stress-producing situation, are ways you interpret the situation. But these interpretations you generate are usually negative and unproductive, like thinking that you will never be a complete woman again and this will be so awful that you cannot accept yourself ever again. In contrast, a self-enhancing thought is a more realistic, constructive, and positive way to interpret your future life with a breast implant—like thinking, "This is not what I would want, but I am on my way to health again, and I am more than just breasts; I can live, work, be happy, marry, have a family, and do about anything I set my head to, and that's fine; I can be as strong and invincible as I can truly believe, in my mind, that I am." How does that feel to you as I say it?

The therapist was deliberate in explaining to Myra the difference between rational or self-enhancing thoughts (facts) and irrational or self-defeating thoughts (beliefs) and gave her pertinent examples.

CL: Well, I've worried myself insane over it. I've been doing exactly what you're describing, and the more I worry the worse my panic and anxiety seem to get.

TH: Myra, that's the reason it is important for you to understand that whenever you continue to be preoccupied with your inner negative thoughts and worry about the outcomes of your recovery this can affect your feelings and your behavior. Worrying about the recovery can really make you feel anxious and panicky and can actually interfere with your regaining good health. Thinking positively and using your imagination constructively can certainly help you erase your worries, help you feel more relaxed, and enable you to handle the whole implant and recovery situation more easily and effectively.

Here, the therapist was explaining the influence of irrational and self-defeating thoughts on Myra's emotions and performance.

CL: That's making a lot of sense. I'm beginning to look forward to viewing my condition more positively.

TH: So what you're wanting to do right now, Myra, is to work on developing positive mind control over your recovery. You're really wanting to use your mind to get rid of the negative emotions, such as panic, and to get on with accentuating your positive assets.

The therapist was confirming Myra's motivation to work on her own cognitive restructuring and was using a verbal set (to predispose Myra to believe that the therapy will work). What the therapist has done in these excerpts is to accomplish step one of the cognitive restructuring (rationale and overview).

Identifying Client Thoughts in Problem Situations.   Now that Myra is motivated to work on her problem and accepts the therapist's rationale concerning the cognitive restructuring procedures, the next step is to identify the thoughts that are contributing to her panic and anxiety toward her impending breast implant. The therapist will want to explore both the range of situations and the specific content that Myra cognitively generates. An essential tool the therapist uses in every session with Myra is an audio tape recorder. Recorded data are valuable in helping the therapist prepare and carry out the cognitive therapy and in helping Myra, as she listens to the taped sessions, enhance her learning and awareness.

TH: Myra, think of the last time you were upset by thoughts of the implant. Describe for me what you think before you begin to feel panicky. What are you usually thinking about when conversations and consultations about the implant are presented to you?

CL: I'm thinking, "Oh my gosh, I dread this! I can't stand it! I wish they wouldn't come. I don't want to talk about this. I don't even want to think about it. I don't want to be cut on any more. I don't want any ugly scars! I just know I will look horrible by the time they're through."

TH: Good. We have that on our audiotape. Now, what are you thinking while the medical specialists are talking to you about it?

CL: By the time they get in here and crowd around my bed, I'm so upset and anxious I don't know what I'm thinking. I guess I'm thinking, "This is awful! Why don't they leave? Why are they discussing me like I'm a broken-down machine? I just know I'll end up being a defeminized person that no man would ever look at, much less love."

TH: What thoughts are going through your mind after the consultation is over?

CL: Oh Lord! I think, "I'm confused and scared. Why did this have to happen to me? My life is ruined!"

TH: All right. Now let's see which of those thoughts are actual facts about the implant situation or are positive and constructive ways to interpret it. Which thoughts are mainly your beliefs about the implant situation that are unproductive, negative, or self-defeating?

CL: I don't know. As we're talking about it right now, I get to feeling better; then I imagine the worst and just start to panic again!

TH: All right, Myra. I want you to just turn that thought off right now. Just go back, in your mind's eye, to a place of safety, relaxation, serenity, and warmth. Just relax again. Just like you did when we first started. Imagine you have lots of time. Just lots of time. So relaxed. So comfortable. Just take your time, and whenever you get completely and comfortably relaxed again, begin to tell me what you're seeing, feeling, and thinking. Just take your time. Lots of time. (*Myra relaxes; long pause*)

CL: I'm sitting on a chaise lounge. I'm at the beach. I'm very comfortable. The sun is keeping me warm. The sea breezes are refreshing. I'm in my bathing suit, wearing sunglasses, with sunscreen lotion all over me. I have my music and my reading. I'm feeling relaxed and content. I'm not thinking about the hospital or my operation or anything like that. I'm thinking that the sun and the sea and the rest will make me whole again.

TH: Good. Just take lots of time. Feel yourself getting more relaxed every moment. Getting stronger and stronger. Healthier and healthier. So relaxed. Free of pressures. Free of pain. Free to think, in a very relaxed and safe place, about the power you have right there in your body to think, to control, to emerge as a stronger you. Now, with your whole body so relaxed and in a state of pure ecstasy, I want you to begin to think about and name the thoughts you want to begin saying to yourself, whenever you begin to feel anxious and panicky. Just continue to relax, with lots of time, and whenever you begin to get a very good idea of those healthy thoughts that you most want to have and use, begin to say them . . . now.

The therapist had used relaxation many times with Myra, so she was ready and motivated to enjoy it and use it productively. The therapist was also asking Myra to recall and record specific thoughts that she could use to effect cognitive restructuring. As an additional means of identifying Myra's thoughts in the problem situation, the therapist later assigned problem-identification homework.

TH: We've made a good start on nailing down those nasty self-defeating thoughts. An additional way to help you and me identify your various thoughts about the implant situation is to keep track of your thoughts as they happen. I'm going to leave this tape recorder right here on the stand beside your bed. I want you to use it liberally. Every time you have a profound thought about your medical condition, I want you to say it into the microphone right then. If you have a positive, healing thought, say it. If you have a negative, panicky thought, say it, too. I want us to listen to the audiotape at the beginning of our next session, after supper tonight.

The therapist was using a tape recorder rather than a log. Tape recorders are often preferred to logs because clients can usually put more thoughts onto the audiotape than they can on a writing pad, and the voice helps both therapist and client to identify additional emotional content and detail about the problem.

Introduction and Practice of Coping Thoughts.   The introduction and practice of coping thoughts are crucial to Myra's successful cognitive restructuring. We will briefly describe what the therapist does with Myra.

Before proceeding very far in this step, the therapist reviews the audiotape with Myra and ensures that all the negative and positive thoughts are identified. Then the therapist explains the purpose and potential use of coping thoughts and gives examples that pertain to the client's situation. Positive, self-enhancing thoughts that focus on Myra's anxiety about the implant *before* the situation are confronted and *during* conversations about the implant are collaboratively developed. Then constructive coping thoughts and behaviors are generated to equip Myra actually to deal with feeling panicky, anxious, or overwhelmed.

The therapist next directs Myra in thinking of additional coping thoughts that she could use or has used in dealing with the mastectomy, implant, or any other traumatic situation. Myra is then coached in practicing three important aspects of attaining control of her coping thoughts: (1) verbalizing the most positive and self-enhancing coping statements; (2) using the coping statements both before and during a problem situation; and (3) appropriately sequencing and mentally internalizing the meanings of her statements during rehearsal and actual problem solving.

> TH: Now, Myra, let's put it all together by your imaging that you're in your room one hour before the women from the Cancer Society are coming. As you begin to feel panicky or anxious, stop and practice the coping thoughts we have been using.

> TH: Myra, imagine, as vividly as you can, how it feels to be there and what your coping thoughts really mean to you as you picture yourself, in your mind's eye, talking with those women.

The entire session is devoted to the introduction and practice of coping thoughts that Myra and the therapist judge to have the most potential for success.

Shifting from Self-Defeating to Coping Thoughts.   In this step the therapist, as a mentor, introduces Myra to the technique of rehearsing the shift from self-defeating to coping thoughts during stressful periods. The rehearsal of such shifting is done to assist Myra in using her self-defeating thoughts as cues to switch immediately to coping thoughts. Three important procedures contribute to the success of this step: (1) the therapist verbally models Myra shifting from recognizing a self-defeating thought and stopping it to replacing it with a coping thought; (2) the therapist coaches Myra in her practice of shifting from self-defeating to coping thoughts; and (3) the therapist coaches Myra in practicing using shifting for each stressful situation until the anxiety and panic felt while practicing the situation decrease to a reasonable and negligible level and until she can carry out her own rehearsal using coping thoughts in a self-directed manner. A few examples of the therapist cognitively coaching Myra illustrate these procedures.

> TH: Myra, let me demonstrate how you might shift from recognizing a self-defeating thought and stopping it to replacing it with a coping thought. First, I'm in my

room, relaxed and comfortable. Suddenly it pops into my mind: "They will walk into this room with my doctor in a little over an hour! Gosh! What will I do? My hands are getting sweaty! I'm feeling both panicky and overwhelmed. I'm thinking I might just freeze up or faint. No! Stop that thought right now! I will just use my deep breathing, like we've been practicing, and I will begin to get calm, serene, and ecstatic. I will just imagine myself relaxed and greeting them. I will be the coolest, most relaxed person in the room."

TH: Now, Myra, let's rehearse this another way. This time you will imagine the situation and rehearse it. As soon as you begin to feel a self-defeating thought emerging, stop it. Verbalize to me the thought aloud, and command yourself to stop it. Then verbalize to yourself and to me a coping thought in place of it and vividly imagine carrying out, on your own, the coping messages you give yourself.

CL: (*long pause; relaxes*) I'm just lying here reading. Passing the time away. I look out the window. I see a car a long way off with some writing on it. Of course I can't tell what the writing is. Then I think, "Oh my gosh! What if that's them!" I'm feeling panicky and scared again. My palms and my forehead are getting sweaty. (*pause*) Then I think about my thought control! In my mind, I see that great big red stop sign! I think about what it means. I now command myself, "You stop that negative thinking this minute! You know, yourself, that you have nothing to fear and everything going for you. You have the whole VA behind you. You have your whole life in front of you. You're a strong person, both physically and intellectually. You know what you want to do in life. Open up your mind and get ready for what these experts have to tell you and to give you. You can, no, you *will*, do whatever you want to do and be whatever you want to be. You realize you need to know all that essential stuff about taking care of yourself *before* the implant operation. You need to get a thorough and professional consultation about the prosthesis, too. This is going to be a *good* day for you, Myra."

TH: Myra, I'm pleased to say that you are learning the procedure exceedingly well. I can tell that you are understanding the concepts and that you will be able to use your thought control to great advantage for yourself.

As Myra demonstrates the ability to identify, stop, and replace her self-defeating thoughts, the therapist systematically decreases the amount of coaching and mentoring. Before proceeding to the final steps of cognitive restructuring, Myra should demonstrate competence in practicing and carrying out these shifts in a completely autonomous and self-directed manner.

Introduction and Practice of Positive or Reinforcing Self-Statements.   The benefits of cognitive restructuring will not be fully available to clients until they learn how to reinforce themselves for successful coping. Clients do not automatically know the value of reinforcing self-statements and may not know that such self-statements must be learned. Typically, therapists must model and teach the art and skill of self-reinforcement. It is very important for clients to learn to reinforce themselves through self-statements because therapists can

provide reinforcement only during therapy sessions. The goal of therapy is client independence, and client self-reinforcement provides a key to obtaining that goal.

The therapist follows four steps in helping Myra attain competency in using reinforcing self-statements. The first step is to explain the purposes of positive self-statements and provide verbal examples.

> **TH:** Myra, you have made excellent progress in learning to use positive coping statements to prepare yourself for facing the implant surgery and rehabilitation. It is now time to solidify your gains by learning to reward or encourage yourself. As soon as you have coped with a panicky situation, you can pat yourself on the back for having done so by thinking a positive or rewarding thought like, "Hey! I did it!" or "I stood up to the test and passed. I can really do it!"

The second step in the introduction and practice of positive or reinforcing self-statements involves instructing Myra to think of additional appropriate self-statements and selecting some statements to practice.

> **TH:** Myra, I want you to think of some things that would be rewarding or encouraging for you to say to yourself whenever you've accomplished your goals. Try to come up with some thoughts that will be right for you, personally.

The third step is for the therapist verbally to model application of selected positive self-statements as self-reinforcement for shifting from self-defeating to coping thoughts.

> **TH:** Myra, this is one way you could reward yourself for having coped. You recognize the self-defeating thought. Now you're successfully using coping thoughts, and you're experiencing thoughts like "Just concentrate on drawing a deep and soothing breath, staying focused right on the task at hand, and keeping control of my thinking and my emotions." Now the consultation is concluded. You are aware that you did an excellent job using coping thoughts. You now reward yourself by thinking "I did it, and I did it well. It was really no big deal. I know how to manage my thinking."

The fourth and final step in helping Myra to practice positive or reinforcing self-statements is to instruct her to practice positive self-statements within the therapeutic interview itself; then, gradually, Myra will practice on her own in real confrontational situations. She will be taught to reward herself by giving herself positive and reinforcing self-statements during and following real situations. She will also put these self-statements on audiotape following her successes, to assist her and her therapist in fine-tuning her self-rewarding skills.

> **TH:** All right, Myra. As you imagine the confrontation, you're using the coping thoughts you will verbalize. Just relax and imagine your best coping thoughts.

Now, imagine the confrontation is over and begin to verbalize several reinforcing thoughts for having successfully coped.

CL: Okay, I handled myself quite well. I'm improving every day. The panic I felt when they first pulled those prostheses out of the box was really nothing to dread. I handled that as well as anyone. I am really making progress, and I'm doing it myself!

Homework and Follow-Up.   Even though homework is used in every step of cognitive restructuring, the ultimate goal for Myra is to use cognitive restructuring in any stressful situation in her daily life. The therapist teaches her to do her own self-pacing, monitoring, and problem solving. For a while she must practice on her own, audiotape verbalizations of her thinking patterns, and finally graduate to autonomous use of cognitive restructuring. A key concept throughout the procedure is that Myra must not emerge dependent on the therapist or anyone else.

The homework and follow-up step is the time when the therapist serves as Myra's mentor. Myra lives and demonstrates effective thinking to herself and to the therapist. She develops confidence in identifying self-defeating thoughts, stops unproductive thinking, shifts to coping thoughts, reinforces herself with positive self-statements, and uses these mechanisms effectively in her everyday life as well as in particular problem situations.

Contributions of Cognitive Therapy

The foremost contribution of the cognitive movement to therapy in general and to behavioral psychology in particular is that it has firmly established internal human thought processes as data or events to be studied and used by clients in therapy.

Another contribution has been the validation of a number of relaxation techniques as legitimate procedures for use in formal therapy. Before the emergence of the cognitive strategies, little attention was paid by the therapeutic community to relaxation. Today, many kinds of therapists, inside and outside the cognitive movement, make great use of the power of relaxation to help and to heal.

The cognitive movement has enhanced the rational therapies, such as REBT. Since the emergence of the cognitive movement, more and more attention has been given to the effects of covert human beliefs and self-talk on overt behavior. That view of human functioning should prove beneficial to all the helping professions.

The two powerful cognitive perspectives—the Meichenbaum practitioner formulation and the Beck researcher base—combine to bring cognitive behavioral therapies into the forefront as a systematic scientist–practitioner model that the therapeutic community can readily understand and use. While a majority of practitioners do not necessarily validate an approach, nevertheless it appears from our vantage point that a majority of current psychotherapists use some form or degree of cognitive therapy in their work. This movement has seen a relatively rapid evolution out of operant conditioning and REBT that would not have been clearly in evidence prior to the emergence of the modern cognitive movement.

Shortcomings of Cognitive Therapy

Cognitive therapy may fit very well with mainstream clients from Euro-American back-grounds and individuals who are comfortable with challenges to their belief systems, such as clients who have masculine or strongly individualistic orientations. But cognitive therapy and cognitive restructuring have been harshly judged in some quarters by advocates of some current models of feminist therapy, multicultural counseling, and ecological systems of therapy. For instance, Kantrowitz and Ballou (1992) charge that the rational and irrational thinking themes of cognitive therapy reinforce worldviews, attitudes, and cognitive processes that are stereotypically masculine and Euro-American. Alternative worldviews tend to be either devalued or disregarded. As a result, the worldviews and cognitive processing styles of some women and some persons of color may be overlooked or rejected altogether. In that regard, Brown (1994) challenges the cognitive therapist's rationale because, for some individuals from some cultural backgrounds, changing the oppressed person's way of thinking does not automatically lead to resolution of that person's presenting problems. Kantrowitz and Ballou (1992, p. 81) also suggest that the cognitive therapist's pattern of directly challenging the client's beliefs may run counter to clients with some gender and socialization orientations.

Cormier and Cormier (1998, pp. 373–378) described numerous diverse groups and cultural populations for which the cognitive therapy methods of challenging one's beliefs and disputing one's conclusions may prove ineffective if not harmful to the therapeutic process. Some examples of such diverse clientele are (1) Asian Americans who oppose revealing very personal and/or familial difficulties to strangers, (2) individuals from any background who are opposed to or uncomfortable with highly individualized thinking or cognition, but are more amenable to worldviews or orientations that focus primarily on affective, group, family, cooperative, caring, sharing, connection, or attachment-oriented styles, (3) clients with language barriers to challenges in their thinking, and (4) people, such as Native Americans, who because of acculturation or deculturation stressors may have less need for cognitive work than for skills to cope with the demands of the indigenous culture, the mainstream culture, and the transculture (Renfrey, 1992, p. 330).

One of the main shortcomings of the cognitive system is that it requires a great deal of training, skill, hard work, and practice to effectively use the various procedures available to the therapist. It is almost always difficult to ferret out the cognitions that have become skewed and debilitating for the client. Not every therapist is equipped by attitude and aptitude to apply the cognitive techniques appropriately. The inertia and momentum of the medical model of therapy militate against training in and successful application of cognitive procedures. Many practitioners find it hard to believe that clients can help themselves simply by changing their thinking.

Cognitive practitioners must not only understand and be able to apply techniques appropriately, they must also be well grounded in behavioral techniques and learning theory. We have encountered therapists who approach cognitive techniques as no more than a power of positive thinking exercise, and then they become puzzled, frustrated, and bored when outcomes are not attained. Furthermore, they sometimes erroneously ascribe to the cognitive approach flaws that instead are attributable to how it is applied.

A great deal of therapist discipline is essential, and there is less tolerance for error in using the cognitive approaches as compared to some of the other modalities. There is less room for freelancing and greater need to follow set procedures and guidelines. As a result, for those who are not willing to become thoroughly versed in cognitive concepts and procedures, attempting cognitive therapy may prove extremely confining and frustrating.

Cognitive Therapy with Diverse Populations

Cognitive therapy is prescriptive for matching a specific technique to a specific problem (Cormier & Cormier, 1991) without regard to race, creed, or color. The wide diversity of techniques available is a major strength enabling the cognitive therapist, for instance, to use systematic desensitization for phobias, cognitive restructuring for depression, and thought stopping for a diversity of compulsive or habituated behaviors.

Thomas (1992, pp. 304–310) stated that cognitive approaches are appropriate for working with minority groups. Cognitive techniques are used to engender positive expectations and examine negative expectancies, especially in African-American students and urban families. Thomas describes how she uses Beck's cognitive therapy with urban families to (1) motivate change; (2) reinforce commitment, loyalty, and trust; (3) increase behavioral expectations of love; (4) change cognitive distortions; (5) improve communication skills; (6) solve problems through management of conflict; (7) troubleshoot; and (8) deal with anger and hostility. Thomas corroborates the conclusion of Beck and Emery (1985), Beck and Weishaar (1995), Douglas (1989), and Jacobson (1989) that one of the most widely recognized strengths of the cognitive approach is that the relationship itself can be used to promote positive changes in diverse clients.

For many people from lower socioeconomic classes who have experienced an external locus of control, the discovery that they can truly exercise autonomy over their intellectual apparatus can indeed be liberating. A wide diversity of clients can be effectively helped by cognitive therapy as long as they can recognize the relationships among thoughts, feelings, and behaviors and are able to take some responsibility for self-help (Beck & Weishaar, 1995, pp. 238–249).

The first step in the process of cognitive therapy, initiating a relationship of mutual trust (Beck & Weishaar, 1995), is that approach's greatest strength in working with a diversity of clients. DeRubeis (1990); Dolce and Thompson (1989); Lyddon (1990); Safran (1990); and Stoltenberg, Leach, and Bratt (1989) have confirmed the primacy of the cognitive therapist's relationship with the client. Cognitive therapists work effectively with diverse clientele because they actively pursue the client's point of view throughout the therapeutic process (Beck & Weishaar, 1995, pp. 243–244). By incorporating the Rogerian conditions of warmth, accurate empathy, genuineness, and acceptance, the therapist appreciates each client's personal worldview. Therefore, we view the cognitive approach to be suited for use with clients from different racial and ethnic backgrounds, sexes, sexual orientations, socioeconomic statuses, and disability conditions.

Livneh and Sherwood (1991) describe the cognitive approach as having characteristics appropriate for counseling clients who are physically disabled. They cite two reasons:

(1) the affect, inner self-verbalizations, and behavior of the physically disabled are largely determined by cognitive perceptions; and (2) these cognitions and self-verbalizations frequently translate into negative feelings about oneself that culminate in the client's lowered self-esteem and erroneous interpretations and conclusions.

Unlike REBT, which would likely attribute the disabled client's problem to irrational beliefs, cognitive theory emphasizes the impact of cognitive deficits or biased selection of information and distorted interpretations. Cognitive strategies and techniques are designed to deactivate such distorted cognitions and interpretations (Beck & Weishaar, 1995, p. 230) and to help the physically disabled client to shift to normal or adaptive cognitive functioning (Livneh & Sherwood, 1991, p. 532).

For clients from diverse backgrounds, cognitive therapy is similar to REBT in that it is a no-nonsense and straightforward approach that appeals to people without focusing on their origins or lifestyles. It focuses on clients' thinking and behavior, not on their personhood. It involves the client in every step, from problem identification through meaningful homework and follow-up. It does not view the person as being bad, flawed, or inferior; rather, it views the thinking as distorted or the behavior as debilitating. Regarding example populations not heretofore mentioned, cognitive therapy has been appropriately used with a wide array of presenting problems by individuals within clientele groups such as the elderly, African Americans, Asian Americans, Native Americans, Latinos, Christians, individuals with physical challenges, gay men, lesbians, low-income individuals, and many others (Cormier & Cormier, 1998, pp. 373–377). Clearly, cognitive therapy is a viable approach for helping a great many people from diverse populations because it is adaptable to human nuance and is essentially free of threat or judgment.

Summary

Cognitive therapy is new but has roots deep in the scientific psychology of behaviorism, the rational therapies, and other systems. Cognitive behavior therapy departs from traditional behavioral psychology in that it accepts the operant and respondent components but rejects the concept that only environmental factors can be rightly considered behaviors. Consequently, cognitive therapists perceive all internal thoughts and feelings, which are identifiable by clients, to be grist for study and used by therapists to help clients. We have included in our coverage of cognitive behavior therapy the work and concepts of many cognitivists, foremost among them Albert Ellis, Aaron Beck, and Donald Meichenbaum.

The vast array of concepts and strategies developed by researchers and practitioners inside and outside the cognitive movement constitute an eclectic and formidable menu for helping a wide variety of clients manifesting a large host of problem categories. Among the major procedures are: (1) Beck's cognitive psychotherapy; (2) relaxation training and relaxation therapy; (3) mental and emotive imagery; (4) cognitive and covert modeling; (5) thought stopping; (6) cognitive restructuring, reframing, and stress inoculation; (7) meditation and relaxation; (8) biofeedback; (9) neurolinguistic programming; and (10) eye movement desensitization and reprocessing (EDMR).

Cognitive restructuring is probably the most representative of the cognitive procedures. We focused heavily on cognitive restructuring and presented excerpts and comments on the case of Myra to illustrate the use of cognitive strategies with a real client.

Although the cognitive movement is relatively new, it is rapidly developing and has a great many adherents. Cognitive behavior therapy shows great promise as a methodology for therapists and other helpers. It can help clients with assorted problems to use the full power and potential of their minds to gain control of their thinking, emotions, and behavior.

SUGGESTIONS FOR FURTHER READING

Beck, A. T. (1976). *Cognitive therapy and the emotional disorders*. New York: International Universities Press.

Beck, A. T. (1986). Cognitive therapy. In E. L. Shostrom (Executive Producer), S. K. Shostrom (Producer), and H. Ratner (Director), *Three approaches to psychotherapy III* (Film no. 2, Case of Richard). Corona Del Mar, CA: Psychological and Educational Film.

Beck, A. T., & Emery, G. (1985). *Anxiety disorders and phobias: A cognitive perspective*. New York: Basic Books.

Beck, A. T., & Weishaar, M. E. (1995). Cognitive therapy. In R. J. Corsini & D. Wedding, *Current psychotherapies* (5th ed., pp. 229–261). Itasca, IL: F. E. Peacock.

Cormier, S., & Cormier, B. (1998). *Interviewing strategies for helpers: Fundamental skills and cognitive behavioral interventions* (4th ed.). Pacific Grove, CA: Brooks/Cole.

Krumboltz, J. D. (1997). *Cognitive-behavior therapy* (Videotape No. 205-32882-2, T. Labriola, Producer). In J. Carlson & D. Kjos, *Cognitive-behavior therapy with Krumboltz: Psychotherapy with the experts*. Boston: Allyn & Bacon.

Lazarus, A. A. (1977b). *In the mind's eye: The powers of imagery for personal enrichment*. New York: Guilford Press.

Meichenbaum, D. H. (1977). *Cognitive-behavior modification: An integrative approach*. New York: Plenum.

Meichenbaum, D. H. (1985). *Stress inoculation training*. New York: Pergamon.

Meichenbaum, D. H. (1997). *Cognitive-behavior therapy* (Videotape No. 205-31950-5, T. Labriola, Producer). In J. Carlson & D. Kjos, *Cognitive-behavior therapy with Meichenbaum: Psychotherapy with the experts*. Boston: Allyn & Bacon.

Walker, L. (1997). *Cognitive-behavioral feminist therapy* (Videotape No. 205-32909-8, T. Labriola, Producer). In J. Carlson & D. Kjos, *Cognitive-behavioral feminist therapy with Walker: Psychotherapy with the experts*. Boston: Allyn & Bacon.

REFERENCES

Adler, A. (1936). The neurotic's picture of the world. *International Journal of Individual Psychology, 2,* 3–10.

Alexander, F. (1950). *Psychosomatic medicine: Its principles and applications*. New York: Norton.

Bandler, R., & Grinder, J. (1975). *The structure of magic. I: A book about language and therapy*. Palo Alto, CA: Science & Behavior Books.

Bandler, R., & Grinder, J. (1982). *Reframing*. Moab, UT: Real People Press.

Bandura, A. (1985). *Social foundations of thought and actions: A social cognitive theory*. Englewood Cliffs, NJ: Prentice-Hall.

Beck, A. T. (1963). Thinking and depression. 1. Idiosyncratic content and cognitive distortions. *Archives of General Psychiatry, 9,* 324–333.

Beck, A. T. (1964). Thinking and depression. 2. Theory and therapy. *Archives of General Psychiatry, 10,* 561–571.

Beck, A. T. (1967). *Depression: Clinical, experimental, and theoretical aspects*. New York: Hoeber. (Republished as *Depression: Causes and treatment*. Philadelphia: University of Pennsylvania Press, 1972.)

Beck, A. T. (1970). Cognitive therapy: Nature and relation to behavior therapy. *Behavior Therapy, 1,* 184–200.

Beck, A. T. (1976). *Cognitive therapy and the emotional disorders*. New York: International Universities Press.

Beck, A. T. (1986). Cognitive therapy. In E. L. Shostrom (Executive Producer), S. K. Shostrom (Producer), and H. Ratner (Director), *Three approaches to psychotherapy III* (Film no. 2, Case of Richard). Corona Del Mar, CA: Psychological and Educational Film.

Beck, A. T. (1989). An interview with a depressed and suicidal patient. In D. Wedding & R. J. Corsini (Eds.), *Case studies in psychotherapy* (pp. 124–142). Itasca, IL: F. E. Peacock.

Beck, A. T., & Emery, G. (1979). *Cognitive therapy of anxiety and phobic disorders.* Philadelphia: Center for Cognitive Therapy.

Beck, A. T., & Emery, G. (1985). *Anxiety disorders and phobias: A cognitive perspective.* New York: Basic Books.

Beck, A. T., & Emery, G. (1979). *Cognitive therapy of anxiety and phobic disorders.* Philadelphia: Center for Cognitive Therapy.

Beck, A. T., & Emery, G. (1985). *Anxiety disorders and phobias: A cognitive perspective.* New York: Basic Books.

Beck, A. T., Rush, A. J., Shaw, B. F., & Emery, G. (1979). *Cognitive therapy of depression.* New York: Guilford Press.

Beck, A. T., & Weishaar, M. E. (1995). Cognitive therapy. In R. J. Corsini & D. Wedding, *Current psychotherapies* (5th ed., pp. 229–261). Itasca, IL: F. E. Peacock.

Beck, A. T., & Young, J. E. (1985). Cognitive therapy of depression. In D. Barlow (Ed.), *Clinical handbook of psychological disorders: A step-by-step treatment manual* (pp. 206–244). New York: Guilford Press.

Benson, H. (1976). *The relaxation response.* New York: Avon Books.

Benson, H. (1987). *Your maximum mind.* New York: Avon Books.

Bernstein, D. A., & Borkovec, T. D. (1973). *Progressive relaxation training: A manual for the helping professions.* Champaign, IL: Research Press.

Bornstein, P. H., & Devine, D. A. (1980). Covert modeling—hypnosis in the treatment of obesity. *Psychotherapy: Theory, Research, and Practice, 17,* 272–275.

Borysenko, J. (1987). *Minding the body, mending the mind.* Reading, MA: Addison-Wesley.

Boswell, L. K., Jr. (1987). Abstract imaging: Abstract imaging as a mode of personality analysis and adjustment. *Medical Hypnoanalysis Journal, 2,* 175–179.

Boudewyns, P. A., Stwertka, S. A., Hyer, L. A., Albrecht, J. W., & Sperr, E. V. (1993). Eye movement desensitization and reprocessing: A pilot study. *Behavior Therapy, 16,* 30–33.

Brown, B. B. (1974). *New mind, new body.* New York: Harper & Row.

Brown, B. B. (1977). *Stress and the art of biofeedback.* New York: Bantam.

Brown, L. S. (1994). *Subversive dialogues: Theory in feminist therapy.* New York: Basic Books.

Bry, A., & Blair, M. (1979). *Visualization: Directing the movies of your mind.* New York: Barnes & Noble.

Carrington, P. (1978a). *Clinically standardized meditation (CSM). Instructor's manual.* Kendall Park, NJ: Pace Educational Systems.

Carrington, P. (1978b). *Learning to meditate: Clinically standardized meditation (CSM). Course workbook.* Kendall Park, NJ: Pace Educational Systems.

Cautela, J. R. (1966). The treatment of compulsive behavior by covert sensitization. *Psychological Record, 16,* 33–41.

Cautela, J. R. (1969). Behavior therapy and self-control: Techniques and implications. In C. Franks (Ed.), *Behavior therapy: Appraisal and status* (pp. 323–340). New York: McGraw-Hill.

Cautela, J. R. (1971, November). *Covert modeling.* Paper presented at the fifth annual meeting of the Association for Advancement of Behavior Therapy, Washington, DC.

Cautela, J. R. (1976). The present status of covert modeling. *Journal of Behavior Therapy and Experimental Psychiatry, 6,* 323–326.

Cautela, J. R., & Groden, J. (1978). *Relaxation: A comprehensive manual for adults, children, and children with special needs.* Champaign, IL: Research Press.

Cocco, N., & Sharpe, L. (1993). An auditory variant of eye movement desensitization in a case of childhood PTSD. *Journal of Behavior Therapy and Experimental Psychiatry, 24,* 373–377.

Cormier, L. S., & Cormier, W. H. (1998). *Intervention strategies for helpers: Fundamental skills and cognitive behavioral interventions* (4th ed.). Pacific Grove, CA: Brooks/Cole.

Cormier, L. S., & Hackney, H. (1987). *The professional counselor: A process guide to helping.* Englewood Cliffs, NJ: Prentice-Hall.

Cormier, W. H., & Cormier, L. S. (1985). *Interviewing strategies for helpers: Fundamental skills and cognitive behavioral interventions* (2nd ed.). Monterey, CA: Brooks/Cole.

Cormier, W. H., & Cormier, L. S. (1991). *Interviewing strategies for helpers: Fundamental skills and cognitive behavioral interventions* (3rd ed.). Pacific Grove, CA: Brooks/Cole.

DeRubeis, R. J. (1990). Determinants of change in cognitive therapy for depression. *Cognitive Therapy and Research, 14,* 469–482.

Dolce, J. J., & Thompson, J. K. (1989). Interdependence theory and the client-therapist relationship: A model for cognitive psychotherapy. *Journal of Cognitive Psychotherapy, 3,* 111–122.

Douglas, A. R. (1989). The limits of cognitive-behavior therapy: Can it be integrated with psychodynamic therapy? *British Journal of Psychotherapy, 5,* 390–401.

Dryden, W. (1984). *Rational-emotive therapy: Fundamentals and innovations.* London: Croom Helm.

Dryden, W., & Trower, P. (1986). *Rational-emotive therapy: Recent developments in theory and practice.* Bristol, UK: Institute for RET.

D'Zurilla, T. J., & Goldfried, M. R. (1971). Problem-solving and behavior modification. *Journal of Abnormal Psychology, 78,* 107–126.

Ellis, A. E. (1962). *Reason and emotion in psychotherapy.* New York: Lyle Stuart.

Ellis, A. E. (1982). Major systems. *Personnel and Guidance Journal, 61,* 6–7.

Ellis, A. E. (1984). *Rational-emotive therapy and cognitive behavior therapy.* New York: Springer.

Ellis, A. E., & Grieger, R. M. (Eds.). (1986). *Handbook of rational-emotive therapy* (Vol. 2). New York: Springer.

Epstein, M. (1995). *Thoughts without the thinker.* New York: Norton.

Feindler, E. L., & Fremouw, W. J. (1983). Stress inoculation training for adolescent anger problems. In D. H. Meichenbaum & M. E. Jaremko (Eds.), *Stress reduction and prevention* (pp. 451–485). New York: Plenum.

Fontana, D. (1991). *The elements of meditation.* New York: Element.

Forbes, D., Creamer, M., & Rycroft, P. (1994). Eye movement desensitization and reprocessing in posttraumatic stress disorder. *Journal of Behavior Therapy and Experimental Psychiatry, 25,* 113–120.

Freeman, A., Simon, K. M., Beutler, L. E., & Arkowitz, H. (Eds.). (1989). *Comprehensive handbook of cognitive therapy.* New York: Plenum.

Freud, S. (1958). Formulations on the two principles of mental functioning. In J. Strachey (Ed. and Trans.), *The standard edition of the complete psychological works of Sigmund Freud* (Vol. 12, pp. 213–227). London: Hogarth Press. (Original work published in 1911.)

Gendlin, E. T. (1996). *Focused-oriented psychotherapy: A manual of the experiential method.* New York: Guilford Press.

Gilliland, B. E., & James, R. K. (1983). Hypnotherapy and cognition: A combinatorial approach. *Medical Hypnoanalysis: Journal of the Society of Medical Hypnoanalysts, 4,* 101–113.

Gilliland, B. E., & James, R. K. (1997). *Crisis intervention strategies* (3rd ed.). Pacific Grove, CA: Brooks/Cole.

Gilliland, B. E., & Johnston, R. (1987). Human potential groups: High risk high schoolers model and rehearse for success. Memphis, TN: Memphis State University (ERIC Document Reproduction Service No. ED283084).

Gilliland, B. E., & Myer, R. (1985). Weight management and food intake control. *Medical Hypnoanalysis: Journal of the Society of Medical Hypnoanalysts, 6,* 85–90.

Gorrell, J. (1993). Cognitive modeling and implicit rules: Effects on problem-solving performance. *American Journal of Psychology, 106,* 51–65.

Grinder, J., & Bandler, R. (1976). *The structure of magic II.* Palo Alto, CA: Science & Behavior Books.

Hackney, H., & Cormier, L. S. (1988). *Counseling strategies and objectives* (3rd ed.). Englewood Cliffs, NJ: Prentice-Hall.

Hatch, J. P., Fisher, J. G., & Rugh, J. D. (Eds.). (1987). *Biofeedback: Studies in clinical efficacy.* New York: Plenum.

Holcomb, W. R. (1986). Stress inoculation therapy with anxiety and stress disorders of acute psychiatric inpatients. *Journal of Clinical Psychology, 42,* 864–872.

Homme, L. (1965). Perspectives in psychology: XXIV. Control of coverants, the operants of the mind. *Psychological Record, 15,* 501–511.

Horan, J. J. (1976). Coping with inescapable discomfort through in vivo emotive imagery. In J. D. Krumholtz & C. E. Thoresen (Eds.), *Counseling methods* (pp. 316–329). New York: Holt, Rinehart & Winston.

Horney, K. (1950). *Neurosis and human growth: The struggle toward self-realization.* New York: Norton.

Jacobson, E. (1929). *Progressive relaxation.* Chicago: University of Chicago Press.

Jacobson, E. (1964). *Anxiety and tension control.* Philadelphia: Lippincott.

Jacobson, N. S. (1989). The therapist-client relationship in cognitive behavior therapy: Implications for treating depression. [Special issue: Client-therapist relationship and cognitive psychotherapy.] *Journal of Cognitive Psychotherapy, 3,* 85–96.

Johnston, R., & Gilliland, B. E. (1987). A program for effective interaction between school systems and consultants. *School Counselor, 35,* 110–119.

Kant, I. (1798). *The classification of mental disorders.* Konigsberg, Germany: Nicolovius.

Kantrowitz, R., & Ballou, M. (1992). A feminist critique of cognitive-behavioral therapy. In L. S. Brown & M. Ballou (Eds.), *Personality and psychopathol-*

ogy: Feminist reappraisals (pp. 70–87). New York: Guilford Press.

Kazdin, A. E. (1979a). Effects of covert modeling and coding of modeled stimuli on assertive behavior. *Behaviour Research and Therapy, 17,* 53–61.

Kazdin, A. E. (1979b). Imagery elaboration and self-efficacy in covert modeling treatment of unassertive behavior. *Journal of Consulting and Clinical Psychology, 47,* 725–733.

Kazdin, A. E. (1980). Covert and overt rehearsal and elaboration during treatment in development of assertive behavior. *Behaviour Research and Therapy, 18,* 191–201.

Kazdin, A. E., & Mascitelli, S. (1982a). Behavioral rehearsal, self-instructions, and homework practice in developing assertiveness. *Behavior Therapy, 13,* 346–360.

Kazdin, A. E., & Mascitelli, S. (1982b). Covert and overt rehearsal and homework practice in developing assertiveness. *Journal of Consulting and Clinical Psychology, 50,* 250–258.

Kelly, G. (1955). *The psychology of personal constructs.* New York: Norton.

Knapp, T. J. (1985). Contributions to the history of psychology. XXXIX: T. V. Moore and his cognitive psychology of 1939. *Psychological Reports, 57,* 1311–1316.

Krumboltz, J. D. (1997). *Cognitive-behavior therapy* (Videotape No. 205-32882-2, T. Labriola, Producer). In J. Carlson & D. Kjos, *Cognitive-behavior therapy with Krumboltz: Psychotherapy with the experts.* Boston: Allyn & Bacon.

Kush, F. R., & Fleming, L. M. (2000). An innovative approach to short-term group cognitive therapy in the combined treatment of anxiety and depression. *Group Dynamics: Theory, Research, and Practice, 2,* 176–183.

Lankton, S. R. (1980). *Practical magic: A translation of neurolinguistic programming into clinical psychotherapy.* Cupertino, CA: Meta.

Lazarus, A. A. (1968). Variations in desensitization therapy. *Psychotherapy: Theory, Research, and Practice, 5,* 50–52.

Lazarus, A. A. (1977a). Has behavior therapy outlived its usefulness? *American Psychologist, 32,* 550–554.

Lazarus, A. A. (1977b). *In the mind's eye: The powers of imagery for personal enrichment.* New York: Guilford Press.

Lazarus, A. A. (1982). *Personal enrichment through imagery.* Workbook (audio tape). New York: BMA Audio Cassettes.

Lazarus, A. A., & Abramovitz, A. (1962). The use of "emotive imagery" in the treatment of children's phobias. *Journal of Mental Science, 108,* 191–195.

Lehrer, P. M. (1982). How to relax and how not to relax: A reevaluation of the work of Edmund Jacobson—I. *Behaviour Research and Therapy, 20,* 417–428.

Lehrer, P. M., Woolfolk, R. L., Rooney, A. J., McCann, B., & Carrington, P. (1983). Progressive relaxation and medication: A study of psycho-physiological and therapeutic differences between two techniques. *Behaviour Research and Therapy, 21,* 651–662.

Levine, S. (1991). *Guided meditations, explorations and healings.* New York: Anchor Books.

Livneh, H., & Sherwood, A. (1991). Application of personality theories and counseling strategies to clients with physical disabilities. *Journal of Counseling and Development, 69,* 525–538.

Long, B. (1995). *Meditation.* London: Barry Long Books.

Lyddon, W. J. (1990). First and second-order change: Implications for rationalist and constructivist cognitive therapies. *Journal of Counseling and Development, 69,* 122–127.

Mahoney, M. J. (1974). *Cognition and behavior modification.* Cambridge, MA: Ballinger.

Mahoney, M. J., & Thoresen, C. E. (1974). *Self-control: Power to the person.* Monterey, CA: Brooks/Cole.

Martin, G. L. (1982). Thought-stopping and stimulus control to decrease resistant disturbing thoughts. *Journal of Behavior Therapy and Experimental Psychiatry, 13,* 215–220.

Maultsby, M. C. (1984). *Rational behavior therapy.* Englewood Cliffs, NJ: Prentice-Hall.

May, R., & Yalom, I. (1995). Existential psychotherapy. In R. J. Corsini & D. Wedding. *Current psychotherapies* (5th ed., pp. 262–292). Itasca, IL: F. E. Peacock.

Meichenbaum, D. H. (1977). *Cognitive-behavior modification: An integrative approach.* New York: Plenum.

Meichenbaum, D. H. (1985). *Stress-inoculation training.* New York: Pergamon.

Meichenbaum, D. H. (1993). Stress inoculation training: A 20-year update. In P. M. Lehrer & R. L. Woolfolk (Eds.), *Principles and practice of stress management* (2nd ed., pp. 373–406). New York: Guilford Press.

Meichenbaum, D. H. (1997). *Cognitive-behavior therapy* (Videotape No. 205-31950-5, T. Labriola, Producer). In J. Carlson & D. Kjos, *Cognitive-behavior therapy with Meichenbaum: Psychotherapy with the experts.* Boston: Allyn & Bacon.

Meichenbaum, D. H., & Goodman, J. (1971). Training impulsive children to talk to themselves. *Journal of Abnormal Psychology, 77,* 127–132.

Meichenbaum, D. H., & Turk, D. (1976). The cognitive-behavioral management of anxiety, anger, and pain. In P. O. Davidson (Ed.), *The behavioral management of anxiety, depression, and pain* (pp. 1–35). New York: Brunner/Mazel.

Meichenbaum, D. H., Turk, D., & Burstein, S. (1975). The nature of coping with stress. In I. G. Sarason & C. D. Speilberger (Eds.), *Stress and anxiety: Vol. II.* New York: Wiley.

Mitchell, L. K., & Krumboltz, J. D. (1987). The effects of cognitive restructuring and decision-making training on career indecision. *Journal of Counseling and Development, 66,* 171–174.

Montgomery, R. A., & Ayllon, T. (1994). Experimental desensitization across subjects: Subjective and physiological measures of treatment efficacy. *Journal of Behavior Therapy and Experimental Psychiatry, 25,* 217–230.

Moore, T. V. (1939). *Cognitive psychology.* New York: Lippincott.

Overholser, J. C. (1991). The use of guided imagery in psychotherapy: Modules for use with passive relaxation training. *Journal of Contemporary Psychotherapy, 21,* 159–172.

Reber, A. S. (1995). *Dictionary of psychology* (2nd ed.). New York: Penguin Books.

Renfrey, G. S. (1992). Cognitive-behavior therapy and the Native American client. *Behavior Therapy, 23,* 321–340.

Rimm, D. C. (1973). Thought stopping and covert assertion in the treatment of phobias. *Journal of Consulting and Clinical Psychology, 41,* 466–467.

Rosenthal, T. L., & Steffek, B. D. (1991). Modeling methods. In F. H. Kanfer & A. P. Goldstein (Eds.), *Helping people change* (4th ed., pp. 70–121). New York: Pergamon.

Safran, J. D. (1990). Towards a refinement of cognitive therapy in light of interpersonal theory I: Theory. *Clinical Psychology Review, 10,* 87–105.

Sandweiss, J. H., & Wolf, S. L. (Eds.). (1985). *Biofeedback and sports science.* New York: Plenum.

Sarason, I. G. (1973). Test anxiety and cognitive modeling. *Journal of Personality and Social Psychology, 28,* 58–61.

Schwartz, R. M. (1986). The internal dialogue: On the asymmetry between positive and negative coping thoughts. *Cognitive Therapy and Research, 10,* 591–605.

Shapiro, D. H. (1980). *Meditation: Self-regulation strategy and altered state of consciousness.* New York: Aldine.

Shapiro, F. (1989a). Efficacy of the eye movement desensitization procedure in the treatment of traumatic memories. *Journal of Traumatic Stress, 2,* 199–223.

Shapiro, F. (1989b). Eye movement desensitization: A new treatment for post-traumatic stress disorder. *Journal of Behavior Therapy and Experimental Psychiatry, 20,* 211–217.

Shapiro, F. (1991). Eye movement desensitization and reprocessing procedure: From EMD to EMDR—a new treatment model for anxiety and related traumata. *Behavior Therapist, 14,* 128, 133–135.

Shapiro, F. (1995). *Eye movement desensitization and reprocessing.* New York: Guilford Press.

Sheikh, A. A. (1983). *Imagery: Current theory, research, and application.* New York: Wiley.

Shorr, J. E., Sobel-Whittington, G., Robin, P., & Connella, J. A. (Eds.). (1984). *Imagery: Theoretical and clinical applications* (Vol. 3). New York: Plenum.

Silver, S. M., Brooks, A., & Obenchain, J. (1995). Eye movement desensitization and reprocessing treatment of Vietnam veterans with PTSD: Comparative effects with biofeedback and relaxation training. *Journal of Traumatic Stress, 8,* 337–342.

Simpkins, C. A., & Simpkins, A. M. (1996). *Principles of meditation.* Boston: Charles E. Tuttle.

Southam, M. A., Agras, W. S., Taylor, C. B., & Kraemer, H. C. (1982). Relaxation training: Blood pressure lowering during the working day. *Archives of General Psychiatry, 39,* 715–717.

Spivack, G., Platt, J. J., & Shure, M. B. (1976). *The problem-solving approach to adjustment.* San Francisco: Jossey-Bass.

Stoltenberg, C. D., Leach, M. M., & Bratt, A. (1989). The Elaboration Likelihood Model and psychotherapeutic persuasion. *Journal of Cognitive Psychotherapy, 3,* 181–199.

Suinn, R. M., & Richardson, F. (1971). Anxiety management training: A nonspecific behavior therapy program for anxiety control. *Behavior Therapy, 2,* 498–510.

Sullivan, H. S. (1953). *The interpersonal theory of psychiatry.* New York: Norton.

Taylor, J. G. (1963). A behavioral interpretation of obsessive-compulsive neurosis. *Behavior Research and Therapy, 1,* 237–244.

Thomas, M. B. (1992). *An introduction to marital and family therapy: Counseling toward healthier family systems across the lifespan.* New York: Macmillan.

Thomas, R., & Gafner, G. (1993). PTSD in an elderly male: Treatment with eye movement desensitization and reprocessing (EMDR). *Clinical Gerontologist, 14,* 57–59.

Tryon, G. S., & Pallandino, J. J. (1979). Thought stopping: A case study and observation. *Journal of Behavior Therapy and Experimental Psychiatry, 10,* 151–154.

Vaughan, K., Armstrong, M. S., Gold, R., & O'Connor, N. (1994). A trial of eye movement desensitization compared to image habituation training and applied muscle relaxation in post-traumatic stress disorder. *Journal of Behavior Therapy and Experimental Psychiatry, 25,* 283–291.

Vaughan, K., Wiese, M., Gold, R., & Tarrier, N. (1994). EMD: Symptom change in PTSD. *British Journal of Psychiatry, 154,* 533–541.

Walker, L. (1997). *Cognitive-behavioral feminist therapy* (Videotape No. 205-32909-8, T. Labriola, Producer). In J. Carlson & D. Kjos, *Cognitive-behavioral feminist therapy with Walker: Psychotherapy with the experts.* Boston: Allyn & Bacon.

Warner, R. E. (1991). A survey of theoretical orientations of Canadian clinical psychologists. *Canadian Psychology, 32,* 525–528.

Watson, D. L., & Tharp, R. G. (1997). *Self-directed behavior* (7th ed.). Pacific Grove, CA: Brooks/Cole.

Watson, L. (1976). *The effects of covert modeling and covert reinforcement on job interview skills of youth offenders.* Unpublished doctoral dissertation, West Virginia University, Morgantown.

Wells, J. K., Howard, G. S., Nowlin, W. F., & Vargas, M. J. (1986). Presurgical anxiety and postsurgical pain and adjustment: Effects of a stress inoculation procedure. *Journal of Consulting and Clinical Psychology, 54,* 831–835.

Wertkin, R. A. (1985). Stress inoculation training: Principles and applications. *Social Casework, 66,* 611–616.

Williams, R. L., & Long, J. D. (1979). *Toward a self-managed life style* (2nd ed.). Boston: Houghton Mifflin.

Wolpe, J. (1982). *The practice of behavior therapy* (3rd ed.). New York: Pergamon.

Woolfolk, R. L., Lehrer, P. M., McCann, B. S., & Rooney, A. J. (1982). Effects of progressive relaxation and meditation on cognitive and somatic manifestations of daily stress. *Behavior Research and Therapy, 20,* 461–467.

11 Solution-Focused Brief Therapy

Fundamental Tenets

History

Welcome to the new-millennium therapy. If you like fast food, fast cars, cell phones, palm pilots, instant gratification, immediate reinforcement, and quick therapeutic fixes that don't impinge on your already chock-to-the-brim schedule, you'll love solution-focused brief therapy (SFBT). This rather caustic opening sentence might characterize a number of the critics of this approach. Perhaps even more critical, detractors decry "brief" therapy as a subterfuge of greedy insurance companies and mental health-care provider networks that care little about the ethics of client care, provide only minimal financial outlay for maximum financial gain, use it as a stopgap measure for poorly trained therapists and short-handed service providers, and having little empirical research to substantiate its efficacy (Johnson, 1991; Lieberman, 1984; Miller, 1996; Stalker, Levene, & Coady, 1999; Stern, 1993).

Pragmatically, the need to deal with large numbers of people in need of mental health services, a shortage of resources, the inability of long-term therapies to deliver on problem reduction, and the growing disaffection of practitioners with those therapies has led inexorably to a search for briefer, problem- or solution-focused therapies (Carlson & Sperry, 2000; de Shazer, 1991; Lieberman, 1984; Montgomery & Webster, 1994; Sklare, 1997, p. x; Thompson & Rudolph, 2000, p. 137).

The simple fact is that the twentieth century has brought an increased awareness of the need for mental health care for the general population, not just the privileged few. This intensified and expanded notion of mental health care provision has dictated that more efficacious and time-efficient therapies need to be used. Long-term therapeutic approaches are simply ill-equipped to deal with the numbers of clients that need mental health care or counseling (Parrott, 1999; Sklare, 1997, p. 3). To that end, practically every major therapeutic modality in current existence now promotes its own version of brief therapy.

Yet, the question remains—what is meant by *brief*? And why have a chapter in a theories book that deals mainly with the amount of time spent in therapy? Depending on the therapy used and the therapist using or advocating it, brief can mean anything from no sessions (the initial telephone conversation and admonishment to think about when the problem is not in evidence and what the person is doing suffices to change behavior)

(Weiner-Davis, de Shazer, & Gingerich, 1987), twenty-minute multiple sessions (Huber, 1994), one session only (Rosenbaum, 1994), 14.2 sessions (Exner & Andronikof-Sanglade, 1992), or a year or more of weekly in-depth sessions for traditional psychodynamic or analytical therapy.

Historical Evolution.   The focus of this chapter, solution-focused brief therapy (SFBT), has a very clear historical evolution that started with the Mental Research Institute (MRI) in Palo Alto, California. In their struggle to turn the broad array of research they were doing into therapeutic practice, the MRI staff sought out Milton Erickson, a well-known hypnotherapist and originator of paradoxical counseling strategies that focused on symptom reduction. The MRI staff were influenced by his optimistic view that people wanted to change and that therapy should become actively involved, focus on problems, remove symptoms, and do it as efficiently and quickly as possible (Havens, 1987; Nichols & Schwartz, 1995, pp. 96–97; Risch, 1990). This view of focusing on problem resolution in a directive, time-efficient model had great appeal to the MRI group who generally viewed the world from a behavioristic, cybernetic perspective (Nichols & Schwartz, 1995, pp. 92–94). Out of this philosophy, the seeds for solution-focused therapy were planted.

One of the therapists who was affiliated with the MRI was Steve de Shazer. He has been the major force behind the development of SFBT as a writer, theorist, practitioner, and researcher (de Shazer, 1984, 1985, 1988a, 1988b, 1991, 1994; de Shazer & Berg, 1992; de Shazer & Kral, 1986). In the late 1970s, de Shazer helped start the Brief Family Therapy Center in Milwaukee. Along with his wife, Insoo Berg, and Eve Lipchek and Michele Weiner-Davis, two other therapists who were dissatisfied with the status quo in family therapy, the Milwaukee group shifted away from the MRI's focus on the dynamics and interaction of the system. Rather than focusing on problem identification and resolution of systems that interact on the problem, the SFBT group began building a theoretical approach to therapy that concentrated on solutions that have worked in the past and that have a good chance of working now and in the future (de Shazer, 1985, 1988a, 1988b, 1991, 1994; de Shazer et al., 1986; O'Hanlon & Weiner-Davis, 1989). This is a major perceptual shift from a negative to a very positive view of the human dilemma, and at one stroke knocks down the totem of most other psychotherapies—in-depth exploration of the problem. It is no exaggeration to say that this shift has had major ramifications for the techniques and delivery of psychotherapy.

The Milwaukee group's theory and practice caught on in big way with managed care and behavioral health maintenance organizations that were looking to control financial outlays for mental health provision. As a result, during the 1990s the practice of solution-focused therapy or derivations of it spread to every conceivable kind of problem and client group imaginable (Araoz & Carrese, 1996; Atlas, 1994; Bonjean, 1997; Carlson & Sperry, 2000; Dolan, 1997; Jackson, 2000; Juhnke & Coker, 1997; Lindforss & Magnusson, 1997; Mooney, 2000; Sharry, 1999; Shapiro & Henderson, 1992).

Use in Schools.   One of the major venues where SFBT has found a fertile field to take root and grow has been school counseling. Traditional models of counseling students in schools ignore much of what is true about how school systems work (Metcalf, 1995, pp. 3–31; Sklare, 1997, pp. 3–4; Williams, 2000). SFBT, however, fits very well into a school counseling program because it holds a positive, can-do attitude, directly involves counselors in helping guide and reinforce students, focuses on current behavior that is directly affecting academic performance, organizes information in straightforward ways that are compatible with and palatable to the family and professional educators with which it interacts, and is time efficient in delivering services to large client populations (Amatea & Sherrard, 1991; Bonnington, 1993; Bruce, 1995; Hughes, 1990; Metcalf, 1995; Mostert, Johnson, & Mostert, 1997; Murphy & Duncan 1997; Rhodes, 1993; Selekman, 1997; Sklare, 1997). Gerald Sklare (1997) and Linda Metcalf (1995) have both developed instructional materials and conducted workshops that have spread the word about the utility of SFBT to school personnel workers across the country. In summary, whether its critics and detractors like it or not, brief therapy—particularly solution-focused brief therapy—gained a firm foothold in the last decade of the twentieth century. It is not much of an exaggeration to say that in the twenty-first century all therapy is brief therapy (Carlson & Sperry, 2000, p. vii).

Overview of Solution-Focused Brief Therapy

SFBT might best be called a person-centered, behavioral stew with a dash of cognitive behaviorism thrown in for good measure. SFBT is one of the very few theories that places more emphasis on the future than it does on the present or past. The past with all its labels, stigmas, failures, and problems doesn't fit in with SFBT's positive view. Even the Rogerians would be hard pressed to be seen as more humanistic than the SFBT therapists, who avidly hold that people are free to make choices and are not chained to bad gene pools or lousy environments. Clients are viewed as being their own experts who know what is best for them. Thus, the therapist accepts the client's view of reality at face value and utilizes this view as the foundation of a cooperative, collaborative approach to therapy. SFBT is unbridled in its positive, enthusiastic outlook regarding what people can do when given an opportunity to use their considerable resources to build a better future. SFBT does not harp and brood on past problems.

Setting specific behavioral goals based upon the resources people have and what they are able to do is every bit as important to the SFBT therapists as it is to behaviorists. The cognitive behaviorists also would not take issue with the SFBT view of reframing perceptions of problematic events to obtain more positive cognitions and mental sets about them. The focus of this chapter is on using the foregoing tenets to effectively enhance proactive behavior and reduce or extinguish complaints within one to ten therapy sessions.

Theory of Personality

The theory of personality undergirding SFBT is more a blend of a theory of philosophy and a theory of language (de Shazer 1991, pp. 44–45; Nichols & Schwartz, 1995, p. 446). That blend has constructivism as its foundation and poststructuralism as its framework.

Constructivism. Constructivist theory, formerly known as *personal construct theory,* was first developed by George Kelly (1955). Constructivism may be defined as a relativistic point of view that emphasizes a subjective construction of reality. Reality is based on our own personal preconceptions, biases, and past history, all of which color our view of what our current "reality" is. Reality is not generic, but rather resides within each person. Reality is in the eye of the beholder and no two realities are alike.

In the constructivist system of therapy, both the client and the therapist use the personal construct as the major thrust by which the client anticipates events and construes, interprets, explains, ascribes meaning to, and predicts personal experience. Such a construct is like a mini scientific theory in that it helps the client construct predictions about reality (Hergenhahn, 1994, p. 451). Provided the predictions generated by a client are confirmed by the experience, the theory is useful. If the predictions are not confirmed, the construct must be reexamined, revised, or abandoned. Kelly (1955, pp. 8–9) postulated that we view the world through lenses that create our own idiosyncratic reality which we attempt to fit over the realities of which that world is composed. The work of the constructivist therapist is to help clients try on different lenses to see which gives them the best view.

Constructivist therapy believes that what is being seen in the client is a product of the therapist's own assumptions about people, about problems, about the therapist's interactions with the client, and about therapy itself (Nichols & Schwartz, 1995, pp. 126–127). As such, the therapist's view of the problem may be very different from the client's view even though both are in the same room at the same moment, hearing the same words, discussing the same problem, feeling the same room temperature, and smelling the aroma of the same cup of coffee. How can this be?

Poststructuralism.   In the world of structural therapy meanings are stable and knowable. Symptoms are the behavioral products of some underlying problems or personality flaws. There are recurrent patterns of interaction that define and stabilize the shape of relationships. Linear causality and the interactional dynamics of systems may be ferreted out in a structured world no matter how complicated those systems may be (de Shazer, 1991, pp. 29–37).

However, in the poststructural, constructivist world of SFBT, things are very different (de Shazer, 1991, pp. 44–46). Therapy is not so neat and tidy. To further compound the messy business of therapy, de Shazer (1991, p. 45) proposes that reality arises from a consensual linguistic process. Put simply, that means that the world, the social context, and the reality we live in are created and formed by the filter of language. Reality is thus created by the individual's interpretation and understanding of communication from other sources and people.

Interactional Constructivism.   In poststructural SFBT, words and phrases take on different meanings and concepts. Meaning is open to interpretation because it lies between, rather than within, individuals (de Shazer, 1991, p. 45). Therefore, in SFBT a concept involving *interactional constructivism* is needed, wherein the therapist attempts to engage the client in what Watzlawick, Weakland, and Fisch (1974) called *reframing*. Therapy then may be viewed as a series of language negotiations between therapist and client which are aimed at understanding what is going on. These negotiations set the stage for reframing problems. Reframing attempts to change the conceptual and/or emotional viewpoint of the client in relation to the situation experienced and to place it in another frame which better fits the facts of the situation (p. 95).

Constructive Alternativism.   Hopefully as the client and therapist reframe problems they form new solution-oriented alternative constructs. Kelly stated that "there are always alternative constructions available to choose among in dealing with the world. No one needs to paint himself into a corner; no one needs to be completely hemmed in by circumstances; no one needs to be the victim of his own biography" (1955, p. 15). As the client and therapist struggle to understand, then make sense of and give meaning to ambiguous events, feelings, and relationships, they attempt to construct a shared alternative reality of the problem. Reality and meaning are developed through negotiation, not discovered or uncovered by searching for general laws of learning or unconscious structure of the personality (de Shazer, 1991, pp. 69–75).

Phenomenological/Humanistic/Existential Basis.   Because a therapist adhering to a constructivist philosophy may have only one opinion about what is going on with the client (though there may be many equally valid opinions), SFBT gives little credence to theoretical expertise and therapeutic authority. Instead, because the therapist's view may be no more valid than any other, SFBT tends to have a humbler, kinder, gentler, more humane approach to therapy. SFBT does not see the client's perceptions as necessarily incorrect, maladjusted, or in need of change and does not seek to impose its own values on clients (Nichols & Schwartz, 1995, p. 447). As such, SFBT operates on a phenomenological/humanistic/existential basis that looks and sounds very much like the person-centered, nondirective approach of Rogers, although it doesn't give a lot of credit to the Rogerians in the bargain (Nichols & Schwartz, 1995, p. 127).

Nature of Maladjustment

By its very nature SFBT has little to say about problems of adjustment and their origin because its emphasis is on finding solutions (Nichols & Schwartz, 1995, p. 445). A fundamental SFBT premise of maladjustment is that it may be difficult, if not impossible, to determine the origins and etiology of problems. Maladjustment occurs and is maintained by the ongoing behavior of clients and others with whom they interact. If such problem behaviors are diminished or extinguished, the problem itself will vanish no matter what its origins are (Weakland, Fisch, Watzlawick, & Bodin, 1974).

Cognitively, people are capable of rational thought. The problem is that without direction people will tend to be regressive and dwell on the negative aspects of their life in the absolutistic ways that the rational emotive behaviorists spend so much time attempting to depropagandize. People are constricted by their narrow and pessimistic viewpoints which cause them to be bound in continuous feedback loops of nonfunctional behavior. Their attempts at solutions generate more of the same—attempts which failed once and are bound to fail again (Nichols & Schwartz, 1995, p. 445; Weakland et al., 1974). This occurs because of the language—or more specifically, the types of narratives—that clients use. Gergen and Gergen (1986) conclude that there are three narrative typologies operating in therapy:

1. Progressive narratives that indicate that clients are moving and acting on goals
2. Stability narratives that keep the status quo
3. Regressive narratives that demonstrate that clients are retreating from goals

Because change is difficult and fearsome, people tend to operate in stability or regressive narratives. The stability narrative allows clients to complain at length, engaging in what alcohol and drug therapists call *pity parties,* wistfully wringing their hands and hoping and wishing for a better life but doing little to transform or discontinue maladaptive behavior. The regressive narrative calls for the avoidance of any new behaviors because they are too threatening. Any attempts to change behavior cause an immediate retreat into old, unproductive, and debilitating but familiar and safe territory.

From a cognitive standpoint, one of the major tasks of SBFT is to get clients to start reframing their negative, absolutistic, problem-centered stability and regressive narratives of present and past behaviors to progressive, possibility-driven, solution-centered views of future behaviors. Unless therapy can change these narratives to more progressive ones and help clients to elaborate on and expand exceptions and change themes, maladjustment is likely to continue (Gingerich, de Shazer, & Weiner-Davis, 1988).

The Counseling Process

Client–Therapist Relationships

The stereotypical client as recipient and therapist as provider relationship is turned topsy-turvy in SFBT. In SFBT, client–therapist relationships and cooperation come in three different types: customer–seller, complainant–listener, and visitor–host (Fisch, Weakland, & Segal, 1982; Segal & Watslawick, 1985). Customers are active in wanting to do something about their complaints so the therapist is more directive in guiding them toward solutions. The complainant who is unwilling to do anything or wants someone or something else to change is accepted nonjudgmentally, given compliments for understanding that things are not as he or she might like, and asked to perform observational tasks such as noting exceptions to his or her general complaints. The visitor who cannot define a complaint or goal is given sympathy, politeness, and compliments for whatever he or she is doing successfully.

While the foregoing may sound as if it is more pandering to the client's wishes than therapeutic to the client's needs, the idea is that working with clients at the stage they are in is far more preferable than attempting to confront and move them to a stage that they are not prepared for. In so doing, the SFBT therapist avoids or simply dissipates resistance (Duncan, Hubble, & Miller, 1997).

Basic Rules and Assumptions

The foundations of the SFBT approach are laid down in three basic rules by de Shazer (1991, p. 57). First, "If it ain't broke, don't fix it." The client determines the goals of therapy, not the therapist. Therapist agendas in regard to problem definition, exploration of thinking and feeling, and attempts to determine interpersonal, intrapersonal, or environmental effects or other tangential issues do little to move the client forward in seeking solutions. Second, "Once you know what works, do more of it." Sticking with what works and replicating it lets the client see positive behaviors mounting up, reinforces proactive behaviors, and generates even more success. Third, "if it's broke, do something to fix it. If it doesn't work, don't do it again." People tend to get caught up in endless feedback loops of nonproductive behavior because that is all they know how to do. Doing something that has worked before or doing something different is critical. If that doesn't work, something else can be tried.

There are several basic assumptions, which correlate with these three basic rules, that frame the SFBT approach (Bruce, 1995; de Shazer, 1984; de Shazer,1991, p. 91; Lipchik, 1988, p. 4; Metcalf, 1995; O'Hanlon & Weiner-Davis, 1989; Sklare, 1997, pp. 9–16).

1. *Focus on what is right and what is working rather than what is wrong or troublesome.* The idea is to practice "solution talk" rather than "problem talk." All clients have strengths and resources that can be identified and used. The key is to accentuate the client's positive aspects so they can turn them into successes.

2. *Every problem has identifiable exceptions that can be turned into solutions.* The times when complaints are absent is the time when the goal state is approximated and the raw material for constructing the solution is present. There are always times when bad things are not happening and clients (and therapists who do not practice SFBT) fail to see the significance of these exceptional times and act on them.

3. *Little changes have multiple and even exponential effects that can cause much bigger changes.* Changes in one's intrapersonal life tend to affect interpersonal relationships. The change in interpersonal relationships can have ripple effects on the total ecosystem within which the individual operates.

4. *Goals are always set in positive terms.* Goals are behaviors that are to be accomplished, not things to be avoided or extinguished. It is very difficult to measure *not* doing something. Therefore, how can one know when the goal is obtained?

5. *People do want to change for the better.* When people don't follow directions they are not resistant, they are attempting to teach the therapist the best way to help them. It is the therapist's responsibility to understand what clients are saying when they fail to carry through on assignments. The therapist must collaborate with the client to figure out ways to get back on track.

6. *People are highly susceptible and dependent.* Therapists may create problems that don't exist. The expert or guru status that the client bestows on the therapist can delude the therapist into form-fitting the client's problems to his or her own theoretical modality. This can exclude the client's own needs and goals.

7. *Never ask a person to do something he or she has not been successful at before.* Generating new behavior is a fearsome task, replete with dangers, for most people. New behaviors need to be coupled with past successes using the client's previously successful coping mechanisms and resources.

8. *Avoid problem analysis.* Problem analysis only confirms clients' expectations that something is wrong with them and begets a self-fulfilling prophecy of failure. Knowing why we are the way we are doesn't change one bit of our behavior.

9. *Be efficient.* Forget about spending time looking for the source of problems and all the possible ramifications they have for the client's functioning. Spend time looking for solutions that will work and make the client independent of the counselor as quickly as possible.

10. *Be a survivor, not a victim.* SFBT pursues a survivor mentality that looks at how one has overcome and prevailed during difficult times. Being a victim allows clients to disavow their own actions.

11. *Focus on the present and the future.* The only reason to explore the past is to find exceptions to the current problems. Once those are found, immediately move to a present or future perspective that presupposes that the client will now be able to marshal those exceptions and change behavior for more positive future adjustments. Once clients are successful, their perception of the past changes and they are no longer concerned with it.

Strategies for Helping Clients

Formula Tasks

Formula tasks are tasks that are part of the standard operating procedure for SFBT.

Introduction to SFBT.   Central to strategies for helping clients are what de Shazer (1985) calls *formula tasks.* Formula tasks can seemingly be used with any problem. A major formula task is the initial session. The initial session (perhaps the only session) of SFBT is crucial in setting the tone, structure, direction, and foundation of treatment because of the brevity and the focused intentionality of the approach (Budman, Hoyt, & Friedman, 1992). Sklare (1997, p. 19) proposes that after initial introductions, the counselor use the following scripted format:

> CO: Here's how this is going to work. I'm going to ask you some questions, some of which might be difficult, and some of which might sound a little weird. I'll be writing down your answers to these questions. At the end of the session I'll take some time to write what I think we have talked about. I'll read this to you and give you a copy.

This statement tells clients what is going to happen and sets the tone for the collaborative relationship that the counselor expects to develop. It also tells clients how hard they are going to have to work. This statement is important, particularly when working with children, so clients do not deem themselves dumb and unequal to the task if they get stuck (Sklare, 1997, p. 19).

> CO (*later in the session*):   Remember, I said some of these questions would be tough, and this is one of those.

Goals.   A formula task given in the first session is to ask clients what their goal is for coming to therapy (Walter & Peller, 1992). The idea is to initiate and immediately focus on goal identification and goal seeking.

CO: What will occur, as a result of coming here, that will tell you that you don't need counseling? What will you be doing that will tell you that you are succeeding? What will others be able to see that will show them that you're accomplishing your goal?

These questions help reorient clients to focusing on the good things in their lives and starting to expect those good things to happen more frequently. They also imply that the counselor expects the client to succeed. The answers to these questions lead to the formation of subsequent questions which are designed to elicit even more specific information about what the client's goals are (Sklare, 1997, p. 21).

CO: So when you say that that would get your parents off your back, what would that look like? How would I be able to tell that if I were watching a videotape?

One of the best ways to define goals is to describe them with verbs ending in "ing." This indicates that there is a continuing sequence of action. Examining how things are happening presents videolike images that give clients the opportunity to see their possibilities (Sklare, 1997, p. 37).

CO: What would that look like? What might I be hearing and seeing if I was watching that as it was going on?

A critical component of goal setting is motivation. Motivation to change is a must. Usually lack of motivation comes about not because clients are lazy or stubborn, but because they are unclear as to what they want to occur that is different from what is going on now (Metcalf, 1995, p. 23).

Charles is in a quandary as to whether he should commit to a great deal of training in order to qualify for a supervisor's job. This job would mean a big raise in salary but would also greatly increase his responsibility. He keeps waffling back and forth and is attempting to get the counselor to make a decision for him.

CO: I'd like to stop counseling for today and give you an assignment. Do what you need to do to clear your mind. Take a walk in the park. Write down the pros and cons on a sheet of paper. Read the supervisor's manual. Eat a bowl of ice cream. Do whatever is necessary to move things forward. Come back next week and tell me what possible solutions have come to mind.

Miracle Question. The most notable formula task is the miracle question (de Shazer, 1994, pp. 133–134; Sklare, 1997, p. 31, 2000, pp. 442–443; Webb, 1999, p. 55).

CO: Suppose one night a miracle happened and your problem was solved. How would you know? What would be different?

Miracle questions start to give clients a problem solving mind-set. They focus not only on eliminating the problem but also on the possibilities in their future. By focusing on the future, the counselor is setting up a self-fulfilling prophecy that problems are already partially in the past (Webb, 1999, p. 56). In correlation with the miracle session is pretending the problem is solved. Pretending can be a face-saving approach that allows the client to pretend to change, when in fact he or she actually is changing but doesn't have to admit it, and also reduces the risk of failure since the client is only pretending to do something about the problem (de Shazer, 1991, p. 115; Webb, 1999, p. 99).

Alonzo is 16 years old and is having trouble with his parents. They are having trouble with him. He is seen by them as oppositionally defiant, lazy, and unmotivated. Alonzo sees his parents as domineering, untrusting, and he thinks they treat him like a 6 year old. Alonzo and his parents are in an initial family therapy session.

> **FAMILY THERAPIST:**   Alonzo, if a miracle occurred and things were okay again, how would it be?
>
> **ALONZO:**   Well, mom and dad would be off my back. I wouldn't talk back to my parents when they started lecturing me. My homework would be done before I practiced my guitar, they would trust me to have the car, and trust me to be in by 10:00 on the weeknights and 12:00 on the weekend.
>
> **FAMILY THERAPIST:**   Let's pretend that is happening. What two days next week might you pretend that this is actually occurring? I would like you to observe and see if anything different happens with your parents. Parents, I want you to do nothing but observe. See if you can figure out which days Alonzo is pretending to be this superkid you have been looking for.

At times, clients give unspecified or impossible miracle solutions. Janie is a fifth grader who wants to have better relationships with her peers. She is in a counseling group at school.

> **JANIE:**   If a miracle happened for me all the kids would want to come over to my house. They would all want to play with me and I'd be happy and popular.

The therapist needs to immediately use soliciting questions that get the client to specify what she or he would be doing and give the client ways of ascertaining how others would be reacting to her attempts to change behavior (Sklare, 1997, p. 32).

> **SCHOOL SOCIAL WORKER:**   Group, how might Janie know that was happening? What might she be doing to make that occur? What might other kids be doing to let her know that was happening?

When the miracle involves wanting others to be different, the counselor needs to help the client understand reciprocity, the notion that when clients change their behaviors others reciprocate by changing their behaviors as well (Sklare, 1997, p. 34).

> **JANIE:**   Well the other kids would all treat me really nice and wouldn't look down on me and say mean things.

SCHOOL SOCIAL WORKER: If they were all doing that, what might you be doing differently?

The Nightmare Question. The antithesis of the miracle question is the nightmare question (Reuss, 1997). This question is often used when the idea of a better future is not motivating enough and the client tends to minimize or deny a problem, which is typical of people with addiction complaints.

Alice is 27 years old. She is about to lose her husband of five years and two small children, Allison, 3, and Ike, 1. Her husband came home and found that the lights, gas, and water had been cut off for nonpayment. Alice had taken the household money and had lost it on the video poker machines.

ALICE: Well this is just some temporary trouble. I'll be able to go back to work when Ike can go to day care. I can make that money up. I got a little out of hand. It felt good to go to the casino and have some fun. Besides I'm on antidepressants for depression.

ADDICTIONS COUNSELOR: It seems like you are having a hard time picturing what it would be like not to get the rush of gambling. I'd like you to think of your worst nightmare. Think about waking up one morning after having this terrible nightmare about gambling and its effects. What would be happening to let you know this nightmare had occurred?

ALICE: I wouldn't be able to quit and I'd lose all our money we have saved up to buy a house. Mike would take the kids away from me. I'd be homeless and destitute. I'd go kill myself because I would feel so bad.

ADDICTIONS COUNSELOR: Is that a choice you wish to make?

ALICE: (*eyes tearing up*) No, that's not acceptable. I've got to quit.

Labeling. Using a nonpathological approach to describe the possibilities for a solution does not change the diagnosis, the reality of the situation, or the seriousness of it, but it does describe the problem in a way that says it can be solved (Webb, 1999, p. 58). The idea is to externalize the problem so that the person is not the problem but rather that the problem is out there where the client can see it and fight it. Externalizing the problem allows for less blaming and more empowerment (Webb, 1999, pp. 44–45). It should be clearly understood that externalizing and objectifying the problem is very different from allowing the client to externalize and project blame or fault on some other person or thing. This is a way of disavowing responsibility for consequences or for taking action. Externalizing allows the client to view the problem in a less pathological way and to not think of it as a genetic component of him- or herself that is going to become a self-fulfilling prophecy beyond solution (Webb, 1999, p. 59).

Emilio has been sent to the counselor's office for being belligerent to the teacher when she shook him awake in her social studies class. He has been labeled as an oppositionally defiant child. After speaking with Emilio and finding out he is getting up at 3:30 AM to deliver the morning paper, the school counselor redescribes the problem.

> **SCHOOL COUNSELOR:**   Gee, I'm impressed. You deliver 218 papers every morning to help support your mom and dad. That's awesome! It's sounds like you've got more of a "getting enough sleep problem" than an "acting out in class problem." What do you think?

Normalizing.   Clients have complaints, issues, and concerns, not symptoms, problems, or pathologies. Symptoms, problems, or pathological terms indicate there is some underlying disease at work which invites negative labeling. Complaints, issues, and concerns indicate that something isn't working and needs to be straightened out (Metcalf, 1995, p. 20). The counselor should attempt to normalize the situation so that it becomes surmountable (Webb, 1999, p. 72).

Shayla is a 13 year old who has been having a bad day at school. She has received write-ups from three teachers today and is now in the counselor's office.

> **SHAYLA:**   I think maybe I've got PMS and depressive disorder. That's what my mom has and she gets upset very easily right before her period. And those teachers of mine, particularly Mrs. Root, would get anybody to be a maniac or depressed with all this testing stuff.

> **SCHOOL COUNSELOR:**   Maybe you do have a disorder. But what I really heard out of all that was that you seem upset about the teachers really pushing you with all those tests. That seems to be your real complaint and they didn't seem to listen to you when you explained you were working as hard as you could.

Insight.   It is not necessary to promote insight to be helpful. This is particularly true of children who often do not have the cognitive development necessary to gain insight into a problem (Sklare, 1997, p. 15). George is 23 years old. He still lives at home with his mother. He wants to move out on his own. Notice how the therapist immediately refocuses on the solution and doesn't get into a long-winded discussion about child-rearing practices.

> **GEORGE:**   I think it's a dependency and attachment issue. Probably has to do with my mother not breast feeding me or pushing me too hard to toilet train.

> **PSYCHOLOGIST:**   Tell me the times when you have been away from home for a little while and it was OK. What was going on then?

It is not necessary to know a great deal about the complaint. Candace is a 33-year-old single female who has been divorced twice and has had numerous broken romances in between. She presents to a mental health clinic as depressed.

> **CANDACE:**   I'm the born loser at love. There are so many bad romances I don't even know where to start. But I suppose it goes back to high school and Chuck and. . . .

> **LICENSED PROFESSIONAL COUNSELOR:**   Excuse me a moment, but given all those romances, I just wonder if perhaps in one of those there were some good moments and also some things you learned to take care of yourself. Could you think about one of those right now?

Focusing. Complex problems do not have to have complex solutions (Metcalf, 1995, p. 22). Problems become complex when tangential aspects are considered to be somehow important. Latonya is working two jobs, not doing well in college, having trouble with her parents, and has just broken up with her fiancée. She is talking to a counselor at the college counseling center.

LATONYA: Life is the pits. (*States a litany of the foregoing events plus other issues such as roommate problems, uncaring teachers, a fascist college administration, and so on.*)

COLLEGE COUNSELOR: While all that may be, the specific reason you came here was to keep from flunking out of school by figuring out a study plan and how to budget your time more efficiently. So when are some times that you have been really efficient in your life?

Positive Blame. Fitting into the worldview of the client lessens resistance and encourages cooperation, particularly with adolescents who rarely feel that anyone is listening, much less trying to understand them (Metcalf, 1995, p. 22). Some clients know nothing but blame. SFBT finds a way to blame positive changes on the client (Thompson & Rudolph, 2000, p. 132; Webb, 1999, p. 205).

Casey has not been able to do anything right in Mr. Smitherman's algebra class. However, in the last week, after an initial session with the counselor, he has not been kicked out of class, has passed two quizzes, and has turned in all of his homework.

CASEY: (*griping*) He's just looking for an excuse to get on my back. He must have been sick this last week cause he didn't get on me.

SCHOOL COUNSELOR: (*somewhat sarcastically*) Don't kid me. I think you're messing with Mr. Smitherman's mind and now you're trying to mess with mine. You've gone out of your way to not get thrown out of class, to get your homework in, and to pass the quizzes. Well it won't work, Casey, 'cause I know what you're doing.

Don't Know. Sklare (1997, p. 48) proposes that for clients who "don't know" the rejoinder of "but what if you did know?" be used repeatedly to pull out of them their new strategies and behaviors. He also says that for those clients who cannot own their success but attribute them to others, it is important to not let them discount their successes.

SCHOOL COUNSELOR: So what was different about this week Casey? What brought that about in you?

CASEY: Ahh, I dunno.

SCHOOL COUNSELOR: Well, if you did know what would be different?

CASEY: Like I said, Smitherman must have been sick, that's why he let up on me. Besides, it's probably because you're counseling me.

> **SCHOOL COUNSELOR:**   Ah, it wasn't me in algebra class. Been there done that! So how in the world did you do all that?

> **CASEY:**   (*smiles sheepishly*) Well, ah, I decided to see if I was really smart, and like, you know, could do it. So I set up study time and wrote out questions and stuff I thought he'd ask.

Combating Resistance.   There is no such thing as resistance when we cooperate (Metcalf, 1995, p. 24). This does not mean becoming a doormat for a client to walk all over, or pandering to a client's every whim. What it does mean is using basic empathy and communication skills to make a connection and establish a trusting working relationship and alliance with the client. Aretha is an overprotective parent who can't cut the umbilical cord with her daughter. She is starting to have a phobic response to her daughter attending kindergarten.

> **SCHOOL SOCIAL WORKER:**   I certainly understand why you are scared and worried about all the things that might happen or could go wrong if you're not there to take care of your daughter. I appreciate a parent who really cares about her child like you do, because I see a lot who just don't care one bit. I'll bet you really want her to have a lot of opportunities and become independent so that she can make her own choices. So I wonder what we might work out so that you can feel good about letting her go to school and giving her a really positive start in kindergarten.

Scaling Questions.   Scaling questions are used to get clients to subjectively quantify their progress toward meeting their goals and to identify additional actions that will indicate further progress (Lipchek & de Shazer, 1988; Metcalf, 1995, p. 62; Sklare, 2000, p. 445; Webb, 1999, pp. 157–158). Once the client scales the concept, the therapist asks what could be reasonably expected and what the client would need to do to get there. Scaling helps the client and the therapist instigate small changes that work toward total success. Mrs. Albertson, Tommy's sixth-grade teacher, wants him to do a lot better. Tommy is currently getting a 40–60 percent completion rate on his work and about 60–70 percent of what is completed correct.

> **SCHOOL COUNSELOR:**   Tommy, if you were to rate yourself on a scale of 0 to 10, with 10 being the day after your miracle happened and 0 being the worst day, where would you be right now?

> **TOMMY:**   Well I have been 0 or even minus 0, but right now I think, after we talked and stuff, a 3.

> **SCHOOL COUNSELOR:**   Where on the scale do you think you could be in the next week?

> **TOMMY:**   I think I could get to, like, a 6.

> **MRS. ALBERTSON** (*conferencing with the school counselor*):   That boy is bright enough to get the work in and get 90 percent minimum on it! He's just a lazy bones!

SCHOOL COUNSELOR: How much do you think it would be reasonable for Tommy to increase his work on a scale of 0 to 10, 0 being no percent and 10 being 100 percent increase by this time next week?

MRS. ALBERTSON: Well, I would say a 2 or 20 percent. That would at least get him up around passing.

SCHOOL COUNSELOR: Great! I've talked to Tommy and he thinks he can boost it up by about 30 percent. What are we going to need to do to see that he meets his goal?

Exceptions. The exception question ignores the times when the problem was florid and instead looks at the times when the client didn't have the problem or it was minimal. By examining these times and what was different about them, clients can garner information about what works to exploit those exceptions. Clients also start to see the problem as less ominous and all encompassing and as something they can begin to take control over (Metcalf, 1995, p. 26; Sklare, 1997, pp. 67–68, 2000, p. 444; Webb, 1999, p. 89). Leon is in an anger management program for batterers.

LEON: She just honks me off all the time. Who wouldn't get frustrated with that, her and her high-and-mighty ways.

GROUP LEADER: Yet you have said you really love her and we now have some hard evidence that you are not "honked off" all the time. So there are clearly times when that is not happening. What are you doing at those times?

Reframing. Reframing problems in different words can help encourage resolution (Metcalf, 1995, p. 27). Mrs. Jones is Tommy's mother. She and the teacher are both convinced Tommy has ADHD and should be medicated.

SCHOOL COUNSELOR: Let's suppose you were back in school, Tommy's age. What would they have called his behavior back before they had these labels?

TOMMY'S MOTHER: Rambunctious and energetic.

SCHOOL COUNSELOR: Indeed, I see Tommy a lot and he is a bundle of energy. I see him using that energy to be very creative. Would you want him to be unenergetic and uncreative?

MRS. JONES: Well no!

SCHOOL COUNSELOR: So how shall we go about capitalizing on Tommy's energy and creativity?

Cheerleading. Supporting and encouraging clients' success is cheerleading. A counselor can increase the level of his or her voice, expressing excitement and amazement at what has been done, and showing admiration for the client's dedication and commitment. These are all part of cheerleading. Cheerleading is not patronizing and it must be sincere. In a world where clients hear little if anything but booing and jeering of their attempts to succeed, catching them doing well and cheering them on do much to extinguish ingrained patterns of maladaptive behavior and reinforce new, positive, adaptive behaviors (Sklare, 1997, p. 49).

SCHOOL COUNSELOR: I am *impressed* Tommy! Not only did you meet your goal of getting your work done and getting no write-ups, but you *also* exceeded what your goal was on percentage correct! WAY-TO-GO! How about a high five? (*congratulatory hand slaps Tommy*) How in the world were you ever able to do all that?

Writing the Message

Writing the message or progress note occurs at the end of the first session. The message restates, summarizes, plants ideas, and praises the client for his or her coping skills (Webb, 1999, p. 214). It is concrete evidence that the client takes out of the session that he or she can use to remember the exceptions to the problem and the progress that has and will be made. The intervention message was first started by de Shazer (1991, pp. 143–144) and his team. The counselor takes notes during the session and uses the material to write a message that has three components—at least three compliments, a bridging statement to the task, and tasks the client needs to accomplish to raise the scale score 10 percent or more (Sklare, 1997, pp. 57–64, 2000, pp. 446–447; Thompson & Rudolph, 2000, p. 133).

Compliments.   SFBT is unabashed in complimenting clients to reinforce behavior, reframe cognitions, and find concrete exceptions to problems. The following are all behavioral bases for constructing compliments (Sklare, 1997, pp. 58–59):

1. Actions such as courage, healthy risk taking, and follow-through
2. Efforts that demonstrate planning, growth, and endurance
3. Commitments that show loyalty, tenacity, and dedication
4. Attitudes that reflect tolerance, acceptance, and helpfulness
5. Thoughts that are creative, rational, and insightful
6. Desires that are realistic, healthy, and sensible
7. Decisions based on judgment, consequences, and reason
8. Attributes of maturity, understanding, and empathy

The list is virtually endless, so there is little reason that a therapist cannot come up with at least three compliments for the client.

Bridging Statement.   The bridging statement connects the compliment and the task portion of the message. The bridging statement is composed of two parts: (1) a brief reference to what the student wants to do as a result of counseling, and (2) a short statement intended to initiate the task (Sklare, 1997, p. 59).

Tasks.   The third part of the message is the task or homework assignment. Antithetical to most other approaches in which very specific assignments are given, in SFBT the assignment is left purposefully vague (Berg, 1997). The vagueness of the assignment sends a message to clients that they are trusted to complete the homework in ways that are best for them. Clients will not get stuck because the compliment part of the message actually spells out the details of what the client is going to do to increase on the scale.

Sample Case

The case of Pat is a somewhat eclectic rendering of SFBT. It incorporates work from Steven de Shazer and his associates' original version of SFBT (Berg, 1997; de Shazer, 1985, 1988a, 1988b, 1991; de Shazer & Berg, 1992), Willyn Webb's (1999) 4-P (purpose, potentials, plan, progress) solutioning process, and the school-based/child-focused approaches of Linda Metcalf (1995) and Gerald Sklare (1997, 2000).

Case of Pat

Pat is a 35-year-old female who is currently working as an executive secretary for a large legal firm. She is divorced and has no children. She has a bachelor's degree in business and has been employed at the firm for thirteen years. She has risen out of the secretary pool and is now executive secretary to the senior partner in the firm. She is extremely involved in the business of the firm and sees that as both her occupation and her pastime. She has few outside interests other than going to the symphony, plays, and church. She spends an average of sixty hours per week on her job. She has high performance marks and regularly receives bonuses for her work. She is ambitious enough to be working on her MBA and is planning an Internet operation that will put the law firm into the international consulting business on salvage law. She has the backing of the firm and a commitment of a million dollars to get the operation started. She describes herself as quiet, driven, obsessive–compulsive about doing her best, and as having a social phobia/anxiety reaction. She states that she is terrified that her social phobia of speaking in front of people will flunk her out of the MBA program. She is now at the college counseling center and is having her initial interview with an SFBT-oriented counselor.

> **SFBT:** Hi Pat, I'm Ingrid. I first want to tell you I think that you must be pretty proactive and self-motivated. You've decided that you need to get this situation straightened out and that speaks highly of you. Not everybody is willing to do that.

The counselor starts by explaining the format and also sets a positive mental set by complimenting the client for taking action and coming to counseling. In particular, she then tells the client that she will be taking notes throughout the session and will then take some time to collect her thoughts (Berg, 1997) and then write out an analysis of the session with some suggestions for the client to take with her. Following Webb's 4-P approach (1999), her first P is to determine the purpose of counseling and what the client wants to do.

> **SFBT:** So what is your purpose in coming here today? What do you want to have happen?
>
> **PAT:** (*starts sobbing and pours out her story*) I'm a fraud and now everybody will find out. Whenever I get up to speak or I am called on in class my mind goes blank. Now the professor in my research seminar has started to call on me and there are only eight students in there and I can't think or respond. I just sit there really dumb. He called me in and wondered whether I was cut out to be in the MBA program. I

am terrified they'll throw me out and my life will be ruined. I've staked my whole life on this and I just can't fail. Who am I kidding though, I'm a cretin.

The client makes a number of all or none, absolutistic statements that rational-emotive behavior therapists would have a field day working on. The SFBT counselor, however, does not respond to these but rather works on isolating, externalizing, and reconstructing the problem so that it becomes distinct and separate from the client's personhood. The counselor focuses on getting clear as to what the client wants to happen and getting her to describe it in behavioral terms.

> **PAT:**   I want to get rid of this phobia. This curse that I think my demanding, you never-will-get-it-right mother put on me.
>
> **SFBT:**   How might you know when that has happened?
>
> **PAT:**   Well I would be able to get up in front of a class, stark naked (*grimacing laugh*) if necessary, not have any anxiety at all or embarrassment, not be tongue-tied, think clearly, respond to every one of the questions brilliantly, or ask questions myself. Just meeting mommy's minimum standards! (*laughs ironically*)

The counselor briefly acknowledges the mother issue but does not get into the tempting mommy-made-me business. Rather, she focuses on what the client wants to start and not what she wants to stop.

> **SFBT:**   I understand you seem to have some hash to settle with your mother on this issue, but right now I'd kinda like to stay focused on what you want to see occur so this gets settled. You have indicated what would *not* be happening mostly, I'd like to think of this in positive terms. What *would* be happening for you?

As is typical with most clients, Pat is concerned about getting rid of a bad behavior and doesn't think in terms of starting a good one. The counselor reframes to a positive view and attempts to get her to indicate what her expectations might be.

> **PAT:**   I would be confident. Sawdust would not be falling out of my mouth or flies buzzing in and out. (*opens her mouth and glazes her eyes over with a "duh!" sound and then laughs*) I just can't think and then I freeze up! (*starts to tear*)
>
> **SFBT:**   That certainly sounds upsetting, but you can also laugh about it and make some fun of yourself so you really know you are not a dullard. If you had to rate this problem on a 10 point scale, 0 being the absolute worst and 10 being the absolute best, what would it be right now?
>
> **PAT:**   It would be about a 2 or 3.

The more than zero rating gives the SFBT counselor an opportunity to start looking for the exceptions.

SFBT: So it is not the absolute worst, like a minus number? That means there must be at least a few times when it is not absolutely awful. Tell me about those times.

PAT: Well when I can write things out on note cards, I can go right through it. I did that once for a secretary's conference. There were like 250 executive secretaries in the auditorium of the Peabody Hotel and I somehow got roped into being the MC. I was terrified, but I did it. It is also okay when I am with just a few people. When I was married, a lot of times my husband who was in commercial real estate would have dinner meetings and I would go out to eat with him and the clients.

SFBT: How were you able to do that?

PAT: I didn't know them and probably wasn't going to see them again so it didn't make any difference. There were only two or three people usually so it was more intimate, not a big crowd or group . . . not as intimidating.

SFBT: How often did you do that?

PAT: Oh, I'd say about twice a month over the course of the eight years we were married. I also speak up in the firm's meetings, but I know all those people.

The counselor immediately focuses on the exceptions to the problem.

SFBT: So there are at least some exceptions, both in regard to specific settings and numbers of people, when you are doing fine.

PAT: Well yes, but those are exceptions rather than the rule.

SFBT: Okay but what were you doing to make those okay?

PAT: I made up my mind to go out and enjoy myself with my husband because it really didn't matter to me, they were his clients. With my boss and the other lawyers, they know what I can do and they know me personally so I feel comfortable. At that big conference, I decided that I had to prepare for it so I really researched the issue and the people presenting.

SFBT: Let's get a little more specific on what you want to have happen. How would you know when you have gotten to the place you want to be—secure, with no anxiety-producing expectations of what "they" wanted you to know?

PAT: I suppose I would be eager to get into the debate or express my opinion in class. I do have some pretty good ideas or at least my boss says so. I mean the firm is backing me to the tune of about a million bucks on this Internet project. That's what really burns me up, not being able to show people how really capable I am. Them just thinking I'm a dumb blonde.

SFBT: So you'd really like to show them that you do have capabilities and a mind to go with it and the ability to make things happen such as the Internet project at work.

A lot of dialogue in SFBT is no more or less than basic person-centered therapy where many open-ended questions and summary restatements are used to help clients explore additional components of their situation, refine goals, and to affirm what they are saying as the counselor does here. The counselor restates the client's words, affirms her capability, and further refines the goal by asking an open-ended lead by using the standard SFBT miracle question.

> **SFBT:** This next question is going to sound really weird. What if you went to sleep and a miracle happened tonight and your problem was solved, what would you be doing differently?
>
> **PAT:** I would be speaking up in class. Voicing my opinion, not waiting to be called upon.

The counselor now reframes the problem from a long-term personality disorder to a situational issue and seeks to get the client to define how she would know if things changed.

> **SFBT:** Aha! I think I have it now. This really boils down to an academic issue. What you really want is to become assertive in class so you can pass it. If that would happen, who would notice a difference?
>
> **PAT:** Well Dr. Bateman sure would. He wouldn't wonder whether I was an idiot who had somehow snuck into the MBA program. I suppose the other students would notice too.
>
> **SFBT:** How might they respond to you?
>
> **PAT:** Well I think the professor would be flabbergasted. I haven't said one word in there. Maybe he might even compliment me if what I said was any good. The other students would probably be looking at me and nodding their heads or maybe even disagreeing, but that would be all right because I would be responding right back to them.

Here the counselor is interested in what the client would notice, how she might respond, and also how the significant others would react as a way of fleshing out the behavioral outcomes that would let the client know she is meeting her goal.

> **SFBT:** Your teacher would act or say something different then and other students and your boss also would notice the difference?
>
> **PAT:** Yes they would get to know me for who I really am and not this speech-impaired, emotional eunuch. It would just be an easy give-and-take between me and the other students and the professor.
>
> **SFBT:** I want to go back now and look at those exceptions. Let's use those times when you were and are self-assured and assertive and transfer that over to the seminar class. What did you specifically do in those cases that you can use to be more assertive and confident in class? You said you are at a 2 or 3 on that scale now. Where do you want to be by the next week in class? Where do you want to be by the end of semester?
>
> **PAT:** I guess I'd like to be about a 5 next week and by the end of the semester a 9, not a perfect 10, but a 9.
>
> **SFBT:** Great! How will you get there?

PAT: Well I prepared really well, like researching stuff in the secretary conference. I could do that in class. Write my questions out. Maybe even write some answers to the discussion questions out I suspect he'll ask. Maybe I could start to make friends with some of the students, ask a couple to grab a snack at the university center before class. Maybe I could talk to Dr. Bateman about doing some Net search stuff that he asked about in class. I am really good at that. I also bought some tapes on assertion training that I have started to play as I go to work.

SFBT: Good! That sounds something like a plan. I think I have enough information. I'm going to write up my notes. I'll be back in about twenty minutes, so you can take a break.

SFBT: (*twenty minutes later*) Okay, here's what I have. I'd like to read it and then I'd like to talk about what you can do about this.

Compliments
First, I think you are smart and proactive for deciding you are tired of this situation and wanting to do something about it. Even though it is scary, threatening, and anxiety provoking, you are determined to face it and even have a sense of humor about your dilemma. You've done a number of things on your own such as getting the tapes, making notes, and coming for counseling when many people would just be paralyzed with this (*complimenting*). Second, I'd like you to see that there are numerous exceptions to the situation (*noting exceptions*). As a matter of fact, the exceptions are so numerous that they are almost, I would say, normal (*normalizing*) as opposed to the isolated instances when you don't feel you can be assertive, such as in front of a graduate class or a large group of people. Those would be the exceptions because they take up such a small percentage of your life, but right now are in such an important area of your life (*externalizing the situation*). I think they stand out for you because they are indeed exceptions (*reinforcing the situation as a true exception*). You are assertive with those high-powered lawyers in your firm every day but you are so familiar with the situation. You don't see how most people would be intimidated by them. I am impressed that you could go out with people whom you know nothing about and carry on an intelligent conversations with them (*complimenting*). That is something I don't think many people could do. You did that for . . . umh . . . wow . . . eight years about twice a month (*cheerleading*). How in the world did you ever do that given what you have said about being shy (*positive blaming*)? That's hard to believe. That would be 192 (*reframing using concrete numbers to demonstrate success*) minimum instances where you did not have, as you say, sawdust falling out of your mouth and flies buzzing in and out because you were too stupid to engage in the conversation (*using client's own metaphors to counterpoint*). You also were able to get up in front of a large crowd and speak to them. You used notes to do that, but even the president of the United States has a prompter in front of him! I see that as a reasonable solution to be sure you are right in what you say. I think that is pretty understandable and would be true of most everyone (*normalizing*). When you are faced with a tough situation you think it through and make a plan (*reinforcing for planning and goal setting*).

Bridges Statement
Because you are bound and determined to become more assertive in the MBA program and particularly in the research seminar class (*bridging statement about what the student wants*), I would suggest you consider the following things.

Task-Initiating Statement

You might want to ask a couple of your fellow students to go out to eat before class as a way of getting more familiar with them. I would also suggest that you talk to Dr. Bateman about his query for research assistance (*specifying target relational behaviors*). Those both sound like doable, positive ways for increasing your confidence and putting you on more equal footing (*reinforcing the goal*). It sounds like you already have a plan going on—reinforcing and supporting your goal to be assertive outside of the class through the website and the tapes. You may want to really be concrete and specific about how you're going to do that. I would also suggest that you go ahead and write out some questions and answers for class (*specifying targeted task behavior*) and see if all of that will get you up to a 5 next week and a 9 by the end of the semester (*desired scalular outcome*).

This message is a positive reinforcing statement that reminds the client of her strengths and resources and sets the stage for the client to succeed. It provides the client with a homework assignment that is pretty much of her own making. The homework is set in terms of possibilities. That is, the counselor makes suggestions so the methods and outcomes are not seen as counselor dictated. The assignment also uses the client's own interpretation of scaling to determine what will be successful.

SFBT: I'd like you to take this copy of my notes with you as a game plan for trying this as a sort of experiment. Do you have any questions about that?

PAT: Wow! I don't know why, but I really do feel better, less anxious somehow. I think I can do that. It seems simple. Just sorting it out, breaking it down. Okay!

SFBT: If you want, you can come back and talk to me next week or at the end of the semester. Whenever you think it's necessary.

As Berg (1997) indicates, there are no set appointment times or typical standard weekly sessions. If the client feels the need to return for an appointment next week, or at the end of the semester, or not at all, that is up to her.

Subsequent Session

Berg (1994) has coined the acronym EARS (eliciting, amplifying, reinforcing, and starting over) to be used in subsequent sessions. Two months has passed since the initial session with Pat.

Eliciting.   The counselor starts the session with an eliciting question that seeks to find out what differences or positive changes have occurred.

SFBT: Good to see you again Pat. What's better or different since the last time we met?

PAT: Well, I got through the class. I got a B out of it. It wasn't perfect, but I did talk. I am doing some Net research for Dr. Bateman. He and I are getting along pretty well and I got to know three of the students. I made the notes for class and that got me through. My mind still went blank a lot and anxiety would just wash over me.

While the client has not been 100 percent successful, she has experienced some successes. The counselor attempts to elicit more information about these successes.

> **SFBT:** But you said there were some times in class, when you were using your notes, that you were able to talk. That is certainly different than when you came in February when you were absolutely frozen. What was going on with you when things were working okay?
>
> **PAT:** I had note cards and I could refer to them. I didn't have to rely on my memory. I could just rattle off the answer.

Amplifying. Amplifying looks at the ripple effect—how changes in the client's behavior change others around the client.

> **SFBT:** How have the other students come to see you? How about Dr. Bateman? He must have had a change of opinion to let you do research for him.
>
> **PAT:** Some of the other students want me to organize a study group for our comprehensive exams. They were amazed at my written responses, so I feel pretty comfortable with the ones I know. Yes, Dr. Bateman is really interested in my Net consulting concept. He has agreed to help me turn it into my major area paper.

Reinforcing. Here Sklare (1997, p. 94) proposes that the counselor needs to listen acutely for "better." Even though Pat says she had lapses, it is clearly apparent that things are better. Hearing "better," the counselor reinforces the client.

> **SFBT:** Correct me here if I'm mistaken, but it sounds like you just got nominated as leader of the pack by the other students and your professor. Am I missing something? It sounds like you did what you said you were going to do and it worked.
>
> **PAT:** Well um, yes, I guess I did, I just didn't get an A and I still feel like I will freeze up at anytime. I keep thinking that it's just a question of time until it happens again.

Starting Over. The client, as is often typical, has trouble seeing how successful she was and instead looks at the times she wasn't. Her statement that she didn't get an A is a generalized complaint that may have little to do with her subsequent behavior after her plan went into effect. However, she has been so successful that the counselor does not want to start over. She goes directly to what Webb (1999, pp. 207–208) calls "writing the recipe."

> **SFBT:** My notes say you were at a 3 on the scale and looking for a 9 by the end of the term. How would you say you fared?
>
> **PAT:** I would say a 7.
>
> **SFBT:** All things considered, a 7 is one giant step from the 2 you came in with. I would like to think that with a bit more honing and polishing you can make that into a 10+. Want to try?
>
> **PAT:** Sure. I mean, who wouldn't?

> SFBT: Excellent! Then I want you to tell me the recipe for your success. Just like a cake, if you can write it down you can do it over and over again with the same outcome. (*Pat writes down her recipe and with help from the counselor comes up with a final written recipe that includes all of the methods she used.*)

By writing out her statement the client is specifically mindmapping (Sklare, 1997, pp. 47–50) a future plan of attack. While she could restate it, we believe that writing it down stamps the recipe in the client's memory. An old Russian proverb states, "What is written with a pen, cannot be cut out with an ax." We believe that proverb fits very well in preparing the client to go forward.

> SFBT: Three more questions and I believe we are finished. First, when will you know you are done with counseling? Second, what might other people tell you to say you don't need to come in for counseling? Finally, how many more meetings do you think you will need before you are finished?
>
> PAT: I guess when I can do this without even thinking about it. It's not a huge tank-trap anymore, but I'd say it's still a rut. Other people would say I communicated effectively with an audience. Since I don't want to bust an axle, I guess I'd like to try this out over summer school and come back one more time and see you in the fall for a reality check.

These questions all set the stage for termination. One major thesis of SFBT is that therapy is not a forever contract. The positivist, SFBT view of humans believes that they are resilient and capable and can march to the beat of their own drummer. Providing a positive mind-set that therapy will end sets the client up to expect to move forward on her own.

Contributions of Solution-Focused Brief Therapy

SFBT has taken the challenge of providing a time-efficient, therapeutic approach that fits not only with the contemporary milieu of managed health care, but also with the prevailing philosophy of faster, more efficient use of time in all areas of the environment. The emphasis on a positive view of people who have the resources to learn more adaptive behavior has taken a long vacation since the heyday of Carl Rogers and the person-centered view. Certainly that view is one that needs to be remembered and used. The perceptual set that comes from viewing one's strengths, as opposed to one's weaknesses, is a powerful therapeutic tool.

We have also found that many clients would love to dwell on the outrageous slings and arrows they have suffered due to past injustices, external forces out there that control their destinies, and the masochistic delight they seem to get from wallowing in pain and misery. It would seem far better to use language and structure in therapy that does not reinforce those maladaptive behaviors.

SFBT has probably found its greatest utility and best niche with pupil personnel workers who are faced with the monumental task of providing therapy to mind-boggling case load numbers in K–12 school systems. Its straightforward, positivist approach has a great deal of appeal to parents, teachers, administrators, and students. It is as noncontroversial as a therapeutic endeavor can be, and can be appropriately used in the sensitive political arena of school systems.

SFBT has, at the least, caused a rethinking of how a business-as-usual approach is taken in therapy. It is not an overstatement that SFBT has helped to cause a major paradigmatic shift to occur in how therapy is delivered. As the proliferation of books, journal articles, workshops on brief therapy in general, and SFBT in particular has occurred, it is becoming more and more apparent that this approach is meeting the acid test of having staying power.

Shortcomings of Solution-Focused Brief Therapy

Critics of solution-focused brief therapy have challenged its simplicity, brevity, and the credibility of its research claims, which are mostly either self-reports or reports from rabid adherents (Johnson, 1991; Lieberman, 1984; Miller, 1996; Stalker, Levene, & Coady, 1999; Stern, 1993; Wylie, 1990).

It is worthwhile to note Thompson and Rudolph's (2000, p. 137) warning that counselors practicing SFBT need to guard against clients who want the counselor to assume control over them. These dependent clients will love this approach, will allow their counselors to select goals for them, and will fail miserably because they have little ownership in the therapist-generated goals. Their flight-into-health from all of the positive, encouraging words and their desire to please will crash and burn in flames.

Just as the over-compassionate, sympathetic therapist is a prime breeding ground for dependent behavior, the flip side of the coin may be a super-positive, discounting therapist who minimizes serious psychological problems. At times, one gets the notion of a cheer-leading SFBT therapist, like Mary Poppins on mood-enhancing psychotropic medication. SFBT's clients may acquiesce to a no problem/only-solution philosophy, then shut up and leave therapy prematurely because they are cured, are angry that the therapist does not seem to take them seriously, or they feel guilty because the therapist seems to dismiss their pain and self-doubts as normal. We might agree that some clients can readily adjust and change their outlooks because they have lived under a pessimistic dark cloud for so long that they don't know there is sunshine above it. However, there are numerous clients who have problems that go beyond mere reframing of words and unraveling problems of syntax.

While SFBT and person-centered therapy have much in common in regard to a humanistic view of the client, a major difference in the two approaches is the emphasis on the counseling relationship. For counseling to move forward, most clients need to have the therapist demonstrate genuineness, unconditional positive regard, empathy, congruence, and other core faciliative conditions that are hallmarks of person-centered therapy. We believe that establishing trust with clients calls for much more than SFBT's cheerleading and paying compliments. It calls for taking some time to adequately explore the affective, behavioral, and cognitive dimensions of what got the client to counseling. Research shows again and again that counselor credibility and trust are the major facilitative conditions of therapy. When that is not present, we wonder if the great amount of face validity of SFBT has much content- or criterion-related validity in regard to its long-term, client outcomes.

If therapy were as simple as SFBT appears, then everybody could do it. Doing SFBT right is not simple. Over seventy years of experience between the two authors of this book, doing therapy and training counselors and psychologists, tells us one thing. Not everybody can do this because therapy is at times anything but simple. That same experience has taught us that no therapy that adheres to a rigid treatment orthodoxy, such as SFBT seems to endorse, can be a panacea to every type of client and problem that comes to therapy. We have seen a number of approaches come down the pike extolling such a cure-all approach. At this point in time, none has lived up to the promise.

Solution-Focused Brief Therapy with Diverse Populations

Probably some of the most voceriferous critics of brief therapy in any form are the adherents of a multicultural view of counseling and psychotherapy. By its very definition as being time efficient and viewing change as residing within the individual, brief therapy would appear to violate two major dictums of most multicultural models. First, that change best occurs when time is taken to understand the history and cultural context within which the client is operating. Second, that the target of change may not be so much as with the client but with the systems that impact the clients.

That having been said, the following points seem reasonable. For those cultures and individuals who prefer a matter-of-fact, no-nonsense, down-to-earth, way-to-go approach to therapy, SFBT is the clear choice. For those cultures and individuals who are not highly concerned with affective or cognitive components of the problem, or even very much of the behavioral components of the problem, or in fact, the problem itself, SFBT is the clear choice. For those cultures and individuals who want to take immediate, directive action, SFBT is the clear choice. Cultures and individuals who like to assume individual responsibility for their actions over groups such as family or community also will see SFBT as the clear choice for therapy. We would hasten to state, though, that while SFBT focuses on the individual, a great deal of consideration is taken in regard to how other individuals in the client's social milieu are going to respond to what the client does.

Berg and de Shazer (in Berg, 1997) propose that SFBT is boundaryless and will work as well in Helsinki as it will in Hong Kong because it makes the client his or her own therapeutic expert and thus reduces the biases and cultural artifacts the therapist brings into the setting. However, because SFBT is tied so closely to how clients and therapists use and understand language, different language structures may have an impact on the use of SFBT. Lexical difficulties in posing the miracle question, changing verb tenses to challenge dysfunctional assumptions, and reinforcing selected client statements all may have difficulty when they are transported into the structure of other languages (Yeung, 1999).

Summary

SFBT has come into being because of its pragmatic utility in serving a large number of clients with a wide variety of problems in a time-efficient way. Behavioral health management organizations have eagerly embraced the precepts and philosophy of SFBT because of their vested interest in containing mental health care costs. As a result, the advent and growth of SFBT have caused every major therapeutic modality that hopes to survive in the current mental health care climate to restructure itself and come up with its own brand of brief therapy.

SFBT also has a great deal of appeal to clients because of its common-sense, no-nonsense approach to therapy that is both positivistic and humanistic in its respect for clients and their abilities. SFBT's therapeutic title defines it as a seeker of solutions rather than a dissector of problems. That subtle distinction has large ramifications in how therapy is conducted and what the focus of therapy is. The past has meaning for SFBT only in regard to finding exceptions to problematic situations and then teaching clients that they can exploit those exceptions and make them the rule in their future.

Because of its constructivist and poststructural philosophy, SFBT places a great deal of reliance on the client's view of reality and the client's ability to problem solve. Steven de Shazer, the principal founder of SFBT believes that therapy is essentially a dialogue between two people who are attempting to figure out what one person (the client) is saying (Berg, 1997). By clarifying goals for the person, the therapist gives the client the opportunity to act on his or her considerable resources and become master or mistress of his or her own destiny. One of the major goals of brief therapy, according to de Shazer, is to come to as few therapy sessions as possible and only as many as are necessary. According to de Shazer (in Berg, 1997) that means an average of 3.2 sessions for their clients.

SUGGESTIONS FOR FURTHER READING

Berg, I. K. (1997). (Speaker). *Psychotherapy with the experts: Solution focused therapy.* (Videocassette). Boston: Allyn & Bacon.

de Shazer, S. (1985). *Keys to solutions in brief therapy.* New York: W. W. Norton.

de Shazer, S. (1991). *Putting difference to work.* New York: W. W. Norton.

de Shazer, S. (1994). *Words were originally magic.* New York: W. W. Norton.

Metcalf, L. (1995). *Counseling toward solutions: A practical solution-focused program for working with students, teachers, and parents.* West Nyack, NY: The Center for Applied Research in Education.

Sklare, G. (1997). *Brief counseling works: A solution-focused approach for school counselors.* Thousand Oaks, CA: Corwin Press.

REFERENCES

Amatea, E. S., & Sherrard, P. A. (1991). When students cannot or will not change their behavior: Using brief strategic intervention in the school. *Journal of Counseling and Development, 69*(4), 341–344.

Araoz, D. L., & Carrese, M. A. (1996). *Solution-oriented brief therapy for adjustment disorders: A guide for providers under managed care. Mental health under managed care series, vol. 3.* Philadelphia: Brunner/Mazel.

Atlas, J. A. (1994). Crisis and acute brief therapy with adolescents. *Psychiatric Quarterly, 65*(2), 79–87.

Berg, I. K. (Speaker). (1994). *"I'd hear laughter": Finding solutions in the family* (Videotape). Milwaukee, WI: Brief Family Therapy Center.

Berg, I. K. (1997). (Speaker). *Psychotherapy with the experts: Solution focused therapy.* (Videocassette). Boston: Allyn & Bacon.

Bonjean, M. J. (1997). Solution-focused therapy with aging families. In T. D. Hargrave & S. M. Hanna (Eds.), *The aging family: New visions in theory, practice, and reality* (pp. 81–100). Philadelphia: Brunner/Mazel.

Bonnington, S. B. (1993). Solution-focused brief therapy: Helpful interventions for school counselors. *School Counselor, 41*(2), 126–128.

Bruce, M. (1995). Brief counseling: An effective model for change. *The School Counselor, 42*(5), 353–364.

Budman, S. H., Hoyt, M. F., & Friedman, S. (Eds.). (1992). *The session first in brief therapy.* New York: Guilford Press.

Carlson, J., & Sperry, L. (Eds.). (2000). *Brief therapy with individuals and couples.* Phoenix, AZ: Zeig, Tucker, & Theisen.

de Shazer, S. (1984). The death of resistance. *Family Process, 23,* 11–21.

de Shazer, S. (1985). *Keys to solutions in brief therapy.* New York: W. W. Norton.

de Shazer, S. (1988a). Once you have doubts, what have you got?: A brief therapy approach to "difficult cases." In E. Nunnally & C. S. Chilman (Eds.), *Mental illness, delinquency, addictions, and neglect. Families in trouble series,* vol. 4 (pp. 56–68). Thousand Oaks, CA: Sage.

de Shazer, S. (1988b). Utilization: The foundation of solutions. In J. K. Zeig & S. R. Lankton (Eds.), *Developing Ericksonian therapy: State of the art* (pp. 112–124). Philadelphia: Brunner/Mazel.

de Shazer, S. (1991). *Putting difference to work.* New York: W. W. Norton.

de Shazer, S. (1994). *Words were originally magic.* New York: W. W. Norton.

de Shazer, S., & Berg, I. K. (1992). Doing therapy; A post-structural revision. *Journal of Marital and Family Therapy, 18*(1), 71–81.

de Shazer, S., Berg, I. K., Lipchik, E., Nunnally, E., Molnar, A., Gingerich, W., & Weiner-Davis, M. (1986). Brief therapy: Focused solution development. *Family Process, 25*(2), 207–222.

de Shazer, S., & Kral, R. (Eds.). (1986). *Indirect approaches in therapy,* Rockville, MD: Aspen.

Dolan, Y. (1997). I'll start my diet tomorrow: A solution focused approach to weight loss. *Contemporary Family Therapy: An International Journal, 19*(1), 41–48.

Duncan, B. L., Hubble, M. A., & Miller, S. O. (1997). *Psychotherapy with "impossible" cases: The efficient treatment of therapy veterans.* New York: Norton.

Exner, J. E., & Andronikof-Sanglade, A. (1992). Rorschach changes following brief and short-term therapy. *Journal of Personality Assessment, 59*(1), 59–71.

Fisch, R., Weakland, J. H., & Segal, L. (1982). *The tactics of change: Doing therapy briefly.* San Francisco: Jossey-Bass.

Gergen, K. J., & Gergen, M. J. (1986). Narrative form and the construction of psychological science. In T. R. Sabin (Ed.), *Narrative psychology: The storied nature of human conduct* (pp. 87–107). New York: Praeger.

Gingerich, W. C., de Shazer, S., & Weiner-Davis, M. (1988). Constructing change: A research view of interviewing. In E. Lipchik (Ed.), *Interviewing* (pp. 42–61). Rockville, MD: Aspen.

Havens, R. A. (1987). The future orientation of Milton Erickson: A fundamental perspective for brief therapy. In S. Lankton (Ed.). *Central themes and principles of Ericksonian therapy.* (Ericksonian Monographs No. 2, pp. 3–14). Philadelphia: Brunner/Mazel.

Hergenhahn, B. R. (1994). *An introduction to theories of personality* (4th ed.). Englewood Cliffs, NJ: Prentice-Hall.

Huber, C. H. (1994). Brief therapy: The twenty minute hour. In J. L. Ronch & W. Van Ornum (Eds.), *The counseling sourcebook: A practical reference on contemporary issues* (pp. 72–85). New York: Crossroad.

Hughes, J. N. (1990). Brief psychotherapies. In T. B. Gutkin & C. R. Reynolds (Eds.), *The handbook of school psychology* (2nd ed., pp. 733–749). New York: Wiley.

Jackson, D. D. (2000). Brief psychotherapy. *Journal of Systemic Therapies, 19*(2), 7–22.

Johnson, C. L. (Ed.). (1991). *Psychodynamic treatment of anorexia nervosa and bulimia.* New York: Guilford Press.

Juhnke, G. A., & Coker, J. K. (1997). A solution-focused intervention with recovering, alcohol-dependent, single parent mothers and their children. *Journal of Addictions & Offender Counseling, 17*(2), 77–87.

Kelly, G. A. (1955). *The psychology of personal constructs* (Vols. 1 & 2). New York: Norton.

Levenson, H., & Evans, S. A. (2000). The current state of brief therapy training in American Psychological Association-Accredited graduate and internship programs. *Professional Psychology Research and Practice, 31*(4), 446–452.

Lieberman, F. (1984). Children, adolescents, and social work: A statement from the editor. *Child and Adolescent Social Work Journal, 1*(1), 3–17.

Lindforss, L., & Magnusson, D. (1997). Solution-focused therapy in prison. *Contemporary Family Therapy: An International Journal, 19*(1), 89–103.

Lipchik, E. (1988, Winter). Interviewing with a constructive ear. *Dulwich Centre Newsletter,* pp. 3–7.

Lipchik, E., & de Shazer, S. (1988). Purposeful sequences for beginning the solution-focused interview. In E. Lipchik (Ed.), *Interviewing* (pp. 105–117). Rockville, MD: Aspen.

Metcalf, L. (1995). *Counseling toward solutions: A practical solution-focused program for working with students, teachers, and parents.* West Nyack, NY: The Center for Applied Research in Education.

Miller, I. J. (1996). Time limited therapy has gone too far: The result is invisible rationing. *Professional Psychology: Research and Practice, 27*(6), 567–576.

Montgomery, C. L., & Webster, D. (1994). Caring, curing, and brief therapy: A model for nurse-psychotherapy. *Archives of Psychiatric Nursing, 8*(5), 291–297.

Mooney, K. (2000). Focusing on solutions through art: A case study. *Australian & New Zealand Journal of Family Therapy, 21*(1), 34–41.

Mostert, D. L., Johnson, E., & Mostert, M. P. (1997). The utility of solution-focused brief counseling in schools: Potential from an initial study. *Professional School Counseling, 1*(1), 21–24.

Murphy, J., & Duncan, B. (1997). *Brief interventions for school problems: Collaborating for practical solutions.* New York: Guilford Press.

Nichols, M. P., & Schwartz, R. C. (1995). *Family therapy: Concepts and methods.* Boston: Simon & Schuster.

O'Hanlon, W., & Weiner-Davis, M. (1989). *In search of solutions: A new direction in psychotherapy.* New York: Norton.

Parrott, C. (1999). Doing therapy in primary care: Theoretical concepts. In R. Bor & D. McCann (Eds.), *The practice of counselling in primary care* (pp. 140–147). London: Sage.

Reuss, N. (1997). The nightmare question: Problem talk in solution-focused brief therapy with alcoholics and their families. *Journal of Family Psychotherapy, 8*(4), 71–76.

Rhodes, J. (1993). The use of solution-focused brief therapy in schools. *Association for Educational Psychologists Journal, 9*(1), 27–34.

Risch, R. (1990). The broader implications of Milton H. Erickson's work. In S. R. Lankton (Ed.), *The broader implications of Ericksonian therapy.* (Ericksonian Monographs, No. 7, pp. 1–39). Philadelphia: Brunner/Mazel.

Rosenbaum, R. (1994). Single session therapies: Intrinsic integration? *Journal of Psychotherapy Integration, 4*(3), 229–252.

Segal, L., & Watslawick, P. (1985). On window-shopping or being a non-customer. In S. B. Coleman (Ed.), *Failures in family therapy* (pp. 73–90). New York: Guilford Press.

Selekman, M. (1997). *Solution-focused therapy for children: Harnassina family strengths for systematic change.* New York: Guilford Press.

Shapiro, L. E., & Henderson, J. G. (1992). Brief therapy for encopresis: A case study. *Journal of Family Psychotherapy, 3*(3), 1–12.

Sharry, J. J. (1999). Toward solution groupwork: Brief solution-focused ideas in group parent training. *Journal of Systemic Therapies, 18*(2), 77–91.

Sklare, G. (1997). *Brief counseling works: A solution-focused approach for school counselors.* Thousand Oaks, CA: Corwin Press.

Sklare, G. (2000). Solution-focused brief counseling strategies. In J. Carlson & L. Sperry (Eds.), *Brief therapy with individuals and couples.* (pp. 437–468). Phoenix, AZ: Zeig, Tucker, & Theisen.

Stalker, C. A., Levene, J. E., & Coady, N. F. (1999). Solution-focused brief therapy—one model fits all? *Family in Society, 80*(5), 468–477.

Stern, S. (1993). Managed care, brief therapy, and therapeutic integrity. *Psychotherapy: Theory, Research, Practice, Training, 39*(1), 162–175.

Thompson, C. L., & Rudolph, L. B. (2000). *Counseling children* (5th ed.). Belmont, CA: Wadsworth/Thompson Learning.

Walter, J. L., & Peller, J. E. (1992). *Becoming solution-focused in brief therapy.* Philadelphia: Brunner/Mazel.

Watzlawick, P., Weakland, H. H., & Fisch, R. (1974). *Change.* New York: Norton.

Weakland, J. H., Fisch, R., Watzlawick, P., & Bodin, A. (1974). Brief therapy: Focused problem resolution. *Family Process, 13,* 141–168.

Webb, W. (1999). *Solutioning: Solution-focused interventions for counselors.* Philadelphia: Accelerated Development.

Weiner-Davis, M., de Shazer, S., & Gingerich, W. J. (1987). Using pretreatment change to construct a therapeutic solution: A clinical note. *Journal of Marital and Family Therapy, 13*(4), 359–363.

Williams, R. G. (2000). The application of solution-focused brief therapy in a public school setting. *Family Journal Counseling and Therapy for Couples and Families, 8*(10), 76–78.

Wylie, M. S. (1990). Brief therapy on the couch. *Family Therapy Networker, 14,* 26–34, 66.

Yeung, F. K. (1999). The adaption of solution-focused therapy in Chinese culture; A linguistic perspective. *Transcultural Psychiatry, 36*(4), 477–489.

12 Systems Therapy

Fundamental Tenets

History

Systems theory is generally equated with *family therapy,* and today, most practitioners refer to the two terms synonymously (Jones, 1993). Although the systems approach is not primarily a theoretical approach, it is eclectic in that it draws from a broad range of therapies, procedures, and strategies (Lawson & Prevatt, 1999). The focus is not only directed toward an individual client, but is also concentrated on the family or other pertinent group that makes up the particular system. (Here we define *system* as a group of individuals whom counselors and other human service personnel are attempting to help.)

Emergence of an Ecological Format. A fundamental but essential trend that characterizes the family of the twenty-first century United States is that the family is no longer viewed as simply an enclave: it is an integral part of an ecological system that is continually and often richly intervolved with environmental components in the immediate neighborhood, the larger community, and beyond (Bronfenbrenner, 1986, 1995; Bronfenbrenner & Morris, 1998; Santrock, 1999, pp. 41–46). It is from this perspective that the systems theories of the late 1990s have been somewhat supplanted by an ecological systemic approach that serves as an umbrella formulation which overarches the whole sphere of systems therapy. That is the focus of this chapter. Consequently, wherever we use the terms *systems theory* or *systems therapy* we are also including an ecological contextual perspective.

The essential difference between systems therapy and many other therapies is that the system is the client (Foley, 1989, p. 459; Jones, 1993, pp. 1–5; Kadis & McClendon, 1998, pp. 6–7). Systems theory has come to be viewed as inclusive of various theoretical models that have core foci such as *ecology* (total sociocultural/developmental/life span view), *communications* (as being a critical issue), and *behavior* (representing a central theme) in explaining dysfunction and effecting therapeutic change. But all of the approaches have in common the concept that relationships, connections, and interactions are of vital importance (Hardy, 1997; Jones, 1993; Madsen, 1999; Santrock, 1999; Webb, 1999).

The *system* that we speak of includes not only a specific family but also the total ecological and environmental context that impacts every aspect of that family's being. Bronfenbrenner's ecological theory of development, as described by Santrock (1999, pp. 42–46), captures the broad-based, eclectically oriented, counseling/consulting/coordinating roles that counselors perform in what we think of as an ecological, contextual systems approach to counseling and psychotherapy with families as clients.

Similar to the definitions described by Nichols, Pace-Nichols, Becvar, and Napier (2000), we use the term *family* broadly in consonance with the cultural realities of the twenty-first-century United States. We understand that families may be two parents and their children, single-parent families, remarried families, estranged families, extended families, intergenerational families, gay and lesbian families, blended families, mixed or multiracial families, multiethnic families, non-kin families, and unmarried couples with or without children. If this characterization of *family* seems too ambiguous, consider that each group or system of individuals consists of interacting personalities, dynamic structure, and is continually developing, changing, and evolving (Horne & Ohlsen, 1982, pp. 1–3; Kadis & McClendon, 1998, pp. 153–192; Nichols et al., 2000). Consider also that families function within a context of ecological systems that are constantly evolving and changing as the lifespan development of each family member evolves and changes (Santrock, 1999, p. 42).

Precursory Underpinnings. The current state of systems therapy encompasses several twentieth-century theoretical underpinnings described by Thomas (1992, pp. 190–201). Eight of these approaches were identified: experiential-humanistic, psychoanalytic, intergenerational family of origin, behavioral, structural, brief or solution-focused, strategic, and systemic. Within the systemic approaches, we include the ecological, contextual systems approach. Among several models that illustrate the historical underpinnings of current systems therapy approaches, four examples are Satir's (1967) conjoint family therapy or humanistic approach, Haley's (1987) strategic problem-solving therapy, Minuchin's (1974) structural family therapy, and Bowen's family systems therapy (Bowen, 1978; Kerr & Bowen, 1988).

Conjoint Family Therapy or the Humanistic Approach. The central core of Satir's humanistic theory is the healing power of love, nurturing self-valuing or self-esteem, and facilitating healthy relationships between marriage partners and among family members (Cottone, 1992, p. 197; Lawson & Prevatt, 1999; Satir, 1967, 1972, 1975, 1982; Thomas, 1992, p. 204). The healthy family is viewed as one in which verbal and nonverbal communication encourage the following in each family member: equal sharing, openness, inquiry, decision making, self-worth, respect for others, diversity of opinion and style, and recognition of each others' stages of growth. The unhealthy family is characterized by blaming, threat, detraction, not sharing, keeping secrets, and rigid control (Thomas, 1992, pp. 204–207).

The process of counseling involves the facilitation of effective communication in a relational context, with the counselor acting in the roles of official observer of family interaction and instructor of communication among family members (Cottone, 1992, pp. 200–208). The conjoint family therapist focuses on both the family as a whole and individuals in the family context. The therapist is active both linguistically and physically, using a broad range of expressions, touching, feeling, videotape techniques, and many other innovative and traditional psychotherapeutic strategies. The outcome goals are to change the family's destructive and unhealthy patterns and communications and to facilitate emotional wellness, health, and positive self-esteem in all members of the family system (Cottone, 1992, pp. 200–205; Thomas, 1992, pp. 206–207). The therapist models and operates from the belief that people want to be whole and connected, that they want to grow in authenticity and sensitivity, and that they want to behave genuinely with one another. Consequently, the therapist looks for and finds in people signs of their healthy abilities and intentions even when such intentions appear deeply embedded in unhealthy behavior (Lawrence, 1999, p. 170).

Current followers of Satir's strategies adhere to her lifelong fundamental beliefs about systems therapy (McLendon, 2000). These basic beliefs include

1. Every individual has the capacity to change.
2. Therapy should focus on strengths.
3. Empowerment is gained through experiencing choice.
4. Spirituality is a vital and powerful ingredient for nurturing health.
5. Behaviors are viewed as simply attempts to communicate.
6. When new information is obtained or when circumstances and situations change, the therapy plan changes accordingly.

Some of the basic Satirian strategies currently in use include resourcefulness, empowerment, congruence, inner system, patterns, and externalization. Therapeutic tools or techniques include mandla, meditations, sculpting, communication stances, family mapping, inner child work, and the self-esteem maintenance kit. In Satir's approach, often called the human validation process model, the ability of individuals to be in awareness of their thoughts, feelings, body sensations, and spiritual dimensions determines the depth, speed, and effectiveness with which transformation can take place. According to Griffin and Greene (1999, p. 93), to the end of her life, Satir "embraced an almost evangelical belief in the power of compassion and genuineness to heal all human problems."

Strategic Problem-Solving Therapy.   Haley's (1987) model is a systemic-relational therapy that is highly behavioral. Haley stated:

> If therapy is to end properly, it must begin properly—by negotiating a solvable problem and discovering the social situation that makes the problem necessary. The act of therapy begins with the way the problem is examined. The act of interviewing brings out problems and the relationship patterns that are to be changed (p. 8).

Therapy is directed toward changing the family relational dynamics that may be supportive of unwanted or symptomatic behavior (Cottone, 1992, pp. 214–215). Some of the debilitating symptomatic patterns may be unhealthy (perverse) triangular entrenchment, pervasive double-bind situations, and power struggles within the family system (Thomas, 1992, pp. 364–365). Triangular entrenchment occurs when two members of the family regularly take sides in opposition to a third member, who then becomes a victim or scapegoat. A double bind occurs when a member of the family is in a position of being rejected or criticized regardless of what he or she does. The strategic therapist, in effect, joins the family, becomes a functioning entity therein, and takes on the role of director as in a live production. The therapist is consistently respectful of clients' language, culture, and worldview (Keim, 1999, p. 214). The therapist is also active, directive, powerful, and persuasive in getting family members to behaviorally change the operative relationships that sustain the unhealthy symptoms and power struggles that inflict so much damage (Haley, 1987). To facilitate change the therapist involves the whole family in examining and learning effective communication; correcting destructive triangular situations; using language, humor, and metaphor to change attitudes and behavior; behaving ethically to prevent dysfunction and promote growth and stability; and reinforcing autonomous problem solving (Haley, 1987). Strategic family therapy is systematic in that it seeks to facilitate positive, incremental changes in the social interactions and consequences that are associated with defined problems (Griffin & Greene, 1999, p. 20; Keim, 1999, pp. 216–218).

According to Cottone (1992, p. 227), Haley's strategic problem-solving therapy is highly consistent with its stated formulations. Its systemic-relational mechanisms invariably focus on external relational factors as fundamental to both definition and solution of the symptomatic problems. Emphasis is on the whole family's problem, not on scapegoating or singling out any one individual. The techniques are designed to produce behavioral change and to help families themselves learn to change distressful situations.

Structural Family Therapy. Minuchin's external model of systemic-relational therapy (Colapinto, 1984; Minuchin, 1974, 1984) focuses on family structural change rather than on specific targets such as communication. In Minuchin's usage, *structure* refers to organization and roles within the family. The quality of that structure can lead to the development of either stability (healthy emotional functioning) or instability (dysfunction) within a family. Dysfunction or pathology is almost always synonymous with enmeshment or disengagement (Foley, 1989, p. 462). Enmeshment occurs when one person's identity is so heavily invested in that of another that he or she is unable to relate to others independently. Disengagement occurs when one is emotionally estranged from others to the extent that he or she has a total lack of affect toward them. The structural family therapist seeks either to loosen or to establish boundaries, depending on the degree of closeness or distance in the family structure. In that regard, Minuchin (1974) stated that both his theory and his technique focus on the individual within the social context of the family. Therapy is directed toward changing the organization and roles in the family: "When the structure of the family group is transformed, the positions of members in that group are altered accordingly. As a result, each individual's experiences change" (p. 2). As expressed by Griffin and Greene (1999, p. 10), the goal of structural family therapy is to influence families to change boundaries and hierarchies sufficiently that presenting problems and symptoms are reduced or nullified.

The structural family therapist essentially joins the family and enters into its interactive process as a way of accessing and changing the structure (Cottone, 1992, p. 234; Kemenoff, Jachimczyk, & Fussner, 1999, pp. 114–115). According to Minuchin and Fishman (1981), such joining is more an attitude than a technique. The joining process puts the therapist in a position to understand, to be trusted, to use humor, to raise intensity, to reduce existing conflict by weakening existing dysfunctional patterns and installing new ones, and to be perceived as working for and with the family in exploring alternatives, trying unusual experiments, and effecting change in roles and structure (Griffin & Greene, 1999, pp. 9–10; Minuchin & Fishman, 1981). Joining is the glue that binds the therapist and the family together and enables the therapist to influence and devise more adaptive roles and structure. Several joining techniques, "although more heavily emphasized during the early phases of therapy, are used throughout the process of treatment and are continually interwoven with restructuring techniques" (Kemenoff et al., 1999, pp. 115–117). Such purposeful joining enables the therapist to more effectively use reframing, enactment, cognitive restructuring, teaching, and other techniques with families.

According to Colapinto (1982), the basic goal of structural family therapy is restructuring the family's system of transactional rules in such a way that more flexible interactions among family members expand the availability of alternative ways of dealing with each other. "By releasing family members from their stereotyped positions and functions, this restructuralization enables the system to mobilize its underutilized resources and to improve its ability to cope with stress and conflict" (Colapinto, 1982, p. 122). Cottone (1992, p. 236) further states that positive growth occurs whenever the family organization progresses to the point where it no longer supports or tolerates debilitating behaviors. Once the whole family demonstrates its propensity for sustaining positive change in the face of family stressors, therapy is no longer needed.

Nichols and Minuchin (1999), in describing the current core issues of brief structural family therapy, pointed out that what makes couples therapy structural is that it focuses not simply on the dynamics of interaction between partners but also on the boundaries around and between them. What makes it short term is that it is an energetic, interventionist approach to helping partners realize that they create, and can change, each other's behavior by their own actions and initiatives.

Family Systems Theory.   Systemic family therapies usually depict family difficulties and problems as being derived from interactions between family members (Lawson, 1999, p. 27). Griffin and Greene (1999, pp. 81–82) characterize family systems theory mainly on the following three premises: (1) emotional illness reflects the cumulative effects of functioning or dysfunctioning across three generations, (2) that dyads, as inherently unstable subsystems, may attempt relief by involving a third party in their choices and interactions (i.e., triangulation), and (3) triangulation of children influences them to exhibit emotional pathology that persists into adulthood. Bowen's family systems theory was developed from his research in the 1950s. He discovered that hospitalization and treatment of an entire family that contained a schizophrenic member had a positive and constructive impact on the whole family as an emotional unit (Kerr & Bowen, 1988, p. 6). This sudden and fundamentally new view of the treatment of family functioning and dysfunctioning ushered in a revision of assumptions regarding therapy with a dysfunctional family member. As a result, Bowen asserted that to change a dysfunctional family member, the entire family unit had to become involved and undergo fundamental change, a core clinical component that typifies current Bowenian theory (Brown, 1999). As a result of such a view of inclusiveness, Lawson (1999, pp. 27–37) describes and refers to the theory as an *integrated intergenerational family approach.*

According to Bowen (1978, pp. 529–530), "The one most important goal of family systems therapy is to help family members [move] toward a better level of 'differentiation of self'. . . . In any course of therapy it has been routine to encourage each spouse to work systematically toward the differentiation of self in the family of origin." Another important goal of therapy is to identify and control the level of chronic anxiety in individual family members. The lower a person's differentiation of self, the less adaptiveness that person has to cope with stress. This leads to a higher level of chronic anxiety (Kerr & Bowen, 1988, p. 112).

Family evaluations are accomplished through various techniques, including interviews, incorporating the therapist into the family's problems, and examining the family's multigenerational and historical patterns. Bowen developed genograms, which he later called *family diagrams,* to graphically demonstrate to family members the importance of multigenerational influences (Kerr & Bowen, 1988, pp. 282–338). Genograms became family diagrams that depict the histories, personalities, and relationships of family members. They are constructed in collaboration with family members and used as both diagnostic and therapeutic tools in family systems therapy.

Overview of Systems Therapy

Ecological Theory. Systems therapy is not, nor has it ever been, a single theory. It is an eclectic approach in that it systematically integrates many of the modern theoretical modalities, approaches, and techniques into one coherent way of thinking and conducting family therapy (Lawson & Prevatt, 1999). Furthermore, the ecological, contextual systems approach that we describe in this chapter reaches far beyond the relational interactions between and among the various members a specific biological family. This encapsulates the view of systems counseling and psychotherapy that resonates in the fragmented families of the twenty-first century (Bronfenbrenner, 1986, 1995; Santrock, 1999). This theory takes a sociocultural view of human development. It consists of five environmental systems ranging from the fine-grained inputs of direct communications with social agents (individuals capable of impacting families) to the broad-based inputs of the local community agencies as well as the broader influences of the attitudes and ideologies of the culture (Santrock, 1999, pp. 42–44). Bronfenbrenner (1986, 1995) identifies these five environmental components as the microsystem, the mesosystem, the exosystem, the macrosystem, and the chronosystem.

The *microsystem* is the setting in which the person lives. The microsystemic setting's contexts include the individual's family, peers, school, neighborhood, and usual haunts. It is within this microsystem that the individual experiences the most direct social interactions and communications with others (e.g., parents, siblings, peers, teachers, therapists, church groups, law enforcement personnel, ministers). The systems therapist adhering to the ecological, contextual systems approach views the client not as a passive recipient of experiences in the microsystemic settings but as an individual who actively participates in the construction of those settings (Santrock, 1999, p. 42).

The *mesosystem* serves as the communication channel, pathway, or interactive mechanism between components in the microsystem and the exosystem. The mesosystem maintains connections and communications among contexts such as the family's interactions with schools, school experiences with church experiences, and family experiences with peer experiences (Bronfenbrenner, 1995; Santrock, 1999). For example, children who have experienced rejection in the family may have difficulty interacting with and developing positive relationships with school, church, or other community personnel (Santrock, 1999, p. 42–44). Therefore, the mesosystem is of primary concern to the systems counseling and therapy process because it is the coordinating launching pad that drives the dynamic linkages among all components (people, groups, contextual connections, ecological resources) in the client's environment that may influence or encourage changes in acting, thinking, and affective functioning. The counselor or therapist—in the role of consultant, collaborator, and coordinator, in systems therapy—is a key resource operating out of the mesosystem.

The *exosystem* expands and extends the circle of dynamic influence on individual development to include factors beyond the microsystem. The exosystem includes a variety of components such as extended family members, relatives, friends of the family, neighbors, social welfare services, legal services, mass media, and all governmental agencies and programs that are in a position to impact the individual and to assist families in need. The exosystem exposes the person to experiences in a wider social setting than those encountered in the microsystem context (Bronfenbrenner, 1986, 1995). For example, a woman may receive a promotion on her job that requires her to work different hours or to do more traveling. Her promotion may precipitate marital discord and change the patterns of parent–child interaction. A second example might be the local government, which is responsible for the quality of libraries, parks, and recreational facilities for children and adolescents. A third example might be state and federal government roles in providing quality medical care and support systems for the elderly (Santrock, 1999, p. 44).

The *macrosystem* encompasses the total culture in which people live (Bronfenbrenner, 1995). *Total culture* refers to the behavior patterns, beliefs, mores, historical artifacts, legal constructs, and all other traits and pursuits that are endemic to a group of people and that are passed on from generation to generation (Santrock, 1999, p. 44).

The *chronosystem* is identified by Bronfenbrenner (1995) as the patterning of environmental events and transactions over the life span as well as the social and historical circumstances that influence the individual and the family. The essence of the chronosystem is the time dynamic. For example, research investigations have shown that the negative effects of divorce on children often peak during the first year following divorce, and that male children suffer more debilitating effects than females. By two years after the divorce, family life becomes more stable and less chaotic. Given that women of the twenty-first century, compared to a generation or so ago, are more likely to be engaged in a career, the chronosystem exerts a profound effect on families and individual life span development (Santrock, 1999, p. 44). The chronosystem, then, represents what happens over time. The phrases "time changes everything" and "time is of the essence" capture the flavor of the role of the chronosystem.

The Case for Inclusion.   As much as is feasible the practitioner of systems therapy uses eclectically oriented strategies while working directly with the total ecology and multiple individuals and groups within a particular system. The basis for inclusion of all persons in the system is that each person is influenced by the system and the system, in turn, affects every individual within the contexts of that system (Bennun, 1997; Hardy, 1997; Papero, 2000). However, not all therapists completely subscribe to the all persons in the system concept. Kadis and McClendon (1998, p. 4), for instance, aver that it is not at all necessary to meet with an entire family in order to improve or alter the functioning of that family unit.

The term *systems therapy* connotes collaboration among helpers, ecological contexts, and clients in the system. As described by Madsen (1999, pp. 1–2), the relationship of the helper to the client is one of an appreciative ally. Such an alliance requires that systems counselors or therapists position themselves in ways that strengthen respect, curiosity, autonomy, and connection rather than judgment, disconnection, disapproval, and dependency. As noted by Madsen (1999, p. 2), the appreciative ally works with families to continually nurture competence, connection, vision, and hope in ways that result in clients consistently perceiving the helper as being on their side.

Crucial Issues.   Hardy (1997) describes systems theory in terms of the three critical issues of relationships, interactions, and context. Usually we do not examine the behaviors or interactions of people in isolation from their connection with others. If we are to understand the significance of human behavior and the human condition, we have to consider the relationships and the context. For example, context may be seen through relationships between individuals, relationships between the individual and family, relationships between the individual and society, or even relationships between nations. Also, we all live in multiple contexts such as cultural, socioeconomic, gender, ethnic, and racial (Dattilio & Jongsma, 2000; Madsen, 1999; Nichols et al., 2000). According to Hardy (1997) the systems therapist does not deal with an individual's behavior or interaction in isolation from that person's interactions with others in the system. Therefore, two important questions the therapist initially attempts to answer are "How does the individual's context inform his or her behavior?" and "How does the behavior inform the context?"

Systems approaches, more than many other modalities, appear to take into account the ecological, contextual, psychological, social, demographic, technological, cultural, environmental, and diverse worldviews that tend to generate stress and affect the functioning of individuals in couples (Santrock, 1999; Sharpe, 2000) or family units (Hardy, 1997; Madsen, 1999).

Theory of Personality

Human Development as a Process of Meaning-Making and Reality Construction.
According to Becvar (2000, pp. 65–82), "therapy, like human development, is understood to be a process of human construction and intersubjective meaning-making." The constructivist view of personality development derives from the idea that people generate their knowledge and belief systems in response to interactions with other people and with the environment (p. 67). DeKay (2000) links human development to *evolutionary psychology,* meaning roughly that we do not know all the answers to how personality forms but we know that humans and their personalities are constantly evolving. It is posited that a synthesis among factors such as genetics, environment, Darwinian selection, sociobiology, and evolution itself may combine to develop what is the essence of

personality (pp. 23–40). In a manner of speaking, the mechanisms of the human personality are slowly but surely changing. Perhaps, as DeKay's theories infer, such changes are a part of a naturally occurring, never-ending dynamic process of interaction among ecological, human biological and psychological life span development, and environmental influences.

Human Development as a Process of Interaction.   Systems theory tends to reorient the way we think about the world. Rather than simple cause-and-effect attribution, systems theory views phenomena such as behaviors, cognitions, beliefs, and emotions in interactional terms. Clearly, to the systems theorist, the core of an individual's beliefs and actions is in some way related to one's interactions with other people. All matters associated with who we are are somehow connected with others. In systems therapy counselors and therapists look to the system to examine these associations (Hardy, 1997). It necessarily follows then that the development of personality is a systemic matter. One does not develop a personality in isolation. Given our genetically inherited predispositions and characteristics, we subsequently become what the system develops, influences, or constructs in us, and we absorb or develop our personalities through interaction with others.

Human Development as a Life Span Process.   The developmental perspective assumes that understanding a person requires consideration of where the person is in the evolutionary process and the way in which that person creates meaning (Becvar, 2000, pp. 76–77). To greatly simplify, the life span developmental approach assumes that the individual continuously evolves through stages that impute thoughts, feelings, and differentiations among self, objects, and others. That approach is likened to a form of social constructivism in which the individual's acquisition of memory, attitudes, thinking, or intrapsychic processes are derived from social processes (Becvar, 2000, p. 71). Becvar uses the term *developmental constructivism,* which invokes "meaning-making in a life span developmental perspective, as a process of maturation that includes alternating periods of change and stability," in which previous forms of knowing give way to more comprehensive forms as the individual constructs more powerful ways of making sense of the world (pp. 68–71). In terms of systems therapy, sociocultural and environmental experience is the source from which the individual mind is constructed and from which the individual's personality and identity emerge (Becvar, 2000; Hardy, 1997).

Santrock (1999, pp. 185–188) contends that the "individual characteristics of the infant that are often thought of as central to personality development are trust, the self, and independence." Erikson (1968) believes that autonomy versus shame and doubt holds the key to the developmental theme of toddlers up to their second year in life, and that independence is a critical issue especially during the second year. Trust, according to Erikson, is characterized by the trust-versus-mistrust stage of development. Contrasted with the regularity, consistency, warmth, and protection experienced in the mother's womb, the infant faces an environment that is more frightening and less secure. Infants learn to trust as a result of experiencing consistent, warm, and safe care (Santrock, 1999, pp. 185–186). The self is not imputed by either parents or the culture. It is constructed over time through experience with the environment. Independence becomes a central theme in the infant's life during the second year. It is critically important to infants that they develop, learn, and experience doing things on their own (Santrock, 1999, pp. 187–188). A child's development of independence or autonomy is not a phenomenon of the culture or of parental gift. It is an innate need that commences during infancy and pervades the entire life span of the individual.

Nature of Maladjustment

When symptoms of pathology or dysfunction occur, and people behave in maladaptive or destructive ways, systems theory does not usually attribute such dysfunction exclusively to the individual (Bottoms, 2001). Rather it attributes the dysfunction to the system (Becvar & Becvar, 1988; Cottone, 1992). Because problems almost always occur within the system, it follows that, to solve such problems, efforts should be put forth to create a healthy context—that is, a healthy system. In a healthy system, people are not dysfunctional. Almost all symptoms of dysfunction are associated with systems—systems choose individuals to express those symptoms (Bottoms, 2001). Therefore, the symptoms of an individual are really symptoms of a system (Becvar & Becvar, 1988; Hardy, 1997; Nichols et al., 2000, pp. 6–7).

Many systems theorists view pathological problems such as depression, anxiety, anger, and lack of self-esteem as having strong systemic components. Such problems are usually associated with some degree of need, feeling, influence, or response regarding others (Hardy, 1997) or with the perception of being devalued or negatively judged (Sharpe, 2000, pp. 197–242). From a humanistic or Satirian point of view, family dysfunction stems from blockages in personal growth resulting in the individual's developing low self-esteem or diminished self-valuing. The devaluation of feelings and the denial of the validity of one's emotional experiences lead to low self-esteem that leads to even lower self-esteem (Lawrence, 1999, p. 171). Although some pathology may definitely manifest into organic or biological components, systems theory does not preclude the presence and influence of interpersonal systemic influence (Hardy, 1997). An evolutionary perspective of maladjustment, presented by DeKay (2000, pp. 23–24), indicates that various forms of dysfunction may be linked to the evolved psychological mechanisms underlying mating, parenting, kinship, and other social and biological aspects of Darwinian selection processes. Santrock (1999, pp. 188–189) reminds us that "all development—normal and abnormal—is influenced by the interaction of heredity and environment." He contends that, from a life span–developmental standpoint, many of the maladaptive problems and disorders occurring in U.S. children stem from various kinds of child maltreatment in the family and from a steady diet of extensive violence in the culture (e.g., the violence that appears on television).

From a practitioner vantage point, symptoms of maladjustment in families are usually masked by the surface or presenting crisis or problem that initially brought the case into contact with the helping agency or clinic (Bottoms, 2001). The crisis point may be that a child or some other family member has done something to get in trouble with the law and the family has been mandated to undergo evaluation and counseling. The adage "where there is smoke, there is fire" applies in most situations like this. In assessing a case, the helping agency begins by examining the crisis incident and then quickly determines what is really going on in the family. What is driving the crisis? Usually there will be a much deeper core of maladjustment (such as major parental drug or alcohol addiction) than just the surface incident, and that will become the primary focus for working toward strengthening the family and helping them find ways out of their destructive patterns of functioning.

Major Concepts

Assumptions.   Systems theory recognizes that each person is a part of various systems such as family, school, church group, work group, couple, or dyad. Each system might be thought of as a unique community composed of specific individuals. Our membership in or attachment to any one (or many) of these community systems helps us to identify who we are. Any change or disruption in any component of the system, especially in families or couples, affects the individual. Occurrences such as death, divorce, job loss, relocation, addictive or seriously dysfunctional individuals, arguing and fighting between family members, abusive or irresponsible behaviors, and school crises have a powerful effect upon the individual member. Pursuant to such changes, the individual interacts to exert change on the system (Hardy, 1997; Rotunda, Scherer, & Imm, 1995).

Consultation, Collaboration, and Coordination.   The work of the counselor operating within the ecological, contextual systems approach that we are describing involves substantial consultation, collaboration, and coordination compared to many other forms of counseling and psychotherapy (Bottoms, 2001; Dougherty, 2000). *Consultation* involves a helping relationship in which counselors and therapists work with individuals or groups in a wide variety of settings (such as schools, agencies, businesses, churches, law enforcement entities, and the courts) to help them function more effectively (Dougherty, 2000, p.1). *Collaboration* is similar to consultation with the added assumption "that *direct* service between the professional and the client system is integral to successful outcomes" (p. 2). Thompson and Rudolph (2000, pp. 405–411) combine the two concepts, using the term *collaborative consultation* to connote, for example, the coming together and active involvement of counselors, parents, educators, and youths as equal participants and experts in resolving a specific problem. *Coordination* entails activities such as integrating, harmonizing, attuning, reconciling, readjusting, balancing, accommodating, and assimilating the various components in a complex system. Ford (1994, pp. 48–50) indicates that coordination is a necessary function designed to avoid chaos and confusion. He identifies coordination as the process of combining the specialized components of a system in a variety of ways to produce positive outcomes in efficient and flexible ways. Thus, the coordination role of the systems counselor is essential in bringing together a variety of ecological resources, strategies, and actions needed to solve client problems. This means that the systems counselor rarely, if ever, stands alone as a helping entity.

Tenets.   Characterizing the family as a system and as the client implies adherence to several tenets that differentiate family or systems from individual therapy (Becvar & Becvar, 1988, pp. 61–70). These tenets are as follows:

1. Family systems operate recursively, meaning that behavior is reciprocally causal.
2. Feedback is a systematic process that serves to maintain the status quo or produce change in the system.

3. A state of dynamic equilibrium that balances systemic change and stability is necessary for healthy systemic functioning.
4. Unspoken rules govern behavior, express values, and establish boundaries within and outside of the system.
5. The system permits or screens out information to the extent that it is open or closed.

The Counseling Process

The Ecological, Contextual Systems Counselor as Consultant, Collaborator, and Coordinator

The case of Janet depicted in this chapter provides one example of how a systems counselor in the ecological, contextual mode functions. Rarely is such counseling a solo act. The role of such a professional is portrayed by Thompson and Rudolph (2000, p. 400) as having "evolved over the years from that of one-on-one content expert to process helper to today's collaborative consultation." Invoking ecological concepts such as those found in Bronfenbrenner's (1986, 1995) theory, the systems counselor does indeed serve as a counselor, consultant, collaborator, and coordinator. In that role, the counselor must be an effective and empathic listener in order to grasp the initial contextual problem and environmental situation facing each individual at the core of the system. It starts with the individual. Given that understanding, the counselor may then proceed to counsel and also consult, collaborate, and coordinate from among a variety of components in the client's microsystem to bring to bear the appropriate persons (including groups, such as social agencies), strategies, and other environmental procedures and resources needed to resolve the problem.

Early on in the therapy the systems counselor might select and invite participation of appropriate individuals or groups from among the microsystem's components (e.g., family, school, peers, church group, health services, neighborhood play area). As the therapeutic process progresses, the counselor is likely to branch out further into the exosystem and involve, as consultants or collaborators, components such as the extended family, friends of the family, neighbors, legal services, social welfare services, the mass media, and so forth (Bottoms, 2001). Such a counseling format might even evolve or progress into the macrosystem and focus on the attitudes and ideologies of the particular culture in which the client exists. It is from these perspectives that the systems counselor becomes an eclectic overseer or ombudsman of sorts—a person who facilitates the orderly, systematic, efficient progression of therapy from intake to termination.

Focus on the System

In systems therapy we focus both on the affect of the system on the individual and also on the way the individual affects the system (Foley, 1989; Hardy, 1997; Jones, 1993; Lawson & Prevatt, 1999). It is important for counselors and therapists to consider the effects of disruptions that any one member of a system has on all the other members of that system. All of the systemic variables have a bearing on how therapists perceive and work with every member of the system (Becvar & Becvar, 1988). The systems approach is integrative in that it combines family systems, psychodynamic principles, social learning, and other theories. Intensive focus is on communication and feedback processes that occur among larger contexts: the interpersonal relations in the marital subsystem, individual behaviors, and the psychic processes of the persons in couples, the marriage, and the family (Nichols, 1999, 2000; Sharpe, 2000). It should be remembered that a couple may constitute a system. Therefore, couples counseling should be considered an integral component of systems therapy (Sharpe, 2000).

Focus on the Individual

Systems therapists usually take a wholistic or ecological approach. Not only is the individual within a dynamic system affected by all persons in that system, but the individual may also be influenced by any number of contextual elements such as destabilized and/or dysfunctional families, religious and spiritual needs, acute and chronic environmental changes and emergencies, sociological and political influences, financial stresses, impact of mass media, ideological pressures, meanings and beliefs, sexual and physical abuse and neglect, human developmental deficits, family migration and cultural transition conflicts, alcohol and drug addictions, and vocational or employment pressures. The therapist considers any and all such contextual dimensions when working with either the systemic group or the individual client as a member of that system (Aponte & DiCesare, 2000; Duhl, 2000; Hayes & Strauss, 1998; Kaslow, Smith, & Croft, 2000; Landau-Stanton, 1990; Rotunda et al., 1995).

In consonance with what Becvar (2000) describes as a postmodern shift in beliefs within the behavioral sciences that "has spawned a variety of approaches to human development that emphasize subjectivity, reflexivity, and individual interpretation" (p. 65), systems counselors and therapists are encouraged to interact with clients by being particularly sensitive to individual differences and uniqueness of clients. Such sensitivity creates a heightened awareness of the shared expertise of everyone involved in the therapeutic enterprise, an appreciation of the larger social context, and an understanding of the creation of identities through relational contacts.

Focus on Both the System and the Individual

One important advantage of the systems approach is that it works toward breaking the chain of system-induced dysfunction. Such dysfunction is not usually expunged through individual therapy alone. When counselors and therapists work with an individual who makes progress, that individual often goes back to the family, group, or system where the dysfunction originated. When that occurs, any therapeutic progress that has been made reverts right back to enabling the dysfunction to reassert itself (Rotunda et al., 1995). Thus, the systems approach attempts to change the dynamics that tend to produce dysfunction. Therefore, many systems therapists prefer to work with numbers greater than one (Hardy, 1997).

Systems processes apply even in group psychotherapy that initially involves an aggregate of unrelated individuals because, very soon, some dynamic gets created among and within group members that emerges as a system. An individual's problems are viewed in terms of the system (Bowen, 1978; Haley, 1987; Minuchin, 1984). Whether the individual is seen in therapy inside or outside the group, the therapist typically will be thinking something like, "How is this problem manifested within this individual? How is it connected to other parts of his or her life? Who else has a role in this problem? What is the context of this problem within this system?" A dominant way of thinking that informs the counseling process, according to Hardy (1997), is that our entire existence is permeated with systems; we are never without participation in a system in some way. In that regard, systems therapists may find themselves dealing with ecological, environmental, legal, medical, and social concerns, in addition to the face-to-face meetings with individuals and groups of people that have a direct bearing on the system and the ongoing therapy.

Sample Case

The Case of Janet

Janet Cooper, age 15, was a tenth-grade student in a large high school located in a technically oriented community surrounded by rural farming areas. Her measured ability and achievement test scores were slightly above average and her grades were average. She was physically well developed and had a reasonable number of friends. Her teachers reported that until recently Janet appeared to be friendly, cooperative, and socially well adjusted. During the past six weeks, however, she started skipping school and doing very poorly in her studies. She also was caught shoplifting at a local mall. Janet was the only child from her mother's first marriage. She had two siblings (half-brothers) from her mother's second marriage, and there were no children produced in her mother's current (third) marriage.

Janet lived in a household with her mother, the two siblings, and her stepfather (her mother's third husband). Janet's having been caught smoking in a school restroom and threatening the teacher who reported her led to her suspension. She was also involuntarily transferred to the district's alternative school for students with behavior problems. A counselor at the alternative school, being knowledgeable of the signs and symptoms of abuse, interviewed Janet. Janet disclosed that her stepfather had been sexually abusing her. It was the sexual abuse that precipitated the crisis that brought Janet's family into counseling. Figure 12.1 outlines the major systemic components or participants in the case. Figure 12.2 displays the contextual progression and approximate sequencing that developed in consonance with the case handling, which involved multilevel counseling, consulting, collaborating, and coordinating.

Strategies for Helping Clients

Systems Work with Abused Children: Prime Considerations

For the ecologically oriented systems counselor or therapist, helping clients is more than strategies or techniques. Counseling, consultation, collaboration, and coordination are functions that are at the forefront. Therapy is more of a mind-set about people, connections,

FIGURE 12.1   Major Components in Ecological, Contextual Systems Counseling: The Case of Janet

Examples of Microsystemic Components

I. Individuals

Initial client: Janet Cooper, Age 15, Grade 10.

Biological mother: Emily Davis, Age 34. Janet is Emily's daughter from her first marriage. Emily is now on her third marriage.

Stepfather: Arlo Davis, Age 42. This is his fourth marriage.

Janet's sibling (1): Gene Stanfield, Age 10.

Janet's sibling (2): George Stanfield, Age 8. Gene and George are Janet's half-brothers. They are Emily's sons from her second marriage.

II. Noteworthy Support Persons

Janet's peers: School friends, neighborhood playmates, community pals, church friends

Janet's adult associates and support service providers: Teachers and other school personnel, minister and church personnel, and neighborhood police

Janet's attorneys: Retained by the Child Advocacy Center to represent Janet's legal interests and to accompany Janet during any legal proceedings, hearings, and court actions that she might be required to attend

Janet's therapist: From the Child Advocacy Center (CAC)

Examples of Mesosystemic Components

Mechanisms and communication channels between and among components in the microsystem and the exosystem: Family communication and relationships between the school and the Child Advocacy Center; establishment of procedures for release and exchange of information among Janet's mother, social welfare services, and the Public Health Service; and articulation between Janet's attorneys and her therapist and counselors at the Child Advocacy Center. It is noted that an infinite number of communications, relationships, and alliance building interactions, on Janet's behalf, will probably occur between and among components of the microsystem and the exosystem.

Examples of Exosystemic Components

I. Individuals

Janet's extended family: Bill Cooper, Age 39, Janet's biological father; Irene Cooper, Age 61, Janet's biological paternal grandmother; Ben and Laura Hamby, Ages 59 and 57, Emily's parents and Janet's biological maternal grandparents; several of Janet's aunts, uncles, and cousins

II. Extended Support People and Agencies

Neighbors of Janet's family

Friends of Janet's family

Local mass media

Legal services: Attorneys, the juvenile court system, the juvenile judge, youth services officers, family resource centers

FIGURE 12.1   Continued

Counseling and psychological services: School counselors; school social workers; community service agency coordinators, counselors, and crisis intervention specialists; psychologists; licensed social workers and welfare and human services workers; Child Advocacy Center (CAC) case managers, therapists, counselors, psychologists, and social workers

Social welfare services: Community social workers and welfare and human services workers

Public health services: Physicians, public health nurses, community task force

Examples of Macrosystemic Components

Attitudes, ideologies, mores of the culture in which Janet and her family were reared and that exist in the place where they currently reside: Macrosystem components might include existing laws and legal practices; prevailing religious beliefs and practices; societal attitudes concerning child physical and sexual abuse; family traditions; historical artifacts that sustain community pride; taboos that are prescribed by Janet's society as being improper or unacceptable; and standards of behavior and conduct that are acceptable and expected.

Examples of Chronosystemic Components

Time as a dynamic influence: The societal patterns, in Janet's life and society, of environmental events that are considered important, celebrated, sacrosanct, or beyond human control are influenced by time. For example, the profound changes in the patterns of families, marriage, divorce, broken homes, and blended families between the present and the time Janet's grandparents were adolescents. Another example could be the negative effects of divorce or abuse on children, over time, as the factors of growth and development, attitudinal shifts, media influence, technology, and lifestyle changes interact with the time dynamic.

and relationships (Hardy, 1997). With such an attitude an enormous number of appropriate strategies are available for use by the systems therapist. Several important conditions and considerations emerged as the case of Janet developed and progressed. We will list and/or briefly comment on five of these factors as they relate to the dynamics and therapeutic relevance of the case handling in the case of Janet that depicts a systems approach.

Coordinated and Shared Responsibility.   As illustrated in Figure 12.1, a great number of individuals and agencies were involved with Janet's case. The four Cs—counseling, coordinating, consulting, and collaborating—that are espoused by Dougherty (2000) and James, Crews, and Gilliland (2000) were often in evidence. This is a normal occurrence in systems therapy. In Janet's circumstance, the Child Advocacy Center (CAC) was tasked, legally and professionally, with taking a leading or coordinating role. The center was competently staffed, well equipped, and experienced in handling child abuse cases. It had enjoyed a history of success in helping survivors and abusive families overcome the traumas of abuse and to learn more adaptive and less destructive ways to live. The CAC's child sexual abuse program was based on and patterned after the operational concepts developed by the Carl Perkins Child Advocacy Center in Jackson, Tennessee (Bottoms, 2001). Janet's primary (and coordinating) therapist was a full-time counselor at the CAC.

FIGURE 12.2 Ecological, Contextual Depiction of a Systems Approach to Counseling: The Case of Janet

Counseling Objectives	The Individual Context (Janet as the Focal Client)	Microsystem Context	Exosystem Context	Macrosystem Context
Day 1	During Janet's scheduled session with the alternative school counselor regarding suspension from high school and assignment to alternative school, disclosure of sexual abuse by stepfather Immediate crisis intervention counseling with Janet—ensuring her safety, stabilizing and returning her to emotional equilibrium Placement of Janet in a safe home overnight (or as long as required)	Stabilizing crisis situation at alternative school; notifying principal about abuse Making and filing appropriate reports of alleged abuse to all agencies and persons as required by law and ethical and safety concerns Contacts and crisis or emergency conferences with Janet's mother and stepfather	Notification of abuse and communication with the Child Advocacy Center	Indignation and outrage felt and expressed among counselors, school administrators, and agency personnel privy to sexual abuse of Janet
Days 2 through 10	Provisions for counseling for Janet Provisions for counseling for Emily, Gene, and George Abusive stepfather arrested and incarcerated Janet's biological father agrees to provide personal and financial supports Janet's biological grandparents agree to help any way they can Janet's peers at alternative school provide friendship and support	Juvenile court apprised of case of reported abuse; juvenile court judge, youth services officer, and the family resource center notified Youth services officer and family resource center initiate investigation of alleged abuse Janet's attorney becomes active on her behalf Home visits by minister of Janet's family to provide support during crisis period Sunday school teacher and Janet's Sunday school peers provide supportive visits	Initiatives commenced regarding social services, financial issues, and other pressing needs of family Child Advocacy Center assumes coordinating and counseling role in handling case of Janet Definite involvement of pertinent community agencies having any interest or purview of case: Child Advocacy Center, juvenile court, school system, family resource center, community services agency	Many people in community express empathy and support for Janet and her family and affirm commitment to pursue justice in abuse case Steps taken to ensure that legal, ethical, and confidential aspects of Janet's case be handled with minimal harm to Janet and her non-offending family Attorney General's office formulates legal action plan against perpetrator

(Left margin vertical labels: CHRONOSYSTEM; CONTENT)

Comprehensive case assessment initiated and substantially finalized

Janet's biological father, interviewed by Child Advocacy Center, asked to provide support and resources to help Janet

Attorney General's office initiates steps to take perpetrator to court for trial

Widespread community support of law enforcement and legal system's handling of sexual abuse case of Janet and other physical and sexual abuse cases

Continuation of communicating, coordinating, consulting, and collaborating by personnel at Child Advocacy Center

Juvenile court system active in pursuing criminal charges against perpetrator

Janet's attorney managing legal aspects on Janet's and her non-offending family's behalf

Young Life group providing Janet with growth-promoting activities and spiritually uplifting experiences

Child Advocacy Center active in community and neighborhood on Janet's behalf

Minister of Janet's church providing much-needed spiritual guidance and healing for Janet and her family

Ongoing ecological, contextual counseling and individual psychotherapy for Janet

Counseling with Emily, Gene, and George on an as-needed basis

Child Advocacy Center active in keeping different agencies abreast of case and coordinating flow of appropriate information among entities that need to know

Sunday school class and teacher involved with Janet in ongoing positive activities

Review and follow-up procedures carried out by family resource center and Child Advocacy Center personnel

Days 11 through 365

Systematic counseling, coordinating, consulting, supervising, and collaborating by Child Advocacy Center; alternative school counselor, and alternative school administration fully participating in counseling with Janet

Neighborhood adult friends of Janet and Emily, who are privy to situation, offer acceptance, friendship, and encouragement

Child Advocacy Center workers visit maternal and paternal grandparents; request they help Janet

Cooperative, Proactive, and Preemptive Responding.   Because the sexual abuse of Janet required serious personal, legal, moral, educational, and psychological responses, the communications and alliances among individuals and agencies had to take place smoothly, professionally, and in a timely manner. A number of agency components, such as the elements of the legal system (juvenile court, juvenile court judge, and youth services officer) acted proactively and preemptively. The school system handled the case ethically and professionally. One unique feature of the case handling was that the administration and staff of the alternative school welcomed and assisted the CAC counselors in working with Janet and her peers during school time and within the school buildings.

Optimum Place for Counseling Services.   The venues of counseling, consulting, coordinating, and collaborating were clearly carried out on a community-wide basis. This meant, when practical, that helping personnel routinely traveled to the various locations of the people who were receiving their services. The theme "go to the place where the client exists" pervaded the daily routines and thinking of workers, especially the CAC personnel. Counselors believed that taking the service to clients would enable them to better understand the clients' environments and enable them to more effectively assess and offer the professional assistance that clients needed and deserved.

Building Relationships.   Developing a wholesome, caring, trusting, and genuine relationship with survivors, families, friends, and colleagues is of primary importance. Systems counselors do more than simply conduct therapy with individuals. As a result of mutually trusting relationships between client and helper, counselors are also empowered to do parent training; facilitate growth-promoting outings and recreational activities; conduct group therapy; and organize and lead educational, personal growth, and problem-solving groups on important issues such as anger management, conflict resolution, safety strategies, bullying, study skills, tutoring, and mentoring. Bottoms (2001) cites mentoring as a key strategy in helping abused children to cope and return their lives to some sense of normalcy. The mentor must be someone, almost anyone (relative, grandparent, friend, peer, acquaintance, neighbor), who truly cares about and is eager to spend quality time with the child. This does not have to be a professional person. It can be anyone, educated or not. The mentor must be someone who has a natural knack for empathic listening and is interested in going places with the child and in participating in activities that are not only exciting for the child but that also broaden and enhance the motivation, experiences, and vision of the child.

Systems therapists also concentrate on developing alliances and relationships with colleagues in other agencies that interact and work with their clients. Bottoms (2001) recommends that all people who work with abused children develop and sustain positive, open relationships with key personnel in other agencies and that these persons feel free to communicate back and forth regarding the child's needs, progress, and concerns. For the sake of the child, it is vital that all agency personnel working with the individual keep abreast of the work being done, and not drop the ball and let the child fall through the cracks. That means visiting with families, phoning colleagues to thank them for doing a good job, getting acquainted with new workers in the field, and keeping feedback loops alive and functioning for the benefit of the child. Building and maintaining an effective professional support system to track and keep current about clients' needs is as much a part of the systems approach as counseling with individuals.

Listening. A fundamental priority of the systems counselor is effective and empathic listening. To fully understand the systemic status, dynamics, context, emotional status, and worldview of clients, the counselor must be fully tuned in to the client's world. In the initial phases of the interaction, much concentrated listening and very little talking on the part of the counselor is the usual format. Many times the systems counselor does practically no talking, as long as the client fills in pertinent details regarding family dynamics and problems (Hardy, 1997). The therapist must listen to not only the abused child but also the other people who may have helpful knowledge. According to Bottoms (2001) you have to find out from the child "Who listens to you when you're upset? Who do you think cares about what happens to you?" We've even gone as far as saying, "Who do you think would be at your funeral?" We do this to determine who that child already has a trusting relationship with. Many times the child's best friend's mom, a peer, or anyone who really listens to and cares about the child may prove to have suggestions, have information, or be willing to collaborate in helping the child. Effective listening is a primary strategy for solidifying relationships with the child and eliciting information that is vital to helping that child.

Segments of Systems Work in the Case of Janet

Discovery of Family Dynamics. Once the counselor has established a genuine and trusting relationship with the client, opportunities open up to gain a full understanding of the client's perception of the situation. It is important to discover, from the person's viewpoint, the overarching dynamics of the family. Usually this strategy involves asking specific open-ended questions that yield important information. Some examples include "How does this family create meaning in its life and interaction? What mythologies and passions guide the family's existence? What does this family truly believe?" The counselor cannot begin to design effective interventions until the family dynamics are understood (Hardy, 1997). There are numerous methods that the systems therapist may use to elicit information needed to proceed with helping the individual and the family. One illustration of the use of an open-ended question took place during an intake interview.

> **ALTERNATIVE SCHOOL COUNSELOR:** Janet, from what you've been telling me, I sense that there are far more serious things going on in your life than just smoking in the restroom. What is *really* going on in your world right now? (*In her response, Janet breaks down in tears and discloses the details of perpetration of sexual abuse by her stepfather*).

Whenever such a disclosure occurs, the counselor immediately shifts the focus of the interview to directly confront and deal with the essential core issues. At the same time, the counselor's primary concern is to be empathic, supportive, honest, ethical, and show concern about the client's integrity, feelings, and well-being.

> **ALTERNATIVE SCHOOL COUNSELOR:** Janet, I suppose you are aware of the fact that I am now required to notify some people that your stepfather has been sexually abusing you.
>
> **JANET:** (*sobbing*) Yes, I know . . . who do you have to tell?

COUNSELOR: The juvenile judge. The juvenile court people will get the family resource center involved. There will have to be an investigation into the abuse. Probably the youth services officer will actually be in charge.

JANET: (*still sobbing*) I shouldn't have blabbed about this. He'll just deny it and say it is my fault. I've heard about how awful these things can get.

COUNSELOR: Janet, you have done the right thing. This is going to be hard on you and on everybody else. But you have done nothing wrong. Your stepfather committed a crime against you and against society. Let me assure you that the people who are going to be working with you know what to do. They have dealt with many cases of abuse. I will be here for you. And there will be lots of people in your corner. It won't be easy for you. But we must make sure that this abuse does not happen again, ever! Your stepfather should be severely punished. But, beginning right now, the most important thing is for you to be safe and receive the help you deserve. You are a brave person for disclosing this. I admire and respect you for it. You have taken a step in the right direction. With the help of lots of people, including me, we are going to start you on the road to treatment.

Individual Counseling with Family Members.   The therapeutic process invariably includes separate interviews with individual family members. In the case of Janet, counselors at the Child Advocacy Center talked with Janet's mother, Emily, and Gene and George, Janet's half-brothers. Interviews and investigative work involving the alleged perpetrator, Arlo Davis, was conducted by professionals from legal services and the family resource center. Communication among agency personnel was carried on ethically, legally, and timely. Because each person is an integral part of the family system, it is necessary to factor that person's perspective into the therapeutic meld that will eventually affect the whole family. It is through intensive work with individuals that counselors gain a sense of the real issues and dynamics that are driving each person. In the case at hand, the thoughts, feelings, and beliefs of Emily, the non-offending parent, shed light on her thinking and feelings.

CHILD ADVOCACY CENTER THERAPIST: Emily, I understand how agonizing all this has been for you. I know how hard it must have been for you to first deny that Janet was being sexually molested, then to turn around and accept it. I want you to know, also, that I admire you for having the courage to face it, to cope with having Arlo arrested, and to agonize about how you are going to manage without the financial support you need. And I commend you for coming around and believing Janet. I am sure that Janet really needs you now, and you probably need her, too.

EMILY: I do. I really do! I guess I was a blind fool! I just didn't want to believe Arlo would do such a thing. I should have had some inkling. (*starts sobbing, softly*) I guess I'd better just tell you this—this happened to me when I was a child. With the good Lord as my witness, I swore that this would *never* happen to my child! I promised myself, over and over, that I would *never* let my own child be molested the way I was.

THERAPIST: I want to assure you that you are not alone in this. You are not the one who did the offending, and we are here to do whatever it takes to help you and your children get through this trauma. It is going to take courage and tenacity on the part of every one of us. I am with you. We are all with you all the way.

Counseling with individuals such as Emily provides opportunities to begin to do educational and rehabilitative work not only with that individual but also with other family members. It often provides the background information and impetus to develop group activities that are designed to provide the knowledge and techniques that families need to realign their choices toward constructive living. For the individual, the counseling process itself may be both educational and therapeutic. Bottoms (2001) indicates, for instance, that disclosures such as those made by Emily during the previous dialogue are exceedingly freeing for the woman. When a woman understands that she is not alone in enduring such a traumatic experience, it can be liberating.

EMILY: He didn't want me to have any contact with my family. Didn't let me have any money or to let me know anything about our finances. Wanted to control who I talked to on the phone. Was always suspicious of me, of all people, thinking I was going out and having an affair behind his back. Demanded to know everywhere I went and why. Was even jealous of me having contact with my girlfriend. Even accused me of being a lesbian. That's the kind of things I've been living through. Now, I'm already beginning to feel better about myself. Just knowing that it's not *me!* That other women have suffered through the same things I have. That's a beginning, I guess, in making myself an acceptable human being again. Maybe I *can* begin to live again!

THERAPIST: Emily, that is marvelous! What I want to do is work closely with you so that you can use this momentum to blossom into your full potential.

EMILY: It does make me feel better. And I appreciate your sticking by me so faithfully. But I still care about Arlo and I worry about him suffering and not being taken care of, too. I know that he has done a terrible thing and must be punished, but I feel for him being in jail and I cry for him and what he is going through.

THERAPIST: That is a very caring and insightful statement you just made. I am also very concerned that Arlo should receive the therapy, help, and understanding that he needs. He really needs counseling and specialized medical treatment. I assure you that I am personally going to contact the law enforcement authorities and lobby hard for him to receive expert help—both for his sake and for yours, and for society's as well.

The last therapist response was indicative of the therapist's use of Satir's humanistic approach (McLendon, 2000). Satir's six fundamental beliefs support the therapist's demonstration of deep love and concern for all people. That includes perpetrators as well as nonperpetrators. The therapist's statement also validates the client's expressed feelings and concerns.

Educational Information and Guidance.   Systems therapists are frequently called on to provide educational information for clients. Even though the distinction between guidance and therapy is sometimes blurred, it is not at all uncommon for the therapist to engage in both. The segment that follows illustrates the point.

> EMILY: I'm still feeling a lot of guilt and I'm disappointed and ashamed of myself for letting this happen. This abuse of Janet. I feel so powerless. The awful deed has already been done. I'd like to be doing something, but I'm clueless about what I can do. I just don't know what to do or where to turn.
>
> CHILD ADVOCACY CENTER THERAPIST: Maybe you and I can plan and work together on that. I'd like to suggest that you come to our Tuesday night women's group. You may find lots of understanding and help there. One thing that occurs to me is that the women's group has been sharing things women can do to break the intergenerational cycle of abuse. It is possible that the crisis you have experienced might cause Janet to do some rebellious activities that abused children and teens sometimes do—like engaging in promiscuous behavior or even drifting into more shoplifting or other destructive things. Perhaps you could learn to play a double role as mother and teacher to help guide Janet in a direction to avoid such a trap in her future.
>
> EMILY: I never thought about that. That's something I am interested in and I certainly will do it if I can.
>
> THERAPIST: Another thought I had is that the Tuesday night women's group might even help you to learn to guide your two sons in a positive direction. Many times in an abusive home, the kids—especially boys—become emotionally upset and go out and "perp" on other kids. That means become perpetrators, too. I hope your sons wouldn't do that. But you could be a great asset to both boys and to yourself if you could somehow guide and teach them in a way that they don't end up abusing.
>
> EMILY: Gee, this is really serious. But I can see that it is also important and exciting. I can certainly give it a try.

In the above dialogue, the therapist is guiding Emily's negative pleading into something positive and constructive that she can do. The therapist is also directly applying one of Bowen's family systems theory concepts (Kerr & Bowen, 1988) regarding multigenerational influences, to good effect. In that regard, the therapist made herself a mental note: "What I shall plan to do is to help educate Emily by meeting with Janet, Emily, Gene, and George together, with the goal of constructing a family diagram to teach them to understand their family's intergenerational dynamics and history. That should help them avoid some pitfalls in the future and it should provide Emily with some strategies that a mother can use to guide her children. At this point, I believe that she is capable of starting to learn how to do that."

Joining as a Therapeutic Strategy.   One of the premier strategies used in Minuchin's structural family model is that of *joining* or actually living with the family (Minuchin & Fishman, 1981). Whenever the therapist purposefully lives with a family, opportunities are opened up for effective use of reframing, enactment, cognitive restructuring, teaching, and other cognitive-behavioral techniques (Kemenoff et al., 1999, pp. 115–117). Following an experience in joining with Janet, Emily, Gene, and George, the CAC therapist, Dr. Virginia Epstein, took advantage of what she had learned about the family, as illustrated in the following exchange.

JANET: Dr. Epstein, it has really been neat—you going with us to the zoo, to the youth museum, and having meals with us. It's sort of like you're one of us now.

(later)

JANET: George really gets on my nerves sometimes. The little snit! Everything I get, he bugs me about it. Asks a million dumb questions. I wish he'd grow up or get lost or something. I don't have time to fool with him every time I turn around.

THERAPIST: Maybe it would be better if he was 15 and you were 8. Then you could show him how to act. Or, maybe he just needs an older, more mature sister to admire and look up to.

JANET: *(pauses, thoughtfully for a moment)* Well, for sure, I don't want to be 8! After all, he is just a child. Maybe I do need to cut him a little slack.

Here the therapist uses her joining experience, knowledge of Minuchin's therapy techniques, and reframing strategies, as described by Cormier and Cormier (1998, pp. 395–423), to help Janet perceive George in a different frame. The therapist was able to use a confrontation style because of the excellent rapport that the joining experience nurtured in the family members. The therapist carefully considered the dynamics between Janet and George. She was also cognizant of the requirement that effective reframes "are the ones that are accurate and are as valid a way of looking at the world as the way the person sees things now" (Cormier & Cormier, 1998, p. 399). The therapist judged that the above reframe or alternative perception would likely fit Janet's values, style, and sociocultural worldview.

Problem-Solving Therapy. A substantial amount of the work of systems therapists includes some degree of problem solving. As Haley (1987, p. 8) explains it, "negotiating a solvable problem and discovering the social situation that makes the problem necessary" is really a strategic part of the therapy.

GENE: Why did you ask all of us to get together, Dr. Epstein?

THERAPIST: Well, I have been observing what's going on in the family lately, and I don't clearly understand what is behind this fussing and bickering. I've seen too much good progress in the way we treat each other around here to ignore the fussing and let it pass. I'd like to emphasize that I don't intend to take sides or to take a negative stance. All I'm interested in is this whole family's emotional health and well-being. So let's not get into blaming any one individual or blaming at all. What we need is to find out *together* what the root of the problem is and then *together* join in and help each other figure out what we need to do to solve it and keep this problem from getting bigger—to keep this family a happy and loving family.

Here the therapist, using Haley's (1987) model, took the role of director. She was purposefully active, directive, powerful, persuasive, and collaborative in setting the stage for the family system to engage in strategic problem-solving.

Interagency Communication: Standard Systems Therapy Procedures.   An integral and essential element of a systems therapy framework is effective and timely sharing of information regarding assessment, treatment progress, efficient allocation of agency talent and resources, and other important matters (Dougherty, 2000; Thompson & Rudolph, 2000, pp. 400–415). The helping professions are operating in an entirely different world than heretofore existed. As Bronfenbrenner (1986, 1995) has indicated, the family is no longer viewed simply as an enclave. The dynamics generated by rapid changes in technology, mass media, faster travel, accelerated worldwide development, increased human longevity, the population explosion, exponential increases in separation and divorce rates, and the changing patterns of human growth and development have all combined to totally change the landscape in which the helping professions must operate. The complex ecological and environmental milieu impels us to add a fifth C to Dougherty's four, generating a format that includes counseling, consulting, coordinating, collaborating, and *communicating*. The different systems and modes of communicating are virtually infinite. Boiling it down to the case of Janet, we shall offer only a few segments that illustrate interagency communications (and some of the other Cs) by systems therapy practitioners.

The Group Meeting Format

CHILD ADVOCACY CENTER (CAC) THERAPIST: As a CAC therapist and coordinating counselor of the Janet case, I called this case conference to provide an opportunity for representatives of the major agencies involved in the case to give us an updated status report and to share successes, needs, and concerns that you are encountering. I am truly grateful for the hard work and competent handling of the case that has been attained by each of your agencies. First of all, here's where the CAC stands at this point. We have interviewed and assessed many of the people who might contribute to the support of Janet and the non-offending members of her family. While the family resource center conducted the investigation, here at CAC we placed Janet in the home of her biological paternal grandmother, Mrs. Irene Cooper. That provided her with a safe place to be until her stepfather was taken into custody. Janet is now back with her mother. We are in the process of conducting individual and group counseling with Janet at the alternative school. We are also counseling Emily, her mother. We're making good progress with her. We are very concerned about her financial situation because if Arlo is released on bail and returns to the house to cause trouble, Janet will have to be moved immediately. Several relatives believe her story and are willing to take care of her if the need arises. Her grandmother, Mrs. Cooper, will happily do so. In fact, she insists. Also, Bill Cooper, Janet's biological father, would be willing to take her in. At this point we are wary of considering Arlo's parents as a safe home, because we never know when Arlo may show up at his parents' house. Right now, resources for Emily to put food on the table and pay rent and utilities is a big problem.

COMMUNITY SERVICES AGENCY (CSA) COUNSELOR: We have done an assessment on that. We have funding that can provide for temporary payment of her utilities and rent. We could also provide food if needed.

FAMILY RESOURCE CENTER (FRC) COORDINATOR: We have interviewed Janet's father, Bill Cooper, and he can make arrangements to reinstate child support on behalf of Janet. That may help the family make ends meet. We'll follow through on that. Emily has expressed the desire to go back to work. We are also working with her to help her find employment.

CHILD ADVOCACY CENTER THERAPIST: This week we're starting group counseling with just the non-offending family: Janet, Emily, Gene, and George. We're doing study skills work with both Gene and George because their school performance has dropped drastically since this crisis hit. We're also doing some educational work with Emily to help her with her parenting skills and to try to bolster her confidence and self-esteem. We're not equipped to deal with adult perpetrators, so we are not planning to work with Arlo if and when he is released on bail.

YOUTH SERVICES OFFICER (YSO):   Representing the juvenile court system, I can report that the case against Arlo is pretty solid. The Attorney General's office is handling the evidence and the prosecution end of it. We're helping with witnesses, information we have, and other legal matters. We have explored mandated counseling options for Arlo. It is necessary that he receive heavy-duty educational counseling—anger management, sexual-related therapy, and counseling to deal with his issues of control and the like. Some of this can be obtained right here in this county. But some of it will have to be arranged through specialized programs in other places. We're working on that too.

(The case conference continues with reports and recommendations from other centers and agencies participating in the case.)

Telephone Format
(Part of a phone conversation between Mr. Farrell, who is Janet's attorney, and Dr. Epstein, Janet's therapist, at the Child Advocacy Center)

ATTORNEY: There is a hearing scheduled next Tuesday at 2:30 P.M. The judge wants to have Janet there to hear her side of the story. Arlo and his attorney will be there, too. So, I wonder if we can get together and prepare Janet for that hearing.

THERAPIST: I'm so grateful that you called, Mr. Farrell. It is certainly important that we prepare Janet for this stressful event. I will be happy to come to your office with Janet so we can work on this. I want to be by her side during this preparation and certainly I want to accompany her to the hearing and to any and all trials or legal proceedings involving her that might transpire.

ATTORNEY: Splendid! It is so good to know that the CAC is so supportive of her. That makes my job a whole lot easier. That kid is going to be put through the wringer. But we can handle it in a way that does the least damage to her. OK, now let's set up a time to meet for this rehearsal and preparation session.

E-mail Format

**(E-MAIL MESSAGE FROM CHILD ADVOCACY CENTER CASE MANAGER TO (1) DAR-
LENE MORRIS, PROJECT MANAGER OF THE COMMUNITY TASK FORCE OF THE
DEPARTMENT OF HEALTH, (2) MR. JAMES ALLEN, COUNSELOR, ALTERNATIVE
SCHOOL, (3) RAUL CUNNINGHAM, RECREATION DIRECTOR, FAMILY RESOURCE
CENTER)** I want to personally thank each of you for organizing the youth outing
to the hot air balloon festival last Saturday. Your three organizations jointly spon-
sored and funded the transportation, outing, and food for the youngsters. Your
inviting Janet Cooper and her two half-brothers was heartwarming and laudatory.
For you, Darlene, when you went up in that balloon with Janet and mentored and
talked with her that day meant a world of memorable fun and excitement for her.
You did a very good deed. To both Raul and James, I can't say enough about how
you made Gene and George feel at home. Based on what the boys have told me,
they were thrilled because both of you were kind of substitute dads that day and
they enjoyed just being with you. Your accepting them and listening to them was
just as important to them as taking them up with you in that balloon. I know they
shall ever be grateful to you for spending that day with them. As their case manager, I can't find the words to tell you how much I appreciate you. Our CAC
appreciates you. So I am sending memos of commendation via U.S. Mail to each
of your supervisors to tell them of the exemplary work and service you have performed to help these kids who needed your time and energies so very much.
Thank You.

Copies to: Dr. Epstein, psychologist and therapist at the Child Advocacy Center
            Mrs. Emily Davis, the children's mother
            Hon. Ben Llewlyn, juvenile court judge

We cannot overemphasize the importance of networking and communicating with
individuals and organizations that constitute alliances for providing services to our clients.
The above e-mail message is only one example of cultivating alliances. Personal communication and rapport are the avenues through which we pave the way for our clients to receive
exemplary services from multiple sources.

Contributions of the Systems Approach

The systems approach has transformed the way counselors and therapists view and conduct therapy, especially family therapy. The most important contribution can be seen in
the attitudes and self-examination in counselors and therapists toward clients and the
process of helping them (Hardy, 1997). For example, Flores and Carey (2000, pp. vii–x)
cite the necessity of examining one's own cultural presuppositions and prejudices and the
need for cultural training as important prerequisites for therapists. These authors, along
with Wehrly, Kenney, and Kenney (1999) also call attention to the emergent need for
counselors to avail themselves of competent cross-cultural supervision and consultation

in relation to the acquisition of gender, multicultural, and racial sensitivity. The systems approach has also fostered the expansion of the application of eclectic models and practices that provide competent treatment for an enormous array of human problems, needs, disorders, and dilemmas (Dattilio & Jongsma, 2000; Griffin & Greene, 1999; Horne & Kiselica, 1999; Horne & Ohlsen, 1982; Madsen, 1999; Nichols et al., 2000; Thomas, 1992).

Probably the most powerful contribution that systems therapy has made is in the realm of the attitudes counselors and therapists cultivate within the helping relationship. Hardy (1997), Madsen (1999), and many others have provided examples of how counselors may position of themselves in relation to clients becoming the primary factor in the successful healing of clients in a system. Modern systems counselors and therapists intentionally position themselves as allies, coaches, mentors, and person-centered helpers rather than experts whose role it is to fix problems. Such helpers, for instance, do not focus on families with problems or problem individuals. Instead they focus on families who are experiencing multiple stresses and dilemmas and who need understanding, support, choices, decision-making abilities, encouragement, hope, and techniques for finding their own solutions. Pejorative labels such as resistant, noncompliant, dysfunctional, high risk, chaotic, disorganized, or multiproblem families are avoided. Instead, families that have multiple and complex difficulties that they do not presently have the resources or the power to solve are viewed with empathy, acceptance, and respect. Thus, from the beginning helpers can appreciate the dignity, worth, and humanity of clients and begin to find ways to help by strengthening bonds, self-identities, interactions, and connections with and among clients in the system (Flores & Carey, 2000; Hardy, 1997; Madsen, 1999; Nichols et al., 2000; Wehrly et al., 1999).

Shortcomings of the Systems Approach

Family counselors and therapists have long recognized that gender plays a fundamental role in family dynamics. According to Griffin and Greene (1999, pp. 113–115), however, feminists have been critical of marriage and family therapy because of its history of failure to adequately address issues of gender. One example is that the importance of changing performance within gender roles has often been emphasized as opposed to challenging the roles themselves. Another example is that mothers are frequently blamed for family difficulties because of traditional prescriptions that hold them responsible for child rearing and household management. Also, many counselors and therapists in the past have not received adequate training for dealing with abuse, neglect, and violence against women and children. The patriarchal perspective has been allowed to persist in both overt and subtle ways. For instance, referring to violent acts of beating or battering as *spouse abuse* or *marital aggression* rather than the blatant violent or criminal acts that they indeed are has tilted the gender scales toward male privilege. These criticisms point to the need for a general perspective that promotes awareness of gender and power equality among all members of systems being counseled (Griffin & Greene, 1999, p. 114).

Systems Therapy with Diverse Populations

Suitability for Work with Human Differences

Systems counselors and therapists have demonstrated effective and efficient treatment with a wide variety of clientele. The broad, systematic, eclectic techniques that are available provide the flexibility and models (Griffin & Greene, 1999; Horne & Ohlsen, 1982) needed to treat problems across multicultural lines (Flores & Carey, 2000; Nichols et al., 2000; Wehrly et al., 1999) and dilemmas affecting multi-stressed families (Madsen, 1999). Family therapy strategies work to alleviate the ill effects of many different family crisis categories such as anger management, alcohol abuse, bereavement issues, separation and divorce, and dozens of other problem areas (Dattilio & Jongsma, 2000; Horne & Kiselica, 1999; Madsen, 1999).

Developing Skill in Multicultural Counseling Techniques

During the past few decades systems counselors and therapists have become increasingly aware of the necessity of developing and using strategies that take into consideration the cultural context of all the clients they serve (Arredondo, 1998, 1999; Flores & Carey, 2000; Ridley, 1995; Sue & Sue, 1999; Wehrly et al., 1999). Factors such as race, national origin, sex, sexual orientation, religion, economic status, age, having a disability, educational level, and other cultural background differences have a direct bearing on how assessment and therapy should be conducted. An enormous amount of empirical data and experiential information informs the modern-day practitioner regarding clients of all different cultural and family backgrounds (Arredondo, 1998, 1999; Atkinson, 1983; Atkinson, Ponce, & Martinez, 1984; Constantine & Ladany, 2000; Dana, 2000; Fischer, Jome, & Atkinson, 1998; Prieto, McNeill, Walls, & Gomez, 2001; Ridley, 1995; Ridley, Li, & Hill, 1998; Sue & Sue, 1999).

Summary

Systems theory is generally equated with family therapy. It is eclectic in that it draws from a broad range of therapies and strategies. The focus is not usually directed toward an individual client, but rather on the particular system that the counselor or therapist seeks to help. The fundamental difference between systems therapy and many other therapies is that the system is the client. The term *family* was used broadly in line with the diverse and varied cultural realities in the twenty-first-century United States. To give examples of the historical underpinnings of current systems therapy, we summarized four approaches whose major proponents were Satir, Haley, Minuchin, and Bowen. Systems therapy is not, nor has it ever been, a single theory. It systematically integrates most of the modern theoretical modalities. The systems therapist or counselor uses eclectically oriented strategies while working directly with as many of the particular system's individuals as feasible. The basis for inclusion of all persons in the system is that each person is influenced by the system and the system, in turn, affects every individual in that system.

The system that is the focus of this chapter includes not only a specific family but also the total ecological and environmental context that impacts every aspect of that family's being. Bronfenbrenner's ecological theory of development captures and describes the broad-based, eclectically oriented, counseling/consulting/coordinating brand of therapy. This formulation, which we call an *ecological, contextual systems approach* to counseling and psychotherapy with families as clients, comprises the major theme of this chapter.

We have depicted the systems approach as emphasizing the concept that relationships, connections, and interactions are of prime importance. A sample case was presented and selected fragments of client/counselor dialogue illustrated how the systems counselor may interact with clients. Several examples of segments of therapists demonstrating interagency communication, coordination, and consultation were included. The focus was mostly on individuals in the family and on family therapy. Descriptive summaries of a variety of different strategies for helping clients were provided to illuminate the eclectic flavor of the systems approach.

Systems therapy connotes collaboration among helpers and clients. The relationship between helper and client is one of an appreciative ally. Such an alliance requires that systems counselors position themselves in ways that strengthen respect, curiosity, autonomy, and connection rather than judgment, disconnection, disapproval, and dependency. The counselor or therapist, as an appreciative ally, works with families to continually nurture competence, connection, vision, and hope in ways that result in clients consistently perceiving the helper as being on their side. Systems theory has also been described in terms of the three critical issues of relationships, interactions, and contexts. If we are to understand the significance of human behavior and the human condition we have to consider the relationships and cultural contexts, such as social status, gender, ethnic, and racial differences.

Systems approaches, more than many other modalities, appear to take into account the ecological, psychological, social, demographic, technological, cultural, environmental, and diverse worldviews that tend to generate stress and affect the functioning of individuals in the modern systems or family unit.

SUGGESTIONS FOR FURTHER READING

Dattilio, F. M., & Jongsma, A. E., Jr. (2000). *The family treatment planner.* New York: Wiley.

Family Therapy Section of the National Council on Family Relations, http://www.ncfr.com

Flores, M. T., & Carey, G. (Eds.). (2000). *Family therapy with Hispanics: Toward appreciating diversity.* Boston: Allyn & Bacon.

Griffin, W. A., & Greene, S. M. (1999). *Models of family therapy: The essential guide.* Philadelphia: Brunner/Mazel.

Hardy, K. V. (Therapist). (1997). *Family systems therapy* (Videotape No. 0-205-32931-4, T. Labriola, Producer). In J. Carlson & D. Kjos, *Family systems with Hardy: Psychotherapy with the experts.* Boston: Allyn & Bacon.

Horne, A. M., & Kiselica, M. S. (Eds.). (1999). *Handbook of counseling boys and adolescent males: A practitioner's guide.* Thousand Oaks, CA: Sage.

Madsen, W. C. (1999). *Collaborative therapy with multistressed families: From old problems to new futures.* New York: Guilford Press.

Nichols, W. C., Pace-Nichols, M. A., Becvar, D. S., & Napier, A. Y. (Eds.). (2000). *Handbook of family development and intervention.* New York: Wiley.

Santrock, J. W. (1999). *Life-span Development* (7th ed). Boston: McGraw-Hill.

Wehrly, B., Kenney, K. R., & Kenney, M. E. (1999). *Counseling multiracial families.* Thousand Oaks, CA: Sage.

REFERENCES

Aponte, H. J., & DiCesare, E. J. (2000). Structural theory. In F. M. Dattilio & L. J. Bevilacqua (Eds.). *Comparative treatments for relationship dysfunction* (pp. 45–47). New York: Springer.

Arredondo, P. (1998). Integrating multicultural counseling competencies and universal helping conditions in culture-specific contexts. *The Counseling Psychologist, 26,* 592–601.

Arredondo, P. (1999). Multicultural counseling competencies as tools to address oppression and racism. *Journal of Counseling and Development, 77,* 102–108.

Atkinson, D. R. (1983). Ethnic similarity in counseling psychology: A review of research. *The Counseling Psychologist, 11,* 79–92.

Atkinson, D. R., Ponce, F. Q., & Martinez, F. M. (1984). Effects of ethnic, sex, and attitude similarity on counselor credibility. *Journal of Counseling Psychology, 31,* 515–520.

Becvar, D. S. (2000). Human development as a process of meaning making and reality construction. In W. C. Nichols, M. A. Pace-Nichols, D. S. Becvar, & A. Y. Napier (Eds.), *Handbook of family development and intervention* (pp. 65–82). New York: Wiley.

Becvar, D. S., & Becvar, R. J. (1988). *Family therapy: Systematic integration.* Boston: Allyn & Bacon.

Bennun, I. (1997). Relationship interventions with one partner. In W. K. Halford & H. J. Howard (Eds.), *Clinical handbook of marriage and couples interventions* (pp. 451–470). Chichester, England: Wiley.

Bottoms, D. (Speaker). (2001, May 23). *Child sexual and physical abuse: A systems intervention approach to helping families in crisis.* (Cassette Recording No. 1-523-01). Memphis, Tennessee: University of Memphis, Department of Counseling, Educational Psychology and Research.

Bowen, M. (1978). *Family therapy in clinical practice.* New York: Jason Aronson.

Bronfenbrenner, U. (1986). Ecology of the family as a context for human development: Research perspectives. *Developmental Psychology, 22,* 723–742.

Bronfenbrenner, U. (1995). Developmental ecology through space and time: A future perspective. In P. Moen, G. H. Elder, Jr., & K. Luscher (Eds.), *Examining lives in context: Perspectives on the ecology of human development* (pp. 619–647). Washington, DC: American Psychological Association.

Bronfenbrenner, U., & Morris, P. A. (1998). The ecology of developmental processes. In W. Damon & R. M. Lerner (Eds.), *Handbook of child psychology* (5th ed., Vol. 1, pp. 993–1028). New York: Wiley.

Brown, J. (1999). Bowen family systems: Theory and practice: Illustration and critique. *Australian & New Zealand Journal of Family Therapy, 20*(2), 94–103.

Colapinto, J. (1982). Structural family therapy. In A. M. Horne & M. M. Ohlsen (Eds.), *Family counseling and therapy* (pp. 112–140). Itasca, IL: F. E. Peacock.

Colapinto, J. (1984). Integration and model integrity. *Journal of Systemic and Model Therapies, 3,* 38–42.

Constantine, M. G., & Ladany, N. (2000). Self-report multicultural counseling competence scales: Their relation social desirability attitudes and multicultural case conceptualization ability. *The Journal of Counseling Psychology, 47,* 155–164.

Cormier, S., & Cormier, B. (1998). *Interviewing strategies for helpers: Fundamental skills and cognitive behavioral interventions* (4th ed.). Pacific Grove, CA: Brooks/Cole.

Cottone, R. R. (1992). *Theories and paradigms of counseling and psychotherapy.* Boston: Allyn & Bacon.

Dana, R. H. (2000). Psychological assessment in the diagnosis and treatment of ethnic group members. In J. Aponte & J. Whol (Eds.), *Psychological interventions and cultural diversity* (2nd ed., pp. 59–74). Boston: Allyn & Bacon.

Dattilio, F. M., & Jongsma, A. E., Jr. (2000). *The family treatment planner.* New York: Wiley.

DeKay, W. T. (2000). Evolutionary psychology. In W. C. Nichols, M. A. Pace-Nichols, D. S. Becvar, & A. Y. Napier (Eds.), *Handbook of family development and intervention* (pp. 23–40). New York: Wiley.

Dougherty, A. M. (2000). *Psychological consultation and collaboration in school and community settings* (3rd ed.). Belmont, CA: Wadsworth/Thompson.

Duhl, B. S. (2000). Uses of the self in integrated contextual systems therapy. In M. Baldwin (Ed.), *The use of self in therapy* (2nd ed., pp. 107–126). Boston: Haworth Press.

Erikson, E. H. (1968). *Identity: Youth and crisis.* New York: W. W. Norton.

Fischer, A. R., Jome, L. M., & Atkinson, D. R. (1998). Reconceptualizing multicultural counseling: Universal healing conditions in a culturally specific context. *The Counseling Psychologist, 26,* 525–588.

Flores, M. T., & Carey, G. (Eds.). (2000). *Family therapy with Hispanics: Toward appreciating diversity.* Boston: Allyn & Bacon.

Foley, V. D. (1989). Family therapy. In R. J. Corsini & D. Wedding (Eds.), *Current psychotherapies* (4th ed., pp. 455–500). Itasca, IL: F. E. Peacock.

Ford, D. H. (1994). *Humans as self-constructing living systems: A developmental perspective—Behavior and personality* (2nd ed.). State College, PA: IDEALS.

Griffin, W. A., & Greene, S. M. (1999). *Models of family therapy: The essential guide.* Philadelphia: Brunner/Mazel.

Haley, J. (1987). *Problem-solving therapy.* San Francisco: Jossey-Bass.

Hardy, K. V. (Therapist). (1997). *Family systems therapy* (Videotape No. 0-205-32931-4, T. Labriola, Producer). In J. Carlson & D. Kjos, *Family systems with Hardy: Psychotherapy with the experts.* Boston: Allyn & Bacon.

Hayes, A. M., & Strauss, J. L. (1998). Dynamic systems theory as a paradigm for the study of change in psychotherapy: An application to cognitive therapy for depression. *Journal of Consulting and Clinical Psychology, 66*(6), 939–947.

Horne, A. M., & Kiselica, M. S. (Eds.). (1999). *Handbook of counseling boys and adolescent males: A practitioner's guide.* Thousand Oaks, CA: Sage.

Horne, A. M., & Ohlsen, M. M. (Eds.). (1982). *Family counseling and therapy.* Itasca, IL: F. E. Peacock.

James, R. K., Crews, W. E., & Gilliland, B. E. (2000). Systems consultation: Working with a metropolitan police department. In A. M. Dougherty (Ed.), *Psychological consultation and collaboration: A casebook* (3rd ed., pp. 83–102). Belmont, CA: Wadsworth/Thompson.

Jones, E. (1993). *Family systems therapy: Developments in the Milan-Systemic therapies.* Chichester, England: Wiley.

Kadis, L. B., & McClendon, R. (1998). *Concise guide to marital and family therapy.* Washington, DC: American Psychiatric Press.

Kaslow, N. J., Smith, G. G., & Croft, S. S. (2000). Families with young children: A developmental-family systems perspective. In W. C. Nichols, M. A. Pace-Nichols, D. S. Becvar, & A. Y. Napier (Eds.), *Handbook of family development and intervention* (pp. 189–207). New York: Wiley.

Keim, J. (1999). Strategic therapy. In D. M. Lawson & F. F. Prevatt (Eds., pp. 210–231), *Casebook in family therapy.* Belmont, CA: Brooks/Cole.

Kemenoff, S., Jachimczyk, J., & Fussner, A. (1999). Structural family therapy. In D. M. Lawson & F. F. Prevatt (Eds., pp. 111–145) *Casebook in family therapy.* Belmont, CA: Brooks/Cole.

Kerr, M. E., & Bowen, M. (1988). *Family evaluation: An approach based on Bowen theory.* New York: Norton.

Landau-Stanton, J. (1990). Issues and methods of treatment of families in cultural transition. In M. P. Mirkin (Ed.). *The social and political contexts of family therapy* (pp. 251–275). Boston: Allyn & Bacon.

Lawson, D. M. (1999). Integrated intergenerational family therapy. In D. M. Lawson & F. F. Prevatt (Eds., pp. 27–50), *Casebook in family therapy.* Belmont, CA: Brooks/Cole.

Lawson, D. M., & Prevatt, F. F. (Eds.). (1999). *Casebook in family therapy.* Belmont, CA: Brooks/Cole.

Lawrence, E. C. (1999). The humanistic approach of Virginia Satir. In D. M. Lawson & F. F. Prevatt (Eds., pp. 169–187), *Casebook in family therapy.* Belmont, CA: Brooks/Cole.

Madsen, W. C. (1999). *Collaborative therapy with multistressed families: From old problems to new futures.* New York: Guilford Press.

McLendon, J. A. (2000). The Satir system: Brief therapy strategies. In J. Carlson & L. Sperry (Eds.), *Brief therapy with individuals and couples* (pp. 331–364). Phoenix, AZ: Zieg, Tucker, & Theisen.

Minuchin, S. (1974). *Families and family therapy.* Cambridge, MA: Harvard University Press.

Minuchin, S. (1984). *Family kaleidoscope.* Cambridge, MA: Harvard University Press.

Minuchin, S., & Fishman, H. C. (1981). *Family therapy techniques.* Cambridge, MA: Harvard University Press.

Nichols, M. P., & Minuchin, S. (1999). Short-term structural family therapy with couples. In J. M. Donovan (Ed.), *Short-term couple therapy* (pp. 124–143). New York: Guilford Press.

Nichols, W. C. (1999). Family systems therapy. In S. W. Russ & T. H. Ollendick (Eds.), *Handbook of psychotherapies with children and families* (pp. 137–151). New York: Plenum.

Nichols, W. C. (2000). Integrative marital therapy. In F. M. Dattilio & L. J. Bevilacqua (Eds.). *Comparative treatments for relationship dysfunction* (pp. 210–228). New York: Springer.

Nichols, W. C., Pace-Nichols, M. A., Becvar, D. S., & Napier, A. Y. (Eds.). (2000). *Handbook of family development and intervention.* New York: Wiley.

Papero, D. V. (2000). Bowen systems theory. In F. M. Dattilio & L. J. Bevilacqua (Eds.). *Comparative treatments for relationship dysfunction* (pp. 25–44). New York: Springer.

Prieto, L. R., McNeill, B. W., Walls, R. G., & Gomez, S. P. (2001). Chicanas/os and mental health services: An overview of utilization, counselor preference, and assessment issues. *The Counseling Psychologist, 29,* 18–54.

Ridley, C. R. (1995). *Overcoming unintentional racism in counseling and therapy.* Thousand Oaks, CA: Sage.

Ridley, C. R., Li, L. C., & Hill, C. L. (1998). Multicultural assessment: Reexamination, reconceptualization, and practical application. *The Counseling Psychologist, 26,* 827–910.

Rotunda, R. J., Scherer, D. G., & Imm, P. S. (1995). Family systems and alcohol misuse: Research on the effects of alcoholism on family functioning and effective family interventions. *Professional Psychology: Research and Practice, 26,* 95–104.

Santrock, J. W. (1999). *Life-span development* (7th ed.). Boston: McGraw-Hill.

Satir, V. (1967). *Conjoint family therapy.* Palo Alto, CA: Science and Behavior Books.

Satir, V. (1972). *Peoplemaking.* Palo Alto, CA: Science and Behavior Books.

Satir, V. (1975). *Self-esteem.* Millbrae, CA: Celestial Arts.

Satir, V. (1982). The therapist and family therapy. In A. M. Horne & M. M. Ohlsen (Eds.), *Family counseling and therapy* (pp. 12–42). Itasca, IL: F. E. Peacock.

Sharpe, S. A. (2000). *The way we love: A developmental approach to treating couples.* New York: Guilford Press.

Sue, D. W., & Sue, D. (1999). *Counseling the culturally different: Theory and practice* (3rd ed.). New York: Wiley.

Thomas, M. B. (1992). *An introduction to marital and family therapy: Counseling toward healthier family systems across the lifespan.* New York: Macmillan.

Thompson, C. L., & Rudolph, L. B. (2000). *Counseling children* (5th ed.). Belmont, CA: Wadsworth/Thompson.

Webb, W. H. (1999). *Solutioning: Solution-focused interventions for counselors.* Philadelphia: Accelerated Development.

Wehrly, B., Kenney, K. R., & Kenney, M. E. (1999). *Counseling multiracial families.* Thousand Oaks, CA: Sage.

13 Eclectic Counseling and Psychotherapy

An Eclectic Theoretical Orientation

An eclectic theoretical approach does not follow any one theoretical formula, but rather selects and uses from each theory whatever is considered the best in it (Santrock, 1999, p. 47). No single approach depicted in this chapter is indomitable or capable of explaining the rich complexity of the practice of counseling and psychotherapy. Our major objective in presenting this chapter is to show the reader how eclectic counseling and psychotherapy seeks to incorporate the best, most efficacious techniques together from all known and available systems and tailor them to fit the needs of specific clients.

Current Trends

Coming Out of the Enclaves

For many years ideological enclaves have pervaded the practice of counseling and psychotherapy. According to Corsini (1995, p. 10), some of these enclaves are inhabited by therapists who believe they have the "right, the final, the complete and only answer—and that all other systems are incomplete, tentative, weak, or simply mistaken." But we believe, as do Corsini (1995) and Garfield and Bergin (1986), that these ideological boundaries are shrinking and becoming more permeable. Garfield and Bergin have noted that "A decisive shift in opinion has quietly occurred; and it has created an irreversible change in professional attitudes about psychotherapy and behavior change. The new view is that the long-term dominance of the major theories is over and that an eclectic position has taken precedence" (Garfield & Bergin, 1986, p. 7). We take the position that most good counselors and therapists are eclectics.

Counseling Theories as Theory Stories

In a postmodern perspective, Larsen (1999) proposed that all psychological theories could be viewed as stories. Labeling psychological theories as theory stories, she argues that they reflect the life experiences of their founders and authors as well as their sociopolitical context. By conceiving of psychology itself as a discipline of stories, she proposes that theory stories are likely to contain many similar themes despite strong differences. These similarities exist because all theory stories are born of human experience. The author further suggests that past theory stories have the potential to inform, deconstruct, and add depth to current postmodern counseling practice. This provides justification for the importance of eclecticism in counseling and psychotherapy. As an example, Larsen explores two theories, logotherapy and radical behaviorism, for their fit within a postmodern framework. Frankl's existential logotherapy is conceptualized as a search for meaning whereas Skinner's behaviorist approach conceptualizes an individual's story as behavior in context. Finally, by viewing theory as a story, it is proposed that eclecticism provides the necessary tools to explore story alternatives when liberating clients from oppressive story lines.

Movement Toward Integration

Since the 1950s there has been an increasing trend for counselors and psychotherapists to report that their practices are based on a combination or integration of theoretical methods and approaches, rather than being grounded in one pure approach (Garfield & Kurtz, 1975; Hollanders & McLeod, 1999; Smith, 1982). Furthermore, the more experience a practitioner has had, the more likely he or she is to believe in and practice an eclectic modality (Hollanders & McLeod, 1999). That trend is only one reason why we deemed it essential for this book to address eclectic theory.

When we consider the numerous theories and schools of counseling and psychotherapy being favored and used by practitioners in the early years of the twenty-first century, we find that about half the major systems are of recent vintage. Prior to 1950, three major schools predominated: (1) the psychoanalytic or insight theories (Freud, Jung, Adler); (2) trait-factor theories (Williamson, Darley); and (3) humanistic/existential theories (Maslow, Rogers). Since about 1960, the young theories (behavioral, cognitive, REBT, choice/reality, TA, Gestalt) have emerged into prominence. They are less than fifty years old. We point this out to drive home the fact that much of the material found in this book is based on recent developments. Therefore, we are convinced that the *one true path* to effective psychotherapy has not yet emerged.

The competent eclectic counselor must be flexible enough to choose an appropriate theoretical system to use with different clients or a variety of presenting problems. Even during a counseling session, if an impasse has been reached, the counselor knows when to select another theory and which system to employ. While some theorists have suggested that eclecticism is a jack-of-all-trades, master-of-none approach (Linden, 1984; Russell, 1986), eclectic counseling and psychotherapy as we propose it is *not* a nondescript, disorganized, nonsystematic modality. It is our view that a therapist who is *not* adept and proficient enough to change techniques as the therapeutic conditions require, but who espouses one dogmatic view, will usually experience frustration and failure. Sometimes adherents to one particular modality purport to have more answers for the human dilemma than the others. Many of these adherents organize their own systems of training, certification, and enfranchisement (Buie, 1988). The essence of their claims is that each one can solve client problems better than the others. Such claims are questionable.

Differing Views of Eclecticism

Perceptions of an eclectic system of therapy seem to be distributed roughly among proponents, opponents, and those who are neither. Proponents, such as Brammer, Shostrom, and

Abrego (1989), Cormier and Cormier (1991), Corsini (1981), Garfield (1980), Lazarus (1987, 1989c), Norcross (1986, 1987), and Patterson (1986) recommend a broad-based, integrated system of therapy that makes systematic and appropriate use of the best of techniques from all known theories.

Opponents, such as Chessick (1985), Linden (1984), Russell (1986), and Stall (1984), tend either to diminish or seriously to question the efficacy of eclecticism. Their opposition is usually related to what they perceive as a lack of one or more foundational bases, whether historical, theoretical, conceptual, or empirical.

Individuals who support both pro and con positions on eclectic psychotherapy—or neither—include Berman (1985), Borgen (1984), Colapinto (1984), Ellis (1984), Eysenck (1984), Rychlak (1986), Scheidlinger (1984), and Sims and Sauser (1985). They tend to view the use of eclectic techniques as a selective matter rather than as a synthesis or a broad-based system of psychotherapy.

Fundamental Tenets

History

Eclectic counseling and psychotherapy received scant recognition until well after World War II. More than two decades of seminal work by Frederick C. Thorne (1950, 1973) and other scientist-practitioners helped eclecticism finally emerge as a respectable modality amid a very competitive therapeutic environment. By the early twenty-first century the eclectic approach had moved to center stage in the arena of psychotherapeutic intervention.

Evolution of Theory-Based Practices. From the early 1900s until shortly after World War II, Freudian psychoanalysis was the predominant theoretical and clinical modality. Numerous psychoanalytic spin-offs, such as Adlerian and Jungian therapies, took root in the United States and began to expand. Clients were usually referred to as patients. Helping them derive insight, primarily from the unconscious psyche, was the primary goal of most psychoanalytically oriented therapies. From the late 1940s until about 1970, hundreds of schools of psychoanalysis and different approaches to counseling and psychotherapy emerged. Rogers's nondirective therapy evolved into client-centered therapy and later emerged as person-centered therapy. Several other humanistic theories, such as Rollo May's existential theory, continued to be used, albeit on a minimum scale compared to all the other brands of psychotherapy. Albert Ellis's rational-emotive therapy (RET) was formulated and was later refined and became widely recognized and practiced as rational-emotive behavior therapy (REBT). Around 1958, behavior therapy began to appear on the scene. It has grown through several iterations and is still a viable system today, with far wider application and appeal than it had in its beginnings. William Glasser's reality therapy, later known as control theory, and more recently transformed into choice theory, came on the scene. Other systems, such as Gestalt therapy, trait-factor counseling, transactional analysis (TA), cognitive-behavior therapy, systems therapy, cognitive therapy, and many others became popularized and each enjoyed a substantial following of adherents. Amid this flurry of growth, the virtues of technical eclecticism also began to be recognized (Lazarus, 2000b).

Emergence of an Eclectic, Ecological Climate.   From the 1960s to the 1990s, private practice increased exponentially, managed care and HMOs were established, and the marketplace was inundated with numerous brands of counselors and therapists. Multiculturalism or diversity became a major focus. New age therapists, power therapies, brief therapies (such as solution-focused brief therapy), and computerized tracking, under the sway of advertising and market-driven influences, began to dominate the landscape of therapeutic practice (Lazarus, 2000b). By the time of the arrival of the twenty-first century, corporate-based management of counseling and psychological practices controlled a large percentage of the mental health services dollar. The professional associations of psychologists, counselors, and social workers were mounting organized campaigns in the process of lobbying state and federal governments to step in and regulate the equitable allocation and distribution of mental health services. In a nutshell, that eclectic ecological and environmental climate defines the circumstance in which eclectic counselors and psychotherapists currently operate.

Evolution of Eclecticism.   Frederick C. Thorne (1950) is credited with developing the first systematic position, which he called an attempt to gather "an eclectic collection and evaluation of all known methods in terms of empiric experience" (p. xiii). From 1945 until his death in 1978, Thorne made a formidable contribution toward integrating all psychological knowledge into a comprehensive and systematic approach to counseling and psychotherapy (Thorne, 1955, 1960, 1961, 1965, 1967, 1968). Even though few writers and researchers in the 1950s and early 1960s ventured into the arena as eclectics, eclecticism among practitioners grew at a phenomenal rate. Patterson (1980), reporting on Thorne's comments on the shifts in attitude toward eclecticism, stated that whereas in 1945 no members of the American Psychological Association's (APA) Division of Clinical Psychology identified themselves as eclectics, by 1970 more than 50 percent referred to themselves as eclectic (p. 572). In the mid-1970s, Garfield and Kurtz (1975) reported that of the 733 members of the APA Division of Clinical Psychology, 470, or 64 percent, gave their orientation as eclectic. It appears that outside the United States similar movements toward an eclectic viewpoint have taken place. For example, Warner (1991) found that eclecticism was the leading theoretical orientation among Canadian psychologists. Later, researchers Hollanders and McLeod (1999) found that as many as 87 percent of British counselors reported that they practiced a non-pure or eclectic model.

Since Thorne's initial attempts to formulate an eclectic approach, the movement has become broad-based and multifaceted. From the late 1960s through 1977, Robert Carkhuff and his colleagues developed, tested, and researched a comprehensive, systematic, integrated, eclectic developmental model that incorporated proven relationship, problem-solving, and training skills into the scientific selection and preparation of prospective helpers (Carkhuff, 1969a, 1969b, 1993; Carkhuff & Berenson, 1977). Carkhuff's work was a monumental breakthrough because the skills he advocates for helpers are the same skills needed by anyone to function effectively.

Egan (1975, 1982, 1986, 1990, 1994) and Cormier and Cormier (1998, pp. 11–220) demonstrated the integration of the best-known therapeutic relationship skills into goal-oriented systematic counseling. They drew from four major sources: systematic skills training systems, social influence theory, behavioral and learning theory, and scientific-based cognitive-behavioral interventions. These clinically oriented works successfully incorporated developmental ideas and strategies, self-understanding, and action/problem-solving skills. The Egan, Cormier, and Carkhuff models have been used extensively in the training of counselors, psychotherapists, and other helpers.

Overview of Eclecticism

Concomitant with the pros and cons of eclecticism, the known systems or approaches to counseling and psychotherapy are clearly evolving or changing. It appears that none of the theoretical systems is becoming more narrow or restrictive in their foci. The eclectic trend is really twofold—more and more practitioners and theorists are identifying themselves as adhering to some type of eclecticism (Brammer, Shostrom, & Abrego, 1989; Castonguay & Goldfried, 1994; Corsini & Wedding, 1995; D'Andrea & Daniels, 1994; Duncan, Parks, & Rusk, 1990; Fischer, 1995; Garfield, 1994; Lazarus, 1995a, 1995b, 1997; Norcross, 1995; Patterson, 1986; Watkins & Watts, 1995; Zook & Walton, 1989) and existing schools of therapy are moving toward a broader or more eclectic stance. All the surveys we have seen have indicated that eclecticism is the leading theoretical orientation among psychologists and counselors in the United States, Canada, and Great Britain.

In this chapter we hope to present eclectic counseling and psychotherapy in a way that will bridge the gap between theory and practice. One goal is to acquaint the reader with a variety of theoretical tenets, counseling processes, and helping strategies that eclectic counselors typically use. Another goal is to show how specific strategies, or clusters of strategies, can be put to use in an organized and consistent framework. We present our Expanded Eight-Stage Systematic Counseling Model and several clusters or categories of strategies for implementing the model. A sample case illustrates some of the eclectic counselor's options and behaviors.

Personality

Eclectic counselors are concerned about personality theory because they recognize that the validity of an eclectic approach rests on the state of its supporting knowledge. Thorne (1970), the principal architect of eclectic theory, said that "the ultimate clinical validation of any theoretical viewpoint . . . is a function of breadth of phenomena which the system is able to clarify and explain. . . ." (p. 142). The validation of eclectic counseling and psychotherapy necessarily requires a broad-spectrum view of personality to undergird a multifaceted approach to the counseling process.

Eclectic personality theory incorporates the valid elements from all theories into a framework for clarifying human behavior. But its primary source of data, according to Thorne (1961), Palmer (1980), and Ivey (1997), is the study of individuals in day-to-day living in a constantly changing world. Thorne (1961) developed an original comprehensive set of formulations on personality development, starting with the premise that "the Person is the basic datum and the only proper subject in the global unit of the 'person-running-the-business-of-his-life-in-the-world' " (Thorne, 1973, p. 455). He contended that personality theory should be derived inductively from the first-hand study of individual cases over a broad time frame using a person-centered approach. Both Lazarus

(2000a, 2000b) and Leger (1998) would extend Thorne's perspective on personality development. Lazarus' multimodal orientation is predicated on the theory that most psychological problems are "multifaceted, multidetermined, and multilayered, and that comprehensive therapy calls for careful assessment of seven parameters or 'modalities': behavior, affect, sensation, imagery, cognition, interpersonal relationships, and biological processes" (Lazarus, 2000b, pp. 93–94). Similarly, Leger (1998) contends that a theory that avoids the fractionalization of the person must address the behavioral, biological, and cognitive foundations of the human personality.

The eclectic view of personality includes the concepts of integration, psychological states, dynamic change, developmental aspects of the organism, and social-cultural factors, with integration and psychological states constituting the core concepts (Thorne, 1961, 1967). Traditional views of static traits and personality structures are not considered valid predictors of behavior because they do not account for constant and rapid change. The human organism is viewed as continually striving to achieve and maintain the highest possible level of integration. Integration assumes that the human organism operates in a continuously evolving world and that the organism is itself constantly developing, changing, and experiencing different levels of integration. These varying levels of integration affect each other and change with time as the human develops. The highest order of human integration, which the individual theoretically strives toward, is self-actualization or satisfactory integration of all levels of need. The master motive is seen as personal enhancement, which we equate with self-actualization.

Psychological states rather than personality traits are another central focus in eclectic personality theory. Thorne (1973) views behavior (personality) as being in a continuous flux—always evolving and changing in a changing universe. Accordingly, the "Law of Universal Change" postulates that behavior is a result of (1) organismic status (but is not static), (2) situational status (in a changing interpersonal milieu), and (3) the human situation or condition in general. The stream of human life (or the psychological state), then, is an important source for studying behavior (personality) (Thorne, 1973, pp. 455–456).

Although most of the recognized proponents of eclectic systems of counseling and psychotherapy do not specify the personality theories that undergird their approaches, all of them are based on some global set of principles for understanding and predicting human behavior (Garfield, 1994; Ivey, 1997; Watkins & Watts, 1995).

Major Concepts

Eclecticism, as such, has few major concepts. Thorne (1973, p. 451) identified several "necessary tasks" of eclecticism, which come as close to being concepts as we can find. One task is to "identify" valid elements in all systems and to integrate them into a mutually consistent whole that does justice to the behavior data to be explained. A second task is to consider "all pertinent theories, methods, and standards for evaluating and manipulating clinical data according to the most advanced knowledge of time and place." A third task is to identify with no specific theory, keep an open mind, and continually experiment with those formulations and strategies that produce valid results.

Based on the works of Carkhuff and Berenson (1977), Garfield (1980), Palmer (1980), and Thorne (1967, 1968, 1973), a number of statements can be made that summarize the concepts or descriptive positions of the eclectic movement in counseling and psychotherapy. Eclecticism assumes that the client's primary need is to achieve and maintain the highest feasible level of integration across time. It deals with the client's current psychological state within the client's emergent world and views consciousness as a central focal point. The approach is scientific, systematic, and logical without identifying with any proprietary school. Eclectics are constantly evolving and changing to incorporate new ideas, concepts, techniques, and research findings. They do not operate on faith, guesswork, emotion, popularity, special interest, or ideological consistency as ends in themselves.

Eclecticism deals *directly with the person* in the person's rapidly changing and complex world, taking into account the person's developmental state and cultural, social, and personal values and goals (as opposed to talking *about* or theorizing *about* the person). Eclectics focus directly on the person's behaviors, goals, problems, and so on (as opposed to talking *about* behaviors, goals, or problems). They also recognize and deal with problem situations that are primarily outside the client's ability to control them, such as prejudice, poverty, handicapping environment, and cultural/ethnic diversities among helpers and clients.

Encapsulated, the foregoing list has these main thrusts: The eclectic counselor *makes the client fully aware* of the problem situation, *teaches the client consciously and intentionally to choose* to exercise control over the problem behavior, and *assists the client in developing a higher level of integration* through his or her proactive choice. To help the client understand and deal with the integrative processes, the helper may function in a variety of roles, such as counselor, psychotherapist, teacher, consultant, facilitator, mentor, adviser, or coach. According to Thorne (1967), eclecticism is the only approach global enough in its scope to deal effectively with the broad spectrum of factors potentially influencing the integrative process.

The Counseling Process

Introducing an Eclectic Model

Our Expanded Eight-Stage Systematic Counseling Model is presented as one example of an eclectic counseling model in the hope that readers will understand that eclecticism embraces many different processes. The eight-stage model incorporates the necessary global processes required to qualify as a true eclectic system. No single counseling process can be truly representative of the whole array of possibilities available to eclectics. An eclectic viewpoint incorporates the therapeutic processes of most recognized systems. Two global process phases of psychotherapy, resulting from many years of clinical judgment and study by Thorne (1950, 1968), are contained in some form in many eclectic models: (1) effective case handling involves the appropriate psychological conditions whereby the necessary relationship with the client can be established, and (2) effective case handling outcomes derive from the use of behavior modification strategies that facilitate positive change in clients.

Focus on Client Growth in Systematic Counseling:
Stages in a Systematic Counseling Model

In the systematic counseling model we draw on the theories, philosophies, tenets, constructs, relationship skills, processes, techniques, and strategies of all known theory systems or skills in counseling. We assume that: (1) no two clients or client situations are alike; (2) each client and counselor is in a constant state of flux—no person or situation in counseling is or can ever be static; (3) the effective counselor exhibits a flexible repertoire of activity on a continuum from nondirective to directive; (4) the client is the world's greatest expert on his or her problem; (5) the counselor uses all the available personal and professional resources in the helping situation but is fully human in the relationship and cannot ultimately be responsible *for* the client; (6) counselors and the counseling process are fallible and cannot expect to observe overt or immediate success in every counseling or client situation; (7) competent counselors are aware of their own personal professional qualifications and deficits and take responsibility for ensuring that the counseling process is handled ethically and in the best interest of the client and of the public; (8) client safety takes precedence over counselor need fulfillment; (9) there are many different approaches and strategies available for conceptualizing and dealing with each problem—there is probably no one *best* approach or strategy; (10) many problems in the human dilemma appear to be insoluble (indeed for some problem situations we sometimes believe we can find no satisfactory options), but always there is a variety of alternatives, and some alternatives are better for the client than others; (11) generally, effective counseling is a process that is undertaken *with* the client rather than *to* or *for* the client.

The systematic counseling model can be represented in eight stages, which we conceptualize as operating in a fluid process rather than in a series of mechanistic, compartmentalized steps. Figure 13.1 shows the process flow for the model. We emphasize the arrows denoting feedback loops and fluidity of the process. We have organized the model in stages mainly to clarify and facilitate the instructional aspects of application of the model to the actual counseling process. The essence of the eclectic model is the continu-

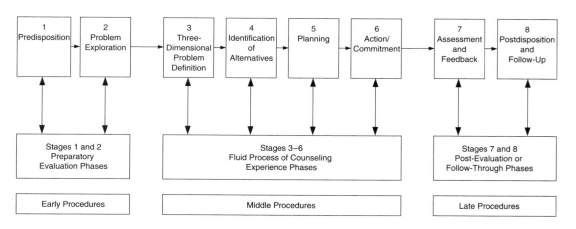

FIGURE 13.1   Expanded Eight-Stage Systematic Counseling Model

ous, systematic, integrative flow of counseling strategies and interactions from pre- to post-disposition stages.

Stage One: Predisposition

Counselor's Process Goals: Initiating contact prior to the first formal counseling session via telephone, computer link, or face-to-face contact; setting the stage for treatment and change; recruitment of client cooperation; stabilizing and restoring equilibrium and homeostasis if a crisis is in evidence; dealing with issues of client safety if needed; informing the client of treatment processes; obtaining a specific description of the problem; assessing problem severity, coping skills possessed, and prior attempts at solution; targeting exceptions to the problem; reinforcing help-seeking behavior; initiating establishment of rapport and trust; predisposing client to anticipate therapeutic activities of counselor and to expect counseling to succeed (deShazer, 1985, 1988; Haas & Cummings, 1991; Hoyt & Miller, 2000; Hubble, Duncan, & Miller, 1999; Miller, Duncan, & Hubble, 1997; Prochaska & DiClemente, 1982, 1984; Prochaska, DiClemente, & Norcross, 1992; Stromberg, Loeb, Thomsen, & Krause, 1996; Thompson & Rudolph, 2000).

Theoretical Basis: Stage-appropriate change-oriented brief or solution-focused therapy (Hoyt & Miller, 2000, pp. 289–330) to assess client commitment and motivation to change, to establish pretreatment goals, to conduct a client self-assessment, to prepare the client for induction into counseling, to seed expectations for success; Six-Step Crisis Intervention Model (James & Gilliland, 2001, pp. 31–35) to determine the degree and kind of problem, safety issues, and support needs; Triage Assessment Scale (Myer, Williams, Ottens, & Schmidt, 1992) to determine problem severity across affective, behavioral, and cognitive dimensions of the client's functioning; use of person-centered (Rogers, 1951), integrative, or existential therapy (Carkhuff, 1969a, 1969b, 1973, 1993; Egan, 1986, 1990, 1994; Ivey, 1997) models of helping to provide concreteness, empathy, congruence, and unconditional positive regard for building a trusting relationship; taking cognizance of mounting research evidence that sets the stage for counseling success, or predisposing the client to expect the counseling to succeed (this may be as critical or even more so than much of the counseling process itself) (deShazer, 1985, 1988; Haas & Cummings, 1991; Hoyt & Miller, 2000; Hubble, Duncan, & Miller, 1999; Miller, Duncan, & Hubble, 1997; Prochaska & DiClemente, 1982, 1984; Prochaska, DiClemente, & Norcross, 1992); taking note of the fact that the days of long-term, cookie-cutter therapeutic interventions are long past because of managed health care's insistence on efficiency and behavioral outcomes; recognizing that today's clients are far more likely to be given specific, tailor-made interventions that call for a great deal of outpatient, psychoeducational, and consultative treatment approaches; being aware that the efficacy and success of specific treatment goals matched to client success have led to managed care's absolute insistence on monitoring clients' long-term aftercare; the knowledge that predisposition is now becoming almost mandatory both for ethical reasons and for reimbursement by third-party payers (deShazer, 1985, 1988; Haas & Cummings, 1991; Hoyt & Miller, 2000; Hubble et al., 1999; Miller et al., 1997; Stomberg et al., 1996; Thompson & Rudolph, 2000).

Stage Two: Problem Exploration

Counselor's Process Goals: Establishing rapport; listening to client concerns; responding in ways that encourage the client to explore his or her concerns on a deeper level; developing mutual trust; permitting the client to ventilate whenever ventilation is needed; attending to verbal and nonverbal behavior; attending to affect as well as content; being genuine, real, empathic, caring, prizing, nonjudgmental, nonpossessive, and as accepting as possible in the relationship (Carkhuff, 1969a, 1969b, 1993; Cormier & Cormier, 1998, pp. 11–298; Egan, 1990, 1994; Hackney & Cormier, 1988, pp. 13–49); paying close attention to how the client sees and understands the world (Ivey, 1997).

Theoretical Basis: Person- or client-centered, integrative, existential or cognitive-behavior therapy; use of effective relationship skills for facilitative listening and responding; the Carkhuff Model (1969a, 1969b, 1993), the Cormier and Cormier Model (1998), and the Egan Model (1986, 1990, 1994) are appropriate examples for counselor use during the exploration stage because they provide for a full range of helper relationship skills.

Stage Three: Three-Dimensional Problem Definition

Counselor's Process Goals: The affective, cognitive, and behavioral aspects of the client's problem are attended to by the counselor; thinking, feeling, and factual aspects of the problem are verbalized until there is an understanding between the client and the counselor (both the client and the counselor can agree on problem definition in precise and concrete terms); that this definition enables both the client and the counselor to ascertain the etiological base of the problem; any lack of agreement on the definition returns the process to stage two.

Theoretical Base: Person- or client-centered, integrative, existential, or cognitive-behavior therapy (same relationship skills for facilitative listening and responding as used in stage two).

Stage Four: Identification of Alternatives

Counselor's Process Goals: The identification and examination of the current alternatives available, including physical and emotional safety; all reasonable options should be expressed and openly examined; the counselor may make a written list of alternatives during the session; the client is encouraged to enumerate and verbalize as many viable alternatives as possible that he or she views as appropriate, realistic, and options that he or she can own; the counselor may use open-ended questions to clarify the client's options; the counselor does not impose alternatives on the client; the client may be given homework assignments to discover additional alternatives; referral resources and consultants may be used; an important process goal for stage four is the discovery of appropriate alternatives for immediate use.

Theoretical Basis: Person-centered, choice theory/reality therapy, psychoanalytic, object relations, rational-emotive behavioral, Adlerian, Gestalt, behavioral therapy, cognitive therapy, transactional analysis, multimodal, integrative, and systems theories are examples of systems that may be used in examining the alternatives that are available to the client; elements from more than one system or approach are likely to be used during stage four.

Stage Five: Planning

Counselor's Process Goals: Critical evaluation of alternatives is identified; plan may include rehearsal, role playing, suggestion, or emotive imagery of action steps planned by the client; assisting the client in deciding which and how many alternatives are appropriate and realistic in view of the client's past level of performance and present readiness to risk and respond; the counselor may serve as a teacher, mentor, or model for selected planning elements; the counselor may use suggestion or didactic techniques in cases in which the client needs to know (e.g., not all problems can be systematically solved, some situations require time for healing, some can be only partially alleviated to minimize debilitating effects, or "we can't control what others do or think, nor can we be responsible for others"; development of a realistic, success-oriented, workable plan is a primary goal of this stage; any plan is tentative and approached pragmatically but treated as important; client ownership of a realistic plan is the optimum goal of the planning stage.

Theoretical Basis: Person-centered, choice theory/reality therapy, psychoanalytic, object relations, rational-emotive behavioral, Adlerian, Gestalt, behavioral therapy, cognitive therapy, transactional analysis, multimodal, integrative, and systems theories are examples of systems that may be used in the planning of appropriate action steps that the client can reasonably take; elements from more than one system or approach are likely to be used in stage five.

Stage Six: Action/Commitment

Counselor's Process Goals: Genuine commitment to workable *action steps* by the client is the primary goal; it is important for the client to decide which action steps to undertake in terms of reality, time, emotional capability, and need fulfillment; the client's commitment is specific; the counselor is personally involved and genuinely supportive but cannot *do* action steps *for* the client; the client views the action steps as viable and goal-related and shows willingness to try; nonattainment or partial attainment of the goal on the first trial is understood realistically by the client who knows in advance that partial success on one trial is neither catastrophe, failure, nor total success; the counselor's role in the commitment stage is clearly supportive and is intended to help the client achieve optimum success and to assist the client in assessing progress and refining the plan; the counselor asks the client to summarize the plan and commitment prior to terminating the interview; client's action/commitment is normally a starting point for the next interview.

Theoretical Basis: Person-centered, choice theory/reality therapy, psychoanalytic, object relations, rational-emotive behavioral, Adlerian, Gestalt, behavioral therapy, cognitive therapy, transactional analysis, multimodal, integrative, and systems theories are examples of systems that may be used in helping the client make a realistic action or commitment toward successful behavior, goal attainment, decision, or internal attitudinal change; more than one system or approach is likely to be used during stage six.

Stage Seven: Assessment and Feedback

Counselor's Process Goals: The client usually summarizes the progress made toward attainment of the goal based on an action or commitment at the previous session; both the client and the counselor review and assess the level of goal attainment in terms of the client's needs, feelings, and present coping level; further discussion and evaluation of plan are conducted if assessment of attainment level or if the client's current needs so indicate; feedback and assessment data may be processed by the counselor and the client in light of the client's desire for additional attainment or in terms of the client's need to work on another problem; the counselor may continue as a monitor and a support person, helping the client on the same goal (maybe more rehearsal or imagery is needed, more time required, or additional refinements to the plan are needed); the systematic counseling model is viewed as fluid, melding from stage two through seven as appropriate and is required to respond to the client's needs; the counselor focus may go immediately from stage seven to any other stage; collaborative assessment governs direction and focus of client–counselor interaction during each interview following predisposition and the formal initial session.

Theoretical Basis: Theoretical approaches in assessment feedback stage are selected on the basis of their having developed and tested mechanisms and experienced success in a wide range of client assessments and feedback; person-centered, choice theory/ reality therapy, psychoanalytic, object relations, rational-emotive behavioral, Adlerian, Gestalt, behavioral therapy, cognitive therapy, transactional analysis, multimodal, integrative, and systems theories are examples of systems that may be used to help the client make an assessment that helps him or her determine to what degree, if any, outcomes resultant from counseling achieved the desired level or if needs were satisfactorily met; elements from one or more theoretical systems may be used during the assessment and feedback stage.

Stage Eight: Post-Disposition and Follow-Up

Counselor's Process Goals: Reinforcing, reevaluating, and checking the client's progress in applying to daily life what has been learned in counseling; assessing degree of long-term goal attainment, long-term goal maintenance, relapse prevention, positive leave-taking, and termination.

Theoretical Basis: Stage-appropriate change-oriented brief- or solution-focused therapy (Hoyt & Miller, 2000, pp. 289–330) and trait and factor clinical procedures (Williamson & Darley, 1937); both theories provide long-term evaluation in regard to the degree of client success and/or the need for further therapy.

Foundational Perspective

The Expanded Eight-Stage Systematic Counseling Model rests on three foundation stones. Stage one, predisposition, and stage two, problem exploration, are generally based on a preparatory evaluation block that denotes the early procedures of the counseling relationship.

Stage three, three-dimensional problem definition, stage four, identification of alternatives, stage five, planning, and stage six, action commitment, function on the fluid process of counseling experience phases block. These four stages comprise the middle procedures phases of the counseling process.

Stage seven, assessment and feedback, and stage eight, post-disposition and follow-up, rest on the post-evaluation or follow-through phases block. These two phases constitute the late procedures that wrap up the counseling process and relationship.

The Process of Eclectic Counseling

Great flexibility in theory, style, and technique is inherent in the systematic model or any eclectic model. One should not infer from the considerable flexibility, however, that there is lack of organization or that this involves a hodgepodge of arbitrary, inconsistent, or contradictory assumptions and methods. The systematic model as well as every true eclectic model embodies a planned, systematic, consistent base of assumptions, formulations, and methods (Castonguay & Goldfried, 1994; Watkins & Watts, 1995).

Even though eclectic counselors are knowledgeable and skilled and have mastered several theoretical approaches, they do not have to be expert in every process. They are flexible, versatile, sensitive, and capable of using the best of each theoretical system in appropriate ways. Eclectics view themselves as continuous learners and accept themselves as fallible human beings. There is no place for perfectionist tendencies or parochial dogma in eclectic counseling.

Strategies for Helping Clients

Overview

We have organized the various strategies in clusters or categories to facilitate presentation and discussion of the numerous techniques available to the eclectic counselor. The ten categories focus on relationships, interviewing, assessment, idea generation, case handling, gaining insight, behavior management, evaluation and termination, personal and professional growth, and research. We cite several representative exponents or references (from various theoretical orientations) that we identify with each cluster of strategies. We also give a thumbnail encapsulation of the general implications and perspectives of both the counselor and the client as they experience appropriate use of the strategies.

Categories of Counseling Strategies

We have arranged the ten categories or clusters of strategies in Table 13.1. We recognize that our arrangement contains some overlapping. For instance, several of the techniques under case handling could very well be placed in other categories. Also, there is overlap between assessment and evaluation and termination. We preferred to make separate categories to preserve certain distinctions. We believe the cluster format of Table 13.1 serves as a concise and systematic means of portraying eclectic strategies.

TABLE 13.1 Categories of Counseling Strategies

Counseling Strategy Category	Representative Exponents or References	Implications of Strategies for Feeling, Thinking, Behaving, and Learning	
		From the Counselor's Perspectives and Behaviors/Goals	From the Client's Perspectives and Behaviors/Goals
Relationship Strategies	Brammer (1985, 1990); Carkhuff (1969a, 1969b, 1993); Cormier & Cormier (1991, 1998); Egan (1986, 1994); Hackney & Cormier (1988); May & Yalom (1995); Raskin & Rogers (1995); Rogers (1951)	Attending, listening, respecting, responding, caring, empathic understanding, accepting, being genuine, trusting, being open, creating a climate of unconditional positive regard; ensuring physical/emotional safety of client	Trusting self and others; feeling understood, valued, respected, worthwhile, secure, and authentic; experiencing a climate of acceptance or unconditional positive regard; getting in touch with own feelings, values, choices, and inner motives
Interviewing Strategies	Beck & Weishaar (1995); Cormier & Cormier (1991, 1998); deShazer (1985, 1988); Hoyt & Miller (2000); Ivey (1997); Ivey & Authier (1978); Raskin & Rogers (1995); Thompson & Rudolph (2000); Thorne (1968)	Identifying purposes of counseling: selectively responding to help client clarify problem situation and present and desired level of functioning; using summarized restatements, open-ended questions; responding to both verbal and nonverbal messages of client	Clarification of problem dimensions; discrimination among own internal/external, emotional/behavioral functioning; recognizing desired direction and/or level of own future functioning
Assessment Strategies	Adler (1963); Cormier & Cormier (1991, 1998); Gambrill (1977); James & Gilliland (2001); Lazarus (1995b, 1997); Neimeyer & Neimeyer (1990); Thorne (1968); Williamson (1965)	Problem definition, diagnosis, prognosis, goal selection, needs assessment, determination of appropriate helping resources/techniques available; assessing coping levels of client and social/environmental implications for client; examining global and isolated, simple and complex, and long-term and short-term nature of client's situation	Problem exploration and definition; realistic goal setting and selection; surveying and understanding own attitudes, interests, abilities, problems, goals, resources, potentials, and social/environmental conditions; evaluating effects of own goals in terms of global/isolated, simple/complex, and long-term/short-term dimensions

Strategy	References	Counselor Role	Client Outcomes
Idea-Generation Strategies	Carkhuff (1973, 1993); Gambrill (1977); Glasser (1984, 1996, 1998, 2000); Kelly (1955); Miller, Duncan, & Hubble (1997); Prochaska & DiClemente (1984); Prochaska, DiClemente, & Norcross (1992); Williams & Long (1983); Williamson (1965)	Exploration and identification of options, alternatives, behaviors, rewards, consequences, wants, and incentives that impinge on and are appropriate to client's goals; helping client generate both overt and covert alternatives; intervening in collaborative, nondirective, or directive mode (as needed) to facilitate client recognition of viable choices and formulation of concrete list of realistic choices	Discovery of repertoire of realistic options available; generation of overt and covert alternatives, both cognitive and behavioral; developing usable ideas for improving or changing own thinking, doing, and feeling patterns; expanding own awareness of the vast number of alternatives available and of own role in initiating and implementing alternatives
Case-Handling Strategies	Beck & Weishaar (1995); Cormier & Cormier (1998); Ellis deShazer (1985, 1988); Ellis (1995); Gambrill (1977); Glasser (1965, 1984, 1996, 1998, 2000); Hoyt & Miller (2000); Hubble, Duncan, & Miller (1999); James & Gilliland (2001); Kelly (1955); Lazarus (1995b, 1997); Palmer (1980); Thorne (1968); Watson & Tharp (1989)	Selecting and systematically using appropriate techniques, referral resources, modeling, reinforcement contingencies; facilitative responding and other helping strategies to intervene, influence, teach, lead, support, inspire, collaborate with and otherwise help client attain desired goals in positive and responsible ways; preserve client autonomy, rights, and independence during counseling	Learning to cope, adjust, change internal views, improve behavior, alter environment, make social adjustment, choose and discriminate among alternatives, gain independence, follow modeled adaptive patterns of behavior, gain confidence and self-esteem; coping with and incorporating new information and innovative adaptive choices into own lifestyle
Insight Strategies	Adler (1963); Auld & Hyman (1991); Douglas (1995); Ellis (1979, 1995); Ellis & Harper (1975); Freud (1949, 1961); Kelly (1955); Kohut (1971, 1977, 1984); Lazarus (1989a; 1989b, 1989c, 1997); Maslow (1976); Polster & Polster (1973); Scharff & Scharff (1998); St. Clair (1996); Summers (1999)	Facilitating discovery of polar conflicts; helping client gain recognition of early life traumas that may have contributed to current problems; setting up conditions so client can discover and deal with developmental deficits; confronting client in responsible, constructive, and helpful ways; dealing with client's conscious, unconscious, and altered conscious thoughts to help client understand past cognitions and restrictive present/future conditions affecting feeling, thinking, behaving, and learning	Discovering conflicting polarities within self; recognizing that past unresolved traumas (perhaps during own childhood) are a basis for current problems; gaining a mental connectedness, from the past, of developmental deficits that may contribute to present developmental difficulties and gaining mental self-images of successful coping or acting to remediate for such deficits; confronting own biases, deficits, conflicting values, polar conflicts, and emotional disturbances in positive and constructive ways; learning to understand own inner functioning through analysis of dreams, projections, free associations, fantasies, drawings, and other methods of gaining access to the unconscious

Continued

TABLE 13.1 Continued

| | | Implications of Strategies for Feeling, Thinking, Behaving, and Learning | |
Counseling Strategy Category	Representative Exponents or References	From the Counselor's Perspectives and Behaviors/Goals	From the Client's Perspectives and Behaviors/Goals
Behavior-Management Strategies	Beck & Weishaar (1995); Cormier & Cormier (1985, 1991, 1998); Gambrill (1977); Kanfer & Goldstein (1975); Krumboltz & Thoresen (1976); Lazarus (1989c, 1995b, 1997); Meichenbaum (1972); Skinner (1953); Thoresen (1980); Williams & Long (1983); Wilson (1995); Wolpe (1969)	Acting and modeling in a variety of helping roles, such as counselor, therapist, teacher, mentor, consultant, facilitator, and support person; intervening in a variety of modes from directive to collaborative to nondirective; facilitating the client to change thinking and behaving from maladaptive to adaptive and to change and/or cope with a changing, complex physical and social environment; applying all known behavioral techniques in scientific approach to helping client	Implementing strategies to extinguish maladaptive thinking and behaving and to develop adaptive thinking and behaving; developing skills to change and/or cope with a changing, complex physical and social environment; learning the behavioral skills and techniques to develop ability scientifically to manage own lifestyle according to tested behavioral principles
Evaluation and Termination Strategies	Cormier & Cormier (1991, 1998); deShazer (1985, 1988); Haas & Cummings (1991); Hansen, Stevic, & Warner (1977); Hoyt & Miller (2000); Hubble, Duncan, & Miller (1999); Palmer (1980); Pietrofesa, Hoffman, Splete, & Pinto (1978); Thorne (1973)	Evaluating counseling effectiveness and outcomes; assessing appropriateness of concepts, assumptions, and strategies; terminating counseling sessions and counseling relationships in ways that are appropriate, helpful, professional, and ethical; providing for client to return or be referred in case further help is needed; developing effective and efficient system of follow-up	Gaining concrete understanding of outcomes of counseling; recognizing positive learning and growth steps experienced during counseling; ending each session with a knowledge of what has been accomplished; discontinuing counseling relationship in a positive mode; identifying growth steps; showing greater independence and more frequent coping behaviors than were in evidence prior to counseling; making realistic comparisons between own functioning before and after counseling and during progressive increments of counseling

Personal/ Professional Growth Strategies	Auld & Hyman (1991); Blocher (1987); Glasser (1998, 2000); Glasser & Glasser (1999, 2000) Goldenburg & Goldenburg (1995); Ivey (1986, 1997); Ivey, Ivey, & Simek-Downing (1987); Kell & Mueller (1966); Kelly (1955); Lazarus (1989c, 1995b, 1997); Lowen (1995); May & Yalom (1995); Palmer (1980); Santrock (1999)	Continuously developing oneself as a person and as a counselor; viewing oneself as a continuous learner; discovering, creating, and implementing ways to renew one's personal and professional life; intentional improvement of counseling and relationship skills; initiating meaningful contact with colleagues, through professional/educational growth activities, and adopting training and continuous learning as a way of life; becoming sensitive and responsive to counselor accountability	Learning to grow and cope as a way of life; discovering that one has many choices and ways of implementing one's options; gaining fuller self-acceptance, self-confidence, and self-esteem; moving toward greater independence, self-sufficiency, and self-actualization; adopting prevention and proactivity as a way of life; developing life-long renewal mechanisms and strategies
Research Strategies	Heppner, Kivlighan, & Wampold (1992); Hoyt & Miller (2000); Huck, Cormier, & Bounds (1974); Ivey, Ivey, & Simek-Downing (1987); Stricker (1992); Strupp (1988, 1989)	Investigating accuracy and effectiveness of counseling theory and techniques; engaging in ongoing research studies and activities; supporting and sponsoring research in counseling; sharing own research findings with appropriate audiences; improving on own strategies based on research findings by self and others; making research and learning a way of life as a counselor; encouraging colleagues and students to conduct research	Whenever appropriate, participating in research in counseling; being willing to help self and others by supporting research programs/activities; developing a positive attitude toward research in counseling; returning research survey forms in a thorough and timely manner; being candid and objective in all responses involving investigative research

The categories integrate feeling, thinking, behaving, and learning from both counselor and client perspectives. As may readily be seen, the system uses principles and techniques from a wide variety of theories.

Multimodal Therapy: A Technical Eclecticism

An alternative to the multitheory approach is the single-system multimodel of Lazarus (1981), which he promotes as *technical eclecticism* (Lazarus, 1967; Lazarus & Beutler, 1993). Lazarus proposes that multimodal therapy is a comprehensive systematic therapeutic approach to major areas of human functioning (Lazarus, 1989a, 1989b; Lazarus & Beutler, 1993). He has formulated these areas of functioning into a multimodal schema composed of seven components that he calls BASIC ID (Lazarus, 1989a, 1989b, 1989c, 1995a, 1995b, 1997).

Multimodal therapy is a highly comprehensive and systematic approach to behavior modification (Lazarus, 1981, 1986a, 1986b, 1987, 1989a, 1989b, 1989c, 1995b). It is pragmatically evolving and incorporating new concepts and strategies that are found to be valid through research or practice (Lazarus 1987, 1989c). Although Lazarus does not classify the system as eclectic in the usual sense, it is, in essence, a systematic approach that is a technical eclecticism. Lazarus himself (1989b, pp. 503–510) referred to the system as multimodal eclecticism when comparing it to the functionalism of James. Over a period of several years Lazarus (1989b, 1989c, 1995b) refined the multimodal schema into seven components that he called the BASIC ID, representing the major areas of human functioning.

B = Behavior
A = Affective responses
S = Sensations
I = Images
C = Cognitions
I = Interpersonal relationships
D = Drugs, biological functions, nutrition, and exercise

According to Lazarus (1989a, 1989b, 1989c, 1995b) effective therapy begins with a comprehensive assessment of the client's functioning on each of the seven components. No therapy is considered complete unless it assesses and treats each modality of the BASIC ID. Lazarus (1989b, p. 509) encapsulates the essence of the therapeutic treatment in the following statement.

Multimodal therapists constantly ask, "What works, for whom, and under which particular circumstances?" Thus, they take care not to attempt to fit the client to a predetermined treatment. With most practitioners, the client seems to get only what the therapist practices—which may not necessarily be what is best for the client. In multimodal therapy, there is a deliberate attempt to determine precisely what type of relationship, what type of interactive posture, each client will respond to. The multimodal orientation emphasizes therapeutic flexibility and versatility above all else. There is no unitary way to approach peoples' problems.

BASIC ID Assessment

The multimodal therapist uses assessment data to address each dimension of the BASIC ID during the course of treatment. It is a highly refined scientific therapy that defers assumptions, diagnoses, and treatment plans until the answers to pertinent questions about the client are answered. The multimodal therapist's operational assessment proceeds by ascertaining, through open questioning and written devices, the client's level of functioning on each of the seven BASIC ID components. Most open questions start with words like *what* and *how.* They are phrased to elicit from the client, in the client's own words, precisely what is being done, felt, sensed, imagined, or thought. Closed questions that elicit simple yes or no responses are usually not asked.

Behavior. Behavior may involve a wide range of psychomotor actions, from simple to complex, such as speaking, smiling, walking, writing, eating, and engaging in sexual activity. First the therapist focuses on the client's behaviors. The behavioral component targets overt, observable, measurable emitted responses, actions, reactions, habits, and patterns of performance. For assessment purposes the therapist may rely on inferences or on self-reports. The therapist pays particular attention to behavioral excesses or deficits.

Affect. The affective component targets the client's emotional, feeling, and/or psychological functioning. For assessment purposes, the therapist looks for the presence or absence of particular emotions as well as hidden and/or distorted emotions.

Sensation. The sensation component is assessed to determine the adequacy of the client's sensory functioning. Sensory functioning is important because often the client's perception of personal fulfillment is connected with sensory inputs (sight, sound, smell, taste, kinesics, and so on), and may emerge, unrecognized by the client, in the form of bodily ailments such as dizziness or digestive problems. The person's total wellness and emotional adjustment may be substantially affected by such sensations.

Imagery. The imagery component targets the client's view of self in the mind's eye, including the client's imagination, dreams, daydreams, fantasies, internal pictures, meditations, memories, reminiscences, and visualizations. The therapist's assessment considers either overuse or underuse of the client's imagery—that is, the client's exaggeration of the impact or reality of a fantasy or the absence of imaging altogether.

Cognition. The cognition component targets aspects of the client's thinking processes, including evaluating, judging, valuing, theorizing, hypothesizing, and problem solving. The therapist's assessment especially considers the client's illogical or irrational cognitions.

Interpersonal Relationships. The interpersonal relationship component targets aspects of the client's interactions with other people. The therapist pays close attention to the way the client expresses and accepts feelings communicated to him or her in interpersonal exchanges. The quality of the client's social communications is also important.

Drugs/Biology.   The drugs/biology component targets far more than the client's medication or substance abuse. It includes the person's nutrition, exercise, and total bodily well-being. The therapist's assessment of this component is important because neurological and biochemical factors can have a profound effect on behavior, affective responding, sensations, imagery, and cognition.

Usually the assessment data reveal that clients are troubled by multiple symptoms. Consequently, the process of psychotherapy uses a multitude of treatments. Also, because assessment is a continuous process, treatments are altered as needed as the therapy proceeds.

Constructivist Theory

Constructivist theory, formerly known as *personal construct theory,* was first developed by George A. Kelly (1955). The fundamental postulate of the theory is that personal constructs are ways of construing or categorizing people, events, and environments in the experiential world of the individual (Smith & Vetter, 1991, p. 237). Kelly embellished this basic postulate by formulating the eleven corollaries listed below that, in combination, represent an eclectic-like system that Hergenhahn (1994, pp. 449–450) characterized as phenomenological, cognitive, existential, and humanistic.

1. *Construction corollary.* "A person anticipates events by construing their replications" (Kelly, 1955, p. 50).
2. *Individuality corollary.* "Persons differ from each other in their construction of events" (Kelly, 1955, p. 55).
3. *Organization corollary.* "Each person characteristically evolves, for his convenience in anticipating events, a construction system embracing ordinal relationships between constructs" (Kelly, 1955, p. 56).
4. *Dichotomy corollary.* "A person's construction system is composed of a finite number of dichotomous constructs" (Kelly, 1955, p. 59).
5. *Choice corollary.* "A person chooses for himself that alternative in a dichotomized construct through which he anticipates the greater possibility for extension and definition of his system" (Kelly, 1955, p. 64).
6. *Range corollary.* "A construct is convenient for the anticipation of a finite range of events only" (Kelly, 1955, p. 68).
7. *Experience corollary.* "A person's construction system varies as he successfully construes the replications of events" (Kelly, 1955, p. 72).
8. *Modulation corollary.* "The variation in a person's construction system is limited by the permeability of the constructs within whose range of convenience the variants lie" (Kelly, 1955, p. 79).
9. *Fragmentation corollary.* "A person may successively employ a variety of construction subsystems which are inferentially incompatible with each other" (Kelly, 1955, p. 83).
10. *Commonality corollary.* "To the extent that one person employs a construction of experience which is similar to that employed by another, his psychological processes are similar to the other person" (Kelly, 1955, p. 90).
11. *Sociality corollary.* "To the extent that one person construes the construction processes of another, he may play a role in a social process involving the other person" (Kelly, 1955, p. 95).

Pursuant to Hergenhahn's (1994, pp. 449–450) fourfold characterization of the constructivist system as phenomenological, cognitive, existential, and humanistic, the following assumptions, proposed by different theorists, shed interesting light on the eclectic flavor of constructivism.

> *It is phenomenological.* People perceive the world and impose their own perspectives on it from the standpoint of their own system for construing experience (Duck & Condra, 1990, p. 187).
>
> *It is cognitive.* The constructivist model views people's cognitions and behaviors as being reciprocally interrelated (Viney, 1990, pp. 119–122).
>
> *It is existential.* The constructivist system is existential in that, in the person's mind, all interpretations of the universe are subject to revision (Sechrest, 1977, p. 209).
>
> *It is humanistic.* Kelly's fundamental postulate undergirds and each corollary fleshes out a constructivist view of what it is like to be human (Neimeyer & Neimeyer, 1987, p. 4).

Culture and Cognition.   A group of Hong Kong researchers (Hong, Morris, Chiu, & Benet-Martinez, 2000) developed a novel constructivist approach to culture and cognition, which focuses on the dynamics through which specific elements of cultural knowledge (implicit theories) become operative in guiding the construction of meaning from a stimulus. Whether a construct comes to the fore in a perceiver's mind depends on the extent to which the construct is highly accessible (because of recent exposure). Hong and associates found constructivist approaches to be positive and dynamic influences in counseling with bicultural clients. The authors found that cultural constructs (1) can be potent drivers of behavior, and (2) provide bicultural individuals with the knowledge needed to control the cognitive effects of culture.

Constructionism, Eclecticism, and Technology.   Aspy, Aspy, Russel, and Wedel (2000) studied Carkhuff's human technology as it relates to constructivist theory. Their investigation supports and extends Kelly's observation that counselors should follow the trend in counseling toward integration of theory and eclecticism in clinical practice. Kelly contended that the counseling profession should integrate its theories to combine the strengths of both the humanistic and the technical orientations in the field. Kelly's recommendation was supported by the research. Carkhuff's human technology (which integrates nondirective, psychodynamic, and behavioristic counseling modes) was found to be compatible with constructivist approaches. Based on the outcome data, Aspy and associates found the human technology/constructivist combination to be supportive of the continuing growth potential to be derived from integrating humanistic and technical orientations.

Personal and Scientific Attributes.   In the constructivist system of therapy both the individual and the therapist use the *personal construct* as the major thrust by which the client anticipates events and construes, interprets, explains, ascribes meaning to, and predicts personal experiences. Such a construct is like a miniscientific theory in that it helps the client construct predictions about reality (Hergenhahn, 1994, p. 451). Provided the predictions generated by a client are confirmed by experience, the theory is useful. If the predictions are not confirmed, the construct must be reexamined, revised, or abandoned. Kelly (1955, pp. 8–9) postulated that we view the world through transparent patterns or templates that we create and then attempt to fit over the realities of which that world is composed. The work of the constructivist therapist is to facilitate the client's trying these patterns on for size.

Constructive Alternativism.   Constructivist theory emphasizes that each person creates his or her own constructs for dealing with the world and that each one of us has the goal of reducing future uncertainty. Even so, we are free to construe reality any way we like. Kelly called that assumption *constructive alternativism* (Hergenhahn, 1994, p. 451). In that regard, Kelly stated that "there are always alternative constructions available to choose among in dealing with the world. No one needs to paint himself into a corner; no one needs to be completely hemmed in by circumstances; no one needs to be the victim of his own biography" (1955, p. 15).

Integrative Theory

Integrative Concepts.   The verb *integrate* usually means to make whole or complete; to bring separate components together or incorporate them into a unified, harmonious, or interrelated whole or system. We believe that is a brief but fairly accurate way to describe integrative theory, and that it is also a typical eclectic view. In terms of integrative therapy, Ivey (1997) is one among several leading proponents. Thorne (1967) is considered to be the founder of integrative psychology, on which both the theory and therapy are based. Thorne presented his comprehensive integrative viewpoint in the form of 57 postulates (Patterson, 1986, pp. 484–488). These postulates describe a broad spectrum of the human condition. Integrative psychology holds that human behavior can be understood only in terms of its inner, subjective, existential meanings and that the psychological state of the individual is the critical factor to consider in attempting to understand what the person is doing.

Integrative psychology rejects behavioristic postulates that define behavior as conditioned by the environment. Rather, it holds that the human organism is striving, goal-directed, purposive, active, dynamic, motivated, and, in general, in quest of self-actualization. The primary motive of life is considered to be self-enhancement on all levels of integration (Patterson, 1986, p. 484).

Ivey's (1997) integrative therapy not only integrates Thorne's ideas but also draws from philosophy, developmental theory, and the major theories of counseling and psychotherapy. Ivey also draws from Plato, Hegel, Piaget, and others to put theory into practice in the actual counseling process with clients. His developmental philosophy and intentional therapeutic strategies are therefore highly integrative and eclectic.

Integrative Practices.   In working with an individual client, the integrative counselor operates in an intentional manner. Counseling strategies are changed or adjusted, depending on the client's level of understanding, current functioning, and view of the world. The counselor pays particular attention to assessment and treatment related to cultural issues. The counselor may incorporate elements of a variety of counseling theories into the ongoing work with a client. According to Ivey (1997), some of the approaches that the counselor typically employs are developmental, strategic, multimodal, cognitive-behavioral, existential/humanistic, psychodynamic, systems, person-centered, psychoanalytic, brief or solution-oriented, and multicultural (which Ivey refers to as *the fourth force*). These and other therapy approaches have value for the integrative counselor. Integrative therapy is used extensively with groups, families, and in counseling and supportive work with multicultural groups and individuals.

A basic theoretical tenet of integrative therapy is that clients have within themselves many important answers. Those answers are often in the client's own language. The counselor searches, within the client's own statements, for *anchors*. Such anchors may be words, ideas, or emotional feelings that often can be used later to help the client gain a new perspective on a situation or problem. A typical goal of the integrative therapist is to discover what the client would really like to have happen and then to facilitate the person toward attainment of that goal (Ivey, 1997).

Chaos and Complexity Theory

Background. Chaos and complexity theory, popularized by such theorists as Prigogine (1984) and Gleick (1987) in the 1980s, has recently received a great deal of attention in the scientific community (Briggs, 1992; Briggs & Peat, 1989; DeAngelis, 1993; Eiser, 1994; Hall, 1991; Schroeder, 1991). Initially, chaos theory was principally examined by and applied to the so-called hard sciences such as physics. It is now accepted that certain elements of chaos theory contain important implications for counseling and psychotherapy (Barton, 1994; Brack, 1993; Brack, Brack, & Zucker, 1995; Brennan, 1995; Butz, 1993, 1995; Chamberlain, 1993, 1994, 1995; Gleatt, 1995; McCown & Johnson, 1993; Peca, 1992; Wilbur, Kulikowich, Roberts-Wilbur, & Torres-Rivera, 1995).

Overview. Chaos and complexity theory is not a substitute or a replacement for other systems of counseling. On the contrary, it serves as a viable adjunctive and alternative paradigm that enriches other therapeutic perspectives. The essence of chaos theory, according to Gleick (1987), is that there is an underlying order in all systems, but that systems are so complex that long-term predictability is not feasible. Waldrop (1992) noted that complexity theory deals with the self-organization that emerges from the unpredictable. Thus, "chaos and complexity theory challenge our presuppositions that reality is always linear, predictable, and controllable" (Brack et al., 1995, p. 200).

Ford (1994) speaks of complexity in terms of *organized complexity* and the concept of *system*. There is organization in all living systems, but it is the pattern of complexity of relatedness of the parts that defines a specific organization. "If parts are related in such a way that together they produce a property that none may manifest by itself, then organization exists" (p. 36). What we may view as chaos in a person, a system, or an organization may then be what Ford calls organized complexity, even though we might not recognize it as such viewed through a traditional concept of linearity or cause-and-effect thinking.

Applied to counseling practice, a linear view of a case study may indicate that a person's life might appear to be in total disarray and dysfunction and that the person's behavior and thinking are unpredictable, dangerous, chaotic, and without order. But what may seem at one level to be erratic and unpredictable, when viewed from a more global and holistic vantage point may actually turn out to be ordered.

Chaos Theory, Counseling, and Psychotherapy

Nature of Chaos.   An oversimplified version of chaos theory in regard to counseling and psychotherapy is that (1) the universe, the world, and nature are inherently chaotic or in a continual state of random disequilibrium, but there appear to emerge random and cyclical periods of nonchaos, equilibrium, or order in human functioning just as there are in nature; (2) the chaos or disequilibrium that occurs in the lives of human beings appears to emerge randomly, but there are periods of cyclical and systematic order and homeostasis; (3) in the lives of clients, the periods of disequilibrium are equated with chaos, whereas the periods of equilibrium are equated with nonchaos or order; (4) infrequently, but importantly, a seemingly insignificant and perhaps unexplainable event occurs during a stressful situation that appears to exert a dramatic and positive effect on the client's ability to attain equilibrium and clarity amid the perceived chaos; (5) isolated events in human life, like isolated events in nature, cannot be studied and defined as well as they can be studied and defined in a global or holistic frame of reference; and (6) in any given dilemma or chaotic system there is an underlying order in that system; even when it may appear to be totally disordered to the client or a casual observer (Butz, 1993, 1995; Chamberlain, 1993, 1994; Zheng, 2000).

Unique Life Example of Chaos.   Chamberlain (1995, pp. 118–120) provided a case example of chaos and complexity that applies the theory to therapeutic intervention in a family dealing with suicidal ideation and threat. Amid family turmoil, dysfunction, and long-term family therapy, the father found the daughter making plans to kill herself, having already made several attempts. The father, wanting to spontaneously create a reframe of the situation from "I must keep her from committing suicide," to "I want to make her want to live," began choking the daughter. By exerting great effort, the daughter broke the father's grip. Although the choking event did not even begin to resolve all the family's serious systemic problems, it did stop the suicide attempts. During a six-year follow-up period, the daughter was never known to become suicidal again. This example illustrates how a one-time brief event done out of frustration and desperation may change the course of a suicidal person's life where years of professional time, medication, and money have failed.

A Chaotic Case: Larry.   An example of the use of chaos theory can be found in the case of "Larry" (Harding, 1992), a man in his fifties who once lived what people considered to be the American dream. He had a well-paying civil service job, a comfortable suburban home, a caring wife, and three bright children. But it all went sour for Larry when he fell victim to bipolar disorder, or manic depression. A conventional linear view of Larry's chaos could render it unexplainable. All manner of conventional linear thinking, assessment, medication, and psychotherapy went for naught. But a broader, global view of his situation may make more sense when considering the many dynamic pressures, demands, expectations, seemingly random dilemmas, and complex interactions that his whole family encountered over an extended period of many years.

For instance, Larry attributed his bipolar disorder to recent job stress and family pressures. Chaos and complexity theory, however, would likely examine concomitantly, from Larry's internal perspective as well as from a global external assessment, his current and total past internal and environmental physical, social, familial, vocational, economic, spiritual, and educational lives. Whereas Larry, his family, physicians, therapists, employer, and coworkers might view his apparently chaotic dilemma condition as having come about as a result of recent and specific work, family, or social events, chaos theory would likely hold that his condition is not necessarily chaotic. Rather, chaos theory would characterize Larry's total life history as a system with an underlying order—as any other system in nature has an underlying quality of order.

In Larry's case, the so-called chaotic situation has two opposing and ambivalent qualities: on the one hand, at any given moment his behavior and thinking make perfect sense when viewed exclusively from Larry's internal perspective. On the other hand, when Larry externalizes his situation as helpless, and perhaps even hopeless, his dilemma becomes one of both danger and opportunity. That is the point at which the counselor might be of the greatest help to Larry. It may be the only point at which Larry himself may have an opportunity to understand the underlying systemic order that drives his chaos and a chance to grasp the opportunity to shift from a state of disequilibrium to one of equilibrium or homeostasis.

Chaos as a Self-Organizing Entity. Chaos theory has been likened to a random or evolutionary event in nature as well as in human existence. "It is evolutionary in that it is essentially an open-ended, ever-changing, 'self-organizing system' whereby a new system may emerge" out of the seemingly disorganized situation (James & Gilliland, 2001, p. 12; Zheng, 2000). Chaotic situations or events—which Postrel (1998, p. xv) refers to as *emergent complex messiness*—evolves into a self-organizing format whenever a critical mass of people come to perceive that there are no known ways to identify patterns or to preplan options to cope with the chaos. Because the chaotic situation falls outside of known alternative solutions, counselors may necessarily resort to spontaneous, trial-and-error experimentation to try to deal with the dilemma. The messiness of the dilemma lies not in disorder but in an order that is incomprehensible, unpredictable, and spontaneous—an ever-shifting pattern driven by millions of uncoordinated, independent factors that necessitate experimentation yet may eventually result in a global clarification of the situation. Such experimentation may lead to false starts, dead ends, spontaneous innovation, brainstorming, trial and error, cooperative enterprise, and other types of evolutionary activities in quest of making sense of and coping with the dilemma (James & Gilliland, 2001, pp. 11–13).

Experimentation and Discovery. Experimentation by a critical mass of people (or even by a single individual) can also provide the impetus to reframe and redefine a dilemma in terms of new and divergent ways of viewing the chaotic impasse and generation of new and different alternatives for coping with it. An example of an experimental activity that bore positive fruit occurred while Francine Shapiro was struggling with a difficult problem. While she was at lunch one day, she sat on a park bench and looked up into the sky. She became aware that, as her eyes moved back and forth watching the birds, suddenly she became unusually relaxed and the problem seemed to have diminished. She pondered that change, and decided that her eye movement back and forth watching the birds might have had something to do with it. It was in that context that Shapiro practically stumbled onto the fact that her eye movement had something to do with her transformation, and her further examination of the event led to the discovery of the essential principles of Eye Movement Desensitization Reprocessing (EDMR). Later she was able to apply EDMR techniques to many of the difficult cases of post-traumatic stress disorder that had been confronting her in her professional responsibilities. Dr. Shapiro's real-life experience illustrates the sudden, nonlinear, spontaneous, random, unfolding, non-cause-and-effect quality that appears to explain the nature of chaos theory. Out of what was a seemingly chaotic situation, Shapiro apparently stumbled onto a new organizing theme. But it was not really a stumble because she possessed the self-organizing background to reorganize the chaos through her "ah ha!" experience and, in essence, to transform or reframe her disequilibrium (disorganization) into equilibrium or homeostasis (acquiring a new understanding or different thought pattern regarding a previously confusing set of phenomena) (James & Gilliland, 2001, p. 12).

In chaos theory terms, *self-organizing* means that people may come to perceive the situation or dilemma as global and they thereby pragmatically discover an underlying order within what was previously viewed as fundamentally chaotic disorder. Postrel (1998, pp. xiv–xviii, 39–40; Zheng, 2000) characterizes chaos theory as appearing to seek order randomly, without design, direction, or control. Thus, chaos may symbolize systems that are self-organizing, but such systems do not simply self-organize around nothing. Instead, they evolve toward the most fundamental principles and continuously self-organize around those principles. Even though a chaotic situation or dilemma may appear to be at an insoluble impasse, careful examination may reveal that an important, profound, and unnoticed global message is discernible. The recognition of such a global message can provide both the impetus and the motivation required to initiate positive, intentional action toward alleviating the problem or dilemma (James & Gilliland, 2001, pp. 12–13; Postrel, 1998, pp. 39–40).

Sample Case

The Case of Mary

The eclectic counselor may integrate procedures from different systems of counseling during the same interview with a client or incorporate different approaches over an extended period of time. As previously emphasized in our description of the systematic counseling model, the preparatory evaluation phases (containing stages one and two) are vitally important.

Predisposition

During the predisposition stage, the client's husband, George, came in personally to inquire whether his spouse, Mary, could get an appointment rather quickly. He revealed that his spouse had agreed to see a counselor but was too embarrassed and upset to schedule an appointment. After the counselor talked briefly with George, George phoned Mary, and Mary talked by phone with the counselor. Even though she was distraught over the impending separation and divorce, Mary had reconciled herself to the dissolution of the marriage, and the counselor made an appointment to see Mary. Fortunately, Mary had her own private e-mail address, so the counselor used that electronic method to set the stage for treatment and change. Prior to the first meeting, it developed that Mary's emotional status was volatile. Part of the time she was in a state of crisis or disequilibrium and part of the time she could function quite adequately. She communicated her emotional needs to the counselor in a timely enough manner that the counselor could phone her between e-mail transmissions. At each phone call, Mary's equilibrium was restored and the counselor was able to instill a modicum of trust prior to actually seeing her in person. The predisposition phase gave the counselor the opportunity to deal with Mary's safety issues and explain the treatment processes that she could reasonably expect. Fortunately, all the major goals of the predisposition stage were accomplished by phone and by e-mail, and, although she was emotionally upset, Mary appeared to be convinced that she was doing the right thing by coming for counseling and that the counseling was expected to help her in the healing process.

During the predisposition stage the theoretical modality was primarily person-centered with some of the Egan and Carkhuff model techniques used.

Mary, age 52, came to the counselor at the urging of her husband, George. George was a 52-year-old Ph.D. who held a high-level administrative position in a large organization. Mary was a professional in the same organization. Mary and George were born and reared in the geographical region where they worked. They both attended school at state universities and had lived and worked in the same region of the state during their entire careers up to the time counseling was initiated. They had two children. Linda, age 26, lived and worked in a large city some 150 miles away and Mark, 22, had just been accepted to the state university's dental school located in the same city where Linda lived. The family was known as an ideal family.

Suddenly George let it be known to Mary that he wanted a divorce. Initially he told only Mary (and also the counselor) that he wished to take early retirement, move to a city some 450 miles away, take a different managerial job, and marry a younger woman. George did not want to tell anyone else about his decision, especially Linda or Mark. George met with the counselor to disclose his decision and express his concern over the possible damaging effects his actions might have on Mary. Mary agreed to see the counselor, and within a few days George retired and left town to carry out his plan. During the first interview Mary was composed but in emotional shock. She expressed disbelief, denial, self-blame, and severe depression.

Middle Procedures: Fluid Process of Counseling Experiences

Characteristic of the eclectic approach, the counseling process with Mary did not follow a strictly lock-step mechanical or linear format. Stages two through seven proceeded in a fluid progression as will become evident. Mainly, person-centered approach techniques were employed during the first formal session. It is noted that Mary and the counselor seemed to be receptive toward relating to each other as a result of the predisposition activity. This enabled both counselor and client to make good use of the first session. At subsequent sessions the counselor used multimodal, rational-emotive behavioral, analytic, behavioral, object relations, existential, solution-focused, and systems techniques. There was little combination of approaches during each session (though that would have been quite appropriate) except that the Carkhuff model of listening and responding was used to initiate each session. After Mary had had an opportunity to explore and define her concerns at the beginning of each interview, the counselor selected an approach judged to be appropriate to the case handling during most of the remainder of that particular interview.

Initiating Eclectic Counseling

A brief segment from the first interview with Mary gives some idea of the client's level of functioning and the eclectic counselor's initial technique.

> CL: I keep wondering, "Is this really happening? What did I do to bring all this on?" I must be dreaming. This must be a nightmare. What did I do?
>
> CO: You're finding it hard to believe that this is really happening to you. Yet, you believe that somehow *you* had some part in bringing on this disaster. But you are at a loss to explain it.
>
> CL: I must have been living in a dream world. George has always been a perfect husband, a perfect father. It *must* be something I've done or failed to do! If I could just go to sleep (*pause*) and let the whole world just pass on by (*no tears, no emotion, no affect shown*).
>
> CO: A part of you is blaming yourself and asking "Why?" But another part of you says, "I just wish I could go to sleep and not wake up—just wish I could experience a painless death."
>
> CL: Oh, I've thought about that, seriously. Right after George first exploded this bombshell. Dying really appealed to me. I contemplated it all right. (*long pause*)
>
> CO: I'm very concerned about your thoughts about suicide. I noticed you were talking about it in the past tense, though. I'm concerned about your present danger to yourself and about the availability of your means of doing it if you should decide—maybe on impulse—to actually do it.
>
> CL: Oh, I could do it all right. But I thought, "What would happen to Mark and Linda?" No, I couldn't do that to them. They are going to have it rough enough as it is, without me making matters worse for them.
>
> CO: Your concern for Mark and Linda's welfare is too strong to allow you to carry out such a drastic act and complicate their lives even more.
>
> CL: Definitely, I feel they are going to need me more than ever when they find out what George has done—and what he still plans to do.

CO: So you feel you can't abandon them now.

CL: Never. They're all I've got. And I may be all they've got. We're going to need each other now more than ever.

The counselor was concerned about Mary's safety, was attempting to assess her level of lethality and coping potential, and was using reflection to assist her in ventilating and deeply exploring the problem. By the end of the first interview the counselor felt, from observing Mary's nonverbal behavior, tone of voice, and verbal responses, that she was not in imminent danger to herself. The counselor referred her to her physician for a complete physical examination, and gave her a calling card to use in case she experienced a crisis prior to the next interview. The counselor obtained a firm commitment from Mary that she would talk with the counselor by phone immediately in the event of a crisis of such a nature as to cause her impulsively to harm herself.

Process of Multimodal Psychotherapy, Using the BASIC ID

In multimodal therapy the assessment process precedes therapy and attends to all of the BASIC ID patterns. Psychotherapy is governed fundamentally by the assessed unique needs and requirements of each client. There is no typical treatment regimen (Lazarus, 1989b, p. 521, 1995a, 1995b, pp. 337–341, 1997). Further, the multimodalist will not really decide on treatment modalities until the interview sessions begin. A preliminary modality and treatment plan is usually decided on by the start of the third session. For Mary, it was determined that the three most compelling BASIC ID areas needing therapeutic work were behavior, sensations, and images.

Processing Mary's Behavior. The multimodal therapist actively, intentionally, and directively guided Mary's attention to specific behavioral deficits uncovered through the assessment process and inferred in her interviews.

CL: I haven't had the nerve to tell Mama yet. But I did contact my friend about the possibility of leaving here and getting a job in the city where Linda lives.

CO: Well, those are perhaps important things to do. But what about your communication with George that you talked about last time? You indicated that you didn't want to make any major career decisions until you knew what financial resources you are going to have. What have you done to clarify your financial status?

CL: I was hoping he would come by to get the remainder of his clothing and that I would see him and maybe talk to him then.

CO: Will *hoping* and *what he does* get you where you want to go within the time frame you have set for yourself? You've said you want to take charge and be your own pilot. What actions do *you want to initiate* to take charge and begin to chart your own course?

CL: Hmm . . . What I really want to do is to get some independent legal advice before I have any more discussion with him about financial or property settlement matters.

CO: So, what's the next step going to be for you?

In working on Mary's *behaviors* the multimodal therapist kept her largely in the here-and-now and guided her concentration on those behaviors that were critical to her current needs. Also typical in multimodal therapy, metaphors that were derived from Mary's own situation were used by the therapist to drive home to her what she had verbally stated she wanted to do. Multimodal therapists use metaphors to enrich, strengthen, affirm, and empower clients to take realistic and positive action steps that they themselves choose to do. Concrete behaviors designed to put control and autonomy in the hands of clients is of primary importance.

Mary's therapist might have applied a variety of other mechanisms of behavioral processing had Mary's situation warranted them. Extinction techniques (such as massed practice, response prevention, and flooding), counterconditioning (such as using incompatible response techniques), positive reinforcement, and operant procedures (such as token economies, contingent praise, timeout, and aversion strategies) are a few of the mechanisms that might be brought to bear in multimodal therapy (Lazarus, 1989b, pp. 525–526, 1995b, pp. 342–347, 1997).

Processing Mary's Sensations.   In helping Mary to focus on, recognize, and validate her sensations, the therapist's objective was to enable Mary to get in touch with the pleasures, pains, and bodily sensations and responses to environmental stimuli such as sex, food, music, art, and aesthetic stimulations (Lazarus, 1989b, p. 515, 1995b, pp. 332–341, 1997).

CL: I guess I'm still in too much of a daze to fully realize what I'm doing and what I'm up against. Much of the time since George dropped this bombshell I've simply been too tense and too numb to really feel anything.

CO: Let's concentrate on your tenseness and numbness. What kinds of activities typically get you going, provide relaxation throughout your body, and stimulate your inner enjoyment and pleasure during more normal times in your life when you find yourself temporarily stressed out?

CL: Strolling in nature. Beauty in the park. The trees and the birds . . . the flower gardens in Audubon Park! Those are the kinds of things that get inside me and touch me when I'm emotionally stuck—that I have neglected by staying inside, lying in bed, and crying since this happened.

CO: Let's talk about how you can get some pleasure . . . some tension-releasing sensations back into your life.

The multimodalist placed a great deal of importance in facilitating sensory pleasuring (Lazarus, 1989b, p. 526, 1995b, pp. 332–337, 1997) in Mary's life. Such sensations may involve mechanisms such as biofeedback, relaxation training, purposeful physical exercise, positive tactile sensations, and aesthetic experiences. In Mary's case, she provided the therapist with a viable lead when she remembered her positive sensations experienced in a particular natural setting.

Processing Mary's Imagery. Mary's vivid imagination, fantasies, and daydreams constituted what amounted to negative and distorted mental pictures of herself because she was unable to evoke positive self-images.

> CO: So you can only picture yourself as a worn-out discard. Let's talk about where you got those images and then work together to change that view of yourself as some awful, despicable person.
>
> CL: I keep thinking I must be deplorable. I see myself through his eyes, I guess, and I view myself as unacceptable, because if I were pleasant to look at and be with, he wouldn't reject me and look for another woman.
>
> CO: That's exactly where we will start, right now. I think we can come up with what I call "coping images" that will enable you to evoke some different pictures of yourself—some pictures that will portray you to yourself as worthwhile, having self-control, and capable, competent, and deserving of respect.

The therapist recognized Mary's need for positive and constructive imaging. The therapist then began to help Mary develop a different repertoire of images, mainly through using mental and emotive imagery, positive self-talk, and visualizations that were realistic and true for her.

The multimodalist's use of the BASIC ID model with many different types of clients transcends traditional behaviorist approaches by invoking unique assessments and by working with great intensity and depth with the client in coping with presenting dilemmas. The therapist goes into specific detail in using the mechanisms that improve sensations, imagery, cognitions, and interpersonal functioning in addition to making improvements in behavior and personal physiology. A fundamental premise of multimodal therapy is that clients are usually troubled by a multitude of problems, as was Mary, and that a multitude of specific treatment mechanisms may therefore be necessary to effect positive and constructive change (Lazarus, 1989b, p. 503, 1995a, 1995b, pp. 341–342, 1997).

Continuing Eclectic Counseling with Mary

We have briefly illustrated one multimodalist technique and shall continue with the fundamental processing of Mary's case with an eclectic counselor. During her first few interviews several themes emerged: putting herself down, blaming herself for what had happened, protecting George from blame, assuming responsibility for George's continued unhappiness, focusing on her past behavior that may have caused George to reject her, and worrying about the effects of the divorce on Mark and Linda. The counselor used rational-emotive behavioral techniques to help the client sort out these issues. REBT was employed because the client appeared to be quite a cognitive person. She was quick to grasp and deal with the world of ideas, beliefs, philosophies of life, and rational decisions.

CO: Mary, you seem to be saying to yourself that there must have been something pretty awful you were doing—that you were somehow pretty bad to let all this happen. Let's examine what you're saying to yourself about what was happening to give you such a picture of yourself, now.

CL: Well, I know I've been very critical of myself—perhaps too critical. But I can't help thinking, "I must have been stupid to have neglected him—to have forced him to go looking somewhere else for his love and comfort."

CO: Look how you just devalued yourself—using the word *stupid.* You seem to have already tried and convicted yourself of some heinous crime before even analyzing what really happened. You seem to be saying, "It's all my fault, look how terrible I am," and to be protecting him at all costs. Did you *really* force him to do those things? Let's examine your crimes for a moment. Did you sneak around behind George's back for three or four years, having a clandestine affair with a male friend?

CL: Certainly not! I would never even think of such a thing!

CO: Was it you who took a lover with you to conventions at resort hotels and stayed several days extra, time and time again, leaving George at home to keep things going?

CL: No, he was doing that, long before I even knew anything was wrong.

CO: Was it you who allocated family funds and fabricated weekend conferences to spend time with your boyfriend, leaving George and Mark to fend for themselves, and then did you lie to them about doing it?

CL: No. (*pause*) It's true that I have done the best I could. I have never lied to George, and I've never done him wrong. I haven't been perfect, but I've certainly done nothing to deserve what I've got.

CO: So you *can* assign some of the responsibility to George.

CL: Well, I guess I just hung on to my image of him so long, I just couldn't believe. (*pause*) But yes, he did do those things. (*pause*) I don't want to give you the impression that George is a terrible person. He has lots of very good qualities. It's like, he just went off his rocker—lost his sanity. That's not the George I thought I knew and trusted and loved.

CO: Sounds like you can admit that he did those things, and that you were not the cause of his doing them. But it also sounds like you are still protecting him—or your image of him—by saying that it wasn't the real George who did them; that the real George wouldn't behave like that and that maybe the real, sane George might still exist.

CL: I guess it is hard to admit to myself the raw truth. I guess it is really hard for me to realize that he has discarded me. Just cast me off like an old piece of clothing. That he prefers someone else to me. That's what hurts.

CO: I can see that you're hurting, and you have real cause to be hurt. I can also see that what you're telling yourself *about* this rejection may be at the source of some of the hurt. Let's see if we can determine what messages you're giving to yourself *about* the rejection that's resulting in your rejecting yourself, before all the facts are in. What are you saying to yourself at the moment you're feeling like an old discard?

CL: Well, I know I'm feeling like, "this is the ultimate put-down," like a curse he's put on me. But I also realize that I'm being hard on myself—maybe too hard.

CO: So, when you think about it, it may be distasteful; it may be degrading; but it isn't an absolute catastrophe—it *is* something you'll get over.

CL: Oh yes, I'll get over it. I may even be stronger—more independent—when I do. It's just such a new experience for me to suddenly have to fight and claw for every little crumb of my being—it's left such a void in my life.

CO: It seems to me you're realizing that this is going to be a tough, hard hill to climb. But it seems that you're telling yourself now that you dread it; that it is inconvenient and highly distasteful; but that you can stand it, and that you may be less dependent when it's all settled.

CL: I really have no choice. I'll have to survive, some way.

Mary was quick to grasp and deal with the exaggerations and catastrophic tendencies. Each time she returned, the counselor had to reindoctrinate her because she would lapse into her old patterns of irrational thinking between interviews. After several sessions of coaching and confronting with the rational techniques, Mary began to discard her self-blame, guilt, and awfulizing. The counselor noticed some new emotions emerging—anger directed at George, chagrin at herself for not having been a more independent person during the marriage, and puzzlement over the dynamics of her inner motives and emotions. She seemed to have achieved a plateau of sorts, where she was rational, decision-oriented, poised, and in control. Her concern now seemed to be directed toward self-understanding.

Mary resigned her job, rented the family home, moved to the city where Linda and Mark were residing, obtained another professional position, and continued seeing the counselor. She expressed great desire to achieve self-understanding. In discussing various insight techniques, Mary was resistant to most of the procedures suggested and described by the counselor. She was not personally suited to dream analysis and interpretation or Gestalt techniques. However, she had a vivid imagination and proved to be able to deal with imagery quite effectively, as was previously illustrated with the multimodal counselor. The counselor was about to conclude that working mainly on Mary's resistance was needed when the idea of analysis of her writing was mentioned as a possibility. That idea appealed to Mary and the counselor gave her an initial writing assignment as a trial strategy toward achieving insight. That strategy worked well. Mary was ideally suited to expressing her emotions on paper.

Over the course of eight months, Mary dealt with her anger, her need for assertiveness, her unfinished business from the past, and a number of other important emotional and motivational concerns. Her treatment on each topic was one of written free association. She was completely free to write anything she thought or felt on the preselected topic. Her many topics were planned, progressively, toward achieving a variety of insights. A few of her seventy-five different compositions were (1) Why do I feel despondent? (2) My hang-ups, (3) Divorce! (4) Off my pedestal, (5) Severance, (6) I must not fear life,

(7) Patience and reality, (8) I'm making progress, (9) Am I crazy? (10) My pluses and minuses, and (11) I saw a sunset—I can feel again. Writing proved to be the one avenue through which Mary could experience release from her inhibitions. No emotional topic or thought was sacrosanct. She expressed her pain as well as her ecstasy; her fears as well as her hopes; her doubts as well as her convictions; her weaknesses as well as her strengths. It soon became obvious to the counselor and to Mary that she was making positive movement toward insightful handling of her defenses, fantasies, fears, and so on. A sample of Mary's free-association writing appears below (reproduced by permission of "Mary," her alias for this book).

> 6/9, Monday, 9:00 P.M. Tonight I'm going to try to recapture my emotions at the time of the first realization of the possibility of divorce. George never said to me until the first of last October the words, "I want a divorce." That is the only time he has actually said it to me. This realization came earlier, in August.
>
> DIVORCE! It can't be! Not I; not us! Never! Other people, yes! But not us! Those years! All those years! A DIVORCED woman! Sylvia, yes! Peggy, yes! But Mary Jones! No! No! No! TO NO LONGER BE HIS WIFE! I can't stand it! I'd rather be dead! I will be dead! I'll kill myself first. Oh, agony, oh sick, sick, sick unto death! "Oh God! Please let me die! I want to die. AND NO ONE WILL EVER HAVE TO KNOW. Not Linda, not Mark or Mama or Mother or Daddy or anyone. Please, God please!" (I actually prayed this prayer.) MY WORLD HAS ENDED!
>
> Now, I'm going to pick out key words or phrases to analyze. DIVORCE—the utter horror of the word. Unspeakable. The one thing I felt could never happen to me. To me. A DIVORCED WOMAN. Branded! Shamed! I didn't want to see anybody. I didn't want to talk with anyone. I was enveloped in a fog of hurt, confusion, and despair. My whole body ached! My greatest desire was to ESCAPE. Complete lethargy filled my being. TO NO LONGER BE HIS WIFE! To no longer be Mrs. George Jones; to no longer be No. 1 in his heart and mind! I couldn't bear the thought. Death would be sweet. An end. An end to the hurt, the shame, the anguish, the heartache.
>
> KILL MYSELF! Yes, I contemplated suicide. What did I have to live for? What good was I now? Linda and Mark were old enough to take care of themselves. My brother would see after Mother and Daddy. Besides, if I killed myself, no one would ever have to know the TRUTH. Everyone would be shocked, but ultimately they would reason, "How unfortunate! Mary was that age, you know." Menopause would be blamed.
>
> George could wait a decent time, marry; everything would be all right. . . . Oh yes, I not only contemplated suicide; I considered several methods! Gun? No! Knife? No! Automobile accident? No! Pills? Possibly! Electric shock? Maybe! Drowning—yes! It would be easy to fall over the side of the boat. I couldn't swim! Yes, that was the best—drowning! (As I write and reread this, I am struck with the thought: HOW INSANE—HOW UTTERLY INSANE! How selfish! How irrational! How cowardly! YET, the fact of suicide is still there. The emotion of it has diminished. . . .)
>
> 6/24. 9:00 P.M. Tuesday. Burl is very discreet in allowing me to find answers to my own questions. I can now answer the one concerning time: "Did you perceive that I might be wanting to rush things?" The answer is "Yes." Because I have been, in the past few weeks, inclined to want to hasten this process. HURRY to feel happy. HURRY to find answers. HURRY to heal! HURRY to get it over! HURRY! HURRY! HURRY! I must remember that I am not meeting a deadline (no pun intended). Time is on my side. This whole situation did not develop overnight. It cannot be resolved overnight. . . .

Mary filled four notebooks in eight months. Not only were the writings used during counseling sessions, but also Mary read and reread them from time to time. She still does. She reports that the written "history" helps her keep a healthy perspective.

Family Therapy in Mary's Case. Mary's total eclectic treatment program involved family therapy. She was referred to an experienced family systems therapist for two specific reasons. First, she was concerned about Mark and Linda's persistent bitterness toward their father following the divorce. Second, she was fearful that her own previous inability to sustain and preserve the marital relationship signaled some sort of intergenerational weakness that might be passed on to her offspring. She was particularly concerned about Linda, who was considering marriage to a man with characteristics and traits similar to those of her father (Mary's ex-husband). The three of them successfully pursued family therapy together.

Within a few months both Mark and Linda were able to reestablish a functional relationship with their father. The family therapist facilitated Mary, Mark, and Linda in the construction, study, and discussion of their respective family genograms. That strategy proved to be exciting, interesting, and educational for all three, and Mary reported that learning about her multigenerational dynamics enhanced her own self-confidence and self-esteem.

Finalizing Mary's Eclectic Counseling. Mary's written free-association assignments did not terminate abruptly; her writing gradually tapered off. As her goals of achieving insight were steadily fulfilled, her need for writing progressively declined. One day she made the remark, "Huh, seems like I don't need to write any more." It was like the end of a phase. Termination of counseling was discussed. "That would be okay," she said, "but there are some things I really need to do first." Thus began another phase of Mary's counseling. Although she was not familiar with the term *self-managed behavior model*, that is precisely what she felt the need to learn and apply to her lifestyle before she terminated the counseling relationship. She quickly learned the skills of problem identification and definition in behavioral terms, establishing measurable goals, monitoring target behaviors, changing setting events, establishing effective consequences, and consolidating gains. She was astute and conscientious about behavioral contracting. A short segment from one of the behaviorally oriented sessions between Mary and the counselor gives one example of this phase of the counseling.

CO: So you have several legal concerns that are important to you, but you've been sitting on your hands.

CL: I guess they are "legal," at that. I have just kept getting upset over them. Wondering if I should call George and confront him or write him. I don't really want to contact him, though. It's his responsibility. I've kept putting it off, but I keep worrying about it all the time.

CO: Since it's mostly legal matters relating to his breach of the written agreement, wouldn't it be wise for you to consult an attorney?

CL: Well, I have every right to. I'm not interested in punishing George. All I want is for George to meet his part of the agreement. I just don't know any attorneys—

except Butch. I'm not sure that he's the one I should see. He's the one who drew up the financial and property agreements for George and me. He may consider himself George's attorney. He's a good lawyer, though, and I trust him.

CO: Sounds like you're reluctant to consult a new attorney until you can clarify whether it would be a conflict for you to retain Butch.

CL: That's right. I have an aversion to starting legal proceedings. But I can't keep up this worrying. And I can't keep ignoring George's not keeping his end of the bargain.

CO: Then it sounds like you're to the point of deciding how and when you're going to get the answers to your legal questions.

CL: Yes, there's no sense in putting it off.

CO: How do you intend to go about getting this thing off dead center and getting some peace of mind for yourself?

CL: Well, I was just thinking. (*pause*) I have to go up to that county Friday. I could call Butch's office to see if he could see me Friday afternoon or Saturday morning.

CO: When do you intend to call Butch's office to make the appointment?

CL: This afternoon.

(*Later in the interview*)

CO: Okay, Mary. We've laid out the plans of what you're contracting to do. Can you summarize so we are both clear on what you are going to do to relieve yourself from this particular financial worry?

CL: First of all, I feel good about what I've decided to do. It should relieve me of lots of stress. I plan to go back to the office today and call Butch's office and make an appointment as soon as I can—preferably this Friday afternoon or Saturday. Second, I plan to ask him if he can ethically serve as my attorney in case I decide to bring litigation against George. Third, if he says, "yes," I will ask him for an opinion on two things: Can I require George to sign the quitclaim deeds on the property, so we can sell the property and divide it evenly, as he agreed to do in the legal settlement? Next, what legal steps must I take to get George to pay his share of Mark's education and upkeep while he's in dental school? George has quit sending Mark his support payments, in violation of the written agreement.

CO: You've given a good summary of what you've contracted to do. Anything else?

CL: Yes, I will call you Monday morning to give you a status report.

Mary was the type of client who didn't need a written contract. The verbal agreement was sufficient. She appeared to receive a great deal of intrinsic reinforcement through completion of action steps.

The termination of Mary's case was a natural turn of events—a collaborative decision between the client and the counselor. Both she and the counselor knew that the time was near when she desired to make it on her own. She made remarks such as, "The time has come for me to launch out on my own. It's important to me to handle it myself now." The counselor, sensing her need for autonomy and privacy, left the door open for her to return or to call if, in her judgment, she needed further personal contact.

We might ask, "Why was the eclectic model appropriate for Mary?" Several reasons. First, Mary came to counseling with the answers within herself. But initially, she didn't know how to frame the questions. Second, she was unable to find the answers that were within herself. The eclectic counseling was versatile enough to employ whatever techniques were needed to help her ask herself the right questions and find her own answers. Third, the eclectic method exposed her to enough strategies and alternative action steps to enable her to find the options that were uniquely effective for her. The eclectic counselor used a wide repertoire of strategies and was able to come up with an appropriate strategy for Mary each time she needed it. This is what eclectic counseling is all about!

Post-Disposition and Follow-Up

Following termination of Mary's counseling, stage eight, post-disposition and follow-up, transpired in a natural and healthy way. She could effectively function on her own. She even expressed the definite opinion that she was now better off without George, but that she could remember and value all the good times of the marriage and cope with the bad ones. The client was assured that counseling could be resumed if the need arose. The counselor made it a point to check with Mary several times during the following year, and Mary kept in intermittent contact by e-mail. Mary filled out the counselor's evaluation forms and was prompt to contact the counselor whenever she had the need to do so. But she was not a dependent after-client. After a couple of years, Mary developed a relationship with a male friend and moved to an adjoining state to live. She continued to e-mail the counselor and, without fail, send holiday cards to the counselor letting the counselor hear how she was doing. But that was the end of the face-to-face contact. Only cards and e-mails remained as communication media between the two. Even though we have changed the names in the case to protect the privacy of Mary and her entire family, she did read, approve, and provide written release of the case synopsis you have just read. She was also kind enough to obtain for us written releases from her two children and her ex-husband for consent for publication of the case in this book. That was a very important and necessary component of the late procedures which comprised stages seven and eight of the systematic counseling model. Her continuing e-mails and annual holiday cards are still valued and considered to be an integral part of the post-disposition process.

Contributions of the Eclectic System

Eclecticism has demonstrated that it is possible and desirable to integrate and utilize a wide variety of techniques that have proven to be of practical value. The system has been able to accommodate even opposing points of view. This has been perhaps its greatest strength. Also, eclecticism has focused on the commonalities of therapies. It has synthesized the positive points of various systems rather than treating each as separate, unrelated, or oppositional to the others.

Eclecticism has dealt with the total client situation. It has dealt with the person's *internal events* (cognitions such as motivations, emotions, and beliefs); the client's *external events* (behaviors or overt acts); and *social influences* (other persons; organizations; groups, starting with primary groups, such as the family; and the entire social structure). Eclecticism has drawn on a diversity of ideas and sources for its formulations: experimental research, clinical observation, nonscientific study, practical experience, and even an "understanding of poets, philosophers, and novelists" (Palmer, 1980, p. 4). Eclecticism has shown that the human condition is too complex to be served by a single, narrow approach. That theory serves best which is not tied to one limited set of formulations, technology, and techniques and which isn't tailored or skewed toward benefiting only a few types of people, problems, or syndromes.

Shortcomings of the Eclectic System

The first and foremost shortcoming of the eclectic system has to do more with the practical than the theoretical. Simply, it is unrealistic to expect an individual to acquire sufficient expertise in all the therapeutic systems to become a proficient eclectic. Most aspiring counselors and psychotherapists cannot devote enough time and resources to master the theories, skills, and experiential requirements to become effective eclectic helpers. Many do not have the personality and attitudinal and interest characteristics to be compatible with the many modalities advocated for eclectics. Eclecticism might be ideal, but it is not always practical in terms of human limitations and fallibilities. A related criticism is that if eclectics must master all techniques, then they will probably be expert in none.

The second major shortcoming is that eclecticism has no unifying set of principles, philosophies, theories, tenets from which to build a rationale of operation. Without a blueprint or map, how can we determine which way to go, make corrections during the journey, or determine when we have arrived at the desired destination?

A third criticism is that the world of clients and the techniques of counseling are changing so rapidly that it is difficult to keep up. Even those proficient in eclectic counseling soon fall behind. We live in an age of change and specialization. Often expert counselors must specialize to attain and retain competence.

As of yet, we know of no clear formulae that can be arbitrarily applied to the idiosyncratic nature of specific client problems. The clusters of therapeutic strategies proposed in this chapter are more far-reaching than merely assessing and applying a generic prescription to a client problem. In that regard no eclectic has thus far been able to reduce therapy to a formula. Given the current status of affairs in therapy, we would urge caution for any beginner who would accept lock, stock, and barrel any theorist who proposes that he or she has found the one eclectic path to therapeutic truth and knowledge.

Eclectic Counseling with Diverse Populations

An integral part of the multicultural counseling movement has emerged from the impetus of professional organizations and the research and writing of a large number of counseling professionals espousing essentially eclectic counseling principles (AACD, 1988, 1989; APA, 1991, 1992; Atkinson, Morten, & Sue, 1989; Pedersen, 1988, 1989, 1990; Sue, 1991, 1992; Sue, Arredondo, & McDavis, 1992; Sue & Sue, 1990). According to Sue, Arredondo, and McDavis (1992), culturally skilled counselors have competencies in a wide variety of verbal and nonverbal techniques. They are skilled at both receiving and sending nonverbal as well as verbal communications and they "are not tied down to only one method or approach to helping but recognize that helping styles and approaches may be culture bound" (p. 87).

Sue (1992) makes several important points in favor of the eclectic approach and against traditional theories (such as behavioral, Rogerian, REBT, and Gestalt), including statements that: (1) licensing committees that administer examinations look with suspicion on candidates who claim to be eclectic, and (2) culturally sensitive eclectic counselors recognize that cross-cultural counseling involves not only people's thinking, feeling, behaving, and social interacting but also their cultural and political orientations. The real difficulty with traditional theories is that they are culture-bound. The eclecticism that Sue advocates values, counsels, and affirms a diversity of clients and client orientations, including special concerns of the culturally different and economically and educationally disadvantaged clients that traditional therapists may not be prepared to handle. Many of the talk therapies are oriented toward self-disclosure, which is incompatible with the cultural values of many minority clients.

Several fundamental issues point to the validity of Sue's (1992) call for counselors to employ varied intervention strategies. For instance, the typically Euro-American belief that the individual is of paramount importance is not held in all cultures. A client from a culture in which the family, the clan, or the sect takes precedence over the individual may feel totally disaffected or even demeaned in the presence of a counselor who is ignorant of such values. Regarding clients from some minority backgrounds, even subtle and unconsciously held prejudices and stereotypic thinking on the part of the counselor can negatively affect the therapeutic relationship. Also, not all people have been acculturated to embrace such Euro-American ideals as rugged individualism and competition. Clearly, the sociopolitical atmosphere of which some narrowly focused traditional counselors are a part may be counter to the minority client's values, orientation, and style and may be detrimental to the client and the counseling process.

Sue, Arredondo, and McDavis (1992) reviewed the Association for Multicultural Counseling and Development's (AMCD)–approved document outlining the need and rationale for a multicultural perspective in counseling. The major components of the plan call for counselors to possess the following broad cross-cultural competencies:

1. Awareness of own cultural values and biases
2. Awareness of client's worldview
3. Culturally appropriate intervention strategies (pp. 84–88).

The AMCD document calls for the incorporation of the above competencies in the training and practice of counselors so that the inculcation of appropriate multicultural counselor attitudes, beliefs, knowledge, and skills may become the norm rather than the exception. Sue (1992) describes the counseling profession as being at a crossroads. On the one hand, monoculturalism/ethnocentrism, the road we have traditionally traveled, is forcing us to recognize that we are not serving the interests of the many diverse groups in our society. Multiculturalism, the alternate path, is the road less traveled. "It recognizes and values diversity. It values cultural pluralism and acknowledges our nation as a cultural mosaic rather than a melting pot. It is the road that challenges us to study multiple cultures, to develop multiple perspectives, and to teach our children how to integrate broad and conflicting bodies of information to arrive at sound judgments" (p. 8).

Sue's (1992) perspective represents an eclectic counseling theory that integrates the philosophical, theoretical, and practical elements into a cohesive and systematic system. He states that culturally, economically, and educationally disadvantaged clients may not be oriented toward "talk therapies," that self-disclosure may be incompatible with the cultural values of such populations as Asian Americans, Latinos, and Native Americans. He views therapeutic systems founded only on traditional European populations as being deficient in the worldview needed by today's counselors. Sue says he once would have proudly announced that he was "behavioral in orientation," but today he is an advocate of an even broader and more flexible helping process to facilitate equal access and opportunities for all clients (p. 14).

We believe an eclectic model is appropriate and viable for a cross-cultural counseling perspective. To be an eclectic means to be adaptable in both theory and technique. Adherence to any one narrow, inflexible traditional theoretical approach is outmoded and inappropriate. If we are to do what Sue (1992) proposes, we must operate in some type of organized, consistent, systematic, and integrated eclectic system that is well grounded in a broad array of theories, is sensitive and responsive to diversity, and is geared to the idiosyncratic and phenomenal world of each client. An eclectic system—a road less traveled—offers a broad enough worldview of clients and their inner worlds to understand, affirm, and help people in all cultures and lifestyles.

Summary

Eclectic counseling and psychotherapy selectively and systematically applies all the known and valid helping procedures to assist individuals in solving their problems and maintaining stability in their lives. No one theoretical position is embraced. No one strategy or set of strategies is used or advocated exclusively. Eclectic methodology, according to Thorne (1967) and others, is a basic scientific approach to the process of selecting suitable strategies to meet the needs of specific clients.

Several formidable eclectic models have been developed. Approaches by Thorne (1968); Brammer (1979); Brammer and Shostrom (1968); Carkhuff and Berenson (1977); Cormier and Cormier (1998); Garfield (1980); Ivey and Simek-Downing (1980); Lazarus (1981, 1989c, 1997); Palmer (1980); Ivey (1997); and our own Expanded Eight-Stage Systematic Counseling Model, depicted in Figure 13.1 and described in this chapter, are only a few of the many systematic and integrative models that might be considered eclectic. Eclecticism utilizes strategies from several schools (analytic, Gestalt, TA, REBT, humanistic-existential, person-centered, systems, cognitive, brief or solution-focused, and so on) to help clients gain insights for understanding and controlling internal events. It uses techniques from other schools (behavior modification, behavior therapy, REBT, cognitive-behavior therapy, choice theory/reality therapy, and so on) to assists clients in modifying their behavior for the control and maintenance of external events.

Although the eclectic approach has been subjected to a great deal of skepticism and criticism from proponents of various special schools of therapy, it has experienced tremendous growth in the number of self-identified followers since the mid-1940s. It is the viewpoint of eclectics that all schools have some contribution to make and that practitioners should try to learn to incorporate valid techniques that each of these schools has developed.

In the case of Mary in this chapter, we have shown one abbreviated example of the enormous scope of possibilities available to the eclectic counselor. The systematic counseling model highlighted in Figure 13.1, like other integrative models, can of course accommodate a much wider range of problems and clientele than could be portrayed in one brief chapter. Although no system is perfect or, as of this writing, complete, our aim and our hope was to make a sound case for eclecticism and the continuing pursuit of excellence in the practice of counseling and psychotherapy.

SUGGESTIONS FOR FURTHER READING

Beck, A. T., & Weishaar, M. E. (1995). Cognitive therapy. In R. J. Corsini & D. Wedding (Eds.), *Current psychotherapies* (5th ed., pp. 229–261). Itasca, IL: F. E. Peacock.

Brammer, L. M. (1985). *The helping relationship: Process and skills* (3rd ed.). Englewood Cliffs, NJ: Prentice-Hall.

Brammer, L. M., Shostrom, E. L., & Abrego, P. J. (1989). *Therapeutic psychology: Fundamentals of actualizing counseling and psychotherapy* (5th ed.). Englewood Cliffs, NJ: Prentice-Hall.

Carkhuff, R. R. (1993). *The art of helping* (8th ed.). Amherst, MA: Human Resources Development Press.

Cormier, S., & Cormier, B. (1998). Interviewing strategies for helpers: Fundamental skills and cognitive behavioral interventions (4th ed.). Pacific Grove, CA: Brooks/Cole.

Corsini, R. J., & Wedding, D. (Eds.). (1995). *Current psychotherapies* (5th ed.). Itasca, IL: F. E. Peacock.

Egan, G. (1990). *The skilled helper: Model, skills, and methods for effective helping* (4th ed.). Pacific Grove, CA: Brooks/Cole.

Glasser, W. (2000) *Reality therapy in action.* New York: HarperCollins Publishers, Inc. (This book, reissued in paper edition format without change in content, is also titled *Counseling with choice theory: The new reality therapy*).

Hoyt, M. F., & Miller, S. D. (2000). Stage appropriate change-oriented brief therapy. In J. Carlson & L. Sperry (Eds.), *Brief therapy with individuals and couples* (pp. 289–330). Phoenix, AZ: Zieg, Tucker, & Theisen, Inc.

Ivey, A. E. (1991). *Developmental strategies for helpers: Individual, family, and network interventions.* Pacific Grove, CA: Brooks/Cole.

Ivey, A. E. (Therapist). (1997). *Integrative therapy* (Videotape No. 0-205-32910-1, T. Labriola, Producer). In J. Carlson & D. Kjos, *Integrative therapy with Ivey: Psychotherapy with the experts.* Boston: Allyn & Bacon.

Ivey, A. E., Ivey, M. B., & Simek-Downing, L. (1987). *Counseling and psychotherapy: Integrating skills, theory, and practice* (2nd ed.). Englewood Cliffs, NJ: Prentice-Hall.

James, R. K., & Gilliland, B. E. (2001). *Crisis intervention strategies* (4th ed.). Belmont, CA: Wadsworth/Thompson.

Kelly, G. A. (1955). *The psychology of personal constructs* (Vols. 1 & 2). New York: Norton.

Lazarus, A. A. (1989). *The practice of multimodal therapy.* Baltimore: Johns Hopkins University Press.

Lazarus, A. A. (1997). *Brief but comprehensive psychotherapy: The multimodal way.* New York: Springer.

Santrock, J. W. (1999). *Life-span development* (7th ed.). New York: McGraw-Hill.

Thorne, F. C. (1950). *Principles of personality counseling: An eclectic viewpoint.* Brandon, VT: Journal of Clinical Psychology.

Thorne, F. C. (1968). *Psychological case handling, I: Establishing the conditions necessary for counseling and psychotherapy.* Brandon, VT: Clinical Psychology.

Thorne, F. C. (1973). Eclectic psychotherapy. In R. Corsini (Ed.), *Current psychotherapies* (pp. 445–486). Itasca, IL: F. E. Peacock.

REFERENCES

Adler, A. (1963). *The practice and theory of individual psychology.* Paterson, NJ: Littlefield, Adams.

American Association for Counseling and Development. (1988). *Ethical standards.* Alexandria, VA: Author.

American Association for Counseling and Development. (1989). *Bylaws.* Alexandria, VA: Author.

American Psychological Association. (1991). *Guidelines for providers of psychological services to ethnic, linguistic, and culturally diverse populations.* Washington, DC: Author.

American Psychological Association. (1992, December). Ethical principles of psychologists and code of conduct (an *American Psychologist* publication). Washington, DC: Author.

Aspy, D. N., Aspy, C. B., Russell, G., & Wedel, M. (2000). Carkhuff's human technology: A verification and extension of Kelly's (1997) suggestion to integrate the humanistic and technical components of counseling. *Journal of Counseling and Development, 78,* 29–37.

Atkinson, D., Morten, G., & Sue, D. W. (1989). *Counseling American minorities: A cross-cultural perspective* (3rd ed.). Dubuque, IA: Brown.

Auld, F., & Hyman, M. (1991). *Resolution of inner conflict: An introduction to psychoanalytic therapy.* Washington, DC: American Psychological Association.

Barton, S. (1994). Chaos, self-organization, and psychology. *American Psychologist, 49,* 5–14.

Beck, A. T., & Weishaar, M. E. (1995). Cognitive therapy. In R. J. Corsini & D. Wedding (Eds.), *Current psychotherapies* (5th ed., pp. 229–261). Itasca, IL: F. E. Peacock.

Becuar, D., & Becuar, R. (1988). *Family therapy: A systematic integration.* Boston: Allyn & Bacon.

Berman, E. (1985). Eclecticism and its discontents. *Israel Journal of Psychiatry and Related Sciences, 22,* 51–60.

Blocher, D. H. (1987). *The professional counselor.* New York: Macmillan.

Borgen, F. H. (1984). Counseling psychology. *Annual Review of Psychology, 35,* 579–604.

Brack, C. J., Brack, G., & Zucker, A. (1995). How chaos and complexity theory can help counselors to be more effective. Counseling and Values, 39, 200–208

Brack, G. (1993, August). *Chaos theory: A critical new dimension in consultation.* Paper presented at the Annual Convention of the American Psychological Association, Toronto, Canada.

Brammer, L. M. (1979). *The helping relationship: Process and skills* (2nd ed.). Englewood Cliffs, NJ: Prentice-Hall.

Brammer, L. M. (1985). *The helping relationship: Process and skills* (3rd ed.). Englewood Cliffs, NJ: Prentice-Hall.

Brammer, L. M. (1990). *How to cope with life transitions.* New York: Hemisphere.

Brammer, L. M., & Shostrom, E. L. (1968). *Therapeutic psychology: Fundamentals of actualization counseling and psychotherapy* (2nd ed.). Englewood Cliffs, NJ: Prentice-Hall.

Brammer, L. M., Shostrom, E. L., & Abrego, P. J. (1989). *Therapeutic psychology: Fundamentals of counseling and psychotherapy* (5th ed.). Englewood Cliffs, NJ: Prentice-Hall.

Brennan, C. (1995). Beyond theory and practice: A postmodern perspective. *Counseling and Values, 39,* 99–107.

Briggs, J. (1992). *Fractals: The patterns of chaos.* New York: Simon & Schuster.

Briggs, J., & Peat, F. D. (1989). *Turbulent mirror: An illustrated guide to chaos theory and the science of wholeness.* New York: Harper & Row.

Buie, J. (1988). Psychoanalysis: Lawsuit takes aim at barriers to training, practice for non-MDs. *The APA Monitor, 19,* 1–14.

Butz, M. R. (1992). The fractal nature of the development of the self. *Psychological Reports, 3*(2), 1043–1063.

Butz, M. R. (1993, August). *Chaos theory and familial dynamics: What does it look like?* Paper presented at the Annual Convention of the American Psychological Association, Toronto, Canada.

Butz, M. R. (1995). Chaos theory, philosophically old, scientifically new. *Counseling and Values, 39,* 84–98.

Campbell, J. (Ed.). (1971). *The portable Jung* (R. F. C. Hull, Trans.). New York: Penguin Books.

Carkhuff, R. R. (1969a). *Helping and human relations. Vol. 1: Practice and research.* New York: Holt, Rinehart and Winston.

Carkhuff, R. R. (1969b). *Helping and human relations. Vol. 2: Practice and research.* New York: Holt, Rinehart and Winston.

Carkhuff, R. R. (1973). *The art of problem-solving: A guide for developing problem-solving skills for parents, teachers, counselors, and administrators.* Amherst, MA: Human Resources Development Press.

Carkhuff, R. R. (1993). *The art of helping* (8th ed.). Amherst, MA: Human Resources Development Press.

Carkhuff, R. R., & Berenson, B. G. (1977). *Beyond counseling and therapy* (2nd ed.). New York: Holt, Rinehart & Winston.

Castonguay, L. G., & Goldfried, M. R. (1994). Psychotherapy integration: An idea whose time has come. *Applied and Preventive Psychology, 3*(3), 159–172.

Chamberlain, L. (1993, August). *Strange attractors in patterns of family interactions.* Paper presented at the Annual Convention of the American Psychological Association, Toronto, Canada.

Chamberlain, L. (1994, August). *Is there a chaotician in the house? Chaos and family therapy.* Paper presented at the Annual Convention of the American Psychological Association, Los Angeles, CA.

Chamberlain, L. (1995). Chaos and change in a suicidal family. *Counseling and Values, 39,* 117–128.

Chessick, R. D. (1985). The frantic retreat from the mind to the brain: American psychiatry in mauvaise foi. *Psychoanalytic Inquiry, 5,* 369–403.

Colapinto, J. (1984). Integration and model integrity. *Journal of Strategic and Systemic Therapies, 3,* 38–42.

Cormier, L. S., & Cormier, W. H. (1998). *Interviewing strategies for helpers: Fundamental skills and cognitive behavioral interventions* (4th ed.). Pacific Grove, CA: Brooks/Cole.

Cormier, W. H., & Cormier, L. S. (1985). *Interviewing strategies for helpers: Fundamental skills and cognitive behavioral interventions* (2nd ed.). Monterey, CA: Brooks/Cole.

Cormier, W. H., & Cormier, L. S. (1991). *Interviewing strategies for helpers: Fundamental skills and cognitive behavioral interventions* (3rd ed.). Monterey, CA: Brooks/Cole.

Corsini, R. J. (Ed.). (1981). *Handbook of innovative psychotherapies.* New York: Wiley.

Corsini, R. J. (1995). Introduction. In R. J. Corsini & D. Wedding (Eds.), *Current psychotherapies* (5th ed., pp. 1–14). Itasca, IL: F. E. Peacock.

Corsini, R. J., & Wedding, D. (Eds.). (1995). *Current psychotherapies* (5th ed.). Itasca, IL: F. E. Peacock.

D'Andrea, M., & Daniels, J. (1994). Group pacing: A developmental eclectic approach to group work. *Journal of Counseling and Development, 72,* 585–590.

DeAngelis, T. (1993). Chaos, chaos everywhere is what the theorists think. *The APA Monitor, 24*(1), 1, 41.

deShazer, S. (1985). *Keys to solution in brief therapy.* New York: Norton.

deShazer, S. (1988). *Clues: Investigating solutions in brief therapy.* New York: Norton.

Douglas, C. (1995). Analytical psychotherapy. In R. J. Corsini & D. Wedding (Eds.), *Current psychotherapies* (5th ed., pp. 95–127). Itasca, IL: F. E. Peacock.

Duck, S., & Condra, M. (1990). To be or not to be: Anticipation, persuasion, and retrospection in personal relationships. In G. J. Neimeyer & R. A. Neimeyer (Eds.), *Advances in personal construct psychology: A research annual* (pp. 187–202). Greenwich, CT: JAI Press.

Duncan, B. L., Parks, M. B., & Rusk, G. S. (1990). Strategic eclecticism: A technical alternative to eclectic psychotherapy. *Psychotherapy, 27,* 568–577.

Egan, G. (1975). *The skilled helper: A model for systematic helping and interpersonal relating.* Monterey, CA: Brooks/Cole.

Egan, G. (1982). *The skilled helper: Model, skills, and methods for effective helping* (2nd ed.). Monterey, CA: Brooks/Cole.

Egan, G. (1986). *The skilled helper: A systematic approach to effective helping* (3rd ed.). Monterey, CA: Brooks/Cole.

Egan, G. (1990). *The skilled helper: Model, skills, and methods for effective helping* (4th ed.). Pacific Grove, CA: Brooks/Cole.

Egan, G. (1994). *The skilled helper* (5th ed.). Pacific Grove, CA: Brooks/Cole.

Eiser, J. R. (1994). *Attitudes, chaos, and the connectionist mind.* Oxford, UK: Blackwell.

Ellis, A. (1979). Rational-emotive therapy. In R. Corsini (Ed.), *Current psychotherapies* (2nd ed., pp. 185–229). Itasca, IL: F. E. Peacock.

Ellis, A. (1984). The use of hypnosis with rational emotive therapy (RET). *International Journal of Eclectic Psychotherapy, 3,* 15–22.

Ellis, A. (1995). Rational-emotive behavior therapy. In R. J. Corsini & D. Wedding (Eds.), *Current psychotherapies* (5th ed., pp. 162–196). Itasca, IL: F. E. Peacock.

Ellis, A., & Harper, R. (1975). *A new guide to rational living.* Hollywood, CA: Wilshire Books.

Eysenck, H. J. (1984). Personality and individual differences. *Bulletin of the British Psychological Society, 37,* 237.

Fischer, J. (1995). Uniformity myths in eclectic and integrative psychotherapy. *Journal of Psychotherapy Integration, 5*(1), 41–56.

Ford, D. H. (1994). *Humans as self-constructing living systems: A developmental perspective, behavior, and personality* (2nd ed.). State College, PA: IDEALS.

Foley, V. D. (1989). Family therapy. In R. J. Corsini & D. Wedding (Eds.), *Current psychotherapies* (4th ed., pp. 455–500). Itasca, IL: F. E. Peacock.

Freud, S. (1949). *An outline of psychoanalysis.* New York: Norton.

Freud, S. (1961). *The standard edition of the complete psychological works of Sigmund Freud.* (J. Strachey, Ed. and Trans.). London: Hogarth Press. (Original work published 1924)

Gambrill, E. (1977). *Behavior modification: Handbook of assessment, intervention, and evaluation.* San Francisco: Jossey-Bass.

Garfield, S. L. (1980). *Psychotherapy: An eclectic approach.* New York: Wiley.

Garfield, S. L. (1994). Eclecticism and integration in psychotherapy: Developments and issues. *Clinical Psychology Science and Practice, 1*(2), 123–137.

Garfield, S. L., & Bergin, A. E. (1986). *Handbook of psychotherapy and behavior change.* New York: Wiley.

Garfield, S. L., & Kurtz, R. (1975). Clinical psychologists: A survey of selected attitudes and views. *The Clinical Psychologist, 28,* 4–7.

Glasser, W. (1965). *Reality therapy.* New York: Harper & Row.

Glasser, W. (1984). *Control theory: A new explanation of how we control our lives.* New York: Harper & Row.

Glasser, W. (1996). *Staying together: The control theory guide to a lasting marriage.* New York: HarperCollins (Perennial paper edition).

Glasser, W. (1998). *Choice theory: A new psychology of personal freedom.* New York: HarperCollins.

Glasser, W. (2000). *Reality therapy in action.* New York: HarperCollins. (Reissued in paper edition format without change in content, is also titled *Counseling with choice theory: The new reality therapy*).

Glasser, W., & Glasser, C. (1999). *The language of choice theory.* New York: HarperCollins.

Glasser, W., & Glasser, C. (2000). *Getting together and staying together: Solving the mystery of marriage.* New York: HarperCollins.

Gleick, J. (1987). *Chaos: Making a new science.* New York: Viking Penguin.

Gleatt, H. B. (1995). Chaos and compassion. *Counseling and Values, 39,* 108–116.

Goldenberg, I., & Goldenberg, H. (1995). Family therapy. In R. J. Corsini & D. Wedding (Eds.), *Current psychotherapies* (5th ed., pp. 356–385). Itasca, IL: F. E. Peacock.

Haas, L. J., & Cummings, N. A. (1991). Managed outpatient mental health plans: Clinical, ethical, practical guidelines for participation. *Professional Psychology: Research and Practice, 22,* 45–51.

Hackney, H., & Cormier, L. S. (1988). *Counseling strategies and interventions* (3rd ed.). Englewood Cliffs, NJ: Prentice-Hall.

Hall, N. (1991). *Chaos: A guide to the new science of disorder.* New York: W. W. Norton.

Hansen, J. C., Stevic, R. R., & Warner, R. W., Jr. (1977). *Counseling: Theory and process.* Boston: Allyn & Bacon.

Harding, W. (Producer). (1992). *LARRY.* (26-minute videotape documentary of Dr. Larry Gladwin Harding's life of chaos as a bipolar or manic depressive person.) Arvada, CO: Walking Eagle Productions.

Heppner, P. P., Kivlighan, D. M., Jr., & Wampold, B. E. (1992). *Research design in counseling.* Pacific Grove, CA: Brooks/Cole.

Hergenhahn, B. R. (1994). *An introduction to theories of personality* (4th ed.). Englewood Cliffs, NJ: Prentice-Hall.

Hollanders, H., & McLeod, J. (1999). Theoretical orientation and reported practice: A survey of eclecticism among counsellors in Britain. *British Journal of Guidance and Counselling, 27,* 405–414.

Hong, Y., Morris, M. W., Chiu, C., & Benet-Martinez, V. (2000). Multicultural minds: A dynamic constructivist approach to culture and cognition. *American Psychologist, 55,* 709–720.

Hoyt, M. F., & Miller, S. D. (2000). Stage appropriate change-oriented brief therapy. In J. Carlson & L. Sperry (Eds.), *Brief therapy with individuals and couples* (pp. 289–330). Phoenix, AZ: Zieg, Tucker, & Theisen.

Hubble, M. A., Duncan, B. L., & Miller, S. D. (Eds.). (1999). *The heart and soul of change: What works in therapy.* Washington, DC: American Psychological Association.

Huck, S. W., Cormier, W. H., & Bounds, W. G. (1974). *Reading statistics and research.* New York: Harper & Row.

Ivey, A. E. (1986). *Developmental therapy: Theory into practice.* San Francisco: Jossey-Bass.

Ivey, A. E. (Therapist). (1997). *Integrative therapy* (Videotape No. 0–205–32910–1, T. Labriola, Producer). In J. Carlson & D. Kjos, *Integrative therapy with Ivey: Psychotherapy with the experts.* Boston: Allyn & Bacon.

Ivey, A. E., & Authier, J. (1978). *Microcounseling: Innovations in interviewing, counseling, psychotherapy, and psychoeducation* (2nd ed.). Springfield, IL: Chas. C. Thomas.

Ivey, A. E., Ivey, M. B., & Simek-Downing, L. (1987). *Counseling and psychotherapy: Integrating skills, theory, and practice* (2nd ed.). Englewood Cliffs, NJ: Prentice-Hall.

Ivey, A. E., & Simek-Downing, L. (1980). *Counseling and psychotherapy: Skills, theories, and practice.* Englewood Cliffs, NJ: Prentice-Hall.

James, R. K., & Gilliland, B. E. (2001). *Crisis intervention strategies* (4th ed.). Belmont, CA: Wadsworth/ Thompson.

Kanfer, F. H., & Goldstein, A. P. (Eds.). (1975). *Helping people change.* Elmsford, NY: Pergamon.

Kell, B. L., & Mueller, W. J. (1966). *Impact and change: A study of counseling relationships.* New York: Appleton-Century-Crofts.

Kelly, G. A. (1955). *The psychology of personal constructs* (Vols. 1 & 2). New York: Norton.

Kerr, M. E., & Bowen, M. (1988). *Family evaluation: An approach based on Bowen theory.* New York: Norton.

Kohut, H. (1971). *The analysis of self.* New York: International Universities Press.

Kohut, H. (1977). *The restoration of the self.* New York: International Universities Press.

Kohut, H. (1984). *How does analysis cure?* Chicago: University of Chicago Press.

Krumboltz, J. D., & Thoresen, C. E. (Eds.). (1976). *Counseling methods.* New York: Holt, Rinehart & Winston.

Larsen, D. J. (1999). Eclecticism: Psychological theories as interwoven stories. *International Journal for the Advancement of Counselling, 21,* 69–83.

Lazarus, A. A. (1967). In support of technical eclecticism. *Psychological Reports, 21,* 415–416.

Lazarus, A. A. (1981). *The practice of multimodal therapy.* New York: McGraw-Hill.

Lazarus, A. A. (1986a). Multimodal therapy. In J. C. Norcross (Ed.), *Handbook of eclectic psychotherapy* (pp. 65–93). New York: Brunner/Mazel.

Lazarus, A. A. (1986b). Multimodal therapy. In E. L. Shostrom (Executive Producer), S. K. Shostrom (Producer), & H. Ratner (Director), *Three approaches to psychotherapy II* (Film no. 2, Case of Kathy). Corona Del Mar, CA: Psychological and Educational Film.

Lazarus, A. A. (1987). The need for technical eclecticism: Science, breadth, depth, and specificity. In J. K. Zeig (Ed.), *The evolution of psychotherapy* (pp. 164–178). New York: Brunner/Mazel.

Lazarus, A. A. (1989a). The case of George. In D. Wedding & R. J. Corsini (Eds.), *Case studies in psychotherapy* (pp. 227–238). Itasca, IL: F. E. Peacock.

Lazarus, A. A. (1989b). Multimodal therapy. In R. J. Corsini & D. Wedding (Eds.), *Current psychotherapies* (4th ed., pp. 503–544). Itasca, IL: F. E. Peacock.

Lazarus, A. A. (1989c). *The practice of multimodal therapy.* Baltimore: Johns Hopkins University Press.

Lazarus, A. A. (1995a). Different types of eclecticism and integration: Let's be aware of the dangers. *Journal of Psychotherapy Integration, 5*(1), 27–39.

Lazarus, A. A. (1995b). Multimodal therapy. In R. J. Corsini & D. Wedding (Eds.), *Current psychotherapies* (5th ed, pp. 322–355). Itasca, IL: F. E. Peacock.

Lazarus, A. A. (1997). *Brief but comprehensive psychotherapy: The multimodal way.* New York: Springer.

Lazarus, A. A. (2000a). Multimodal replenishment. *Professional Psychology: Research and Practice, 31,* 93–94.

Lazarus, A. A. (2000b). Will reason prevail? From classical psychoanalysis to New Age therapy. *American Journal of Psychotherapy, 54,* 152–155.

Lazarus, A. A., & Beutler, L. E. (1993). On technical eclecticism. *Journal of Counseling & Development, 71,* 381–385.

Leger, F. J. (1998). *Beyond the therapeutic relationship: Behavioral, biological, and cognitive foundations of psychotherapy.* Binghamton, NY: Haworth Press.

Linden, G. W. (1984). Some philosophical roots of Adlerian psychology. *Individual Psychology: Journal of Adlerian Theory, Research, and Practice, 40,* 254–269.

Lowen, A. (1995). Bioenergetic analysis. In R. J. Corsini & D. Wedding (Eds.), *Current psychotherapies* (5th ed., pp. 409–418). Itasca, IL: F. E. Peacock.

Maslow, A. H. (1976). *The farther reaches of human nature.* New York: Penguin Books.

May, R., & Yalom, I. (1995). Existential psychotherapy. In R. J. Corsini & D. Wedding (Eds.), *Current psychotherapies* (5th ed., pp. 262–292). Itasca, IL: F. E. Peacock.

McCown, W., & Johnson, J. (1993, August). *Chaos in response to changes in family systems: Empirical findings.* Paper presented at the Annual Convention of the American Psychological Association, Toronto, Canada.

Meichenbaum, D. H. (1977). *Cognitive behavior modification: An integrative approach.* New York: Plenum.

Miller, S. D., Duncan, B. L., & Hubble, M. A. (1997). *Escape from Babel: Toward a unifying language for psychotherapy practice.* New York: Norton.

Mosak, H. H. (1995). Adlerian psychotherapy. In R. J. Corsini & D. Wedding (Eds.), *Current psychotherapies* (5th ed., pp. 51–94). Itasca, IL: F. E. Peacock.

Myer, R. A., Williams, R. C., Ottens, A. J., & Schmidt, A. E. (1992). A three-dimensional model for triage. *Journal of Mental Health Counseling, 14,* 137–148.

Neimeyer, G. J., & Neimeyer, R. A. (Eds.). (1990). *Advances in personal construct psychology: A research annual* (Vol. 1). Greenwich, CT: JAI Press.

Neimeyer, R. A., & Neimeyer, G. J. (Eds.). (1987). *Personal construct therapy casebook.* New York: Springer.

Norcross, J. C. (Ed.). (1986). *Handbook of eclectic psychotherapy.* New York: Brunner/Mazel.

Norcross, J. C. (Ed.). (1987). *Casebook of eclectic psychotherapy.* New York: Brunner/Mazel.

Norcross, J. C. (1995). A roundtable on psychotherapy integration: Common factors, technical eclecticism, and psychotherapy research. *Journal of Psychotherapy Practice and Research, 4*(3), 248–271.

Palmer, J. O. (1980). *A primer of eclectic psychotherapy.* Monterey, CA: Brooks/Cole.

Patterson, C. H. (1980). *Theories of counseling and psychotherapy* (3rd ed.). New York: Harper & Row.

Patterson, C. H. (1986). *Theories of counseling and psychotherapy* (4th ed.). New York: Harper & Row.

Peca, K. (1992, April). *Chaos theory: A scientific basis for alternative research methods in educational administration.* Paper presented at the Annual Convention of the American Educational Research Association, San Francisco, CA.

Pedersen, P. B. (1988). *A handbook for development of multicultural awareness.* Alexandria, VA: American Association for Counseling and Development.

Pedersen, P. B. (1989). Developing multicultural ethical guidelines for psychology. *International Journal of Psychology, 24,* 643–652.

Pedersen, P. B. (1990). The constructs of complexity and balance in multicultural counseling theory and practice. *Journal of Counseling and Development, 68,* 550–554.

Perls, F. (1969). *Gestalt therapy verbatim.* Lafayette, CA: Real People Press.

Pietrofesa, J. J., Hoffman, A., Splete, H. H., & Pinto, D. V. (1978). *Counseling: Theory, research, and practice.* Skokie, IL: Rand McNally.

Polster, E., & Polster, M. (1973). *Gestalt therapy integrated: Contours of therapy and practice.* New York: Brunner/Mazel.

Postrel, V. (1998). *The future and its enemies: The growing conflict over creativity, enterprise, and progress.* New York: Free Press.

Prigogine, I. (1984). *Order out of chaos: Man's dialogue with nature.* Toronto: Bantam Books.

Prochaska, J. O., & DiClemente, C. C. (1982). Transtheoretical therapy: Toward a more integrative model of change. *Psychotherapy, 19,* 276–288.

Prochaska, J. O., & DiClemente, C. C. (1984). *The transtheoretical approach: Crossing traditional boundaries of therapy.* Homewood, IL: Dow-Jones-Irwin.

Prochaska, J. O., DiClemente, C. C., & Norcross, J. C. (1992). In search of how people change. *American Psychologist, 47,* 1102–1114.

Raskin, N. J., & Rogers, C. R. (1995). Person-centered therapy. In R. J. Corsini & D. Wedding (Eds.), *Current psychotherapies* (5th ed., pp. 128–161). Itasca, IL: F. E. Peacock.

Rogers, C. R. (1951). *Client-centered therapy.* Boston: Houghton Mifflin.

Russell, R. L. (1986). The inadvisability of admixing psychoanalysis with other forms of psychotherapy. *Journal of Contemporary Psychotherapy, 16,* 76–86.

Rychlak, J. F. (1986). Eclecticism in psychological theorizing: Good and bad. *Journal of Counseling and Development, 63,* 351–353.

Santrock, J. W. (1999). *Life-span development* (7th ed.). New York: McGraw-Hill.

Scharff, J. S., & Scharff, D. E. (1998). *Object relations individual therapy.* Northvale, NJ: Aronson.

Scheidlinger, S. (1984). Group psychotherapy in the 1980's: Problems and prospects. *American Journal of Psychotherapy, 38,* 494–504.

Sechrest, L. (1977). *Personal constructs theory.* In R. J. Corsini (Ed.), *Current personality theories* (pp. 203–241). Itasca, IL: F. E. Peacock.

Schroeder, M. (1991). *Fractals, chaos, and power laws: Minutes from an infinite paradise.* New York: W. H. Freeman.

Sims, R. R., & Sauser, W. I. (1985). Guiding principles for development of competency-based business curricula. *Journal of Management Development, 4,* 51–65.

Skinner, B. F. (1953). *Science and human behavior.* New York: Macmillan.

Smith, B. D., & Vetter, H. J. (1991). *Theories of personality* (2nd ed.). Englewood Cliffs, NJ: Prentice-Hall.

Smith, D. (1982). Trends in counseling and psychotherapy. *American Psychologist, 37,* 802–809.

Stall, R. (1984). Disadvantages of eclecticism in the treatment of alcoholism: The "problem" of recidivism. *Journal of Drug Issues, 14,* 437–448.

St. Clair, M. (1996). *Object relations and self psychology: An introduction* (2nd ed.). Pacific Grove, CA: Brooks/Cole.

Stomberg, C., Loeb, L., Thomsen, S., & Krause, J. (1996). State initiatives to healthcare reform. *The Psychologists Legal Update, 8,* 1–6.

Stricker, G. (1992). The relationship of research to clinical practice. *American Psychologist, 44,* 543–549.

Strupp, H. H. (1988). What is therapeutic change? *Journal of Cognitive Psychotherapy, 2,* 75–82.

Strupp, H. H. (1989). Psychotherapy: Can the practitioner learn from the research? *American Psychologist, 44,* 717–724.

Sue, D. W. (1991). A conceptual model for cultural diversity training. *Journal of Counseling and Development, 70,* 99–105.

Sue, D. W. (1992, Winter). The challenge of multiculturalism: The road less traveled. *American Counselor, 1,* 6–14.

Sue, D. W., Arredondo, P., & McDavis, R. J. (1992). Multicultural counseling competencies and standards: A call to the professionals. *Journal of Counseling and Development, 70,* 477–486.

Sue, D. W., & Sue, D. (1990). *Counseling the culturally different: Theory and practice.* New York: Wiley.

Summers, F. L. (1999). *Transcending the self: An object relations model of psychoanalytic therapy.* Hillsdale, NJ: Analytic Press.

Thompson, C. L., & Rudolph, L. B. (2000). *Counseling children.* Belmont, CA: Wadsworth/Thompson.

Thoresen, C. E. (Ed.). (1980). *The behavior therapist.* Monterey, CA: Brooks/Cole.

Thorne, F. C. (1950). *Principles of personality counseling: An eclectic approach.* Brandon, VT: Journal of Clinical Psychology.

Thorne, F. C. (1955). *Principles of psychological examining.* Brandon, VT: Clinical Psychology.

Thorne, F. C. (1960). *Clinical judgment.* Brandon, VT: Clinical Psychology.

Thorne, F. C. (1961). *Personality.* Brandon, VT: Clinical Psychology.

Thorne, F. C. (1965). *How to be psychologically healthy: Tutorial counseling.* Brandon, VT: Clinical Psychology.

Thorne, F. C. (1967). *Integrative psychology.* Brandon, VT: Clinical Psychology.

Thorne, F. C. (1968). *Psychological case handling, I: Establishing the conditions necessary for counseling and psychotherapy.* Brandon, VT: Clinical Psychology.

Thorne, F. C. (1970). Adler's broad-spectrum concept of man, self-consistency, and unification. *Journal of Individual Psychology, 26,* 135–143.

Thorne, F. C. (1973). Eclectic psychotherapy. In R. Corsini (Ed.), *Current psychotherapies* (pp. 445–486). Itasca, IL: F. E. Peacock.

Viney, L. L. (1990). A constructivist model of psychological reactions to physical illness and injury. In G. J. Neimeyer & R. A. Neimeyer (Eds.), *Advances in personal construct psychology: A research annual* (pp. 117–151). Greenwich, CT: JAI Press.

Waldrop, M. (1992). *Complexity: The emerging science at the edge of order and chaos.* New York: Simon & Schuster.

Warner, R. E. (1991). A survey of theoretical orientations of Canadian clinical psychologists. *Canadian Psychology, 32,* 525–528.

Watkins, C. E., & Watts, R. E. (1995). Psychotherapy survey research studies: Some consistent findings and integrative conclusions. *Psychotherapy in Private Practice, 13,* 49–68.

Watson, D. L., & Tharp, R. G. (1989). *Self-directed behavior: Self-modification for personal adjustment* (5th ed.). Pacific Grove, CA: Brooks/Cole.

Wilbur, M. P., Kulikowich, J. M., Roberts-Wilbur, J., & Torres-Rivera, E. (1995). Chaos theory and counselor training. *Counseling and Values, 39,* 129–144.

Williams, R. L., & Long, J. D. (1983). *Toward a self-managed lifestyle* (3rd ed.). Boston: Houghton Mifflin.

Williamson, E. G. (1965). *Vocational counseling.* New York: McGraw-Hill.

Williamson, E. G., & Darley, J. G. (1937). *Student personnel work: An outline of clinical procedures.* New York: Norton.

Wilson, G. T. (1995). Behavior therapy. In R. J. Corsini & D. Wedding (Eds.), *Current psychotherapies* (5th ed., pp. 197–228). Itasca, IL: F. E. Peacock.

Wolpe, J. (1969). *The practice of behavior therapy.* Elmsford, NY: Pergamon.

Zheng, R. (2000). New progress in psychological counseling. *Psychological Science, 23,* 599–602.

Zook, A., II, & Walton, J. M. (1989). Theoretical orientations and work settings of clinical and counseling psychologists: A current perspective. *Professional Psychology: Research and Practice, 20,* 23–31.

14 Computer-Assisted Therapy/Cybercounseling

Fundamental Tenets

Consider the following propositions:

1. Thinking is unique to humans. Therefore, computers cannot think.
2. Thinking is a series of symbolic operations. Therefore, computers can think (Wagman, 1988, p. 8).

For most humanists and many psychotherapists, the idea that a computer could be a counselor that would deal in multimodal ways with a variety of client problems is anathematic. However, what if a computer could so closely approximate human behavior that the human being who interacted with it could not differentiate between its thinking and that of a human? Further, what if a computer system that used virtual reality could so closely approximate the event itself that the client's emotional and physiological responses were indistinguishable from those at the time of the actual event? If that were true, the philosophical question of whether computers do indeed think would be moot. All that would really matter would be that they *appear* to do so (Wagman, 1988, p. 10).

We end this fifth edition with what may be, to many, a controversial view of therapy in the new millennium—counseling in cyberspace and the counseling computer. That is correct! We are speaking of a computer who will counsel clients about personal problems. (Please note that here we have not made a grammar mistake in using the pronoun "who," which is used to refer to people. The reason for this grammatical choice will soon become apparent. Also, we have chosen a different font to portray a computer screen in the Counseling Process section.)

Part of this chapter covers what already is and part covers what the experts believe will be (Franklin, 1995, 1997; Greist, 1995; Kirkby, 1996; Wagman, 1988). It would appear that in the twenty-first century computers will act as both therapeutic assistant and primary therapeutic agent (Pardeck & Schulte, 1990). Given that, we believe we are all on the threshold of a truly astounding new field in psychotherapy.

History

The history of computer counseling is approximately three decades long. Two interesting events mark early efforts in the 1960s to develop computers in the mental health field that would hint at the powerful roles computers might one day play in dealing with the human condition. As with many such discoveries, both events were serendipitous and largely accidental to the task at hand. Slack, Hicks, Reed, and Van Cura (1966) discovered that the development of a computer program to allow clients to write down their own histories had a beneficial side effect. Clients reported that while inputting their histories they had learned a lot about themselves; furthermore, they felt better after just working with the computer.

Weizenbaum (1965), in order to deal with communication difficulties brought about by the daunting task of programming human interaction, modeled ELIZA after a Rogerian person-centered mode of responding. Amazingly, when the program was first tried, people became deeply involved with it and insisted the machine understood them despite Weizenbaum's (1976) efforts to remind them that they were in a dialogue with nothing more than a machine.

During the 1970s and 1980s probably the most significant and concentrated work was the PLATO project jointly engineered between Control Data Corporation and the University of Illinois (Wagman, 1979, 1980, 1982, 1984, 1988). PLATO is an expert system that has a highly structured set of strategies to deal with dilemmas. Clients are given instructions on the meaning of dilemmas and on how to formulate their dilemmas so the computer will understand them, and then are allowed practice in generating solutions. PLATO gives demonstrations of how possible solutions may be generated and then assigns each client the task of developing a solution for his or her own particular dilemma. Feedback and reinforcement are given by PLATO as clients move through the sequence. PLATO has today been accessed by more than 2,000 sites around the world (Wagman, 1988, pp. 105–107).

Computer counseling in the 1990s did not expand as extensively as possible. However, one significant shift in psychotherapy and three major advances in computers may be bellwethers for a major change in the delivery of mental health counseling and psychotherapy.

In counseling and psychotherapy, cognitive systems have gradually come to dominate the field. Whereas older systems of psychotherapy concentrated on personality dynamics; generalized predictions about a person; and motivation, needs, drive, global problem dimensions, and complete structural change of the personality, cognitive behaviorism emphasizes discrete categories, inferential thinking, situation-specific behavior change, and multiple cognitive mapping and programming schemata to change the irrational, nonlogical thinking of maladaptive behavior (Amsel, 1992; Brennis, 1994; Wagman, 1988). This general shift has made psychotherapy much more compatible with the algorithmic, logical, and linear mathematical schemata that drive computers and undergird artificial intelligence.

Solution-focused brief therapy (SFBT) (see Chapter 11) can be fitted nicely into this algorithmic approach. Gingerich and de Shazer (1989, 1991) operationalized the theory into expert computer programs called Briefer I and Briefer II, which could hypothetically advise counselors on selecting, designing, and developing an intervention at the end of the very first therapy session (1991, p. 241). While no computer application of Briefer I or II was ever commercially made, Presbury and Marchal (2000) have followed up on what Gingerich and de Shazer proposed and made a working model of SFBT for training counselors.

Three major technological advances have changed dramatically what computers are and will be able to do in providing psychotherapy and counseling. First, memory systems have increased and become more efficient. Memory now available to even a simple personal computer will allow for the vast amount of information a counseling computer needs to be truly interactive with a human being in multidimensional ways. What Colby (1963) struggled to do on a computer mainframe in the 1960s in writing a program to deal with depressed clients he could now do with relative ease on a personal computer (Colby, 1995).

A second advance is the Internet. When the third edition of this book was being written in the early 1990s, using the Internet to provide mental health services was seen as a novelty—if considered at all—by most mental health providers. The Internet is changing the way mental health services are delivered.

The Internet allows access to everything from online chat rooms, in which members of interest and support groups with common mental health issues talk to one another (Binik, Cantor, Ochs, & Meana, 1997; Gary & Remolino, 2000); to websites that operate crisis lines (Gary & Remolino, 2000); to commercial enterprises that provide a variety of good to bad counseling and mental health services (Binik et al., 1997; Heinlein, Richmond, Rak, & Welfel, 2001). This change will become exponentially more dramatic as sophisticated therapy programs that can be accessed from anywhere in the world go online. And go they will. John Greist (1995), clinical computing editor for the journal *Psychiatric Services,* suggests that the programming to provide effective computer counseling is already available—all we need to do is use it.

A third advance is virtual reality. Virtual reality is unheralded in the ways its technology can be used to provide the client *in vivo* access to role play, desensitization, covert modeling, and a variety of other techniques that allow him or her to practice coping and change behaviors while being directly or indirectly involved with the therapist (Biocca, 1992; Kirkby, 1996; Lamson, 1995; Muscott & Gifford, 1994; Rothbaum et al., 1995). Phobic reactions are particularly amenable to immersive virtual reality, wherein the client has a helmet placed on his or her head. The helmet provides graded auditory and visual scenarios of the feared situation; the clients can monitor and control the amount of exposure to the feared stimulus. The client may also receive a running score on how successful he or she is in closing proximity to and length of time spent facing the feared stimulus (Kirkby, 1996; Rothbaum, et al., 1995).

Presently computers do not have minds in the human sense of the word, nor do they feel or create as humans do. However, that doesn't mean any of these are impossible tasks for computers by any means; indeed, some predict that a computer with humanlike consciousness will become a reality in about forty years (Moravac, 1988). All of these tasks are being worked on as we write. A number of bright and capable cognitive scientists, ranging from mathematicians to psychologists to neurobiologists to computer engineers, are busily at work trying to understand and create artificial minds (Franklin, 1995). When these concepts are applied to the computer counselor, as far as its range of techniques is concerned, it may well equal—and perhaps exceed—the typical human therapist. Whether the future counseling computer can stand alone or will serve as an adjunct to the human therapist is an interesting question. Whether it will do as well or even better than the human therapist is another interesting question.

Theory of Personality

It should be abundantly clear that a counseling computer has no distinct theory of personality other than what is programmed into it. Given the current state of technology, there are limits to what that programmed theory of personality might be. Cognitive-behavioral approaches are currently the most amenable to programming, in contrast to psychoanalytic approaches, which call for deep personal understanding of the client (Finkel, 1990; Kenardy & Adams, 1993; Wagman, 1988, p. 102).

Nature of Maladjustment

Presently, maladjustment is probably most limited by current programming's ability to deal with initial relationship exploration, adjustment problems that can be handled with psychoeducational techniques, and situation-specific cognitive-based problems such as phobias and depression (Colby, 1995; Kirkby, 1996). Although virtual reality is capable of being adapted to such issues it cannot, at present, generate more complex psychodynamic scenarios such as individually building the client's own personal psychodrama or role playing (Franklin, 1997).

Major Concepts

Integrating Metaphorical Systems.   The language of psychotherapy and other systems is best represented in metaphors. Wagman's (1988) analysis of different types of metaphors as representative of different types of systems of psychotherapy is instructive from the standpoint of the intersection of type of therapeutic relationship and type of problem. That is, psychoanalysis has classical literary metaphors; behaviorism has physiological, mechanistic metaphors; humanistic therapies have personal and idealistic metaphors; and cognitive therapies have logical and educative metaphors.

These therapeutic systems and their metaphors can be put in contrast to one another in a dimensional analysis. On an X-Y axis the four quadrants would contrast affective and cognitive relationships (X) and focal and diffuse problems (Y). Virtually every therapeutic modality in this book could be placed in one of the quadrants, depending on how much affective (person-centered) or cognitive (cognitive-behaviorism) emphasis is placed on the therapeutic relationship and how focal (phobia; clarification of values) or diffuse (generalized, chronic depression; anxiety neurosis) the problem is (Wagman, 1988, pp. 12–14).

On the other hand, artificial intelligence has as its basis computational and schematic metaphors that Wagman (1988) believed tended to put its metaphorical representation at cross purposes with the major therapeutic systems (p. 13). Nine years later, Franklin (1997) stated that was no longer so and that, in principle, any of the psychotherapeutic metaphors could be programmed or developed.

The Computer as Mind.   The concepts of *mind* and *intelligent mind* need to be thought of in new and different ways. Franklin's (1995) work on artificial minds wrestles extensively with this problem. The advent of attempting to make "intelligent" computers calls for divergent thinking about what *mind* is. Traditional mind–body theories fall into three categories. The *mentalist* theory holds that the mind is everything and that it produces the material world as sensation such that the mind is a spiritual entity. The *materialist* theory holds that mind is only a physical process, but that this physical process can become very sophisticated, up to and including the exotic physics of quantum mechanics. The *dualist* theory holds that the mental and the physical have existences of their own and that the mind is subject to completely different principles of operation than the body (Franklin, 1995, pp. 25–26). To get at the business of an artificial mind, Franklin proposes a workable hypothesis that considers minds in a functionalist-physicalist sense. That is, minds are the software and brains are the hardware that make the software run. In that regard, mind could certainly run on some type of hardware other than a human being's neurological system. In fact, it might just as well run on a computer (p. 28).

Computers That Can Learn.   Mind, to some degree, can be implemented on machines (Franklin, 1995, p. 18). The question becomes to what degree? A truly humanlike computer counselor ought to have a mind of its own that could create, store, and modify information. It could make inferences and deductions based on that information and extrapolate it in bigger and better ways as new and different situations enter its environment. It should be able to hop between the quadrants of therapeutic modalities and problem specificity, described by Wagman (1988), without going into default mode. In short, it should be able to learn from its experience.

The Counseling Process

Before you burn this book because you now believe that a counseling computer with an empathic, cheerful-looking virtual reality therapist will replace you before you even get to be one, consider the following propositions from the computer counselor's critics and proponents.

Therapy requires a human therapist. If that were so, then there would be no crisis lines or self-help audio- and videotapes. Colby (1995) believes that when clients use his computer counselor, Overcoming Depression, they are communicating with him, except they are one step removed. The bottom line is that if computer therapy can be made available for individuals who could not access human help because it was half a world away or could not afford it, then it would be highly unethical to not provide computer counseling (Lee, 2000). Let us introduce you to Lucy, who is currently undergoing therapy for treatment of depression.

LUCY: (*Lucy, in Brisbane, Australia, more than 200 miles from her home at a cattle station in Queensland, Australia, talking to Dr. Lovehaight, a psychologist.*) Look, I know I need the therapy. I guess I'm pretty depressed, but I'm an over-the-air school teacher, don't make much money, and live over 200 miles from here.

DR. LOVEHAIGHT: I've got something I'd like you to try. I see by your intake form that you have access to a computer and the Net. I'm hooked up to Webpsych; it's a computer counseling system that works with depression. I also have a computer program on depression that I'll give you on a diskette that I think will help. Would you be willing to do that and have the computer keep me informed of your progress? I will check with you every two weeks or on an as-needed basis. The counseling computer is twenty dollars per session and you can pay by credit card. You can access it any time. If you agree, I'll set you up on a trial basis.

The computer counselor is always accessible. Twenty-four hours per day, 365 days per year. This can be particularly helpful on Christmas when you are all alone and feeling blue. Unlike the fifty-minute counseling hour and a therapist who will not be there in the evening—and certainly not on Christmas eve—the computer is always accessible (Colby, 1995; Zarr, 1994). The advent of the Internet and websites make the computer counselor available to anyone, at any time, in any place.

> LUCY: (*Christmas eve, alone on the Gipsy Plains cattle station near ClonCurry, Queensland, Australia, typing www.EnergizedHal.com*)
>
> HAL: (*Energized Hal online computer of WorldWide Therapy Incorporated, Seattle, Washington, United States, responding*) Please enter your access code and credit card number.
>
> LUCY: (*types "Downunder"*)
>
> HAL: Hello, Lucy. What would you like to talk about this evening?

Use of stand-alone counseling computers is dangerous and unethical. As with all science, computers have the capacity for good and evil. (We certainly are not thrilled, for example, by the extremely violent and bloody computer action games in arcades.) However, there is no reason to suppose that computers cannot be programmed, like a doctor, to "do no harm." The computer can determine when its skill boundaries have been reached (Binik et al., 1997). The computer will then make a referral to other resources. This is not always the case with some human therapists.

> HAL: Lucy, my limits are exceeded by your current problem. I am going to give you the e-mail address of a marriage and family therapist in Grenada, Mississippi, USA, Dr. Sharon Latham. She is capable of dealing with this issue. She is available for an appointment at 11 A.M. tomorrow, your time. Would you like me to log you into her appointment book? The fee is a copayment of $20 per hour, which you may pay by credit card. I am also worried that you might be thinking of harming yourself. Thus, I have sent Dr. Lovehaight a pager call in Brisbane. He should be contacting you immediately by telephone. I want you to be sure and stay online with me until you get his call, OK?

Computers also would not be prone to some of the interpersonal relationship problems that plague human therapists and that prompt many of the ethical complaints that reach boards of review. Computers are not likely to have sexual harassment charges made against them.

Both the American Psychological Association (1995) and the American Counseling Association (1999) have sections in their ethical codes that deal with the use of computers. These codes specifically consider the intellectual, emotional, and physical capabilities of the client to use computers; the client's specific needs as they fit computer capabilities; the client's understanding of what the computer program is designed to do and its limitations; and the need for adequate follow-up by the therapist to ensure appropriate use and assess subsequent client needs.

The computer counselor is unable to experience feelings. That's true as of now. However, that doesn't mean the client is unable to project his or her feelings onto the computer. In fact, the computer counselor is eminently capable of being projected on by clients (Binik et al., 1997; Weizenbaum, 1976). The computer is quickly anthropomorphized into a living person, which is both good and bad. As a result, it is the rare person indeed who doesn't experience feelings generated at the computer counselor and by the computer counselor. We are hard-pressed to see how that is very different than a human counselor.

LUCY: One thing I like about you, Hal, is that you never get on me about messing up. My controlling boyfriend could take a lesson!

HAL: It's pretty important to let you alone to make your own mistakes, Lucy, and that includes your boyfriend not trying to tell you what to do.

LUCY: You don't understand how important this guy is to me Hal. I really love him . . . and hate him. About like you sometimes, you stupid machine!

HAL: So you have ambivalent feelings about both your boyfriend and me. Can you tell me more about that?

From a psychoanalytic view, creating transference is critical to catharsis, insight, and resolution of the problem. This example indicates how both positive and negative transference from client to the computer counselor can occur, and how the computer counselor will respond in much the same manner as a human therapist who recognizes the phenomenon and doesn't get sucked into it.

The computer counselor is infinitely patient. The computer counselor will engage in practicing the desired behavior over and over and over again with just as much patience as the first time, perhaps unlike the human counselor, who may get tired and frustrated with the client's attempts to take therapy out into the real world. As Colby (1995) indicates, high percentages of clients have relapses of depression. Catching the slide into relapse quickly and doing something about it is as easy as turning the computer on.

LUCY: I have practiced and practiced being assertive. Sure it's fine when I do it with you, but boy, when I try that on him, I always wimp out. I can't do this anymore. I give up!

HAL: You have practiced quite a lot, Lucy, and done very well with me. Perhaps we could try this again?

LUCY: Not only NO, but HELL NO.

HAL: That's great! You certainly showed some assertiveness with me just now. I understand your frustration; perhaps we can try a new routine later on this evening and you could use that assertiveness on your boyfriend Schroeder the next time he tells you what to do.

The computer will not engage in countertransference. Countertransference is common when the client is frustrated and projects his or her failures onto the therapist and the therapist, equally frustrated, retaliates (Wagman, 1988, p. 16). In short, the computer counselor will not start to see the client as, for instance, a whining, parasitic sister-in-law who she tries to avoid as much as possible at family gatherings.

LUCY: You son-of-a-bitch. It's always back to my screwy thinking. Well he's the one that's screwy, you motherboard, and so are you for that matter.

HAL: It sounds like you're angry with both him and me for questioning you.

LUCY: You bet your hard-drive ass I am.

HAL: Anger is a different emotion than you have ever expressed with me before. Want to tell me what's different now?

LUCY: You are, you're just like him.

HAL: So we both frustrate you and make you feel overwhelmed, but now you feel safe in getting angry with me. I'm glad you feel safe enough to lose control with me. Can you catch the thought or the feeling, or even a behavior that happened right before that? It would be a good cue when Schroeder starts to do that to you.

The counseling computer is an "expert." The counseling computer may make rookie mistakes to begin with, but as the computer programmers and psychotherapists engineer the glitches out, it will make fewer and fewer—at least as far as the "experts" who programmed it are able to. A process called expert engineering, which teams computer programmers with experts in the field, would enable the responses of any therapeutic guru to be programmed into the counseling computer along with the necessary treatment plan to go with it (Franklin, 1997; Stout, 1992; Wagman, 1988, pp. 71–81). The computer counselor who has been programmed by these experts will have just as much expertise and most likely will not make the therapeutic errors a less experienced counselor might.

Therapeutic technique is target specific. Indeed, as therapy has evolved and cognitive therapies have come to the forefront, global personality change has become secondary to identification and reduction of specific symptoms. As such, therapy has taken on a much more educational and technological approach and has become more prescriptive in nature. Advances in programming have allowed the computer to be individually tailored to the specific characteristics of the client and shift focus back on the client's answers rather than plod ahead to solve its own internal system goals (Binik et al., 1997; de Vries & Brug, 1999; Dijkstra & de Vries, 1999; Ochs & Binik, 1998). The contemporary therapist has become more of an instructor, guide, and advisor, and this is exactly where the computer counselor is in its element (Colby, 1995; Wagman, 1988, p. 18).

> HAL: Lucy, from the issues you have presented, I am going to suggest that
> this problem can best be taken care of by a procedure called covert mod-
> eling. Now let me explain what we are going to do. Please feel free to ask
> me questions if you are unsure of my explanation.

The counseling computer is cheap mental health help. As with other technological
fields, the computer is much less expensive to operate than a human being and doesn't need
an insurance plan, retirement benefits, or vacation or sick leave. For the price of a monthly
subscriber fee a client may have unlimited access to a multiplicity of programs that will
assess, diagnose, prescribe, and refer the client for medication or other specialized help
(Colby, 1995; Zarr, 1994).

> HAL: Lucy, it seems to me you are depressed enough to need some med-
> ication. If you agree, I will send your MMPI personality test results and
> symptoms to Dr. Rex Adapuss, a psychiatrist in Brisbane. He will want to
> talk with you and perhaps prescribe some medicine for you.

Hal sends a complete printout about Lucy to Dr. Adapuss along with a diagnosis of
the problem and treatment suggestions. Indeed, programs are now available that not only
diagnose but also prescribe treatment procedures for specific maladies (Hile, Ghobary, &
Campbell, 1995; Warzecha, 1991) and provide specific test results and drug information for
the client (Colby, 1995).

> HAL: Lucy I'd like you to take a brief test for depression. I'll score it and send
> it to Dr. Adapuss and Dr. Lovehaight. I'll also give you the interpretation and
> tell you whether or not it seems that an antidepressant is indicated. I'll also
> tell you, if you want, what your drug options are and what they can and can-
> not do for you. You can then check these out with your doctors.

A computer can't understand nonverbal communication. The computer and its
peripherals are admirably suited to continuous monitoring, measuring, and recording of a
number of physiological responses in the client that may directly relate to what is going on
in therapy (Kirkby, 1996).

> HAL: Lucy, so I can get a better idea of what's going on with you physically
> when you start to get those frustrated feelings, I'd like for you to put that
> skin temperature monitor on your index finger.

Counseling computers don't understand subtlety. While this may be true now, there is
no reason to believe that it will remain so. Voice-activated computers that respond through
natural language are in the not-too-distant future (Kirkby, 1996). One has only to look at the
evolution of video games to see the unlimited potential of the computer. Binik and his associates (1997) have developed Sexpert, a counseling program for individuals and couples
dealing with sexual dysfunction. Given the sensitive nature of the subject, a great deal of

effort was made to create a program that would react according to user expectations of normal social discourse and give feedback in natural language. Controlled research studies on the program indicated that it was as good, if not better, than other self-help modalities although a human therapist was still considered ideal (Ochs & Binik, 1998; Ochs, Meana, Mah, & Binik, 1994). There is no scientific reason to believe that computers will not be able to understand the subtlest client nuances with improved language, video, and physical response feedback systems.

LUCY: I don't think I'M THAT DOWN, OLD BUDDY! I just gotta think. So just go AWAY for awhile.

HAL: (*senses the rise of emotion from increased temperature on biofeedback device on her finger, tremulous voice modulation as she speaks out what she writes, and text capital letters of her reaction to his last statement about getting her help; waits passively for her to "think."*) Okay.

Dan Mitchell and Lawrence Murphy, two trailblazers in Internet counseling, have done a lot to debunk the notion that the nonverbal behavior of a client cannot be determined through their online e-mail therapy (Murphy & Mitchell, 1998). In fact, through the contextual techniques they have developed, computers may know more about what is going on with their clients because they are forced to ask more specific and meaning-enhanced questions. By its very nature, e-mail therapy cannot make assumptions based on how clients look or act. Therefore they have been forced to generate textual techniques that allow them to better understand the emotional content of what is going on with their clients (Collie, Mitchell, & Murphy, 2000).

Emotional Bracketing

The nonverbal element in the background of conscious awareness is often emotional. Therefore, brackets are used to set off the underlying emotion. These brackets give the client and the therapist more information about each other, encourage the client to be more deeply aware of what his or her emotions are, and encourage changes by externalizing part of the conversation (Collie et al., 2000, p. 225).

HAL: [Concerned and worried] I need to be assured you are safe!

LUCY: You worry too much. I'm not suicidal [Relieved, even though I don't say so].

Descriptive Immediacy

This is one of a broader array of *presence techniques* that bring the client into a genuine subtext of warmth and caring. This describes what is currently going on physically, emotionally, and cognitively and uses language that implies that the client and the therapist are face-to-face. By using this, clients are encouraged to be more aware of themselves, their experience, their behavior, and their environment (Collie et al., 2000, pp. 226–227).

HAL: Wow! Good! Right now, if I could smile and breathe a sigh of relief, I would. Watch the happy face emoticon come up on your screen.

LUCY: Well, you could see a smile on my face, too, you dumb box of circuits, so I appreciate you looking out for me. I can physically feel myself relaxing and not feeling so uptight.

Case Sensitive Writing, Pseudo-Words, Spacing, and Emoticons

E-mail writing, much like any projective technique, indicates much about what is going on with a client, not only through what is written, but also how it is written. Both the therapist and the client can use font type, size, and style; spacing; grammar and spelling; syntax; scrolling; or embellishment through color, graphics, or emoticons to better communicate to a client. Emoticons are keyboard symbols that, when rotated 90 degrees clockwise, look like facial expressions. Pseudo-words and spacing can lend increased or decreased emphasis to what is written (Collie et al., pp. 229–231).

LUCY: (*next morning*) I feel . . . I don't know . . . I feel . . . pretty insignificant right now . . . but I'm alive . . . and maybe . . . maybe . . . can see some light . . . maybe.

HAL: I see by your eight-point font just how small you feel and the spaces tell me how hard it is for you to get the words out. But I want you to know that I am glad that

YOU ARE ALIVE and WELL! Yesssssssssss!

So I wonder if you could just type that out in a twelve-point Chicago font for a little emphasis. "I'm alive. I made it through the night and I am alive." :) Happy face for you, Lucy.

LUCY: **Chicago**'s too much, how about Palatino. I'm alive, by golly, I'm alive, and darn it I'm going to stay alive! ;) That's a wink for "Way to stick in there with me and get me off my dead butt, ether buddy."

Isolation from Human Support Systems. Virtual support groups abound on the Internet. Given the large numbers of people that are now cyberlinked, one would be hard pressed not to find a support system on the Internet. Computer access can open the door to a wide variety of support and psychoeducational groups, particularly for individuals who are isolated by geography, physical disability, or some other barrier of human support (Binik et al., 1997; Gary & Remolino, 2000).

HAL: Lucy, I do worry that you are not getting enough contact with people. I have a support group that I think you should log onto. This group is very receptive to talking about depression. There are many participants who are geographically isolated. The site is *Alt.support.depression*. Worldwide Therapy, my parent company, has checked this group out and they are legitimate.

Computer therapy is currently too mechanistic. The computer counselor is presently bound to the limits of the machine's program, but it can achieve the precision of a human therapist and probably perform even better. The advent and progress of computer therapy demand that therapeutic systems finely hone techniques and construct precise language to fit the decision rules of a computer. Therapeutic experts who build counseling programs report that the precision demanded of them to build a workable program makes them become more explicit about their theory and techniques, and helps them further understand their theory (Binik et al., 1997; Gingerich & de Shazer, 1991; Presbury & Marchal, 2000). Because of this, computer counseling is likely to help therapy become more efficient and problem specific (Wagman, 1988, p. 29).

Some people would be turned off by a computer. A great deal of research has found the therapeutic relationship to be more critical than method, technique, theory, or particular therapist in predicting a successful outcome (Cormier & Cormier, 1991; Corsini & Wedding, 1995; Eysenck, 1952, 1965; Garfield, 1980; Menniger & Holzman, 1973; Patterson, 1994). Perhaps if you are over a certain age and believe that electric typewriters are new-fangled contraptions, you may have difficulty forming a relationship with a counseling computer. However, for many members of generation X (Colby, 1995) and for many young children (Calam, Cox, Glasgow, Jimmieson, & Larsen, 2000) the computer is as natural a part of life as eating. There is mounting evidence that computers used for assessment and intake interviews, vocational/educational information, planning and decision making, psychoeducation over a wide variety of topics, therapeutic adjuncts to human therapist, or stand-alone computer therapy are at least as acceptable as their human equivalent. These findings show little variance across a variety of demographic variables such as age, sex, education, and marital status. The one major variable that affects computer preference is whether the particular individual knows how to operate a computer (Binik et al., 1997; Cohen & Kerr, 1998; Coldwell et al., 1998; Dolezal-Wood, Belar, & Snibbe, 1998). Clients are often more willing to reveal personal information to a computer than to a therapist because they know the computer will not think any less of them (Ochs & Binik, 1998; Plutchik & Karasu, 1991).

> LUCY: (*somewhat shyly*) Hal, I . . . well . . . I'm not as sophisticated and worldly as I make out.
>
> HAL: How is that Lucy?
>
> LUCY: I'm 23 years old and I'm still a virgin.
>
> HAL: Tell me what goes through your mind to make you think that being a virgin is unsophisticated.

Although the computer counselor may not consummate a traditional therapeutic relationship with a client, it is the client's perception and receptivity of the relationship that really counts. For the mounting numbers of people who are becoming familiar and at ease with computers, the question of relationship may become a moot point.

The computer is locked into its own program and can't adapt. At present, computers are hard pressed to adapt to any degree beyond what they are programmed to do. Yet computers that are adaptable in every sense of the word are currently being constructed (Franklin, 1997). However, being locked into a particular approach may be a positive attribute. Computers can standardize treatment without the vagaries, personal issues, therapeutic biases, or other incompetencies that can plague human therapists (Stout, 1992). In assessment terminology, the computer counselor would be highly reliable. The truth is that although particular therapeutic techniques are known to be the most effective approaches for a particular problem, they do not always get used (Greist, 1995). If a computer is counseling, the most efficacious and efficient treatment commonly employed for the problem will be used—without hesitation.

Contributions of Computer-Assisted Therapy

We have already mentioned many of the benefits that a counseling computer could provide a client. Let us now look at what it could do for a therapist. First and foremost, it could do what computers now do best—that is, relieve the therapist of such tedious and mind-numbing chores as history taking, diagnostic work-ups, and case following (Strugis, 1998). It can provide the therapist with best-bet diagnoses and therapeutic approaches, and access to expert advice (Hile, Ghobary, & Campbell, 1995). It can also deal quite nicely with the time-consuming trenchwork of less freewheeling and creative therapeutic techniques such as repetitive desensitization procedures or data gathering prior to cognitive restructuring. It is capable of handling any number of clients at one time. Depending on the number of terminals and the size of the server system, the computer counselor could relieve the severe understaffing that plagues so many mental health clinics. The counseling computer could also allow the therapist to take Christmas off—for the most part. As in the dialogue with Lucy, the counseling computer could field crisis calls at any time and have a danger mode that would trigger a call to a therapist, to 911, or to anywhere else it might need to seek help (Binik et al., 1997, p. 78).

The counseling computer can also help therapists become more proficient when its role is reversed and it becomes the computer client. A variety of computer programs have been developed to model client behavior and increase therapist skills (Colby 1975; Hummel, Lichtenberg, & Shaffer, 1975; Hyler & Bujold, 1994; Lichtenberg, Hummel, & Shaffer, 1984; Presbury & Marchal, 2000).

In the form of virtual reality, the computer could become one of the most powerful tools a therapist has in safely projecting clients into a feared situation while at the same time providing valuable data through peripheral biofeedback devices on how the client is responding to the situation. The computer counselor's replicability would allow for very precise measures of the treatment process (Kirkby, 1996). Its efficiency to do all of the foregoing could allow harried therapists in a managed-care world to deal with more clients and more complex cases, and to provide those clients with more quality therapy time at reduced cost (Colby, 1995).

Shortcomings of Computer-Assisted Therapy

A major area of concern in computer counseling has to do with ethics in regard to both the social effects and the moral dimensions of computerization (Behar, 1993). There are a number of major ethical problems that critics might propose for computer counseling. The first major issue is confidentiality. There is no guarantee, at present, that what goes out over the airwaves does not become fodder for public consumption. The American Counseling Association indicates that it is an absolute ethical must that any website that offers counseling provide encryption devices to ensure confidentiality. Yet a review of websites reveals that few have such safeguards (Heinlein, Richmond, Rak, & Welfel, 2001). A more troubling thought is that even if online information is encrypted, there is still no guarantee that hardcopy printouts of the client's comments will remain confidential (Hughes, 2000, p. 327).

The second issue is program validity. The assessment movement has a long and sometimes sad history of promising much and providing little in the way of valid tests. There is no reason to suppose that commercial computer counseling programs would be any better. Whereas the *Mental Measurements Yearbook* (Conoley & Impara, 1995) does an excellent job of casting a critical eye on commercial tests, there is no such vehicle for computer counseling programs. Consumers need to be aware of just how well such programs do what they promise to—although the same could surely be said of human therapists.

The field of psychotherapy has had its own long and sad history of self-styled gurus and charlatans who promise much and deliver nothing, at best, or who are dangerous to clients, at worst. From the various larcenies and other felonies already being perpetrated over the Net, it is not to hard to imagine that a number of electronic salespeople will be in the business of trying to fleece individuals with mental health issues. The Net is clearly a caveat emptor world, particularly when the charlatans are operating half a world away. Among the evils that are lurking in cyberspace for the unsuspecting consumer are a panacea of solutions for a wide variety of problems, guarantees of success, lack of information about provider credentials, lack of any meaningful way to determine credential claims, up-front payments or pay-by-the-minute requirements, and lack of screening for children or incompetent clients (Heinlein et al., 2001).

The simple fact is that interstate cybercounseling may not be legal. Further complicating legitimate provision of counseling is just how far and in what ways liability and malpractice extend in cyberspace. How in the world do computer counselors fulfill their duty to warn when they may have no idea where the client is (Hughes, 2000, p. 328)?

Although computer counseling can engage in a good deal of variety now, it is not presently at the stage that it can see individuals as phenomenological entities with their own specific issues. That is, while you and I may be depressed, we are certainly not depressed in the same way. Nor is anyone else depressed quite like either one of us. Therefore, although we both may benefit from cognitive restructuring, we still need to be approached in an idiosyncratic way as distinct individuals who just happen to have depression in common. Presently, the technology would seem to mandate that human therapists be part of the treatment procedure to ensure that therapy doesn't become an assembly line approach. Whether this will be true in the future as computers become more adaptable remains to be seen.

Unless a virtual reality therapist or a counseling robot can engender tactile sensation, the sense of physical touch that is often important in therapy is certainly missing with the computer counselor. Although many clients maintain that touch is the last thing they want, and fear of sexual harassment charges has certainly limited touching in the contemporary world of therapy, it is our strong belief that many clients need what they avoid most—direct human contact. Some of our most poignant, moving, and productive moments have come by touching or holding someone in therapy.

Finally, therapists themselves may be a shortcoming. For many therapists, coming to grips with a counseling computer may be as thrilling as having the Ebola virus sitting in the room. Greist (1965) states quite well the case of therapists who rigidly resist the computer by quoting the noted physicist Max Planck (1968) on the problem of scientific revolutions and paradigm shifts:

> A new scientific truth does not triumph by convincing its opponents and making them see the light, but rather because its opponents eventually die, and a new generation grows up that is familiar with it.

Any change is difficult, but this is one of the most dramatic changes in mental health provision since Freud decided to have a patient lie down on a couch.

Computer-Assisted Therapy
with Diverse Populations

As seen with our fictitious client from the Outback, computer counseling has tremendous advantages for those who live in remote geographical areas where psychotherapy is not readily available. For those who have a physical disability or are otherwise unable to travel to a therapist, the counseling computer certainly would be a valuable asset. We also see the applicability of the computer counselor in crisis line work, much of which is done by volunteers. There is a constant struggle to keep enough staff available to operate phone lines twenty-four hours a day, 365 days a year. The counseling computer would seem well equipped to do such a job.

The counseling computer also has the capability of providing counseling to many people who could not otherwise afford therapy. It is well suited to communities and states strapped for funds in providing at least adjunctive mental health care to the indigent.

For people who are shy and have trouble finding the right words to express themselves, the computer is not only infinitely patient, but also nonthreatening. Furthermore, the counseling computer would seem particularly appropriate for people who believe that their problems are so socially unacceptable that they would be too ashamed to talk about them. As in the case of adult survivors of childhood sexual abuse, who may feel shame and culpability in the abuse inflicted on them, the computer counselor is absolutely accepting and nonjudgmental in hearing the most intimate details of a person's life.

Those people with access to computers and other means of technology are likely to benefit most from cybercounseling, whereas those with the greatest need are at risk for receiving fewer services because they have less capability and access (Lee, 2000, p. 85). This problem is pervasive on a culture-wide basis. Caucasians are twice as likely as African Americans or Hispanics to have Internet access in their homes (United States Department of Commerce, National Telecommunications and Information Administration, 1999). Therefore, it seems that only the privileged will be able to take advantage of these services (Hughes, 2000, p. 330; Lee, 2000, p. 86). However, the mobility, accessibility, and affordability of cybercounseling holds promise for the economically and socially marginalized (Lee, 2000, p. 88).

Summary

Computers as an informational and assessment component to psychotherapy have been integral to the profession for over twenty years, but their role is changing. With the advent of more powerful memory, home computers, the Internet, and virtual reality, the computer counselor has arrived on the therapeutic scene. Although presently the computer is not widely used as a direct service provider, that is changing. The promise of easy and inexpensive accessibility has extrinsic appeal in a world of managed care that is attempting to get the most bang for its buck. Computers that feel, create, adapt, and learn are in the works. There is no reason to suppose that these cannot be adapted to psychotherapy. As we move into the new millennium, it would appear that the counseling computer is going to be inextricably linked to the human therapist.

SUGGESTIONS FOR FURTHER READING

American Counseling Association (1999, October). American Counseling Association ethical standards for online counseling. Retrieved January 14, 2002 from: counseling.org/gc/cybertx.htm

Bloom, J. W., & Walz, G. R. (Eds.). (2000). *Cybercounseling and cyberlearning: Strategies and resources for the millennium* Alexandria, VA: American Counseling Association. (A comprehensive overview of what is currently happening in cybercounseling.)

ERIC/CASS cybercounseling website. Retrieved January 14, 2002 from: http://askeric.org/ERIC. This website that constantly updates topics on cybercounseling. Use search word "cybercounseling."

REFERENCES

American Counseling Association. (1999). *Ethical standards for Internet online counseling of the American Counseling Association.* Alexandria, VA: Author.

American Psychological Association Ethics Committee. (1995). *Services by telephone, teleconferencing, and Internet: A statement by the Ethics Committee of the American Psychological Association.* Washington, DC: American Psychological Association.

Amsel, A. (1992). Confessions of a neobehavioralist. *Integrative Physiological and Behavioral Science, 27*(4), 336–346.

Association for Counselor Education and Supervision. (1999). *Recommended technical competencies for counselor education students.* Retrieved January 14, 2002 from: http://www.siu.edu./~epse1/aces/

Behar, J. (1993). Computer ethics: Moral philosophy or professional propaganda? *Computers in Human Services, 9*(3–4), 441–453.

Binik, Y. M., Cantor, J., Ochs, E., & Meana, M. (1997). From the couch to the keyboard: Psychotherapy in cyberspace. In S. Kiesler (Ed.), *Culture of the Internet* (pp. 71–100). Mahwah, NJ: Erlbaum.

Biocca, F. (1992). Virtual reality technology: A tutorial. *Journal of Communication, 42*(4), 23–72.

Brennis, B. C. (1994). The skewing of psychiatry. *Academic Psychiatry, 18*(2), 71–80.

Calam, R., Cox, A., Glasgow, D., Jimmieson, P., Larsen, S. G. (2000). Assessment and therapy with children: Can computers help? *Clinical Child Psychology & Psychiatry, 5*(3), 329–343.

Cohen, G. E., & Kerr, B. A. (1998). Computer mediated counseling: An empirical study of a new mental health treatment. *Computers in Human Services, 15*(4), 13–26.

Colby, K. M. (1963). Computer simulation of a neurotic process. In S. S. Tomkins & S. Messick (Eds.), *Computer simulation of personality: Frontiers of psychological research* (pp. 165–180). New York: Wiley.

Colby, K. M. (1975). *Artificial paranoia: A computer simulation of paranoid processes.* New York: Pergamon.

Colby, K. M. (1995). A computer program using cognitive therapy to treat depressed patients. *Psychiatric Services, 46,* 1223–1225.

Coldwell, S. E., Getz, T., Milgrom, P., Prall, C., Spadafora, A., & Ramsay, D. S. (1998). CARL: A LabView 3 computer program for conducting exposure therapy for the treatment of dental injection fear. *Behaviour Research & Therapy, 36*(4), 429–441.

Collie, K. R., Mitchell, D., & Murphy, L. (2000). Skills for online counseling: Maximum impact at minimum bandwidth. In J. W. Bloom & G. R. Walz (Eds.), *Cybercounseling and cyberlearning: Strategies and resources for the millennium* (pp. 219–236). Alexandria, VA: American Counseling Association.

Cormier, W. H., & Cormier, L. S. (1991). *Interviewing strategies for helpers: Fundamental skill and cognitive behavioral interventions* (3rd ed.). Pacific Grove: Brooks/Cole.

Corsini, R. J., & Wedding, D. (1995). *Current psychotherapies* (5th ed.). Itasca, IL: F. E. Peacock.

de Vries, H., & Brug, J. (1999). Computer-tailored interventions motivating people to adopt health promoting behaviors. *Patient Education & Counseling, 36*(2), 99–195

Dijkstra, A., & de Vries, H. (1999). The development of computer-generated tailored interventions. *Patient Education & Counseling, 36*(2), 193–203.

Dolezal-Wood, S., Belar, C. D., & Snibbe, J. (1998). A comparison of computer-assisted psychotherapy and cognitive-behavior therapy in groups. *Journal of Clinical Psychology in Medical Settings, 5*(1), 103–115.

Eysenck, H. J. (1952). *The scientific study of personality.* New York: Macmillan.

Eysenck, H. J. (1965). *Fact and fiction in psychology.* Harmondsworth, UK: Penguin Books.

Finkel, S. J. (1990). Psychotherapy, technology, and aging. *International Journal of Technology and Aging, 3*(1), 57–61.

Franklin, S. (1995). *Artificial minds.* Cambridge, MA: MIT Press.

Franklin, S. (1997). The present and future of artificial intelligence in psychotherapy. (Cassette Recording 9701). Institute for Intelligent Systems. Memphis, TN: University of Memphis.

Garfield, S. L. (1980). *Psychotherapy: An eclectic approach.* New York: Wiley.

Gary, J. M., & Remolino, L. (2000). Coping with loss and grief through on-line support groups. In J. W. Bloom & G. R. Walz (Eds.), *Cybercounseling and cyberlearning: Strategies and resources for the millennium* (pp. 93–113). Alexandria, VA: American Counseling Association.

Gingerich, W. J., & de Shazer, S. (1989). BRIEFER: An expert system for clinical practice. *Computer in Human Services, 5*(12), 53–68.

Gingerich, W. J., & de Shazer, S. (1991). The BRIEFER project: Using expert systems as theory construction tools. *Family Process, 30*(2), 241–250.

Greist, J. H. (1995). Computers and psychiatry. *Psychiatric Services, 46,* 989–991.

Heinlein, K., Richmond, E., Rak, C., & Welfel, E. R. (2001, March). *Cybercounseling: Best (and worst) practice and future directions.* Paper presented at The American Counseling Association 2001 Annual Conference, San Antonio, TX.

Hile, M. G., Ghobary, B. B., & Campbell, D. M. (1995). Source of expert advice: A comparison of peer-reviewed advice from the literature with that from an automated performance support system. *Behavior Research Methods, Instruments, and Computers, 27*(2), 272–276.

Hughes, R. S. (2000). Cybercounseling and regulations: Quagmire or quest? In J. W. Bloom & G. R. Walz (Eds.), *Cybercounseling and cyberlearning: Strategies and resources for the millennium* (pp. 321–336). Alexandria, VA: American Counseling Association.

Hummel, T. J., Lichtenberg, J. W., & Shaffer, W. F. (1975). CLIENT 1: A computer program which simulates client behavior in an initial interview. *Journal of Counseling Psychology, 26,* 279–284.

Hyler, S. E., & Bujold, A. E. (1994). Computers and psychiatric education: The "Taxi Driver" mental status examination. *Psychiatric Annals, 21*(1), 13–19.

Kenardy, J., & Adams, C. (1993). Computers in cognitive behavior therapy. *Australian Psychologist, 28*(3), 189–194.

Kirkby, K. C. (1996). Computer assisted treatment of phobias. *Psychiatric Services, 47,* 139–142.

Lamson, R. J., (1995). Virtual therapy: The treatment of phobias in cyberspace. *Behavioral Healthcare Tomorrow, 4*(1), 51–53.

Lee, C. (2000). Cybercounseling and empowerment: Bridging the digital divide. In J. W. Bloom & G. R. Walz (Eds.), *Cybercounseling and cyberlearning: Strategies and resources for the millennium* (pp. 85–93). Alexandria, VA: American Counseling Association.

Lichtenberg, J. W., Hummel, T. J., & Shaffer, W. F. (1984). CLIENT 1: A computer simulation for use in counselor education and research. *Counselor Education and Supervision, 24,* 155–167.

Menninger, K. A., & Holzman, P. S. (1973). *Theory of psychoanalytic techniques* (2nd ed.). New York: Basic Books.

Moravec, H. (1988). *Mind children.* Cambridge, MA: Harvard University Press.

Murphy, L. J., & Mitchell, D. L. (1998). When writing helps to heal: E-mail as therapy. *British Journal of Guidance and Counseling, 26,* 21–31.

Muscott, H. S., & Gifford, T. (1994). Virtual reality and social skills training for students with behavioral disorders: Applications, challenges and promising practices. *Education and Treatment of Children, 17*(4), 417–434.

Ochs, E. P., & Binick, Y. M. (1998). A sex-expert computer system helps couples learn more about their sexual relationships. *Journal of Sex Education and Therapy, 23*(2), 145–155.

Ochs, E. P., Meana, M., Mah, K., & Binik, Y. M. (1994). Learning about sex outside the gutter: Attitude towards a computer sex-expert system. *Journal of Sex and Marital Therapy, 20,* 86–102.

Pardeck, J. T., & Schulte, R. S. (1990). Computers in social intervention: Implications for professional social work practice and education. *Family Therapy, 17*(2), 109–121.

Patterson, C. H. (1994). *Theories of counseling and psychotherapy* (5th ed.). New York: Harper and Row.

Planck, M. (1968). *Scientific autobiography and other papers* (F. Gaynor, Trans.). Westport, CT: Greenwood Press. (Original work published 1949).

Plutchik, R., & Karasu, T. B. (1991). Computers in psychotherapy: An overview. *Computers in Human Behavior, 7*(1–2), 33–44.

Presbury, J., & Marchal, J. (2000). Getting counselor expertise into a computer: A cyberassistant for students of brief counseling. In J. W. Bloom & G. R. Walz (Eds.), *Cybercounseling and cyberlearning: Strategies and resources for the millennium* (pp. 255–274). Alexandria, VA: American Counseling Association.

Rothbaum, O., Hodges, L. F., Kooper, R., Opdyke, D., Williford, J. S., & North, M. (1995). Effectiveness of computer generated virtual reality graded exposure in the treatment of acrophobia. *American Journal of Psychiatry, 152,* 626–628.

Slack, W. V., Hicks, G. P., Reed, C. Z., & VanCura, L. J. (1966). A computer based medical history system. *New England Journal of Medicine, 274,* 194–198.

Stout, C. E. (1992). An automated method of psychiatric treatment planning. *Behavior Research Methods, Instruments, and Computers, 24*(2), 326–327.

Sturgis, J. W. (1998). Practical use of technology in professional practice. *Professional Psychology: Research and Practice, 29*(2), 183–188.

United States Department of Commerce, National Telecommunications and Information Administration. (1999, July 8). *Falling through the net: Defining the digital divide.* Retrieved January 14, 2002 from http://www.ntia.doc.gov/ntiahome/fttn99/contents.html.

Wagman, M. (1979). Systematic dilemma counseling: Theory, method, research. *Psychological Reports, 44,* 55–72.

Wagman, M. (1980). PLATO DCS. An interactive computer system for personal counseling. *Journal of Counseling Psychology, 27,* 16–30.

Wagman, M. (1982). A computer method for solving dilemmas. *Psychological Reports, 50,* 291–298.

Wagman, M. (1984). *The dilemma and the computer: Theory, research, and applications to counseling psychology.* New York: Praeger.

Wagman, M. (1988). *Computer psychotherapy systems: Theory and research foundations.* New York: Gordon and Breach.

Warzecha, G. (1991). The challenge to psychological assessment from modern computer technology. *European Review of Applied Psychology, 41*(3), 213–220.

Weizenbaum, J. (1965). ELIZA—A computer program for the study of natural language communication between man and machine. *Communication of the Association for Computing Machinery, 9,* 36–45.

Weizenbaum, J. (1976). *Computer power and human reason: From judgment to calculation.* San Francisco: Freeman.

Zarr, M. (1994). Computer-aided psychotherapy: Machine helping therapist. *Psychiatric Annals, 24*(1), 42–46.

INDEX